THE INDUS RIVERS

THE INDUS RIVERS

A Study of the Effects of Partition

by Aloys Arthur Michel

New Haven and London, Yale University Press, 1967

Acknowledgments

Permission to quote the indicated copyrighted material is gratefully acknowledged to the following: Columbia University Press, New York, for the quotations from Paul W. Paustian, *Canal Irrigation in the Punjab,* 1930; to Ernest Benn Limited, London, Frederick A. Praeger, Inc., New York, and Ian Stephens for the quotations from Ian Stephens, *Pakistan,* 2nd ed., 1964; to David McKay Company, Inc., New York, for the quotations from Louis Fischer's Introduction to the First American Edition of Maulana Abul Kalam Azad, *India Wins Freedom,* New York, Longmans, Green and Co., 1960; Dr. Nafis Ahmad and the Editorial Board of the *Oriental Geographer,* Dacca, East Pakistan Geographical Society, for the quotations from Kazi S. Ahmad, "Canal Water Problem," *Oriental Geographer, 2* (January 1958); to Michael Edwardes for the quotation from his book *The Necessary Hell: John and Henry Lawrence and the Indian Empire,* London, Cassell, 1958; to the American Geographical Society, New York, for the quotations from F. J. Fowler, "Some Problems of Water Distribution between East and West Punjab," *The Geographical Review, 40* (1950); to George Allen & Unwin Limited, London, for the quotations from Khushwant Singh, *The Sikhs,* 1953; to Harcourt, Brace & World, Inc., New York, for the quotations from Humphrey Evans, *Thimayya of India: A Soldier's Life,* 1960, and to both them and Weidenfeld and Nicholson Limited, London, for those from Leonard Mosley, *The Last Days of the British Raj,* 1962; to William Heinemann Limited, London, and The Viking Press, New York, for the quotations from C. R. Attlee, *As It Happened,* 1954; to David E. Lilienthal and Crowell Collier and Macmillan, Inc., New York, for the quotations from David E. Lilienthal, "Another 'Korea' in the Making?" *Collier's, 128* (August 4, 1951); to A. M. R. Montagu for the quotations from his "Presidential Address to the Punjab Engineering Congress, 33rd Session, 1946"; to Frederick A. Prager, Inc., New York, and to Pall Mall Press, London, for the quotations from Hugh Tinker, *India and Pakistan: A Political Analysis,* 1962; to the Princeton University Press, Princeton, New Jersey, for the quotations from V. P. Menon, *The Transfer of Power in India,* 1957; and to S. S. Kirmani, Chief Engineer, Indus Basin Project, Lahore, Pakistan, who originated the term "The Indus Rivers."

For Connie
and "Idu Khan"

Introductory Note

by *A. M. R. Montagu, C.I.E, F.C.G.I., M.I.C.E*
Chief Engineer and Secretary to Government of the Punjab,
Public Works Department, Irrigation Branch, 1943–47

I feel it is a privilege to supply a brief foreword to the author's work on the Indus Basin. Such small contribution as I have been able to provide has been made possible by thirty-five years of service in the Irrigation Branch of the Punjab Public Works Department, within the area of the Indus Basin, on the canals and river works which figure so prominently in the relatively recent history of Northern India.

Those of us who served in that great department were naturally concerned with the detailed design, construction, and operation of the canals and the river control works. We had little leisure to follow political controversies. Professor Michel has had the inestimable advantage of detachment and has brought to his investigation an open mind and a clarity of judgment together with a keen interest in his subject. My own service terminated in February 1947. From that date onwards, I was simply an "informed" member of the public, keenly interested in what was happening in India/Pakistan, but no better informed as to events and their underlying causes than any one else not directly concerned. But there are two chapters upon which I may be allowed to comment.

Chapter 3 should convey to the reader something of the technical world in which we lived, the fascination of changing bare "pat" or "jungal" into areas of varied crops; the early morning inspections on horseback, the nostalgia of wood smoke in the evenings when we met the local cultivators to listen to their difficulties and disputes over water rights and supplies.

Chapter 5 is on a different plane. No one who did not live through that period of uncertainty, suspicion, threat and counterthreat can appreciate the bewilderment of the ordinary folk and the anxiety and worry of the official, whatever his status. In Chapter 5, for the first time, I have read a dispassionate and comprehensive account of the negotiations which ultimately led to Partition. Rightly or wrongly, it seems to me that all concerned were in the grip of impersonal developments which were beyond the wit of man to control. Man had released the whirlwind—and men had to live through the resulting disaster.

With so much fascinating material at one's disposal, one is inevitably inclined to remark upon those portions with which one is personally acquainted. I found the author's account of the origin and growth of the Colony system particularly interesting. When I joined the Service in 1914, the Triple Canals Project (Upper Jhelum, Upper Chenab, and Lower Bari Doab Canals) had just been completed and colonization was in full swing. It is worth noting that the system remained unchanged, save in minor details, during the whole of my service. It was successful beyond expectation, agriculturally and financially. The originators built better than they knew and their intense zeal and care were amply justified.

The author's narrative of post-Partition developments is the most lucid I have read. In particular, his account of the task of boundary delineation which Radcliffe undertook goes far to acquit him (Radcliffe) of responsibility for the results. It would be profitless to attempt to allocate this responsibility; the task was impossible of accomplishment in the time available. But I am only a technician. Water follows immutable laws of nature. Man makes his own laws as he goes along—and immediately breaks them. I prefer water. Successfully or not, the British did their best and found satisfaction and reward in so doing.

This volume deals with one limited area of the Indian subcontinent and events over a short period of its history. The area is important to its peoples, and the period covers immense changes in their material and social conditions. To all interested in the degree and manner of such changes, this volume will make fascinating reading.

London, November 20, 1966

Introductory Note

by Lt. Gen. Emerson C. Itschner, Ret.
Chief, Corps of Engineers, U.S. Army, 1956–61
and Chief Technical Adviser, Indus Basin Project,
West Pakistan Water and Power Development Authority, 1961–64

Professor Michel's absorbing story of Pakistan's epic struggle to maintain its vitally important agricultural economy is an account of that nation's heroic effort to continue to use water supplies for irrigation equivalent to those which it has rightfully employed for a century. He describes a two-pronged endeavor: one to neutralize the effects of the diversion to India of stream flows in the three eastern Indus River tributaries, and the second a battle against nature to prevent the loss of irrigated land caused by water-logging and salinity. He makes it clear, but I would like to add my emphasis, that the generally poor and underprivileged Pakistani people are determined, dedicated, patriotic, and highly intelligent. They number among them many of the world's most knowledgeable irrigation engineers. Unfortunately, their country's physical resources are not equal to the capability of the people to exploit them.

The Indus Basin Project (IBP) is a brilliant and practical engineering solution to the problems resulting from the diversion of flows from the eastern Indus tributaries to India. While many competent people from several nations participated in its conception and implementation, the greatest share of the credit should go to Lt. General Raymond A. Wheeler, then engineer consultant for the World Bank, and Mr. S. S. Kirmani, now Chief Engineer, IBP, Water and Power Development Authority of West Pakistan (WAPDA). The latter had a desk in General Wheeler's office during the critical years when the project was being formulated. Mr. Rashid Kazi, whose promotion to Secretary of Irrigation vacated the position which Mr. Kirmani filled, is another extremely competent engineer who played an important role in the early phases of the construction project. Mr. Ghulam Ishaq, as Chairman of WAPDA, handled his responsibilities with exceptional tact, perception, and wisdom.

So much controversy has centered around Tarbela Dam that I feel that a comment is appropriate. Tarbela definitely is not a good dam site and I doubt that it would be built in the United States. We must recognize, however, that it is the best site available in the Indus which will meet the requirements of the IBP. I am thoroughly convinced that the Consortium of Nations in the "Indus Basin Club" promised Pakistan to support the Tarbela Dam, although not by name.

During Professor Michel's stay in Pakistan I had the opportunity to observe closely his research methods. He traveled every place where information regarding West Pakistan's water problems could be obtained. He devoted much time to studying the numerous reports and other publications produced by WAPDA, the Irrigation Department of West Pakistan, and other governmental agencies. He became acquainted with the staffs and consultants of these organizations, as well as those of the World Bank. I was actually awed by his thoroughness.

Professor Michel's book, in my opinion, is accurate, complete, authoritative. I doubt if further research would supplement the history of Pakistan's water problems and their solution since Partition. The Indus Basin has long needed a geographer and a historian. In Professor Michel it now has one.

Portland, Oregon, November 28, 1966

Author's Preface

This book represents both a fulfillment and a beginning.

Ten years ago, as a doctoral candidate in search of a dissertation subject, I suggested to my mentor, the late Professor John Ewing Orchard of Columbia University, that I would like to examine the interplay between the irrigation system and the regional economy of the Indus Basin. Dr. Orchard, who knew the subcontinent at first hand, diplomatically suggested that any comprehensive study of the Indus Basin irrigation system would prove too large and too complex for a doctoral dissertation. (At times during the preparation of this book I have thought that it might prove too large and too complex for one man in one lifetime.) Instead, he suggested that I go to Afghanistan where several smaller basins, including those of the Helmand River and of the Kabul tributary of the Indus, could serve for a more limited regional analysis of the impact of modern irrigation techniques upon traditional agricultural economies and of such irrigation-induced problems as waterlogging and salinity. Furthermore, any study of the Indus Basin made in 1957–58 would have lacked the guidelines presented by the Indus Waters Treaty of 1960 and of the Indus Basin Project (in West Pakistan) and the Bhakra-Beas-Rajasthan Project (in India), which were designed or redesigned in conformity with that Treaty. I shall always be grateful to Dr. Orchard for his wise suggestion, and to the people and Government of Afghanistan for their hospitality and cooperation. My introduction to the conditions of rural life, the problems of climates and soils, and the promise of irrigation and regional planning in South Central Asia was highly rewarding in itself and an excellent preparation for my later work in West Pakistan and northern India.

Although I was able to carry out a preliminary reconnaissance of the Pakistani and Indian portions of the Indus Basin in 1957–58, most of the field work on which this study is based was conducted between August 1963 and May 1964. For reasons which the reader can well appreciate, the latter work had to concentrate on either the Pakistani or the Indian portion of the Basin. Because most of the water, most of the land, and most of the projects are concentrated in West Pakistan, because Pakistan has gone much further with a groundwater program, and because the success or failure of the new programs is relatively more critical to Pakistan as a whole than to India, Pakistan was chosen. But within the limits of time and mobility in the field, I have attempted to give the Indian projects an adequate treatment. In the next study of what I regard as a twenty-year series, it should be possible to evaluate the still-pending Indian decisions on the proposed Beas-Sutlej Link and particularly on the relative advantage of expanding still further into Rajasthan rather than concentrating water on the existing canal commands in the Indian portion of the Indus Basin. An account will also have to be made of the effects of the partitioning of the Indian Punjab on November 1, 1966.

As any scholar must, I have tried to preserve impartiality in evaluating the attitudes and positions of both nations in the struggle over Partition, in Kashmir, and in the Indus Waters Dispute. Unavoidably, some readers will feel that I have slighted India or Pakistan—or perhaps both. Some reviewers have criticized portions of the manuscript as being "pro-Pakistan," others as being "too hard on Pakistan." For the present, I am content to settle for that. I accept full responsibility for the opinions expressed and for any errors that remain despite my efforts and those of the learned persons to whom I have submitted these portions.

Obviously, for a work of this scope I am indebted to a great many institutions and persons. Because the list is so long, and because specific acknowledgment might prove embarrassing to some, I cannot include all of them by name. But the contributions of the following organizations and individuals have been so great that no general expression of thanks would be adequate.

I wish to express my gratitude to Yale University for granting me a leave of absence during the academic year 1963–64 and also for the award of a Junior Faculty Fellowship. For supplementary assistance, thanks are due to the American Council of Learned Societies and to the Concilium on International Studies of Yale University.

Two distinguished civil engineers, both of whom could long since have rested on their laurels but both of whom are still actively pursuing their careers, have been a source of assistance and inspiration to me. Mr. A. M. R. Montagu, formerly Chief Engineer, Irrigation, Punjab, has contributed greatly to my account of the evolution of the irrigation system prior to 1947. Lt. Gen. Emerson C. Itschner, formerly Chief of the Corps of Engineers, U. S. Army, and later Chief Technical Adviser, Indus Basin Project, facilitated and encouraged my work in West Pakistan. Both of these gentlemen have been kind enough to read the manuscript and to contribute introductory notes. Lt. Gen. Raymond A. Wheeler, also a retired Chief of the Corps of Engineers and Engineering Adviser to the World Bank during and after the negotiations of the Indus Waters Treaty, read an early version of Chapter 6. Sir Kenelm Guinness, another of the Bank's chief negotiators for the Treaty, in his personal capacity read the penultimate versions of Chapters 6 and 7 and made a number of helpful criticisms. Mr. David E. Lilienthal, who in 1951 inspired those negotiations, has graciously allowed me to read the proofs of the third volume of his *Journals*, which deals in part with those negotiations. John B. Drisko of Tippetts-Abbett-McCarthy-Stratton, New York, has been an invaluable guide throughout my work. Mr. Drisko; R. J. Tipton, President, Tipton and Kalmbach, Denver; and David W. Greenman, also of Tipton and Kalmbach, have read and criticized large portions of Chapters 6 through 9. Mr. Greenman and Dr. Milton Fireman, of the University of California at Davis (who was then associated with Tipton and Kalmbach), were also of considerable assistance to me in my field work as well as being excellent companions.

Dr. Roger Revelle, now Director of the Center for Population Studies, Harvard University Medical School, and Dr. Abdus Salam,

Science Adviser to the President of Pakistan, have provided insights into the groundwater and reclamation program. Professor Mark W. Leiserson, Project Director of the Yale University Pakistan Project; Professor Robert P. Burden of the Revelle Panel and the Harvard Water Program; and Professor Henry C. Hart of the University of Wisconsin's Indian Studies Program have read and constructively criticized the manuscript.

Sir Cyril (now Viscount) Radcliffe was kind enough to answer my questions concerning the program and the records of the Punjab Boundary Commission in 1947, and both Sir Evan Jenkins (then Governor of the Punjab) and Sir George Abell (then Private Secretary to Lord Mountbatten) granted me interviews in London. The staff of the old India Office Library (now the Commonwealth Relations Office Library) in London, and Mr. M. J. Moir in particular, were extremely helpful in my archival research. Mr. Ferris J. Stephens, of the American Oriental Society Library at Yale, greatly facilitated my use of their extensive collection of Indian District Gazetteers.

Of the many persons who assisted me in Pakistan, I should like to thank especially Mr. G. Mueenuddin, C.S.P., who headed the Pakistani delegation during most of the Treaty negotiations, and Mrs. Barbara Mueenuddin; Mr. K. Ghafoor Ahmad, Deputy Secretary of the West Pakistan Water and Power Development Authority; and Mr. S. S. Kirmani, Chief Engineer, Indus Basin Project. Without the assistance of these persons, the field research would have been impossible.

The following officials of the West Pakistan Government, of its semiautonomous agencies, and of the Central Government of Pakistan made significant contributions to my study:
West Pakistan Water and Power Development Authority (WAPDA)

Administration and Coordination Wing: Mr. Hamid Jalal, Director, Public Relations; Mr. Raziuddin, Assistant Director, Press Information; and Major S. N. Hasan, Assistant Director, Publications (now Director, Public Relations)

Development and Coordination Division, Planning and Investigations Directorate: Mr. S. Monawar Ali, Director-General, and Mr. S. Mumtaz Ali, Assistant Director, Statistics

Indus Basin Project Division: Mr. Riaz Nazir Tarar, Technical

Officer; Mir Bashar Khan, Chief Engineer, Mangla Dam; and Mr. Sultan M. Naim, Chief Engineer, Tarbela Dam

Ground Water and Reclamation Division: Mr. Sayyid Hamid, Chief Engineer, and Mr. Muhammad Badruddin, Superintending Engineer

Water and Soils Investigation Division: Mr. S. M. Said, Chief Engineer; Mr. Zamir-uddin Kidwai, Superintending Geologist; and Mr. H. S. Zaidi, Superintending Research Officer

West Pakistan Irrigation and Power Department

Mr. A. Rashid Kazi, Secretary; Dr. Mushtaq Ahmad, Director, Irrigation Research Institute; Dr. Nazir Ahmad, Physicist, I.R.I.; Dr. R. M. Firdausi, Section Officer, I.R.I.; and Mr. S. M. Abdul Hayye, Librarian, Public Works Department Library

West Pakistan Agricultural Development Corporation

Mr. Ahmad Hassan, Chief Engineer and Adviser, Irrigation; Dr. M. Altaf Hussain, Director, Planning and Evaluation; Dr. Ali Asghar, Director, Extension and Training; and Lt. Col. S. W. H. Jafarey, Chairman, Thal Development Authority

West Pakistan Board of Revenue

Mr. Sultan Maqsood, C.S.P., Officer on Special Duty

Government of Pakistan, Ministry of Agriculture and Works

Mr. M. A. Cheema, C.S.P., Joint Secretary and former Secretary General of the Food and Agriculture Commission; and Mr. A. H. Khokhar, Deputy Commissioner, Agricultural Census Organization

The following members of firms employed as consultants by WAPDA for the Indus Basin Project, for groundwater development and reclamation, and for regional and overall master planning were (in addition to those mentioned above) of assistance to me in my research in West Pakistan:

Harza Engineering Company International: Messrs. W. C. Boegli, R. E. Helgeson, M. Maasland, C. H. Studebaker, and Col. J. U. Moorhead

Hunting Technical Services, Ltd.: Mr. A. P. S. Forbes and Mr. P. E. Taylor

Tipton and Kalmbach, Inc.: Dr. Wayne Hinish and Dr. Mohammad Iqbal

Messrs. D. Gene Reese, Paul W. Bedard, James J. Maslowski, Emory G. Roberts, and Eugene W. Whitman of the U.S. Agency for

International Development, Lahore, also contributed valuable information and guidance. Consul General David M. Bane, and Consul and Commercial Officer Donald F. Haher did all in their power to assist my research.

Mr. John K. Black, Agricultural Economist at the U. S. Department of the Interior, Bureau of Reclamation, was kind enough to read the portions of Chapters 7 and 8 dealing with the projects in India. Dr. H. L. Uppal, Director of the Irrigation and Power Research Institute, Amritsar, made time for me in a very busy schedule, and he and his assistants greatly facilitated my all-too-short field work in India. Thanks are also due to my old friend, Sardar Kapoor Singh, Chairman of the Punjab Legislative Council, Chandigarh, and to Mr. Ragbir Singh, Executive Engineer, Gurdaspur Division, for their gracious hospitality. Mr. O. P. Mehta, Undersecretary to Government Punjab (India), Beas Project Administration, facilitated my visit to the Pong Project.

Professionally and personally, I should like to thank my colleagues in the Department of Geography, University of the Panjab, Lahore, especially the Chairman, Professor Kazi S. Ahmad, and Dr. Rashid Ahmad Malik, both of whom have contributed to the study of the Indus Basin, as have my colleagues at the Department of Geography, Punjab University, Chandigarh, in particular the Chairman, Dr. Gurdev Singh Gosal and his assistant Mr. G. Radhakrishan, all of whom provided guidance and stimulating discussions in my work.

Sincere thanks are also due to Miss Jane V. Olson of the Yale University Press and to Miss Casey Miller for their painstaking work in editing the manuscript, to Mrs. Sally Sullivan for designing the book, and to Mrs. Dorothy deFontaine for her splendid and patient work on the maps.

As is customary, I absolve all of the foregoing from any responsibility for errors which may remain in the book, and particularly for any of the opinions I have felt free to express. I trust that they will absolve me in return. On a purely personal level, I want to add a word of appreciation to Mr. and Mrs. William S. Brinigar, but for whom the field work could never have been begun, and to Dr. and Mrs. Philip K. Russell, without whom it might well have ended in tragedy.

Aloys A. Michel

New Haven, Conn.
June 1966
xvi

Contents

Introductory Note by A. M. R. Montagu   vii

Introductory Note by Lt. Gen. Emerson C. Itschner   ix

Author's Preface   xi

List of Tables   xxi

List of Maps   xxiii

List of Abbreviations   xxiv

1. Prologue   1

   The Legacy of Partition   1

   The Scope of This Study   11

2. The Indus Rivers and the Indus Plains   22

   Rivers and Mountains   22

   Rivers and Plains   29

   The Indus Plains   36

3. Canals and Colonies: Engineers and Administrators   46

   Precursors   46

   The British Raj   51

   The First British Canal   58

   Motives   65

   The Sirhind Canal   71

   Administrative Doubts   73

   The Second Wave of Canal Building   76

   A Stock-Taking Interlude   81

   The First Integrated System: The Triple Canals Project   90

	The Sutlej Valley Project	93
4.	The Indus Waters Dispute Before Partition	99
	Sind: "The Unhappy Valley"	99
	Irrigation in Sind: Sukkur	104
	Foundations of the Dispute	111
	Sind-Punjab Disputes: The Bhakra, Trimmu, and Thal Projects	118
	Trimmu and Thal	123
	Bhakra Again	128
5.	Partition	134
	The Cabinet Mission Plan	135
	Mountbatten and Menon	149
	The Positions of the Sikhs	159
	The Punjab Boundary Commission	162
	The Sikh Proposal	169
	Radcliffe's Line and Alternatives	176
	The Position in the Manjha and the Bist-Jullundur Doab	185
6.	The Indus Waters Dispute from Partition to the Treaty (1947–60)	195
	The Irrigation Crisis of April 1948	195
	Post-Partition Projects	205
	Engineers, Lawyers, and an Occasional Statesman	219
	The Indus Waters Treaty and the Development Fund Agreement	254
7.	Implementing the Treaty	268
	The Indus Basin Project (West Pakistan)	268
	IBP: Mangla and Tarbela	283
	IBP: The Tarbela Crisis	295
	The Bhakra-Beas-Rajasthan Project (India)	316
8.	Reorganizing to Develop the Indus Basin	341
	Effects of Independence	341
	West Pakistan: WAPDA and Its Associates	348
	India: The Center and the States	364
	Bringing Development to the Farmers	383
9.	The Groundwater Programs	444
	Precursors	444
	Tubewells in the Punjab	452
	Waterlogging	455

Contents

	The Modern, Massive Approach in West Pakistan	463
	The Revelle Approach	476
	Evaluation and Alternatives	489
	The Indian Experience in East Punjab	509
10.	Prospects for Future Development	515
	A Brief Retrospect	515
	Economic and Political Outlook: India and Pakistan	520
	Prospects for Irrigation and Reclamation Programs in West Pakistan	532
	Appendix: The Indus Waters Treaty of 1960	557
	Bibliography	547
	Index	573

List of Tables

1. Catchment Areas and Runoff of the Indus Rivers   33
2. Cost of Principal Productive Irrigation Works to the End of March 1903   81
3. Rainfall, Runoff, and Utilization for Irrigation in River Basins of Northern India   83
4. Data on Irrigation in Certain Projects in West Pakistan, 1958–59   112
5. Percentages of Sikhs and Muslims in the Divisions and Districts of the Former British Punjab According to Censuses of 1931 and 1941   172
6. Percentages of Sikhs and Muslims in Certain Districts and Tahsils of the Former British Punjab According to Censuses of 1931 and 1941   187
7. The Bhakra-Beas-Rajasthan Scheme in India   208
8. Indian and Pakistani Plans for Use of the Waters of the Indus Rivers as Submitted to the World Bank in 1953   231
9. Comparison of the Bank Proposal for Divison of the Indus Rivers (February 1954) with the Plans Submitted by India and Pakistan (October 1953)   239
10. Pledges by the "Friendly Governments" and Loans Promised by the U.S.A. and World Bank to Pakistan and India Toward the Costs of a Waters Settlement in the Indus Basin   251

11. Comparison of Estimates by Indus Basin Advisory Board, World Bank Consultants, and WAPDA Consultants for the Indus Basin Project, West Pakistan, by Components 252
12. Phase I of the Indus Basin Project 279
13. Phase II of the Indus Basin Project 281
14. Comparison of the Major Dams in the Indus Basin (West Pakistan and India) 288
15. New Irrigation in East Punjab Made Possible by the Bhakra Canal System 318
16. Projected Releases from Pong and Bhakra Reservoirs to Meet the Needs of Punjab and Rajasthan at Harike Barrage 325
17. Projected Irrigation under the Rajasthan Canal 332
18. Composition of Supervisory Boards, Bhakra Project 376
19. Composition of Supervisory Organizations, Beas Project 384
20. Parallel Organizations in the Government of West Pakistan 388
21. Size Distribution and Fragmentation of Farms in West Pakistan According to the 1960 Census of Agriculture 405
22. Assumed Crop Responses in Project Areas under the Revelle and Harza-WAPDA Programs 506
23. Comparison of Areas and Costs for the Initial Stages of the Revelle and Harza Programs 506
24. Indus Plains Surface and Groundwater Supplies as Envisaged by the Harza and Revelle Programs 537

List of Maps

Maps drawn by Dorothy deFontaine

1. The Indus Basin at the Time of Partition   xxvi–xxvii
2. Catchment Areas of the Indus Rivers   20–21
3. Development of the Indus Basin Irrigation System
   to 1960   44–45
4. Percentages of Muslims and Sikhs in the Districts
   of the British Punjab According to the Censuses of
   1941 and 1931   142–43
5. The Central Punjab, Showing the Relation of the
   Partition Line to the Muslim and Sikh Population
   by Tahsil and to the Irrigation and Railway Systems   150–51
6. The Indus Basin Project in West Pakistan   266–67
7. The Bhakra-Beas-Rajasthan Project in India   286
8. The Groundwater Projects in West Pakistan
   a. Location of the Early Tubewell Projects in the
      Chaj, Rechna, and Bari Doabs   441
   b. Tentative Priority Assigned to Groundwater and
      Reclamation Projects by the Harza Report   443

List of Abbreviations

ADC	Agricultural Development Corporation (West Pakistan)
A.I.D.	Agency for International Development (U.S.A.)
BBRP	Bhakra-Beas-Rajasthan Project (India)
BRBD Link	Bambanwala-Ravi-Bedian-Dipalpur Link
CBDC	Central Bari Doab Channels (Canals)
C.C.A.	Culturable Commanded Area
CE	Chief Engineer
C-J Link	Chasma-Jhelum Link
C.S.P.	Civil Service of Pakistan
Cusecs	Cubic feet per second
D.C.	Deputy Commissioner
F.A.C.	Food and Agriculture Commission (Pakistan)
IBAB	Indus Basin Advisory Board
IBRD	International Bank for Reconstruction and Development (World Bank)
IBP	Indus Basin Project (West Pakistan)
I.C.A.	International Cooperation Administration (U.S.A.)
I.D.E.	Institute of Development Economics (Karachi)
LBDC	Lower Bari Doab Canal
LCC	Lower Chenab Canal
LJC	Lower Jhelum Canal
M-B Link	Mailsi-Bahawal Link

M-R Link	Marala-Ravi Link
P.E.P.S.U.	Patiala and East Punjab States Union
PIDC	Pakistan Industrial Development Corporation
P.I.U.	Produce Index Unit
Q-B Link	Qadirabad-Balloki Link
R.C.D.	Regional Cooperation for Development (Pakistan, Iran, Turkey)
R-Q Link	Rasul-Qadirabad Link
SCARP	Salinity Control and Reclamation Project
S-M Link	Sidhnai-Mailsi Link
S.V.P.	Sutlej Valley Project
T and K	Tipton and Kalmbach
TAMS	Tippetts-Abbett-McCarthy-Stratton
T.C.P.	Triple Canals Project
T.D.A.	Thal Development Authority (West Pakistan)
T-P Link	Taunsa-Panjnad Link
T-S Link	Trimmu-Sidhnai Link
T-S-M-B Link	Trimmu-Sidhnai-Mailsi-Bahawal Link
UBDC	Upper Bari Doab Canal
UCC	Upper Chenab Canal
UJC	Upper Jhelum Canal
U.P.	United Provinces (India)
U.S.G.S.	United States Geological Survey
WAPDA	Water and Power Development Authority (West Pakistan)
WASID	Water and Soils Investigation Division (West Pakistan WAPDA)
WJC	Western Jumna Canal
XEN	Executive Engineer

Note: Definitions of technical and vernacular terms in the text will be found at either the first entry or the one marked "def." in the Index.

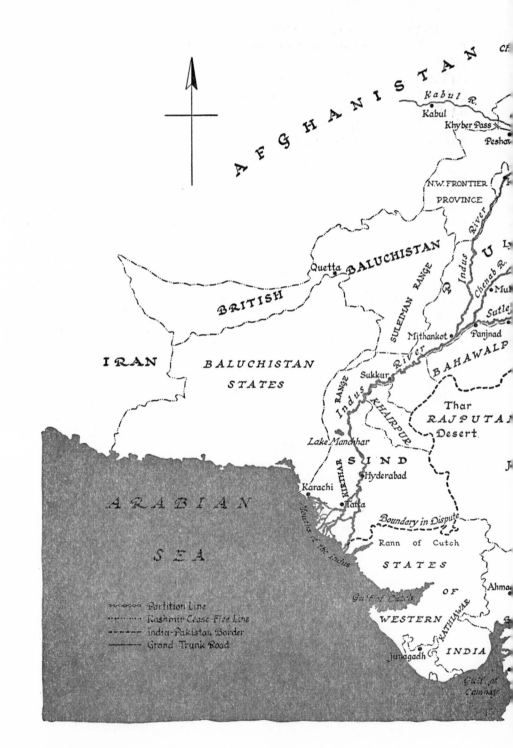

AFGHANISTAN

CF

Kabul R.
Kabul
Khyber Pass
Peshav

N.W. FRONTIER
PROVINCE

Quetta
BALUCHISTAN
BRITISH
SULEIMAN RANGE
Indus River
Chenab R.
U Ly
Mu

BALUCHISTAN
STATES

IRAN

KIRTHAR RANGE
Mithankot
Panjnad
Sutlej
BAHAWALP

Sukkur
Indus River
KHAIRPUR
Thar
RAJPUTAN
Desert

Lake Manchhar

SIND
Hyderabad

KIRTHAR RANGE
Karachi
Tatta

Mouths of the Indus

Boundary in Dispute

Rann of Cutch

ARABIAN

SEA

STATES
Je
OF

Ahma
Gulf of Cutch

WESTERN
KATHIAWAR
INDIA
Junagadh
*Gulf of
Cambay*

~~~~ Partition Line
.... Kashmir Cease-Fire Line
------ India-Pakistan Border
——— Grand Trunk Road

The Indus Basin at the time of Partition

1. Prologue

*"And the king said, Divide the living child in two,
and give half to the one, and half to the other."*
                                                                    —1 Kings, 3

The Legacy of Partition

On August 15, 1947, the British partitioned a subcontinent containing one-sixth of the world's people into the modern nations of Pakistan and India. Eighteen years later, the undeclared war over Kashmir served as an unpleasant reminder to the world that Partition and Independence had left much unfinished business in the subcontinent. For Indian independence, when it finally came, came swiftly and was not handled in the tidy fashion that later became a pattern for Britain's other colonies. Though victorious in World War II, the British in 1946 and 1947 were plagued with political and military problems in Germany, Greece, Turkey, Palestine, Iran, and Malaya as well as in the subcontinent, where the repatriated members of the Indian National Army, which had fought for the Japanese, were being greeted as heroes and where the morale of even the British was none too good. In England the Labour Party, though conscious of its repeated pledges to India, was anxious to get along with reconstruction and with the building of a socialist society. Thus, within the space of a few months, the phrase "Quit India" was transformed

1

from an Indian National Congress slogan to a policy of the British Government.

Nevertheless, the transfer of power in India cannot fairly be described as abrupt. "Representative government" had been evolving toward "self-government" for almost forty years, from Edward VII's proclamation of 1908 through the Morley-Minto Reforms (Indian Councils Act) of 1909, the Montagu-Chelmsford Reforms embodied in the Government of India Act of 1919 (taking effect from 1921), and the recommendations of the Simon Commission of 1927–30 and the Round Table Conferences of 1931, which led to the Government of India Act of 1935 (taking effect from 1937). After 1937, the provinces of British India enjoyed a considerable amount of local autonomy under popularly elected ministries but with British-appointed governors. This was not enough to satisfy the Indian National Congress, some of whose leaders tried to capitalize on the crisis which developed after Japan had entered the war, and particularly after the fall of Singapore and Rangoon, by demanding "Independence Now." Sir Stafford Cripps' mission in the spring of 1942, offering dominion status at the end of the war, met with no acceptance from Congress. Gandhi, in fact, described the offer as "a post-dated check on a failing bank." Churchill's remark that he had not become the King's First Minister to preside over the liquidation of the British Empire summed up the attitude of most Conservative leaders, but Clement Attlee, who took over as Prime Minister in July 1945 and who had been a member of the Simon Commission, saw matters in an entirely different light. Nevertheless, it was not until March 1946 that the Labour Government sent Cripps back to India with the Cabinet Mission, whose work led, indirectly to be sure, to Independence seventeen months later (see Chapter 5 for the details).

Although the Cabinet Mission ultimately failed to achieve agreement, by the time it left India at the end of June 1946, it had at least succeeded in convincing the Indian leaders that the Labour Government was in earnest and that "self-government" would indeed mean independence. But that independence would mean partition did not become clear until almost a year later. The Muslim community in British India had enjoyed separate representation since the Morley-Minto Reforms. But it was not until the Lahore Resolution of March 1940 (at a time when the Congress had withdrawn its members from the provincial ministries) that the Muslim League, still angered over its treatment by Congress in forming those ministries after the 1937 elections, formally adopted a policy demanding independence of both the British and the Hindu Raj.

Although the Muslim League would have settled for the Cabinet Mission plan, the compulsory grouping features of which offered an eventual way to achieve an independent Pakistan by secession, Nehru in July 1946 scuttled the last clear hope for a unified, though federal, India. Thereafter, "things came unstuck" in an alarming fashion, aggravated by riots among the religious communities, starting in Bengal and Bihar between Muslims and Hindus and spreading to northwestern India, where the Sikhs became involved. When the London Conference in December 1946 failed to reconcile the parties, Attlee decided to send out a new Viceroy, Lord Louis Mountbatten, who announced upon his arrival in March 1947 that he would be the last Viceroy, and that independence would be conferred by June 1948. Ten weeks later, on June 3, 1947, the Government in London announced its acceptance of a plan drafted by V. P. Menon, Mountbatten's Constitutional Adviser, and endorsed by the Viceroy, the Congress, the Muslim League, and Sikh leaders. The Menon Plan meant partition. On June 4, Mountbatten suggested that independence might be conferred as early as August 15, 1947, allowing only ten additional weeks to make all constitutional and administrative arrangements, including a division of assets, records, military and civil service personnel and equipment, and the drawing of boundaries in the Punjab and Bengal-Assam. The boundaries would be drawn by a Partition *Commission,* the remainder of the work would be done by committees under the supervision of a Partition *Council.*

Unfortunately, the work of the Partition Commission had to await decisions on the part of the legislative assemblies of the Punjab and Bengal that they wanted their provinces to be divided. By the time those decisions were reached, and two separate Boundary Commissions, one for each province, had been constituted, it was June 30. Sir Cyril Radcliffe, the British jurist who headed both provincial Boundary Commissions and the Partition Commission, did not arrive in Delhi until July 8. Even then, formal proceedings had to await the enactment of the Indian Independence Bill by Parliament and

3

its signing by the King on July 18. Thus less than one month remained before the dates fixed for the transfer of power. Whether the Boundary Awards were actually ready by August 10 or not until August 14 is a matter of dispute, but there is no question that they were not made public until August 17, two days *after* Independence, thus aggravating the confusion, hardship, and loss of life among service personnel and communal refugees trying to find their way to their coreligionists in India or Pakistan. Although the exact numbers will never be known, the minimal estimates are that 200,000 or 300,000 people were killed in a migration that eventually involved at least ten million persons in the Indus Basin and perhaps another half million in Bengal. Hundreds of thousands were wounded or maimed for life, and an incalculable number of infants and children were lost or abandoned. The trauma of Partition has left an ineradicable mark not only on Indo-Pakistani relations but upon the lives and feelings of millions of Indians and Pakistanis.

On the face of it, it would certainly seem that Partition could have been accomplished in a less hasty and less violent manner; that the boundaries could have been drawn more carefully had six months been allowed instead of six weeks; that the Boundary Awards could have been published before, rather than after, Independence was proclaimed; that the Indian Army and Civil Service could have been separated into Hindu-Sikh and Muslim elements before rather than during the transfer of power; that sufficient safeguards for the transfer of populations could have been organized; that in particular the Punjab Boundary Force, in size and disposition, could have been less inadequate for its monumental task; and that the transfer of power and population might have been made during the autumn or spring fallow period rather than in the heat, rain, and mud of late summer, with the untended crops going to waste in the fields.

The defenders of those responsible argue that mayhem was inevitable; that delay would only have made it worse; that it was unbearably hot in Delhi and Lahore while the Boundary Commission worked (it always is when the monsoon is late, as it was that year); that the Congress leaders would have preferred jail or mutiny to postponement (but did they require acceleration?); that the communal mood by then was one of revenge, not rapprochement; and even that some extremist Sikh leaders welcomed the bloody migration of their people

4

from the West Punjab, with its accompanying attrition, as a means of consolidating the faithful in a single region of India where their political strength would be enhanced, while the martyrdom of some served as a reaffirmation of Sikh particularism.

In any event, as Partition was carried out, neither the Boundary Awards of the Partition Commission nor the decisions of the Partition Council and its Arbitral Tribunal, which dealt with the division of the assets and equipment of British India between the new nations, could settle all the initial and potential disputes between India and Pakistan. Lack of time was a major factor, but another was that both the Partition Commission and the Partition Council were dealing only with British India. The Princely States, which had never been absorbed into British territory and whose relations with the Crown and the Viceroy were governed by direct treaties, could not be assigned to either India or Pakistan in this fashion. In legal theory, the paramountcy of the Crown would lapse with Independence, and each state would be free to join India or Pakistan or to remain aloof as it saw fit. In fact, most of the rulers were persuaded by Lord Mountbatten to accede to one dominion or the other by August 15.

But three states did remain aloof: Hyderabad, in south central India; Junagadh, on the Kathiawar coast between Karachi and Bombay; and Kashmir. Junagadh, a tiny state with a Hindu majority and a Muslim ruler, attempted to accede to Pakistan and the accession was accepted despite the lack of a common border; but Junagadh was occupied by Indian forces in September 1947, and the accession was reversed. Hyderabad, a huge state with a Hindu majority but a politically dominant Muslim minority and a Muslim ruler, attempted to remain independent; but Hyderabad was occupied by Indian forces in the "police action" of September 1948.

Kashmir, of course, had a Muslim majority and a Hindu ruler. The Maharaja delayed his decision until October 1947, when, faced in the area around Poonch with a rebellion of Muslims, who quickly received the support of volunteer tribesmen from northwestern Pakistan, he acceded to India. Indian forces were flown into Srinagar and proceeded to push the rebels and their allies out of the Vale of Kashmir. By the late spring of 1948, Pakistani forces had been formally committed to the defense of what had been proclaimed as "Azad," or Free, Kashmir, with results that are only too well known.

The cease-fire line proposed by the United Nations in August 1948 was finally accepted by both India and Pakistan in December of that year. But Pakistan did not withdraw her forces from Azad Kashmir as called for in the August UN resolution, thus giving India an excuse for refusing to proceed with the plebiscite envisaged by that resolution and the further resolution of January 1949.

For almost seventeen years, apart from occasional skirmishes, Indian and Pakistani forces faced each other across the UN-patrolled cease-fire line, which became in effect an unofficial and unrecognized extension of the Indo-Pakistan border from a point midway between the Chenab and Jhelum rivers to a point in Ladakh beyond the Shyok tributary of the Indus (see Map 1). In the fall of 1962, Chinese forces occupied portions of eastern Ladakh, pushing the Indians out of areas which they claim are a part of Kashmir and hence of India. In 1963–64, Pakistan and China agreed upon and demarcated a boundary in northern Kashmir as far as the Karakorum Pass, despite Indian claims that Pakistan was surrendering part of Indian territory. Then, in August 1965, Azad Kashmiris and Pakistan "irregulars" again crossed the line, followed in September by Indian and Pakistani troops, who ignored both the cease-fire line in Jammu-Kashmir and the international border (Partition Line) between the Ravi and Sutlej rivers. Other incursions occurred far to the south, across the accepted and demarcated boundary between Indian Rajasthan and the old Sind province of West Pakistan. Pursuant to the Tashkent agreement of January 1966, both the international boundary and the Kashmir cease-fire line were restored by the end of February, but the Kashmir Dispute still appears to be a long way from solution. We shall have to refer to it frequently in the course of this study.

A second major dispute related to the waters of the Ravi and Sutlej rivers. The international border devised by the Punjab Boundary Commission (see Chapter 5 and Maps 4 and 5) ran, with minor exceptions, along the Ujh tributary of the Ravi and the Ravi itself, then across the Bari Doab to the Sutlej above Ferozepore, and then, with more significant exceptions, down the Sutlej to a point just above the Suleimanke headworks. (With the accession of Bahawalpur and Khairpur to Pakistan, the borders of these states and that of the province of Sind became the international boundary from Suleimanke down to the Rann of Cutch.) Thus India was left with the upper course of the Sutlej and the entire course of its Beas affluent. India received the upper Ravi and the headwaters of the Chenab; to India also went the Ferozepore headworks on the Sutlej and the Madhopur headworks on the Ravi, both of which served canals leading into Pakistan.

With the occupation of southeastern Jammu-Kashmir, India obtained control of both sides of the Ravi in the reaches where it formed the boundary between the pre-Partition Punjab Province and the Punjab Hill States, to the south, and Jammu-Kashmir to the north. India also attained control of the Chenab through Jammu-Kashmir to the cease-fire line above the Marala headworks. Because the Jhelum rises inside Kashmir, India's occupation of the Vale gave her control of the Jhelum's headwaters and its course through Lake Wular down to a point beyond Uri. Finally, in Ladakh, India acquired the head reaches of the Indus itself from the point where it crosses the disputed Tibetan border to a point near Kargil where it flows into Azad Kashmir. By occupying Azad Kashmir and the Gilgit Agency, however, Pakistan secured both the remainder of the Indus' course and the vital reach of the Jhelum leading to the Mangla headworks.

Thus the combination of the Partition boundary and the Kashmir cease-fire line, one de jure and the other de facto, gave India control of the headwaters of the Indus and four of its Punjab tributaries, plus the entire course of the Beas. The situation produced by the Partition Line in itself was enough to cause trouble. Radcliffe realized this and had made an attempt, before he drew that line, to get India and Pakistan to agree to provide for continued operation of the irrigation system of the Punjab as a unit (see Chapter 5). But he was rebuffed and had to content himself with expressing, in the Boundary Award, the hope that some arrangement would be made for joint control. There is internal evidence in the published Punjab Boundary Award that Radcliffe took the irrigation system into consideration, but that communal majority considerations and the desire to leave some canal-irrigated lands to the Sikhs, who bore the brunt of Partition, prevailed. At any rate, although some possible alternatives are discussed in Chapter 5, no conceivable boundary line based on communal majorities could have avoided bisecting the irrigation system and leaving some areas in the West Punjab (Pakistan) de-

7

pendent on headworks in the East Punjab (India). A "Standstill Agreement" for maintaining the pre-Partition allocation of water to West Pakistan was actually signed in December 1947, but it expired on March 31, 1948, the same day on which the Arbitral Tribunal went out of existence. The next day, April 1, 1948, India cut off supplies on the canals leading into West Pakistan. Had the Arbitral Tribunal continued in existence, the dispute over canal waters could have been referred to it. As it was, it evolved into a dispute over all of the water in all of the Indus Rivers, and required twelve years and the good offices of the World Bank before it was settled by the Indus Waters Treaty of 1960.

The Jammu-Kashmir situation enormously complicated the problem of the waters dispute by giving India control over the Chenab and Jhelum rivers, which furnish no irrigation in India and very little in Jammu-Kashmir, but upon which the West Punjab and indeed all of West Pakistan are heavily dependent. Pakistan must have realized this from the start, and it may not be entirely a coincidence that the formal commitment of Pakistani forces to the Kashmir struggle came in May 1948, the month after India had cut off supplies from Madhopur and Ferozepore. Of course, many other factors played a part, but the timing is suggestive of the degree to which the Kashmir Dispute and the Indus Waters Dispute were intertwined.

When the Indus Waters Treaty was signed, hopes were expressed that a Kashmir settlement might soon be reached in the new climate of cooperation. Such hopes unfortunately proved unfounded, basically because of the essential difference between the two disputes. In agreeing to recognize Pakistan's right in perpetuity to virtually all of the waters of the three western rivers (Indus, Jhelum, and Chenab), India was really giving away only one stream, the Chenab, that she could really use herself (by diversion into the Ravi or Beas). She was gaining undisputed possession of the waters of the three eastern rivers (Ravi, Beas, and Sutlej) in perpetuity after the Transition Period ends in 1970 or at the latest in 1973. These are the rivers that are really useful to India, and the Indus Waters Treaty gives her the right to dry them up entirely if she so chooses.

The Treaty deals only with water, and it was studiously worded to avoid sanctioning either nation's claim to Kashmir or any portion thereof. Even in the accompanying Indus Basin Development Fund

Agreement (see Chapter 6), to which India is *not* a party, Pakistan's
Mangla Dam on the Jhelum, which extends into Azad Kashmir, is
not mentioned by name. The Kashmir Dispute, on the other hand,
is a dispute over territory and essentially over the population of
that territory. It is a highly emotional dispute, colored not only by
centuries of Hindu-Muslim rivalry in the subcontinent but by mem-
ories of the atrocities perpetrated by Hindus, Muslims, and Sikhs at
the time of Partition as well as by the fighting in Jammu-Kashmir
in 1948 and 1965. In contrast to the Indus Waters Treaty negotiations, which aside from occasional press releases were conducted
in secrecy and the record of which is still confidential, the positions
of India and Pakistan with respect to Kashmir have been the subject
of publicity and propaganda for eighteen years. The waters dispute
left room for maneuver. It represented an area where the expertise
of engineers and the ingenuity of lawyers and statesmen could be
coupled with the incentives of international financing to produce a
settlement.

The Kashmir Dispute, at least at the time of writing, seems to have
congealed into fixed positions with no room for maneuver. This is
especially true in the respective positions over the plebiscite from
which neither party can retreat without enormous loss of face. In
theory, the Kashmir Dispute might be resolved in the same way the
Muslim-Hindu dispute was solved in 1947, by partition along communal majority lines. Such a partition would give Pakistan the Vale
of Kashmir and the western areas and leave India in possession of
most of Jammu and Ladakh. Such a partition would have little
effect upon the Indus Waters Treaty arrangements. In fact it might
even lead to development of the Dhiangarh dam site on the Chenab,
which is now barred to Pakistan by the Kashmir cease-fire line although nearly all of the water is hers. The engineers of both countries
are perfectly capable of working out a Dhiangarh project that would
include the enhanced supplies for the Jammu area envisaged by the
Treaty (see Chapter 6). But it would have to be predicated on a
general Kashmir settlement, which is turn would have to be predicated on mutual trust, the quality most conspicuously absent in
Indo-Pakistani relations.

The Indus Waters Treaty itself, of course, is based on mutual
trust, and it is worth noting that although both the Kashmir cease-

fire line and the international boundary or Partition Line were repeatedly violated in September 1965, neither nation took this opportunity to denounce the Treaty. Nor were there any direct attacks on irrigation facilities, despite—or perhaps because of—the extreme and increasing vulnerability of both countries in this respect. The destruction of the Bhakra Dam or the Sukkur Barrage would be a far greater catastrophe to India or Pakistan than the casualties suffered in the "September War." The fact that the Treaty, and the irrigation works, survived this crucial test is evidence of their mutual value to each nation.

But it must be said that, in a paradoxical manner, the Treaty is also an example of mutual distrust. For the negotiations, suggested by David E. Lilienthal in 1951, and begun with the good offices of the World Bank in 1952, were initially directed to achieving a reintegration of the Indus Basin irrigation system. By 1954 it had become apparent that neither party trusted the other sufficiently to construct and operate an integrated system. At this impasse, both parties asked the Bank to make a recommendation, and the Bank suggested the partition of the waters. That India accepted almost immediately is further evidence that the western rivers are geographically of little use to her even if she remains in Kashmir. But it took six more years to convince Pakistan that, especially without the Kashmir courses of the Jhelum and Chenab, the three western rivers could satisfy her needs. And then she agreed to the plan only after storage facilities on the Jhelum and Indus had been incorporated and arrangements had been made with the World Bank and six "friendly Governments" to underwrite the cost of the "replacement works" plus some "development" features for Pakistan (and a dam on the Beas for India).

The purpose of the Indus Waters Treaty of 1960 is not to restore the regional economic unity of the Indus Basin nor even to reintegrate the irrigation system. On the contrary, it envisages the permanent division of both the Basin and the system: the Treaty and the accompanying financial arrangements contemplate the construction of two integrated irrigation systems where one previously existed. In so doing, they confirm the economic division between Pakistan and India, and the rupture of the infrastructure of communications, transportation, trade, and finance. By the time the works of the

Indus Basin Project in West Pakistan and the initial structures of the Bhakra-Beas-Rajasthan Project in India are completed, around 1980, the partition of the Indus Basin will be impressed upon the landscape in concrete, crushed rock, rolled earth, and brick canal linings—structures as indelible as the Great Wall of China. It may be admitted that this partition of the Basin, like the partition of the subcontinent itself, is economically costly and theoretically indefensible, but it is here to stay, barring the conquest of the entire subcontinental portion of the Basin by one of the parties or by an outside power.

The Scope of This Study

To the geographer as well as to the historian, the Partition of 1947 and the Indus Waters Treaty of 1960 represent bench marks in the political and economic development of the Indus Basin. And the irrigation system itself provides a unique framework within which to trace and analyze the regional evolution. For if modern geography can be defined as the analysis of man's interaction with his physical environment, in time and in space, then the analysis of the evolution of irrigation and of an irrigation-based infrastructure in the Indus Basin furnishes an ideal field of endeavor for the economic or regional geographer. Irrigation is one of the best examples of how man has been able simultaneously to adapt to and modify an initially hostile environment. The study of its modern evolution in the Indus Basin provides a case-book example of the interaction of man and nature over time in an environment that has been radically metamorphosed over the short period of little more than one century.

As in most subhumid regions of the earth, water in the Indus Basin is more valuable than land. Had it not been for the modern irrigation network developed after the annexation of Sind and the Punjab to British India in the 1840s, much of what is now the economic heart of West Pakistan would have remained essentially a semidesert. True, there were many inundation canals serving floodplain areas along the major streams and permitting the cultivation of one crop of wheat or even rice per year. There were also areas in the foothills and on the Potwar Plateau north of the Jhelum that received, in most years, enough rainfall for one sparse crop of wheat, sorghum, millet, pulses, or oilseeds. But the *doabs,* or areas between the rivers, were inhabited only by pastoralists or bandits, and the desert margins east and west of the Indus were practically devoid of habitation.

Without the modern irrigation system inaugurated by the British in the nineteenth century, there would have been scarcely twenty million persons in West Pakistan by the time of the Partition, instead of the thirty-five million in 1947 or the nearly fifty million today. Karachi would have remained what it was in 1843, an overgrown fishing village. Without irrigation, Hyderabad, Multan, and even Lahore could hardly have grown much larger than they were a century ago, and Lyallpur and Montgomery would never have been called into existence. The British would have improved the Grand Trunk Road from Delhi to Peshawar for the same strategic, administrative, and commercial reasons that led the Moguls to lay it out originally, and a railway might have followed for the same reasons. But there would have been little point in connecting Karachi to Multan and Lahore, or in building the railways and highways that laced the doabs after the Canal Colonies were started. The Punjab would never have become the granary of northern India, nor could rice, sugarcane, and cotton production have been developed to their present proportions.

Without the irrigation system, the problem of partition would have been much simpler even in communal terms. The Sikhs would never have had a reason to leave their homelands to migrate to Sargodha, Lyallpur, Montgomery, and Multan and to take up new lands in the Canal Colonies. Except for the Sikhs around Lahore and Sheikhupura, the Muslim predominance in West Punjab would have been even greater, within a much smaller total population, than Sir Cyril Radcliffe found it. The Partition Line might have been drawn very much as it was in 1947, but the exodus from West Pakistan would have been much reduced. With less communal intermixture and with less of the economic jealousy that underlay much of the communal strife, the Punjab massacres before and immediately after Partition might have been avoided. No waters dispute would have ensued, because without the modern irrigation system the value of water would have been minimal and the prospect of diverting the flows nonexistent.

So it is not too much to say that modern irrigation provided the framework around which both West Pakistan and those portions of the Indian Punjab west of the Beas and south of the Sutlej, together with northern Rajasthan, grew to their present economic importance. Each new canal was followed by a migration, by the foundation of new towns, including the *mandi,* or market towns, deliberately spaced along the roads and railways to serve an irrigated hinterland, and by the development of a modern infrastructure of transportation and trade. Although the nineteenth-century projects in the Punjab and Sind were isolated schemes, from 1901 onward efforts were concerted to integrate the system both within and between the provinces. By 1947 a functioning economy had come into being based essentially on the integrated operation of the irrigation system. And by 1947 a master plan had been devised and initialed by the Chief Engineers of Punjab and Sind, the implementation of which would have led to an enlarged coordinated network ranging all the way from the rim stations at the foothills to the Arabian Sea, and served by a major storage dam on the Sutlej (see Chapter 4). For better or for worse, Partition wrecked that plan and destroyed that unity, partly by cutting off border villages from their market towns, roads, and railways, but more fundamentally by producing a disruption in the supplies of grain, sugar, and cotton moving from the Canal Colonies to what had become the East Punjab, and of water supplies flowing from India into West Pakistan. In the sense that water is more valuable than land, Pakistan had the greater problem, and the early link canals (see Chapter 6) were its inadequate response. But India, deprived of the West Punjab granary, had to turn to the nonperennial irrigated areas south of the Sutlej and to the desert margins of Rajasthan in the attempt to replace the lost crop acreage. Thus each country was forced to devise a fundamental reordering of the irrigation system in the attempt not only to compensate for the effects of Partition but to cope with a staggering population growth, which even by 1947 had begun to limit the ability of the *undivided* Punjab to provide food and fiber surplusses *beyond* its borders. For these reasons, a study of the regional effects of Partition must be focused upon the Punjab but can neglect neither the adjoining regions of Sind and Rajasthan nor the larger questions of national developmental policies.

In modern geographical theory, a *region* is no longer regarded as an absolute entity but as a conceptual tool. A region may be defined to suit the purposes of the investigator, generally in terms of one or more variables that remain nearly constant throughout its areal extent. Few geographers would question that, in terms of physical features, the Indus Basin below the rim stations, where the streams emerge from the foothills onto the Indus Plains, comes as close to an ideal geographical region as any area of comparable size in the world. As we shall see in Chapter 2, the virtual absence of intervening hills, the minimal amount of local relief due to erosion, the nearly constant slope toward the sea, and the very slight gradations in climatic and vegetative patterns over the Indus Plains make them an almost homogeneous region for agricultural purposes and for the development of an economy based primarily upon irrigation agriculture. The pattern and regime (seasonal rise and fall) of the rivers themselves, combined with the pattern of the landforms they have created, served to suggest irrigation agriculture to men in the Basin for five thousand years or more. The form of this irrigation depended, of course, on the technology available, but the same technology could be applied from one end of the Indus Plains to the other.

Thus the Indus Plains offered to man a set of nearly homogeneous physical geographic conditions that eventually allowed him to develop there the largest contiguous irrigation system in the world. For this development, three things were essential: political control of most or all of the Basin; a technology sufficiently advanced to cope with the magnitudes involved; and a population large enough to construct, operate, and maintain the works, to cultivate the fields, and to provide a market for the produce. All of these prerequisites were achieved by 1850 when the British, having annexed Sind and the Punjab and concluded treaty arrangements with the neighboring Princely States, began to consider how the abundant water of the rivers could be applied to the "Crown Waste Lands" to produce food for the famine-prone areas of northern India and fiber for mills from Multan to Manchester. At the same period, the engineering technology developed in England's Industrial Revolution provided inspiration for the design and construction of canals having a capacity and length previously inconceivable in India or anywhere else in the world. The translation of this technology from the navigation canals of England to the irrigation canals of the subcontinent could not be literal. Particularly in the field of hydraulics much had to be learned by experiment and by experience. Costly mistakes were made, but the lessons were learned and a new science took shape.

In the realm of administration, too, new arrangements had to be developed for routing canals from British-controlled headworks through the territory of Princely States and back again, and for assigning water rights. An elaborate system of fiscal administration had to be devised, from the initial estimating of costs and revenues needed to obtain sanction for public works through the assessment and collection of water dues. Methods for recruiting, settling, and succoring colonists had to be developed for the Canal Colonies established when water was brought to the wastelands. But by the start of this century, irrigation of the Crown Waste Lands had proved to be a financial success, and engineering technology had reached a point where water could be shunted almost at will across the breadth of the doabs. At the same time it had become apparent that there were limits to the bounty of nature, and that there might not be sufficient water to allow the engineers and colonizers to do everything they had in mind. The primary consideration again became a political one: which districts, provinces, and states ought to benefit from what water there was? The solution embodied in the Triple Canals Project of 1905–15 paved the way for the Sutlej Valley Project of the 1920s. By that time, new materials and new techniques, combined with the potential shortage of water, had resulted in plans for the first storage dam in the Indus Basin at Bhakra. But water disputes between the provinces of Sind and Punjab delayed its construction until after Partition, and then it served quite different areas and purposes. By 1947, however, a vast new project on the lower Indus, at Sukkur, had become a reality, designed to serve an area larger than that of any other single irrigation command in the world.

Meanwhile, the inevitable and insidious companion of any irrigation network constructed without a drainage system had risen to threaten both the Punjab and Sind. In some years, waterlogging and salinization removed more land from cultivation than was added. Again, new technology seemed to offer the answer in the form of deep tubewells (driven wells lined with pipe "tubes" and fitted with pumps) that would not only lower the water table but provide additional supplies of fresh groundwater for leaching out the salts and increasing allocations to crops. But the cost was great, and new problems of well deterioration arose to confront the engineers and planners. Thus the architects of irrigation development in the Indus Basil once again found themselves on the frontier of technology with little or no experience elsewhere to guide them.

The history of irrigation technology as well as of irrigation development in the Indus Basin is a vital aspect of this study. Meaningful consideration of the effects of Partition and of the Indus Waters Treaty cannot be divorced from a consideration of what went before. The arguments and data of the Treaty negotiators were in many respects the same as those used in the Sind-Punjab disputes. The engineering solutions that made an agreement possible were modeled on those employed in the Triple Canals Project. The authors of the Treaty, and the planners and engineers who are now implementing it in Lahore and Chandigarh, Rawalpindi and Delhi, Mangla and Pong, are not writing on a blank surface. Their task is to incorporate what exists, most of which was designed for a unified Basin, into two expanded networks that will serve its parts as efficiently as possible within the existing political framework (and to make such allowances as they can for any future change in Kashmir).

Political boundaries have always set limits to the work of irrigation engineers and administrative planners, just as physical geographic considerations have. From 1849 to 1947, the men working in the Indus Basin had an incomparable field of operations encompassing a minimum of physical and political obstacles. Nowhere else on earth had nature provided such lavish quantities of water that could be tapped without reservoir storage for gravity distribution. At no other period in history was such an area subject to the political control of a power that could develop and bring to bear the advanced technology and the financial resources necessary to place over 35 million contiguous acres of cultivable land under canal command, of which 26 million acres were annually irrigated at the time of Partition.

What has changed since 1947 is that the sphere of planning, and hence the number of alternatives available within the natural limitations, has been reduced. Yet the goal remains the same: to make the most of the water at hand within the territory available. Prior to

Partition, intraregional boundaries and interests gave way, often slowly, often reluctantly, but almost invariably, to the broader interests of the subcontinental portion of the Basin as a whole. Since Partition, not only has the sphere of planning and operations been reduced for the engineers, but there has also been a reassertion of intraregional claims and interests at the administrative level. Thus, at the same time that new techniques have emerged to enlarge the possibilities for development, new political boundaries and pressures have come forth to restrict it.

In studying the Indus Plains irrigation system and its role in regional development, we cannot neglect either changes in technology or changes in political power. Nor would we want to. So many interwoven themes, illustrating the interaction of modern man with his ageless environment, make this a fascinating study in historical geography, reaching far back into the past and looking ahead to the foreseeable future—to the completion of the Indus Basin Project and the Bhakra-Beas-Rajasthan Project and beyond. Yet despite the attractiveness and promise of the subject, some limitations must be imposed. To trace the evolution of the modern irrigation system and of the economic organization it supported and shaped from 1850 to 1947 would itself represent a lifetime's work for any scholar. To measure, in addition, the impact of Partition and of the projects envisaged by the Indus Waters Treaty, which cannot be completed and in operation much before 1980, is indeed an enormous undertaking. But at least a start can be made. Indeed, the opportunity compels the effort, and the attractiveness may excuse the presumption. The Indus Plains need the attention of the geographer and of the historian.

Fortunately, much of the earlier work has been completed, some of it extremely well. The British were fascinated by the Punjab, and few provinces received such excellent historical attention, not only with respect to political and administrative affairs but especially regarding the agricultural-economic history including the development of the Canal Colonies and of the revenue administration that went with it. The decade of the 1920s, which saw the establishment of the Punjab Board of Economic Enquiry, was especially fruitful in these latter respects. Hubert Calvert's studies, *The Wealth and Welfare of the Punjab* (Lahore, 1922), *Agricultural Holdings in the Punjab* (Lahore, 1925), and *Size and Distribution of Agricultural Holdings* (Lahore, 1928) represent pioneering achievements in the collection and analysis of agrarian data. Sir Malcolm Darling's classic *The Punjab Peasant in Prosperity and Debt* (Oxford University Press, 1925), and Hugh K. Trevaskis' equally fine *The Land of the Five Rivers* (Oxford University Press, 1928) provide, respectively, an analysis of the situation and problems of the cultivator and an economic history of the Punjab up to the time (1890) when the first Canal Colonies were being established. Both Darling and Trevaskis had the incomparable advantage of long service in the Indian Civil Service in the Punjab, although their experience did not equip them to deal specifically with the effects of modern irrigation on the agricultural economy. In turn, the irrigation engineers had their own historians in men such as R. B. Buckley, E. B. Bellais, and D. G. Harris, though these men dealt essentially with the technical side of the projects.

The first real attempt to deal with the economic impact of irrigation was made in Paul W. Paustian's *Canal Irrigation in the Punjab* (Columbia University Press, 1930), but Paustian was as much concerned with the fiscal returns of the projects themselves as with their economic impact, and he carried his study only through the Triple Canals Project. With the exception of Rashid Ahmad Malik's excellent study entitled *Irrigation Development and Land Occupance in the Upper Indus Basin* (a doctoral dissertation published by Malik at Indiana University in August 1963), there has been no attempt to trace the interrelations between the irrigation system and the regional economy since Paustian's. And no work at all has attempted to deal specifically with the regional effects, as manifested through the irrigation system, of political changes (i.e. the increasing autonomy in irrigation matters of the provinces after 1919 and 1935, the Sind-Punjab disputes, Partition, and the Indus Waters Treaty) or of new technology applied in recent decades (i.e. the ability to construct mass concrete and rolled-fill dams, the use of link canals, and the employment of tubewells for both drainage and irrigation purposes).

The present book represents an attempt to lay a foundation for such a study, to present the background for an inquiry that should continue for at least two decades. One cannot appreciate what is occurring in the Indus Basin today, or what is likely to occur there by 1980 or by the end of this century, without understanding what has taken place since 1849. But because the period up to about 1930 has already been well covered, only those background features that seem directly relevant to the post-Partition developments will be stressed here. As new projects are completed, and as the statistical services mature, much more will be possible in the way of comparative regional economic analyses. Much that can now only be hinted at in qualitative or descriptive fashion should later become susceptible of quantitative analysis. As the benefits of the new projects become manifest, especially if these benefits are not immediately consumed by a still-burgeoning population, it is to be hoped that more time and effort will be devoted to compiling the raw materials on which a quantitative analysis must be based. Also, as the events of Partition and of the "September War" of 1965 recede still further, and as some modus vivendi is worked out in or around Kashmir, one hopes that freedom of access to places and to information in the Basin will be further enhanced.

Because most of the water, most of the irrigated land, and most of the current projects lie in the Pakistani portion of the Indus Basin, and because the success or failure of the new schemes (including the groundwater program that is almost entirely confined to the Pakistani portion) is relatively more crucial to Pakistan than to India, this initial effort is concerned mainly with that portion of the subcontinent. It is also true that the program for surface water development in the Pakistani portion is currently more definite than that in the Indian portion. By the time the next study appears, however, it should be possible not only to evaluate some of the initial effects of the Indus Basin Project in West Pakistan but to assess the decisions made by India with respect to the proposed Beas-Sutlej Link and the further extension of the Rajasthan Canal.

It is only natural that the focus of our attention falls on the Punjab in the recent past and present, for this is where the Partition Line runs and where most of the works have been or will be constructed. But we cannot limit our consideration thereto in either time or space. The relevant threads run out into the high Himalayas and into the geological past. They run from the Vale of Kashmir to the deserts of Rajasthan and the deltaic lands of Sind. In the words of one of the principal architects of the Indus Waters Treaty (though uttered in an entirely different context), they run "wherever the Indus waters flow."

U. S. S. R.

PAMIR RANGES

AFGHANISTAN

HINDU KUSH

China-Pakistan-1963

KARAKORUM RANGE

Hunza

Tirich Mir

Rakaposhi

K2

Chitral

Gilgit

Karakorum P

Sazin

Bunji

Shigar R.

Khapalu

KOHISTAN RANGES

Skardu

Chilas

Nanga Parbat

LADAKH RANGE

Kunar R.

Swat R.

Rotkai

Darband

L. Wular

Shyok R.

Kabul River

Warsak Dam

Tarbela

Srinagar

Kargil

Leh

Unai Pass

Kabul

Jalalabad
Khyber Pass

Peshawar
Kohat

Attock

Haro R.

Rawalpindi

PIR PANJAL RANGE

ZASKAR RANGE

Zaskar R.

Nyom

SAFED KUH

Soan R.

Dhiangarh
Riasi

Mangla

Chenab R.

Bannu

Kalabagh

Jinnah B.

SALT RANGE

PABBI HILLS

Jammu

Thein

Bhaga R.

Chandra R.

Kurram R.

Jhelum R.

Rasul

Maralab B.

Rohtang Pass

Tank R.

Thal

Doab

Chaj
Doab

Chenab R.

KIRANA HILLS

Rechna
Doab

Ravi R.

Madhopur B.

Qong B.

Doab

Mandi

ShipkiLa

Larji

Gomal R.

Chiniot

Lyallpur

Amritsar

Mandi Plain

Bhakra Dam

Simla

SULEIMAN RANGE

Taunsa B.

Trimmu B.
Shorkot

Bari
Beas

Lahore

Kapurthala

Rupar B.

Harappa

Harike B.

Ferozepore B.

Indus River

Multan

Old bed of

Sutlej R.

Chandigarh

Panjnad Barrage

Old bed of Ghaggar (or Hakra)

Mithankot

Yamuna (Jumna) R.

Delhi

Ganga Gang.

0   100   200   300

Statute Miles

Map 2. *Catchment areas of the Indus Rivers. (Note: The conventional map symbol for a dam has been reversed on this and subsequent maps to indicate a barrage, which is a rather different structure.)*

2. The Indus Rivers and the Indus Plains[1]

Rivers and Mountains

The physical geography of the Indus Basin presents numerous problems of interpretation; its geology even more. Various theories have been advanced to explain the remarkable fact that the Indus rises well to the north of the main range of the Himalayas and flows around it to the northwest, just as the Tsangpo-Brahmaputra, rising very near the Indus, flows around the Himalayas to the southeast. The general alignment of the Indus and Brahmaputra troughs has led to speculation that both rivers were once part of a single trans-Himalayan stream, though where this stream had its sources and how it flowed is still subject to debate. In 1919, both E. H. Pascoe and G. E. Pilgrim, working independently, suggested that at the end of the Tertiary, i.e. before the Himalayas were raised to their present heights, one great trans-Himalayan stream flowed to the northwest while a second master stream paralleled it at the foot of the rising mountains.[2] Helmuth de Terra, writing in 1934, held that the pre-Pleistocene trans-Himalayan drainage was from northwest

1. Portions of this chapter have appeared in *Indus* (Journal of the West Pakistan Water and Power Development Authority, Lahore), *6* (March, 1965), 6–17.
2. For a discussion of the Pascoe and Pilgrim theories, see O. H. K. Spate, *India and Pakistan: A General and Regional Geography* (2nd ed. London, Methuen, 1957), pp. 29–33.

22

to southeast, and dispensed with the need for a sub-Himalayan master stream.[3] Unfortunately, geological research in the Western Himalayas has always been extremely sparse, and virtually nothing has been done since 1940. In Nepal, on the other hand, the Swiss geologist Toni Hagen was able to work almost continuously from 1950 to 1958. He has contributed a consistent and highly persuasive account of the origins of the Eastern Himalayas.[4] Hagen accepts the idea of a trans-Himalayan master stream, but is noncommittal as to its direction.

For our purposes, the most important features of the Himalayan orogeny are that the ranges are among the youngest mountains on earth, that they were raised with (geologically speaking) considerable speed, and that they attained their present elevations only in the Pleistocene period, i.e. within the last one million years. The fundamental cause of the Himalayan orogeny was the southward movement of the ancient hard core of Asia—the Asian Block, or, as some geologists have termed it, after its center in eastern Siberia, the Angaran Shield—toward the South Indian Block. The latter, sometimes called the Deccan Shield, is represented in its northerly portions by the Aravalli Range, which Hagen terms "the oldest mountain range on earth, about 1200 million years old." This southward movement began about seventy million years ago, compressing the sediments of what the nineteenth-century geologist Eduard Suess had named the "Tethys Sea" between the blocks. The central part of the sea was raised up and folded over toward the south to form what Hagen terms the "Tibetan highland rim," later to become the "Tibetan Marginal Mountains" (see Map 2), the northernmost range of the Himalayan system. This range divided the Tethys into a northern "Tibetan Sea" and a southern "Himalayan Sea," becoming the watershed between them. The remarkable thing is that, except for the Tsangpo-Brahmaputra, it is *still* the watershed, for streams

3. Helmuth de Terra, "Physiographic Results of a Recent Survey in Little Tibet [Ladakh]," *Geographical Review, 24* (1934), 12–41.
4. For the detailed report of Hagen's work, see Toni Hagen et al., *Mount Everest* (London, Oxford University Press, 1963). For a more popular account, illustrated with the author's magnificent photographs, see Toni Hagen, *Nepal* (Berne, Kummerly and Frey, 1961). Both studies include excellent diagrams and maps. Unfortunately, no one yet has produced a similar study of the Western Himalayas and Karakorums.

rising south of the Tibetan Marginal Mountains cut through the Main Himalayas, the Lesser Himalayas, and the Siwaliks to reach the Ganges and the sea.[5]

During the pluvial epochs of the next fifty million years, when the Asian monsoonal system may be presumed to have acted more or less as it does today, the erosional effects on the outer slopes of the Tibetan highland rim resulted in the deposition of enormous quantities of sediments in the Himalayan Sea. Then came another push from the north, resulting in the overthrusting of a series of "nappes" (which may for convenience be thought of as waves of rock, frozen just as they break) toward the south. This phase apparently took place over a period from fifteen to seven million years ago, during which the south-flowing rivers were able to maintain their courses across the rising mountains by exploiting ancient zones of weakness where the nappes had been split into sections. Although the Tibetan Marginal Mountains still remained the watershed, the raising of the nappes between them and the sea naturally reduced the force of the monsoonal impact and thereby the quantities of water that flowed from their slopes.[6]

In the final stages, which may have begun as recently as 600,000 years ago (within the Pleistocene period of the great ice ages), the Tibetan basin and the Marginal Mountains were raised simultaneously. The latter achieved approximately their present elevations averaging 20,000 feet, high enough to intercept the full force of the monsoons and to convert the newly formed Tibetan Plateau into a near-desert. With the raising of the Tibetan Plateau, the streams that had drained the Marginal Mountains northward into the Tibetan Sea found their course blocked, and were diverted east or west.[7] Thus, presumably, was formed that trans-Himalayan master stream about which there has been so much speculation. (Possibly, also, the master stream assisted in the drainage of the Tibetan Sea, a task that would have increased its down-cutting power enormously.) Then, as the Main Himalayas were raised to roughly their present heights by the compression of the nappe roots beneath them, the trans-Himalayan master stream was apparently split into two by the

5. Hagen et al., *Mount Everest,* pp. 32–38.
6. Ibid., pp. 39–42.
7. Ibid., p. 43.

creation of the Kailas Range, with each branch forced to detour around the ends of the system in order to reach the sea.

The Main Himalayas at first replaced the Tibetan Marginal Mountains as the recipients of the full force of the monsoon, and the south-flowing streams were able to maintain their courses by down-cutting as the Siwaliks began to arise. But when the Lesser Himalayas (the Mahabharat Range in Nepal) were elevated, less than 200,000 years ago, some of these rivers were ponded back behind them, forming huge lakes. Eventually, the water rose high enough to find outlets to the south (aided, of course, by the work of the truncated rivers cutting back through the Lesser Himalayas), and the lakes were drained, leaving the level basins found today around Katmandu and Pokhara in Nepal. South-flowing streams cutting through the Siwaliks had no difficulty in maintaining their courses because that frontal range was never high enough to shut off precipitation in their source areas. Yet the uplift of the Himalayas, including the Siwaliks, is apparently still continuing, offset by rapid erosion of course, and earthquakes are by no means uncommon as a result.[8]

Thus, thanks mainly to eight years of concentrated effort by Toni Hagen, we have a well-substantiated account of the development of the Eastern Himalayas and of their drainage system. To the north-west, however, much remains to be explained. The main question concerns the course of the upper Indus and of its longest tributary, the Sutlej, for these two rivers rise within 80 miles of each other yet envelop the entire Western Himalayas before they meet near Mithankot, well out on the plains and over 600 air miles to the west. In its course to join the Indus, the Sutlej collects the drainage of all the shorter streams rising in or cutting through the Main Himalayas, including the drainage of the Vale of Kashmir, around Srinagar and Lake Wular, which is an old lake basin very much like the basins in Nepal. (The Beas joins the Sutlej directly; the Jhelum and Ravi join what is called the Chenab, which in turn unites with the Sutlej to form the Panjnad above Mithankot; but we may disregard the local names for the present.) In symmetrical fashion to the east, the Tsangpo-Brahmaputra and the Ganges envelop virtually the entire Eastern Himalayas, and the Ganges collects the

8. Ibid., pp. 65–78.

intervening drainage. And again, the Tsangpo and the Ganges rise within 80 miles of each other and of the sources of the Indus and Sutlej!

To explain this remarkable pattern, we must again direct our attention to the Kailas Range overlooking the twin lakes of Manasarowar and Rakas. For although Mount Kailas (22,028 feet), which lies midway between the world's two highest mountains, Everest (29,028 feet) and K2 in the Karakorams (28,250 feet), is considerably lower than either of them, the Kailas Range forms one of the great water divides of Asia. Northwest of this range, water flows 2,000 miles via the Indus to reach the Arabian Sea. Southeast, drainage via the Tsangpo-Brahmaputra leads over 1,700 miles to the Bay of Bengal. To the southwest, Lakes Manasarowar and Rakas feed the Sutlej, while directly south of the lakes rises the Karnali tributary of the Ghagra and Ganges. Small wonder that Mount Kailas is sacred to Buddhists and Hindus, who regard it as Siva's paradise, walk in pilgrimage around it, and forbid its being climbed.

The Kailas Range thus holds the key to Himalayan drainage, and its elevation in the very recent geological past would explain the symmetry to east and west. A difficulty is presented in the apparent continuity of the Kailas and Ladakh ranges, since the Ladakh Range is now generally accepted as part of the Karakoram system which, with the Hindu Kush, antedates the Himalayas. But Helmuth de Terra, after his reconnaissance in Ladakh, held that the topographical alignment is misleading, and that there is no structural connection between the Ladkh and Kailas ranges. In de Terra's estimation, the Indus above Leh, or for that matter above the confluence of the Gilgit River, has not cut through *any* of the Himalayan ranges. "The peculiar short deflection of its course that takes place east of Nyoma is not a transverse valley but merely a bend following the re-entrant of the Ladakh Range."[9] If de Terra is correct, then the pre-Pleistocene drainage was from northwest to southeast, with the Indus flowing from Gilgit along the base of the Karakoram-Ladakh ranges, and then into the Tsangpo-Brahmaputra north of the Kailas region and of the Tibetan Marginal Mountains. The separation of the systems would, therefore, be assigned to the uplift of the Kailas region during

9. De Terra, p. 40.

26

the very recent Pleistocene, with the Tsangpo shifting its headwaters to the southeastern slopes of the new Kailas range.

An alernative explanation is based on the apparent structural continuity of the Indus-Tsangpo trough between the Main Himalayas on the one hand and the Tibetan Plateau and Kailas-Ladakh-Karakoram ranges on the other.[10] It should be noted that this "structural depression" (the old Ladakh-Lhasa trade route followed it) is now occupied in descending order by the Manasarowar Lakes, the uppermost Sutlej, and the Gartang River, with the Indus coming into it only above Tashigong. In other words, this alternate theory assumes that the pre-Pleistocene Indus-Tsangpo flowed south of Kailas, with subsequent uplift separating the two watersheds. Which, if either, of these explanations is correct can only be determined after intensive field investigations in areas that are now barred to Western scientists (see Map 2).

In any case, there would seem to be little doubt that the present, almost imperceptible watershed between the Ganges and Indus drainage is very recent in origin. Here the key seems to lie in the shifting or migration of stream beds across the alluvium of the plains, and the key role to have been played by the Jumna and a former stream (possibly the legendary Sarasvati) the course of which is now marked by the bed known as the Ghaggar in the Indian Punjab and Rajasthan, and as the Hakra in Pakistan Bahawalpur, that parallels the Sutlej toward the Indus. The enormous amounts of detritus brought down by the Punjab Rivers and the present affluents of the Ganges are more than sufficient to explain stream blockage and shifting without invoking tectonic forces, and capture of one stream by another is well attested. The Beas, for example, was captured by the Sutlej at the end of the eighteenth century. Its old course from near Harike to the Chenab above Panjnad is well marked in the landscape of the southern Pakistan Punjab, with the town of Kasur and a series of villages still lining its "banks." The Ghaggar, which is used in part by modern canals and which has begun to flow again as water tables have risen, may very well represent the former course of such a truncated river. Spate suggests that it could have been fed either by the Sutlej, itself occupying a different channel, or by the Jumna.[11]

10. Spate, p. 31.
11. Ibid.

If it was the Jumna, then the Jumna clearly has been captured by the Ganges.

The Ganges itself has been pushed southward by the detritus brought down by its Himalayan affluents. Similarly, the lower Indus has in places been pushed eastward (away from the site of Mohenjo Daro, for example) by outwash from the Kirthar and Suleiman ranges (see Map 1). Where not so encumbered, the Indus follows the general tendency of rivers in the Northern Hemisphere to work to their right, a tendency believed to be due to the rotation of the earth. The Eastern Nara bed (see Map 3) in the desert of Khairpur and Sind below Sukkur, now used for a canal, may represent an earlier course of the Indus itself, or possibly an extension of the Ghaggar-Hakra toward the sea. But where a river in the process of deepening its bed encounters rock, it usually ceases its lateral movement and expends its effort on down-cutting. The Indus has thus become "fixed" on transverse rock ledges at Hyderabad and Sukkur, where it has cut a short gorge at least 35 feet below its lowest seasonal surface level.

The rivers of the Punjab, on the other hand, once they have left their rim stations in the Siwaliks to emerge onto the plains, generally encounter no such ledges. Only the Chenab is "fixed" at Chiniot where it has cut into the buried ridge of the Kirana Hills, themselves outliers of the Aravalli Range. The other Punjab streams, flowing at gradients of only a foot or so per mile across unconsolidated sediments they themselves have deposited, are free to obey the rule of rivers in the Northern Hemisphere. That is, they tend to undercut their right-hand banks and to leave floodplains behind on the left. Thus, the Chenab has abandoned Multan and the Ravi has abandoned Harrappa and, quite recently, the oldest part of the city of Lahore. The cross sections of the Punjab river valleys, with their high interfluves, old abandoned floodplains, and recent or active floodplains, as well as the existence of abandoned river channels such as those of the Beas and Ghaggar, have had a determining influence on the layout of the canal systems.

To recapitulate, then, we have seen that from a point near Mount Kailas in the central Himalayas, two master streams that apparently were once continuous now drain in opposite directions and pass around the ends of the Main Himalayan Range. Many of their tributaries, however, cut right through the Himalayas, and apparently did so during most of the mountain-building stages. Two great tributaries in particular, the Sutlej and the Ganges, rise within 80 miles of their respective master streams. But before they join them, the tributaries collect the drainage of the entire Himalayan front. Thus, the Indus and Tsangpo-Brahmaputra envelop the north of the Himalayas; any drainage that escapes them passes into the enclosed basins of Tibet with their ephemeral, salty lakes. The Indus also collects the drainage of the Karakorams, and, via its only long right-hand affluent, the Kabul, with *its* Chitral-Kunar tributary, of the Hindu Kush. Beyond the Indus Basin to the north and west, water passes into the enclosed basins of Soviet Central Asia or of Seistan on the Afghan-Iranian border.

Rivers and Plains

The total area of the Indus Basin has recently been computed at 364,700 square miles,[12] which is larger than the area of West Pakistan (310,043 square miles including the interior basins of Baluchistan and the Makran Coast, with its short streams that very occasionally flow into the Arabian Sea) and only slightly less than the combined areas of East and West Pakistan (365,529 square miles). Of the total Basin, some 160,400 square miles lie in the highlands of Tibet, Kashmir, Afghanistan, and West Pakistan. The rest comprises the Indus Plains, one of the most homogeneous physiographic regions on earth. The Indus Plains might be described as a vast example of the piedmont alluvial plains to be found at the foot of the San Bernardino or San Gabriel ranges in southern California. But in size they are closer to the Great Plains from Denver, Colorado, north to the Canadian border and east to St. Louis. Indeed, the Missouri River system in the United States bears many topographic similarities to the Indus system, in addition to being of the same order of magnitude.

The depth of the alluvial deposits is unknown over most of the

12. Harza Engineering Company International, *A Program for Water and Power Development in West Pakistan, 1963–1975, Prepared for Water and Power Development Authority of West Pakistan,* "Supporting Studies—An Appraisal of Resources and Potential Development" (Lahore, September 1963), p. I-7. This study will be cited hereafter merely as "Harza Report."

Indus Basin, but there is good reason to believe that it averages a mile or more. As has already been mentioned, the alluvium was laid down over earlier marine deposits as the land rose and the Tethys and Himalayan seas dried up. Thus, in many areas, the unconsolidated materials capable of holding and transmitting water may be even deeper than one mile. Nevertheless, extensions of the Aravalli Range and its outliers, such as the Kirana Hills, come close to and even protrude above the present surface. Some investigators have assigned to these buried or nearly buried ranges a significant role in impeding the subterranean drainage, but it is doubtful that they have more than a local effect.[13] Indeed, although there are stratigraphic differences in the type of material deposited—that is, although clays, silts, sands, gravels, and various sizes and combinations of these vary in a vertical direction and sometimes form large horizontal lenses—in the broadest sense the Indus Plains may be regarded as one vast and fairly homogeneous aquifer, a sort of vast sponge, capable of absorbing runoff from the foothills as well as rainfall and seepage from the rivers and canals that cross them, and of transmitting this subterranean flow downslope to the Arabian Sea.

The water table or top level of this vast reservoir varies with distance from the foothills and from the rivers and canals, as well as with local alterations in the nature of the matrix, and it varies from season to season and year to year. Recent investigations in the Pakistan Punjab have been sufficiently detailed to allow preparation of contour maps showing depth to water table, and comparisons with older data from wells indicate its general rise since irrigation was introduced.[14] Variations in the salt content of the groundwater have also been charted over much of the Punjab, and similar groundwater surveys are now being carried out along the lower Indus in Sind. The groundwater reservoir apparently represents at least ten times the annual runoff of the Indus Rivers, and in many areas offers an additional source of irrigation water when tapped by tubewells. Con-

13. D. W. Greenman, W. V. Swarzenski, and G. D. Bennett, "The Ground-Water Hydrology of the Punjab, West Pakistan" (West Pakistan Water and Power Development Authority, Water and Soils Investigation Division, Bulletin No. 6) (Lahore, WAPDA, 1963), pp. 34–35; and Zamir-uddin Kidwai, "Geology of Rechna and Chaj Doabs, West Pakistan" (West Pakistan WAPDA, WASID, Bulletin No. 5) (Lahore, WAPDA, n.d.), pp. 24–25.
14. Greenman et al., Maps 11, 12, 16–20.

trol of the water-table level by means of pumping from wells or by drains is also essential to the success of the surface-water irrigation, for in many areas the salt-carrying groundwater has risen perilously close to the surface. These problems and potentialities of groundwater are discussed in Chapter 9. For the present, it is enough to emphasize that we must always conceive the land-water relationships in the Indus Basin in the vertical as well as in the horizontal dimension, and apply this vertical analysis to groundwater as well as to surface flows. But let us now return to consider those surface flows.

Where the Indus is formed, in the shadow of Kailas, it is at an elevation of over 15,000 feet. Where it receives the Gartang, and turns northwest in the "structural trough" mentioned above, it has fallen less than 2,000 feet. Near Leh in Ladakh it crosses the 12,000-foot contour. Southwest of K2, it receives the Shyok and then, at Skardu, the Shigar. Here the Indus is still 1,400 miles from its mouth and 7,500 feet high. Twenty-five miles below Skardu, the Indus enters its 300-mile gorge, in the course of which it falls 6,000 feet for an average gradient of 20 feet per mile. In making this descent, the Indus reaches its northernmost point (35° 51' or virtually the same latitude as K2) at an elevation of about 4,500 feet. After receiving the Gilgit and Astor rivers in the vicinity of Bunji, the Indus turns west just north of Nanga Parbat and continues this trend past Chilas and Sazin. It then describes another "S" around the Kohistan ranges representing the Pir Panjal, or Lesser Himalayas. This brings it to the possible dam site at Kotkai. Then the Indus turns south through the Siwaliks, where it passes the dam sites at Darband and Tarbela. At Tarbela, the Indus has descended to a level of 1,300 feet, but it is still 1,100 miles from its mouth. Although the river has now finished with the Himalayas, it still has the outliers of the Hindu Kush, represented by the Safed Kuh, and the Suleiman and Salt ranges to contend with. These are met and breached in the 100 miles between Attock and Kalabagh.[15] At Attock the Indus receives the Kabul River from the right, and between Attock and Kalabagh the Haro and Soan rivers from the left. Three miles below Kalabagh it meets the first barrage (Jinnah Barrage). The old minimum recorded level at the

15. Historically, Attock has been considered the rim station because the Indus gauge has been maintained there for ninety-five years. But Kalabagh, where the Indus finally emerges onto the plains, is really entitled to the distinction.

Kalabagh gauge (before the barrage covered it) was about 680 feet above sea level. Since the distance from the Jinnah Barrage to the Arabian Sea is about 950 miles, the average gradient of the Indus for approximately the lower half of its entire course is less than 9 inches per mile. From Mithankot, where the Panjnad (combined streams of the Punjab) joins the Indus, the latter has an average gradient of less than 6 inches per mile.

The course of the Sutlej is less complicated than that of the Indus. We have already discussed some of the features of its upper reaches, concerning which there is still no geological certainty.[16] But in general the Sutlej acts as a transverse Himalayan stream, apparently exploiting an ancient fault line in its gorge below Shipki La. This course brings it to the Inner Siwaliks at the Bhakra site (1,200 feet above sea level). But the rim station on the Sutlej is at Rupar, where it cuts through the last of the foothills and emerges onto the plains. From Rupar to Mithankot is a distance of almost 550 river miles, over which the Sutlej falls only 560 feet, making an average gradient of 1 foot per mile.[17]

Between Rupar and Ferozepore, the Sutlej collects the drainage of the Beas. The Beas used to flow all the way to the Chenab above Panjnad, but was captured late in the eighteenth century by the Sutlej near Harike. Thus, the Beas is the shortest of the Punjab Rivers (only 247 miles long) although the contribution it makes is a very respectable one (see Table 1, Catchment Areas and Runoff of the Indus Rivers). The Beas at Mandi Plain (near Kapurthala and not to be confused with Mandi on its Himalayan course) had an average annual runoff of 13 million acre feet between 1922 and 1961, compared to 14 million acre feet for the Sutlej at Rupar and only 7 million acre feet for the Ravi at Madhopur. The Beas rises near the Rohtang Pass at the southeastern end of the Pir Panjal Range. Its headwaters are closely hemmed in by those of the Sutlej to the south and east and of the Ravi and the Chandra tributary of the Chenab to the west and north. In fact, the Chandra narrowly cuts off

16. See above, pp. 25–27, and Spate, p. 33.
17. The Indus Waters Treaty of 1960 (see Appendix I, Article I, "Definitions") defines the Panjnad as part of the Chenab because the Sutlej is awarded to India. For convenience, however, we are treating the Panjnad as a prolongation of the Sutlej. Geographically, either treatment can be justified.

Rivers and Plains

Table 1. Catchment Areas and Runoff of the Indus Rivers[a]

River	Gauging Station	Catchment Area (square miles)	Average Annual Runoff, 1922–61 (million acre feet)
Sutlej	Rupar	18,550	14
Beas	Mandi Plain[b]	6,500	13
Ravi	Madhopur	3,100	7
Chenab	Marala	11,400	26
Jhelum	Mangla	12,900	23
Kabul	Warsak	26,000[c]	17.4[c]
Indus	Attock[d]	102,000	93

a. Source: Harza Report, pp. I-12, IV-6; S. S. Kirmani, "Sediment Problems in the Indus Basin, Part I: Sedimentation in Reservoirs," Proceedings of the West Pakistan Engineering Congress, 43 (Lahore, West Pakistan Engineering Congress, 1959), Paper No. 336, 9.

b. Mandi Plain, west of Kapurthala, is the historic gauging station for the Beas. The rim station is really at Pong, where the catchment area is 4,850 square miles.

c. Figures for the Kabul River (and its Swat tributary, which contributes another 5 million acre feet below Warsak) are included in those for the Indus at Attock.

d. Attock is the historic gauging station. The rim station should really be Kalabagh, where the catchment area is 103,800 square miles.

the Beas from all but the Pin Parbati massif of the Main Himalayas.[18]

The rim station for the Beas may be said to be at Pong, near Talwara (Hoshiarpur District, see Map 7) where the river cuts through the Siwaliks. Construction of a storage dam at Pong, comparable in position to Bhakra, is now under way.

> The drainage area of the river above Pong damsite is about 4,850 square miles, of which [only] 300 square miles is under permanent snow cover in the high Himalayas. The drainage area above Larji [where the Beas begins to cut through the Pir Panjal Range, or Lesser Himalayas] is about 1,830 square miles. . . .
>
> In the [Beas] river basin above Larji there is little evidence of large or frequent floods. . . . The streams appear to be fed largely by snowmelt runoff from the higher elevations. . . . It

18. The two streams pass within 6 linear miles; a diversion dam and tunnel were proposed prior to the signing of the Indus Waters Treaty (see Chapters 6 and 7). Now India has given up this scheme in favor of a 24-mile link, involving two tunnels, between the Beas at Pandoh, at the end of its gorge through the Lesser Himalayas, and the Sutlej.

appears that the major flood-producing area lies on the north
side of the Beas River from Pong damsite easterly to the vicinity
of Jogindar Nagar, an area which comprises about one-half the
total length of the watershed. Also, it appears that the rain-fed
runoff from the drainage area lying in the high country east of
the river from Manali to Larji is a minor part of the total runoff at Pong.[19]

The fact that the Beas draws, from a relatively small catchment
area practically limited to the Lesser Himalayas and Siwaliks, a
runoff almost as great as that which the Sutlej collects all the way
from Lake Manasarowar, is indicative of the impact of the monsoon
on the front ranges.

Like the Beas, the Ravi does not penetrate the Main Himalayas.
In fact, its catchment area is limited to the southwestern slopes of the
Pir Panjal Range (Lesser Himalayas), and it is also closely circumscribed by the Chandra-Chenab. Thus, its runoff at the rim station,
Madhopur, is only half that of the Beas or Sutlej, and it is also the
most seasonal of the Punjab Rivers. One perennial irrigation scheme,
the Upper Bari Doab Canal, sufficed to dry up its middle course until
it was linked with the Chenab. A storage dam at Thein, 13 miles above
Madhopur, is now being considered by India. Compared to the Beas,
the Ravi has a long course, traveling 435 miles from Madhopur to its
junction with the Chenab above Multan. Over this course, it falls
almost exactly 1 foot per mile.

The two remaining Punjab Rivers, Chenab and Jhelum, have certain similarities. At their rim stations, Marala and Mangla respectively, their average annual runoff (26 and 23 million acre feet respectively over the period 1922–61) is roughly the same. Their lengths
differ, 600 miles for the Chenab and 450 for the Jhelum, but their
courses have an interesting parallelism. Both drain the Main Himalayas to the northwest, as does the Indus, then turn south, west, south
again, and finally southwest from the rim stations until they converge
at Trimmu. When the geology of the Pir Panjal Range is fully understood, it may be determined that the upper Chenab once flowed into

19. Bureau of Reclamation, United States Department of the Interior, *Evaluation of Engineering and Economic Feasibility, Beas and Rajasthan Projects,
Northern India*, Report Prepared by the United States Department of the Interior, Bureau of Reclamation, for AID, Agency for International Development,
Department of State, U.S.A. (Washington, D.C., July 1963), pp. 152–53.

the upper Jhelum. As it is, the Chenab now flows through Jammu, and the Jhelum rises inside the Vale of Kashmir. The sources of the Chenab are the Chandra, which as we have seen cuts into but not through the Main Himalayas, and the Bhaga, which has a similar course. Drainage beyond the Chenab sources is either to the Sutlej or to the Indus.

The Chenab and the Jhelum each offers a dam site within Jammu-Kashmir. The Chenab site at Dhiangarh, north of Riasi, would be of some value to Pakistan. Use of the site on the Jhelum, where it leaves Lake Wular and cuts through the Pir Panjal Range, might involve flooding much of the Vale. Lack of a well-defined reservoir also inhibits damming the Chenab at Chiniot, where it cuts through the Kirana Hills (see page 28). But the course of the Jhelum through the zone where the Salt Range meets the Siwaliks offers a good dam site, at Mangla, which is now being developed by Pakistan under the Indus Basin Project (see Map 3). The Mangla Dam, located at the rim station, includes the Kishanganga and Kunhar tributaries of the Jhelum in its storage.[20]

Aside from the five rivers of the Punjab, the Indus has only one other major affluent. This is the Kabul River which, rising in the 10,000-foot Unai Pass of the southern Hindu Kush, drains eastern Afghanistan over the fractured edge of the Iranian Plateau and into the Indus at Attock. Where it crosses the Afghan-Pakistan boundary, just north of the Khyber Pass, the Kabul has drained an area of some 26,000 square miles.[21] It should be noted, however, that much of this catchment area is in Pakistan, for the Chitral River, which rises northeast of Tirich Mir (25,230 feet, the highest peak of the Hindu Kush) flows for some 200 miles in Pakistan before it crosses into Afghanistan and, under the name Kunar, joins the Kabul below Jalalabad. Again, between the Afghan border and Attock, the Kabul receives the Swat, which itself drains some 9,000 square miles[22] and provides almost one-fourth of the 23.1 million acre feet which the

20. No mention is made here of the possibilities for tributary or off-channel storages, which are discussed in Chapters 6 and 7. The principal sites include several on the Haro and Soan tributaries of the Indus, one at Rohtas on the Kahan tributary of the Jhelum beow Mangla, and one each on the Monawar Tavi and Jammu Tavi affluents of the Chenab above Marala (on the unlikely assumption that Jammu becomes Pakistani territory).
21. Harza Report, p. IV-6.
22. Ibid.

Kabul contributes to the Indus at Attock. It should be noted, however, that the Kabul's contribution is as great as that of the Jhelum,
and far greater than that of any other Indus tributary except the
Chenab (see Table 1).

The other right-hand affluents of the Indus (Kohat, Kurram, Tank,
Gomal, etc.) make minor contributions. In fact, the streams draining
the "Sibi reentrant," where the plains extend northward between the
Suleiman and Kirthar ranges toward the Bolan Pass, do not even
reach the Indus. Thus it may be said that for the 625 miles from
Mithankot to the sea, the Indus is in effect an "exotic" stream like the
Nile below the Atbara juncture, i.e. it has no perennial tributaries
and flows across a region where it could not maintain itself were
it not for the vast contributions received upstream.

The Indus Plains

Although the whole of the Indus Basin below the rim stations is
topographically quite homogeneous, with only the Kirana Hills and
the limestone ridges at Sukkur and Hyderabad to interrupt the flow
of the rivers, there is nevertheless a real distinction to be made between the lower, "Nilotic," course of the Indus and the divided regions of the doabs upstream. Some have suggested that the fundamental difference lies in the fact that from Mithankot to the sea the
Indus flows, for the most part, between natural levees and thus has
raised itself above the general level of its floodplain. But this characteristic of the lower Indus is foreshadowed in sections of each of
the tributaries, and even along stretches of the Indus itself between
Kalabagh and Mithankot. Natural levees are characteristic of all "mature" or aggrading streams, and so are found on all of the Indus
Rivers below the rim stations in certain reaches. Thus each of the
Punjab streams foretells, in its own course, the pattern of the lower
Indus with its braided channel, meanders, cutoffs, and abandoned
channels. Indeed, the formation of natural levees probably provided
the inspiration for the earliest irrigation works at Harappa on the
Ravi as well as at Mohenjo Daro on the Indus, as well as for much
more recent works on the Sutlej, Jhelum, and Chenab.

So perhaps it would be preferable to say that the course of the
lower Indus is physically distinguished first by the exotic character

of the stream and second by the predominance of natural levees, now supplemented by artificial bunds built and maintained at considerable cost along a line sufficiently removed from the natural levees of the principal low-water channel(s) to provide a reasonable hope of containing the river in flood. In winter, the lower Indus may appear less like a river than a series of pools, each from 1,000 to 4,000 feet wide and several miles in length, connected by channels only 4 to 6 feet deep over the intervening bars. But the Indus rises rapidly in spring, and by summer, when the monsoon arrives to reinforce the snow-melt, it may be several miles wide and retained only by the bunds. After the British annexation of Sind in 1843 (see Chapter 4) flood-control measures received far more attention than irrigation works, and by the turn of the century the 330-odd miles of channel from Kashmor to the delta were almost completely diked on the right bank and two-thirds diked on the left.[23] The bunds have since been completed along virtually the entire length of the lower Indus from Mithankot to the delta. But such works are also to be found above Mithankot, so that although the width of the active floodplain is remarkable, one can hardly single out either natural levees or artificial bunds as a unique characteristic of the lower Indus.

Nor do climatic conditions provide any absolute demarcation between the upper and lower Indus Plains. There are climatic changes, of course, over this vast region. But the change over the 63 miles from Karachi to Tatta, being the change from a coastal to an inland station (though one which still receives some maritime modification),[24] is much greater than that over the 61 miles from Tatta to Sukkur or over the 251 miles from Tatta to Hyderabad. In fact, in any given season the differences in temperature between Hyderabad and Lahore (693 miles apart) are apt to be smaller than those between Tatta and Karachi.

Except in the coastal and submontane zones, the Indus Plains are pretty much a climatic unit. As in any monsoonal region, differences in elevation are more significant than latitude or, except in the first

23. *Gazetteer of the Province of Sind,* compiled by E. H. Aitken (2 vols. Karachi, Printed for Government, 1907), *A,* 10, 14.
24. An unmistakable indication of villages that receive some climatic amelioration from the sea are the ventilators to be found on rooftops as far inland as Hyderabad. These ventilators resemble chimney pots, with the single opening facing southwest to catch the breeze.

20 miles or so, distance from the sea. Because the gradient of the Indus Plains is less than one foot per mile, the traveler by road or rail is conscious of only a very gradual change in any season. Of the Indus Plains meteorological stations, Jacobabad, northwest of Sukkur, experiences the highest absolute temperatures and the lowest average annual rainfall. But on an afternoon in June, when it may be 120°F. in Jacobabad, it is likely to be 110°F., or even 115°F. in both Hyderabad and Multan, and not much cooler in Lyallpur or Lahore. Winter differentials are greater and are reflected to some degree in the natural vegetation and cropping patterns. Light frosts are experienced in Lahore and occasionally even in Multan, though never in Hyderabad or Karachi. Winter rainfall is not unknown in Jacobabad, though it gets at least 3 of its 4 inches in the months of June, July, and August—and it must be emphasized that these are mean annual figures reflecting both occasional downpours of 1 inch in an hour or two and long periods with no rain at all. Hyderabad and Multan, about equally distant from Jacobabad to the south and northeast respectively, each get an annual average of 6 or 7 inches. Lyallpur receives about 14, Lahore nearly 20, and Sialkot is close enough to the foothills to get about 35 inches of rain—again an average of forty years or more of records. In the Indian portion of the Indus Plains, Chandigarh is analogous to Sialkot, and Amritsar and Ferozepore to Lahore, but as one moves south into Rajasthan, rainfall declines and temperatures increase more rapidly than they do along the Sutlej-Panjnad-Indus axis.

It is another characteristic of the Indus Plains that, in any given season, variations in local weather conditions (day to day or hour to hour) may exceed the differences between one end of the Plains and the other. Thus a monsoonal downpour or a dust storm will temporarily create a far greater change in Lahore or in Hyderabad than that which normally prevails because of their 600-foot difference in elevation or 6-degree difference in latitude.

Within the Indus Plains, there are subtle differences in the landscape and particularly in the vegetation pattern. The salt-tolerant date palm, to cite one example, is found in groves all along the lower Indus floodplain. In the southern Punjab, however, it reaches its cold-tolerant limit beyond which it will not bear fruit, and so it is grown far less widely, and only as an ornamental, to the north and east. In the central Punjab, the *babul,* or acacia (*Acacia arabica*), largely supersedes the palm, though the acacia is characteristic of the lower Indus as well. The *sissu,* or shisham (*Dalbergia sissoo*), first becomes prominent in Khairpur and extends all over the Punjab and into the foothills, where it is joined by the deodar (*Cedrus deodara*). All of these natural changes over the plains are gradual, and generalities would be misleading. Nor does the cropping pattern offer a clear distinction. Rice is grown in the submontane tract and wheat in Sind, both well within their climatic limits. The same is true of sugarcane and cotton. What determines the cropping pattern is availability of water, soil fertility and drainability, and access to market. Citrus cultivation extends intermittently from Karachi to Peshawar and eastward into India. To draw a line, somewhere about Multan, at the average southern limit of frost would be an arbirtary oversimplification with no direct correspondence to the natural or introduced vegetation pattern.

Even the man-made landscapes have great similarity, for the land-survey system based on the irrigation network, in which holdings are divided into *chaks* or blocks served by the watercourses, has been extended from the Crown Waste Lands in the center of the Punjab doabs to equivalent areas in Sind and even to state-owned lands in Bahawalpur and Khairpur. The post-Partition developments in the Thal Doab and under the Gudu and Ghulam Mohammad barrage commands in Sind have emphasized this similarity, as did the greatest of them all, the Sukkur development beginning in the 1930s and not yet complete. The Canal Colony landscape, not uninteresting in itself but monotonous in its seemingly endless repetition over thousands of square miles, may now be found from within 50 miles of the foothills to within 50 miles of the coast. In the "dry districts" of the north and northeast (Rawalpindi, parts of Jhelum and Gujrat, Sialkot, Gurdaspur, Hoshiarpur, Ambala; see Map 5), settled long before the Canal Colonies and dependent primarily upon rainfall and wells, one finds the same sort of feudal village common to medieval Europe and originating in the same needs. Hilltops crowned by forts, with the houses clustering tightly for protection, mark the districts that were longest settled—and longest "unsettled" due to the depredations of warlords and bandits. Again, in parts of Bahawalpur, Khairpur, and Sind, including part of the delta country, the amirs had built up a system of fiefdoms worked by tenants who were virtually serfs and supported by inundation irrigation for centuries or even millennia before the modern works were introduced. Here the regular *chak* system could not be superimposed, and one still finds large areas where, despite the recent impact of land reforms, the boundaries are still highly irregular and the feudal pattern evident. Multan, Shor Kot, Chiniot, and Lahore are ancient bastions and entrepots, as are Sukkur and Hyderabad. But for hundreds of miles in between, especially away from the rivers, the villages of the Plains are all but indistinguishable.

Village patterns and house types are also common to both the Punjab and the lower Indus. The former vary according to whether the village is ancient, in which case the pattern is chaotic; or "modern," in which case it conforms, more or less but rather less than more, to the rectangular patterns prescribed in the colonization manuals. House types may be more indicative of where settlers came from than of any local styles, again with modifications in the coastal areas and in the foothills where wood is more plentiful. Adobe construction is predominant, with straw or reed roofs becoming more common toward the south. Architecture will, of course, reflect local differences in income, but it is a poor guide to regional differentiation.

Yet the difference between the Punjab and the lower Indus exists and is evident to the traveler, although it cannot be quantified or specified. The greatest change seems to occur to the southwest of Multan. Once the Chenab is crossed into the lower Thal Doab, with its date-palm oases, one feels that he is in the "South." In the last analysis, we are forced to be subjective in drawing a line between the Punjab and the "lower Indus," so perhaps the best we can do is to accept the confluence of the Panjnad with the Indus at Mithankot as the division. True, the political boundaries of both the former Punjab Province and the State of Bahawalpur extended further downstream, to Kashmor. But these were nineteenth-century accommodations, and they do not correspond to any physical features.

At any rate, and subject to all of the preceding qualifications and hesitations, for the purposes of this study we shall use "lower Indus" to refer to the course of the river from Mithankot to the sea, "middle Indus" for the stretch from Mithankot to Kalabagh, and "upper Indus" for the gorge reaches, including Attock and Tarbela and areas upstream. "Punjab" we had better leave in its older historic sense, including all areas to the *east* of the Indus above Mithankot. It should be noted that this *excludes* the Dera Ghazi Khan District of the *Derajat* (so named from the camping grounds of the Afghan chiefs, Ismail, Futteh, and Ghazi, during their invasions in the eighteenth century), which was politically united to the Punjab by the Sikhs and the British only in the nineteenth century. It *includes* the Potwar Plateau area (Rawalpindi, Attock, and Jhelum districts), which was intermittently held by the power controlling the Punjab (Mogul or Sikh) prior to the coming of the British. The eastern boundary of the Punjab also shifted historically, but we may most conveniently include the present (mid 1966) Indian State of (East) Punjab, extending to the Jumna but not including the Delhi District. Where a more restricted use of the term "Punjab" is employed, this is indicated in the text or in a footnote.

"Indus Plains" is defined simply in the physiographic sense as including all of the region tributary to the Indus from the rim stations (Rupar, Pong, Madhopur, Marala, Mangla, and Kalabagh, not Attock) to the sea. In the latter portion of the book, we shall refer to the "Northern Zone" and "Southern Zone" of the Indus Plains. Those terms have been evolved for planning purposes by the West Pakistan Water and Power Development Authority (which is known throughout the province simply as "WAPDA"). The division is based upon canal commands and accordingly the dividing line runs through the Gudu Barrage (see Maps 6 and 8b) rather than through Mithankot, where we divide the "lower Indus" from the "middle Indus."

"Indus Rivers" will mean, unless otherwise specified, only the major perennial rivers that cross the Plains and that are the subject of the Indus Waters Treaty, i.e. the Indus and its five Punjab tributaries.[25] "Punjab Rivers," as the very word implies ("Punjab" or "Panjab" is derived from the Persian-Urdu words *panj* for "five" and *ab* for "water" or "river") are the five streams whose combined waters form the Panjnad, which delivers them to the Indus.

---

25. The Kabul is excluded, for most purposes of this study, because it neither crosses the Indus Plains nor was it a subject of the Indus Waters Dispute. It is not beyond the realm of possibility that a dispute may someday arise between Pakistan and Afghanistan over the waters of the Kabul and its major affluent, the Chitral-Kunar. For the role of the Kabul river within Afghanistan, see Aloys Arthur Michel, *The Kabul, Kunduz, and Helmand Valleys and the National Economy of Afghanistan* (Washington, D.C., National Academy of Sciences—National Research Council, 1959).

By custom dating from Mogul times, each of the interfluves between the Punjab Rivers is called a *doab* (*do* means "two") and has a
name derived from those of the bounding rivers. Thus the area between the Beas and the Sutlej is known as the "Bist Doab," that between the Beas and the Ravi as the "Bari Doab," that between the
Ravi and the Chenab as the "Rechna Doab," and that between the
Chenab and the Jhelum as the "Chaj Doab" (in older works also
referred to as the "Jech Doab"). The interfluve between the Indus
and the Jhelum-Chenab was long known as the "Sind Sagar Doab"
or "Desert of the Indus" but is now called the "Thal Doab."

So vast did the Indus appear to the Aryan invaders of the subcontinent that they gave it the Sanskrit word "Sindhu," meaning "ocean,"
from which "Indus" is derived. Not yet having seen the ocean, the
Aryans apparently thought that the "Sindhu" deserved the same title
they later applied to the sea itself. The name is also preserved in
that of the southernmost province of the Indus Basin.

A review of the above definitions will indicate that despite the
geographer's traditional predilection for emphasizing physical factors, and his usual delight in finding coincidences or correspondences
between physical features and man-made boundaries, most of the
regional terms we shall employ in this study reflect political-adminis-
trative and historical factors as much as physical ones. Relatively
distinct physical features, the Indus Rivers, serve to define two sides
of each doab, but one has to be arbitrary in defining the third, or
upper, side. One can choose a contour or an isohyet (a line joining
places of equal average rainfall), but one will not find such a boundary demarcated on the ground. By selecting the rim stations to mark
the upper boundary of the Indus Plains, we have chosen points which
are both clearly demarcated and of enormous practical significance.
Yet to assume that a "closing line" joining the adjacent rim stations
would mark the upper end of each doab would be only a crude approximation, for nature does not work in straight lines.

The other boundaries that cross the rivers cause us the most difficulty. In the gently sloping region of the Indus Plains, no physical
boundary stands out between the rim stations and the coast. Thus,
while we are on safe physical ground in dividing the upper from the
middle Indus at the Kalabagh rim station, the division between the

middle and the lower Indus at Mithankot is less clearcut; it may look clear enough on a map or from a plane, but it is not distinct on the ground. Hence the need to rely on historical, administrative, or operational definitions. It is far more satisfactory to define the Punjab as it existed at a given date than to search for elusive or nonexistent physical boundaries. For purposes of planning, engineering, and administration of the irrigation system and the economy based thereon, the only boundaries that make sense are those of the canal commands. Thus it may be said that the dividing line between the Northern Zone and the Southern Zone of the Indus Plains in Pakistan, though hardly arbitrary, is purely man-made. The Kashmor reach of the Indus was undistinguished by any transverse feature until the Gudu Barrage was built. Now that barrage, and the canal networks based on it, mark a sudden change between desert and sown.

Thus the first man-made diversion of Indus water below the Mithankot confluence, rather than that confluence itself, becomes the more significant boundary for this study. Indeed, this definition of the single most important regional boundary within Pakistan's Indus Plains today foreshadows our whole discussion of the Indus Waters Dispute and typifies one of the main themes of this study: that in a region where water is scarcer than land, any change made by man in the distribution of water is as important as any natural transition in the landscape and may be more important than a change in a political or administrative boundary. Under a given sovereignty within the Indus Basin, the latter premise would seem incontestable. It follows that since modern irrigation was introduced the engineers have on the whole played as important a role as the administrators in influencing the life and fortunes of the region.

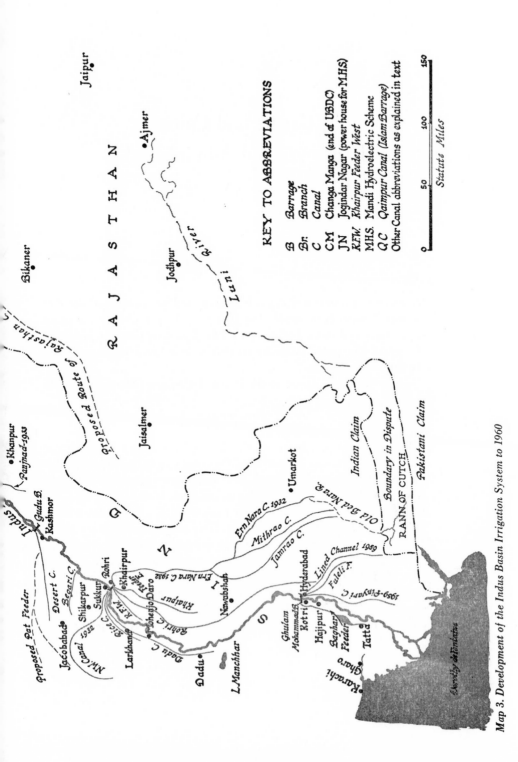

KEY TO ABBREVIATIONS

B   Barrage
Br.   Branch
C   Canal
CM   Changa Manga (end of UBDC)
JN   Jogindar Nagar (power house for MHS)
KFW   Khairpur Feeder West
MHS   Mandi Hydroelectric Scheme
QC   Qaimpur Canal (Islam Barrage)
Other Canal abbreviations as explained in text

Statute Miles
0   50   100   150

Map 3. Development of the Indus Basin Irrigation System to 1960

3. Canals and Colonies:
Engineers and Administrators

"Irrigation is a new and difficult science, and the wonder is, not that mistakes have been made, but that they have not been far more numerous and more serious. . . . The first essential is a profound belief in the possibilities of irrigation and great boldness in attacking the problems."
—Col. S. L. Jacob to the Indian Irrigation Commission, 1902

Precursors

The geographical pattern of the Indus Rivers, and in particular those of the Punjab, along with the very gentle gradients of the streams, floodplains, and doabs, provided a natural setting and stimulus for irrigation. Below the rim stations, these sediment-laden streams usually flow in beds higher than the level of their floodplains. This results from the fact that each time they overflow their banks they deposit the heavier and coarser sediments first, carrying only the finer sands and silts to any distance from the stream. Thus, as in ancient China, Egypt, and Mesopotamia, the rivers themselves taught man how to irrigate land. By breaching the banks, or "natural levees," and providing shallow channels to direct the floods, it was possible to bring the water to fields on the lower-lying portions of the floodplain. Of course, this can be done only during high-water periods, and so "inundation irrigation" is limited, in the Indus Basin, to the summer season, the period of *kharif* crops. Although the rivers have since shifted their courses and all trace of canals has been obliterated, it seems indisputable that both Mohenjo Daro on the lower Indus and Harappa on the Ravi were supported by irrigation agriculture some 5,000 years ago.

It was soon discovered that the period of flood irrigation could be extended by building small diversion structures at the head of each canal. Even though these structures did not extend across the whole river, they served to pond back the water sufficiently to raise its level. But of course the structures were swept away by the next year's flood and had to be replaced. Often the flood created new breaches in the natural levees, obliterating the small canals, and covering the field with coarse and uncultivable deposits. Inundation irrigation was (and still is in a few portions of the Indus Basin) a precarious means of agriculture. It was limited both seasonally and areally, and its temporary structures demanded labor at just the time when fields needed plowing, leveling, and seeding. But for millennia the techniques and materials at hand permitted no improvement. As late as 1872, the following description was still valid:

> The chief inundation canals of India are found in the basin of the Indus and of its five tributaries. . . . The higher land on each bank, which is from 10 to 50 feet above the general level of these valleys, is called the *bhangar*, the lower land the *khadir*. The *bhangar* lands form the *doabs*, as they are called, lying between the six rivers; they are fertile in themselves, but cultivation depends entirely on the scanty rain, or, if artificial irrigation is not provided, on laborious irrigation by mechanical means from wells which are often 60 and 70 feet in depth. The *khadir* lands are generally fertile, but the *bhangar* lands, though formed of good soil, are to a considerable extent covered with grass or brushwood, or entirely waste. As the rivers converge into the single stream of the Indus, near Mithankot, the *bhangar* lands gradually disappear and the low *khadir* extends right across between the rivers. Some of the inundation canals of the Punjab lie in the *khadir* of the higher reaches of

the Sutlej and the Jhelum, but the majority of them . . . are in the area bordering on the confluence of the rivers with the Indus. The district of Multan, lying between the Sutlej and the Chenab, where rain hardly ever falls, is rendered beautifully fertile by a series of inundation canals, taken from both rivers, which are said to have been originally constructed by the Afghan rulers left by Aurunzib [Aurangzeb, sixth Mogul emperor, who reigned 1658–1707]. In the Derajat on the right bank of the Indus, above Mithankot, there is a group of twelve inundation canals which have been constructed since the British rule, and in Muzzuffarghar [southeastern Sind Sagar Doab, now called Thal Doab, along the Chenab] a corresponding group irrigates a tract some 12 miles broad on the left bank. The Upper Sutlej inundation canals are in the central portion of the doab lying between the Sutlej and the Ravi rivers. Here the face of the country is covered with traces of former life and prosperity. The cause of decay was due to the loss of water-supply consequent upon the diversion of the river Beas, which formerly had an independent course to the Chenab, fertilising the land on either bank. But in 1790 it was diverted into the Sutlej [i.e. it was captured by the Sutlej in the course of the natural migration of that river near Harike], and its old bed became a dry ravine with a complicated system of deserted watercourses. A new system of inundation canals has been carried into this tract from the Sutlej. The inundation canals of the Punjab aggregate some 2,500 miles in length, and irrigate more than one million acres.[1]

There were also extensive systems of inundation canals in Bahawalpur State, taking off from the Sutlej and Panjnad, and in Sind, dependent upon the Indus. At Hyderabad, the Amirs of Sind dammed

1. Robert B. Buckley, C.S.I., *The Irrigation Works of India* (2nd ed., London, E. & F. N. Spon, 1905), pp. 10–11. Buckley drew his account from the *Report on East India Progress and Condition, 1872–3*, printed June 2, 1874, for the House of Commons. The reader should note that the low *khadir* lands, subject to flooding, are also called *bet*, while the high *bhangar* lands, especially those in the centers of the doabs, are also called *bar*. Thus the center of the Bari Doab around the present city of Montgomery was known as the Ganji Bar. In order to avoid confusion, we shall in general restrict ourselves to the terms "bar" and "doab," and contrast the former with the term "floodplain."

a side channel of the Indus and converted it into an inundation canal; this was the precursor of the perennial Fuleli Canal.

The next stage in the evolution of irrigation was the construction of perennial, or two-season, canals having permanent headworks that could withstand the flood flows of the rivers. It must be emphasized that these headworks either did not extend across the entire stream or were constructed first as "weirs" and later as "barrages" (or weirs surmounted by movable gates) that allowed the floods to pass over their crests. In no sense were they dams designed to hold back and store a large portion of the flood. Only in the mid-twentieth century did it become feasible or desirable to construct storage dams on any of the Indus Rivers. The function of the weir or barrage is merely to "head up" the water sufficiently, in times of low flow, so that it will pass into the intake or "head regulator" of the canal, while allowing virtually unobstructed flow in times of flood.

Perennial irrigation in India may have begun as early as A.D. 300 when the Grand Anicut of Madras was dammed by a structure of stone, cut and fitted without benefit of mortar. But its beginnings in the Punjab are a thousand years more recent. In the fourteenth century, Firoz Shah Tughluk desired to irrigate a hunting estate in Hissar, 100 miles northwest of Delhi. To satisfy his whim, a canal was built all the way from the Jumna. The Emperor Akbar (reigned 1556–1605) around 1568 decided to restore this canal and to allow some of its water to be used for crop irrigation. Again, under Shah Jahan (reigned 1628–58), the Mogul engineer Ali Mardan Khan extended this precursor of the Western Jumna Canal to irrigate lands northwest of Delhi and also brought a branch canal into the city where it watered the grounds of the imperial palace (the Red Fort of today). Although this was a perennial canal, it had no permanent headworks, and there was no barrage in the Jumna.[2]

The first perennial canal on any of the Indus Rivers was built under Shah Jahan's predecessor, Jahangir (reigned 1605–27), who spent much of his reign in enforced exile at Lahore. For emergencies as well as for entertainment, Jahangir had a fortress and hunting lodge across the Ravi at Sheikhupura. Nearby, at the Hiran Minar,

2. A. M. R. Montagu, "Presidential Address to the Punjab Engineering Congress, 33rd Session, 1946," in *Proceedings of the Punjab Engineering Congress, 33rd Session, 1946*, p. ii.

he built a pleasure garden around a large, walled-in tank or reservoir. To feed this reservoir, the emperor caused a canal to be dug some 50 miles to a site on the Ravi where a small, year-round water supply could be obtained.

Jahangir's example was followed by his son, Shah Jahan, who also was fond of Lahore. To irrigate the Shalamar Gardens outside that city, Shah Jahan had a canal known as the "Huslie" built on the left bank of the Ravi around 1633. In the period of Sikh rule (1763–1849) a branch of this canal was carried into Amritsar to fill the tank at the Golden Temple. Some crop irrigation was also provided, producing a revenue of about 85,000 rupees per year at the time the British arrived.[3]

This was the situation as the British found it. To appreciate their enormous contribution, not only to irrigation in the Indus Basin and in India as a whole but to the development of modern irrigation engineering, one must realize that the British had had virtually no experience in the field. Obviously, irrigation is unnecessary in the British Isles (although some "supplementary" sprinkler irrigation is now employed in East Anglia). Nor was it used in the portions of North America, South Africa, or Australia colonized by Great Britain prior to 1849. True, the British, and particularly the British Army, had been in a position to examine the irrigation works in Egypt some forty years before they moved into the Sind or Punjab. But the Egyptians were practicing a system of inundation irrigation made feasible, reliable, and indeed almost automatic by the remarkable regularity of the Nile flood. Perennial irrigation was not introduced into Egypt until 1861 with the completion of the Mohammed Ali Barrage at the head of the Nile delta.

Thus the British engineers in India were, one might say, "writing the book" where perennial irrigation was concerned. They did not, of course, write on a blank sheet. They had the existing inundation systems and a few perennial Mogul works to examine. The British

3. Ibid., p. iii. *The Report of the Indian Irrigation Commission, 1901–03* (4 vols., Calcutta, Office of the Superintendent of Government Printing, India, 1903), *1*, 9, para. 39, states that the Huslie Canal had a length of 130 miles and a capacity of 150 cubic feet per second. The British usage is to abbreviate "cubic feet per second" as "cusecs," whereas American engineers use "c.f.s." Since the British system has been preserved in the subcontinent, we shall use "cusecs" henceforth.

restored the Western Jumna Canal in 1821 and fitted it with a permanent headworks in 1836. They sent fact-finding missions to
northern Italy, southern France, Spain, and northwest Africa to
investigate the perennial systems in use there. To do full justice to all
precursors, it may even be pointed out that some of the irrigation
techniques that originated in the Middle East and were carried across
the Mediterranean by the Arabs and Moors were reintroduced by the
British into India. Nevertheless, a great deal had to be learned anew,
much of it by trial and error in the field, more by careful experiment
in the laboratory and model station. But by the time the Union Jack
came down in Lahore, British engineers had not only given the Indus
Basin the most extensive irrigation system in the world; they had
developed most of the formulas now used everywhere in canal construction and operation.

The British Raj

Before describing what the British built, we must understand how
they operated, for colonial administration in India was evolving just
as was irrigation practice. The history of administrative evolution
in India can of course merely be sketched here. A detailed and
definitive, though discontinuous, account will be found in Volumes
5 and 6 of *The Cambridge History of India*, edited by H. D. Dodwell
(Cambridge, England, Cambridge University Press, 1929 and 1932)
and a short summary, carrying the account to and beyond Independence, in the Indian Institute of Public Administration's *The Organisation of the Government of India* (Bombay, Asia Publishing House,
1958).

To begin with, it should be recalled that until the Indian Mutiny
of 1857 (actually until November 1, 1858), British rule in India was
administered through the mechanism of the East India Company.
Indeed, it was not until 1813 that Parliament clearly asserted British
sovereignty in India. From the last day of 1600, when Queen Eliza-
beth granted certain merchants of London a monopoly of trade
eastwards from the Cape of Good Hope to the Straits of Magellan,
through the reorganization of the Company in 1702–09, to 1773 when
Parliament enacted the Regulating Act, no provision had been made
by the Crown for governing India. Instead, the Company had been

allowed to manage its own affairs, to fight wars, to conquer territory, and to conclude treaties with the Mogul emperors and other Indian rulers. In legal theory, the Company's conquests belonged to the Crown while its concessions, including the right to collect taxes and customs duties in various parts of India, belonged to the Company. But in fact the Company's officers and shareholders were so influential at the British Court and in Parliament that that body had not attempted to interfere with so powerful and private an enterprise. The Company's affairs in England were managed by a twenty-four-member Court of Directors, elected by the larger shareholders but more or less self-perpetuating. In India, the Company's holdings had been grouped around three major centers, Madras (founded in 1639), Bombay (which had replaced Surat in 1687), and Calcutta (founded in 1690). In each of these places, the Company had a major fort, a good port, storehouses and trading facilities, and a staff of civil and military "servants." In each center, the Company's affairs were managed by a council of senior servants, and although the president of the council was generally known as the "Governor," the territories or "Governments" were usually referred to as "Presidencies." The Company's contractual, or covenanted, "servants" in India ran its political, military and commercial affairs in so profitable a fashion, both for the shareholders and for themselves, that appointments in the Company's service were considered the most lucrative form of patronage and contributed to the Company's vast influence at home. Indeed, by the middle of the eighteenth century, since England was obviously not running the Company, some wondered whether the Company was instead running England.

But in the 1750s and 1760s, reports of peculation, corruption, and mismanagement in India had become so notorious that when, due to a purely temporary stringency, the Company had to apply to the Crown for a loan in 1772, Parliament took the occasion to investigate the Company's affairs and to pass the Regulating Act of 1773. The Act set forth the terms of office of members of the Court of Directors and attempted to ensure a rotation among them. It also required the Company to submit all correspondence from India to officers of the Crown. With respect to administration in India, the Regulating Act made the Governor of Bengal at Calcutta a "Governor-General" with powers over the Governors of Bombay and Madras in matters of peace and war. But it also ordained that the Governor-General could act only in conformity with the decisions of his Council, which the Act increased to four members, and it gave him the deciding vote only in case of a tie. Thus the Governor-General could be forced to execute a decision against which he had voted.

The Regulating Act did not work well, and in 1784 it was replaced by Pitt's India Act which reduced the Governor-General's Council to three members and strengthened his control over the subordinate Presidencies of Bombay and Madras. (It was not until 1786 that he got the power to overrule his Council.) In England, the Act of 1784 established a Board of Control, including two members of the Cabinet whose approval was required for all but strictly commercial orders by the Company's Court of Directors to its servants in India. This act clearly made the British Government ultimately responsible for the conduct of political and military affairs in India, but it was not until 1813 that Parliament, in renewing the Company's charter, proclaimed the sovereignty of the Crown over the Company territories in India. Henceforth, the Governor-General was no longer styled the servant of the Mogul emperor, and the Company's tribute to the emperor was no longer presented in the Governor-General's name. At the same time, the Company's exclusive trading privileges were revoked by Parliament, and twenty years later its commercial activities were completely terminated. Thus, by 1833 the Company was in effect, if not in name, merely the agency of the British Government for the administration of the British territories in India. By this time, the Company's power had gradually been extended up the Ganges from Bengal, Bihar (and Orissa) through Benares to Agra. It bypassed Oudh but surrounded Delhi where the titular Mogul emperor was maintained on his throne so that the Company might clothe its acts in his weakening authority and avail itself of his diminishing prestige and influence with the princes. Scattered among and between the Company's holdings was a congeries of "native states" whose rulers, Hindu, Sikh, or Muslim, stood in direct treaty relation with the Company. Most of these treaties incorporated the principle of "lapse": that upon the death of a ruler without an heir, his territory would escheat to the Company. The Company placed its "Residents" at the courts of the more important princes, as it did at the imperial court in Delhi.

The political map of India looked in 1857, as indeed it did ninety years later, like the patchwork quilt of the Holy Roman Empire, with the native or Princely States set into a background of British India. The paramount power lay in Calcutta, seat of the Governor-General *of India* as the Act of 1833 had styled him. To ease his task as Governor of the Bengal Presidency, the areas from Benares to Agra were in 1836 constituted the North Western Provinces (not to be confused with the North West Frontier Province, along the Afghan border, established only in 1932) under a Lieutenant-Governor subordinate to the Bengal Government. When the Punjab was annexed to the Presidency in 1849, it was first placed under a Board of Administration and then, in 1853, under a Chief Commissioner. After the Mutiny, the Punjab became a Lieutenant-Governor's province, like the North Western Provinces, within the Bengal Presidency. Oudh was annexed to the Presidency in 1856, setting the stage for the Mutiny, and was placed under a Chief Commissioner. (In 1877 Oudh was incorporated into the North Western Provinces, which became the United Provinces of Agra and Oudh in 1902 and which are the Uttar Pradesh of today's India.) Meanwhile, to relieve the Governor-General of the burden of ruling them directly, in 1854 the older territories of the Presidency (Bengal, Bihar and Orissa, and Assam which was added in 1827) were placed under a Lieutenant-Governor of the "Lower Provinces." Thus, by the time of the Mutiny, the Governor-General of India was ruling the subordinate Presidencies of Madras and Bombay through their Governors, and his own Presidency of Bengal through Lieutenant-Governors and Chief Commissioners.

In the Bengal Presidency the Lieutenant-Governors and Chief Commissioners ruled over a series of Commissioners of Divisions, and the Commissioners in turn over the Deputy Commissioners in charge of Districts. The pattern in the subordinate presidencies of Madras and Bombay was somewhat different, and there were no Lieutenant-Governors in those provinces. After Sind had been annexed to the Bombay Government for four years, however, it was constituted a Commissioner's subprovince and divided into districts like those of the Bengal Presidency rather than the collectorates into which the rest of the Bombay Presidency was divided. The term "province" was used rather indiscriminantly, and applied to Lieutenant-Governor's provinces, such as the North Western Provinces after 1836, Bengal after 1854, and the Punjab after 1859; to Chief Commissioner's provinces, such as the Punjab from 1853 to 1859; and even to a Commissioner's subprovince, such as Sind after 1847. Not until the Act of 1919 (1935 for Sind) were all of these made Governor's provinces, and the terms "Government of Bengal," "Government of Bombay," and "Government of Madras" were used interchangeably with "Presidency" until that date.

The Mutiny of 1857 resulted in the Act of 1858 which transferred the Government of India directly to the Crown. The Act abolished the East India Company with its Court of Directors and replaced the Board of Control with the Council of India. The Council was to advise the new Secretary of State for India both in governing British India and in relations with the Princely States. The Secretary of State acted, from 1858 to 1947, through the Governor-General of India, who was given the additional title of Viceroy to signify the new relation of the Crown to the Government of India. By the Act of 1875, the title "Empress of India" was added to Queen Victoria's style. But there were no changes in the administrative arrangements in India itself.

British penetration of the Indus Basin may be dated from 1809 when the Government of India accepted the allegiance of the Sikh rulers between the Jumna and the Sutlej rivers, extending its protection to them in return for the right of escheat. Gradually, the "cis-Sutlej" territories that lapsed were organized into the new district of Ambala.[4] That the rulers of these states, including the relatively strong Maharaja of Patiala, accepted this condition was due to their fear of Ranjit Singh, the "Lion of the Punjab," whose control of the area from the Sutlej to and beyond the Indus was strengthened by an army of over 30,000 men, led and trained by European (mainly French and Italian) officers and equipped with excellent weapons. After discussions with the Governor-General at Rupar on the Sutlej, Ranjit Singh himself agreed, though with considerable reluctance, to accept the Sutlej as his southeastern boundary. Ranjit Singh's motive, in

4. Hugh K. Trevaskis, *The Land of the Five Rivers* (London, Oxford University Press, 1928), p. 195. The adoption of the term "cis-Sutlej" is indicative of the fact that the British, unlike other conquerors of northern India, were moving from southeast to northwest.

signing the Treaty of Lahore, does not appear to have been fear of
the British but rather hope for their support against the Afghans and
possibly against the Amirs of Sind. In any event, and despite his dis-
appointment on both scores, Ranjit Sing faithfully observed the
treaty for thirty years until his death in 1839.

Ranjit Singh died just as a joint Sikh-British force was moving
through the Khyber toward Kabul while another British force, based
upon Sind, was moving up through Quetta toward Kandahar. Initial
successes were followed by the disastrous withdrawal from Kabul in
January 1842. Although the British subsequently reoccupied the
Afghan capital, their temporary defeat by Asian troops had a far-
reaching impact upon the Indian Army and contributed to the spirit
of revolt that reached its climax in 1857 (after another indifferent
performance by the British in the Crimean War). The unprovoked
and weakly opposed annexation of Sind in 1843, carried out by Sir
Charles Napier with the troops that had withdrawn from Kandahar,
did nothing to restore British prestige. But it brought the British
permanently into the lower Indus. Sind was attached to the Government of Bombay, a situation that persisted until the Government of
India Act of 1935 went into effect.

The death of Ranjit Singh plunged the Punjab into political chaos.
Intrigue and assassinations placed a series of inept rulers on the
throne, culminating in the installation of a boy, Dhulip Singh, dominated by his mother, Rani Jindan, and her lover, Lal Singh. To divert
attention from internal troubles, these last two persuaded the Sikh
Durbar to launch their army across the Sutlej against the British.
The First Sikh War which followed was marked by incompetent
leadership on both sides, but it ended in the defeat of the Sikh army
at Sabraon near Harike on February 10, 1846. The cis-Sutlej Sikh
rulers had not proved conspicuously loyal, and the British seized this
opportunity to absorb most of their states, installing a Commissioner
at Ambala and organizing the additional districts of Thanesar, Ludhiana, and Ferozepore.[5] Furthermore, by the Treaty of Byrowal, December 16, 1846, the Sikhs were forced to cede the territory in the
Bist Doab between the Sutlej and the Beas, where the "trans-Sutlej"
districts of Jullundur, Hoshiarpur, and Kangra were established un-

5. Ibid., p. 207. See also Khushwant Singh, *A History of the Sikhs* (Princeton, Princeton University Press, 1963).

der John Lawrence as Commissioner at Jullundur (see Maps 4 and 5).
Rani Jindan at Lahore was compelled to accept, first, a British Resident in the person of John's brother, Henry Lawrence, and then in
1848 a set of Assistants to the Resident who in effect began to govern
the country. A Sikh "revolt" began at Multan in April 1848, but the
British were disposed to await cold weather before taking decisive
action. They then engaged the Sikh Army in two battles in the Chaj
Doab (at Chilianwala near Rasul, January 13, 1849, and at Gujrat,
February 22, 1849) and succeeded in inflicting a decisive defeat in
the second. The Sikh "revolt" gave Governor-General Dalhousie the
excuse he had been waiting for. The Sikh army was disbanded; the
Punjab was formally annexed, divided into districts and commis-
sionerships with the trans- and cis-Sutlej districts included; and a
Board of Administration, including both Lawrences and, shortly,
Robert Montgomery, was established to rule the new province.[6]

Except for the remaining Princely States below the Beas and in
the hills, the whole of one of India's most fertile and best-watered
regions had thus been brought together under what was probably
the most vigorous and talented administration produced by the East
India Company. This was true not only of the Lawrences (Henry
left the Punjab early in 1853, his brother John having been appointed
sole Chief Commissioner), but of the other young men who served
as commissioners and deputy commissioners. The administrative system was still evolving, and, in the Punjab at least, still remained
flexible:

> The Punjab was a Non-Regulation Province, i.e., the Regula-
> tions of Government were administered in the spirit and not
> in the letter. This method permitted an essentially empirical ap-
> proach to the problems of everyday administration. The prin-
> ciples characterizing the Non-Regulation system adopted by John

6. Trevaskis, pp. 207–12. In February 1858, following the suppression of the
Mutiny, the Delhi Territory, which had been under military administration, was
transferred to the Punjab, perhaps in recognition of John Lawrence's vigorous
action in sending troops and supplies for the recapture of the city. Two additional commissionerships, Delhi and Hissar, were organized. The Delhi District
was removed from Punjab jurisdiction early in this century after the decision
to create New Delhi and make it the imperial capital. The Western Jumna Canal
remained under the Public Works Department of the Punjab, but inasmuch as
the Jumna is not an Indus River we shall not be directly concerned with it here.

Lawrence were simple. First, the country was divided into Districts small enough to make it possible for the officer in charge to know it intimately. Secondly, every civil officer held judicial, fiscal, and magisterial power, concentrating in his person authority and undivided responsibility. Thirdly, the laws and procedure used were of the simplest kind, based, as far as possible, on native customs and institutions.[7]

The proof of the quality of the early British rule in the Punjab lies in the fact that not only did the province not rise in the Mutiny of 1857, but that it served as the base from which Delhi was recaptured in September of that year. When the Crown took over from the East India Company in November 1858, and the Governor-General became a Viceroy as well, no changes were made in the personnel at Lahore. Instead, on January 1, 1859, John Lawrence's post was elevated to the rank of Lieutenant-Governor. Lawrence soon returned to England and a seat in the Council of India, which had replaced the Board of Control. In 1864, John Lawrence came back to India as Viceroy.

The First British Canal

The annexation and consolidation of the Punjab in March 1849 set the stage for the construction of the canal system that is our main concern. In fact, plans for canal building were initiated during the Regency with the cooperation of the Sikh Durbar:

> Soon after the treaty of Byrowal the Resident at Lahore studied the feasibility of enlarging the Shah Nahur or Huslie Canal which intersected the upper portion of the doab. By permission of the Right Honourable Lord Hardinge, the then Governor-General, Lieutenant Anderson, Captain (now Major) Longden, and Lieutenant Hodson were deputed, under Lieutenant-Colonel Napier's [Robert Napier, not Sir Charles, the "conqueror" of Sind] own supervision, to survey and examine the line. These local inquiries were interrupted by the Mooltan insurrection, but not until a considerable portion of both the upper Baree and Rechna Doabs had been roughly but scientifically examined, and Colonel Napier had devised schemes

7. Michael Edwardes, *The Necessary Hell: John and Henry Lawrence and the Indian Empire* (London, Cassell, 1958), p. 131.

of two great canals, one from the Ravee, the other from the Chenab river.

After the annexation the Board [i.e. the Board of Administration in Lahore] lost no time in soliciting the sanction of the Most Noble the Marquis of Dalhousie to the furtherance of the former project. This sanction was accorded by his lordship, who was pleased to manifest an interest in the plan, and to satisfy himself of its feasibility by visiting the proposed canal head.

During the winter of 1849–50, Colonel Napier, the civil engineer, deputed an efficient staff of engineers, headed by Lieutenant Dyas [J. H. Dyas, later Chief Engineer, Punjab], to conduct scientific investigations previous to maturing the project in detail. By the close of this season a complete map was made of the whole doab (regarding the topography of which no information had been hitherto available), levels and cross-sections were taken; the nature of the ground, its surface, its drainage, and its undulations, the capabilities of the existing canal were all precisely ascertained.

Two distinct conclusions resulted from these inquiries: first, that the Huslie Canal must be superseded; second, that a new canal, with three branches, should be conducted through the entire length of the doab. . . .

The central line is to be 247 miles in length. It will commence from that point where the river Ravee debouches from the lowest of the Himalayan Ranges [the Siwaliks at Madhopur], thence, cutting through a high bank, it will cross two mountain torrents, till it gains the tablelands; then it will traverse the heart of the Manjha [the Sikh homeland in the northern portion of the Bari Doab] passing near the great cities of Deenanuggur [actually, a rather small village north of Gurdaspur], Buttala, and Umritsar; thence, striking into the deeps of the wildest wastes of the lower doab, and running past the ruined cities, tanks, temples, and canals, all of which it is to vivify and regenerate, it will join the Ravee 56 miles above Mooltan.[8]

8. *General Report on the Administration of the Punjab, for the Years 1849–50 and 1850–51* (London, Printed for the Court of Directors of the East-India Company by J. and H. Cox [Brothers], 1854), paras. 352–54 and 357, 93–94.

This report is cited at length for several reasons. It describes in contemporary language the genesis of the first modern canal on the Indus Rivers, the Upper Bari Doab Canal (UBDC henceforth). It indicates the type of personnel the East India Company had available for this sort of work: military engineers, trained for the most part in its academy at Addiscombe. Above all, it shows the enthusiasm with which the new rulers of the Punjab took to their work, how eager they were "to vivify and regenerate" the "wildest wastes" and the "ruined cities." It also demonstrates a certain naïveté concerning works of this sort. With the exception of Napier and Dyas, who had worked on the Western Jumna Canal improvements, none of these men had had any previous experience in canal construction. Yet in one cold season "a complete map was made of the whole doab . . . levels and cross-sections were taken; the nature of the ground, its surface, its drainage, and its undulations, the capabilities of the existing canal were all precisely ascertained." Lord Dalhousie satisfied himself of the feasibility of the project merely by visiting the proposed canal head in November 1851, and sanctioned immediate commencement of the work. The first estimate of the flow of the Ravi near Madhopur was made in February 1848, when the discharge "was found to be 2,752 cubic feet per second, and as the river was then pronounced by the people residing on its banks to be at its lowest, that quantity was considered to be the minimum discharge."[9] Yet in December 1851, just after the completion and sanctioning of the plans, the discharge fell to 2,016 cubic feet per second ("cusecs" henceforth).[10] "But the occurrence of such extreme drought is so rare," stated Colonel Napier, "and the period of its duration so short, that it cannot have any material influence on the return of the canal."[11]

Thus, with no clear idea of the minimum flow of the Ravi, a canal requiring 3,000 cusecs at the intake and designed to extend in its main line for a distance of 247 miles was sanctioned and begun.

9. Ibid., "Appendix: Report on the Punjab (Civil Works) by R. Napier, Lieutenant-Colonel, Civil Engineer, Punjab, Section IV, 'Baree Doab Canals,'" para. 30, p. 156.

10. Ibid., para. 32, p. 157. (By 1905, the minimum recorded flow of the Ravi was down to 1,200 cusecs. Buckley, p. 17.)

11. *General Report . . . 1849–50 and 1850–51*, "Appendix, Report on the Punjab (Civil Works)," Section IV, para. 32, p. 157.

Irrigation was to be provided over the first 180 miles of the main line, beyond which the canal was to be used for navigation up to the point where it was to rejoin the Ravi 56 miles above Multan. In actuality, the UBDC had to be terminated or "tailed out" at Changa Manga, about 100 miles short of its goal. The UBDC was finally opened in 1859, and irrigation commenced in 1861. At first, no distributaries were provided. "Irrigation was carried out by a system of cuts in the main canal."[12]

There were other difficulties with the UBDC. It had been designed with an excessive slope (4.22 feet per statute mile, or 4 feet per canal mile of 5,000 feet) and so began to erode its bed just as a river will do. A second problem was that the UBDC had no proper headworks because it was feared that the Ravi in flood would destroy them. Instead, only a side channel of the river was provided with a weir having movable shutters, and at right angles to this was the head regulator of the canal, "with archways which may be closed at pleasure," i.e. by means of gates.[13]

The UBDC, like other canals in India, was designed for continuous operation at or near full capacity during the irrigation season, rather than for the intermittent operation and varying flows characteristic of canals in the western United States. Under such conditions, it was highly desirable that the Indian canals have a "stable" or "permanent" regime, i.e. that silting and scouring ultimately balance. "Since the silt in the river varies from day to day and season to season, the silt in the off-taking canal does the same though the variation is not so wide. The canal is (or should be) so designed that the tendency to scour in the clear water periods (winter) offsets the tendency to silt in the summer when the river carries a heavy silt load. Channels which remain 'stable' over long periods of time are said to have a mean stable regime."[14]

The development of the stable-regime concept and of design formulas for achieving it must rank as another fundamental contribution

12. Montagu, p. iii.
13. *General Report . . . 1849–50 and 1850–51,* "Appendix: Report on Punjab (Civil Works)," Section IV, para. 4, p. 155.
14. Personal communication dated March 16, 1965, from Mr. A. M. R. Montagu, Chief Engineer and Secretary to Government, Punjab, Public Works Department, Irrigation Branch, 1943–47, and now Consultant, Sir M. MacDonald and Partners, Chartered Civil Engineers, London.

to irrigation engineering by the British in India. The pioneering research was conducted by R. C. Kennedy (from 1904 to 1906 Chief Engineer and Joint Secretary to Government, Punjab, Irrigation Branch) who in 1895 published his critical velocity formula $V_o = Cd^{0.64}$ based on measurements in "stable" reaches of the UBDC. Kennedy found that V_o, the velocity that can be maintained without causing either silting or scouring, to depend on d, the depth in feet, and C, a coefficient reflecting the nature of the materials eroded. For the UBDC, Kennedy found $C = 0.84$. For other canals, different values of the coefficient C and of the exponent of d were developed. Later more sophisticated formulas, taking account of width as well as depth of channel, character of the silt, and other factors, were proposed by others in India and elsewhere, notably by Gerald Lacey of the United Provinces Irrigation Branch. Lacey's work has, in turn, been subjected to further analysis and modification.[15]

At this point, it is also desirable to make a clarification in terms. The proper distinction between a "weir" and a "barrage" is as follows. Both consist of low, masonry structures built at right angles to the direction of stream flow and designed to be submerged in times of flood. Both are designed to "head up" water in times of low flow to such a level that it will enter a canal intake. But in the early weirs there was nothing above the crest of the masonry to provide further regulation, and when water reached that level it was immediately lost downstream. Later weirs were equipped with "needles" (wooden beams perhaps 4 feet long and 4 or 5 inches square) set vertically in grooves along the crest, or with wooden or metal "shutters" fixed in a vertical position for an added height of perhaps 4 or 6 feet (the early shutters were made of wood; later iron shutters 6 feet long and 18 inches wide were substituted). This additional height allowed for a higher pond level and for more flexibility in regulating it. It was even possible by opening only certain sections to shift the main flow of the stream, and hence much of the silt, from one side to another. But removing the needles or shutters by hand in times of flood was a dangerous business. Ultimately a type of

15. See Ivan E. Houk, *Irrigation Engineering* (2 vols. New York, John Wiley and Sons, 1956), 2, 100–01, and S. S. Kirmani, "Design of Silt Stable Canals," *Proceedings of the West Pakistan Engineering Congress,* 47 (1963, Paper No. 355), 1–68, esp. 3–9.

hinged shutter was designed that interlocked with the adjointing shutters by levers. By pulling a triggering mechanism, a whole set of shutters extending from one pier to the next could be dropped, domino fashion. But they still had to be reset by hand from a river boat having a block and tackle on the bow.

The "barrage," in which the needles or shutters were replaced by a large vertical gate set between the piers, was a vast improvement. The gates ran in vertical tracks and could be raised or lowered by means of winches located on a metal superstructure or "over bridge." At first the winches were turned mechanically like capstans, but later they were fitted with electric motors. This enhanced both the degree and speed of regulation, and made it possible to build lower, shorter masonry weirs, since most or all of the ponding function was performed by the gates in their lowered position. Thus a barrage is actually a gated weir. The first barrage built as such in the Punjab was that at Balloki, the headworks for the Lower Bari Doab Canal (opened in 1913).

The "head regulator" or "intake structure" for a canal is set at right angles to the weir or barrage. The regulators were always gated structures, at first employing wooden and later metal gates.

The term "headworks" properly includes both the weir or barrage and the head regulator.

The term "dam" indicates a structure designed to store water for a considerable period of time, above and beyond the "heading up" function of a weir or barrage. Normally, water never flows over a dam but may be released around or through it in tunnels or penstocks. The water may be used to turn turbines to generate electricity, or for irrigation, or both. Prior to 1950, the only dams in the Indus Basin were connected with hydroelectric schemes (such as the one in Mandi State near Jogindar Nagar), with flood protection works, or with reservoirs for municipal water supply. There was no storage for irrigation purposes until the Warsak, Bhakra, Rawal, and Mangla dams were built.[16]

16. For parts of the foregoing explanation I am much indebted to Mr. A. M. R. Montagu, who graciously reviewed this and the next chapter. See also Government of West Pakistan, Public Works Department, Irrigation Branch, *Manual of Irrigation Practice* (1st ed., reprinted 1963, Lahore, Superintendent Government Printing, West Pakistan, 1963), Chap. 1, "Definitions."

Experience soon showed that the headworks of the UBDC was inadequate. Timber floated down the side channel and blocked the intake. Between 1869 and 1872, therefore, a permanent shuttered weir was constructed across the entire river, and a new gated intake provided for the canal. Then it was discovered that this intake silted up with the coarse materials brought down by the Ravi, a problem that was soon found to be common to other rim station headworks located in the zone where the stream gradient suddenly decreases and hence where deposition is most rapid. The siltation problem led to experiments with permanent training works (bunds or jetties) designed to shift the main bed of the river away from the intake, and finally to the construction of a divide groyne extending upstream from the barrage. The divide groyne created between itself and the canal intake a "pond" of relatively calm water in which the silt could settle rather than passing into the canal. The problem was thus relieved, but not solved.

The UBDC had its difficulties, but it was a pioneer work and necessarily experimental. With the exception of the improvements to the Western Jumna Canal and (from 1848) the Ganges Canal, the British in North India had had no experience with canal construction or operation. There was no experience anywhere in the subcontinent with a rim station headworks lying in the most difficult zone for stream and silt control. The Public Works Department of the Punjab, founded in 1849 under Robert Napier, can be said to have cut its teeth on the UBDC. Furthermore, it had other responsibilities: road and bridge building,[17] military works, and the construction of offices, dwellings, and rest houses for the civil and military administration of the Punjab. (In 1866, the Public Works Department of the Punjab was divided into three branches, the Military Works Branch, the Civil Works Branch including Irrigation, and the Railway Branch. In 1869, the Civil Works Branch was subdivided into the Buildings and Roads Branch and the Irrigation Branch. In 1895, the functions of the Military Works Branch were

17. Notably along the Grand Trunk Road (see Map 1), which was to be extended across the Punjab from Ludhiana to Peshawar, thus crossing all of the Indus Rivers. A branch from Lahore to Ferozepore entailed a second crossing of the Sutlej. In most cases only boat bridges were provided until the railroad arrived, whereupon one bridge was built to serve both. The road from Lahore to Multan was also under construction in the 1850s.

transferred to the Army, and in 1905 the railway works were transferred to an all-India Railways Board. The Buildings and Roads Branch and the Irrigation Branch remained as the two components of the provincial Public Works Department until 1928 when the Public Health Circle was created. An Electricity and Industries Department was established in the early 1930s. This organization continued until after Partition.)

On the whole, the UBDC represented a good start and served, along with the other public works, to demonstrate to the Punjabis that the new administration was capable of doing much for their welfare. This visible proof of improvement under the British, along with the relative ease of military movements along the new roads, undoubtedly contributed to the quiescence of the Punjab during the Mutiny.

Motives

We should now pause to consider the motives that lay behind the canal-construction program. At one extreme, we may cite British self-interest in improving the agricultural value, and thus the revenue-producing capacity, of the lands they had annexed. The project for the UBDC included a careful, though inevitably erroneous, calculation of the proceeds to be derived,[18] which certainly influenced the Government in sanctioning it. At the other extreme, the enthusiasm of the young administrators and engineers was aroused by the promising "lay of the land":

> The capabilities of the Punjab for canal irrigation are notorious. It is intersected by great rivers; it is bounded on two sides by hills whence pour down countless rivulets; the general surface of the land slopes southward, with a considerable gradient. These facts at once proclaim it to be a country eminently adapted for canals. Nearly all the dynasties which have ruled over the Five Rivers have done something for irrigation; nearly every district possesses flowing canals, or else the ruins of ancient water-courses.[19]

18. *General Report . . . 1849–50 and 1850–51,* para. 363, p. 96.
19. Ibid., para. 348, p. 92.

The professional urge to "do something for irrigation" and to demonstrate that European science could far excel anything that had been done before undoubtedly inspired the Public Works Department in its far-reaching schemes.

Yet neither of these motives appears to have been deciding. Rather, there were two other influences that took precedence. One of these was endemic to all of India: the fear of famine. The famine of 1837-38 had spurred the improvement of the Western Jumna Canal, and its memory was fresh in the Punjab ten years later. The other motive, and apparently the predominant one, was peculiar to the time and place. We have noted that the Sikh Army was defeated in 1846 and disbanded in 1849. The British policy (which was regretted in 1857) was to replace the Sikh levies with sepoys brought from Bengal. This action turned thousands of able-bodied men, accustomed to discipline, loose on the countryside. Some of them immediately took up brigandage; others sat in the villages and grumbled. The Government's solution to the problem, not very different from that adopted by certain countries in the 1930s, was to employ the men on public works and then, where possible, to settle them on the lands benefited by the new canals.[20] Although later canal projects emphasized the economic advantages to be gained from bringing new lands, particularly the Crown Waste Lands, under cultivation and from the introduction of new cash crops such as cotton, contemporary accounts leave no doubt that the *decisive* motive in building the UBDC was to give employment to the Sikh Army veterans.[21]

20. The first British attempt to found a colony in the Punjab came in 1818 at the end of the Pindari campaign when it was sought by means of "grants of land in Hariana and Battiana [i.e. Rohtak, Hissar, and areas west toward Bikaner] both to provide for the troopers of nine disbanded regiments of Rohilla Cavalry and Irregular Horse and at the same time to establish a *quasi*-military colony along the frontier of the British territories in imitation of the Roman plan." The attempt failed because of the grantees' reluctance to remain in so distant and unsettled a country. (L. French, I.C.S., *The Panjab Colony Manual* [Lahore, Civil and Military Gazette Press, 1907], p. 1.) The Hissar colonies were not Canal Colonies, i.e. no canal irrigation was provided, a fact that may have contributed to their failure. But they did provide a precedent for the use of disbanded troops in colonization of wastelands, a precedent of some value along the UBDC and of much greater importance in later projects.

21. It should be noted that the American Civil War, which curtailed Liverpool's cotton supply, was still a decade in the future and that when it came the British turned first to Egypt (where the Mohammed Ali Barrage had just been

The inception of the second Punjab canal, the Sirhind, which also involved the construction of a rim station headworks, brought new problems to both the administrators and the engineers. Administrators up to the level of the Viceroy and the Secretary of State for India were involved because the proposal came in 1861 from the Maharaja of Patiala through whose territory the canal, in part, would run. The Maharaja's proposal took the form of an offer to bear the costs of surveying and project preparation if the British would furnish the personnel to do the work. He also proposed to pay for the works constructed within his territory. The British accepted his offer and detailed Captain Crofton of the Royal Engineers, who had had many years of experience on the Western Jumna and UBDC canals, to carry out surveys in 1861–63. Patiala was one of the cis-Sutlej Sikh states that had proved to be conspicuously loyal during the Mutiny, providing troops and supplies for the recapture of Delhi. Thus the British were particularly well-disposed toward the Maharaja, and his proposal met with a much warmer reception than a similar one made shortly thereafter by the Maharaja of Jammu and Kashmir for a perennial canal originating in his terri-

completed) to make good the cotton deficiency, and only secondarily to India. Furthermore, the Punjab was originally considered too cold for cotton, and when Indian production was expanded, the Bombay Government took the lead with plantations in Gujarat and southern Sind. "That the Punjab will ever prove a productive cotton country, or one on which we could always depend for even a moderate supply, I very much doubt; like many other useful Plants, which flourish almost spontaneously in the more kindly climate of the Lower Provinces, it generally falls a victim, on the eve of attaining maturity, to the rigours of a winter, often sudden as it is severe. . . . To so natural a cause, can we suggest any remedy? 1st. To me it appears that a more hardy description of plant might be introduced; with that object I now forward a few seeds of a particular sort, *said* [italics in original] to endure the cold of this part of India, and as the solitary bush from which they were gathered is now four or five years old, the assertion appears probable. [This seed originally came from the Deccan and had been planted in a Punjab garden.] . . . I am told that either March or June will answer for the sowings. I should prefer the former as likely to furnish the *earlier* crop; however both should be tried." Lt. W. H. Lowther, Note "On Cotton" dated 27 August 1851, *Proceedings of the Sixth Meeting of the Agri-Horticultural Society of Lahore, 14 October 1851, in Proceedings of the Agri-Horticultural Society of the Punjab from May to 31 December, 1851,* Lahore, Lahore Chronicle Press, 1852. The Society was founded on May 16, 1851, with the encouragement of Henry Lawrence and is responsible for the botanical garden that now surrounds Henry Lawrence Hall and John Lawrence Hall in Lahore and is known as the *Bagh-i-Jinnah.*

tory and extending into the Rechna Doab.[22] In the latter case, the British expressed preference for an inundation canal, with its head in their own territory, over a perennial one beginning in the Maharaja's territory. (When the Upper Chenab Canal was finally built, however, the engineers attempted to have their cake and eat it too by designing a perennial canal with its headworks at Marala outside Jammu territory. This site selection has caused a great deal of trouble, as we shall see.)

So one might assume that the guiding principle in joint British-Princely State projects was who controlled the headworks. It might also be pointed out that the British had Patiala surrounded, whereas Jammu-Kashmir was a frontier state. But nothing in the contemporary proceedings indicates that the British kept out of Jammu for fear that they could not control the headworks. On the contrary, D. F. McLeod, then Financial Commissioner of the Punjab, in commenting on Crofton's proposal, asserted the supreme right of Government "necessarily resulting from its position as lord of the great rivers" to levy a duty on water whether supplied to the Princely States or to British India and "as paramount power" to build headworks for its canals wherever it chose, "if needful, on payment of a

22. On September 26, 1864, the Secretary in the Public Works Department, Punjab, told the Executive Engineer on Special Duty, Rechna Doab Canals, "Though it is unquestionable that a canal of the more complete description [i.e. a perennial canal with its headworks in Jammu] for this Doab, as for the Baree Doab, is most desirable, His Honour the Lieutenant Governor desires you to restrict attention at present to works of irrigation which can be executed within our own territory." (Government of the Punjab, "Proceedings in the Public Works Department during the month of September, 1864, Agricultural Proceeding No. 20," dated 26 September 1864, from the Secretary to Government, Punjab, in the Public Works Department to the Executive Engineer on Special Duty, Rechna Doab Canals [London, India Office Library], p. 102.)

Contrast this with the attitude expressed by the same official concerning the Patiala (Sirhind) project: "on the propriety of alienating any part of the water of a river flowing through British territory the Lieutenant Governor concurs with the view that while 'it would be unreasonable to give up the whole of the water to lands not our own, yet it is proper to allow the native states, *under circumstances like those in the present case* [italics supplied], to share, on well adjusted conditions, in the benefits of the water.'" (Government of the Punjab, "Proceedings in the Public Works Department during the month of December, 1864, Agricultural Proceeding No. 3," dated 16 December 1864, from the Secretary to Government, Punjab, in the Public Works Department to the Government of India, Public Works Department [London, India Office Library], p. 71.)

just consideration in return."[23] But McLeod saw the wisdom of
reciprocity in such dealings:

> Passing from the financial to the purely political aspect of
> the question, I regard our relation toward the Native States
> as so closely connecting our interests with theirs in this matter,
> that the dictates of prudence as well as of generosity appear
> to me to require us to act in a spirit of liberal reciprocity. . . .
> I do not think that we could consistently enforce the claim if
> we were to refuse to grant a like privilege, under befitting
> circumstances, to adjoining Native States. It may not be out of
> place also if I remark that, the intimate connection of interest
> which such participation would establish between our Govern-
> ment and theirs, in a matter of the very greatest and yearly-
> increasing importance, could hardly fail to be productive of
> the most beneficial results.[24]

But the most disinterested statement of Government policy in canal
construction came from Captain J. H. Dyas, who from his position
as Executive Engineer in charge of building the UBDC had risen to
become Director of Canals in the Punjab. Commenting on Crofton's
proposal, Dyas wrote:

> Looking as an Engineer merely at the question of the employ-
> ment for irrigation of the water of any river, and assuming that
> no special reasons exist for irrigating any particular tract, I
> am of opinion that the best line for a canal is that from which
> the largest extent of country can be irrigated at the smallest
> cost, irrespective of the name or nature of the existing Govern-
> ment of the country in question.
> If a larger extent of Putiala than of British territory can be
> irrigated from the Sutlej with the same quantity of water at a
> smaller cost, then it would appear to me that the Sutlej was

23. "Memorandum dated 26 April 1864 by D. F. McLeod, Financial Commissioner, Punjab, on proposed system of canals to be taken from the Sutlej near
Kirutpore . . . as surveyed and reported on by Captain James Crofton, Royal
Engineers," in Government of the Punjab, "Agricultural Proceeding No. 3,"
dated 16 December 1864, p. 83.
24. Ibid., pp. 83–84.

intended for the irrigation of Putiala, and I would run the canal accordingly.

Governments are always liable to change, but a properly made canal will endure for centuries, if not for all time, and every Government is equally interested in its maintenance.[25]

Although there may be, in the phrase "the largest extent of country can be irrigated at the smallest cost," the same inherent contradiction as in the Utilitarians' "greatest good for the greatest number," no prince, and indeed no inhabitant of a Princely State, could quarrel with a policy so fairly stated.

It may be noted for future reference that Crofton's report, though greatly praised by his superiors, was not very definite on the questions of cost and amortization of the proposed canal, a deficiency pointed out by McLeod.[26] But by the spring of 1868, the general scheme submitted by the Punjab Government had been accepted by the Government of India, and, although the estimate of cost was still "confessedly rough" at "something over two millions sterling," the Punjab Government was authorized to proceed with more exact designs and estimates, land acquisition, and negotiations with Patiala.[27] Later that year, the Government of India approved the commencement of construction in anticipation of formal sanction from the Secretary of State for India, and even though the exact estimates had not been submitted. When these came in, they amounted to 8,753,444 rupees or 875,344 pounds, and the returns were estimated at 10 per cent on the outlay.[28] A treaty was signed with

25. "Memorandum dated 22 October, 1862, by Captain J. H. Dyas on Captain Crofton's Preliminary Report of the Sutlej Canal Project," in Government of the Punjab, Agricultural Proceeding No. 3, dated 16 December 1864, p. 82. The Government of India adopted a similar policy: "the only project which should be entertained by the Government of India, is the best that can be devised irrespective of the territorial boundaries." (Quoted in Montagu, "Presidential Address," p. iv.)

26. "Memorandum dated 26 April 1864 by D. F. McLeod," in Government of the Punjab, Agricultural Proceeding No. 3, dated 16 December 1864, p. 85.

27. Government of India, Public Works Department (Irrigation), "Letter No. 62 (Public Works) to the Secretary of State for India," dated April 20, 1868, in India, Public Works Department, Letters Received, 1868, *15*, (London, India Office Library), 149.

28. Government of India, Public Works Department (Irrigation), "Letter No. 90 (Public Works) to the Secretary of State for India," dated 30 June 1870, in

Sirhind Canal

Patiala and work on the Sirhind Canal, as it was now named, commenced in 1869. The administrators had, for the time being, done their part; it now lay with the engineers to do theirs.

The Sirhind Canal

As with the UBDC, the main problem of the Sirhind Canal was the design of the headworks. The topographical situation at Rupar was generally similar to that at Madhopur. Both are "rim stations" in the true sense of the word, places where the Sutlej and the Ravi emerge from the Siwaliks to start their long journeys across the Indus Plains. It will be recalled that in 1869 there was no weir across the Ravi at Madhopur. The original designers had considered one unnecessary, and though experience had since shown them to be wrong, the new intake was yet to be built. At Rupar the need to have a weir across the entire Sutlej was clear from the beginning, but there was no direct precedent for such a work. True, between 1836 and 1855, Captain (later Sir) Arthur Cotton had built three masonry weirs in Madras across the Coleroon distributary of the Cauvery, across the Godaveri, and across the Kistna, but all of these were built at or near the head of the deltas and all of them were built on beds of hard sand. No one in India or abroad had built a weir across a major stream at its rim station, where the river in flood brings down heavy boulders and unassorted gravels, sands, and silts, and where the foundation materials are accordingly irregular and highly permeable:

> the Rupar weir was certainly a bold experiment on a large scale. The theory of construction of masonry works on permeable foundations did not exist and there was nothing else in the world which could guide the designers save a few somewhat similar works on a very much smaller scale in Southern Europe.

India, Public Works Department, Letters Received, 1870, *17* (London, India Office Library), 229. At this time, the Indian rupee was maintained at 10 to the pound sterling. The first figure would, in the subcontinent, be written Rupees 87,53,444, corresponding to Rupees 87 lakhs, 53 thousand, 444, but we shall adopt the system used in the text as offering "the least confusion to the most readers."

Under such conditions, it is not surprising that some serious mistakes were made.[29]

Perhaps the main error was that a depth of only 2 feet was provided for collecting silt in the pocket at the intake of the canal. Furthermore, because the relatively steep gradient on the UBDC had induced erosion, designers of the Sirhind Canal reduced its slope to 30 per cent of that of the UBDC. "The canal was opened in 1882 and in view of the care which the designers and constructors had taken to induce the worst possible silting conditions, it is not surprising that heavy silt and all the troubles arising therefrom, were experienced immediately."[30] For the next ten years, silt continued to build up both in the pocket and in the canal, thus radically reducing the capacity of the canal below the 1,000 cusecs it was designed to carry. Finally, in the mid 1890s, it appeared that the canal might silt up completely: "it looked very much as if the silt trouble had killed the Sirhind Canal and that the canal might have to be abandoned."[31] However,

> Colonel Ottley, the Chief Engineer at the time, . . . decided to modify the headworks on lines which have since become standard. A divide groyne one thousand feet long was constructed upstream of the undersluices so as to form a distinct though limited silt trap in front of the canal head regulator. Deposits of silt herein were to be scoured out by opening the undersluices. The waterway of the head regulator was increased so permitting a false cill to be inserted above the permanent cill, thus in effect increasing the depth of the undersluice pocket and passing top water only into the canal. At this stage, the regulator cill was 12 feet above the floor of the undersluices instead of 2 feet in the original design. The "still pond" system of regulation was introduced which, with minor modifications, is today the standard method of regulation at the older canal headworks in the Province [pre-Partition Punjab].[32]

29. Montagu, "Presidential Address," p. v.
30. Ibid.
31. Ibid.
32. Ibid, pp. v–vi.

Administrative Doubts

Meanwhile, the administrators were also having their problems. In December 1872 the Secretary of State for India had sent to the Governor-General a biting complaint citing experience with four separate recent canal irrigation projects, "all of which were originally proposed as highly productive but which were found in the course of construction, or after completion, to be signal failures." The Government of India was requested to apply "a proportionately radical remedy" to prevent irrigation schemes, designed to "benefit the people of India, not more by their direct influence in agriculture than indirectly by causing a largely augmented flow into the national exchequer," from turning into failures. The Secretary of State concluded:

> unless very much more thought has in general been bestowed upon them than those specially adverted to above would seem to have received, it is only too probable that the thirty millions sterling which have been provisionally accepted as the amount in round numbers required within the current decade for the extension of irrigation, may eventually prove to have been expended, not in diminution, but in augmentation, of the national debt of India.[33]

Seldom was the India Office so caustic in its criticism of the work of its emissaries, even in political matters. The Government of India dutifully circulated the admonition to the local governments "with the request that every precaution may be exercised in submitting projects for Irrigation works in future."[34] So unpromising was the climate that a project for the irrigation of the Rechna Doab, though carefully drawn by E. O. Palmer, was not even submitted by the Punjab Government.

33. This selection and the quotations in the preceding paragraphs are extracts from paragraph 5 of the "Dispatch from the Secretary of State for India to the Government of India, No. 114, dated 18 December 1872," quoted in Government of the Punjab, "Punjab Irrigation Proceedings, March, 1873, Proceeding No. 7" (London, India Office Library), pp. 42–43.

34. Ibid., p. 43.

Nor did the situation improve over the next decade. The Western Jumna Canal, although it continued to pay its way, was producing severe waterlogging and salinization of the lands it served. The UBDC was still eroding its bed, and a proper distribution system had yet to be built. No sooner was the Sirhind Canal opened in 1882 than the above-described errors in its construction became evident.[35]

In the meantime, however, a change was occurring in the motivation behind canal construction. The Punjab had now enjoyed the Pax Britannica for over three decades, or two generations in the social order of the subcontinent. Although the population of the Punjab in 1849 can merely be surmised, a backward extrapolation from the censuses of 1868 and 1881 would place it in the vicinity of 15,000,000 persons. (The census of 1868 returned 16,250,000, and that of 1881, 17,270,000.[36]) Under these conditions, each passing year increased the danger of famine unless the agricultural production could be increased at least as rapidly as population.

In 1878, a severe famine hit North India, and forced the Government of India to reconsider its attitude toward irrigation projects. Local governments were invited to submit new schemes, and in 1882 the Punjab offered three suggestions: (1) a canal to be drawn from the Sidhnai stretch of the lower Ravi; (2) a new Chenab Canal project; and (3) the Lower Sohag and Para canals to be drawn from the Sutlej below Ferozepore.[37] The first two evolved into perennial canals; the Lower Sohag and Para remained only inundation schemes, although they watered almost 100,000 acres of wasteland and served in the Pakpattan area as the basis for one of the earliest new settlement schemes.[38]

It should be noted that none of the perennial schemes introduced

35. Montagu, "Presidential Address," p. vi.
36. Paul W. Paustian, *Canal Irrigation in the Punjab* (New York, Columbia University Press, 1930), p. 80.
37. Montagu, "Presidential Address," p. vi.
38. Paustian, pp. 50–51. We shall deal primarily with the perennial canal schemes through which the significant advances in irrigation techniques and in the settlement of new lands were achieved. After the annexation of the Punjab, the British renovated many of the old inundation canals, notably those around Multan, those on the Punjab bank of the Sutlej, and those on both sides of the Indus between Dera Ismail Khan and Dera Ghazi Khan (the Derajat region and the lower Thal or, as the region between the Indus and the Jhelum-Chenab was called in those days, the "Sind Sagar" Doab). Although many of these projects proved to be financial successes, they were of comparatively small scale and did not lead to the settlement of great numbers of people or to the develop-

into the Punjab up to 1882 involved any substantial extension of irrigation to new lands. On the contrary, the Western Jumna, Upper Bari Doab, and Sirhind canal systems primarily served lands long settled and cultivated in the eastern or upper portions of the doabs. Thus, their effect was to intensify both cultivation and crowding.

Had the original UBDC scheme been carried out as planned, irrigation would have been brought to much of the wasteland in the central Bari Doab. The same was true of the Rechna Doab canal scheme which was aborted in 1873. Ten years later, both the Government of the Punjab and the Government of India reverted to plans that would bring water to the wastelands and allow them to be settled with surplus population from the upper doab "dry" districts, i.e. districts with some well, but little or no canal, irrigation. Such an approach had three distinct advantages: (1) it would relieve crowding and hence danger of famine in the settled districts; (2) it would bring into cultivation, and thus revenue-production, vast tracts of wasteland that were inhabited only by the lawless nomads and *junglis*;[39] and (3) the fertile lands thus brought into production

---

ment of an economic infrastructure of the magnitude called forth by the perennial systems.

The development of colonization, "settlement," and revenue procedures in the Punjab has been so thoroughly traced by French, Trevaskis, Paustian, and Sir Malcolm Darling that only the important outlines are given here. More will be said on the subject in Chapter 8. The reader is especially referred to Darling's *The Punjab Peasant in Prosperity and Debt* (4th ed., London and Bombay, Oxford University Press and Geoffrey Cumberlege, 1947), to Rashid A. Malik, *Irrigation Development and Land Occupance in the Upper Indus Basin* (Bloomington, Indiana University doctoral dissertation published by the author, August, 1963), and to Sir James M. Douie, I.C.S., *Punjab Settlement Manual* (5th ed., issued in 1961, Lahore, Superintendent Government Printing, West Pakistan, 1962). It should be noted that "settlement" in British India meant cadastral surveying and revenue assessment rather than "colonization." A specialized study on revenue administration in the Punjab is currently under preparation by P. H. M. van den Dungen of the History Department, Institute of Advanced Studies, Australian National University, Canberra.

39. The Western notion that equates "jungle" with tropical rain forest is erroneous, although widespread. The word "jungle," which apparently is of Persian origin and was first applied to the dense forests south of the Caspian Sea, came into the English language from the monsoonal regions of the subcontinent and especially from the subhumid *bar* "uplands" (see n. 1 above) of the central Punjab doabs. There it connoted a brush and coarse grass vegetation, useful only for the grazing of camels and, to some extent, of sheep, goats, and cattle. Its advantages for concealment were great, and hence the *bar* wastelands became the haunt of fugitives and robbers as well as of the unruly herdsmen. These inhabitants of the "jungle" were indiscriminately known as *junglis*.

could be expected, eventually, to produce a surplus of grain which, provided adequate transportation was furnished, could be shipped back to the densely settled districts not only of the eastern Punjab but even into the Ganges Valley and the Central Provinces. This was the inception of the concept of the Punjab as the granary of India. It is to be noted, however, that the idea of producing cash crops other than grain (e.g. cotton and sugarcane) did not yet enter into consideration. Famine relief and valuation of Crown Waste Lands were the motives behind the second wave of perennial canal projects in the Punjab.

The Second Wave of Canal Building

The Sidhnai Canal Project was a small one, since the water available was limited to the "regenerated" supply of the Ravi between Madhopur and the new headworks built at Theyraj (about 45 miles northeast of Multan). The scheme was first proposed in 1856 when it was still believed that the UBDC could be tailed into the Ravi a few miles upstream of Theyraj. As revived in 1882, the Sidhnai Canal Project was to serve 351,000 acres, of which 206,000 comprised wastelands belonging to the Crown. The importance of the scheme lay not so much in the area to be irrigated as in the fact that it served, as had the Lower Sohag and Para inundation schemes, as an experiment in the migration of agriculturalists from the eastern Punjab and in devising settlement procedures for them. The site selected was at the head of a remarkably straight reach of the Ravi, known as the "Sidhnai."[40] Work was initiated in December 1883, and the Sidhnai Canal opened in May 1886. Three additional short canals were added by 1891. Although designed for perennial irrigation, the "regenerated" flow of the Ravi (due to seepage from the bed and banks and the contribution of any intermediate *nallas*, or

40. There are several theories for the origin of this seven-mile stretch, so unusual in a meandering stream of the Indus Plains. The best explanation is that the river was artificially straightened by order of a ruler of Multan who hoped thereby to keep the Ravi, in its natural rightward migration, from abandoning his city—a vain effort. The peasants at Sidhnai still point to the date palms that line the river and say that the workers who straightened the channel were fed on dates brought up from Multan. In spitting out the pits, the laborers are said to have planted the palms!

intermittent streams) proved insufficient, and the canals had to be closed for a varying period each winter. This condition was finally corrected in the Haveli project of 1937–39 by bringing additional water from the Chenab. But its existence in the 1890s had a great influence on the inception of the Triple Canals Project.

The third scheme entertained by the Punjab Government in the 1880s was one for irrigating the central Rechna Doab. We have seen that the 1862 proposal of the Maharaja of Jammu and Kashmir, as well as the 1872 scheme put forward by the engineer E. O. Palmer, both of which called for irrigating the entire doab, had been denied consideration. Indeed, the problem of an efficient headworks for the upper Rechna Doab was to plague engineers for another eighty years.

The project that was finally adopted in 1891 called for irrigating the huge area of 1,100,000 acres by means of the largest canal— 8,000 cusecs—yet constructed in India. The proposal estimated the return at 11.46 per cent by 1909–10 and 15.64 per cent by 1914–15, including both direct and indirect revenues. In actuality, thanks to the Triple Canals Project of 1905–15, the Lower Chenab Canal has come to irrigate 2.9 million acres and to carry up to 11,500 cusecs. With the exception of some post-Partition canals on the Indus, it remains the largest canal in the subcontinent. Its financial success was far in excess of even the optimistic expectations.[41]

With the Chenab Canal, the British had achieved both an administrative and an engineering breakthrough. The administrative success came through the application of the settlement and revenue techniques worked out at Pakpattan and at Sidhnai. Popham Young was immortalized in local folklore for his settlement work, although the largest town in the project was named for James Lyall, a former Financial Commissioner who was Lieutenant Governor of the Punjab when the project was initiated. If low incidence of rural debt is any measure, the Lyallpur District today is the most prosperous in the West Punjab.[42]

41. French, *The Panjab Colony Manual,* pp. 22–24. See also Deva Singh, *Colonization in the Rechna Doab* (Lahore, Punjab Government Record Office Publications, Monograph No. 7, 1930).

42. Government of Pakistan, Ministry of Agriculture and Works, Agricultural Census Organization, *1960 Pakistan Census of Agriculture,* 2 vols., *1, West Pakistan* (Karachi, Government of Pakistan, October 1963), Report I, Table 37, "Farms Reporting Debt, Classified by Size of Debt and by Size of Farm," 606–20.

The engineering success was due to the incorporation of the techniques and prototypes that had been developed at Madhopur and Rupar, with none of the handicaps. The structure built at Khanki, 10 miles below Wazirabad on the Chenab, incorporated a shuttered weir 4,097 feet long divided by piers into eight bays. Hinged iron shutters which could be dropped, a whole bay at a time, thanks to a dovetailed tripping device, were provided to control the river level and its direction.[43] On the left bank, a gated canal intake was built at right angles to a series of twelve undersluices which could be used for flushing silt downstream. A deep pond served to settle the silt before it could enter the canal. Protective and training works extended along the left bank, while the line of the weir was carried by a bund for nearly 4 miles to the right margin of the floodplain.

Thus part of the success of the Khanki weir was due to its scale. The Indus Rivers were now being approached with assurance rather than with timidity.[44] But it should be noted that the Khanki weir had great site advantages over its predecessors. It was not, as were Madhopur and Rupar, a rim station weir which had to accommodate the heavier alluvial deposits dropped by a river suddenly emerging from the mountains onto the plains. Nor was it, like Sidhnai, a headworks dependent upon the regenerated flow of a river already fully tapped for irrigation upstream. Khanki, some 40 miles from the foothills, could abstract from the full water flow of the Chenab without having to contend with any of its heavier silt.

On the other hand, the distribution system did include one dubious feature not formerly adopted on such a scale:

As indicated in footnote 38, Sir Malcolm Darling devoted an entire book to the significance of rural debt in the Punjab.

43. Buckley, p. 18.

44. It should be explained that before the Khanki weir was constructed, a smaller headworks was built in 1887 for the Ramnagar inundation canal. This was quickly silted up and abandoned. But the Ramnagar failure may be blamed on administrative rather than engineering hesitance. The Irrigation Branch of the Public Works Department was ready, as the Palmer scheme demonstrated, to tackle the whole river on a perennial basis. Perhaps the value of the Ramnagar scheme was that it convinced the Government that parsimony was poor economy. In the event, the Khanki Project incorporated the Ramnagar Canal and turned failure into success. See Deva Singh, pp. 11–12; French, pp. 21–22; and Paustian, p. 55.

The canals are so aligned that it is not possible to escape surplus water back into the river; there is, consequently, a difficulty in disposing of any surplus volume flowing in the channel. Those who are conversant with the regulation of water in a large canal system will appreciate the anxiety of an engineer, who knows that a canal above him is bringing down over 10,000 cusecs, and that he must, some way or another, arrange to dispose of it. On the Chenab Canal seven depressions in the ground have been selected and surrounded with earthen banks: these form reservoirs into which it is possible to divert surplus waters in an emergency.[45]

This method of disposing of surplus canal water was well-designed to aggravate the problem of seepage from the irrigation system with its consequent high water tables and salinization of soils (see Chapters 2 and 9).

When the Lower Chenab Canal (as it was subsequently termed) was opened in 1892, it irrigated 150,000 acres. Work on the three branches and distributaries went forward rapidly, and by 1900 it was irrigating over one million acres.[46] Meanwhile, the skills learned at Khanki had already been applied 32 miles away, across the Chaj Doab, at Rasul. Here a weir that is almost a twin of the one at Khanki was thrown across the Jhelum in record time (actual construction required only from October 1899 to May 1901). Rasul weir is 4,100 feet long, or three feet longer than Khanki. Like its predecessor, it is divided into eight bays provided with hinged iron shutters, and the line of the weir is also continued by a long bund to the edge of the former floodplain on the right side. The undersluices, divide groyne, and canal intake are also similar to those at Khanki. But there is one difference. Rasul marks the point where the Jhelum cuts around the western end of the Pabbi Hills, which may be considered an eastern outlier of the Salt Range. Thus, the left-hand bank of the river is high, in contrast to the situation at Khanki, and the weir has actually diverted the Jhelum to the southeast from its former bed, which was barred by the bund. This slight diversion,

45. Buckley, p. 18.
46. Montagu, "Presidential Address," p. vii.

which actually facilitated construction, plus the presence of the Pabbi Hills and part of the Potwar Plateau between the weir and the rim station at Mangla, have created a more serious silting problem at Rasul, even though the reach of the Jhelum is as great as that of the Chenab between Khanki and Marala.

The (Lower) Jhelum Canal is considerably smaller than the Lower Chenab Canal, having a capacity of only 4,000 cusecs. But the lower part of the Chaj Doab is proportionally much smaller than the lower part of the Rechna, and the canal was *originally* designed to irrigate only 787,418 acres, or three-fourths the duty of the Lower Chenab Canal but with half the designed flow.[47]

Thus, by the year 1901, each of the Punjab Rivers except the Beas[48] had been tapped to support an extensive irrigation system. The Sutlej and the Ravi had rim-station headworks; that on the Ravi was draining the river dry in most seasons, leaving only re-generated flow for the Sidhnai system. All engineering problems appeared to have been solved. Colonization and settlement work was well in hand, and revenues from the newer systems were more than making good any deficits on the old. The Punjab was producing grain surpluses in most years and was beginning to assume its role as the granary of northern India. Everything called for extending the systems and reaping even larger returns. The general financial picture at the end of the second wave of canal building is shown in Table 2.

47. Buckley, p. 18. Paustian, pp. 58–59, gives an interesting account of how, for the first time, the Punjab Government encountered difficulties with local landowners over incorporating the Shahpur Inundation Canals into the Lower Jhelum system and finally, in 1916, abandoned the attempt at some cost to itself. The Government of West Pakistan overcame these difficulties in the 1950s and subsequently completed the Shahpur Branch more or less along the lines origi-nally planned.

48. The Bist-Jullundur Doab between the Beas and Sutlej was too small an area and received, relatively, too much rainfall to warrant the construction of a modern irrigation system in the British period, although some improvements were made to the inundation canals. Another reason for reluctance lay in the plans to use Beas water below Harike, in conjunction with Sutlej water, for irrigating the southern Punjab and Bahawalpur State. Not until 1954, when the Rupar headworks were remodeled for the Bhakra Project, was a Bist Doab Canal opened to provide restricted perennial irrigation south of Jullundur (see Chap. 7).

Table 2. Cost of Principal Productive Irrigation Works
to the End of March, 1903[a]

Name of Works	Approximate Full Discharge of Canals [cusecs]	Area Irrigable [acres]	Cost [rupees]	Cost per Acre Irrigable [rupees]
Western Jumna Canal	6,400	809,000	17,251,501	21
[Upper] Bari Doab Canal	6,500	849,000	19,585,680	23
Sirhind Canal	8,200	1,170,000	24,652,228	21
Upper Sutlej (including				
Lower Sohag and Para Canals)	—	349,700	1,701,510	5
[Lower] Chenab Canal	10,800	1,600,000	27,509,322	17
Sidhnai Canal	2,400	195,000	1,291,905	6
[Lower] Jhelum Canal	3,800	266,500	11,468,942	43

a. Source: Buckley, p. 310. The Lower Chenab and Lower Jhelum canals had not yet reached their maximum acreages.

A Stock-Taking Interlude

Although at the turn of the century the sky over the Punjab seemed rosy for irrigation, the proverbial small cloud was in evidence. Or, to mix the metaphor, the absence of clouds was beginning to pose a problem. A shortage of water, in the places where it was most needed for irrigation expansion, required analysis of the entire provincial situation and planning on at least a regional basis before further construction was undertaken.

The problem of a water shortage had not been unforeseen, of course. The first modern canal built in the Punjab, the UBDC, had demonstrated all too clearly that it was literally possible to dry up a major river in the cool season by building a weir to feed a perennial canal. But the great advantage of weir or barrage type of irrigation (i.e. diversion without storage) in the Indus Basin was that the dry period was usually short and that some 75,000 square miles of snow-clad mountains provided a natural reservoir during most of the time between monsoons. Both climate and topography combined to make irrigation cheap. Thanks to the gentle gradients and the sub-parallel courses of the five Punjab rivers, a minimal amount of works in the plains served to bring water to the hundreds of thousands or even millions of acres under the command of each barrage. But, once the easy and obvious barrage sites had been tapped, the next obvious step, storage dams in the mountains which could retain the monsoon's surplus water for use in the following dry season, required a much more difficult and costly undertaking. By 1901, irrigation in the Punjab seemed to have reached a new level of magnitude, both in engineering and in the administrative-fiscal sectors. Furthermore, another serious famine had occurred in 1899–1901, emphasizing the need to extend the "breadbasket" for northern India. The situation was not dissimilar in other provinces where irrigation had begun to play a major role in the economy.[49]

It was therefore eminently suitable that a review and evaluation of progress to date be made, and that careful plans be devised for future development. Accordingly, the Governor-General, Lord Curzon, established a "Commission Appointed to Report on the Irrigation of India as a Protection Against Famine." Under the presidency of Sir Colin C. Scott-Moncrieff, the Commission was directed to:

(1) ascertain the utility of irrigation under local conditions of agriculture;

(2) report on the extent to which irrigation has been provided by the States, and the results thereof;

(3) determine the scope which exists for further extensions of State irrigation works;

(4) consider the extent to which local capacities for irrigation have already been utilised by private individuals;

(5) consider the character and utility of the works on which relief labour has been employed during the late famine [1899–1901]; to make recommendations, wherever possible, either for the completion or definite abandonment of such works as have not been completed.[50]

49. The preeminence of the Punjab in irrigation at this time may be seen both from the fact that of 11.2 million acres irrigated by major canals in the Indian Empire (including Princely States) in 1900–01, 4.6 million were in the Punjab (Madras ranked second with 2.9 million acres and United Provinces third with 1.9 million), and that of the total capital outlay on irrigation works up to 1900–01, some 3.66 million rupees, expenditures in the Punjab represented almost 30 per cent. *(Report of the Indian Irrigation Commission, 1901–03, 1*, para. 77, p. 21.)

50. Ibid., *1*, Preface, para. 1, p. (1).

The Commission convened at Lahore on October 28, 1901; on October 30 it was present at Rasul for the formal opening of the (Lower) Jhelum Canal; and it then proceeded on tour throughout India. (The selection of the most pleasant season of the year for the tour of the Irrigation Commission may be contrasted with the season chosen, forty-six years later, for the work of the Punjab and Bengal Boundary Commissions; see Chapter 1.) In each province visited, a temporary member, familiar with the region, traveled with the Commission. For the Punjab, this was James Wilson, then Settlement Commissioner.

Table 3. Rainfall, Runoff, and Utilization for Irrigation
in River Basins of Northern India[a]

	All-India (excluding Burma, Assam, East Bengal)	*Indus-Luni[b] Basins*	*G a n g e s* *B a s i n*	
			Above Benares	*Below Benares*
Area [square miles]	1,434,000	450,000	192,000	205,500
Rainfall [average year, billion cubic feet]	125.00	20.00	16.75	27.25
Surface flow [average year, billion cubic feet]	51.00	5.85	6.00	11.50
Utilized in irrigation [billion cubic feet]	6.75	1.75	0.60	1.35

a. Source: *Report of the Indian Irrigation Commission, 1901–03, 1,* diagram facing p. 14.

b. The Luni is a nonperennial stream that collects the drainage of southern Rajputana (Ajmer and Jodhpur but not Jaipur or Udaipur) and occasionally flows into the Rann of Cutch, which is today more dry land than swamp, and which has not reached the sea in at least 300 years (J. Abbott, *Sind: A Re-Interpretation of the Unhappy Valley* [London, 1924] Ch. IV). While the Luni Basin adds some 85,000 square miles to the area of the Indus Basin in this tabulation, it does not significantly increase the rainfall, surface flow, or amount utilized in irrigation. The Commission probably included the Luni because their tour took them from Sukkur to Jaipur and Ajmer. The Rajputana Agency, at the turn of the century, included 113,000 square miles, of which 1,172,000 *acres,* or only 18,300 square miles, were irrigated; most of these fell in the upper Ganges Basin rather in the Luni. (*Report of the Indian Irrigation Commission, 1901–03, 1,* 12, para. 48.)

In its report, the Commission presented the data shown in Table 3 concerning the supplies and utilization of water in the subcontinent, the Indus Basin, and the adjoining densely populated and famine-prone areas of the United Provinces. On the basis of its estimates, the Commission concluded that in the Indus Basin, "under exceptionally favourable conditions," only 9 per cent of the total rainfall, or 30 per cent of the surface flow, was retained for artificial irrigation.

> If all the works which are now conceived to be possible in the Punjab and Sind are constructed, although they may absorb an additional half billion cubic feet, not a single large tract that is especially liable to famine will be affected thereby, and 60 per cent of the surface water will still run to waste in the sea. No human skill or ingenuity will carry any portion of this volume of $3\frac{1}{2}$ billion cubic feet to the high-lying plains of Jaipur [actually in the upper Ganges Basin] and Marwar [in the Luni Basin], or over the ridge of the Indus Valley to famine-stricken tracts in other parts of India.[51]

Since the water could not be transferred out of the Indus Basin, the obvious answer was to utilize as much of it as possible inside the Basin, produce a grain surplus there, and "export" this to the surrounding, famine-liable regions. To do so required further extensions of the transportation system. But it also required some method of utilizing at least half a billion cubic feet of the four billion running to waste in the sea. Storage dams were proposed but seemed prohibitively expensive. Barrages across the lower Indus, feeding perennial canals in Sind which as yet had only inundation systems, were feasible but also extremely costly due to the proportions of the lower Indus in flood. The Punjab was the obvious place for expansion. The Commission saw it as the region best adapted for extensive irrigation from perennial canals, and the one that had made the greatest progress but still had the greatest room for expansion. There was no province in which the direct profits of irrigation works had been so high or in which new works promised so much.[52] But only two rivers offered the water: the Indus itself, which could serve the Derajat or the unpromising Sind Sagar Doab (Thal) regions of the Punjab; or the Sutlej, unharnessed below Rupar and receiving the Beas at Harike.

For irrigation of Crown Waste Lands on the Ganji Bar of the

51. Ibid., *1*, para. 70, p. 18.
52. Ibid., *2*, "Provincial," Ch. 14, "The Punjab," para. 1, p. 1.

lower Bari Doab—areas which had been promised Ravi water in the original UBDC plan but which the Ravi proved unable to supply— the Punjab Government now looked to the Sutlej. So did local land-owners whose appetite had been teased by both the UBDC and Sidhnai projects. But these claims were vigorously disputed by the owners of riparian floodplain lands along the Sutlej in the southern Punjab and in Bahawalpur State, who had only inundation canals to serve their needs. Taking Beas-Sutlej water to feed the central por-tions of the doab would not only deprive these owners of any hope for perennial irrigation, but it would reduce the inundation supplies in years of low runoff. Furthermore, running a canal from the Sutlej onto the higher *bar* uplands in the doab to the north would mean running it across the old bed and floodplain of the Beas, a consider-able expense as well as a departure from the well-established prece-dent of using the Punjab streams to irrigate the doabs on their left-hand banks.[53]

The solution to this impasse came in one of those flashes of creative genius that, in other branches of engineering, might have been recog-nized as a "contribution to the art" and rewarded by grant of a patent. In retrospect, the idea is deceptively simple, yet it not only solved the dilemma of its day to the complete satisfaction of all parties but provided the model for the solution of the Indus Waters Dispute half a century later. The solution lay in transferring water from the western rivers to the eastern by means of contour, or "link," canals built across the slope of the land (i.e. almost along the contours), and which could also provide some irrigation en route. Whether the idea originated in one mind or whether, like so many other inventions, it occurred simultaneously to several persons strug-gling with the problem is yet to be determined. The official records give the credit to two officials, James Wilson, the Settlement Com-missioner of the Punjab who served as the temporary member of the Irrigation Commission in that province and who proposed the idea in a memorandum dated October 22, 1901, and Colonel S. L. Jacob, retired Chief Engineer of the Punjab, who submitted a memorandum to the Commission from England supporting Wilson's proposal.

After reminding his readers that all the Punjab Rivers, including

53. Ibid., 2, Ch. 14, para. 28, p. 13. See also the "Sketch Map of Proposals Relating to the Lower Bari Doab Project" between pp. 16–17.

the Indus, bend westward from the rim stations, "possibly due to the effect of the rotation of the earth," and that this deflection brings the Indus and the Jhelum up against hilly country where little land could be commanded for irrigation, Wilson pointed out that it was both logical and economical to continue the practice of using the Punjab streams to irrigate the low-lying *khadir* lands to their left:

> [The Jhelum and Chenab] still have a large surplus of water available, which cannot be used to irrigate the comparatively high land of the Sind-Sagar Doab Thal and must run to waste unless it is employed to irrigate the Lower Bari Doab. In order to do this it must be carried across the Ravi, but this can present no great engineering difficulty, as the Ravi is not a large river; its channel is often dry in the winter, and it would be easy to control its floods in summer (reduced by the amount taken into the Bari Doab Canal) by a weir which would divert them into the canal crossing the valley from the Chenab, or pass them on down its own channel. Even a high-level aqueduct across the Ravi would not be impossible. This would leave the whole of the water of the combined Sutlej and Beas available for the irrigation of the great tract to the south-east, which must otherwise remain forever a desert.[54]

What Wilson had in mind was a barrage across the Chenab below its junction with the Jhelum at Trimmu (this is the scheme embodied in the 1937 Haveli project, discussed below), with a canal cut across the lower Chaj to the Ravi. But he added:

> It might also be found possible, at some future time, to extend the eastern branch of the present Chenab Canal across the Ravi higher up to irrigate that portion of the Bari Doab which lies in the Montgomery District.[55]

Colonel Jacob's contribution lay not only in lending his prestige to Wilson's proposal (for Wilson was not an engineer) but in recasting it into a form that would solve the problem of the upper

54. J. Wilson, "Note on the Means of Irrigation of the Lower Bari Doab," in *Report of the Indian Irrigation Commission, 1901–03, 4,* Appendix, "Selected Evidence," p. 32.
55. Ibid.

Chaj and Rechna doabs as well as that of the lower Bari Doab. Referring to the lower Bari Doab, Jacob wrote:

> It is admitted that it is an easier scheme to irrigate this land from the Sutlej, and also that there are difficulties in the alternative scheme. Nevertheless, the ultimate benefits to the country as a whole by the alternative scheme are so much greater than by the scheme as prepared, while the difficulties are far from insuperable, so the Sutlej should certainly not be drawn upon for this project. . . . The alternative scheme is as follows: make a channel from the Chenab river [at Marala, not Khanki] to the Ravi, and take out a canal from the Ravi [at Balloki] to irrigate the Lower Doab. Then, to make up the deficiency in the Chenab supply, make a channel from the Jhelum [at Mangla] to the Chenab [at Khanki], and take out a channel from the Chenab to supply the lower part of the Chenab Canal [ultimately found unnecessary]. Aqueducts over these big rivers are out of the question, on account of the expense and the great height to which they would have to be raised to clear the floods, etc.; but the method of dropping the water into the river and taking it out again presents no such difficulty.[56]

Colonel Jacob also took the occasion to chide the administrators for their former conservatism with respect to extensive irrigation projects, pointing out that wherever the original project had been enlarged, usually at the behest of the superintending engineer involved, it had met with success. "Let a bolder policy now take the place of the former caution, for experience has shown that this can be safely done." Jacob felt that inundation irrigation was "an excellent device in an early stage of civilization" but should never be allowed to stand in the way of a modern, perennial canal. He ridiculed the objection raised on behalf of Sind by officials of the Bombay Government that heavier withdrawals for irrigation would impair navigation. "The waste of water that would be necessitated by keeping up navigation is out of all proportion to its value. It would be like keeping an elephant to draw a go-cart. Navigation on the

56. Colonel S. L. Jacob, "Paper on Irrigation and Famine Prevention in the Punjab (1st May 1902)," in *Report of the Indian Irrigation Commission, 1901–03, 4*, p. 45. Locations ultimately selected have been interpolated.

rivers in the Punjab or Sind is doomed, and it is useless to try and save it. Navigable canals do not answer in North India, and traffic will have to be by railway."[57]

And Jacob ridiculed the notion that there was insufficient water. Even without storage, there was plenty of water in the Indus Rivers, especially if water duties (the amount of land that a cubic foot of water is to irrigate) were increased, as Jacob urged, and waste through absorption diminished. (Jacob feared overirrigation both because it entailed waste of water and because he was well aware of the danger of waterlogging. Although the policy of maximizing water duties, which prevailed as long as the British remained in India, has been criticized on economic grounds, there is no doubt that it retarded waterlogging of poorly drained lands, and that the connection was early recognized. On the other hand, Wilson and others felt that the water table should be deliberately raised to the point where it could be tapped by wells, thereby saving surface water supplies for districts where wells were impracticable.[58] The implications of this line of reasoning are discussed further in Chapter 9.)

Despite Jacob's prestige, the Irrigation Commission was not immediately convinced by his and Wilson's argument. Assuming that any new diversion from the Sutlej had to be below Rupar and probably below Harike to take advantage of Beas water (the Nangal site did not enter the picture since there was no suggestion of building a storage dam at Bhakra), the Commission pointed out that any left-hand canal from the Sutlej would serve only a small portion of British territory. Most of the command would lie in the northwest corner of Bikaner and in Bahawalpur, Princely States "from which Government could not recover as large a share of the profits of irrigation as it is able to do when canals are carried into crown waste." The Commission considered the desolate sand hills of Bahawalpur "as unpromising a field for the extension of irrigation as the Sind-Sagar Thal," which it was proposed to irrigate from the Indus—a

57. Ibid., p. 44 (all quotations in this paragraph). For a fascinating account of the failure of navigation in the Punjab, see Faqir Chand, Arrora, *Commerce by River in the Punjab, or a Survey of the Activities of the Marine Department of the Government of the Punjab (1861–62 to 1871–72)* (Lahore, Punjab Government Record Office Publications, Monograph No. 9, 1930).

58. J. Wilson, "Note on Future Irrigation Policy in the Punjab," in *Report of the Indian Irrigation Commission, 1901–03, 4*, p. 35.

proposal the Commission recommended be held in abeyance until the problem of the lower part of the Bari Doab was solved. Despite its misgivings, and with unusual modesty and rare prescience, the Commission hesitated to recommend a right-bank Sutlej canal for the Lower Bari Doab Project "which, whatever its merits, will have the effect of rendering it impossible for our successors for all time to utilize the waters of the Sutlej for extensions of irrigation on its left bank. However unpromising such extensions may now appear, a time may come, in a more or less distant future, when the pressure of population and many other causes may justify their construction."[59] The Commission therefore recommended to the Government of India, in December 1902, that the project for a right-hand supply of Sutlej water to the lower Bari Doab be held in abeyance until the whole question of transfer from the western rivers had been thoroughly investigated. The Commission singled out the problem of getting Jhelum water into the Chenab above Khanki as being the crucial one.

Meanwhile, the Punjab Government was carrying out its own detailed investigations. It was obvious from the difference in levels that no canal from Rasul could be brought into the Chenab above Khanki, and it was doubtful that the Jhelum at Rasul could provide the 3,000 cusecs that eventually had to reach the lower Bari Doab. A proposal from the Resident and State Engineer in Kashmir to place a dam below Lake Wular, capable of storing 20 billion cubic feet of water, was eventually ruled out, in part because it revived the old problem of dependence upon a Princely State; but it did serve to focus attention upon the reach of the Jhelum above Rasul.[60] Here the problem was that of circumventing the Pabbi Hills southeast of the Jhelum. What finally turned the trick was the discovery that at Mangla the Jhelum flowed across a broad ledge of

59. *Report of the Indian Irrigation Commission, 1901–03, 2*, Ch. 14, paras. 35–36, p. 17, for all quotations in this paragraph.

60. That Col. Jacob's invitation to "think big" had not been lost on the Commission is shown by their penultimate comment on this proposal: "The fact that the future extensions of irrigation in Bikaner or Bahawalpur may depend on the construction of a storage work in Kashmir, is a signal illustration of the width of view from which large irrigation projects must now be regarded, and of the extent and character of the investigations which they involve." (Ibid., para. 38, p. 18.)

bedrock that could serve as a natural weir. (Practicality was hotly disputed at the time, but the scheme proved to be eminently feasible.) The savings on weir construction could thus be applied to the costly cut through the high bank (longer than that at Madhopur) and to the series of cuts, fills, and level crossings of *nallas* (intermittent streams) necessary to bring the canal down to the plains near Rasul. The Mangla headworks did involve compromising any idea of complete British control because the intake and first 15 miles of the canal had to be placed in Jammu-Kashmir. But the advantages in being able to activate the Triple Canals Project were so great that the problem of political control—which by this time had really become a chimera—was overlooked.

The First Integrated System: The Triple Canals Project

After interim determinations by Sir Thomas Higham (a retired Chief Engineer and a member of the Commission) finally demonstrated that the lower Bari Doab could in winter be irrigated only from the Jhelum and not from either the Ravi or the Chenab, John Benton of the Punjab Irrigation Branch prepared detailed plans and estimates for the Triple Canals Project, which was sanctioned by the Government of India in 1905. Construction of the UJC and UCC began in that year, and of the LBDC in 1907. Buoyed by the report of the Indian Irrigation Commission and the confident predictions of engineers such as Jacob and Higham, the Punjab Irrigation Branch moved into the Triple Canals Project with such the same enthusiasm as accompanied the construction of the Panama Canal at the same period (1907–14).

By locating the intake of the Upper Jhelum Canal (UJC) at Mangla, it was not only possible to deliver water into the Chenab just above the existing Khanki Barrage, but to provide 345,000 new acres in the upper Chaj Doab with irrigation on the way. (The UJC has only one branch, which extends some 37 miles down-doab.) It was calculated that the 8,500-cusec UJC would deliver enough water to Khanki to allow the extraction of 11,742 cusecs from the Chenab at Marala. From that headworks, an Upper Chenab Canal (UCC) could irrigate 650,000 acres in the upper Rechna Doab and still deliver enough water to the Ravi for the irrigation of the lower Bari Doab. To perform this feat, the UCC was designed with a capacity of 11,742 cusecs, the largest capacity in the subcontinent, and it has actually carried almost 15,500.[61] The site finally chosen for crossing the Ravi was Balloki, and the means selected was a barrage (gated weir) designed as a "level crossing." The UCC tailed into the Ravi over a masonry drop on its right or high bank, and the Lower Bari Doab Canal (LBDC) took off directly opposite. Thus the cost of either a syphon or an aqueduct was avoided, and the regenerated supply of the Ravi (if any, and along with some of its silt) was picked up on the way. The LBDC had a capacity of 6,750 cusecs at its intake and was designed to irrigate 878,000 acres, although the actual irrigation reached 1,494,000 acres within thirty years.[62] The LBDC extends from Balloki within filled-in embankments diagonally across the Ravi floodplain until it reaches the higher lands of the doab, the Ganji Bar. From Renala Khurd onward it parallels both the railway and the highway through Montgomery toward Multan, terminating with its last branch, the Jahania, south of Khanewal. Thus the old dream of irrigating the Bari Doab from the foothills to Multan was finally realized.

Of the three headworks employed in the Triple Canals Project, that at Mangla was unique in that it required no weir, the previously mentioned natural bar of shingle and boulders in the bed of the Jhelum serving the purpose. The design of the Balloki headworks was also an innovation in that it incorporated the first proper barrage, as distinguished from a weir (see above, p. 62) built in the Punjab. The Balloki Barrage was 1,646 feet long, divided into thirty-five 40-foot bays by masonry piers each 7.25 feet wide. Each bay had a steel gate operated by winches from the overhead bridge. Being 140 miles downstream from the Madhopur headworks, the siltation problem at Balloki was not serious until, in the 1950s, a second intake was added for a link canal. Even then most of the silt apparently came from the banks of the link. But the Marala site on the Chenab was different. For this rim station headworks a design similar to that at Madhopur was employed. As already mentioned on page 77, a rim-station headworks for the first Rechna Doab Canal had been abandoned in favor of Khanki. It was pointed out at that time (1872–77) that the logical place for a rim-station headworks on the Chenab lay within Jammu territory. Placing it just outside,

61. Montagu, "Presidential Address," p. ix.
62. Ibid.

at Marala, obviated the political problem both in 1905 and again in 1947 when India occupied southern Jammu, but it raised a serious physical problem. For Marala lies just below the conjunction of the Chenab with two mountain torrents, the Jammu Tavi and the Monawar Tavi, which bring down enormous quantities of sediment in flood. Siltation problems were always serious at Marala and became critical in the 1950s when, as at Balloki, a second intake was added for a link canal.

Considerable attention has been devoted to the Triple Canals Project and to the related proceedings of the Indian Irrigation Commission because the project and the discussions that led to it are landmarks in the development of irrigation in the Indus Basin. The work of the Commission represents the first attempt to plan on a basinwide basis. Although the Triple Canals Project represented the integration of only three of the Punjab Rivers,[63] it was evolved in the effort to preserve the Beas-Sutlej for irrigation in northeastern Bikaner and Bahawalpur as well as in southernmost Punjab. The Commission also considered projects for irrigating the Sind Sagar (or Thal) Doab from the Indus and/or from the Chenab (below

---

63. Operational control of the five linked canals (UJC, LJC, UCC, LCC, and LBDC) was a fascinating problem, the solution of which led to the development of a "shares program." (Although physically linked to the system, neither the UBDC nor the Sidhnai Canal participated in this allocation. The UBDC had a right by prior appropriation to all the water it could use from the upper Ravi at Madhopur. Sidhnai, on the other hand, was a sort of residuary legatee, dependent mainly upon regeneration.)

The shares of the five linked canals for the low-water or *rabi* (cool season cropping) period were therefore worked out by the Superintending Engineers of the circles concerned who met annually "in Lahore before the rabi crop began and in the light of lengthening experience, drew up a 'turns' programme, which ultimately crystallised into a permanent system of dividing up available supplies in Jhelum and Chenab Rivers between the Five Linked Canals. The programme was sent to Ex. En. [Executive Engineer] Mangla to implement as the executive officer on the first canal on the first river. He reminded the other controlling officers on the other four canals when changes were due and he received all the headworks gauges and discharges daily to ensure that the programme was being correctly followed." (Personal communication from A. M. R. Montagu, March 16, 1965.) A complete and separate canal telegraph system was in existence by this time for such coordination purposes and for emergency warnings of floods and failures.

The much more complicated problems involved in allocating flows after the Indus Basin Project with its eight additional link canals is completed will probably necessitate computer programing from an operations center, probably located in Lahore.

Trimmu) and recommended that they be held in abeyance until the Triple Canals Project was finished. To the Commission were presented the misgivings of Sind, then part of the Bombay Government, that withdrawals in the Punjab would prejudice existing inundation works and proposed perennial systems along the lower Indus. As we have seen, these protests were brushed aside by enthusiasts such as Colonel Jacob who maintained that, even were the capital and the equipment at hand to harness the Indus itself, most of its water would, in the absence of storage dams, flow unused to the sea.

Perhaps the greatest contributions of the Indian Irrigation Commission of 1901–03 were the recognition that irrigation technology had come of age in India and that henceforth no large-scale projects could be undertaken without consideration of the interests of all regions, and consultation among all the parties concerned. In its tentative reservation of the Beas-Sutlej waters for the left-hand riparians, the Commission had indirectly endorsed Sind's claim to be heard before any more major withdrawals were made. From now on, both engineers and administrators would be governed by a quasi-judicial assessment of their projects. The principle enunciated by Captain J. H. Dyas in 1862 when water appeared to be a "free good," that "the best line for a canal is that from which the largest extent of country can be irrigated at the smallest cost, irrespective of the name or nature of the existing Government of the country in question," was now modified by the concept that each riparian, upstream or down, was entitled to a fair share in the allotment of water, which might not after all be unlimited in supply.[64]

The Sutlej Valley Project

Between the completion of the Triple Canals Project and the commencement of the next integrated project in the Indus Basin, that on the Sutlej, many men of the Irrigation Branch were called to service in World War I, notably in the Mesopotamian campaign

64. A somewhat different assessment of the work of the Commission with regard to Sind is included in the centennial history of the Public Works Department of the Punjab-West Pakistan: "That body [the Indian Irrigation Commission of 1901–03] did not quite realize the necessity of converting the inundation canals of Sind into weir-controlled supplies, but it advocated extension of irrigation." *(Hundred Years of P.W.D.,* ed. Mubashir Hasan [Lahore, Publication Committee of P.W.D. Centennial, October 1963], p. 28.)

of the Indian Army, and in the frontier skirmishes of the Third Afghan War (1919). Meanwhile, under the impetus of the deliberations of the Irrigation Commission and the inquiries it set in motion, surveys along the Sutlej had begun in 1906. Discussions among the Government of India, the Punjab Government, and the states of Bikaner and Bahawalpur led to agreement at Delhi in 1919.[65] The project was prepared in 1920 and sanctioned in 1921.

The Sutlej Valley Project called for the construction of four new barrages:

1. Ferozepore, from which three canals offtake:
   a. The Bikaner Canal, serving areas in that state on the left bank, the first lined canal in the Indus Basin; perennial
   b. The Eastern Canal, also on the left bank, serving areas in the cis-Sutlej Punjab (Ferozepore District) and a morsel of northeastern Bahawalpur State; nonperennial but replacing most of the Grey system of inundation canals
   c. The Dipalpur Canal, on the right bank, serving areas in the southern Lahore and Montgomery districts which were formerly either Crown Waste or served by inundation canals such as the old Lower Sohag, which was incorporated; nonperennial

65. The 1919 agreement envisaged that 62.2 per cent of the States' and 50.7 per cent of the British culturable lands commanded by perennial canals would be irrigated each year. The envisaged intensity under nonperennial canals was 50 per cent for both. As we shall see in Chapter 4, it was later found necessary to revise these intensities because of insufficient water supplies.

The Government of India Act of 1919, which became effective in 1921, granted partial autonomy to the provinces in irrigation as well as in other matters. "Before 1919, no major irrigation work could be undertaken without the sanction of the Secretary of State, who was advised through the Government of India by the Inspector General of Irrigation and a public works secretariat with an experienced engineer at its head. All matters of dispute between the provinces or states were referred to the Secretary of State, whose decision was final. After 1919, irrigation became a provincial but reserved subject [i.e. the Central Government retained certain powers]. All irrigation projects affecting more than one province or costing more than Rs 5 million, however, had to be recommended by the Government of India to the Secretary of State for sanction." (United Nations Economic Commission for Asia and the Far East, *Multiple-Purpose River Basin Development*, Part 2B, "Water Resource Development in Burma, India and Pakistan" [Flood Control Series No. 11] [Bangkok, UNECAFE, December, 1956], p. 70.) Projects costing less than Rs 5 million and affecting only one province were referred only to the Government of India, and the Governor-General gave direct sanction. *(Hundred Years of P.W.D.,* p. 31.)

94

2. Suleimanki, from which three canals offtake:
    a. The Eastern Sadiqia Canal, on the left bank, providing perennial irrigation for eastern Bahawalpur State
    b. The Fordwah Canal, also on the left bank, providing nonperennial irrigation to areas in Bahawalpur formerly served by an inundation canal
    c. The Pakpattan Canal, on the right bank, which commands areas south of those served by the LBDC and replaced inundation canals with a perennial supply
3. Islam (originally called Pallah), from which three canals offtake:
    a. The Mailsi Canal on the right bank, which, although nonperennial, finally completed the modern irrigation of the Bari Doab begun in 1859
    b. The Qaimpur Canal on the left bank, which has the distinction of being the shortest main canal (as distinguished from a branch canal or a distributary, neither of which offtake from a headworks) in the subcontinent—its length is only 7 miles; nonperennial
    c. The Bahawal Canal, which runs for 48 miles toward Bahawalpur City before branching into the nonperennial Ahmadpur branch and the perennial Desert Branch
4. Panjnad, below the confluence of the Sutlej with the Chenab, which feeds two canals, both on the left bank:
    a. The Abbasia Canal, a short canal running due south (later extended toward the southwest to feed the tail ends of the branches of the Panjnad Canal) ; perennial
    b. The Panjnad Canal, which parallels the river at a distance of some 4 miles for 45 miles, in the course of which it sends off two branches to the south, and then bifurcates into the Sadiq and Dallas branches; part perennial

When the Sutlej Valley Project was undertaken, it was regarded as a more or less cut-and-dried job of engineering. The broad experience gained in constructing and operating the Triple Canals Project was to be applied to the Sutlej with little modification. A new zone was established within the Irrigation Branch, and a new post of Chief Engineer (the third) created to direct it. Four divisions were set up, corresponding to the four headworks, and Executive Engineers ("XENs") were appointed to carry out the construction, which proceeded more or less simultaneously at the three upper barrages, all of which were completed by the end of 1927. Work at Panjnad did not get under way until 1927.

All went well until the summer of 1929. The heavy monsoon of that year produced an extraordinary flood, calculated at 228,000 cusecs at Islam on August 24. Although the barrage had been designed to pass 300,000 cusecs, the bays were wide—60 feet between piers—and thus the whole barrage was a relatively light structure. Undermining of the downstream apron and pier foundations caused the collapse of the six central bays.[66] The undermining was caused not so much by the enormous runoff as by the fact that the water had dropped most of its silt in the deep, wide pond upstream. The clear water emerging from the barrage scoured or "degraded" the bed downstream. This in turn led to "piping" of the subsoil below the structure and the progressive removal of the sand and soil grains and finally to the collapse of the six bays of the barrage.[67] Such an experience was unprecedented, and led to an unprecedented effort. Before the summer of 1930, the six bays that had collapsed were replaced with eleven bays with a span of only 29 feet each, new piers and aprons of reinforced concrete were built, and a 9-inch cover of reinforced concrete was applied over most of the weir to increase both weight and strength.

Although the Panjnad Barrage was well along by the spring of 1930, the Islam Enquiry Committee recommended that fourteen more 60-foot bays be added to the right flank of the thirty-three existing 60-foot bays. This modification did not, in itself, do much to strengthen the barrage, but it did serve to spread the load and to increase the barrage's flood-passing capacity from 600,000 to 700,-000 cusecs. (The summer flood of 1929 had peaked at Panjnad on

66. The destruction was quite symmetrical: of the twenty-four bays, Nos. 11–16 collapsed. Bays 1–4 and 21–24 were in the intake pockets for the canals and thus somewhat secured by the divide groynes, as were the adjoining bays, Nos. 5–10 to 17–20.

67. Personal communication from A. M. R. Montagu, August 2, 1965. Mr. Montagu, who at the time of the Islam disaster was Under-Secretary (Construction) in the Public Works Department, adds: "The three weirs at Ferozepur, Suleimanki and Islam were designed in ignorance of 'degradation' of the downstream bed. The degradation resulted in an increase in the 'exit velocity' of the subsoil seepage which, in turn, led to piping and the removal of soil beneath the apron at Islam. The weir did not blow up; it collapsed."

September 5 at 550,000 cusecs.) More significantly, by reducing the depth at which flood water would pass over the lengthened barrage, the danger of undermining the downstream apron was reduced. Subsequently, modifications were also made at Suleimanke and Ferozepore, the more urgent in the latter case because there the barrage piers also support the railway bridge that replaces the Kaisar-i-Hind bridge on the Kasur-Ferozepore line a short distance upstream. (The railway has not been in use since Partition.)

The Panjnad barrage was completed in time to supply water for the spring-sown (kharif) crops in 1933. The total construction cost of the Sutlej Valley Project had reached Rs 213,074,375, or half again as much as was sanctioned in 1921 (Rs 145,990,433).[68] Although a gross total of 3,400,000 acres (of which 3,300,000 acres were culturable) were commanded by perennial canals in the project, and 5,747,547 gross acres (of which 3,195,000 acres were culturable) by nonperennial canals, it soon became obvious that supplies of water from the Beas-Sutlej, which had been more carefully measured beginning in 1921, would not be sufficient to provide the anticipated intensities of irrigation. For lands in Bahawalpur fed from the Beas-Sutlej, the perennial intensity would be only 52.7 per cent of the gross commanded area instead of 62.5 per cent; in the Punjab, only 50.3 per cent instead of 55.75 per cent. Nonperennial intensities would be only 39.6 per cent instead of 50.0 per cent in Bahawalpur and only 35.5 per cent instead of 50.0 per cent in the Punjab. Only Bikaner and the Bahawalpur lands fed from the Chenab-Sutlej below Panjnad would get their promised water.[69] By 1935, the Punjab and Bahawalpur were accordingly becoming disenchanted with run-of-the-river irrigation.

The years 1933–35 mark another turning point in the irrigation of the Indus Basin. Except for the Haveli Project (with its headworks

68. *Hundred Years of P.W.D.*, p. 35.
69. The Panjnad barrage and canal system were constructed as part of the Sutlej Valley Project, but they were not entitled to an allocation of Beas-Sutlej water during the low-water season. Instead, Panjnad was entitled only to regeneration supplies in the Sutlej and to any supplies coming via the Chenab from the Ravi, Chenab, and Jhelum. Thus, although Panjnad was part of the Sutlej Valley *Project*, it was not part of the Sutlej Valley Canals *system* with respect to allocations. (Personal communication from A. M. R. Montagu, August 2, 1965.)

at Trimmu, the Jhelum-Chenab confluence), sanction of which was being disputed by Sind, the situation was now in reality what it had seemed to be in 1900: extensions of irrigation in the doabs between the Punjab Rivers, or in the lands south of the Sutlej, would require either upstream storage or diversions from the Indus across the Sind Sagar (Thal) Doab. Except for its southeastern margins, which were included in the Haveli Project, the Thal itself could be irrigated only from the Indus. Diversion from the Indus required, under the policy established by the Indian Irrigation Commission of 1901–03, the assent of Sind. The policy was reaffirmed by the Government of India Act of 1919, which required that irrigation projects concerning more than one province be referred to the Governor-General. Sind, which in 1932 had just opened its *first* barrage (the Lloyd Barrage at Sukkur) and its *first* perennial canal system, was in no mood to consent either to the diversion of water from the Indus or to storage projects that would lead to increased withdrawals of water from the Punjab rivers. Thus Sind, whose interests at this time were still represented by the Bombay Government,[70] took strong exception to any withdrawals, or any changes in the river regimes, that might affect its inundation canals above or below the Sukkur command.

70. The Government of India Act of 1935, which took effect in 1937, made Sind a separate province and greatly increased provincial autonomy. "With the introduction of provincial autonomy in 1937, both irrigation and electricity came under provincial jurisdiction. The Central Government came into the picture only if a province made a formal complaint against another regarding interference with its water supplies. In such cases of dispute, the Governor-General was authorized to appoint a commission to investigate the matter and submit a report, on which the Governor-General was authorized to pass final orders, unless any party desired that the dispute be referred to His Majesty in Council for final orders. The procedure laid down for this purpose in sections 130 to 134 of the Government of India Act, 1935, was involved and was not easy to implement. Divergent and conflicting interests could not be resolved quickly, and the pace of river valley development was greatly retarded." (UNECAFE, *Multiple-Purpose River Basin Development*, Part 2B, p. 70.) This change of procedure explains why the early Sind-Punjab disputes were referred to committees of the Central Board of Irrigation whereas after 1937 they had to be referred to a Commission appointed by the Governor-General. As we shall see in Chapter 4, the delays encountered with the Bhakra Project, some but by no means all of which were procedural, were of fundamental significance to the Indus Waters Dispute.

4. The Indus Waters Dispute
Before Partition

"Governments are always liable to change, but a properly made canal will endure for centuries, if not for all time, and every Government is equally interested in its maintenance."

—Capt. J. H. Dyas, 1862

The dispute over allocation of irrigation water within the Indus Basin did not begin in 1947. We have already seen that one of the main tasks of the Indian Irrigation Commission of 1901–03 was to discover a method by which the irrigation of the Bari Doab could be completed without detriment to the left-hand riparians along the Sutlej. The tripartite agreement of 1919 among the Punjab, Bikaner, and Bahawalpur paved the way for sanction and construction of the Sutlej Valley Project, but it said nothing about the rights of the downstream Indus riparians: Khairpur State and Sind, which was still a part of the Bombay Government (about to become the Bombay Province).

Sind: "The Unhappy Valley"

A brief digression on the geographic and historic position of Sind is in order. If the Punjab was the "fair-haired boy" of British India, then Sind was in many respects the stepchild. We have seen in Chapter 3 how Sind was annexed in 1843, more or less as an afterthought and in a fit of pique by the British after the withdrawal from Afghanistan. Sind soon (1847) was made a subprovince under the Bombay Government, where it remained until implementation of the Government of India Act of 1935.

In contrast to the Punjab, with its through-flowing streams, delightful hill stations, Mogul-Sikh heritage and monuments, and industrious peasantry, there was little to attract or inspire the British administrator in Sind. The glories, and even the site, of ancient Debal had been lost among the marshlands of the Indus delta; Tatta's channel had silted up, and the city lay in ruins; Hyderabad and Sukkur, though not without renown, could hardly compare with Lahore and Amritsar; and Karachi was a mere fishing village. Both the coastal and the river ports were long prone to epidemics of plague, and the large areas of standing water in the delta and along the lower Indus make malaria endemic to the region. The new administrators tried hard both to remove the causes of Sind's unhappiness by means of civil works and an orderly, just administration, and to improve its reputation through their historical research and report writing:

> For some time after the British occupation the climate of Sind was believed to be preeminently unhealthy. Our first experiences of it were unhappy. When the army for Afghanistan was passing through the Province [sic] in 1839 the sickness in the camp at Tatta was so terrible as to leave no doubt in the popular mind that the whole of the lakh and twenty-five thousand [125,000] Pirs buried on the Makhli hill [at Tatta] had been stirred to vengeance by the desecration of their tombs; and in the autumn of 1843 more than two-thirds of Sir Charles Napier's forces were prostrated. But ampler experience has shown that Sind is, upon the whole, a healthy country.[1]

1. *Gazetteer of the Province of Sind*, compiled by E. H. Aitken, *A*, 486. See also J. Abbott, I.C.S., *Sind: A Re-Interpretation of the Unhappy Valley* (Bombay and London, Humphrey Milford and Oxford University Press, 1924). Incidentally, Abbott believed that Tatta and Debal were one and the same.

An interesting comparison might be drawn between the reports of United States' officers contrasting conditions in and around Vera Cruz with those on the plateau of Mexico, and the reports of British officers contrasting Karachi and the lower Indus with the Punjab, both written at the same period.

Sind: "The Unhappy Valley"

But the fundamental question was whether Sind could be developed into a desirable abode in its own right or whether it was destined to remain only a passageway, a torment to be passed through as quickly as possible, between the Punjab and the sea. The fact that Sind was attached to, and for ninety years remained with, the Bombay Government is one indication that its connections with the Punjab, though always acknowledged and sometimes extolled, were not deemed of sufficient importance to warrant a more integrated administration. Both the history of transportation development in Sind and the consecutive reports of the administrators indicate that the commercial expectations for Sind progressively diminished. When the first Gazetteer of Sind was written in 1907, the author stated:

> Those who think that we are unduly vainglorious about our Province [sic] and its port [Karachi], should acquaint themselves with a little of what was said and written by the pioneers of British commerce in Sind, and they would learn to admire the chastened and moderate tone of her merchants at the present day. We only speak of Karachi as the natural outlet for the produce of Punjab and the north of India. They spoke thus: "Kurrachee is a position of very great importance, whether regarded in a commercial, a political, or a military point of view. In a commercial point of view it may be defined as the gate of Central Asia and is likely to become to India what Liverpool is to England." The fact is that, before there were any railways in India, a river like the Indus seemed to give to the Province that possessed it an advantage which defied competition. And for many years the Indus had been a main channel of the commerce of Central Asia. But it presented certain serious obstacles. The navigation of its mouths was both difficult and dangerous and its current was so strong that the passage of boats up stream was incredibly slow. Accordingly, as soon as Karachi became a commercial port (about the middle of the 18th century) a good deal of the trade began to avoid the river and take the land route between Karachi and Shikarpur. Shikarpur during its subjection to the Afghans [approximately 1750 to 1824] had become by far the greatest commercial city in Sind. Its merchants and bankers had relations with all the principal marts of

Central Asia. . . . in Bombay it was supposed that the only obstacles to the flow of the commerce of Asia up and down the Indus was the barbaric narrow-mindedness of the Mirs [of Sind] and accordingly some of our earliest treaties with them were directed to opening up the navigation of the river. Natturally, when it came into our own power, that seemed the great thing to do. . . . But the mouths of the Indus proved quite impracticable and were soon abandoned. Our troops and stores either took the road to Tatta, or Kotri, or were conveyed from Kiamari to Ghizri [now southwest and southeast suburbs of Karachi], there put into country boats and taken up the creek to Gharo, whence camels carried them 25 miles further to Tatta. Hence sprang the bold conception of a railway from Karachi to Kotri. By the cooperation of the two great agencies, a railway and steam boats, the trade of India was destined to be developed. . . . But all these devices were swept aside forever by the opening of the Indus Valley Railway from Kotri to Khanpur in 1878. At once the Indus ceased to be a channel of commerce and the trade by road withered away. The trade of Shikarpur is not now considered worth registering and no account is taken of the traffic on the Indus, excepting of the inconsiderable quantity of a few simple commodities which comes down from the Punjab by water to take rail at Sukkur or Kotri. The commercial heart of Sind, the Punjab and United Provinces and British Baluchistan is Karachi, and the North Western and Jodhpur-Bikaner Railways are the arteries and veins.[2]

2. *Gazetteer of the Province of Sind, A,* 366–67. The compiler of the gazetteer attributes the statement in quotes to W. P. Andrew, *The Indus and Its Provinces* (London, Wm. H. Allen, 1857). But on page 49 of that work, Andrew in turn attributes the quotation to Thornton's *Gazetteer of India,* and adds another comment from the *Friend of India:* "From the Sutlej to the Oxus, whoever wishes to communicate with any place beyond the sea, must pass through Kurrachee. It occupies a position scarcely less favourable to commerce than that of Alexandria." Andrew held influential positions as chairman of the boards of directors of the Scinde and Punjab Railway Companies and of the Indus Steam Flotilla. It was he who had proposed connecting the Karachi-Kotri Line to the Multan-Lahore-Amritsar Line by efficient steamer navigation on the Indus. (See Arrora, *Commerce by River in the Punjab.*) But the fallacy in comparing the position of Karachi to that of Alexandria lay in the regime of the Indus as compared to that of the Nile, and in the fact that in the mid-nineteenth century, despite the introduction of stern-wheelers modeled on the Mississippi types, it

Sind: "The Unhappy Valley"

Although any such generalization is open to dispute, it probably would be fair to say that the rapid introduction of railway transport after the annexation of Sind did more to retard than to advance the economic development of places intermediate between Karachi and Mithankot or Multan. The Karachi-Kotri line was opened in 1861. In 1878, a line along the right or western bank was completed from Kotri to Sukkur, where a ferry transferred the cars (wagons) to the line from Rohri via Khanpur to Multan, Lahore, Amritsar, and Delhi. As a result of the westward migration of the Indus (see Chapter 2), the Kotri-Sukkur line was continually subjected to washouts in the flood seasons, so a left-bank linking Hyderabad with Rohri was built between 1892 and 1896. The Sukkur ferry was replaced by the famous Lansdowne cantilever bridge in 1889, and the Kotri ferry by a bridge in 1900, after which the east-bank railway became the main line between Karachi and the Punjab. Kotri-Hyderabad and Sukkur-Rohri of course gained importance as ferry crossings and rail junctions, but their break-of-bulk function (i.e. shift from one means of conveyance to another) was limited in both time and extent. Thus the lower Indus provides another illustration of the principle that a railroad does not benefit a region through which it passes unless that region also contributes to and takes from its traffic. This phenomenon may be illustrated by the fact that in 1884–85 there was no municipality in Sind with a population of over 100,000, and only six with over 10,000. Twenty years later, Karachi had about 120,000 but there were still only six cities in Sind with between 10,000 and 100,000 persons.[3]

---

proved impossible to build a steamboat of sufficient power to ascend the river without making the engines so heavy as to require a draft too deep to navigate the shallow and constantly shifting channels of the lower Indus. Thus, whereas the Nile Valley as a whole still relies on alternating rail and steamboat service, the Indus got rid of the latter as early as possible (in 1871 above Sukkur, including the Punjab tributaries, and in 1878 between Sukkur and Kotri).

3. *Gazetteer of the Province of Sind, A,* 468. The trade of Karachi increased from Rs 1,221,600 in 1842–43 to Rs 21,592,000 in 1857–58, during the Mutiny, and under the pressure of cotton exports during the American Civil War to Rs 66,628,106 in 1863–64. With the end of that war, Karachi's trade fell to Rs 14,180,956 and recovered its former level only after the completion of the Indus Valley Railway in 1878. By 1882–83 it had reached Rs 70,770,838. "From that time the trade of Karachi has advanced rapidly with the extension of railway communication *and irrigation* and the improvement of the harbour." (Ibid., pp. 368–69. Italics supplied, and the Western decimal system introduced.)

In brief, the Indus Valley railway served Karachi and the Punjab, just as the Syr Darya railway, completed in 1906, served Orenburg and the Tashkent region.[4] Neither provided much help to the areas in between until those areas were provided with modern irrigation facilities and thus could contribute more produce to the rail traffic. It is to these facilities in Sind that we must now return.

Irrigation in Sind: Sukkur

One must not hold the impression that Sind was devoid of irrigation improvements until the construction of the Sukkur system. The point is that the very magnitude of the lower Indus, with its shifting beds, deterred the engineers from undertaking any perennial system that would entail the construction of a barrage across the river. But the old inundation canals, many of which utilized former or inactive channels of the Indus, were greatly improved long before they were "switched over to weir control," to use the engineering parlance.

A canal department was firmly established in Sind from 1851 on. It began restoring the Begari Canal above Sukkur in 1852–53 and the Fuleli Canal below Hyderabad in 1856. A small amount of perennial irrigation was actually provided by connecting the Gohar Canal in Shikarpur to the active Western Nara branch of the Indus after 1856, and in 1863 the Eastern Nara Canal was improved and a cut made through the Rohri ridge to supply it. The Mithrao Canal west of the Eastern Nara was activated with considerable difficulty by 1879. Additional new canals were completed, and old ones rebuilt, upstream at Kashmor (Desert Canal, serving 190,000 acres) and midway between Kashmor and Sukkur (Begari Canal, serving 276,310 acres), as well as in the delta region. Thus, the frameworks for the irrigation systems now under command of (i.e. capable of being served by gravity flow from) the Gudu, Sukkur, and Hyderabad barrages were already in existence, primarily on an inundation basis, by the turn of the century when Sind possessed no less than 7,441

Whereas only ten sailing ships had entered Karachi harbor in 1854–55, and 155 square-riggers and steamships in 1863–64, by 1904–05 some 450 vessels used Karachi's facilities. (Ibid., pp. 370–71.)

4. For comparison see Robert N. Taaffe, *Rail Transportation and the Economic Development of Soviet Central Asia* (Chicago, University of Chicago, Department of Geography, Research Paper No. 64, 1960).

miles of canals, commanding 9.5 million acres and actually irrigating some 2.5 or 2.7 million acres per year (of which, however, less than 10 per cent could be double-cropped). At this time, the Punjab was irrigating over 4.6 million acres from perennial canals, plus another million on an inundation basis.[5]

Nor should it be thought that the engineers and administrators of Sind were remiss in calling attention to the possibilities of perennial irrigation. In particular, the advantages of the Sukkur-Rohri site, where a limestone ridge crosses the valley and from which a gravity canal could be made to utilize the Eastern Nara bed all the way to Hyderabad, were urged. The Rohri proposal was first made in 1847, again in 1858, 1867, and 1869. Finally, in 1871, the Government of India authorized the Bombay Government to draft a scheme for perennial irrigation in Sind. But in 1873, presumably in view of the difficulties encountered with the UBDC and Sirhind Canals (see Chapter 3), the Governor-General decided against perennial irrigation in Sind on economic grounds. The Rohri project was not again raised until 1890, again abandoned in 1891, and finally submitted to the Indian Irrigation Commission of 1901–03).[6]

In its report, the Indian Irrigation Commission advocated remodeling and rationalizing (i.e. straightening and simplifying to reduce losses and improve efficiency) the existing inundation system to the extent that private ownership of lands and canals would permit, and then went on to state:

> The question has however been raised whether something more than this may not be done in Sind; and whether the time was not now coming for making the existing canals perennial by the construction of weirs across the Indus, similar to those which we have already recommended in the case of the Sutlej. Sir Evan James, the late Commissioner of Sind, referred to this subject, in the last review of the operations on the Sind canals which he wrote before leaving the province, and *called attention to the possible effect on the canals of the opening of the new perennial canals in the Punjab*. We need hardly point out that

5. *Hundred Years of P.W.D.*, Mubashir Hasan, ed., pp. 10–14, and *Report of the Indian Irrigation Commission, 1901–03, 2, 5, 10, 39.*
6. *Hundred Years of P.W.D.*, p. 27.

the construction of weirs across the shifting bed of the Indus, in its passage through the Sind delta, is quite a different thing from putting weirs across its tributary the Sutlej. Not only would the cost and difficulties, both of first construction and of subsequent maintenance, be immeasurably greater, but *the necessity is less urgent.* The Indus in Sind contains the combined waters of all the Punjab rivers, and is naturally a much less uncertain source of supply for inundation canals than any of its tributaries. The differences between a bad and a good year are much less marked; and many of the most important canals in Sind— the Sukkur, the Eastern Nara systems, and the Fuleli—have moderate perennial supplies, which are generally sufficient for present requirements, though better or more assured supplies would no doubt render further extensions of these systems possible.[7]

Concerning the Sukkur-Rohri site, the Commission had before it a memorandum prepared by Mr. E. F. Dawson, Secretary to the River Indus Commission, who had investigated it in 1900. Contrary to the popular belief, Dawson's tests indicated that the Rohri ridge was not the best site for a barrage. Even in the season of minimum flow, the water level of the Indus was 36 feet above bedrock in the central 700 feet of the channel, and its minimum flow was 30,000 cusecs. Since there was no way to divert it during construction, building the weir in or immediately above the Rohri "gorge" would prove an impossible task. A site further upstream or further down would involve both a longer barrage and very expensive river training works (bunds or jetties designed to contain and direct the flow).[8]

As far as existing Sind cultivation is concerned heroic measures are not required, and there is as we have shown great room for extending existing cultivation by working on existing meth-

7. *Report of the Indian Irrigation Commission, 1901–03,* 2, p. 42. Italics added. With respect to Sir Evan James' concern, the Commission stated, "It is the opinion of the Sind Irrigation Officers who came before us, that the supplies to the canals have not been appreciably affected by the withdrawals from the Punjab rivers."

8. Ibid., p. 44. It may be noted that the 4,725-foot Sukkur Barrage, as finally constructed, was located two miles below the ridge and was built on alluvial deposits, not rock.

ods. These considerations, *to which may be added an apprehension that cultivators would not be forthcoming,* for any great or rapid extension of cultivation in Sind, have hitherto had such weight that the idea of harnessing the Indus has never been seriously considered. . . . There is no doubt that some site in the vicinity of the Rohri gorge would be most suitable for a weir across the Indus. . . . it would apparently be feasible, by means of two great main canals taking off from the right and left banks above the weir, to feed all the remaining irrigation systems in Sind, with the exception of the Karachi systems which take off from the Indus below Kotri. From no lower point in the river could such a command be obtained of the existing systems. A vast scheme of this kind appears to be feasible, but there are many practical considerations which would perhaps render it desirable to reduce its scope.[9]

Although the Commission did not advocate an attempt to irrigate all of the lower Indus from Sukkur, it did feel that any project based on a barrage at that point would have to be large enough, and to include enough new land, to render it remunerative:

It seems to us therefore that if the idea of a weir across the Indus is ever seriously entertained, the scope of the scheme must be very much wider than Mr. Dawson has contemplated; and that, apart from steadying the supply in as many of the existing canal systems as possible, it should provide for something like half a million or a million acres of new irrigation. If this were done it is quite possible that an expenditure of even 4 crores [40 million rupees] might be contemplated, and with some prospect of a remunerative return. . . . A Scheme of this kind will deserve, and will no doubt receive, serious consideration some years hence, but we are not impressed with its immediate importance. *Sind is not liable to famine; it is not thickly populated; the rates that can be realized for irrigation are not high; and there is still considerable scope for the extension of irrigation on general lines without resort to more heroic measures.* We think, however, that the Civil and Irrigation officers in Sind

9. Ibid., p. 43. Italics added.

should endeavour to determine definitely what are the areas in Sind that could be irrigated either by means of extensions of existing systems, or by perennial canals taking off from the Indus. . . . it should be possible to prepare a general plan, showing clearly the position of the six million acres of cultivable waste which are said to exist in Sind, and the possibilities of extending irrigation into these areas. The question of an Indus weir should not in the meanwhile be dropped. An attempt should be made to collect all the data and information that are necessary before a judgment can be formed by the best experts on either the feasibility of the project or its cost, and if something more is then known than at present of the areas into which proposed perennial canals may be advantageously extended, it may be possible to formulate a sound scheme which will have every prospect of success.[10]

In summary, then, the Indian Irrigation Commission saw no urgency in extending perennial irrigation in Sind. The region was not a famine area, and it lay too far, by rail or sea, from the famine-prone districts of the United Provinces, Bihar, and Bengal which the Punjab "granary" was in a superior position to supply (see Chapter 3). A perennial scheme would have to be large to be remunerative, there was a question of whether settlers would take up any new lands, and there were even questions as to where sufficient laborers could be obtained. There was no exact information on the area that could be irrigated nor on the best site for the proposed barrage. In all of this reasoning we may detect signs of the "funnel" nature of the Sind economy alluded to above: Sind was a region through which much passed, including the Indian Irrigation Commission on its tour, but in which little stayed. Had the Commission extended its tour down the Indus from Sukkur, instead of striking

10. Ibid., pp. 44–45. Italics added. Instead of the half million or million acres of new cultivation anticipated by the Commission, the Sukkur Barrage commands 3.8 million acres of new culturable lands (in addition to 3.6 million acres previously cultivated). The total area annually irrigated is now around 5.5 million acres, including .5 million which are double-cropped. Sukkur is the largest irrigation scheme on earth and is still expanding. Instead of the 40 million rupees anticipated, however, it has already cost well over 200 million. Even at that, the per acre cost of less than 40 rupees is very low for projects in the subcontinent or elsewhere in the world's arid zone.

out for Jaipur and central India, their verdict *might* have been different. To their credit, however, goes the fact that they did not foreclose the possibility of perennial irrigation in Sind but rather, as they did with the Sutlej problem, referred it for further study:

> At last in 1904, Dr. Summers, Superintending Engineer in Sind, obtained permission to make extensive surveys for a canal from Rohri. Investigations in 1906 showed that three weirs were needed across the Indus at Mithan Kot [site of the present Gudu Barrage], Sukkur [Rohri] and Kotri [Hyderabad, site of the present Ghulam Mohammad Barrage] to save the economy of this tract. Sukkur was to get the first priority.
>
> Dr. Summers submitted his Rohri Canal Project in 1910. A barrage across the Indus up stream of Sukkur gorge with the Rohri Canal and the Eastern Nara Canal on the left and one canal on the right bank were proposed to serve a GCA [gross commanded area] of 6.2 million acres. . . . Later, to reduce the expense, Dr. Summers modified his project to include a barrage and the Rohri Canal only. . . . A high-powered Technical Committee which examined this scheme in London expressed the view that the project was not productive. A protective project was not considered necessary as *there appeared to be no marked effect on the inundation canals due to higher withdrawals in the Punjab area, as some seemed to suspect.* The Committee, however, recommended that more data be collected and the entire [sic] kept in readiness *in case Sind may be adversely affected in future to an extent to need protective measures.*

Meanwhile irrigation through weir-controlled canals was rapidly developing in the Punjab and in the United Provinces of India. Sind could not boast even one perennial canal and there was loud clamour for regular supplies. The Bombay Government reacted to the growing public unrest by starting work on another scheme. In 1916, Mr. Musto was specially detailed for the preparation of a detailed project with the assistance of revenue and irrigation officers. Necessary work was, however, interrupted by the first World War and could not be completed before October, 1919. In the new plan the right and left bank areas were given equal claims on the river water. Without a weir it was feared, left bank inundation canals would adversely affect the high lands on the right. The project was considered productive and made wider in scope by increasing the gross commanded area to 6.54 million acres at a cost of Rs. 183.6 million.[11]

The Sukkur Project was submitted to the Secretary of State for India in London in December 1920, received its preliminary approval from him in June 1921, and its final sanction from him in April 1923. Thus the long struggle by the engineers and administrators of Sind to obtain a perennial irrigation system was finally rewarded by the authorization of the largest scheme yet undertaken in India or, for that matter, anywhere in the world. Construction began in July 1923, and the Sukkur Barrage was formally dedicated on January 13, 1932. Irrigation began in June 1932 and is still expanding. Close to 7.5 million culturable commanded acres could eventually be served, provided water is available, of which only some 520,000 would remain on a nonperennial basis.

From the administrative standpoint, it is worth noting that despite the provisions of the Government of India Act of 1919, which increased provincial autonomy and transferred ultimate responsibility for approval of irrigation projects from the Secretary of State to the Viceroy, both the Sukkur and the Sutlej Valley projects were initiated and sanctioned under the old system. Reference to Chapter 3, page 94 (and footnote 65 thereto) will indicate that the Sutlej Valley Project received its final sanction from the Secretary of State in 1921. Whether there was any suggestion of a quid pro quo arrangement for Sind on the one hand and the Sutlej riparians on the other must remain a matter of conjecture until 1971 when, under the fifty-year-rule of the India Office Library in London, the relevant files should be opened to the public. At any rate, we have seen that Sind was *not* a party to the tripartite Punjab-Bikaner-Bahawalpur agreement that cleared the way for the Sutlej Valley Project. And we shall see that both Sind and the Punjab subsequently behaved as though neither had been consulted regarding the other's project.

11. *Hundred Years of P.W.D.*, pp. 28–29. Italics added. This account indicates some of the resentment which Sind felt regarding its irrigation position by 1920. For more recent estimates of acreages and costs, see the preceding footnote.

Foundations of the Dispute

With the nearly simultaneous sanction and construction of both the Sutlej Valley Project and the Sukkur Project, conflict of interest over the Indus Rivers became explicit rather than implicit. To understand why this was true, we must examine more carefully the meaning of the terms "perennial," "nonperennial," and "inundation" irrigation. In common usage, perennial and nonperennial are contrasted, and inundation irrigation is also contrasted with perennial, implying that it is the same as nonperennial. This is not quite the case. Inundation irrigation, as discussed at the start of Chapter 3, really means irrigation based on the run, or level, of the river. In some cases, as in small portions of Sind prior to the construction of the Sukkur Barrage, inundation irrigation may actually *be* perennial irrigation. That is, if the supply in the river is substantial, even in the low runoff season, and if the lay of the land is favorable, it is sometimes possible to bring yearround water supplies to limited acreages. Or, it may be possible to bring supplies to a crop for a few weeks after planting, before the river drops below the inundation-canal intake. Depending upon the soil's ability to retain the moisture, this water, which may be augmented later in the season with well supplies, may be sufficient for a quick-maturing grain or pulse crop with inherently low water requirements. This practice in the subcontinent is known as *sailaba* or *bosi-rabi* cropping (contrasted with *sailab* cultivation, which means planting a crop on the floodplain after the waters have receded), and it always refers to a *rabi*, or cool-season, crop sown early in the fall after the water levels have begun to fall. If the soils are right, *sailaba* cropping works in most years because evaporation rates fall at the same time and because the crop is ready for harvest before the warm spring winds dessicate it. But the practice is uncertain.

Thus, there are intermediate forms between perennial and nonperennial irrigation, and inundation irrigation *may* be perennial in restricted areas and in certain years. The true converse of inundation is weir- or barrage-controlled irrigation, although here too there are intermediary forms where a temporary, or even a permanent, weir may be built part way into a stream to divert low water supplies into an "inundation" canal, or where a head regulator is provided to prevent too much water from entering such a canal in flood periods. For our purposes, however, we may contrast barrage-controlled with inundation irrigation, and perennial with nonperennial irrigation.

The Sutlej Valley Project and the Sukkur Project converted vast areas of inundation irrigated lands to barrage-controlled lands. To a great extent, this meant conversion of nonperennial to perennial irrigation, i.e. from one crop per year (the summer, flood-season, *kharif* crop) to two (adding the winter, low-water-season, *rabi* crop).[12] But we have seen that even the Sukkur Project contains half a million acres of nonperennial lands (kharif but not rabi) while in the S.V.P. there is actually more nonperennial than perennially ir-rffiigated land. Table 4, based on a recent year in which runoff was abundant, shows the actual situation.

Table 4. Data on Irrigation in Certain Projects in West Pakistan, 1958–59[a]

Canal or System	Culturable Commanded Areas (1,000 Acres)			Areas Irrigated (1,000 Acres)		
	Perennial	Non-perennial	Total	Rabi	Kharif	Total
Sutlej Valley	2,169	2,815	4,984	2,202	1,813	4,015
Panjnad and Abbasia[b]	512	937	1,449	597	646	1,243
Sukkur Command	6,958	520	7,478	2,705	2,543	5,248

a. Source: Harza Report, Appendix A, Table A-3, p. A-14. Data for October 1958 through September 1959.

b. The Panjnad headworks is not officially included in the Sutlej Valley system. See Chap. 3, n. 69.

12. A. M. R. Montagu puts it quite succinctly: "A 'non-perennial' canal strictly speaking, is one that opens on the first day of the *Kharif* crop and closes on the last day required to water the *Kharif* crop. Generally speaking, non-perennial canals irrigate areas in which *rabi* water is considered unnecessary or harmful, i.e. riverain tracts with a high water table or areas in which water logging is incipient." (Personal communication, March 16, 1965.)

On the other hand, even the distinction between perennial and nonperennial canals and water supplies does not invariably correspond to that between areas which grow two crops per year and those which grow only one, for a rabi crop may be watered mainly by wells but in part by canals: "On non-perennial channels, the last waterings in the *Kharif* season are frequently used to prepare areas for *rabi* cultivation. Similarly the first watering in the following *Kharif* may be used to mature the tail end of the preceding *rabi* crop. . . ." (Personal communication from A. M. R. Montagu, August 2, 1965.)

Examination of the figures in Table 4 indicates that in a year of heavy runoff somewhat more land was actually irrigated in the low-water season than in the flood season in both the S.V.P. and the Sukkur Project. The explanation for this seeming paradox is two-fold: (1) water use is more efficient in the winter because evapotranspiration is lower (the actual water use in 1958–59 in the S.V.P. was 8.21 million acre feet in kharif and 4.27 million acre feet in rabi; in the Sukkur Project it was 12.71 million acre feet in kharif and 9.53 million acre feet in rabi); and (2) the winter (rabi) crops such as wheat and pulses may be more valuable in terms of water and labor input, and in terms of return per acre, than the summer (kharif) crops such as rice and cotton.

But is not the whole logic of perennial irrigation that one should be able to secure two crops per year? In theory, yes. But in practice it is often not possible to plant two crops on the same piece of land each year *even if water is available.* For one thing, the maturing period of one crop may be too long to allow another to follow it in the same year, especially when the time required for harvesting, gleaning, plowing, leveling, and bunding the fields, and preplanting irrigation is added (assuming that the work is not mechanized). This is true of rice and is notorious with sugarcane when the crop is ratooned, i.e. allowed to occupy the same field for three years or more during which several cuttings are made. Even cotton, a kharif crop, is often left standing in the fields until December or January in order to make three or four pickings, after which it is too late to sow a rabi crop.

But the basic reason why a shift from nonperennial to perennial irrigation does not double the area annually cropped is that the soils cannot stand it. In the absence of cheap and abundant fertilizers, fields under command of a perennial barrage must often be fallowed for one or more seasons to allow the soil to regain some natural fertility, especially after a heavy-feeding crop such as cotton has been grown. For these reasons, the total area actually irrigated in the S.V.P. in 1958–59 was only some 80 per cent of the commanded culturable area. In the Sukkur command the percentage was only 70, but here the fact that the distribution network has not been completed must be taken into account.

It must also be emphasized that no perennial or nonperennial irrigation project is ever designed to irrigate all of its culturable commanded area. Under the tripartite agreement for the S.V.P., the annual "intensity" or ratio of areas guaranteed a supply to the total culturable commanded area was only 50 per cent for areas served by nonperennial canals and only 50.7 to 62.2 per cent, respectively, for the British and the States' land under perennial canals. Each canal is authorized a "share capacity" based on this intensity: thus the perennial canals of the S.V.P. were intended to run at full capacity during the kharif season and at only half capacity during rabi. The nonperennial canals were not supposed to run at all during rabi, although they were authorized to take up to 150 per cent of their kharif share capacities when the flood runoff allowed.[13]

By 1935, the 1920 estimates of culturable commanded areas under the S.V.P., including Panjnad, were sharply reduced and the intensities, except for Bikaner State (which acceded to India at Partition), were accordingly raised. This fact, together with the exigencies of the post-Partition agricultural situation in West Pakistan and the excellent water supply in 1958–59, accounts for the high actual intensities achieved in that year. It should also be noted that in 1958–59 the planned regulation of Sutlej runoff by the Bhakra Dam had not yet begun so that the situation in the S.V.P. was still comparable to that on the other Indus Rivers. The development of storage facilities on the Jhelum and the Indus itself, as provided in the Indus Waters Treaty and Fund Agreement, will of course radically alter the situation by allowing the surplus flood from one kharif season to be carried over not only to the next rabi season but, if necessary, to make good any failure in the monsoon of the following kharif. But in the period under discussion no storage was available, and the only benefit of the barrage system was to raise the winter runoff to a level where it could normally be expected to feed, at the indicated intensity, the perennial canals and the lands they served.

At this point the reader may have come to the logical conclusion that once perennial, barrage-controlled irrigation had been introduced into the Punjab and Sind, the only problem in the Indus

13. *Completion Report with Schedules and Financial Forecast (British Areas Only) of the Sutlej Valley Project* (Lahore, Superintendent Government Printing, Punjab, 1935). This report includes the Panjnad scheme (see Chap. 3, n. 69).

Basin involved the allocation of the water supplies for the rabi crops. But a consideration of the agricultural cycle will show that it was not quite that simple. The traditional division of the agricultural and irrigation year into the kharif period (April 1 to September 30) and the rabi period (October 1 to March 31) has to be elaborated into a division among the kharif-sowing period (April through August), the kharif-maturing and rabi-sowing period (September to mid-December), and the rabi-maturing period (mid-December through March). Seen in this light, the critical irrigation phases overlap the second and third periods and the third and first periods.

There is generally no problem with water supplies for kharif maturing. But if the monsoon is weak, or if it ends early, the fall in the rivers and canals may be so rapid that insufficient supplies are available in November and early December for rabi sowing. During most of the rabi-maturing period, runoff is at a minimum, but so is evapotranspiration. The most critical phase begins in late February and March and continues until the rapidly rising temperatures produce a corresponding rise in the rate of snowmelt. Runoff increases accordingly, and by May 1 there is usually enough water in the rivers and canals to supply the needs of the newly sown kharif crops. But the evapotranspiration rate also rises dramatically, and by the middle of June, despite the continued rise in the rivers due to snowmelt, the monsoon is eagerly awaited to offset this tremendous loss of water. If the monsoon is delayed, or begins in a feeble fashion, there may not be enough water to meet the growing demands of the kharif crops (rice, cotton, sugarcane). Thus, irrigation agriculture in the Indus Basin is not "safe" in most years until after the first of July (although storage dams and tubewells are now changing this situation).

The foregoing analysis, though complicated, is necessary in order to explain why the critical phases in the irrigation of the Indus Basin do not neatly fall into the rabi or cold season as one might anticipate. During the cold weather, and up to March or April, most of the rabi crops can mature with little additional water, provided that they are well started, i.e. that the summer monsoon has been a good one and that the water level in the rivers and canals does not drop too rapidly in the fall. But the kharif crops, even if well started in April or May, have to get through a fiery furnace until the monsoon comes, via the rivers and canals, to their rescue. The following description of agriculture in Sind prior to the construction of the Sukkur Project makes this abundantly clear:

> There are two main cultivating seasons, *kharif* and *rabi*. The former extends normally from June to October and coincides for the first three months with the height of the inundation. The month for sowing is usually June, though occasionally seed and especially rice seed is put in in May, and if the rise of the river to a high and steady level happens to be late, sowing not infrequently takes place in July. Kharif crops are usually harvested in October. According to a popular formula, *Juari* [*jowar*, which is sorghum, or great millet] requires . . . 4 months to reach maturity and *bajri* [*bajra* is small millet] . . . 3 months; cotton on the other hand does not yield the final picking under . . . nearly 7 months. The rabi season ordinarily comprises the period from October to March, though sowing may occur from September until early December and reaping may go on into April.
>
> In the desert and on the hills, though the seasons are the same, the farmer's operations, depending entirely on rain, vary with its variableness. *Kharif* sowing can rarely begin till well on in July and there is little or no rabi.[14]

What perennial irrigation meant to Sind, therefore, was not so much a second season (though it did greatly expand the area under rabi crops—wheat, rape, pulses) but the possibility of a longer sea-

---

14. *Gazetteer of the Province of Sind, A,* 224–25. In 1904–05, rice was by far the most important crop grown in Sind, with nearly one million acres devoted to it. "It is almost the only thing that can be grown in the annually inundated lands within the Delta of the Indus." (Ibid., p. 226.) *Bajri* and wheat ranked second and third, followed by pulses. Oilseed crops (*jambo,* rape, and sesame) occupied less than 300,000 acres in all, and cotton 217,602, "but the quality is said to be about the worst produced in India. It only commands a price because it is found useful on the continent for mixing with wool or making imitation woollens. Attempts to introduce better varieties, of longer staple, have met with little success because they take longer to come to maturity, and *since they cannot be sown until the inundation sets in,* about May or June, the winter frosts nip them before the crop is ready for gathering. *The extension of perennial irrigation is,* however, *removing this last difficulty* and very promising experiments have been made during the last two years with Egyptian cotton." (Ibid., p. 227. Italics supplied.) This is a clear exposition of the value of perennial irrigation, and hence a longer kharif period, for cotton cultivation in Sind.

son, i.e. an earlier start on the kharif crops (cotton, rice, bajra, jowar, maize, sesame), and on cotton in particular. For this very reason, Sind was more interested in obtaining a maximum of water in April, May, and June for kharif sowing that it was in increasing the amount of irrigation in the rabi season. But, as we have seen, in the absence of storage reservoirs, this late-spring period was the critical phase for all of the Indus Basin. Until the Sukkur Project was sanctioned, Sind depended primarily on late kharif sowings, as the last quotation indicates. Sind was concerned about upstream withdrawals, to be sure, but its concern was mainly theoretical, especially as no firm evidence could be produced to show that these withdrawals interfered in any way with the traditional water requirements of Sind. But once Sukkur was under construction, Sind's interest in every drop of water flowing in the Indus Rivers between the melting of the snows on the Himalayas and Karakorums and the arrival of the monsoon became actual and vital. This transformation of Sind's interest, which occurred in the 1920s, marks the inception of the Indus Waters Dispute.

Partition changed the parties to the dispute, or rather put three parties where two had been, but it did not change the interests or, fundamentally, the arguments. From 1947 to 1960, the Government of Pakistan had to argue Sind's case, plus Bahawalpur's and part of the Punjab's, while the Government of India inherited the remainder of the Punjab's and all of Rajasthan's (including Bikaner). As we shall see, neither Independence nor the one-unit rule introduced into West Pakistan in 1955 served to eliminate the dispute between the upper and lower regions (now termed Northern and Southern Zones by the engineers and planners) of the Indus Plains within that country. That Sind and West Punjab could make common cause against India did not eliminate the conflict of interest between them, a conflict that is inherent in the physical geography of the Indus Plains (see Chapter 2).

To trace in detail an argument that continued for almost forty years between Sind and the Punjab, West and East, is fortunately for both author and reader beyond the scope of the present work. Certain landmark determinations and agreements must be discussed, however, because they allowed the development of certain key projects prior to Partition, and in addition laid a foundation for the post-Partition dispute and the settlement of 1960.

Sind-Punjab Disputes: The Bhakra, Trimmu, and Thal Projects

When the Government of India submitted the Sukkur Barrage Project for sanction to the Secretary of State in 1920, it admitted

> that the data available were insufficient to enable an accurate determination to be made of the effect on the discharge of the Indus at Sukkur of the withdrawals proposed for the Sutlej Valley Project in the Punjab, but it was possible to show that, even assuming the worst conditions, the shortage at Sukkur was not likely to be greater than could be surmounted by care and economy in distribution. "We consider, therefore, that both the Sukkur and the Sutlej Valley schemes can safely be constructed at the same time, and that there will, when the Sutlej Valley scheme is in full operation, be sufficient water in the Indus at Sukkur to provide fully for the Sukkur scheme. We are instituting a comprehensive system of discharge stations, which, in due time, will admit of a more detailed study of the effect of the withdrawals in the Punjab on the Indus at Sukkur, but it will be some years before useful deductions can be drawn from the observations recorded, and we trust that you will not consider it necessary to defer the construction of this great project or of the Sutlej Valley scheme in the meantime."

The institution of a comprehensive system of discharge stations was undertaken on the advice of Sir Thomas Ward, the then Inspector-General of Irrigation. In a note dated the 10th December 1920, he urged the importance of a full investigation into the supplies of the Indus and its tributaries. "Prima facie," he stated, "it is logical to assume that the abstraction of water from the tributaries of the Indus must necessarily diminish the volume passing Sukkur, but it is quite possible that this diminution is to some extent compensated for by seepage back into the river, during the *rabi* season, of a portion of the enormous withdrawals made by the Punjab during the *kharif*. Unfortunately the data available are too meagre to permit of a definite conclusion being arrived at on the subject. Such records of discharges as exist have, however, been carefully examined and analysed, and, on the information before them the Government of India are satisfied that the Sutlej Valley Project can be put in hand without prejudicing the supplies necessary to secure the area of irrigation contemplated on the Sukkur Canals. More than this it is impossible to assert, and the question of the collection of reliable data for the disposal of the problem has become one of the first urgency. *It will obviously be necessary, once construction commences on the Sukkur scheme, for any future projects put forward by the Punjab to be very carefully examined in relation to the possible effects of further withdrawals from the tributaries of the Indus upon the rights to irrigation from the Sukkur Canals upon which the Government of Bombay are now entering.* I have no hesitation in saying that the data for such an examination do not at present exist, and that, unless steps are immediately taken to collect and collate them, endless difficulty is likely to ensue. Almost all the controversies which have up to date taken place in India in respect of questions of water rights have been directly attributable to the fact that adequate figures were not forthcoming and that consequently recourse had to be had to indirect deductions and presumptions; the only method of averting such controversies is to have at hand reliable information on the factors in the case."[15]

The data collected from 1921 on formed the basis not only for determination of the early Sind-Punjab disputes but for the negotiation of the Indus Waters Treaty, 1952–60.

Upon learning of the Secretary of State's sanction of the Sukkur Project in April 1923, the Government of the Punjab apparently concluded that Sind had won the first round. At any rate, it wanted to stake its claim in no uncertain manner, and therefore entered a protest to the restriction of further withdrawals from both the Indus and the upstream tributaries.[16]

15. Indus Basin Working Party, Draft Outline as Prepared by the Indian Designee, *Comprehensive Long-Range Plan for the Most Effective Utilization of the Water Resources of the Indus Basin*, presented to the Working Party on October 6, 1953 (New Delhi, The Manager, Government of India Press, 1954), Annexure I, "Engineering Data," pp. 29–30. Italics added.

16. Ibid., p. 30, and *Hundred Years of P.W.D.*, p. 36.

The Government of Bombay strongly objected to this attitude on the part of the Punjab Government. They laid stress upon the statement of Sir Thomas Ward that all future Punjab schemes would have to be examined carefully in relation to possible effects at Sukkur. They complained that they had not been consulted when the Sutlej Valley Project was under consideration and feared that the supplies available at Sukkur would be considerably less than those on which the Sukkur Project had been framed.[17]

What was bothering the Punjab Government was that it had three more projects in mind for the Punjab Rivers, and it did not want the sanctioning of Sukkur to serve as a guarantee to Sind in perpetuity of the allocation of enough water to run the project at the stated intensities. From an objective standpoint, however, it is difficult to see what else the sanctioning could have represented.

Of Punjab's three schemes, that for the Bhakra Dam on the Sutlej was to be the most far-reaching. The logic of the Bhakra scheme was simple. No further water could be diverted from the Sutlej without upstream storage that could carry the excess runoff of one kharif period over to the succeeding rabi and to the following kharif-sowing period. If need be, such a reservoir could hold more than one season's excess runoff. This would be the first storage dam, as contrasted to a barrage or weir, in the Indus Basin. An eminently suitable site existed at Bhakra, where the Sutlej cuts through the Siwaliks, and a diversion barrage could be placed between Bhakra and Rupar, the headworks of the Sirhind Canal. Water from this headworks would be led between the distribution systems of the Sirhind and Western Jumna canals into the famine-prone districts of Hissar and Rohtak and on to areas of Rajasthan (including Bikaner) south of the Ferozepore system. As the Bhakra Dam Project was prepared in 1919–21, it called for a 405-foot dam, storing 2.76 million acre feet of water (twice the mean annual runoff at Rupar, although this figure had not been carefully determined at the time). This scheme was referred to a committee of experts by the Government of India. Taking into account the costs of a dam and the anticipated evapora-

17. Indus Basin Working Party, Draft Outline as Prepared by the Indian Designee, Annexure I, p. 30.

tion and seepage losses, it would have been a costly scheme at the time, though far less costly than as actually built after Partition.

The second project was an old one. It called for the irrigation of the Sind Sagar (Thal) Doab between the Indus and the Jhelum. Irrigation of the western side of this doab, from the Indus at Mari, was first proposed in 1873. The Indian Irrigation Commission of 1901–03 had considered the Thal Doab unpromising (see Chapter 3), however, and the Punjab Government let it wait until 1919 when it was again submitted, presumably to stake out a claim to Indus water above Sukkur.

The third project concerned the eastern side of the Thal as well as areas in the lower Rechna and Bari doabs. Since it was fore-shadowed in the Wilson-Jacob evidence before the Indian Irrigation Commission (see Chapter 3), one might characterize it as unfinished business relating to the Triple Canals Project, which on the one hand adversely affected the low-water levels and supplies for inundation canals along the lower Chenab, and on the other made no use of the regenerated supplies below Khanki on the Chenab and Rasul on the Jhelum. The logical place for a headworks, therefore, was about 2 miles below the Jhelum-Chenab confluence at Trimmu; but since this lay upstream of the Panjnad (Chenab-Sutlej) confluence, the Indian Irrigation Commission had insisted that the scheme be put off until the Triple Canals Project had been worked out. When it was put forth in 1915 as a project to improve inundation irrigation on both sides of the Chenab, Bahawalpur State objected, since withdrawals might affect supplies at or below Panjnad, and the scheme was again deferred. As we shall see shortly, Bahawalpur was temporarily satis-fied by the design of the Panjnad system (built as part of the Sutlej Valley Project but not directly entitled to share in Beas-Sutlej water). But Sind stepped in to object to both the Trimmu and the Thal projects as potential threats to the Sukkur scheme, and for essen-tially the same reasons she objected to the Bhakra storage scheme.[18]

From 1923 on, then, the Punjab Government was in effect attack-ing Sind on three fronts, Bhakra, Thal, and Trimmu, whichever seemed the most promising at the moment, while Sind was purely on the defensive with nothing further to propose until the Sukkur

18. Ibid., p. 27, and *Hundred Years of P.W.D.*, p. 36.

scheme was completed. At first, Punjab urged the Thal Project in various forms, but lost both her argument with the Central Government (February 1926) and her appeal to the Secretary of State, who agreed that experience with the actual working of the S.V.P. and Sukkur was needed before any decision could be made.[19]

In June 1928 the Indus Discharge Committee, established in September 1921 to coordinate the gauge measurements instituted by the Inspector General of Irrigation, Sir Thomas Ward, found on the basis of seven years' data that the regeneration gains and seepage and evaporation losses in between the various headworks were a key factor in the system. In its 1929 report, the Indus Discharge Committee agreed that the data were still insufficient to draw any conclusions regarding the Thal Project, but suggested that a limited rabi supply of 1,250 cusecs, and a kharif supply of 7,750 cusecs, might be made available for Trimmu. Not content with this small gain, Punjab again resumed the offensive on the Bhakra front. The committee of experts to which the Bhakra scheme had been referred had reported favorably on the site and had greatly enlarged the scheme to encompass a 500-foot high dam with a storage capacity of 4.75 million acre feet. Confronted with this sizable attack, the Government of Sind shifted its defense by arguing that even if the Bhakra Project on the Sutlej would not reduce the *volume* of water available at Sukkur, it would lower the flood level and thus have a deleterious effect upon the inundation canals that had their headworks between Mithankot and Sukkur. Furthermore, by reducing the volume of water in the annual floods of the Sutlej-Panjnad-Indus, a storage reservoir at Bhakra would increase the amount of silt deposited in the Mithankot-Sukkur stretch, raise the level of the bed of the Indus, and thus silt up or cut off the inundation canals' intakes.[20]

Unfortunately for Sind these arguments were mutually contradictory, and when the Indus Discharge Committee submitted them for investigation by two engineers, H. W. Nicholson from Punjab and W. L. C. Trench from Sind, they were forced to agree that the inundation canals above Sukkur would not be adversely affected so long as the Sukkur Barrage ponded back a considerable amount of water

19. Indus Basin Working Party, Draft Outline as Prepared by the Indian Designee, Annexure I, p. 31.
20. Ibid., pp. 31–32.

and maintained a certain level, while the inundation canals below Sukkur might even benefit. After some further argument, the Government of Bombay withdrew its objections to the Bhakra Project on March 27, 1934. But instead of proceeding with construction at once, Punjab proceeded to redesign Bhakra once again and meanwhile to press the Thal and Trimmu projects![21]

Trimmu and Thal

In order to proceed with Trimmu, the Punjab had to persuade the Government of India to allocate more than the rabi supply of 1,250 cusecs offered by the Indus Discharge Committee in 1929. But increased withdrawals from the combined Jhelum-Chenab would adversely affect supplies available at Panjnad for Bahawalpur, and might affect bed and water levels and supplies along the Indus above Sukkur. The critical phase in early kharif, described above, came into the picture too, because Bikaner had already requested the other Sutlej Valley Project partners to occasionally "give up a share of their water from nonperennial canals to avoid serious consequences in that State."[22] Fortunately, Bahawalpur could do so because the areas actually suitable for irrigation in its territory were smaller than those originally assumed, but Bahawalpur was in no mood to jeopardize further its kharif supplies at Panjnad as an enlarged Trimmu Project threatened to do.

The Thal Project involved only Indus water, and directly concerned only Punjab, Khairpur (with its inundation canals on the Indus), and Sind. There never was any dispute about kharif-maturing or even rabi supplies, but, as we have seen, there was considerable concern in Khairpur and Sind about the supplies for kharif sowing, during which phase even the mighty Indus, without storage facilities, might not be able to meet their needs. Indirectly, Bikaner and Bahawalpur were also involved, lest withdrawals by Punjab from the Indus in the kharif-sowing phase require them to make up the difference from the Sutlej under the "guarantee" to Sind. Even the North West Frontier Province, which included inundation canals above Dera Ismail Khan on the Indus, as well as canals based on the

21. Ibid., pp. 32, 34.
22. Ibid., p. 32.

Kabul and its tributary the Swat, might be affected by a Thal project with its headworks at Kalabagh unless a prescriptive right of prior use were recognized. And even if it were, an implicit or explicit guarantee to the lower riparians would limit or preclude future upstream expansion.

Thus one can see that by 1935 the Indus Basin irrigation system had become so completely integrated that no fewer than six parties had to be consulted before any new withdrawals could be authorized anywhere. The development foreseen, and the principles laid down, by the Indian Irrigation Commission of 1901–03 had borne fruit over the ensuing three decades.

Faced with this multiplicity of interests and proposals, the Government of India in 1935 turned to the Central Board of Irrigation and asked it to convene a Committee on Distribution of the Waters of the Indus to recommend an allocation that might be "acceptable and equitable to all parties concerned." The Committee, also referred to as "The Indus Committee, 1935" or, from the name of its chairman, as the "Anderson Committee," met in New Delhi from March 1 to 8 and in Simla from June 17 to 20, and submitted its final report on September 16, 1935. The alacrity with which the Anderson Committee performed its work is misleading; its report fills three volumes with histories of the projects, briefs submitted by the parties, proceedings, and findings. But the findings were fairly simple and represented a compromise in which all parties secured something, with Punjab receiving the most. Sind obtained more water at Sukkur, Bahawalpur more at Panjnad, and Bikaner more at Ferozepore (from the Gang, or Bikaner, Canal). Bahawalpur had its allowances from Suleimanke and Islam reduced to permit greater withdrawals from Ferozepore and Panjnad. The Punjab got more water at Suleimanke, plus final authorization to proceed with the Thal Project, and at Trimmu where the rabi allowance was raised to 2,750 cusecs though the kharif allocation remained at 7,750 cusecs.

Since Punjab could not make use of this additional quantity of Jhelum-Chenab water in rabi, it altered the Trimmu scheme to incorporate a link, known as the Haveli from a town it passed, which would cut across the lower Rechna Doab, providing perennial command for some 183,000 culturable acres and nonperennial command for another 83,000 culturable acres on the way, and then deliver at least 700 cusecs to the Ravi just above Sidhnai. This transfer not only firmed up the supply at Sidhnai, which had been chronically short inasmuch as it depended on Ravi water below Balloki, but allowed the diversion of an additional 700 cusecs of Ravi water from Balloki into the LBDC and thence, via a new short link (Montgomery-Pakpattan), from the LBDC into the Pakpattan Canal to provide additional irrigation in areas formerly supplied exclusively from the Sutlej. Thus, the "link principle" inaugurated in the Triple Canals Project was revived, though on a much smaller scale, in the revised Trimmu scheme, which henceforth became known as the Haveli Project.

The Haveli Project was sanctioned in July 1937. The Government of India Act of 1935 having come into effect, the Punjab Government was able to give sanction in its own right.[23] Work was begun immediately and, although the Haveli Canal had to be lined throughout its length because of its abnormally flat slope (an unlined canal would have resulted in velocities so low that the silt deposited would have blocked the canal; even as it was, the Haveli experienced some siltation problems), the canal was formally opened in April 1939. To save time and some cost, modern earthmoving equipment was employed. Another cost-saving feature was the use of "box-type" floor for the weir: a network of concrete boxes was laid, the boxes were filled with sand, and the whole was then sealed with a continuous concrete slab. This box design, which reduces the need for concrete, was the innovation of A. N. Khosla (whom we shall meet again in Chapter 6) who also applied his theory of subsoil flow in designing the floor and the pile lines of the weir and aprons.[24]

Except for the extension of Haveli water to the Sidhnai system, the areas irrigated were those proposed as early as 1915: the extreme lower end of the Rechna Doab by the Haveli Canal, and the east-central margin of the Thal Doab by the Rangpur Canal, which replaced many inundation canals along the Chenab but which remains nonperennial, serving 347,000 acres. Including the areas fed in the Sidhnai system, the Haveli Project serves 1,358,000 acres,

23. Ibid., p. 33.
24. *Hundred Years of P.W.D.*, pp. 36–37, and a personal communication from A. M. R. Montagu, September 6, 1965.

roughly half perennial and half nonperennial. Over the past quarter century, however, the Haveli Canal has had a deleterious effect in adjacent areas, for it blocks down-doab drainage and, together with the Chenab and Ravi, forms a small triangle into which, despite the lining of the canal, water seeps from all sides. This has produced not only waterlogging but also one of the most severe salinity conditions in the Indus Basin groundwater.

The Thal Project was simpler in concept than the Haveli, but less promising. In fact, it was the first major project undertaken in the Basin for which an economic justification, based on direct benefits, could not be made.[25] For this reason, the Indian Irrigation Commission of 1901–03 and later committees had shied away from it, and it is questionable whether it would have been sanctioned in 1937 had the Act of 1935 not delegated responsibility to the provinces. The basic difficulty lay in the topography of the Thal Doab, formerly called the Sind Sagar or "Desert of the Indus." The rise from the floodplain of the Indus to the sand hills of the Thal is an abrupt one in most places, and command had therefore to be established high upstream. Kalabagh offered a good site, and from there it would also be possible to bring a canal around the foothills of the Salt Range toward the Jhelum, irrigating some good alluvial fan soils on the way. But the western margin of the Thal was so cut up by sand hills and partly anchored dunes, and the middle (used in an east-west sense) portion consisted of such unrelieved desert, that the Thal seemed unpromising. Scattered settlers had long eked out a living by cultivating the longitudinal depressions, or *pattis,* which lay between the ranges of dunes in the western part of the Thal, but by and large the Thal Doab was the realm of the camel herder or the brigand. It did not even have many *junglis* (see Chapter 3, n. 39) and though the caravan trails across the Thal, connecting places like Multan and Jhang Maghiana with the Derajat and the North West Frontier, were ancient, the doab as a whole had too small a population to warrant any famine-relief measures and too uncertain a potential to justify colonization until other areas had been exhausted. In fact, between 1877–78 and 1929 (when the Sind Sagar Doab Colonization Act was repealed) the Punjab Government had

25. Indus Basin Working Party, Draft Outline as Prepared by the Indian Designee, Annexure I, pp. 26, 33.

reserved some 2 million acres of Thal land for grazing use only. The floodplain margins of the Thal, especially in the southern Muzaffargarh District where the Panjnad and Indus converge, were of course exceptions to this, having a fairly dense population which had supported itself by inundation irrigation since time immemorial.

With a view to doing something, eventually, with the Thal, the Sind Sagar Doab Colonization Act was passed in 1901, permitting the Punjab Government to take possession of about 1.5 million acres in the Bhakkar and Leiah tahsils for development and settlement when a canal could be constructed. A project was prepared in 1919 calling for a 14,000-cusec canal with its intake at Kalabagh. But, as we have seen, Thal was again set aside, partly for lack of Indus discharge data, until the Sutlej Valley Project and the Sukkur Project could be worked out. Furthermore, the Sukkur sanction placed limitations on upstream withdrawals. Although the Punjab protested this state of affairs, it did revise its Thal Project downward in 1925, asking for only 6,750 cusecs. Even this was not allowed, and the Indus Discharge Committee deferred consideration for a decade until more information was available.[26] Meanwhile, popular pressure had in 1929 forced the repeal of the Colonization Act, threatening the Punjab Government with the loss of its reserved lands. Hence the desire to obtain approval for a Thal project despite the physical obstacles.

The Anderson Committee of 1935 approved a 6,000-cusec capacity for the Thal Canal but allocated it only 2,000 cusecs of flow for December, i.e. the rabi-sowing phase. The Thal Project of 1936 accordingly called for a culturable commanded area of 1,039,000 acres, and this was sanctioned by the Punjab Government in the following year. But by the time the Irrigation Branch had completed the Haveli Project and could start on Thal, further data indicated that more water would be available from Kalabagh. Thus the canal was to be built with sufficient cross section to carry 10,000 cusecs, though the flow would be held to 6,000 at first. The design of the barrage just below Kalabagh was to be similar to that at Trimmu, i.e. built on the box principle, but as World War II created a shortage of steel reinforcing rods, it had to be changed to the solid gravity type. The barrage was completed by 1942, when work on the project was in-

26. *Hundred Years of P.W.D.*, p. 38.

terrupted due to war conditions. It was resumed in 1944, and the Thal Mainline Upper Canal, lined throughout its length, was completed down to below Mianwali where it trifurcates. The Mainline Lower, also lined, continues southward, parallel to the Indus, for another 100 miles. The short Dullewalla branch extends about 20 miles southeast of the trifurcation, while the branch now called the Muhajir runs east at the foot of the Salt Range to the vicinity of Juharabad.[27]

Only small portions of the Mainline Lower and Muhajir branches had been completed when the project was commissioned. The last British Governor of the Punjab, Sir Evan Jenkins, dedicated the barrage in February 1947, naming it the Glancy Barrage after his predecessor. At this point, Partition caught up with irrigation development in the Punjab, and in the Indus Basin as a whole.

The Thal Project in many ways is symbolic of the changes Partition brought, even though its area lay far from the boundary between India and West Pakistan. Two names indicate this symbolism: the Glancy Barrage is now called the Mohammad Ali Jinnah Barrage in honor of the founder of Pakistan, and the eastern branch canal has been named the Muhajir in honor of the refugees from India who were settled in its command. Despite Thal's physical limitations, Pakistan was fortunate in having the project in an advanced stage of readiness when Partition came. Its existence gave the West Punjab a place to settle refugees almost from the start. In contrast, although the Sukkur system was still being expanded in the late 1940s, so much land had already been taken up that Sind was not able immediately to move any substantial number of refugees away from the miserably overcrowded fringes of Karachi. We shall return to the post-Partition role of the Thal Project in Chapter 6.

Bhakra Again

It is a principle of international law that treaties are to be observed *rebus sic stantibus*, i.e. if conditions remain the same. This principle is most frequently cited as an excuse for not observing treaties, inasmuch as conditions rarely do remain the same. Thus it was with the Sind-Punjab agreement concerning the Bhakra Project.

It will be recalled that Sind had finally accepted the Nicholson-

27. Ibid., p. 39.

Trench recommendations of 1929, and in 1934 withdrew its objections to a 500-foot high dam with a storage of 4.75 million acre feet on the Sutlej at Bhakra. But Punjab had not acted on the project, proceeding instead with Trimmu (Haveli) and Thal. Both of these projects had involved further negotiations with Sind, and had necessitated the appointment of the Anderson Committee of 1935. On this basis alone, Sind might have claimed that conditions had altered, since all three projects were interrelated. But when, starting in 1939, the Punjab redesigned Bhakra a third time, calling for a smaller reservoir (4 million acre feet) but more use of Sutlej water for the S.V.P. which was still experiencing shortages in the late kharif season, the Government of Sind (which had superseded the Government of Bombay in 1937) was well within its rights in complaining to the Governor-General. Inasmuch as both Sind and Punjab were now separate provinces, and inasmuch as irrigation was now a provincial rather than a central matter, the Governor-General could not refer the complaint to another committee of the Central Board of Irrigation. Instead it was necessary to convene a special, quasi-judicial commission, known as the Indus Commission, under the chairmanship of Mr. Justice B. N. Rau but with two engineers as members.

The Indus Commission was appointed in September of 1941 and did not submit its report until July 1942. The Central Government was not represented, and the proceedings were conducted more or less on the adversary basis with Sind in the position of plaintiff and Punjab as defendant. For reasons with which the reader is now familiar, Sind's case and the Punjab's defense were presented in separate parts for kharif and rabi. In addition, the Report includes a general introduction that furnished not only a history of irrigation in the Indus Basin but a comprehensive review of international law on the subject of riparian rights. Not finding sufficient precedents in the cases on international rivers, the Commission reviewed the work of the United States Supreme Court in deciding interstate disputes, notably those on the Colorado River. Separate treatment was also accorded to the issue of "consequential modifications," or how much change one province might make in project designs without basically altering the premises on which an award had been made, to the problem of costs, and to the rights reserved to the Governor-General under the Act of 1935 to decide interprovincial disputes over water use. In sum, the report of the Indus Commission was the most far-reaching examination of irrigation in the Indus Basin since that of the Indian Irrigation Commission forty years before. This was so because Sind, having learned something of Punjab's tactics, not only complained about the Bhakra Project under contemplation, the Haveli Project already in operation, and the Thal Project under construction, but tried to guess what future projects the Punjab might have in mind. These included:

(4) 24 storage reservoirs with an assumed capacity of 500,000 acre-feet each, on the affluents of the Indus, Jhelum, Chenab, Ravi, Beas, and Sutlej rivers and one of them, the Woolar Lake Scheme on the Jhelum itself, said to be in contemplation and

(5) feeders to transfer water (subject to certain conditions) from the Ravi to the Beas and from the Chenab to the Beas with a total assumed withdrawal of 23,000 cusecs, said to be in contemplation.[28]

In other words, Sind was attempting to use the Indus Commission as a sort of equity proceeding and to have the Punjab enjoined from further interference with its water supply. Punjab's first argument in defense was a demurrer, stating that it contemplated subsidiary storage of only 3.5 million acre feet (item 4) instead of the 12 million acre feet assumed by Sind, and (item 5) desired only (a) a link of 700-cusec capacity from the LBDC to the Pakpattan Canal (the Montgomery-Pakpattan Link, already constructed as part of the Haveli Project) and a link of 5,000-cusec capacity from Balloki on the Ravi to Suleimanki on the Sutlej (built by Pakistan after Partition). Thus, the Punjab admitted to contemplating *over at least the next forty years* feeders with a combined capacity of only 5,700 cusecs rather than the 23,000 suggested by Sind, and the Commission (whose sigh of relief is almost audible in the record) decided to limit itself to that.[29]

28. Report of the Indus Commission, Part 1, General, *Complaint of Sind and Projects Complained of under Section 130 of the Government of India Act of 1935* (6 parts, Lahore, reprinted by the Superintendent of Government Printing, Punjab, 1950), p. 1.

29. Ibid., pp. 1–2. Punjab may have been contemplating both the Marala-Ravi and Balloki-Suleimanke links (see Chap. 6) in order to ease the situation in the Sutlej Valley Canal system in early kharif, while Bhakra was looked upon to ease it in late kharif. See *Hundred Years of P.W.D.*, p. 61.

It was enough. The 3.5 million acre feet of subsidiary storages under item 4 entailed either seven storage sites on the Beas affluents (with a total capacity of 2.065 million acre feet) or a single storage site on the Beas itself (with a capacity of 2 million acre feet; this has evolved into the present Pong Dam which India is building as allowed by the Indus Waters Treaty) plus four storages on the affluents of the Ravi and the Chenab, plus the Wular Lake storage on the Jhelum with a total capacity of 1.4 million acre feet. (These have evolved into the single Thein Dam on the Ravi, which India plans to build, and the Mangla Dam on the Jhelum, which Pakistan is completing under the Treaty.)

The principal proceedings of the Commission, of course, were those relating to the Bhakra Project. The Commission noted that although Sind had accepted the Bhakra Project as described in the Nicholson-Trench report,

> as Punjab now proposes to design Bhakra, though its capacity would be smaller (4 as against 4.75 million acre feet) it would draw water for the reservoir late in the kharif season (since priority in withdrawals is assigned to the Sutlej Valley Canals) when the levels are falling and so might burden the Sind inundation canals.[30]

Broadly speaking, Sind's first complaint was that the effects of the Bhakra Dam Project and the other projects contemplated by the Punjab, when super-imposed upon the full effects of the Thal and Haveli Projects and of certain older projects already executed, would be to cause "such lowering of water levels both in Upper and Lower Sind during the months of May to October inclusive as will seriously affect the efficient working of the Sind's inundation canals." Sind's second complaint, in substance, was that the Thal and Haveli Projects, when taken in conjunction with certain orders passed by the Government of India, in 1937, on the recommendation of the Anderson Committee, would create a serious shortage of water at Sukkur in the *rabi* or winter season (October to March inclusive) and would interfere with the proper working of the Barrage Project in Sind.[31]

30. Report of the Indus Commission, Part 1, pp. 6–7.
31. Indus Basin Working Party, Draft Outline as Prepared by the Indian Designee, Annexure I, p. 34.

On the whole, and with many qualifications, the findings of the Indus Commission were favorable to Sind, especially with respect to the kharif case:

> the withdrawals necessary for the Punjab projects . . . are likely to cause material injury to Sind's inundation canals, particularly in the month of September.[32]

Like the Indian Irrigation Commission before it, the Indus Commission was constructive in its recommendations:

> A final apportionment of the Indus system, to be practicable, would probably require the construction of two new barrages in Sind, at Gudu and Hajipur [both have since been built, although the Hajipur site was superseded by that at Kotri-Hyderabad].[33]

This being so, the Commission recommended that Punjab in particular make a contribution toward the cost of these works.

Neither Sind nor Punjab accepted the findings and recommendations of the Indus Commission, and both appealed to the Government of India against them. Although the matter was actually referred to London, and although a draft agreement between the Chief Engineers of Sind and Punjab was actually prepared in September 1945,[34] political events had now overtaken both engineers and administrators in British India. With the end of the war in Europe and the Far East, and the advent of the Labour Government in Britain, it was realized that Indian independence, and possibly partition, were around the corner. Decisions on irrigation schemes and allocation of water within the Indus Basin were losing priority to decisions on constituent assemblies, interim governments, and boundaries.

Before embarking on the preceding long discussion of the various Sind-Punjab disputes from 1923 to 1945, we pointed out their rele-

32. Ibid., p. 35.
33. Report of the Indus Commission Part 1, p. 26.
34. "The [draft] agreement involved construction of a barrage (Gudu) across the Indus in upper Sind, construction of link canals with capacities up to 19,300 cusecs from the Chenab and Ravi Rivers to the Sutlej [i.e. the Marala-Ravi and Balloki-Suleimanke links], and construction of two storage reservoirs—Bhakra on the Sutlej and Wular Lake on the Jhelum." (Harza Report, p. A-3.) There was no agreement regarding the financial aspects.

vance to the Indus Waters Dispute following Partition and later noted that Pakistan inherited all of Sind's case and part of Punjab's, whereas India inherited the remainder of Punjab's case along with that of Bikaner. It is interesting to speculate on what might have been the situation at the time of Partition and during the negotiations of the Indus Waters Treaty had the Punjab, in 1934, gone forward with Bhakra on the basis of Sind's acceptance of the Nicholson-Trench Report. Had Bhakra been built before, which is to say in lieu of Trimmu (Haveli) and Thal over the decade 1934–44, the center of gravity of irrigation in the Indus Basin would have been pulled to the east and to the south. Difficult as it was to draw a partition line through the Punjab in 1947, it would have been even harder had the Bhakra Project then been in existence. Perhaps it is not too much to say that the existence of Bhakra in 1947 would have telescoped the granting of independence and the signing of a waters treaty between India and Pakistan. Years of frustration and negotiation, and several false starts on emergency diversion and link-canal schemes, might have been avoided. A treaty on water rights and canal operations coincident with Partition (as was indeed suggested by Sir Cyril Radcliffe; see Chapter 5) might have preserved the essential unity of the Indus Basin for irrigation purposes. At the least, the construction of the Indus Basin Project in West Pakistan, and of the projects that have followed Bhakra in India, could have been started much earlier and at considerable savings.

But such speculation is moot in view of the postponement of the Bhakra Project to after Partition and in view of the events of 1946–47 which form the subject of the next chapter. In these years, engineers and administrators deferred to statesmen and politicians, and we must now do the same. But since we shall return to the growth of the irrigation system in later chapters, it is well to bear in mind how many of the post-Partition and Treaty projects were already on the drawing boards at Partition, five years before earnest Treaty negotiations were begun and thirteen years before the Treaty was signed. The negotiators who met in Washington in 1952 under World Bank auspices did not start from scratch. They began with the background of the Sind-Punjab disputes and of the findings and recommendations of Nicholson and Trench, the Anderson Committee, and the Indus (Rau) Commission.

5. Partition

"If you can keep your head when all about you,
Are losing theirs and blaming it on you;
If you can trust yourself when all men doubt you,
But make allowance for their doubting, too...."
                                            —Rudyard Kipling

Although the definitive history of the partition of India has yet to be written, the many first-person accounts and tentative historical treatments available make it unnecessary for us to trace in great detail the political events and negotiations of 1946–47.[1] We are more

1. For the reader who wishes a fuller account of these events, yet who desires to avoid any one-sided presentation, it is suggested that the three following works, taken together, will produce the desired result:

a. Ian Stephens, *Pakistan* (2nd ed., London, Ernest Benn, 1964). This is perhaps the best concise account, eminently readable, up to scholarly standards, written by a first-hand observer of events in 1946–47 who had access to those in high places, and despite its title and slight pro-Muslim bias, quite fair to all concerned.

b. V. P. Menon, *The Transfer of Power in India* (Princeton: Princeton University Press, 1957). The fundamental work on the subject, as close to an official version as one is likely to get, written by a person with access to the records (many of which are reproduced in the appendixes) and who, more than any other individual, was responsible for the shape that Independence and Partition finally took; though written by a Hindu, it is up to scholarly standards and can be criticized only for what is omitted; the pro-Indian bias will serve to counteract Stephens' pro-Muslim leanings.

interested in effects than in causes, and in any case discussion of the latter, however fascinating it may be, cannot yet be carried on in either a fully informed or a fully objective manner. Nevertheless, for the purposes of this study it will be highly useful to review not only the actual Partition and its results, but the possible alternatives and their implicit effects upon the irrigation-based structure of the Indus Basin.

The Cabinet Mission Plan

Realistically, these alternatives fall into two categories: (1) the Cabinet Mission Plan transmitted by the Viceroy, Lord Wavell, to the Congress Party and Muslim League leaders in May 1947, which would presumably have averted most of the economic dislocations, at least temporarily, and (2) alternatives to the Boundary Line actually drawn in the Punjab at Partition, which might have done less harm to the respective Indian and Pakistani sections.[2]

---

c. Penderel Moon, *Divide and Quit* (London, Chatto and Windus, 1961). Written by a former British Civil Servant who in 1947 was in the service of the Muslim State of Bahawalpur but who confesses to a slight pro-Sikh bias; the author had access to many of the principals involved in the events of 1946–47 and was directly concerned with the aftermath of Partition in Bahawalpur; his book offers many unusual and perceptive insights.

Khushwant Singh's novel, *Train to Pakistan* (London, Chatto and Windus, 1956) is also recommended as the best treatment of what Partition meant on the village level; it brings home the ultimate tragedy of 1947 in a manner no factual treatment can.

For a contemporary analysis by a geographer, see O. H. K. Spate, "The Partition of India and the Prospects of Pakistan," *Geographical Review, 38* (1948), 5–29.

2. The so-called "Wavell Plan" of phased withdrawal by the British, which was discussed in London in December 1946, was in no sense a political settlement. It probably should not even be attributed to Lord Wavell. (See Stephens, pp. 122–25.) There was, however, another plan suggested by Wavell to the Secretary of State for India early in 1946, based on the results of the provincial elections which had just been held. Wavell desired "(a) to secure a reasonably efficient Executive Council, with representatives of the principal parties on a proportional basis, which would carry on the Government of India during the interim period; (b) to form a constitution-making body which would produce a workable and acceptable constitution; and (c) to bring about governments in the provinces on a coalition basis as far as possible." (Menon, *Transfer*, p. 233.) Wavell was prepared to go ahead, if necessary, without the Muslim League and to tell Mohammad Ali Jinnah that there was no possibility of a "Pakistan" into which large numbers of non-Muslims would be coerced. "The

The Cabinet Mission consisted of three men, two of whom had considerable experience in Indian affairs—Sir Stafford Cripps, Labourite President of the Board of Trade who in 1942 had conducted the fruitless negotiations with the Indian political leaders, and Lord Pethick-Lawrence, the Secretary of State for India; the third member was Mr. A. M. Alexander, First Lord of the Admiralty. The Mission arrived in New Delhi on March 24, 1946, and after almost two months of discussions issued its "Plan" on May 16.

The essence of the Cabinet Mission Plan was the creation of a federal government for India in which the proposed central authority, a "Union of India" including both British India and the Princely States, would have responsibility only for communications, defense, and foreign affairs. All other subjects would have been vested in the provinces, and these provinces would have been grouped to take cognizance of the communal divisions: Group A comprising the Hindu-majority provinces of central and southern India; Group B consisting of the northwestern, Muslim-majority provinces of Punjab, Sind, N.W.F.P., and British Baluchistan; and Group C comprising Bengal and Assam where Hindus and Muslims were inextricably mixed. Yet the Plan ignored the almost inextricable mixture of Muslims with Hindus, and particularly with Sikhs, in the Punjab. The groups of provinces would have had executives and legislatures to determine in common such matters as the separate provinces might delegate to them.

Had the Cabinet Mission Plan been adopted, and had the grouping taken place as foreseen, the essential unity of the Indus Basin irrigation system might have been preserved within Group B. It is true that the Princely States (such as Bahawalpur, Khairpur, Patiala, and Kapurthala, to mention only the major states in the Basin) would

---

effect of this would be that *at least two divisions of the Punjab* [italics supplied; the divisions indicated were those of Ambala and Jullundur, which did finally end up in India] and almost the whole of West Bengal, including Calcutta, would have to be allowed to join the Indian Union. The attractiveness of Pakistan to the Muslims would thus largely disappear and only 'the husk,' in Jinnah's own words [a "moth-eaten Pakistan" according to Nehru] would remain. It was possible that such a plan might induce the League to remain in an all-India federation." This "Wavell Plan" was never publicly announced. Instead, on receipt of it, the British Government decided to send out the Cabinet Mission. But it is apparent that the "Wavell Plan" of early 1946 anticipated both the Cabinet Mission Plan and the actual Partition lines of August 1947.

not have been compelled to join the Groups, but they probably would have done so. It is also true that the Plan would have allowed any province to secede at a later date from its Group, though not from the Union, but the Punjab with its Muslim majority probably would not have done so. It is also true that the individual provinces could have retained the already considerable autonomy with respect to irrigation works which they enjoyed under the Government of India Act of 1935, but it is likely that this would have been one of the first subjects delegated to the Group executives. On the other hand, as Jawaharlal Nehru pointed out at his famous press conference on July 10, 1946, the Plan did not provide any central authority to settle interprovincial or intergroup disputes. This could indeed have been a stumbling block, although the Union's responsibility for maintaining the roads, operating the railways, and ensuring freedom and security of movement among the provinces, states, and groups might logically, even in the absence of a pre-Independence formal agreement, have evolved into such authority.

But these conjectures are only that. The Cabinet Mission Plan fell through even before the Mission left India on June 29, 1946. It is true that both the Muslim League and the Indian National Congress had "accepted" the statement of May 16. But each had done so with reservations, and their reservations quickly proved irreconcilable.

The Muslim League accepted the Mission Plan because it contained the germ of Pakistan and the seeds of partition. The Mission had rejected the League's claim for a completely independent Pakistan consisting of the six provinces in Groups B and C. It had done so because such a Pakistan would have included the Hindus of Bengal and Assam and the Hindus and Sikhs of the Punjab. The Mission had also rejected the suggestion of a smaller Pakistan, excluding the East Punjab (Ambala and Jullundur divisions) and excluding most of Assam and Western Bengal with Calcutta. At that time, such a "moth-eaten" Pakistan was also unacceptable to the Muslim League.

> The Delegation [Cabinet Mission] themselves were convinced that any solution which involved a radical partition of the Punjab and Bengal would be contrary to the wishes and interests of a very large proportion of the inhabitants of those

137

provinces; moreover, any division of the Punjab would of necessity divide the Sikhs.[3]

But the Mission Plan did give the Muslim League the immediate prospect of controlling the affairs of Groups B and C, and it further allowed for ultimate secession from the Union in its provision for "a reconsideration of the constitutions of the Union and of the groups after an initial period of ten years and at ten-yearly intervals thereafter" upon the initiative of any province by a majority vote of its own legislature.[4] Thus, from the standpoint of the League, it offered both a bird in the hand and a bird in the bush.

The very features that made the Mission Plan acceptable to the League made it unacceptable to the Indian National Congress, and particularly to Nehru with his twin convictions that a secular Congress Party could rule a united India without communal discord, and that a strong central government was essential for economic planning and development. Congress particularly disliked the compulsory grouping of provinces for the purpose of drawing up a constitution, even though the Plan provided for any province to opt out of its group by majority vote of its own legislature at any time after the first elections held pursuant to the new constitution. Congress tried to get the Mission to accept its interpretation that grouping in the constituent assembly was to be voluntary. Since compulsory grouping in the initial stages was the core of the plan, and the only basis on which the Muslin League would accept it, the Mission explicitly rejected Congress' interpretation on May 25, 1946. Nevertheless, Congress made its "acceptance" on June 25 contingent on this reservation, and on July 10 Nehru, who had just assumed the Congress presidency from Maulana Azad, stated in a press conference, "We are not bound by a single thing except that we have decided for the moment to go to the Constituent Assembly."[5]

3. Menon, *Transfer*, p. 264.
4. "Statement of Cabinet Mission and Viceroy, 16 May 1964," quoted in Menon, *Transfer*, Appendix IV, at p. 470.
5. Menon, *Transfer*, p. 280. The following passages are quoted from pp. 280–81: "Speaking at a press conference Nehru admitted that, in agreeing to go into the Constituent Assembly, the Congress had inevitably agreed to a certain process of going into it, i.e. the election of candidates; 'but what we do there we are entirely and absolutely free to determine.' Referring to the two provisos laid down by the Mission, namely proper arrangements for minorities

In his introduction to the first American edition of Maulana Azad's *India Wins Freedom,* Louis Fischer, the biographer of Gandhi (who was, up to June 1947, a firm opponent of partition, and then acquiesced only with great reluctance), writes of this same press conference:

> The event was a Nehru press interview in Bombay. I attended that fateful question-and-answer period and when it ended I said to Nehru in the presence of Mrs. Vijaya Lakshmi Pandit, his sister, "You have changed the entire basis of the agreement with England."
>
> He smiled and replied, "I am fully aware of that."
>
> Nehru had told the assembled journalists that the Congress party, of which he, Gandhi, Azad and Patel were the leaders, would not be bound by the Cabinet Mission's confederation plan. Actually the All-India Congress Committee had met in the same city of Bombay only two days earlier under Nehru's chairmanship and in Gandhi's presence and voted for the plan. This is fully documented in the minutes; Azad, who participated in the discussions, bears witness to it.[6]

On the other hand, a conviction that the federal form of government proposed by the Cabinet Mission Plan would have been too weak for effective planning and development may have played a role in Nehru's action. Fischer goes on to quote the official transcript

---

and a treaty between India and England, he stressed that he would have no treaty with the British Government if they sought to impose anything upon India; as for the minorities, it was a domestic problem and 'we shall no doubt succeed in solving it. We accept no outsider's interference in it, certainly not the British Government's interference, and therefore these two limiting factors to the sovereignty of the Constituent Assembly are not accepted by us.' . . . Dealing with the powers of the proposed Union Centre, Nehru said that defence and communications would embrace a large number of industries necessary for their support. Foreign affairs must inevitably include foreign trade policy. It was equally inevitable that the Union must raise its finances by taxation, rather than by any system of contributions or doles from the provinces. Further, the Centre must obviously control currency and credit; and there must be an overall authority to settle inter-provincial disputes and to deal with administrative or economic breakdowns."

6. Maulana Abul Kalam Azad, *India Wins Freedom* (New York and London, Longmans, Green and Co., 1960), Introduction by Louis Fischer, p. xvii. (Used by permission of David McKay Company, Inc.)

of another press conference held by Nehru in 1959 shortly after the (posthumous) publication of Azad's work. Nehru was asked whether he thought that partition could have been avoided. In his reply he stated:

> Because we were anxious naturally to make good, after Independence, in the political and economic spheres and others—planning and all that—and we felt that if there was some kind of a compulsory union carried on, it would prevent—all our energies would be spent in these inner tugs of war. Whether that was a right analysis or a wrong analysis, I cannot say. I am only saying that it had a powerful effect in our thinking. And, even in the course of the interim Government, we had proposed the appointment of a Planning Commission. It had been opposed by the Moslem League representatives. So that, in every such matter where economic considerations and planning came in, we were likely to come up against inner pulls in different directions. That was, I think—this overwhelming sensation that any kind of a union, if it came about, would first of all not put an end to these inner pulls, secondly, it would leave the Federal Government so weak—with the transfer of power to its various constituent units— the Central Federation would be so weak, that it would not be able to act properly or adopt any effective economic measures. These were the real reasons which ultimately induced us to agree [to Partition]. It was a very, very difficult choice—you can well imagine—and it is frightfully difficult to say now what one could do if one had the same choice. It is very difficult to say; it is very difficult because of what happened subsequently—the terrible things that happened—because when we decided on partition, I do not think any of us ever thought that there would be this terror of mutual killing after the partition. It was in a sense to avoid that, that we decided on partition. So we paid a double price for it, first, you might say, politically, ideologically, second, the actual thing happened that we tried to avoid.

> So, how can I judge how far I was responsible? Mine was certainly part of the responsibility, and Maulana Sahib [Maulana Azad] may be completely right in thinking that I acted wrongly. Only I would say this, that Maulana Sahib thinks too much in

individual terms, sometimes, not in terms of historic forces at work. Individuals make a difference and have made a difference but sometimes individuals are only symbols of forces at work.[7]

How much of this answer, given thirteen years after the event, represented Nehru's thinking in 1946 even Nehru himself admitted he could not recall. Certainly many other factors entered into the decision to refuse to accept compulsory grouping of provinces into Muslim and Hindu areas under a limited federal center. Tolstoian determinism of the type cited by Nehru may have been one factor. But in this study we are concerned only with the practical alternatives to a partition of the irrigation system and associated economic and social organization of the Indus Basin. Examined from this standpoint and employing only the relevant criteria cited by Nehru —economic considerations and planning—it would appear that preserving the irrigation system and infrastructure intact within the Group B provinces would have been preferable to splitting it down the middle of the Punjab. Of course, in 1946 Nehru could hardly have foreseen just where the Partition Line would be drawn.

Ian Stephens, who in 1946 was the editor of the British-owned Indian newspaper the *Statesman*, ascribes Nehru's remarks, and his failure to appreciate the true communal situation in 1946, as "in large part due to his intellectual standpoint as a Western-style Socialist and an agnostic, . . . which led him to suppose that the Indian communal problem, since it was of religious origin, either did not exist, or at any rate was fundamentally much less important than most people imagined."[8]

In Parliament, on July 18, both Sir Stafford Cripps and Lord Pethick-Lawrence again rejected Congress' interpretation of what had been agreed, but to no avail. Although the Congress Party never formally withdrew its "acceptance" of the Mission Plan, its reservation on grouping, coupled with Nehru's statements and a fundamental difference over the composition and manner of formation of the Interim Government, led the Muslim League to withdraw its own acceptance on July 29. At the same time, the League called for "direct

7. Ibid., pp. xxiii–xxiv. The reader should bear in mind that the quotation, with its many ellipses, is the verbatim transcript of a press conference.
8. Stephens, p. 101.

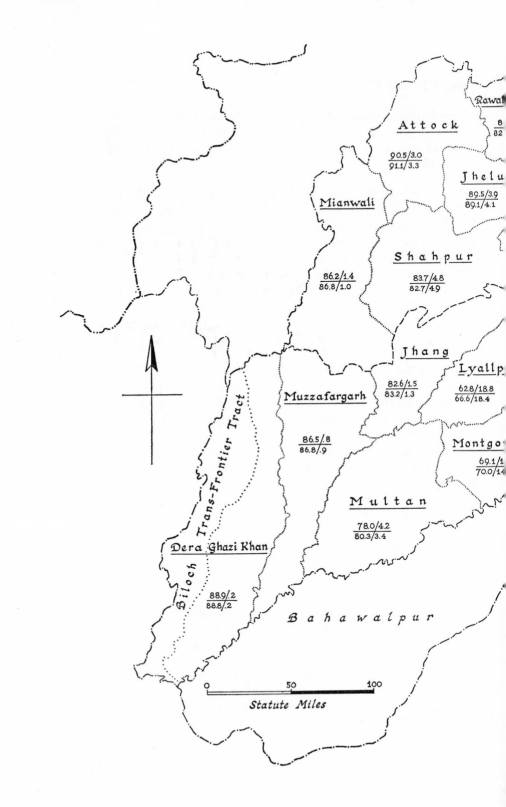

Rawal

Attock

$\frac{8}{82}$

$\frac{90.5/3.0}{91.1/3.3}$

Jhelu

$\frac{89.5/3.9}{89.1/4.1}$

Mianwali

Shahpur

$\frac{86.2/1.4}{86.8/1.0}$

$\frac{83.7/4.8}{82.7/4.9}$

Jhang

Lyallp

$\frac{82.6/1.5}{83.2/1.3}$

$\frac{62.8/18.8}{66.6/18.4}$

Muzzafargarh

Montgo

$\frac{86.5/.8}{86.8/.9}$

$\frac{69.1/1}{70.0/14}$

Multan

$\frac{78.0/4.2}{80.3/3.4}$

Dera Ghazi Khan

$\frac{88.9/.2}{88.8/.2}$

Biloch Trans-Frontier Tract

Bahawalpur

0   50   100

Statute Miles

jrat
6.4
5.4

Sialkot
62.1/11.7
62.2/9.7

Gurdaspur
50.2/19.2
50.8/18.4

Chamba

Kangra
5.1/.6
5.1/.3

Mandi

nwala
70.4/10.9
70.8/9.7

khupura
6/18.9
0/17.2

Amritsar
46.5/36.1
47.0/35.8

Hoshiarpur
32.5/16.9
31.8/16.8

Bilaspur

Suket

Lahore
60.7/18.3
59.2/17.7

Kapurthala

45.2/26.4
44.5/26.5

Kapi

Jullundur

Simla
18.2/2.7
15.8/2.1

Ferozepore
Faridkot

Ludhiana
36.9/41.7
35.3/46.5

Maler Kotla

Ambala

Sirmur

45.1/33.7
44.6/33.6

31.6/18.4
31.1/20.9

Patiala

Karnal
30.6/2.0
30.5/2.0

ikaner

Hissar

28.3/6.0
28.2/6.1

Rohtak
17.2/.2
17.1/.1

Delhi

Jind

Punjab States indicated in italics.
ome minor states in Patiala and
he Simla Hills are omitted.
ames of Muslim majority dis-
ricts are underlined.

Patiala

Gurgaon
33.5/.1
32.7/.1

%Muslims   %Sikhs
1941   /   1941
1931   1931

Percentages of Muslims and Sikhs in the districts of the British Punjab
g to the censuses of 1941 and 1931

action" to secure Pakistan, and soon proclaimed August 16 as "Direct Action Day." On July 31, Mohammad Ali Jinnah, who charged that both the Viceroy and the Cabinet Mission had gone back on their pledges to the Muslim League, rejected Wavell's summons to join the proposed Interim Government.

There is no need to trace in any detail the painful bargaining that continued throughout the remainder of 1946 nor the communal massacres that formed a background to it. Menon, Stephens, and the British journalist Leonard Mosley have already done so. Let it just be said that, although Wavell, in consultation with Pethick-Lawrence, had allowed Congress to form an Interim Government on September 2, and had gotten the Muslin League into it on October 26, no progress was made in convening the Constituent Assembly. Jinnah and the Muslim League continued to call for partition and withdrawal by the British, and held that the Constituent Assembly could do no good.

On November 20, the Viceroy announced the first meeting of the Assembly for December 9, but the communal situation (Stephens aptly terms it "civil war") was such that Wavell feared that actually convening the Assembly would intensify the slaughter that had begun in Calcutta on "Direct Action Day" and then spread from Bengal into Bihar. When the Viceroy intimated this fear to him, Pethick-Lawrence suggested that he bring the leaders of the parties to London for further consultations.[9] Finally, on December 2, 1946, Lord Wavell, Nehru, Baldev Singh (the Sikh member of the Interim Government), Jinnah, and Liaquat Ali Khan, Jinnah's closest associate and a member of the Interim Government, arrived in London. Four days of discussion produced only a statement by the British Government on December 6 that:

> Should a constitution come to be framed by a Constituent Assembly in which a large section of the Indian population had not been represented, His Majesty's Government could not of course contemplate—as the Congress have stated they would not contemplate—forcing such a constitution upon any unwilling parts of the country.[10]

9. Menon, *Transfer*, p. 324.
10. Quoted in Menon, *Transfer*, at p. 330.

What this meant, in effect, was that the Muslin League could secure Pakistan, and partition, by boycotting the Constituent Assembly, and this it proceeded to do, both in December and at a second session in late January. Hamstrung by the League boycott, Nehru on February 13 wrote to the Viceroy demanding that the Muslim League members be asked to resign from the Interim Government. This seemed to bring matters in India to a head, and Wavell accordingly referred the matter to London. Actually, unknown to the parties in India, the British Government by mid-February 1947 had reached an independent decision on the next step in India. Attlee writes:

> I had come to the conclusion that it was useless to try to get agreement by discussion between the leaders of the rival communities. Unless these men were faced with the urgency of a time limit, there would always be procrastination. As long as Britain held power it was always possible to attribute failure to her. Indians must be faced with the fact that in a short space of time they would have responsibility thrust upon them. I did not think that the chances of success were very good but I thought that there was one man who might pull it off.[11]

The man he had in mind was Lord Louis Mountbatten.

Ian Stephens argues convincingly that Attlee had already reached his decision back in December 1946, after the fruitless talks with Wavell and the Indian leaders in London, and that Mountbatten was asked to undertake the Viceroyalty as early as December 18, 1946, while Wavell was still in England. At what point Wavell was informed is not clear, though Leonard Mosley, who sees in Wavell the victim of a Congress plot, believed that it was not until the morning of February 19, 1947.[12] Attlee is not specific as to dates, but he does include this revealing passage:

> I recalled Lord Wavell [in December 1946] in order to discuss the whole position with him. No progress had been made since the return of the Cabinet Mission and Lord Wavell and his chief Service advisers were despondent and could only

11. C. R. Attlee, *As It Happened* (London, William Heinemann, and New York, The Viking Press, 1954), p. 183.
12. Leonard Mosley, *The Last Days of the British Raj* (New York, Harcourt, Brace & World, 1962), p. 52.

suggest a progressive retirement from India province by province [the so-called "Wavell Plan" discussed above in footnote 2], which was, in my view, a counsel of despair. I had great admiration for Lord Wavell, both as a soldier and a man, but I did not think that he was likely to find a solution. I do not think that he and the Indian [sic] could really understand each other. New men were needed for a new policy.[13]

Recent writers such as Mosley and Stephens have been kinder to Wavell than was Attlee, and Maulana Azad expresses great admiration for him. The ultimate verdict may well be that Wavell had indeed outlasted his usefulness, but that the transfer of the Viceroyalty was handled as poorly as the transfer of power itself, six months later.

Of course it is important to consider the situation as it appeared from London as well as in New Delhi. It is easy to forget, twenty years after the event, what Britain faced between 1945 and 1948. There was not only the problem of rebuilding (and transforming to Labourite socialism) a domestic economy run down and heavily damaged by the war, but of facing a lingering series of commitments in Germany, Greece and Turkey, Palestine, Iran, Malaya and the Far East, in addition to India. Thus, the Labour Government regarded the granting of independence to India not only as the fulfillment of a pledge (Attlee himself had been a member of the Indian Statutory Commission [Simon Commission] whose work in 1927–29 laid the foundations of the Government of India Act of 1935) but as a means of ridding itself of an expensive burden.

Furthermore, any decision to prolong British administration in India beyond a year or two would have meant rebuilding the British component of the Indian Civil Service and assigning more British officers and troops to the Indian Army. Stephens points out that between April 1947 and April 1948 the number of British officers in the Indian Army was scheduled to drop from 11,400 to 4,000, while in the upper ranks of the Indian Civil Service the number of British had declined from 2,900 in 1935 to about 1,600 by early 1947.[14] Sentiment for demobilization, punctuated by the "strike-

13. Attlee, p. 183.
14. Stephens, pp. 125–26.

mutinies" in early 1946, was running high in both British and Indian units of the services, and the morale of the Indian forces had been dealt a serious blow by the popular and political support given to the returning veterans of the collaborationist Indian National Army.

For the British Government to have decided, in view of the failure of the Cabinet Mission and subsequent negotiations, to postpone Indian Independence would have required, if any qualified civil servants were to be recruited and trained, a long-range commitment. Breaking faith with the well-publicized and oft-repeated promises would quite possibly have meant trying to hold India by force as the Dutch were trying to hold Indonesia and the French, Indochina. Seen from the standpoint of Britain's domestic and other international problems, it was unthinkable. If the Cabinet Mission accomplished anything, it seemed to have persuaded all but the most incredulous Congress and League politicians of the fact that Britain was not only willing but indeed eager to "Quit India."

Thus, when on February 20, 1947, the Labour Government announced June 1948 as the latest date for the transfer of power, they were only giving official form to an unavoidable decision. June 1948, sixteen months after the announcement, allowed a reasonable period for further discussion, negotiation, and orderly arrangements. August 15, 1947, less than six months later, did not.

The combined effect in India of Attlee's choice of Mountbatten and the June time limit was as stunning as that produced in London the previous summer by the rejections of the Cabinet Mission Plan. But, despite Attlee's later-expressed opinion that, "New men were needed for a new policy," there was no new policy. Rather, the Parliamentary statement merely repeated the old positions and aspirations:

His Majesty's Government are anxious to hand over their responsibilities to a Government which, resting on the sure foundation of the support of the people, is capable of maintaining peace and administering India with justice and efficiency. It is therefore essential that all parties should sink their differences in order that they may be ready to shoulder the great responsibilities which will come upon them next year.

147

10. After months of hard work by the Cabinet Mission a great measure of agreement was obtained as to the method by which a constitution should be worked out. This was embodied in their statements of May last. His Majesty's Government there agreed to recommend to Parliament a constitution worked out in accordance with the proposals made therein by a fully representative Constituent Assembly. But if it should appear that such a constitution will not have been worked out by a fully representative Assembly before the time mentioned in paragraph 7 [not later than June 1948], His Majesty's Government will have to consider to whom the powers of the central Government in British India should be handed over, on the due date, whether as a whole to some form of central Government for British India, or in some areas to the existing provincial Governments, or in such other way as may seem most reasonable and in the best interests of the Indian people. . . .

12. In regard to the Indian States, as was explicitly stated by the Cabinet Mission, His Majesty's Government do not intend to hand over their powers and obligations under paramountcy to any Government of British India. It is not intended to bring paramountcy, as a system, to a conclusion earlier than the date of the final transfer of power, but it is contemplated that for the intervening period the relations of the Crown with the individual States may be adjusted by agreement.[15]

That Mountbatten, whatever his confidential instructions may have been, brought no new policy with him to India is further attested in Menon's account:

Before his departure for India Lord Mountbatten had been given a directive by Prime Minister Attlee as to the broad lines of policy which he was to follow.

The objective of His Majesty's Government was to obtain a unitary Government for British India and the Indian States, if possible within the British Commonwealth, through the medium of a Constituent Assembly set up in accordance with the Cab-

15. "Statement Made by Prime Minister Attlee in the House of Commons, 20 February 1947—'Indian Policy,'" quoted in Menon, *Transfer*, Appendix IX, at pp. 506–09.

inet Mission Plan. Since, however, the basis of the Cabinet
Mission Plan was agreement between the two major parties,
there could be no question of compulsion [italics supplied; see
the statement of December 6, 1946, quoted above]; and if Lord
Mountbatten by 1 October 1947 found that there was no prospect of reaching a settlement on the basis of a unitary Government, he was to report the steps which he considered should
be taken for the handing over of power on the due date.[16]

Thus Mountbatten was expected to take up essentially where Wavell
left off; his only additional "powers" were the terminal date of June
1948 and his own particular abilities.

Mountbatten and Menon

In the month between the February 20 announcement and Mountbatten's arrival in New Delhi on March 22, 1947, Wavell understandably took no action on Nehru's demand that the Muslim League be
expelled from the Interim Government. Nor did the League come into
the Constituent Assembly. But meanwhile the communal killings had
moved into the Punjab.

The skirmish line of the "civil war" spreading across North India
had actually reached the Punjab and the North West Frontier Province in January, for the first time directly affecting the Sikhs. In the
first days of March, the Government of the Punjab (a coalition which
had excluded members of the largest provincial party, the Muslim
League) resigned. Large-scale attacks on the Sikh community shortly
ensued.[17] The effects of the January and March killings on the Sikhs
are well described by Khushwant Singh, the Sikh historian:

Although it would be foolish to attempt to estimate the number
of people killed, in judging the subsequent trend of Sikh politics
it should be remembered that after January 1947 the one factor

16. Menon, *Tranfer*, p. 351.
17. The "causes" included the inconsistent behavior of the Unionist Muslim
Premier Khizr Hyat Khan, first in arresting hundreds of League demonstrators,
then in releasing them, and finally in resigning. The immediate result was the
assumption by the Governor, Sir Evan Jenkins, of direct administration of the
Province on March 5, 1947. The ultimate result, it may be said, was partition of
the Punjab.

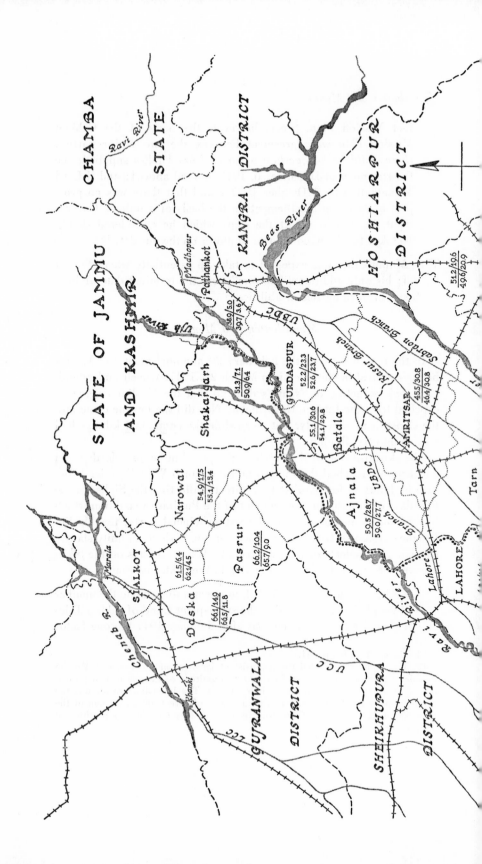

CHAMBA STATE

Ravi River

STATE OF JAMMU AND KASHMIR

KANGRA DISTRICT

Beas River

HOSHIARPUR DISTRICT

Ujh River

Madhopur
Pathankot

38.9/5.0
39.7/3.6

UBDC

51.3/7.1
50.9/6.4

Shakargarh

52.2/23.3
52.6/23.7

GURDASPUR

512/10.6
49.6/20.9

Sabraon Branch

55.1/30.6
54.1/29.8

Batala

Kasur Branch

455/30.8
464/30.8

AMRITSAR

Narowal

54.9/17.5
55.1/15.4

Pasrur

66.2/10.4
65.7/9.0

Ajnala

UBDC

59.5/28.7
59.0/27.7

Tarn

Lahore Branch

61.5/6.4
62.1/4.5

S. IALKOT

Daska

66.1/14.9
66.5/11.8

Marala

Chenab R.

Khanki

Ravi River

LAHORE

GUJRANWALA DISTRICT

UCC

227

SHEIKHUPURA DISTRICT

LAHORE DISTRICT

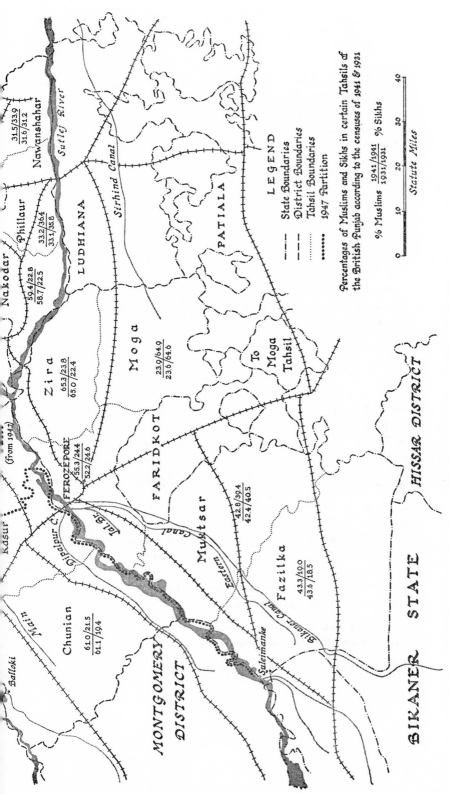

Map 5. The Central Punjab, showing the relation of the Partition Line to the Muslim and Sikh population by Tahsil and to the irrigation and railway systems

which coloured the Sikh outlook was a sense of insecurity from associating with the Muslims.

Atrocity stories were circulated among the Sikhs all over the Punjab and the number of victims no doubt vastly exaggerated. But the Sikhs could not get away from the feeling that the reason for the assaults on them could not be retaliation for the killings in Bihar—because there were no Sikhs in Bihar—but because the Muslims did not want them in what was going to be Pakistan. . . .

The answer to the question "Why did the Sikhs want partition when it would inevitably divide the community into two?" lies in the riots in the winter of 1946–47. . . . by the beginning of 1947 all Sikhs had come to the conclusion that, since they could not prevent Pakistan, the best they could do was to save as much of the province as they could from going into Muslim hands.[18]

Primarily because of the communal strife which began in Calcutta on "Direct Action Day," August 16, 1946, and which, since the beginning of 1947, had started to affect the Punjab, it was actually impossible for Mountbatten to pick up the situation as it stood either when the Cabinet Mission had left India at the end of July or even when the leaders of the Indian parties (the term "party" is employed to designate the Indian National Congress, which called itself a "Party" only after Independence; the Muslim League; and the Sikh factions) left London in early December. The situation had changed in all of northern India, and it had changed radically in the two areas where the rival communities were most inextricably interwoven: Bengal and the Punjab. Thus Mountbatten quickly came to realize that he would have to go beyond the Cabinet Mission Plan with its groups of whole provinces and consider the unpleasant alternative of partitioning not only India but Bengal and the Punjab as well. Within a month, he had summoned the governors of all the provinces and put before them a plan which:

provided that the members of the Legislative Assemblies of Bengal and the Punjab should meet separately in two parts, i.e.

18. Khushwant Singh, *The Sikhs* (London, George Allen and Unwin, 1953), pp. 151–52. The reader should note especially the last clause.

representatives of the predominantly Muslim areas, and representatives of the predominantly non-Muslim areas; and if both sections of each of these Assemblies voted for partition, then that province would be partitioned.[19]

The reaction of the governors directly concerned was negative. The Governor of Bengal, who was ill, sent his advice against partition of the province. Sir Evan Jenkins, who was governing the Punjab by direct administration as the result of the March riots,

> had always held the view that partition of the Punjab would be disastrous. Crude population figures were not necessarily the only criterion. Within the districts the communities were not evenly distributed and the city and town populations often had a different communal composition from that of the adjoining countryside. In some districts the population of tehsils differed widely. In his view, partition would not solve the minorities problem, since the divided provinces would still have considerable and probably discontented minorities.[20]

In the light of what happened in August and September, Jenkins' view was not only correct; it was an understatement.

Yet what alternative was there? The idea of partitioning provinces was not a new one. It had always been inherent in the concept of Pakistan and in the concept of a Sikh state of "Khalistan." It lay embedded in the communal geography of the Punjab and Bengal.

19. Menon, *Transfer*, pp. 353–54. The reader may question the heavy reliance upon Menon in this analysis. Five reasons amply justify it: (1) Menon, though a Hindu and a close friend of Vallabhbhai Patel, one of the key leaders of Congress, was a ranking member of the Viceroy's staff, serving both Wavell and Mountbatten as Reforms Secretary, or Constitutional Adviser; (2) in this capacity, he had access to virtually all of the documents and was a party to most of the negotiations; (3) he has written the most detailed and best documented account of the transfer of power; (4) although some other writers have questioned or disagreed with Menon's interpretations, all have relied heavily upon him and none has seriously questioned his facts; and (5) the final Partition Plan was in large measure Menon's own creation.

20. Menon, *Transfer*, p. 354. Sir Evan, who had served Lord Wavell as Private and Personal Secretary from 1943 to 1946 when he was appointed Governor of the Punjab, was not new to the province. He had had twenty-six years of experience in the I.C.S., of which more than half had been spent in the Punjab. He knew his province and he knew his censuses.

To trace the evolution of the idea of dividing the Punjab along communal lines would be worthwhile, but it would be another study in itself and cannot be done here. Let it just be recalled that the idea had been mooted in Wavell's suggestion of early 1946, which had brought out the Cabinet Mission (see page 135, footnote 2); that it was suggested to the Cabinet Mission by Baldev Singh and other Sikh leaders;[21] that the Cabinet Mission had proposed it to Jinnah as a riposte to his demand for a sovereign, independent Pakistan composed of six entire provinces (those which became Groups B and C of the Cabinet Mission Plan); and that Jinnah had indicated he would consider negotiating on boundaries *if* Congress first accepted the principle of an independent Pakistan, which Congress of course would not.[22]

So partition of provinces was not a new idea; rather it was a nightmare which had been kept in the background by all the parties until the spring of 1947. But now it came to the fore as the only alternative to the impasse. As Menon says:

> The greater the insistence by Jinnah on his province-wise Pakistan, the stronger was the Congress demand that he should not be allowed to carry unwilling minorities with him. Nehru, for instance, in a public speech on 20 April declared: "The Muslim League can have Pakistan, if they wish to have it, but on the condition that they do not take away other parts of India which do not wish to join Pakistan."[23]

But perhaps the more authoritative pronouncement was that made by Rajendra Prasad, President of the Constituent Assembly, when the Assembly met on April 28, still without Muslim League participation:

> While we have accepted [sic] the Cabinet Mission's Statement of May 16, 1946, . . . it may be that the Union may not comprise all provinces. . . . This may mean not only the division of India, but a division of some provinces.[24]

21. Menon, *Transfer*, pp. 242–43.
22. Ibid., pp. 242–51 passim.
23. Ibid., p. 354.
24. Quoted by Menon, ibid., p. 355.

Late in April the Hindu and Sikh members of the Punjab Legislative Assembly, the Constituent Assembly, and the Central Assembly all met in Delhi and resolved that the only solution lay in an equitable division of the province, assuring to its non-Muslim population the land and assets to which they were entitled and assuring the "preservation of the integrity and homogeneity of the Sikh community."[25] Six weeks later, in his press conference on June 4, Mountbatten referred to this meeting and said that he had been very much surprised that the Sikh community had asked Congress to put forward the resolution on the part of the Punjab members. He said that he had "spent a great deal of time seeing whether there was any solution which would keep the Sikh community more together. I am not a miracle worker and I have not found that solution."[26] There was none.

The remaining developments are quickly told. Faced with the reactions of his governors, with continued communal riots, with new statements by the various political leaders—Jinnah still insisted on six complete provinces; Sikh extremists demanded "Khalistan"; the Pathans were talking about an independent N.W.F.P.; and Suhrawardy and Sarat Chandra Bose came out for a sovereign, independent Bengal—Mountbatten revised his plan and sent it off to London on May 2, asking for immediate action. The Mountbatten plan apparently called for handing over sovereignty to the individual provinces, allowing them to recombine at will.[27] If so, it never got off the ground. The British Government sent it back in a significantly revised form, the exact terms of which are not known. But in the meantime, Mountbatten had gone to Simla, in the cooler hill country, accompanied by Menon and later jointed by Nehru. Before Nehru arrived, Menon had an opportunity to explain to the Viceroy a plan which he himself had worked out the previous winter (with the con-

25. Menon, *Transfer*, p. 356.
26. Quoted in Stephens, p. 171. See also Alan Campbell-Johnson, *Mission with Mountbatten* (London, Robert Hale, 1951), pp. 108–09. When a Sikh correspondent asked the Viceroy whether a property qualification would be a factor in partition, Mountbatten replied, "His Majesty's Government could hardly be expected to subscribe to a Partition on the basis of landed property—least of all the present Government."
27. Menon, *Transfer*, pp. 357–58, and Stephens, p. 161.

currence of Vallabhbhai Patel, the Congress leader from Bombay) as an alternative to the Cabinet Mission Plan. Menon, as Reforms Secretary (Constitutional Adviser) to the Viceroy, had at that time been authorized by Lord Wavell to communicate the outlines of his plan to the Secretary of State, Pethick-Lawrence. The essence of the plan was transfer of power to two independent central governments on the basis of Dominion status and on the assumption that Jinnah, in getting a completely sovereign Pakistan from the start, could not ask for the inclusion of the non-Muslim portions of the Punjab, Bengal, and Assam. Menon indicates that Mountbatten had seen the scheme in London before he left. At any rate, Mountbatten now authorized Menon to discuss his plan with Nehru, and Nehru indicated that he was not unalterably opposed to Dominion status. Nehru, apparently, had also been worn down by the continual delays, party bickerings, and the repeated references of all proposals to London.[28]

At this point, on May 10, the revised Mountbatten plan was returned from London. That night Mountbatten tried it out on Nehru, who would have none of it, as it encouraged fragmentation of the provinces and the states: the "Balkanization of India" he termed it when Mountbatten asked him to put his objections into writing. Whereupon Mountbatten authorized Menon to put *his* plan in writing., which he did in "two or three hours." It was shown to Nehru, who termed it "not unacceptable" to Congress. (Patel had already indicated his endorsement of the Dominion principle.) Thus is history made.[29]

The amazing thing about the Menon Plan, promulgated as it was by the Viceroy and his Hindu Reforms Secretary in consultation with the Congress President, is not so much that the British Government accepted it in place of a plan it had just approved on the Viceroy's submission, but that the Muslim League accepted it. (Perhaps this affair provides evidence of the value of a retreat to a hill station from the broiling heat of the Indian plains in May.) At any rate, before Mountbatten took the Menon Plan to London on May 18, he had already obtained the tacit acceptance of Nehru, Patel, Baldev Singh, Jinnah, and Liaquat Ali Khan. Mountbatten returned on May 31 with the approval of the Cabinet, which had drawn up a state-

28. Menon, *Transfer*, pp. 358–60.
29. Ibid., pp. 360–65.

ment to be issued as soon as the Indian political leaders formally accepted the plan. On June 3 they did, and in London the statement of the British Government was immediately made public. That very evening Mountbatten, Nehru, Jinnah, and Baldev Singh spoke on All-India radio to explain the plan to the public. On June 4, Mountbatten discussed it at a press conference, proposing for the first time that power be transferred by the middle of August.[30] The same day, Gandhi reluctantly accepted the principle of partition and advised Congress to approve the plan. It did so on June 14, but the Muslim League had beaten them to it on June 10!

The mechanism of the Menon Plan as embodied in the British Government's Statement of June 3, 1947, was fairly straightforward. The Muslim League representatives were in effect invited to form a second Constituent Assembly, that for Pakistan. Meanwhile, the provincial Legislative Assemblies of Bengal and the Punjab would be asked to meet in two sections, one representing the Muslim-majority districts and the other the remaining districts. Each section would vote on whether the province should be partitioned, and if *either* so decided by a simple majority, partition would take place. If the decision for partition was reached, then each section would decide which Constituent Assembly (India or Pakistan) it would join. The key to subsequent developments in the Indus Basin lay in the following paragraph:

> 9. For the immediate purpose of deciding on the issue of partition, the members of the Legislative Assemblies of Bengal and the Punjab will sit in two parts according to Muslim-majority districts (as laid down in the Appendix) and non-Muslim majority districts. *This is only a preliminary step of a purely temporary nature, as it is evident that for the purposes of a final partition of these provinces a detailed investigation of boundary questions will be needed;* and, as soon as a decision involving partition has been taken for either province, a Boundary Commission will be set up by the Governor-General, *the membership and terms of reference of which will be settled in consultation with those concerned.* It will be instructed to demarcate the boundaries of the two parts of the Punjab *on the basis of ascer-*

30. Ibid., p. 382, and Campbell-Johnson, p. 109.

taining the contiguous majority areas of Muslims and non-Muslims. It will also be instructed to take into account other factors. Similar instructions will be given to the Bengal Boundary Commission. *Until the report of a Boundary Commission has been put into effect, the provisional boundaries indicated in the Appendix will be used.*[31]

The Statement specified that for purposes of determining the communal majorities of *districts,* the 1941 census figures would be considered authoritative. On this basis, the Appendix to the Statement identified the Muslim-majority districts of the Punjab as follows:[32]

Lahore Division: Gujranwala, Gurdaspur, Lahore, Sheikhupura, Sialkot

Rawalpindi Division: Attock, Gujrat, Jhelum, Mianwali, Rawalpindi, Shahpur

Multan Division: Dera Ghazi Khan, Jhang, Lyallpur, Montgomery, Multan, Muzaffargarh.

The Statement provided that, in the event of a decision to partition Bengal, a referendum would be held in the adjoining Muslim-majority district of Sylhet in Assam to determine whether the district favored amalgamation with Muslim Eastern Bengal.

Thus, thirteen months after the Cabinet Mission Plan had been announced, and just two months before independence was granted, the British Government, the Government of India, and the Indian party leaders had come around to a diametrically opposite approach: no federal union, but two independent, sovereign Dominions; no three-tiered grouping of whole provinces, but a partitioning of three (including Assam); no coalition group and central governments, based on painfully wrought compromises, but, in essence, a country for the Muslim League and a country for the Congress Party. If one looks for reasons for this about-face, three would seem predominant: (1) the continuing and spreading communal "civil war"; (2) the failure of the Constituent Assembly to function; (3) the weariness and frustration of all concerned in the protracted negotiations.

Perhaps the most telling evidence of the effects of the year of frus-

31. "Statement Made by His Majesty's Government, 3 June 1947," quoted in Menon, *Transfer,* Appendix X, at p. 512. Italics added.
32. Ibid., quoted at p. 515.

tration was the change in the attitude of the Sikhs, the single community that would be most direly affected by partition. Because the main consideration in dividing the Punjab was the presence of the Sikh community, it is worth noting the key turns in the evolution of their thinking over 1946–47.

The Positions of the Sikhs

First of all, it should be stressed that, despite their relatively small numbers (5,691,447, or 1.47 per cent of the 386,666,623 persons in all of India in 1941; fewer than the Christians who numbered 6,040,665, or 1.63 per cent) and relative geographical concentration (71.6 per cent of the Sikhs lived in the Punjab and Punjab States, comprising 14.29 per cent of the total population there), the Sikhs were not a united community. Many of the writers on Partition have stressed that Mountbatten and his advisers, with the exception of George Abell, who served as Personal Secretary to the Governor-General, had little knowledge of the Punjab and underestimated the importance of the Sikhs.[33] But few have stressed how complicated the Sikh picture was. Sardar Baldev Singh, who served in the Interim Government and as the Sikh spokesman in the June 1947 negotiations, represented the most influential Sikh party, the Akalis.[34] But even the Akalis were split into three or more camps. At the "neutralist" center of the Akali camps was one led by Master Tara Singh, himself a convert from Hinduism, who spent much of his time trying to keep peace among the others. Outside the Akali groups entirely were the Congress Sikhs and the Sikh Communists, who at times had supported the Muslim League.[35]

33. See, for example, Stephens, pp. 131–32.
34. "The strength of the Akali party could be judged from the fact that in 1946, four of the five Sikh members of the Constituent Assembly were Akalis; Baldev Singh, Defence Minister in Mr. Nehru's Interim Government was an Akali; twenty out of thirty-three Sikh seats in the Punjab Legislative Assembly prior to partition were held by the Akali Party and the only Sikh Minister in the Provincial Government was their nominee; of the 168 members of the S.G.P.C. [Shiromani Gurdwara Parbandhak Committee, the board which administered the Sikh places of worship or *gurdwaras*] 140 were Akalis." (Khushwant Singh, *The Sikhs*, pp. 140–41.
35. "An overwhelming majority of the Communist party in the pre-Partition Punjab were Sikhs." (Ibid., p. 145.) For the purpose of fighting the 1946 provincial elections, the Akali Sikhs formed a Panthic Unity Board and made com-

Thus no one, not even Baldev Singh who was then a "neutralist" with close ties to Tara Singh, could speak for the Sikh community as a whole. Recognizing this, but on the grounds that he was then a member of the Punjab Government, the Cabinet Mission had interviewed Baldev Singh separately from three other Akali leaders. But the four Sikhs had offered four different suggestions.[36]

Despite their differences, however, the Sikh reaction to the Cabinet Mission Plan was uniformly negative. They feared submergence in the Muslim-majority Group B. (In many respects, the Sikh attitude at this point paralleled that of the Muslim League; they preferred a separate state to submergence in a larger whole, so long as the separation would not hopelessly sever them.) On June 10, 1946, the Sikh Panthic Board rejected the Cabinet Mission Plan, and it was not until Congress promised to take up their cause that they agreed to enter the Constituent Assembly.[37]

Baldev Singh entered the Interim Government when it was formed on September 2, and as we have seen, accompanied Nehru to London in December. He was a participant in discussions with Mountbatten before the fateful days in Simla at the beginning of May 1947, and Mountbatten had shown him the Menon Plan before he took it to London on May 18. When, after his return, Mountbatten explained the plan to the party leaders on June 2–3, Baldev Singh had accepted it, and he joined with the Viceroy, Nehru, and Jinnah in the broadcast on the evening of June 3.[38] In doing all this, Baldev Singh un-

---

mon cause with the Congress Sikhs against the Communists. Their success in the elections, followed by the events of Partition, led to the temporary eclipse (up to 1952) of the Communist Sikhs.

36. Menon, *Transfer,* pp. 242–43.

37. Early in July 1946, Baldev Singh wrote to Attlee asking for his personal intervention on behalf of the Sikh community by extending to them the possibility of opting out of the Muslim area. Attlee's reply stated that this was impossible, but he hoped that the Sikhs would enter the Constituent Assembly where they could argue their case. (Menon, *Transfer,* pp. 290–91.)

38. "[On June 2] Baldev Singh, on behalf of the Sikhs, accepted the principle of partition as laid down in the plan, but stressed that care should be taken to meet their demands when framing the terms of reference for the Boundary Commission. . . . [On June 3] Baldev Singh desired that instructions to the Boundary Commission should be included in His Majesty's Government Statement, but the Viceroy persuaded him not to press the point." (Menon, *Transfer,* pp. 376–77.) The omission of formal instructions proved to be highly significant.

In his press conference of June 4, "Referring to the position of the Sikhs, the

doubtedly was influenced by the action of the Sikh legislators who at the end of April 1947 had joined with their Hindu colleagues in calling for partition of the Punjab (see above), as well as by later consultations with many of them. But he did not, and could not, speak for all Sikhs. There is considerable evidence for the fact that, prior to June 3, Master Tara Singh and Gyani Kartar Singh, leader of another Akali faction, had told the Viceroy or his aides that the Sikh community, which had asked for and endorsed partition, was not going to take it lying down.[39] In other words, some of the Sikh factions, embittered and infuriated by the treatment of their co-religionists at Muslim hands in early 1946, were conspiring, even before the Menon Plan had been formally accepted and promulgated, to make sure that partition went their way.

Later in June, two of the militant Sikh bodies, "private armies" in effect, amalgamated.[40] By early July, Sir Evan Jenkins, Governor of the Punjab, seems to have been in possession of such alarming reports from the C.I.D. (Criminal Intelligence Division of the Punjab Police) that he met with George Abell, representing the Viceroy, to warn him that the Sikhs were in a very dangerous mood. He also sent to Mountbatten a confidential report which Leonard Mosley quotes, in part, as follows:

"Gianni Khartar Singh came to see me today [July 10]. . . . He said he had come to see me about the Indian Independence

---

Viceroy said that they were so distributed that any partition of the Punjab would inevitably divide them. It was sad to think that the partition of the Punjab, which the Sikhs themselves desired, could not avoid splitting them to a greater or lesser degree. The exact degree of split would be left to the Boundary Commission, on which they would of course be represented." (Menon, *Transfer,* p. 379; see also p. 373.) In Stephens' account of this press conference (p. 171) he quotes Mountbatten as follows: "I found that it was mainly at the request of the Sikh community that the Congress had put forward the resolution on the partition of the Punjab. I was not aware of all the details, and when I sent for the map, and studied the distribution of the Sikh population, I was astounded to find that the plan which they had produced divided this community into two almost equal parts. I have spent a great deal of time seeing whether there was any solution which would keep the Sikh community more together. I am not a miracle worker and I have not found that solution."

39. Stephens, p. 172, and sources cited there. Khushwant Singh, in *The Sikhs,* p. 151, credits Master Tara Singh with touching off the March 1947 riots in Lahore.

40. Stephens, p. 174

Bill and the Boundary Commission . . . He said that in the Punjab there would have to be an exchange of populations on a large scale. Were the British ready to enforce this? He doubted if they were, and if no regard was paid to Sikh solidarity a fight was inevitable. The British had said for years that they intended to protect the minorities and what had happened? The present situation was a clear breach of faith by the British. . . .

"Gianni then said neither [he nor Baldev Singh] had viewed partition *as being based on population alone. The Sikhs were entitled to their own land* just as much as the Hindus or the Muslims. They must have their shrine at Nankana Sahib [in the Sheikhupura District], *at least one canal system,* and finally arrangements must be made so as to bring at least three-quarters of the Sikh population from West to East Punjab. *Property must be taken into account* as well as population in the exchange, as the Sikhs on the whole were better off than the Muslims. Gianni said that unless it was recognised by His Majesty's Government, the Viceroy and the Party leaders that the fate of the Sikhs was a vital issue, there would be trouble . . . they would be obliged to fight . . . that the Sikhs realised that they would be in a bad position, but would have to fight on revolutionary lines by murdering officials, cutting railway lines, destroying canal headworks and so on."[41]

The other communities were less explicit than the Sikhs, but both Hindu and Muslim "private armies" were also preparing to take to the field. This, then, was the atmosphere in which the Punjab Boundary Commission met.

The Punjab Boundary Commission

Once the Indian parties had accepted the Menon Plan, the procedure laid down in the Statement of June 3 was quickly run through. By the end of June, the Punjab Legislative Assembly had met (under strong police guard because of the disorders) and voted 91 to 77 to join a new Constituent Assembly, i.e. that for Pakistan. Then, predictably, the members from the Muslim majority areas, meeting separately, decided 69 to 27 against partition, while the members from

41. Mosley, pp. 205–06. Italics added.

the non-Muslim majority areas decided 50 to 22 for partition with the East Punjab joining the Constituent Assembly for India.[42]

The Legislative Assembly of Sind also decided by 30 to 20 to join Pakistan. In the North West Frontier Province a referendum was finally held between July 6 and 17 after Khan Abdul Ghaffar Khan, the pro-Congress "Red Shirt" leader, had failed in his efforts (endorsed by the Government of Afghanistan) to include a third choice, that of an independent "Pushtunistan." Ghaffar Khan and his followers boycotted the voting, and there has been a controversy ever since over whether more eligible voters abstained or went to the polls. According to Menon, slightly over half of the electorate voted for Pakistan.[43] No plebiscite could be organized in British Baluchistan, but the Muslim Shahi *jirga* (tribal council) met and unanimously decided for Pakistan.[44] Thus, except for Chitral, Dir, and Swat, the westernmost boundaries of Pakistan were established, and Jinnah had three of the six provinces he had set out to obtain. The referendum in Sylhet District gave him a small part of a fourth, Assam.

The next step under the Statement was the appointment of a Partition Commission to divide the Punjab and Bengal. Sir Cyril Radcliffe, the British jurist who had been invited to serve as Chairman of the Partition Commission by the British Government, arrived in New Delhi on July 8. Thus, he had five weeks in which to partition two provinces, although curiously there was no requirement in the Statement concerning the time in which a decision had to be reached or when it had to be announced. Thus arose the incredible circumstance that the boundaries were made public only on August 17, two days after Independence, a state of affairs that produced considerable criticism at the time and since.

To assist him in his work, Radcliffe had a separate Boundary Commission for each province.[45] That for the Punjab consisted of four

42. Menon, *Transfer*, p. 388.
43. Ibid., p. 389.
44. Ibid., p. 388.
45. The Boundary Commissions, although constituted by the Governor-General on June 30, 1947, could not hold any formal proceedings until the Indian Independence Bill had been passed by Parliament. The bill, drafted largely by V. P. Menon in his capacity as Reforms Secretary, was introduced into Parliament on July 4. It was passed by the House of Commons on July 15, by the House of Lords the next day, and signed by the King on July 18. Although this was

justices of the Indian High Court: two Muslims, one Hindu, and one Sikh. But obviously Radcliffe had not only the deciding vote but the whole decision, for none of the justices could risk the opprobrium of lending his support to a decision that was bound to affect cruelly many of his own people.[46] Radcliffe, who later performed a similar task in recommending a partition for Cyprus, had one outstanding qualification for his grave responsibility: knowing little about India, he could be accepted by both sides as impartial.

But even a complete stranger to the Punjab could see from a glance at the map that the irrigation system represented its physiological structure, and the water of the Indus Rivers its lifeblood. According to Leonard Mosley, Radcliffe realized full well that, as far as the Punjab was concerned, continued integration of the irrigation system, at least on a functional basis, was of fundamental importance:

> Radcliffe immediately contacted the Viceroy and told him that he would like to submit a proposition to Jinnah and Nehru. Whatever he decided as to the lines of demarcation, he said, would it not be a good idea if both the leaders agreed at once, before the announcement of his Award, that the Punjab Water System should be a joint venture run by both countries. It would thus safeguard the interests of both peoples and form a basis of co-operation which might prove fruitful in the years to come.
>
> He was rewarded for his suggestion by a joint Muslim-Hindu rebuke. Jinnah told him to get on with his job and inferred that he would rather have Pakistan deserts than fertile fields watered by courtesy of Hindus. Nehru curtly informed him that what India did with India's rivers was India's affair. Both leaders were obviously furious with him and hinted that he was playing politics. It was his one and only attempt to try to make a constructive suggestion.[47]

extraordinarily quick for such important legislation, the delay made it impossible for Sir Cyril to be present at the public sittings in either Bengal or the Punjab, which had to be held concurrently.

46. The Sikh member, J. Teja Singh, had lost several close relatives in the January killings, and, according to several accounts, could not even bear to be in the same room with the Muslim members.

47. Mosley, p. 199. Asked to comment on Mosley's statement, Lord Radcliffe replied, "In general terms it would be true to say that, when I was working on

Radcliffe's position was further weakened by the terms of reference of his Commission:

> The Boundary Commission is instructed to demarcate the boundaries of the two parts of the Punjab on the basis of ascertaining the contiguous majority areas of Muslims and non-Muslims. In so doing, it will also take into account other factors.[48]

That was all. Nowhere was the meaning of "other factors" explained, although Baldev Singh had requested this (see page 160, n. 38), nor was any guidance furnished as to what weight, separately or combined, was to be given to the "other factors" relative to the communal majority factor. Thus, in effect, Radcliffe was told to partition on the basis of "contiguous majority areas of Muslims and non-Muslims," although the use of the general term "areas" rather than the specific term "districts" or "tahsils" left room for adjustments, as we shall see. In the Punjab, with its Sikh population scattered throughout the Canal Colonies to and beyond the Jhelum, where administrative officers had been sending them for sixty years and more, and with its urban population often strikingly different in communal makeup from that of the adjoining rural areas, the term "contiguous majority area" was subject to widely differing interpretations.

But the overriding consideration was time, or rather the lack of it. Even on the premise that the Punjab, and with it the irrigation system, had to be divided on communal lines, five weeks was an impossibly short time to do a thorough job. Worse than that, it allowed no time at all to move the Sikhs and Hindus east of the boundary, exchanging places with Muslims from the East Punjab, before Independence placed the members of each community under the juris-

---

the Punjab line, I was deeply impressed—as anyone concerned would be—by the great importance of not allowing the physical division of territory to sterilize the working of the interrelated irrigation systems." (Personal communication to the author, March 28, 1965.) Radcliffe's Secretary on the Punjab Boundary Commission, H. C. Beaumont, was a member of the I.C.S. and had considerable experience in the Punjab and a resultant familiarity with its problems.

48. *Gazette of India, Extraordinary*, New Delhi, Sunday, August 17, 1947, Government of India, Legislative Department (Reforms), Notification, No. F. 68/47-R, "Report of the Punjab Boundary Commission to His Excellency the Governor-General," p. 1,066. The wording is the same as in the Statement of June 3 (see pp. 157–58).

diction of a hostile or indifferent government. Perhaps worse than hostility or indifference, it was bound to be a disorganized government, whose personnel themselves would be engaged in moving to new districts and positions, often across the Partition Line, or in rescuing their own relatives and friends from the opposite side. The warnings were clear, and every district officer in the Punjab—British, Sikh, Muslim, or Hindu—knew or strongly suspected that Independence and Partition—with the accompanying confusion, migration, and opportunities for plunder and revenge—would bring bloodshed to equal or surpass what had occurred in January and March. It is incorrect to assert either that the Government of India was unaware of the situation in the Punjab or that Mountbatten and his associates completely disregarded the warnings, in particular those of Sir Evan Jenkins, Governor of the Province. Mosley mentions several suggestions that were put forward in July and early August to avert or at least lessen the bloodshed. Jenkins in particular was urging early publication of the Awards, or at least of their general outlines, to allow rational population movements to get under way.[49] According to Mosley, Jenkins even suggested going beyond the terms of reference and the competence of the Boundary Commission and arranging an exchange of populations between the Montgomery and Lyallpur districts, concentrating Sikhs in the former and Muslims in the latter. Thus, each would get a major Canal Colony. Lahore would have to go to Pakistan anyway, but it would be well if Nehru and Patel would publicly waive their claim to it in advance of the partition in order to clarify the situation for the migrants. It was also suggested that Nankana Sahib, the great shrine of the Sikhs west of Lahore (across the Ravi in Sheikhupura District), be declared by Jinnah a "sort of Vatican."[50]

But of all these suggestions, the only one that was adopted was that of Sir Claude Auchinleck, then Commander-in-Chief of the Indian Army and scheduled to serve, for a short time after Independence, as Supreme Commander of the Joint Defence Council of India and

49. It is instructive to note that the only "leak" of the Awards was that Calcutta would be excluded from East Bengal (Stephens, p. 180). Why a similar leak could not have been made with respect to Lahore can only be speculated.
50. Mosley, pp. 211–12.

Pakistan, and that was to to set up a Punjab Boundary Force to keep peace in the Province. This decision was announced on July 23, and the Punjab Boundary Force of some 50,000 officers and men took to the field from August 1. But, with the exception of a few hundred British and Gurkhas, its members were to have their loyalties tested to the breaking point.[51]

By the time the Punjab Boundary Commission publicly convened at Lahore, the local atmosphere was approaching that of an armed camp surrounded by a sea of insurrection:

> In Lahore alone in seven days the fire brigades were called out to 167 fires. From an airplane at night, one could pick out the villages by the flames of the burning huts.[52]

From August 1 on, Master Tara Singh was publicly calling on the Sikhs to "arise and once more destroy the Moghul invader." On August 5, Mountbatten presented to Nehru, Patel, Jinnah, and Liaquat Ali Khan, a C.I.D. officer sent by Jenkins with evidence that the Sikhs were planning to blow up the canal system in West Punjab, attack trains on their way to Pakistan, and even to assassinate Jinnah in Karachi on August 14. Jinnah and Liaquat Ali Khan called for the arrest of Tara Singh and other implicated Sikh leaders. But the

51. The core of the Punjab Boundary Force was the Indian 4th Division, which had fought with great distinction in Africa and Italy during World War II. Like all Indian Army units since the Mutiny of 1857, the 4th Division was composed of members of all communities. The Division's commanding officer, Major General Rees, was made commander of the Boundary Force, but he had advisers from each country: Brigadier Digambhar Singh, a Sikh, for India, and Colonel Ayub Khan, who is now President of Pakistan. India's alternate adviser, Brigadier Thimayya, who subsequently served as Chairman of the United Nations Repatriation Commission in Korea and as the Chief of the Indian Army Staff, has given a heartrending account of the impossible task confronting the Boundary Force: "Once we arrived, we restored order quickly enough, but often the worst was over by then, and meanwhile rioting would have broken out elsewhere. Transport was always a problem. The force was lucky to collect three or four lorries at a time to carry the troops, let alone the thousands of refugees who needed to be moved from a danger zone or who needed food and medicine." (Humphrey Evans, *Thimayya of India: A Soldier's Life*, New York, Harcourt, Brace, 1960, p. 250; see pp. 253–54, and the account of the situation at Sheikhupura, pp. 258–61, which was symbolic of occurrences all over the Punjab, East and West.) Penderel Moon's account of the troubles in Bahawalpur, and Khushwant Singh's novel, are also extremely lucid on the slaughter.

52. Mosley, p. 213.

British demurred on the grounds that Independence would set them free again.[53]

We shall make only incidental reference to the horrible events that accompanied Partition in the Punjab. The story is well known and needs no reemphasis here. What concerns us is what decision Radcliffe reached, in the context; how he reached it; and how it affected the irrigation-based Punjab economy. It will also be instructive to examine what possible alternatives were at hand, even as late as August 1, 1947.

With respect to procedure, we can do no better than to quote Radcliffe in the Report of the Punjab Boundary Commission:

> The public sittings of the Commission took place at Lahore, and extended from Monday the 21st of July 1947, to Thursday the 31st of July 1947, inclusive, with the exception of Sunday, the 27th of July. The main arguments were conducted by counsel on behalf of the Indian National Congress, the Muslim League, and the Sikh members of the Punjab Legislative Assembly: but a number of other interested parties appeared and argued before the Commission. In view of the fact that I was acting also as Chairman of the Bengal Boundary Commission, whose proceedings were taking place simultaneously with the proceedings of the Punjab Boundary Commission, I did not attend the public sittings in person, but *made arrangements to study daily the record of the proceedings and of all material submitted for our consideration.*[54]

The reader is requested to take particular note of the last sentence, and especially of the portion in italics. It indicates that Radcliffe was so pressed for time that he could not even preside in person over the proceedings of the Punjab Boundary Commission in Lahore, which, though unfortunate, is hardly surprising in the circumstances. It also indicates that a record of the proceedings was made and submitted to him each day. This record consisted of a shorthand transcript of

53. Ibid., pp. 214–15; see also Menon, *Transfer,* p. 411: "In the absence of definite proof, which no one was able to deduce, Lord Mountbatten took the advice of the existing Governor [Sir Evan Jenkins] and the Governors-designate of West and East Pakistan [sic; should be "Punjab"] and decided it would be of no avail to arrest the Sikh leaders."

54. *Gazette of India, Extraordinary,* August 17, 1947, p. 1066. Italics added.

the hearings and arguments, along with copies of all petitions and suggestions made to the Commission. As such, it represents an invaluable historical source, if it is still in existence. No one, not even Lord Radcliffe or his Secretary on the Partition Commission, H. C. Beaumont, knows what became of it. The best guess is that it remains in the Secretariat Office in New Delhi, where Mr. Beaumont deposited it at Sir Cyril's request in 1947. Sir Cyril's personal notes, memoranda, and drafts were all destroyed at that time.[55]

The Sikh Proposal

We are left, therefore, only with those materials that were submitted to the Punjab Boundary Commission and also published. Of these the most useful and instructive is the Memorandum signed by thirty-two of the thirty-three Sikh members of the Punjab Legislative Assembly, the group that had joined with members of the Constituent and Central Assemblies in April to recommend partition (see above, page 155) and that had later voted for Partition and to join the Constituent Assembly for India (above, page 163). Because the Sikhs, as a community, stood to lose—and did lose—the most by Partition, their approach to the drawing of a boundary raised all of the issues involved in a most urgent fashion.

The Sikh Memorandum begins by recalling that the Cabinet Mission had rejected the demand of the Muslim League for a separate State of Pakistan because, among other things:

> every argument that can be used in favour of Pakistan can equally be used in favour of the exclusion of non-Muslim areas from Pakistan . . . the division of the Punjab, on population basis, would split the Sikhs on both sides of the boundary, and that such a split would obviously be detrimental to the Sikhs.

The Memorandum then repeats the terms of reference of the Boundary Commission (see above, p. 165) and continues:

> An exhaustive account of factors which may be included in the phrase "other factors" may not be possible. But whenever the question of a boundary line has arisen in the recent past in

55. Personal communication from Lord Radcliffe to the author, March 28, 1965.

Europe or other countries, race, religion, language, history, economic considerations, geographical contiguity, influence of national prejudice and the needs of national defence have been taken to be some of the factors that conspire to indicate the best frontiers of any state.[56]

The Memorandum next reviews the historical growth of the Punjab, first as a Sikh state under Ranjit Singh and then as a British administrative unit. It notes that in 1941 the British Punjab had a recorded population of 28,418,819, but makes the charge that the census of 1941 was notoriously inaccurate because each community tried to swell the importance of its own group and to diminish that of its rivals through bogus entries and omissions, with a view to increasing its own representation in the Provincial Assembly and Government.[57]

Thus, the Sikh legislators argued that the 1931 census was more accurate, and further claimed that of the 14,929,896 Muslims recorded in the Punjab in that year, 4,695,957 were "not rooted in the soil but essentially of a floating character," a charge hard to prove or disprove. Yet the Sikhs admitted that whether one took the 1931 or the 1941 figures, the Muslim population of the British Punjab amounted to 57 per cent and fell only to 52 or 53 per cent, respec-

56. *The Sikh Memorandum to the Punjab Boundary Commission,* ed. Harnam Singh (Lahore, The Mercantile Press, 1947), p. 2.

57. Few serious students of Indian politics would question this charge. Nor was it a new phenomenon in 1941. (See the *Census of India, 1931, Vol. 17, Punjab* [2 parts, Lahore, Civil & Military Gazette Press, 1933], Part I, "Language," p. 271, for a description of another attempt to manipulate the census results for political ends.) But in 1941 the Muslim League was still smarting from its experience in being excluded from provincial governments by the Congress majority after the elections of 1937. The League, and the other parties in response, were anxious to increase the recorded strength of their community in the next census because this would give them increased representation in the next elections. Although the Lahore "Pakistan" resolution of March 1940 preceded the 1941 census, the Muslim League was not necessarily looking forward to Partition and an independent state in this attempt to skew the census results; it was enough for it to look back to 1937. On the other hand, although the League was probably more successful than the Sikh parties or the Congress in its efforts, one could argue that since all the parties tried to exaggerate, the *relative* standing of the various communities was not seriously altered. To meet all objections, however, we have used the results of both censuses in analyzing the alternative forms that Partition might have taken.

tively, if one included the Punjab States.[58] But if one excluded the areas of the northern and western Punjab beyond the Jhelum, as well as the Multan and Jhang districts where the Sikh (and Hindu) population was less than 5 per cent of the total, the non-Muslim population rose to a majority: 11,184,886 out of 21,946,446 even by the 1941 census results. Excluding the Chaj Doab as well, the non-Muslim majority increased to 10,885,834 out of 20,077,452.[59]

Thus the Sikhs were asking for a diagonal, northeast to southwest, partition that would leave them in possession of most of those Canal Colonies to which their fathers and grandfathers had moved at the invitation of the British colonization officers after 1890. In the last analysis, they would write off the Chaj Doab and the Sidhnai Project in the Multan District, but they wanted to keep most of the Lower Chenab Project, especially the prosperous Lyallpur District, as well as most of the areas served by the Triple Canals Project, including the Montgomery District.

To support their argument, the Sikh legislators presented the 1941 census data on the Sikh percentage of population in the districts that lay, wholly or in part, south and east of the Chenab. Although they had attacked the reliability of the 1941 census, it is hard to understand why they did so, because the proportion of Sikhs was *higher* in these districts than it had been in 1931 with only three significant exceptions: Montgomery, Ludhiana, and Ambala. A comparison of the 1931 data with those for 1941 shows, if anything, a slight *westward* shift in Sikh strength. Thus, except that it weakened their claim to Montgomery, one would have thought that the Sikh legislators would have left the 1941 figures unquestioned.

But the real weakness in the Sikh argument was that in almost every district south and east of the Chenab the proportion of Muslims was higher than that of Sikhs. This is shown in Table 5 (and on Map 4) where the data on Sikh and Muslim strengths, by division

---

58. *Sikh Memorandum*, p. 6. The official figures are as follows:

Muslim Population as Per Cent of Total	*1931*	*1941*
All Punjab	52.40	53.22
British Punjab	56.54	57.07
Punjab States	32.53	34.67

Source: Same as for Table 5, p. 172.

59. *Sikh Memorandum*, p. 6.

Table 5. Percentages of Sikhs and Muslims in Divisions and Districts of the Former British Punjab According to Censuses of 1931 and 1941[a]

| | Sikhs | | Muslims | |
	1931	1941	1931	1941
Lahore Division	18.86	19.98	58.01	58.18
Amritsar District	35.80	36.14	46.96	46.50
Gurdaspur District	18.38	19.18	50.80	50.23
Gujranwala District	9.73	10.87	70.82	70.39
Lahore District	17.72	18.29	59.18	60.69
Sheikhupura District	17.15	18.85	64.01	63.62
Sialkot District	9.69	11.70	62.23	62.10
Jullundur Division	24.45	24.32	33.41	34.53
Ferozepore District	33.55	33.68	44.56	45.08
Hoshiarpur District	16.78	16.92	31.79	32.48
Jullundur District	26.45	26.44	44.46	45.17
Kangra District	.30	.57	5.05	5.09
Ludhiana District	46.52	41.69	35.03	36.92
Ambala Division	5.63	5.12	27.72	28.07
Ambala District	20.94	18.44	31.07	31.64
Gurgaon District	.07	.07	32.74	33.49
Hissar District	6.13	6.03	28.21	28.33
Karnal District	1.99	2.00	30.46	30.58
Rohtak District	.07	.15	17.11	17.22
Simla District	2.07	2.67	15.79	18.20
Multan Division	8.10	8.15	76.23	75.43
Dera Ghazi Khan District[b]	.15	.17	88.80	88.90
Jhang District	1.28	1.49	83.16	82.58
Lyallpur District	18.36	18.81	66.62	62.82
Montgomery District	14.82	13.91	69.77	69.07
Multan District	3.36	4.15	80.26	77.96
Muzaffargarh District	.90	.83	86.79	86.52
Rawalpindi Division	4.76	4.98	85.88	85.52
Attock District	3.34	2.97	91.07	90.52
Gujrat District	6.42	6.35	85.29	85.60
Jhelum District	4.07	3.92	89.10	89.51
Mianwali District	1.03	1.36	86.77	86.17
Rawalpindi District	6.50	8.16	82.76	80.00
Shahpur District	4.88	4.81	82.72	83.67

a. Sources: *Census of India, 1931, Vol. 17, Punjab* (Lahore, Civil & Military Gazette Press, 1933), Part II, "Tables," Table XVI, "Religion," pp. 278–79; and *Census of India, 1941, Vol. 6, Punjab* (Delhi, The Manager of Publications, 1941), Table XIII, "Community," pp. 41–45, Subsidiary Table (ii), "Distribution of the Main Communities by Districts (1941)," pp. 48–49, and Provincial Table II, "Population of Districts and Tehsils by Communities, pp. 57–63. There are a few minor, nonsystematic discrepancies between the official data for 1941 and the figures quoted in the Sikh Memorandum.

b. Includes Biloch Trans-Frontier Tract.

and district, are indicated for the four divisions claimed by the Sikh legislators (excepting the Multan and Jhang districts of the Multan Division) and for the Rawalpindi Division which the Memorandum omitted because "Sikhs formed 4.98 per cent of total population before the March Massacre and thus in the demarcation of the two parts of the Punjab they cannot lay claim on population basis alone to any part of the Rawalpindi Division."[60]

The figures in the last column of Table 5 indicate the strength of the Muslim community in 1941 on a district and divisional basis. They also show the strength of the argument for Pakistan on a *religious* basis. The terms of reference of the Boundary Commission distinguished between Muslim majority and non-Muslim areas; all non-Muslim groups including Christians and Parsees (who a priori might with equal logic be placed in a Muslim *or* in a Hindu state) were joined with the Hindus, Jains, and Ad-Dharmis[61] on the basis that Pakistan was to be a religious state whereas India was to remain secular. Not that excluding the Christians and Parsees, or including them with Muslims, would have made any difference. As Table 5 indicates, there was only one district (Gurdaspur) in all of the British Punjab where either the Muslim or the non-Muslim majority was less than 3.5 per cent above or below 50 per cent. The Christian plus Parsee population exceeded this 3.5 per cent in only seven districts: Gurdaspur, Gujranwala, Lahore, Sheikhupura, Sialkot, Simla, and Lyallpur. In all of these except Simla, the Muslims could make good their claim on their own. (That they did not make it good in Gurdaspur is another matter, discussed fully below.) In Simla, Christians plus Parsees comprised 4 per cent, not enough to affect matters one way or another.[62]

In short, the difference between the Muslim demand for Pakistan and the Sikh demands, whether for a separate state or for special consideration in drawing the Indian boundary in the Punjab, was a

60. Ibid., p. 23.
61. The "Ad-Dharmis" were adherents of the "original," i.e. pre-Hindu, religion who, beginning with the 1931 census, began to insist on being recorded under this name rather than as Hindus or "Others." They were members of the "depressed classes" or "scheduled castes," formerly called "untouchables," who despite the efforts of Gandhi despaired of obtaining any improvement in their lot through the Congress Party and began to strike out on their own, refusing to be classified as Hindus.
62. Sources same as for Table 5.

matter both of numbers and of distribution. The Muslims could stand or fall on their own; the Sikhs were so "diluted" that under the terms of reference of the Boundary Commission they had to rely on the total non-Muslim strength even in districts such as Amritsar, Ferozepore, and Ludhiana where they alone comprised a third or more of the population. On any purely statistical basis, their argument was weak. Although their minimum demand—partition along the Chenab excluding the Multan and Jhang districts—would have brought 95 per cent of the 3,767,401 Sikhs of the British Punjab into India, it would also have placed 2.7 times as many Muslims— 10,360,454 or 63.89 per cent of the Muslim population of the British Punjab—there too!

Realizing, no doubt, that a strictly communal division would go against their interests, the Sikh legislators urged "other factors":

> the Sikh community is concentrated in Jullundur and Lahore Divisions and Montgomery and Lyallpur districts of the Multan Division. These areas form one contiguous tract and it is in this tract that the Sikhs have played, and must continue to play, the most important role in the life of the province. . . .
> The Sikhs are mainly concentrated in the two central Divisions of the Punjab and the colony districts of Montgomery and Lyallpur. In this area the Sikhs have vital essential agricultural interests. In fact the agricultural economy of the Jullundur and Lahore Divisions of the Punjab and colony areas depends very largely upon the labour that the Sikhs have put in this area. . . .
> In Lahore District the Sikhs pay Rs. 8,41,921 out of a total land revenue of Rs. 14,19,455; in Amritsar they pay Rs. 11,94,574 out of a total of Rs. 15,77,131. Sikh share in the annual land revenue of the Lahore Division is 46 per cent.[63]

In pointing to their economic interests in and their contribution to the economy of the Lahore and Jullundur divisions and the Montgomery and Lyallpur districts, the Sikhs were on unassailable ground. Most Pakistanis would today concede the historic contributions of

63. *Sikh Memorandum,* pp. 23, 26–27. To substantiate the economic argument, the Sikh legislators cited Malcolm Darling, *The Punjab Peasant in Prosperity and Debt,* pp. 41, 122. They also put forth certain historical and legal arguments which are considered in the next section of this chapter.

the Sikh colonists in the Canal Colonies. But once the "other factors" issue was raised, it had to be carried to its logical conclusion. If the economic contributions of the Sikhs were weighed along with their population distribution, the net economic effect on a divided Punjab had to be considered.

What would partition along the lines proposed by the Sikh legislators have meant to the regional economy of the Punjab? It would have given to India the city of Lahore. Because the Jat Sikh of the Punjab is primarily a rural dweller and cultivator, inclusion of Lahore in India would have brought 418,599 Muslims along with 161,349 Hindus and only 30,143 Sikhs.[64] But the economic implications would have been equally anomalous. With Lahore, India would have received the center of North Western Railway operations. The only possible alternative rail junction and classification center for a West Pakistan shorn of Lahore would have been Multan. From Multan, Pakistan would have had to rely on the Khanewal-Sidhnai Bridge-Jhang Maghiana-Chenab Bridge-Sargodha rail line to link the Lower Indus with Gujrat, Jhelum, and Rawalpindi. Instead of cutting the Lahore-Amritsar, Sialkot-Amritsar, and Kasur-Ferozepore lines, the Sikh proposal would have severed all the up- and down-doab lines connecting Multan to Montgomery, Multan via Shorkot Road (where some adjustment would have had to be made) to Sheikhupura, Lyallpur, and Wazirabad, and, in the southern Bari Doab, Lodhran to Pakpattan. Although shorn of the Potwar Plateau (the area around Rawalpindi) and the North West Frontier portions, the hinterland served by Lahore would have included most of the Punjab wheat and cotton areas, and the best of them. Pakistan would have been left with only the down-doab areas of the Multan and Jhang districts, plus the smallest of the doabs (Chaj) and the largest (Thal) with its large desert. Along with the Sikhs, the economic heart of West Pakistan would have gone to India. Aside from small beachheads east of the Chenab, West Pakistan would have consisted of Sind (plus Khairpur and Bahawalpur states, no doubt), Baluchistan, the North West Frontier Province, the Thal and Chaj doabs, and the

64. *Census of India, 1941, Vol. 1, India* (Delhi, The Manager, Government of India Publication Branch, 1949), Part I, Table IV, "Cities Classified by Population with Variation Since 1891," pp. 76–83, and Table V, "Towns Arranged Territorially with Population by Communities," pp. 85–94.

Rawalpindi Districts: except for the "Nilotic" portion of the Indus, the irrigated beachheads, and the flourishing Chaj Doab, almost all desert, mountain, and eroded plateau!

As a final measure of the Sikh proposal, let us apply the yardstick of the irrigation system itself. West Pakistan would have received Sukkur and Kalabagh. It would have kept the linked Haveli-Sidhnai systems. India would have received not only the Madhopur and Rupar headworks, but all of the systems (UBDC and Sirhind) served by them. The Sutlej Valley Project would have been truncated between Suleimanke and Islam. Although only the Pakpattan Canal distribution would have been seriously affected (to about the same degree as the UBDC was by the actual Partition), the same situation as now exists at Ferozepore would have been created instead at Suleimanke, since it is safe to assume that Bahawalpur would have opted for Pakistan.

The effect of the Sikh proposal on the Triple Canals Project would have been disastrous (in the assumed absence of any agreement on water allocations and some authority to enforce them). Of the five headworks upon whose integrated operation the whole scheme depends (see Chapter 3, pages 90 ff.), two (Mangla and Rasul) would have gone to Pakistan, one (Balloki) to India, and two (Marala and Khanki) would have been split through the middle. Since, as has been explained, the entire Triple Canals Project operation ultimately depends on Mangla, the Sikh proposal would have left the key to the irrigation of their treasured lands in Lyallpur and Montgomery districts in the hands of a disgruntled (to say the least) Pakistan.

Viewed in the light of its effect on the irrigation system, the Sikh proposal would have created a far worse situation than that which actually resulted from Partition. How much weight this consideration carried with Sir Cyril Radcliffe may never be known. But one can say this for his Award: despite his rebuff by Nehru and Jinnah when he raised the question of irrigation in the Punjab, the Award did preserve intact its single most important system, that of the Triple Canals Project.

Radcliffe's Line and Alternatives

Once the Sikh claim to a line along the Chenab plus the Lyallpur and Montgomery districts had been ruled out, the next real questions were where to divide the Rechna and Bari doabs: from the irrigation standpoint, what to do with the Upper Bari Doab and the Sutlej Valley Project systems. That S.V.P. would be divided was almost a foregone conclusion, since it was apparent that the two states of Bahawalpur and Bikaner, over whose disposition Radcliffe had no jurisdiction, would opt respectively for Pakistan and India.[65] With Bahawalpur would go the southern portions of the Islam headworks. At Suleimanke, both sides of the headworks lay in Punjab territory (the Bahawalpur border beginning just downstream on the southern bank; compare this situation with that at Marala, Chapter 3, page 68 and Map 5). But the left-hand canals served only Bahawalpur, and once it was decided that the Montgomery District would go to Pakistan, the disposition of the headworks was determined. Radcliffe tried to make this clear in his Award, but the actual delimitation at Suleimanke resulted from armed clashes between India and Pakistani forces, leaving part of the upstream training works on the left bank in Indian hands, rather than from the logic laid down by Radcliffe:

> It is my intention that this boundary line should ensure that the canal headworks at Suleimanke will fall within the territorial jurisdiction of the West Punjab. If the existing delimitation of the boundaries of Montgomery District does not ensure this, I award to the West Punjab so much of the territory concerned as covers the headworks, and the boundary shall be adjusted accordingly.[66]

Upstream from Suleimanke the problem grew more difficult. Here the Sutlej marked, in general, the boundary between the Ferozepore

65. Although Penderel Moon, p. 107, reports that Congress was making overtures to the Nawab of Bahawalpur (just as the Muslim League was to the Maharaja of Jodhpur), this seems a safe inference. In 1941, Bahawalpur had 1,098,812 Muslims in a total population of 1,341,209 *(Census of India, 1941, Vol. 6, Punjab* [Delhi, The Manager of Publications, 1941], Table 13, "Community," pp. 42–45) and the ruler was a Muslim. Bikaner had a Hindu majority and its Maharaja was one of the most pro-Congress and pro-Indian Union of the princes; he had taken Bikaner into the Constituent Assembly (see Campbell-Johnson, pp. 43–44). It might also be noted that *all* of the Panjnad headworks lay in the Punjab, which had a bridgehead south of the Sutlej-Chenab at the confluence. Since the headworks served only areas in Bahawalpur, accession of that state to India would have created problems at all four of the Sutlej Valley Project headworks.

66. *Gazette of India, Extraordinary,* August 17, 1947, Annexure A, Section 5, p. 1,069.

District to the southeast and the Montgomery and Lahore districts to the northwest. But at the site of the Ferozepore headworks, the Ferozepore District had a small "bridgehead" north of the Sutlej which included the right side of the barrage and the headworks of the Dipalpur Canal. And—a fact that Radcliffe might have overlooked in the press of his work—about five miles above Ferozepore, the Lahore District included an equally small "bridgehead" *south* of the Sutlej, perhaps the result of a change in the meandering mainstream from one bed to another within the recent past.

Four parties were interested in the Ferozepore headworks: Pakistan, India, Bikaner, and to a slight extent Bahawalpur (see Chapter 3, page 94). Since he had no jurisdiction with respect to the Princely States, although he could hardly ignore their existence and proclivities, Radcliffe dealt with their claims as follows:

> 8. Certain representations were addressed to the Commission on behalf of the States of Bikaner and Bahawalpur, both of which States were interested in canals whose headworks were situated in the Punjab Province. I have taken the view that an interest of this sort can not weigh directly in the question before us as to the division of the Punjab between the Indian Union and Pakistan since the territorial division of the province does not affect rights of private property, and *I think I am entitled to assume with confidence that any agreement* that either of those States has made with the Provisional Government as to the sharing of water from those canals or otherwise will be respected by whatever Government hereafter assumes jurisdiction over the headworks concerned.[67]

For both India and Pakistan, Ferozepore represented a test of whether the "contiguous majority area" principle or the "other factors" mentioned in the terms of reference were to prevail. Although the Ferozepore District as a whole was predominantly non-Muslim (54.92 per cent in the 1941 census; 55.44 in 1931), the two northern tahsils, Ferozepore itself and Zira (see Map 5) were Muslim-majority areas (Ferozepore, 55.25 in 1941, 52.20 in 1931; Zira, 65.26 in 1941,

67. Ibid., p. 1,067. Italics supplied. As far as Bahawalpur was concerned, the statement refers also to Suleimanke. At both places Radcliffe's assumption was, unfortunately, unwarranted.

65.02 in 1931). The Fazilka tahsil, which extended southwest along the Sutlej to the Bahawalpur border, was non-Muslim by 56.72 per cent in 1941 (56.36 per cent in 1931).[68] Thus the question arose of whether a *district* should be partitioned. It arose also, as we shall see, with respect to the Gurdaspur District north of Amritsar, and it arose in Bengal. Under the terms of the Boundary Commission, Radcliffe clearly had authority to partition Ferozepore District and to award the two Muslim-majority tahsils to Pakistan on a "contiguous majority" basis, especially as neither the Sutlej nor any non-Muslim tahsil separated them from the Lahore District.

But here "other factors" came forward. Awarding the Ferozepore tahsil to Pakistan would preserve the unity of the Sutlej Valley Project as far as headworks were concerned. It would place parts of the Fazilka tahsil and Bikaner State that were served by the Eastern and Bikaner canals downstream of a headworks in Pakistan, but in view of what Radcliffe felt himself "entitled to assume with confidence," this should have posed no objection. In fact, assuming that the Lahore and Montgomery districts would go to Pakistan, areas served by the headworks would be partitioned no matter what he did with the Ferozepore tahsil. These areas were roughly equal in size: 981,000 culturable commanded acres under the Dipalpur Canal on the right bank; 1,080,316 culturable commanded acres under the Eastern and Bikaner canals on the left bank (though the 650,588 acres served by the Bikaner Canal were perennial and hence more valuable). But the "other factors" extended beyond irrigation considerations.

First of all, the city of Ferozepore, though in a Muslim-majority tahsil, had a non-Muslim majority: 44,112 non-Muslims out of a 1941 population of 82,502.[69] Second, Ferozepore city was a major cantonment area. In 1941, the combined civil and military population of Ferozepore cantonment was slightly larger than that of the Lahore cantonment and second only to Rawalpindi in the whole Punjab. Third, Ferozepore city was a major junction point where

68. Figures for tahsils in 1941 calculated from *Census of India, 1941, Vol. 6, Punjab*, Provincial Table II, "Population of Districts and Tehsils by Communities," pp. 58–63. Figures for 1931 calculated from the respective District Gazetteers issued in the mid-1930s, Part B, Table 16 in all cases.
69. Sources same as in n. 64.

four railway lines and three highways met to cross on the barrage-cum-bridge toward Kasur and Lahore. Awarding Ferozepore to Pakistan would have been, with respect to traffic south of the Sutlej, comparable to awarding Lahore to India. Finally, and perhaps most importantly, Ferozepore was the major military bastion south of the Sutlej, guarding the strategic stretch below the Beas confluence where three major battles had been fought between the British and the Sikhs in 1845–46 (at Mudki, Firoz Shah, and Sabraon). Whether or not Radcliffe had any doubts about the degree of cooperation which he felt entitled to assume, the award to Pakistan of this bastion south of the Sutlej would have conferred a decided military advantage to her.

Thus, it would appear that in the case of Ferozepore District, "other factors" militated against a partition of the district that would have given the Muslim-majority tahsils, with the headworks and the city and cantonment areas, to Pakistan. In fact, Radcliffe went even further in an evident effort to keep control of the entire headworks under one state. For he specified:

> The district boundaries, and not the actual course of the Sutlej River, shall in each case constitute the boundary between the East and West Punjab.[70]

Yet the curious aspect of this Ferozepore award is that, possibly through oversight, Radcliffe created the very type of situation he was anxious to avoid. For, as has been pointed out, upstream of the Ferozepore headworks the boundary of the Lahore District crossed to the southern bank of the Sutlej, and the Award gave Pakistan a bridgehead *south* of the river! Here Pakistan could have constructed a new barrage to serve the Dipalpur Canal and incidentally to "short-circuit" Ferozepore headworks entirely, thus placing the Bikaner and Eastern canals below a new headworks entirely in Pakistani territory. Fear that Pakistan would do just that contributed, along with the requirements of the Bhakra-Beas-Rajasthan scheme, to the construction by India, in 1948–52, of the Harike Barrage upstream of the Pakistan bridgehead and just below the confluence of the Beas with the Sutlej. Since 1952, the Bikaner Canal has been served from

70. *Gazette of India, Extraordinary*, August 17, 1947, Annexure A, Section 4, p. 1,069.

Harike via the Ferozepore Feeder Canal, and not from the Ferozepore headworks at all (see Map 7). Under the Indus Waters Treaty (Annexure H) Pakistan will supply the Dipalpur Canal entirely from the Bambanwala-Ravi-Bedian-Dipalpur (BRBD) Link after the transition period, and the Ferozepore headworks will then serve only the small Eastern Canal. Only after India had started work on Harike did Pakistan, in 1949, commence construction of the BRBD Link which, as finally completed in 1958, gave her an alternative means of supplying the Dipalpur Canal should the Indians again cut off supplies from Ferozepore, as they did in April 1948.

Hindsight is notoriously better than foresight, but in the light of post-Partition developments one may ask whether it would not have been preferable to have made "the actual course of the Sutlej River" the boundary at Ferozepore. This would, in effect, have exchanged the Ferozepore District bridgehead north of the Sutlej for the Lahore District bridgehead south of it. It would have placed the boundary in the middle of the Ferozepore Barrage, but since Radcliffe was confident that the agreements regarding sharing of the water would be respected by the successor states, why did he not provide this visible evidence of his trust? Since a headworks has to be run as a unit, would it not have been preferable to induce the parties to cooperate by giving each of them half of it rather than to place one of them in a position to cut off supplies to the other? Alternatively, if Radcliffe suspected that what actually occurred in the spring of 1948 (when India cut off supplies to the Dipalpur Canal as well as to the Lahore and Main branches of the UBDC) might occur, would it not have been preferable to give the *entire* headworks to Pakistan to balance the award of the Madhopur headworks (of the UBDC in the Gurdaspur District) to India? Thus each country would have held one headworks serving, in part, the other's territory, and the likelihood of a unilateral closure would have been diminished.[71] In any case, this is one instance in which more time for consideration of the

71. Mosley, p. 230, recounts the story of the "rough sketch map" which was supposedly taken down over the telephone on August 8, 1947, and forwarded to Sir Evan Jenkins, showing not only the headworks but the towns of Ferozepore and Zira on the Pakistani side. The idea that the Award was changed at the last moment is widely current in Pakistan. If true, then it indicates that Radcliffe was thinking in terms of partitioning the Ferozepore District as well as the Gurdaspur District, perhaps on a tit-for-tat basis.

detailed boundary, and even for consultation with the Irrigation Branch as to possible effects, would have been most desirable. It certainly would have reduced the scope of and facilitated the negotiations in the Indus Waters Dispute.

Apart from the Ferozepore District, Muslims were in a clear minority (37 per cent or less in 1941) in all districts of the Punjab *south* of the Sutlej. Indeed, aside from Ferozepore and Zira, there were only two other tahsils south of that river that had Muslim majorities, and these, Firozpur-Jhirka and Nuh,[72] lay in the southern part of the Gurgaon District, to the south of Delhi, where they really represented the beginnings of the Muslim concentrations of the United Provinces rather than of the Punjab. Nor, incidentally, was there any Muslim-majority Punjab state south of the Sutlej that was liable to be cut off by the award of the surrounding territory to India.[73] Thus, except in the Ferozepore District, the Radcliffe award south of the Sutlej cannot be challenged. Radcliffe himself says:

> 9. The task of delimiting a boundary in the Punjab is a difficult one. The claims of the respective parties ranged over a wide field of territory, but in my judgment the truly debatable ground in the end proved to be *in and around the area between the Beas and Sutlej rivers on the one hand, and the river Ravi on the other.* The fixing of a boundary in this area was further complicated *by the existence of canal systems,* so vital to the life of the Punjab but *developed only under the conception of a single administration, and of systems of road and rail communication, which have been planned in the same way.* There was also the stubborn geographical fact of the respective situa-

72. *Census of India, 1941, Vol. 6, Punjab,* Provincial Table II, pp. 58–63. Calculations made by the author.

73. Although Radcliffe had nothing to do with the question of the Punjab States and their probable accession to India or Pakistan, he must have noted that although Bahawalpur had a Muslim majority of 81.94 per cent in 1941 (81.17 per cent in 1931) none of the other states south of the Sutlej had more than 40 per cent Muslims. Malerkotla, with 38.45 per cent Muslims (37.82 per cent in 1931), had the most. Patiala, the largest and most influential, had only 22.55 per cent Muslims in 1941 (22.39 in 1931). But there was one state between the Sutlej and the Ravi that had a Muslim majority. Kapurthala, with 316,757 persons, 56.35 per cent Muslim in 1941 (56.59 in 1931), lay awkwardly just to the southeast of the Amritsar District, between it and the Jullundur District. But Kapurthala, like most of the Punjab States, had a Sikh ruler.

tions of Lahore and Amritsar, and the claims to each or both of those cities which each side vigorously maintained. . . .

10. I have long hesitated over those not inconsiderable areas each of the Sutlej River [Ferozepore and Zira tahsils] and in the angle of the Beas and Sutlej Rivers [Jullundur and Nakodar tahsils] in which Muslim *majorities* are found. But on the whole I have come to the conclusion that it would be in the true interests of neither state to extend the territories of the West Punjab to a strip on the far side of the Sutlej and that *there are factors such as the disruption of railway communications and water systems that ought in this instance to displace the primary claims of contiguous majorities.* But I must call attention to the fact that the Dipalpur Canal, which serves areas in the West Punjab, takes off from the Ferozepore headworks and I find it difficult to envisage *a satisfactory demarcation of boundary at this point that is not accompanied by some arrangement for joint control* of the intake of the different canals dependent on these headworks.[74]

Nor can one really question the Award north of the Ravi. The Sikh claim to the Chenab as a boundary, whatever its historic merits, was vitiated by regional infrastructure considerations as well as by the census figures. Muslims were in a clear majority of 60 per cent or more in all districts north of the Ravi, and in only four tahsils in this whole region did their majority fall below 60 per cent.[75] Even in the Nankana Sahib tahsil of Sheikhupura District, with its great Sikh shrine, the Muslim majority was over 74 per cent and Sikh strength only 13.42 per cent.

Thus Radcliffe's problem came down to the area between the Sutlej and the Ravi, and presumably to the area east of the Lahore District since, as we have seen, both the "contiguous majority"

74. *Gazette of India, Extraordinary,* August 17, 1947, p. 1,067. Italics added.
75. *Census of India, 1941, Vol. 6, Punjab,* Provincial Table II, pp. 58–63. Calculations made by the author. With the following exceptions, Muslims also comprised a majority of 60 per cent or more in all *tahsils* north of the Ravi: Narowal Tahsil (Sialkot District), 54.93 per cent Muslim; Sheikhupura Tahsil (Sheikhupura District), 53.40 per cent Muslim; Lyallpur Tahsil (Lyallpur District), 54.52 per cent Muslim; and Jaranwala Tahsil (Lyallpur District), 57.15 per cent Muslim.

principle and "other factors," economic and political, dictated that Lahore go to Pakistan. But the area comprising the Lahore, Amritsar, Gurdaspur, Hoshiarpur, and Jullundur districts represented the heart of the Sikh community, centered on the shrines of Amritsar and Tarn Taran to the south. This was true despite all we have said concerning the dispersion or "dilution" of Sikhs in the Punjab. By 1947 the Sikh community, as a result of the historical growth of Sikhism, the development of Ranjit Singh's state (see Chapter 3), and of the migration of Sikhs into the Canal Colonies, extended like a wedge between the Chenab and the Sutlej. South of the Sutlej the Sikhs were numerous only in the Ambala, Ludhiana, and Ferozepore districts, plus the cis-Sutlej states of Patiala, Malerkotla, Nabha, and Jind. Further south the population was predominantly Hindu, with the Muslim minority much larger than the Sikh.

But the five districts named above had in 1941 a total Sikh population of 1,539,687, or about 41 per cent of the 3,757,401 Sikhs in the British Punjab. The remaining 59 per cent were scattered, with almost half (28 per cent) south of the Sutlej (principally in the Ferozepore and Ludhiana districts) and the remainder to the north and west of the Lahore District (primarily in the Canal Colonies.)[76] Once it was decided to deny the Sikh claim to areas beyond the Ravi and to the Lyallpur and Montgomery districts, and once it was decided to award all of the cis-Sutlej Punjab to India, Radcliffe's attention was perforce focused on these five districts, comprising the old "Manjha" of the Bari Doab and the "Bist-Jullundur" Doab between the Beas and the Sutlej. But here was a situation to challenge a Solomon.

76. In 1941, 1,060,957 Sikhs lived in the Ferozepore and Ludhiana districts and in the Ambala Division of the British Punjab south of the Sutlej; some 399,254 in the Sialkot, Gujranwala, and Sheikhupura districts of the Lahore Division; 234,071 in the Rawalpindi Division; and 518,623 in the Multan Division, 437,801 of whom were in the Montgomery and Lyallpur districts. In addition there were some 1,378,784 Sikhs in the Punjab States, most of them (896,021) in Patiala. Since only a few, small states lay north of the Sutlej, it would be correct to say that the river divided the *entire* Sikh community of the Punjab almost evenly, with about 2.3 million Sikhs south of the river and about 2.8 million north of it. (The total Sikh population of the British Punjab and Punjab States was 5,116,185 in 1941.) But as far as the Sikh population of the British Punjab was concerned—and this was what Radcliffe had to deal with—whatever geographical concentration it exhibited in 1947 lay in the five mentioned districts.

The Position in the Manjha and Bist-Jullundur Doab

The situation confronting Radcliffe in the five districts between the Ravi and the Sutlej was the result of the historical-legal development of the Sikh state under Ranjit Singh. Before examining population statistics, which merely reflect this development, it is necessary to discuss briefly the bases of the Sikh claim for special consideration at least in these five districts. For in the Sikh view this territory comprised the area "guaranteed" to Ranjit Singh by the Treaty of Lahore, which was concluded after the Rupar conference of 1809 (see Chapter 3) and faithfully observed by him until his death thirty years later. During this period, the Jhang and Multan districts and the trans-Jhelum Punjab (territories which the Sikhs were willing to abandon) were conquered by Ranjit Singh. They were afterward retained by the British in the Punjab "for administrative convenience."[77] Although the Agreement of Bhyrowal (December 16, 1846) had recognized British annexation of the trans-Sutlej districts (Jullundur, Hoshiarpur, and Kangra) and allowed the British to establish their Residency at Lahore, the Sikh legislators maintained that it had also bound the British to preserve the territorial integrity of the Sikh state beyond the Beas. In the Sikh view, the rebellion of the Sikh-appointed governor of Multan, which began in April 1848 and gave the British an excuse to annex the remainder of the Punjab in the following year, was not a rebellion *by* the Sikh Durbar at Lahore but the revolt of an outlying province *against* both the Durbar and the British Resident.[78] Thus in the Sikh view, which had certain similarities to the arguments being advanced by the Government of Afghanistan with respect to the Durand Line and the North West Frontier Province, at the lapse of British sovereignty they were entitled to the restoration of their state, at least within the limits held by Ranjit Singh in 1809.

Although the historical-legal argument of the Sikhs, and especially that part relating to the Treaty of Bhyrowal and the 1849 annexation, probably had little influence a century later on the Gov-

---

77. *Sikh Memorandum*, p. 4
78. Ibid., pp. 14–15.

ernment of India in general or Radcliffe in particular, the British were undoubtedly conscious of their debt to the Sikh "nation." As is their custom, the British had treated their defeated foes with magnanimity in 1846 (allowing them to keep their horses, though not their arms), and the Sikhs had repaid the kindness by their loyalty during the Mutiny of 1857. Indeed, most historians would agree that had Lahore risen, and had Sikh levies refused to aid the British, the relief of Delhi would have been impossible and the Mutiny might have succeeded. Further contributions had been made by Sikh members of the Indian Army in both World Wars and in a series of other campaigns.

It was also clear in 1947 that the Sikh community had no future in Pakistan. Although Jinnah had never attacked the Sikhs per se, and had even stated that they were free to remain in Pakistan, he had done nothing to encourage them to do so. The communal killings had effectively demonstrated that, if the Sikh community was to survive, it would require a substantial territorial base within the Indian Union. The Manjha plus the Bist-Jullundur Doab and the districts (and states) south of the Sutlej would provide such a base. But, for the reasons described above, the city of Lahore and most of its district would have to go to Pakistan. Despite its historic role as the site of Ranjit Singh's capital and of the tomb of Arjun (1563–1606), the martyred fifth Guru, Lahore city had only 30,143 Sikhs in a total population of 632,136. Amritsar, to the east, was even more sacred to the Sikhs. Though the city had 183,696 Muslims and only 58,620 Sikhs in a total population of 389,581,[79] it was, with its Golden Temple, the Sikh "Vatican." Furthermore, it lay in a non-Muslim-majority district.

So the logical solution seemed to be to run the boundary between Lahore and Amritsar. But what complicated matters was the fact that if the "contiguous majority" principle was applied on a *tahsil* basis, Muslim-majority tahsils plus the Muslim-majority but Sikh-ruled State of Kapurthala completely encircled the three non-Muslim tahsils of the Amritsar District. In the Lahore district, all tahsils had

79. *Census of India, 1941, Vol. 1, India,* Table V, pp. 85–94. It should again be noted that the Sikh Jat of the Punjab was essentially a rural dweller and farmer, and hence Sikh strength in the countryside was considerably higher than in the cities.

Muslim majorities, while in the Hoshiarpur District all tahsils were non-Muslim. The situation is indicated on Map 5 and in Table 6.

Table 6. Percentages of Sikhs and Muslims in Certain Districts and Tahsils of the Former British Punjab According to Censuses of 1931 and 1941[a]

| | *Sikhs* | | *Muslims* | |
	1931	*1941*	*1931*	*1941*
Amritsar District	35.80	36.14	46.97	46.50
Amritsar Tahsil	30.82	30.83	46.40	45.49
Tarn Taran Tahsil	50.01	51.48	40.55	40.69
Ajnala Tahsil	27.73	28.68	58.95	59.46
Gurdaspur District	18.38	19.18	50.80	50.23[b]
Gurdaspur Tahsil	23.67	23.32	52.62	52.16
Batala Tahsil	29.75	30.62	54.07	55.07
Pathankot Tahsil	3.59	4.95	39.72	38.89
Shakargarh Tahsil				
(north of the Ravi)	6.36	7.06	50.87	51.32
Jullundur District	26.45	26.44	44.46	45.17
Jullundur Tahsil	20.91	19.64	49.62	51.16
Nawanshahar Tahsil	31.19	18.05	31.61	31.54
Phillaur Tahsil	35.83	36.35	33.13	33.19
Nakodar Tahsil	22.48	22.75	58.72	59.41
Kapurthala State	22.79	25.93	56.59	56.35

a. Sources: Percentages for districts and Kapurthala State for both years from *Census of India, 1941, Vol. 6, Punjab,* Subsidiary Table (ii), "Distribution of the Main Communities by Districts," pp. 48–49.

Percentages for tahsils for 1941 calculated from ibid., Provincial Table I, "Area and Population of Tehsils," pp. 52–55, and Provincial Table II, "Population of Districts and Tehsils by Communities," pp. 57–63.

Percentages for tahsils in 1931 calculated from the respective District Gazetteers, Part B, Table 16 in all cases.

Figures are given for 1931 as well as 1941 because of allegations that the communities tried to inflate their importance in the latter census for political advantages.

b. With respect to the official figures for the crucial Gurdaspur District, it should be noted that there is a discrepancy between the percentages given in Subsidiary Table (ii) and the results obtained in calculating percentages from the figures in Provincial Table II. On the basis of the latter figures, the Muslim population would be 51.14 per cent rather than 50.23, and the Sikh percentage would remain 19.18.

Reference to the map will show that although the Sikh-ruled Kapurthala State separated the Muslim-majority tahsils of the Jullundur District (Jullundur and Nakodar) from the Muslim-majority tahsils of the Gurdaspur District (Batala, Shakargarh, Pathankot), the Nakodar tahsil was contiguous, across the Sutlej, with the Muslim-majority Zira and Ferozepore tahsils of the Ferozepore District. If Radcliffe interpreted the "contiguous majority" principle to apply only to whole districts, then he could award the entire Jullundur District to India, as he did with Ferozepore, and thus avoid a Pakistani salient extending south and east of the Amritsar District. By the same logic he could avoid detaching the Muslim-majority Ajnala tahsil from the Amritsar District and awarding it to Pakistan. But then logical consistency would demand that he award the Gurdaspur District in total to Pakistan. Gurdaspur had a slight but definite Muslim majority as a whole, and four of its five tahsils were Muslim.

But in Gurdaspur "other factors" came into consideration as they had in Ferozepore, and irrigation was one of them. The Gurdaspur District included the headworks of the Upper Bari Doab Canal at Madhopur, as well as the bifurcations of the Main, Kasur, and Sabraon branches of that canal. As far as canal-irrigated land is concerned, Gurdaspur itself was practically a "dry" district, i.e. a foothill district largely dependent upon rainfall and well irrigation. Although 71 per cent of its total area was actually cultivated in 1941, only 33 per cent of the cultivated area was irrigated by any means.[80] Of this irrigated area, wells supplied about 57 per cent and canals only 42 per cent, and the canal irrigation was nonperennial, limited to the kharif period.[81]

Perennial irrigation in the UBDC system began only after the branches crossed into the Amritsar District, though even here some areas had only kharif supplies. In the ten-year period 1922–23 to 1931–32, for which figures are available from the District Gazetteers, the average area irrigation by the UBDC system in the Gurdaspur District was only about 90,000 acres, compared with 418,000 acres in the Amritsar District and 792,000 acres in the Lahore District. In percentage terms, the three districts served by the UBDC system contained about 7, 32, and 61 per cent, respectively, of the lands

80. *Census of India, 1941, Vol. 6, Punjab,* Subsidiary Table (i), "Density, Water-supply and Crops," p. 4.
81. *Census of India, 1931, Vol. 17, Punjab,* Part I, p. 38 and map opposite.

served (but the relative importance increased even more down-doab because part of the lands in the Amritsar District and all of those in the Lahore District received perennial irrigation while none of those in Gurdaspur did). In other words, control of the UBDC system was more important to the Lahore District than it was to either or both the Gurdaspur and Amritsar districts, and this was emphasized when one considered that a city of 632,136 persons (as compared with Amritsar's population of 389,581) was deriving much of its municipal water supply from the Lahore branch.[82]

Thus if irrigation considerations were taken in combination with communal population, Radcliffe would have been amply justified in awarding both the Gurdaspur and Lahore districts to Pakistan, and with them control of the UBDC headworks and of over two-thirds of the area served by the system. True, 418,000 acres in the Amritsar District would then have been dependent upon supplies from Madhopur, but (a) this was less than half the nonperennial acreage served by the Dipalpur Canal whose headworks at Ferozepore were awarded to India, and (b) on both the Lahore and Main branches of the UBDC there would have been no way for Pakistan to serve the Lahore District from Madhopur without serving the Amritsar District and city en route (though Pakistan could have cut supplies to the portions of the Amritsar District served by the Kasur and Sabraon branches).

Thus the argument from the irrigation standpoint would appear to have reinforced that from the population standpoint: if the principle of "contiguous majorities" applied to districts as a whole, then it would have been quite logical and quite consistent to award Ferozepore, Amritsar, and Jullundur to India, and Gurdaspur to Pakistan; if irrigation considerations were to take precedence, why not give the Madhopur headworks to Pakistan, since the area served was mainly in the Lahore District, since Pakistan could not supply Lahore without supplying Amritsar on the way, and since—if Pakistan were to inferfere with supplies on the two southern branches —India could retaliate by cutting off supplies from the Ferozepore headworks to the Dipalpur Canal?

82. If the cantonments are included, the figures are 671,659 and 391,010 respectively. Of course both cities used tubewells as well, especially for drinking water; but the canals brought the main supplies (see Chap. 9).

Yet the straightforward logic of communal and irrigation considerations in Gurdaspur was apparently vitiated by still further "other
factors." Gurdaspur included the only road linking the Eastern
Punjab, and hence India, with Jammu and Kashmir, and the only
bridge (on the Madhopur Barrage) over the Ravi above Lahore.
The railways from Amritsar and Jullundur met at Pathankot, with
a branch to Madhopur, although there was no rail connection across
the river here (one was under construction in 1965). Had Radcliffe
awarded Gurdaspur to Pakistan, there would have been no land
communication between India and Jammu-Kashmir.

Radcliffe's solution between the Sutlej and the Ravi involved the
partitioning of districts, a solution he had avoided in Ferozepore.
The Shakargarh tahsil north of the Ravi in the Gurdaspur District
went to Pakistan, the three remaining tahsils, including Pathankot
with the headworks and the bridge, to India. In the Lahore District,
even a tahsil was partitioned: the eastern two-thirds of Kasur tahsil
were awarded to India, presumably on considerations of keeping
intact the areas served by the Kasur and Sabraon branches of the
UBDC. This Kasur award slightly strengthened the irrigation basis
of the Gurdaspur-Madhopur award, but in view of the contradictory
award at Ferozepore, it is hard to accept irrigation factors as
primary. Radcliffe stated:

> I have not found it possible to preserve undivided the irriga-
> tion system of the Upper Bari Doab Canal, which extends from
> Madhopur in the Pathankot Tahsil to the western boundary of
> the district of Lahore, although I have made small arrange-
> ments of the Lahore-Amritsar boundary to mitigate some of the
> consequences of this severance; nor can I see any means of
> preserving under one territorial jurisdiction the Mandi Hydro-
> electric Scheme. . . . I think it only right to express the hope
> that, where the drawing of a boundary line cannot avoid dis-
> rupting such unitary services as canal irrigation, railways, and
> electric power transmission, a solution may be found by agree-
> ment between the two States, for some joint control over what
> has hitherto been a valuable common service.[83]

Why, then, was the Gurdaspur award made as it was? On the
population basis it was anomalous not only in that the district as a

83. *Gazette of India, Extraordinary,* August 17, 1947, pp. 1,067–68.

whole had a Muslim majority but in that the Muslim majority in the Shakargarh tahsil, which went to Pakistan, was only slightly higher than in the district as a whole and somewhat lower than in the Batala and Gurdaspur tahsils which went to India. That the Pathankot tahsil (see Table 6 and Map 5) had a significantly lower percentage of Muslims may partially justify *its* disposition, but hardly that of Batala and Gurdaspur tahsils.

Many well-informed Pakistanis believe that the Gurdaspur award was made to provide India with access to Jammu-Kashmir. They believe that, as in the "sketch-map" story on Ferozepore (see above, page 181, footnote 71) this was an instance where Radcliffe was influenced by the Government of India and perhaps by a Mountbatten miffed at Jinnah's refusal to invite him to serve as Governor-General of Pakistan after Independence. Menon is silent on this point. Stephens alludes to it, but is skeptical.[84] Leonard Mosley, otherwise highly critical of the last Viceroy, discusses it and concludes that Mountbatten, at least, did not interfere in any way.[85]

To tie the Gurdaspur award to the Kashmir situation *may* represent ex post facto reasoning. It should be recalled that up until October of 1947 many of Pakistan's leaders believed that Kashmir's Hindu Maharaja would have to accede to them in deference to the wishes of his about 77 per cent Muslim population. It was only when he announced his accession to India at the end of October, and Indian troops began moving into Kashmir, that India's contiguity to Jammu-Kashmir assumed strategic importance. And even then it should be remembered that as far as the Vale is concerned, i.e. Kashmir proper rather than Jammu, the route from Madhopur via the Banihal Pass to Srinagar was not, in the autumn of 1947 or for several years thereafter, adequate to support military operations. Possession of Gurdaspur and the Madhopur barrage-bridge did contribute to Indian occupation of Jammu itself, and even of Poonch, south of the Pir Panjal Range (see Map 2), but it was not until the completion of the Banihal tunnel and the rebuilding of the Banihal road that the Vale of Kashmir could be supplied by India on the

---

84. "Or again if, as most Pakistanis believe—wrongly in this author's view—Lord Mountbatten or his entourage somehow influenced Sir Cyril Radcliffe towards finalising his Punjab Boundary Award detrimentally to Pakistan, then it follows that the award might have been different had he at the time been Governor-General-Designate of both Dominions." (Stephens, p. 177.)

85. Mosley, pp. 230–31.

ground. As Sheikh Mohammad Abdullah has pointed out,[86] in the fall of 1947 Pakistan controlled the lowland route into the Vale, that along the Jhelum River from Muzaffarabad via Uri to Baramula. Frustration over the failure to make adequate use of this route must not be allowed to obscure its value in comparison to that over the Banihal Pass, and accordingly to inflate in retrospect the strategic value to India, *in the autumn of 1947,* of Gurdaspur with Madhopur. Which is not to say that their strategic value has not increased considerably in the past twenty years!

But the Gurdaspur award would rankle in the Pakistani breast even had Kashmir been secured. Some officers of the Civil Service of Pakistan recall that Muslim members of the Indian Civil Service were actually sent into Gurdaspur prior to Independence in anticipation of the whole district's being awarded to Pakistan. Gurdaspur was, of course, recognized as a Muslim-majority district both in the Statement of June 3—but as "only a preliminary step of a purely temporary nature" until "the report of a Boundary Commission has been put into effect" (see above, page 157)—and in the Indian Independence Act of July 18.[87] Thus the posting of Muslim civil servants may easily have been a well-intentioned administrative faux pas on the part of superior officers completely in ignorance of the Radcliffe Award. But this explanation will hardly assuage the feelings of those civil servants of Pakistan who actually ran up the new Pakistan flag (derived from the banner of the Muslim League) in Gurdaspur on August 15, proceeded to take over the administration, and then on August 17, with the publication of the Award, were sent packing and scurrying for the new border (along with thousands of Muslims not only from Gurdaspur but from Hoshiarpur, Jullundur, Kapurthala, and Amritsar as well).

Again, for the purposes of this analysis, the timing of the announcement of the Award (which was quite clearly Mountbatten's responsibility) and the consequences that stemmed therefrom have to be distinguished from the substance of the Award (which was Cyril Radcliffe's responsibility). In retrospect, the substance appears inconsistent. There does not seem any way to reconcile the Feroze-

---

86. "Kashmir, India and Pakistan," *Foreign Affairs, 43* (1965), 529.

87. Second Schedule, "Districts Provisionally Included in the New Province of West Punjab," quoted in Menon, Appendix XI, at p. 531.

pore award with that at Gurdaspur, on the basis either of contiguous communal majorities or on the basis of irrigation considerations. If the irrigation factor was strong enough at Gurdaspur to vitiate the communal majority principle to the extent of partitioning a Muslim-majority district and awarding not only the non-Muslim Pathankot tahsil but two Muslim-majority tahsils to India, then the irrigation consideration should have prevailed at Ferozepore at least to the extent of giving Pakistan control of the right-hand portion of the headworks with the intake of the Dipalpur Canal. In other words, if the Ravi was the logical boundary in the Gurdaspur District, then the Sutlej was the logical boundary in Ferozepore. Such an arrangement would have *forced* the parties to cooperate from the start, and might have set a precedent that would have obviated the need to partition and divorce the Indus Rivers in 1960. Alternatively, by giving Pakistan control of *either* Ferozepore or Madhopur (and either award could have been justified on a communal-majority principle, the former on a contiguous-tahsil basis, the latter on a contiguous-district basis), each party would have had some leverage against unilateral closure by the other. This would certainly have placed Pakistan in a stronger bargaining position with respect to the Indus Waters Treaty of 1960, and would probably have shortened and simplified the negotiations.

At any rate, under the Treaty both the Sutlej and the Ravi will become Indian rivers, and the irrigation disadvantages of the Radcliffe Award, as far as Pakistan is concerned, will be submerged in the much larger operations of the Indus Basin Project. Even the Kashmir dispute may one day be settled, and, if settlement takes the form of partition along communal lines, India may keep Jammu, or at least that portion of it east of the Chenab River. In that event India will have a legitimate need for the connection via Madhopur, and the Radcliffe Award will turn out to be logical after all.

The Punjab Boundary Line of 1947 was probably not the best that could have been drawn, at least from the standpoint of the irrigation system of the upper Indus Plains. But to assume that the line was drawn, or altered, in a deliberate effort to thwart Pakistan seems unwarranted on the basis of the (admittedly incomplete) information now available. More particularly, to conclude that an original award, more favorable to Pakistan in Ferozepore, was subsequently changed, or that the Gurdaspur award was "gerrymandered" so as to give India access to Kashmir, is certainly to view matters in the harshest light of *Realpolitik. Perhaps* it was so, but the available evidence is only circumstantial. Other interpretations can equally well be placed upon it. Under these circumstances, one need not resort to any "special devil" theory of history. The pressures under which Radcliffe had to operate suffice to explain why his Award was not as consistent and logical as one drawn up over a longer period might have been. Unless and until we have more ample disclosures from those involved (and each passing year makes this less likely), we may leave the issue of the Radcliffe Award as he himself tried to leave it: as an award, not a judgment.

In concluding this long discussion of the Partition Award, it is fortunate that we can quote Lord Radcliffe himself:

> The many factors that bore upon each problem were not ponderable in their effect upon each other. The effective weight given to each was a matter of judgment, which the circumstances threw it upon me to form; *each decision at each point was debatable and formed of necessity under great pressure of time, conditions and with knowledge that, in any ideal sense, was deficient.* I decided therefore that it was in the best interests of everyone that I should leave the matter as an Award, conditioned by the terms of reference that were set me, instead of trying to argue it or elaborate upon it further. . . . I believe my decision was right, at any rate at the time and for the time: but, of course, the whole experience was unprecedented and terrible.[88]

88. Personal communication to the author, March 28, 1965. Italics added.

6. The Indus Waters Dispute from Partition to the Treaty (1947-60)

The Irrigation Crisis of April 1948

The haste with which Partition was accomplished did not allow sufficient time for the division of assets between the two new Dominions. Accordingly, both the Partition Council and the Arbitral Tribunal were continued in existence after August 15, 1947.[1] Thus there continued to be a formal mechanism for the arbitration of disputes up until March 31, 1948, the end of the fiscal year in use in both India and Pakistan at that time. March 31, 1948, was chosen

1. The Partition Council, which is not to be confused with the Partition Commission headed by Lord Radcliffe (see Chap. 5), dealt with such matters as division of assets and liabilities, of staff and records, revenues, currency and coinage, and with questions of foreign relations and the armed forces. It worked through a Steering Committee, under which were ten expert panels of officials, and, as a last resort, through the Arbitral Tribunal which consisted of one Indian, one Pakistani, and one Englishman. (See Chap. 1, p. 5; Menon, *The Transfer of Power In India*, pp. 397–98; and E. W. R. Lumby, *The Transfer of Power in India 1945-7* [New York, Frederick A. Praeger, 1954], pp. 200–01.) It is interesting to note that in the division of the assets of the Punjab, West Punjab was considered to be entitled to 60 per cent of the assets of the undivided province (terms of reference of Committee B of the Arbitral Tribunal).

as the terminal date of the initial "Standstill Agreement" signed on December 18, 1947, which provided among other things that the pre-Partition allocation of water in the Indus Basin irrigation system would be maintained. On April 1, 1948, India shut off water supplies from Ferozepore headworks to the Dipalpur Canal and to the Pakistani portions of the Lahore and Main branches of the UBDC (see Map 5), alleging that Pakistan had failed to renew the Standstill Agreement. As Professor Kazi S. Ahmad remarks with justifiable bitterness:

> There was no water dispute to be referred to the Arbital Tribunal set up by the British Parliament to settle disputes arising out of partition till 31st March, 1948, when the Tribunal ceased to exist. The dispute arose on the very next day, 1st of April, 1948.[2]

By India's action, about 5.5 per cent of the sown area (and almost 8 per cent of the culturable commanded area) in West Pakistan at that time found itself without water at the beginning of the critical kharif-sowing phase (see Chapter 4, page 115). The city of Lahore was simultaneously deprived of the main source of municipal water, and, incidentally, distribution to West Pakistan of power from the Mandi Hydroelectric scheme (see Chapter 5, page 190 and Map 3) was also cut off.

What lay behind India's action at this time? Certainly many factors played a part. Perhaps the least important of these was that Pakistan had imposed an export duty on raw jute leaving East Bengal for the jute mills in West Bengal (India). Of far more importance was the situation in Kashmir, a situation which is largely beyond the scope of this study but which underlay almost every action and position taken by either country in the Indus Basin from this point forward. Although in the spring of 1948 India was not yet confronted with the *official* presence of the Pakistan Armed Forces in Kashmir, she was certainly anxious to take every measure to bring pressure on Pakistan to withdraw her "volunteers" and her

2. Kazi S. Ahmad, "Canal Water Problem," *Oriental Geographer, 2* (1958), 34. Prof. Ahmad also cites the report of the Punjab Boundary Commission to the effect that there was no question of varying the authorized shares of water to which the zones of the various canals were entitled. (Ibid., p. 33; see also Chap. above; pp. 178, 181, and 190.)

violent objections to Kashmir's accession to India. A further, fundamental factor also operated. Certain of the Indian leaders were completely unreconciled to the emergence of Pakistan as an independent state (some still are). They had gone along with Partition as the only way to secure Independence, but once Pakistan had been established, they felt entitled to use every means at their disposal to wreck her economy, to demonstrate that she could not succeed alone, and thus to bring her back to India. Denial of vital irrigation water would be one way to expedite the process. Finally, and perhaps most directly, the canal closures of April 1948 were an assertion of India's claim to all the water in all the rivers that flowed through her territory. At one stroke the closures not only destroyed the hopes expressed by Radcliffe in his Award, but they implemented the sentiment attributed by Mosley to Nehru, "that what India did with India's rivers was India's affair."[3]

But were they in fact "India's rivers"? The Radcliffe Award certainly indicated that they were not. But the law of water use in the Indus Basin had never been very clear. We have seen that in 1941–42 the Rau Commission had to go beyond Indian and even international precedents and cite some decisions of the United States' Supreme Court in an effort to settle the Sind-Punjab disputes. Now that India and Pakistan were independent nations, international law would seem to apply—in the absence of any treaty on the subject. But what was the law and who was to enforce it? Professor Ahmad notes:

> The Council of the Institute of International Law in 1911 (Madrid) decided that a state is forbidden to stop or divert the flow of a river which runs from its own to a neighboring state but likewise to make such use of the water of the river as either causes danger to the neighbouring state or prevents it from making proper use of the flow of the river on its part. Barcelona Convention (1921) to which India was a signatory provides regulations with regard to the utilization of flow of the rivers—"No state is allowed to alter the natural conditions of its own territory to the disadvantage of the natural conditions of the territory of a neighbouring state." However, the convention was unilaterally abrogated by India in April, 1956.[4]

3. See Chap. 5, p. 164.
4. Ahmad, "Canal Water Problem," p. 33.

In an excellent and thorough analysis of the problem in the Punjab, presented at the Annual Meeting of the Institute of British Geographers at Cambridge in January 1950, Professor F. J. Fowler of the University of Leeds summarized the situation as follows:

> The distribution of river water for irrigation canals has been determined by several principles. There is, for example, the law of riparian rights, by which the owner of land contiguous to a stream has proprietary rights. In India this law has not been upheld in practice, or there could have been no large-scale diversion of water for irrigation. Then there is the doctrine of prior appropriation, by which the first user of water acquires a priority right, whether or not his land is contiguous to the stream. Finally, there is the *principle of equitable distribution, which regards a river as an indivisible unit to be developed for the benefit of the maximum number of people regardless of territorial boundaries.* In India this principle was recognized in the early days of British administration, and it has been adopted under numerous international treaties the world over.
>
> In India, though the most important rivers flow through more than one administrative unit, there has been no statutory law on water rights, but the policy of equitable distribution could be enforced by the central government, since it had executive power to impose its decisions in all interprovincial and interstate disputes. Under the India Act of 1935, which came into force in April, 1937, irrigation became a purely provincial matter, though provision was made for the appointment of commissions to investigate complaints relating to water rights and irrigation. This change did nothing to facilitate the settlement of disputes, and the frequent deadlocks and frustrations that occurred indicate the desirability of a centralized, all-India, policy that nevertheless permits local freedom of action in constructing irrigation works.[5]

We have seen (Chapter 3, page 69) that as early as 1862 irrigation officers in the Punjab were enunciating the principle of equitable distribution: "the best line for a canal is that from which the largest

5. F. J. Fowler, "Some Problems of Water Distribution between East and West Punjab," *Geographical Review, 40* (1950), 583–84. Italics added.

extent of country can be irrigated at the smallest cost, irrespective of the name or nature of the existing Government of the country in question"; and that this policy was subsequently adopted by the Government of India.[6] The proceedings and recommendations of the Indian Irrigation Commission of 1901–03 (see Chapter 3, pages 82-93) were also based on the principle of equitable distribution. But that principle cannot be applied on an absolute and unqualified basis. First of all, it contains an inherent contradiction in that it is logically impossible to balance a greater good for fewer people against a lesser good for more people. Secondly, as any irrigation system is developed, and certainly one as large as that of the Indus Basin, the doctrine of prior appropriation must inevitably come to play an increasing role. For how can one justify abandoning earlier systems and taking water away from regions and people who have used it for decades even if the same amount of water might do more good for more people in newer projects elsewhere? The fact, for example, that the UBDC was not included in the shares program of the five linked canals (see Chapter 3, page 92, n. 63) but continued to draw by prior appropriation or "prior allocation" all the water it could use from the Ravi, is an illustration of this fact.[7] So are the persistent efforts by Sind after 1923 to outguess and forestall Punjab lest a prior allocation to that province diminish the share that Sind would enjoy under equitable distribution. As the Indo-Pakistan waters dispute developed, it also became a question whether a prior allocation had to be an actual use or whether an agreement or project sanction was sufficient to constitute such an allocation. It is correct to say that equitable distribution was the guiding principle in the Indus Basin under British rule, but it must also be said that, because the irrigation system grew piecemeal rather than from one single fiat, prior allocation played an important modifying role.

6. "Memorandum dated 22 October, 1862, by Captain J. H. Dyas on Captain Crofton's Preliminary Report of the Sutlej Canal Project," in Government of the Punjab, Agricultural Proceeding No. 3, p. 82; and A. M. R. Montagu, "Presidentail Address," p. iv.

7. In the literature of the Indus Waters Dispute, the terms "prior allocation" and "prior appropriation" are used interchangeably. "Prior appropriation" is sounder from the legal standpoint, but it seems to convey that use has actually been made of the water. "Prior allocation" conveys that the water has been allotted, whether or not use has actually been made of it, i.e. whether or not the rights so conferred have "been entered into." We shall generally use "prior allocation" because of the role that "sanctioned" uses played in the dispute.

But what India was asserting, in April 1948, at least by implication, was neither of these doctrines but rather that of upstream riparian, proprietary rights. There was no historical basis for such an assertion, but neither was there a treaty. In effect, India was saying that Partition and Independence had created a new situation, and that she could proceed from any a priori basis she chose. India could maintain that, on the one hand, she had succeeded to the rights of British India as a sovereign state but that, on the other, since there had been no sovereign Pakistan before 1947, there could be no responsibilities of a successor state toward Pakistan. It was a nice, comforting position, but fortunately for Pakistan it ultimately proved untenable.

Just how nice this Indian position was for the East Punjab, in 1948, may be seen from a short analysis of the situation. Although the recommendations of the Indus (Rau) Commission had not been put into effect, and although the 1945 agreement between the Chief Engineers of Punjab and Sind had never been formalized, the pre-Partition Punjab would hardly have been allowed to proceed with the Bhakra Project without paying to Sind at least some of the costs of one or two new barrages (at Gudu and Kotri-Hyderabad) on the lower Indus. Pre-Partition Punjab would have been subject to limitations on the size of Bhakra and on its operation—limitations reflecting the requirements not only of Sind but of the Sutlej Valley Project below Ferozepore. After Partition, East Punjab was relieved of any of these requirements—at least if the Indian legal position could be made to stick. Furthermore, since no *additional* supplies had to be allocated to West Punjab or Bahawalpur, the Bhakra Project could be redesigned yet another time and Sutlej water allocated to new areas in Rajasthan (India).[8] Nor, in the Indian view, could Pakistan prevent her from proceeding with any of a series of proposed schemes to divert Beas water into the Sutlej (above Bhakra), Ravi water into

8. The final design of the Bhakra Project emerged in the late 1940s and early 1950s. Although the revised project per se included only the Bhakra Dam, the Nangal Barrage, and the Bhakra Main Line (offtaking at Nangal) and Bist Doab (offtaking at Rupar Barrage) canals, it cannot be separated from the Harike Barrage, built 1948–52 to redistribute Sutlej (and ultimately Beas and Ravi) water in Ferozepore and Rajasthan. All this will be explained in the text, but the reader should bear in mind that henceforth "Bhakra Project" really subsumes the Bhakra, Beas, and Rajasthan projects in India unless a more limited meaning is specified.

the Beas (at Madhopur), or Chenab water (via the proposed Marhu Tunnel) into the Ravi. There would, of course, be no point in proceeding with the Wular Lake scheme in Kashmir since a dam of any size would inundate more land (possibly including Srinagar) than could be commanded above the point where the Jhelum passed into "Azad" Kashmir.[9] Yet possession of the site was another means of intimidating Pakistan, since a dam there could ruin the entire Triple Canals Project. Similarly, a dam constructed on the Chenab at Dhiangarh, north of Jammu, would enable India to withhold water from Marala. It was a beautiful position, one later summed up very simply by one of the chief Pakistani negotiators of the Indus Waters Treaty: "India held all the cards."

The position of West Pakistan was accordingly dismal. At Ferozepore and Madhopur India could, immediately, cut off supplies to the Sutlej Valley Project and the Upper Bari Doab Canal, and had done so. By proceeding with Bhakra, Pong, and Thein dams on the Sutlej, Beas, and Ravi, she could dry up the three eastern rivers. There were even possibilities of diversions from the Chenab and, if Indian hostility reached a climax, from the Jhelum. The hopes of West Punjab for enhanced supplies in the S.V.P., and even for traditional supplies north of the Sutlej, were dashed. Bhakra would be built, but for Indian purposes only. As for Sind, instead of having some help from the prosperous, pre-Partition Punjab toward the construction of the lower Indus barrages, she would have to look to a new government, struggling for its very life in Karachi, for aid. True, Sind could still demand an equitable distribution of *Indus* water, and object to completion of the Thal Project or commencement of Taunsa (between Kalabagh and Gudu) until she got some relief. But what had seemed within grasp in 1945 was now almost a forlorn hope.

Pakistan's bargaining position in the spring of 1948 was feeble.

9. The "Azad" or "Free" Kashmir State was proclaimed in the winter of 1947–48 by the Muslims of northern and western Jammu-Kashmir who were seeking to throw off the rule of the Maharajah and to expel the Indian forces from the Vale and eastern Jammu. Azad Kashmir has not technically been incorporated into Pakistan at any point, for such an action would vitiate Pakistan's demand for a plebiscite in the entire State of Jammu-Kashmir. There is, however, a local government for Azad Kashmir in Muzaffarabad, at the angle of the Jhelum below Uri, and external relations (including permission to visit the territory) are handled by the Department of Home and Kashmir Affairs of the West Pakistan Government, as are the affairs of the Gilgit Agency to the north.

Her one firm recourse was war, and there were those who advocated it. But if she could not officially use her army in Kashmir as yet, she could hardly use it in the Bari Doab where all the strategic advantage lay with India.[10] Indeed, a declaration of war by Pakistan in April 1948 might well have led to the extinction of the new state. Neither could she face the kharif season without water for 5.5 per cent of her cropland—not in a year when hundreds of thousands of refugees still lay in camps where they had to be fed, and when UNRRA and the United States had their hands full elsewhere.

So Pakistan dispatched a ministerial delegation to New Delhi to negotiate for restoration of the canal waters. The Indians struck a hard bargain. They wanted recognition of their rights to all of the waters in the eastern rivers (Sutlej, Beas, and Ravi), and they wanted Pakistan to pay for such water as the Indians supplied to her until such a time as Pakistan could find replacement. The Indians proclaimed their purpose ultimately to use all the water in the eastern rivers, but since this could not be done immediately, Pakistan would have time to develop alternative supplies. India claimed that inasmuch as Pakistan had agreed, in the Standstill Agreement of December 1947, to pay water dues, this was tantamount to recognition by Pakistan of India's proprietary right. The Pakistanis insisted that these payments had been for the costs of operating and maintaining the irrigation works, not payment for the water, which belonged to Pakistan by right of prior allocation. Nevertheless, the agreement signed in New Delhi on May 4, 1948, required West Punjab to deposit in the Reserve Bank of India a sum specified by the Prime Minister of India. The text of this "Inter-Dominion Agreement" is worth quoting in full:

A dispute has arisen between the East and West Punjab Governments regarding the supply by East Punjab of water to the Central Bari Doab [i.e. those portions of the UBDC that are in Pakistan] and the Depalpur [sic] Canals in West Punjab. The contention of the East Punjab Government is that under

10. On the Kashmir situation in 1947–48, see Stephens, *Pakistan*, Chap. 15 and the sources quoted therein; also J. B. Das Gupta, *Indo-Pakistan Relations 1947–1955* (Amsterdam, Djambatan, 1958), Chaps. III–IV. The danger of an Indian riposte in the Bari Doab to any Pakistani threat in Kashmir was amply demonstrated in September 1965.

the Punjab Partition (Apportionment of Assets and Liabilities) Order, 1947, and the Arbitral Award the proprietary rights in the waters of the rivers in East Punjab vest wholly in the East Punjab Government and that the West Punjab Government cannot claim any share of these waters as a right. The West Punjab Government disputes this contention, its view being that the point has conclusively been decided in its favour by implication by the Arbitral Award and that in accordance with international law and equity, West Punjab has a right to the waters of the East Punjab rivers.

2. The East Punjab Government has revived the flow of water into these canals on certain conditions of which two are disputed by West Punjab. One, which arises out of the contention in paragraph 1, is the right to the levy of seigniorage charges for water and the other is the question of the capital cost of the Madhavpur [Madhopur] Head Works and carrier channels to be taken into account.

3. The East and West Punjab Governments are anxious that this question should be settled in a spirit of goodwill and friendship. Without prejudice to its legal rights in the matter the East Punjab Government has assured the West Punjab Government that it has no intention suddenly to withhold water from West Punjab without giving it time to tap alternative sources. The West Punjab Government on its part recognises the natural anxiety of the East Punjab Government to discharge the obligation to develop areas where water is scarce and which were under-developed in relation to parts of West Punjab.

4. Apart, therefore, from the question of law involved, the Governments are anxious to approach the problem in a practical spirit on the basis of the East Punjab Government progressively diminishing its supply to these canals in order to give reasonable time to enable the West Punjab Government to tap alternative sources.

5. The West Punjab Government has agreed to deposit immediately in the Reserve Bank such *ad hoc* sum as may be specified by the Prime Minister of India. Out of this sum, that Government agrees to the immediate transfer to East Punjab Government of sums over which there is no dispute.

6. After an examination by each party of the legal issues, of the method of estimating the cost of water to be supplied by the East Punjab Government and of the technical survey of water resources and the means of using them for supply to these canals, the two Governments agree that further meetings between their representatives should take place.

7. The Dominion Governments of India and Pakistan accept the above terms and express the hope that a friendly solution will be reached.[11]

Underlying the respective positions set forth above were certain historical and economic considerations, the significance of which for each of the parties had been sharpened by the recent events of Partition. Writing in 1950, Professor Fowler summarized these as follows:

India argues that it was the policy of the united Punjab to develop irrigation in the western part, where there was a large area of crown wasteland capable of yielding a quick financial return, and that this postponed development in the eastern part, where the land was privately owned and where no major project was constructed after the opening of the Sirhind Canal in 1882; that the Canal Colonies in the west were developed in part by Hindus and Sikhs, who were forced to emigrate to India after the partition; and that only a small proportion of the revenue derived from irrigation, only a small share of the water supplies of the rivers, and only a fraction of the canal-irrigated cropped area of the united Punjab remain in East Punjab. These arguments cannot be assailed, but it must be emphasized that the western part was not developed for the exclusive benefit of that part but for the whole Punjab: a principal objective of the colonization policy was to benefit the eastern part by relieving pressure of population in its more congested areas, and the financial return accruing to the Punjab government was shared indirectly by all parts of the province.[12]

11. "Inter-Dominion Agreement on the Canal Water Dispute signed at New Delhi on 4th May 1948," reprinted in Annexure A of the Indus Waters Treaty, 1960.
12. Fowler, p. 588.

The position of the East Punjab thus echoes the arguments made by the Sikhs at the time of Partition for some property compensation for members of their community forced to leave West Punjab. Exaction of water payments by the Sikh-dominated East Punjab Government might therefore be viewed as a later attempt to achieve, however indirectly, such compensation.

Post-Partition Projects

Although the Inter-Dominion Agreement of May 1948 did not settle anything, it at least blocked out the arguments and provided a modus vivendi until 1960 when it was superseded by the Indus Waters Treaty. With a few temporary exceptions (notably in the winter of 1953–54 when the first Pakistan-United States arms agreement was under consideration, and during an impasse in the Treaty negotiations), the Inter-Dominion Agreement was observed faithfully by India, and it might even be cited as an example to demonstrate that the irrigation system of the Indus Basin could have continued to be operated as a unit. But—although it was not for another six years that this was openly admitted—integrated operation was dead in principle from April 1, 1948. The canal closures had been a rude shock to Pakistan. India's terms for reopening them had been another. Whenever a Westerner would suggest, sometimes with a hint of condescension, that the two "bad boys" were brothers and should forget their quarrels and live and work together, the Pakistani was as apt to cite the canal closures as he was to cite Kashmir. After all, had not India made it clear that she wanted *all* of the rivers' water? Had she not given Pakistan merely a respite to find "alternative sources," and that at a price? Why should she change her mind when time was on her side?

A further indication of Indian intentions came later in 1948 when work was begun on the Harike Barrage, upstream of Ferozepore at the juncture of the Beas and the Sutlej. Indians will say that they had to build Harike for fear that Pakistan would "short-circuit" Ferozepore by building a barrage five miles upstream, where the Radcliffe Award, by specifying the Lahore District boundary rather than the course of the Sutlej as the Partition Line, had given Pakistan both sides of the river. Pakistanis will maintain that they had no such intention (or financial capability) in 1948, and that Harike was built to give India added capacity to cut off the whole S.V.P. The core of the matter is that Harike had to be built as part of the larger Bhakra-Beas-Rajasthan Project in which Sutlej waters stored by Bhakra (plus later increments from the Beas dam at Pong and the Ravi dam at Thein) would be diverted from the Sutlej at Harike and sent on their 400-mile journey into the Thar Desert via the Rajasthan Canal offtaking at that barrage. In the meantime, two other canals would be built from Harike: the Ferozepore Feeder, which took over the supply of the Bikaner Canal from Ferozepore headworks, and the Sirhind Feeder which increased supplies to the lower end of the Sirhind (Rupar headworks) distribution system, making possible higher intensities on the upper reaches of that system (see Map 7).

The Harike Barrage was completed in 1952. Although the Sutlej should, in theory, have a high right bank at this point, the confluence of the Beas apparently pushes the Sutlej to the left. It will be recalled from Chapter 2 that up to the 1790s the Beas had an independent channel to the north of the Sutlej from a point just upstream of Harike to the *Chenab* above Panjnad. Thus, part of the right-hand floodplain and the high right bank at Harike are actually those formed by the migrating Beas, and a mile-long bund had to be built on the right bank, from which no canals offtake. From right to left the barrage itself has twenty-eight bays, each with vertical, electrically operated gates, followed by a divide-groyne including a fish ladder and the undersluices, set 5 feet below the sill of the barrage, for washing silt away from the canal intakes. The Ferozepore and Sirhind feeders have a combined intake with a capacity of about 7,000 cusecs. They bifurcate after some 6 miles. Both are lined with concrete and tiles. An 18,500-cusec intake for the Rajasthan Feeder Canal was built at the same time as the barrage, but its gates were sealed with masonry until the feeder and part of the Rajasthan Canal were ready for use. In the spring of 1964, the masonry was removed and metal gates installed. Some kharif irrigation was provided in 1964 along the upper reaches of the Rajasthan Canal, using supplies released from Bhakra.

Work on the Bhakra Project itself is officially dated from 1946, when some preliminary work on the Nangal Barrage was started.

But work at the Bhakra dam site was not begun until April 1948 (a significant date) when excavation of the two diversion tunnels started. The Sutlej was diverted in October 1954 and, after building the upstream and downstream coffer dams and excavating the foundations to a depth of 260 feet below the normal river level, the laying of the concrete began in November 1955. Storage of Sutlej water began with the kharif of 1958, and the concreting was essentially finished late in 1961 when the dam reached its full height of 740 feet above the deepest foundation. As finally executed, the Bhakra Dam has a total storage capacity of 8 million acre feet, and a live storage capacity of 6.3 million acre feet, or about 40 percent of the average annual runoff of the Sutlej at the dam site (13.33 m.a.f.). Because of heavy irrigation and power requirements, it has not yet been possible to fill the Bhakra reservoir, nor is it anticipated that this can be achieved until after the Beas-Sutlej diversion via the Pandoh Tunnel or some alternative is completed, raising the average annual flow into the Bhakra reservoir from 13.33 m.a.f. to perhaps 17.15 m.a.f.[13] Ultimately, with the Pong Dam on the Beas (now under construction), the Thein Dam on the Ravi (in the investigation stage), the existing Ravi-Beas Link at Madhopur, and the Beas-Sutlej Tunnel Link at Pandoh (plus two additional dams whose sites are being investigated on the Beas and Sutlej), the system could provide about 32.5 m.a.f. in an average year (25.5 m.a.f. in the dependable—26 in 39—year) of which the distribution would be as indicated in Table 7.

Even based on minimum supplies, the Bhakra-Beas-Rajasthan scheme would nearly triple the amount of water being used for irrigation in the Indian portions of the Indus Basin as compared with the pre-Partition period. Prior to Partition, canals in the Indian portions used 9 million acre feet of water and irrigated some 5 million acres. By 1988, when it is expected that the Bhakra-Beas-Rajasthan scheme will reach its ultimate development, a total of about 15 million acres will be irrigated each year, of which 6.5 million acres represent new additions under the Bhakra Project proper and 3.5 million acres new additions under the Beas-Rajasthan portions.

The Bhakra-Beas-Rajasthan scheme is of an order of magnitude

13. Bureau of Reclamation, United States Department of the Interior, *Beas and Rajasthan Projects*, pp. 21–23.

Table 7. The Bhakra-Beas-Rajasthan Scheme in India[a]

Canal System	Headworks	Basic Requirement and Supplies in Millions of Acre Feet		
		Basic Requirement	*Mean Yearly Supply*	*Dependable Yearly Supply*
"Kashmir" Canal	Madhopur	0.743	0.639	0.523
UBDC in India	Madhopur	3.785	3.511	3.180
Bikaner Canal via Ferozepore Feeder and lower Sirhind system via Sirhind Feeder	Harike	3.681	3.663	2.914
Rajasthan Canal	Harike	8.858	8.818	6.506
Upper Sirhind system; Bhakra Main Line in East Punjab; and Bist Doab Canal	Rupar	15.652	15.532	12.138
Tail of Bhakra Main Branch in Rajasthan	Rupar	0.423	0.304	0.225
Totals		33.142	32.467	25.486

a. Source: Bureau of Reclamation, United States Department of the Interior, *Beas and Rajasthan Projects*, pp. 23, 164.

comparable to that of the Indus Basin Project in West Pakistan, and will accordingly receive fuller discussion in Chapter 7. But the outlines have been sketched here because it should be realized that India, and the East Punjab in particular, was able to proceed with the first phase of the scheme, that of the Bhakra Project proper, during the period 1948–60 while the various negotiations that led to the Treaty were in progress. Indeed, the Harike Barrage was completed in 1952 when the negotiators first met under World Bank auspices. By July 1954, while the parties had before them the first plan submitted by the Bank, the Nangal Barrage on the Sutlej had been opened, the Rupar headworks had been remodeled to provide a new intake for the Bist-Jullundur Doab Canal on the right bank, and the Madhopur headworks had been remodeled both for the small, right-bank "Kashmir" Canal (actually serving a small area in Jammu) and for the newly completed Ravi-Beas Link on the left bank. Thus, there was no question of a "standstill" on the Indian side; a physical partition of the Indus Basin irrigation system was being built into the landscape.

Meanwhile, what were the Pakistanis doing? As far as the West Punjab was concerned, the immediate response to the events of the spring of 1948 and to India's start on the Harike Barrage was the design of a small link canal (initial capacity 5,000 cusecs) for emergency use should the May 4 agreement not be observed. This canal takes off from the Upper Chenab Canal at Bombanwala, passes under the Ravi River in a siphon near the border, and feeds the Lahore Branch of the UBDC near Batapur (on the Lahore-Wagah road), then continues to Bedian where it feeds the Main Branch of the UBDC (see Map 6). Later, when the Marala-Ravi (M-R) Link was built (1954–56) it was found possible to divert some 5,000 of its 22,000 cusecs into the Bombanwala Link via a cross link north of the Ravi, and thanks to this increase, to extend the Bombanwala Link from Bedian down to the Dipalpur Canal, thus ensuring that even if India again closed the Ferozepore intake some water would be available along the latter canal. The Bombanwala-Ravi-Bedian-Dipalpur, or BRBD Link was finally completed in 1958. It should be pointed out that such a link was never contemplated prior to Partition, and that its construction was an emergency measure and a considerable burden to the West Punjab. It will serve a vital purpose within the Indus Basin Project, however, since after 1970 or 1973, when India is entitled to abstract all of the water of the Ravi, Beas, and Sutlej, the BRBD Link will be the only means of supplying the "Central" Bari Doab Canal (as those portions of the Upper Bari Doab Canal in Pakistan are now called by the Pakistanis; the Indians and the Indus Waters Treaty refer to the Central Bari Doab "Channels") and the Dipalpur Canal.

It will be recalled that the Inter-Dominion Agreement of May 1948 called upon Pakistan to develop alternative sources of water for the Central Bari Doab and Dipalpur canals (sic). But the BRBD Link hardly served this purpose, for its use implied abstraction of water from the Upper Chenab Canal. Furthermore, since India envisaged increased withdrawals from the Sutlej, the West Punjab (and Bahawalpur) had to find a means of supplying the canals offtaking from Suleimanke and Islam headworks. This was the old problem of shortages in the S.V.P. which had led to the appointment of the Anderson Committee and the Indus (Rau) Commission. In 1939, the Punjab was proposing to solve the problem by building the Bhakra Dam, which would ease the situation in late kharif, and a link of 5,000-cusec capacity from Balloki on the Ravi to Suleimanke on the Sutlej, which would help in early kharif.[14] Ten years later, the West Punjab knew it would get no help from Bhakra, but reverted to the Balloki-Suleimanke (B-S) Link plan in conjunction with another from Marala headworks to the Ravi River above the BRBD syphon. The B-S Link was constructed between 1951 and 1954 with a nominal capacity of 15,000 cusecs (never realized in operation) and an intake at the Balloki Barrage just above the intake for the LBDC. But it was obvious that the B-S Link alone would not solve the problems of Suleimanke and Islam because of uncertain supplies in the Ravi below Madhopur, and especially because by the time it was finished India had completed the Ravi-Beas Link at Madhopur, increasing withdrawals there from 6,500 to 12,000 cusecs not including 350 cusecs for the "Kashmir" Canal. So, in September 1953 work was started on the Marala-Ravi (M-R) Link to transfer water from the Chenab into the Ravi (17,000 cusecs, of which 15,000 are again abstracted at Balloki). The M-R Link was completed in 1956, although like the B-S Link it could not be run at full design capacity.

Both the M-R Link and the B-S Link have been plagued by siltation problems, in the former case principally because of its location at a rim station and just below the confluence of two hill torrents with the Marala Barrage unable to pass the silt, in the latter case because of inadequate design, the haste with which it was brought into operation, and the lack of lining in the upper reaches. The B-S Link was seriously damaged in the flood of 1956. Both links are being remodeled under the Indus Basin Project. But neither, in the absence of the Indus Basin Project, would have provided an "alternative source" of water for Pakistan in the sense of the Inter-Dominion Agreement. The M-R and B-S links served to provide some help for the S.V.P. in early kharif, because the Chenab rises earlier than the

14. See Chap. 4, p. 130 and n. 29. It is most likely that Punjab was contemplating the Marala-Rabi Link in 1939, although it did not present it to the Rau Commission. The Balloki-Suleimanke Link, however, could hardly have functioned without additional supplies for the Ravi from the Chenab.

Sutlej or Beas (or Ravi for that matter). But the real "alternative sources" toward which Punjab had looked prior to Partition were the Bhakra Dam and possibly the Dhiangarh Dam. After 1948, Punjab had to look elsewhere, in particular toward the Jhelum, where a storage site (Mangla) was available and, so long as the position in Azad Kashmir could be held, in safe hands. From Mangla, using the principle developed in the Triple Canals Project, additional link canals could be built to transfer *stored* Jhelum water to the Chenab, Ravi, and Sutlej. This was the inception of the Indus Basin Project. As far as West Punjab was concerned, a storage dam at Mangla could, at considerable cost it is true, be made to replace the lost Bhakra Project.

But to use stored Jhelum water just for replacement would be a step backward as far as the West Punjab engineers were concerned. They felt that, inasmuch as the entire existing irrigation system was sustained by run of the river diversion without storage, an investment in storage facilities could be justified only if it led to enlargement, i.e. "development," of the system rather than just "replacement." To reserve stored Jhelum water for development while replacing the lost Bhakra supplies merely by diversion, the West Punjab engineers proposed an "Upper Indus Link" that would cut across the Potwar Plateau (see Map 3) and tie in to the Triple Canals Project (and thus the new links) at Mangla. Built through the heavily dissected Potwar area, such a link would have been extremely expensive, and the idea was abandoned in the course of the Treaty negotiations.

But what of Sind? Sind had always regarded the Bhakra Project as a threat, and even as a subprovince of the Bombay Government she had managed to delay and circumscribe it with conditions. Now that Bhakra was to be carried out by India, and presumably without any of the compensation which the Indus (Rau) Commission had led Sind to expect from the undivided Punjab, the position of Sind from the hydrological and financial points of view seemed to have deteriorated. Certainly if Punjab placed a storage dam on the Jhelum designed to retain water for diversion through links to the Punjab canals, Sind's position would be even worse.

But Sind's political position after Independence was enhanced considerably. Not only did the province bulk much larger in West Pakistan than it ever had in undivided India, but—largely for strategic reasons—its capital, Karachi, had been chosen as the national capital. Sind, which under British rule had been almost a stepchild (see Chapter 4), had now come into its own. Punjab, the former fair-haired boy, had not only been torn asunder in Partition and in the flight of refugees, but lay under the immediate menace of the Indian Armed Forces in East Punjab and Kashmir. The very factors of isolation, principally the Thar Desert, which had rendered Sind eccentric to the mainstream of economic life in northern India, made her relatively secure after Partition. Lahore, from historical and cultural premises the logical capital of Pakistan, and with a population of almost 700,000 persons, lay three hours' march from the Indian border and thus lost pride of place to Karachi, a city of 425,000 with barely a century of significance.

Thus, although Partition and Independence had deprived Sind of any hope of financial assistance from East Punjab toward the cost of barrage-building on the lower Indus, it had elevated the political position of the province within West Pakistan. Any capital area inevitably benefits from its position. The first fruit as far as Sind was concerned was the Ghulam Mohammad Barrage, which was sanctioned in 1947 and on which work began in earnest in 1950. The estimated cost of the entire scheme in 1947 was 210.5 million rupees; it was revised upward to 240 million when the design of the barrage and channels was changed by the then Chief Engineer, T. A. W. Foy, in 1951. By 1956, when the barrage had been completed, the cost had risen to 350.2 million, and by 1959 to 391 million rupees.[15] For this sum of money, the Government of Pakistan built a barrage some 3,034 feet long across the Indus near Hyderabad (see Map 3), practically at the head of the Indus delta, plus a distribution system aggregating over 2,500 miles in length which superseded the existing inundation canals:

> The area under the command of this project is about 33.9 lakh [3,390,000] acres gross area and forms [the] southern part of the Sind alluvial belt. It is deltaic in nature with a gentle slope of 1:8,000 to 1:10,000 towards the sea. . . . The command has been limited mostly to the land higher than RL 5 [5 feet

15. *Hundred Years of P.W.D.*, ed. Mubashir Hasan, p. 43.

above mean high tide]. Land up to RL 8 gets occasionally flooded in high tide during Monsoons.[16]

The culturable commanded area under the Ghulam Mohammad Barrage is some 2.81 million acres, of which 1.97 million are non-perennial and 839,000 perennial. By 1960–61, 891,000 acres were actually irrigated as compared with 520,000 acres irrigated by inundation canals in an average year before the barrage was constructed.

Construction of the Ghulam Mohammad Barrage provided employment as well as irrigated lands for some of the hundreds of thousands of refugees (many of whom arrived by ship from areas in west and south India, including Hyderabad State) who crowded into the Karachi area after Partition. It also provided a pure water supply for the city of Hyderabad, and by extension through the artificial Kalri Lake on the right bank, about 500 cusecs for consumption in Karachi. Aside from that, it has proved an almost unmitigated failure. It would have been far better for Pakistan had the Ghulam Mohammad Barrage never been built. The key to the problem lies in the phrase (which would be humorous were it not so tragic) in the above quotation, "a gentle slope of 1:8,000 to 1:10,000 toward the sea. This is indeed a gentle slope, not for a canal but for drainage purposes. And it is a slope toward the sea, which means both that a local base level is established below which drainage is impossible, and that saline water penetrates into the project from the ocean. In short, it is not hard to distribute irrigation water in the Ghulam Mohammad command, but it is practically impossible to remove it. Not only is surface water of the worst quality—the effluent of the whole Indus Basin—being applied to the soil, but it immediately encounters brackish, if not saline, subsurface waters. The water table is so high and the slope is so low that surface drains can hardly be dug, and the subsoil water is so poor that tubewell supplies are next to worthless. We shall return to the Ghulam Mohammad problem in our discussion of groundwater in Chapter 9. For the present, the point to be made is that Sind's first irrigation project after Independence was ill-conceived in the extreme and, although this was not realized for almost a decade, it did make Sind highly recalcitrant toward

16. Ibid., pp. 42–43.

the end of the Indus Waters Treaty negotiations, and afterward when the Tarbela Dam project seemed to be in jeopardy.[17] For Tarbela, or a storage dam somewhere on the Indus above Attock, came to mean to Sind what at first Bhakra and later Mangla meant to the West Punjab: the only hope of maintaining existing irrigation systems and of expanding irrigation at a rate in excess of population growth *and* the annual loss of acreage due to water-logging and salinity.

But we are getting ahead of ourselves. Sanction and construction of the Ghulam Mohammad Barrage did satisfy Sind in the late 1940s and early 1950s. The threat posed by India to the West Punjab canals meant little to Sind (though the threat of Bhakra did), and Sind readily assented to the enlargement of the Thal Project by Punjab in 1949, raising the culturable commanded area from 1,039,-000 acres to 1,473,000 acres, and raising the minimum rabi flow from 2,000 to 3,383 cusecs.[18] As was indicated in Chapter 4, the Thal Project was of utmost importance in enabling Pakistan, particularly the West Punjab, to resettle her refugees long before anything was available in the Ghulam Mohammad command (though there was some land available under Sukkur). It has been estimated that by the end of 1955 some 33,712 *families* had been settled in 640 new Thal villages, and that 450,000 acres had been brought under cultivation by irrigation, thanks largely to the efforts of the Thal Development Authority established by Pakistan in 1949.[19]

Sind was also quite accommodating when in 1952 Punjab revived the scheme for a barrage across the Indus at Taunsa, irrigating lands both in the southwestern Thal Doab (Muzaffargarh District) and in the Derajat or trans-Indus Punjab (Dera Ghazi Khan District). The

17. Of course, from October 14, 1955 onward, after the "One Unit Plan" went into effect, there was no Sind Province, but rather two divisions—Hyderabad and Khairpur—plus the District of Karachi. But there still were Sindhis (as well as Punjabis), and we shall continue to use the term in its geographical and historical sense. Nor does it seem necessary to resort in this study to the current official jargon of "former Sind," "former Punjab," etc., used in Pakistan to describe the provinces as they were between 1947 and 1955.

18. *Hundred Years of P.W.D.*, pp. 38–39.

19. The history of the Thal Project has been analyzed in detail by Dr. Rashid A. Malik, now Lecturer in Geography at the University of the Panjab, Lahore, in his published doctoral dissertation, *Irrigation Development and Land Occupance in the Upper Indus Basin* (Bloomington, Indiana, August, 1963), pp. 195–236.

Taunsa scheme had been proposed as early as 1936, but shelved in favor of Thal, which seemed relatively more promising. Had it been pressed, there is no doubt that Sind would have objected to it on the same grounds as Thal, Trimmu, and Bhakra. When, in 1945, the Railways Department and the Buildings and Roads Branch of the Public Works Department were seeking a site for a new crossing of the Indus on the Delhi-Lahore-Quetta highway, and for the long-promised extension of the railway to the best bank of the Indus, they offered to join with the Irrigation Branch in building a single bridge-barrage. A project was prepared in 1947 calling for a barrage at Taunsa, designed to carry both road and railway and to replace the inundation canals downstream with two large nonperennial canals, one on either bank. But again the Thal Project seemed more urgent and more promising, and Taunsa was deferred. It was revived and revised in 1952, sanctioned in 1953, and construction began in the latter year. Financial stringencies dictated both that a gravity weir rather than a raft design be employed (to reduce the cost of reinforcing steel, which had to be imported) and that the project be carried out in stages. It was again revised in 1956 when the cost was reduced from 310 million rupees to 165 million by eliminating some hydroelectric and tubewell features. By 1958 the 4,346-foot barrage had been completed, and in the kharif of 1960 the left-bank Muzaffargarh Canal went into operation with a culturable commanded area of 714,000 acres, of which 528,000 acres represented lands formerly irrigated by inundation. The culturable commanded area under the Dera Ghazi Khan Canal on the right bank is now about 878,000 acres, of which about 145,000 are new lands; another 390,-000 acres of new culturable commanded area may be added if and when the third stage, bringing the Dera Gazi Khan Canal up to Kashmor, is built. Both Taunsa canals are nonperennial, and the maximum withdrawals are limited to 20,000 cusecs if available, Sukkur and Kalabagh having priority of withdrawal. This was the tentative agreement worked out in 1945, and it was insisted upon by Sind in 1953—another example of Sind's determination to augment her claims to equitable distribution by specific agreements as to prior allocation (and another example of the inevitable qualification of the former principle by the latter).[20]

20. Data on Taunsa are from *Hundred Years of P.W.D.*, pp. 40–42.

Not that one should suppose that Sind was so enamored with the Ghulam Mohammad Project that she allowed West Punjab to proceed with all of the projects envisaged by the Indus (Rau) Commission and the 1945 Sind-Punjab Chief Engineers' Agreement (see Chapter 4, page 000 and footnote 34) without the financial compensation envisaged therein. But on the one hand Sind realized that to the extent that central, rather than provincial, funds were going into the costly Ghulam Mohammad Project, Punjab was making a larger contribution than Sind. And on the other hand Sind was only waiting for completion of the Ghulam Mohammad Barrage in order to start work on the even more expensive Gudu Barrage upstream at Kashmor.

The Gudu Project was conceived in Sind in 1940 as part of the riposte to Punjab's Bhakra Project and, as we have seen in Chapter 4, was endorsed by the Indus (Rau) Commission along with the Ghulam Mohammad Project as a means of securing to Sind her equitable distribution of the Indus Waters. A barrage in upper Sind was also mentioned in the 1945 Chief Engineers' Agreement. The project was prepared in 1946–47 by the Sind Government, envisaging a culturable commanded area of 2.295 million acres at a cost of 176.5 million rupees. A barrage of 4,445 feet across the Indus about 55 miles below the Panjnad confluence at Mithankot (the site suggested by the Indian Irrigation Commission of 1901–03), with two canals on the right bank and one on the left, were proposed. The project was sanctioned after Partition, but had to be delayed for financial reasons until after Ghulam Mohammad was finished. Construction was begun in 1955, and the barrage completed in April 1962. (The project was transferred to the West Pakistan Water and Power Development Authority, known as WAPDA, when that organization was established in 1958.) Including the Pat Feeder, which was tacked on to the project in order to irrigate about 500,000 acres in the Quetta and Kalat divisions (Baluchistan), the project has a cultural commanded area of 3,017,184 acres, all nonperennial, as compared with 950,000 acres irrigated from inundation canals before Gudu's construction. Withdrawals are limited to 9.827 million acre feet annually in order to protect the Sukkur and Ghulam Mohammad commands. The project is not yet completed, but the cost has been revised upward to 477,800,000 rupees partly due to the inflation of prices and wages produced by the Indus Basin Project. Still, Gudu seems to be in a much better position than Ghulam Mohammad, except for some salinized areas in Khairpur along the Ghotki Canal, and the financial outlook is optimistic.[21]

Thus, within a span of seven or eight years after Partition and the Inter-Dominion Agreement of May 1948, India and Pakistan were firmly committed to projects for the separate utilization of the waters of the Indus Basin. By 1955, the Harike and Nangal barrages were completed, the Rupar and Madhopur headworks were remodeled, the Ravi-Beas Link was in operation, and concrete was being poured at Bhakra. By 1955, Ghulam Mohammad Barrage was completed, Gudu begun, and Taunsa was well along. The B-S Link was nominally completed, the M-R Link under construction, and the BRBD Link about to be extended. The curious thing is that, with the exception of Harike Barrage and the BRBD Link, all of these projects had been suggested prior to Partition and with the object of preserving and enhancing the integrated irrigation of the Indus Basin. Yet in those two projects lay all of the difference. For Harike Barrage represented not only the diversion of Sutlej-Beas-Ravi water to nonriparian Rajasthan (there was sufficient precedent for that in the Bikaner Canal), but the potential subtraction of water which had by prior allocation (actual or promised) been "guaranteed" to West Pakistan. And the BRBD Link was built solely in order to offset, by diversion from the Upper Chenab Canal, any future withholding of traditional water supplies by India. Although the pre-Partition Punjab had developed and litigated the Bhakra Project primarily for its own use, the post-Partition incorporation of a revised Bhakra scheme into the Bhakra-Beas-Rajasthan Project (signified by the 1955 Interstate Agreement among East Punjab, Rajasthan, and Indian-dominated Kashmir and by India's denunciation of the Barcelona Convention in 1956) demonstrated that Partition and Independence had fundamentally ALTERED the historical development of water use within the Indus Basin.[22] Yet on the technical grounds

21. *Ibid.*, pp. 46–49.
22. The 1955 Interstate Agreement provided that the first 15.85 million acre feet of water developed over and above traditional uses on the Sutlej, Beas, and Ravi would be allocated as follows: Punjab, 7.2 m.a.f., Rajasthan, 8 m.a.f., and (Indian-held) Kashmir, 0.65 m.a.f. Any additional supplies developed would be divided pro rata between Punjab and Rajasthan, Kashmir's share remaining at 0.65 (presumably even if India were to acquire Azad Kashmir). Himachal

that neither the Indus (Rau) Commission recommendations nor the Sind-Punjab Chief Engineers' agreement of 1945 had been implemented, India could, and did, argue that there had been neither a formalized agreement nor an overall, integrated plan for the development of the Indus Basin. The statement of the Indian Designee, submitted to the Indus Basin Working Party (World Bank) in October 1953, makes this abundantly clear:

> [In the postwar period, 1945–47] a number of other new projects were under consideration and were being investigated; *no overall plan for the Indus system as a whole was, however, under contemplation.* The main reason for this was that under the Government of India Act, 1935, the development of irrigation was a subject under the control of Provincial Governments. Each Provincial Government were therefore concerned only in so far as they could benefit from a particular river or stream. Naturally, *some of the Indian States* [i.e. those which in the post-Independence period were gradually formed into the present state of Rajasthan] *were comparatively* weak, both in political status and administrative capacity, [and] had little chance of taking up new projects, unless a river was actually passing through a State.[23]

Pradesh, which had been formed out of the former Punjab Hill States and which includes part of the Bhakra and other reservoir sites, was a party to the agreement but received no allocation as it had no areas susceptible to irrigation. P.E.P.S.U. (Patiala and East Punjab States Union) had been incorporated into the (East) Punjab State in 1955. (See Bureau of Reclamation, p. 21.) The re-partitioning of the Indian Punjab in November 1966 will require the renegotiation of this agreement.

It could be argued that the water would remain in the Indus Basin, even though the Rajasthan Canal alignment is well south of the old Hakra bed, in Bahawalpur (See Chap. 2, p. 27, and Chap. 3, p. 83, Table 3, n. b), but there is no question that the incorporation of the Rajasthan Project fundamentally altered the pre-Partition Bhakra scheme. A small amount of Indus Basin water will, however, be made available for use in the Ganges Basin since the Bhakra Project envisages some exchange with the Western Jumna Canal system in the Delhi District.

23. Indus Basin Working Party, Draft Outline as Prepared by the Indian Designee, p. 35. Italics added.

Engineers, Lawyers, and an Occasional Statesman

We have seen that, to all intents and purposes, integrated development of the irrigation system and associated infrastructure in the
Indus Basin came to an end with the irrigation crises of April 1948
and the ensuing Inter-Dominion Agreement of May 1948. India's
actions, and her assertion of the doctrine of proprietary rights, were
ample indication of her position. Pakistan, although she continued
to assert her rights by prior allocation and equitable distribution,
was in no position to enforce them, even by war. She did attempt to
bring her case to the International Court of Justice in June 1949,
but India refused to go along with such an action. Instead, India
urged that the Inter-Dominion Agreement be made permanent. The
Agreement had provided for further meetings, and the first of these
was held in March 1950, but without result. Although the United
Nations had come into Kashmir, arranging a cease-fire and promising a plebiscite, that situation had not improved. It continued to
hang like Damocles' sword over Indo-Pakistan relations. Finally, in
September 1949 Pakistan had refused to go along with Great Britain,
India, and other members of the Sterling Bloc in devaluing her
currency—on the grounds that such action would impede her economic development program. The Indian reaction was to refuse to
recognize the Pakistani rupee at the old value and to impose an
economic blockade on Pakistan that lasted until the end of 1950.[24]

Into this situation, in February 1951, came David E. Lilienthal on
a fact-finding tour sponsored by *Collier's* magazine. Lilienthal, who
had served as perhaps the most influential, and certainly the most
famous, member and chairman of the Tennessee Valley Authority,
and who had recently resigned as chairman of the U.S. Atomic
Energy Commission, had agreed to write a series of articles for
Collier's bringing his experience and judgments to the attention of
the American people. He wanted in particular to visit India where
enthusiasm for the T.V.A. type of development (treating a river or a
basin as a unit) was high and where Nehru had invited him to
come as a personal guest. According to Lilienthal's *Journals,* the idea
of including Pakistan was suggested by Walter Lippman, who pointed

24. Stephens, *Pakistan*, p. 226.

out, first, that in the prevailing political situation Pakistan would be sure to take umbrage at being bypassed, and, second, that in his (Lippman's) opinion the core of the Kashmir dispute was the struggle for control of the rivers flowing from that state into West Pakistan.[25] Lippman therefore urged Lilienthal to go to Pakistan and to attempt to bring his experience and persuasion to bear on the Indus waters problem. Although Lilienthal did not discuss this problem as such with Liaquat Ali Khan or Nehru, it was very much on his mind during his tour of the subcontinent, which included a visit to the Bhakra Project. To Lilienthal, as to so many outsiders at the time, the situation in the Indus Basin seemed irrational. Why should these two "new" nations, struggling with such severe economic and demographic problems, frustrate their own development by devoting an inordinate share of their resources to preparations for a war over Kashmir? Why could they not bury their differences and get on with the job of economic development?

When Lilienthal reached Hawaii, on the way home, he sketched out an article for *Collier's* in which he stressed the seriousness of the Kashmir situation and its relation to the waters dispute. In the article, which appeared in the August 4, 1951 issue, Lilienthal drew the following realistic conclusions:

a. "As a practical matter" religious considerations could not be excluded from any plebiscite in Kashmir, as India insisted they must be.

b. "The controversy over Kashmir has been so heated that the real issue has largely been lost sight of. The real issue is *not* the plebiscite, but how best to promote and insure peace and a sense of a community in the Indo-Pakistan subcontinent; how best to avoid a UN situation that will create another, though different, 'Korea.'"

c. "The Kashmir issue, *as an issue in itself,* may not be solvable, now, short of war. But the surrounding tensions can be reduced, one

25. David E. Lilienthal, *The Journals of David E. Lilienthal, 3,* "Venturesome Years, 1950–55" (New York, Evanston, and London, Harper and Row, 1966, pp. 54–55; 64–65). In mid-June of 1966, Mr. Lilienthal generously permitted the present author to read the galley proofs of the third volume of his *Journals.* Mr. Lilienthal has also granted permission to quote extensively from his historic article in *Collier's,* which must be regarded as the starting point of negotiations in the Indus Waters Dispute despite the subsequent modifications of his suggested terms of reference.

by one. It may then be possible to solve the matter of Kashmir's political future."[26]

Perhaps not so realistically, Lilienthal insisted that any steps toward reconciliation "be predicated upon the fullest acceptance on all sides of substantially these two propositions":

> "The partition of the subcontinent into Pakistan and India is accepted as a final and permanent thing. If Pakistan feels that India or the United Nations or the U.S.A. is seeking by indirection to return Pakistan (piecemeal, perhaps) to India, she will meet every proposal with distrust and fear.
>
> Pakistan and India do not accept an armed truce as the natural relation, but that they integrate their economic and cultural life, and become dependent on each other as neighbors, as are Canada and the United States, for instance.[27]

Lilienthal then went on to state that Pakistan's legal position, even though it might bring a decision in her favor by the World Court if India agreed to submit the case, was inadequate for the great issues of maintaining peace and providing sufficient food for the people of the Indus Basin.

> Such a legal decision would not prevent the waste of most of the precious waters of the Indus, it would further antagonize India, and it certainly would not start these two countries down the road of active partnership in developing their common resource, the six rivers on which their millions depend for their livelihood and their future. But Pakistan's position, though inadequate, should be the *starting* point, should be accepted as a minimum, without question.
>
> The starting point should be, then, to set to rest Pakistan's fears of deprivation and a return to desert. Her present use of water should be confirmed by India, *provided* she works together with India (as I believe she would) in a joint use of this truly international river basin on an engineering basis that would also (as the facts make clear it can) assure India's future use as well.

26. David E. Lilienthal, "Another 'Korea' in the Making?" *Collier's, 128* (August 4, 1951), 56–57. Italics in the original.
27. Ibid., p. 58.

The urgent problem is how to store up now wasted waters, so they can be fed down and distributed by engineering works and canals, and used by both countries, rather than permitted to flow to the sea unused. This is not a religious or political problem, but a feasible engineering and business problem for which there is plenty of precedent and relevant experience.

This objective, however, cannot be achieved by the countries working separately; the river pays no attention to partition—the Indus, she "just keeps rolling along" through Kashmir and India and Pakistan. The whole Indus system must be developed as a unit—designed, built and operated as a unit, as is the seven-state TVA system back in the U.S.

Jointly financed (perhaps with World Bank help) an Indus Engineering Corporation, with representation by technical men of India, Pakistan and the World Bank, can readily work out an operating scheme for storing water wherever dams can best store it, and for diverting and distributing water.

Once the scheme is designed, the works can be operated by an Indo-Pakistan Agency, or by a supranational international agency such as the Schuman Plan provides in Europe, or by some special corporation like the Port of New York Authority, or some comparable scheme.

Such a plan could certainly be financed, for this now worthless unirrigated land would, with water, become immensely productive and valuable; the increased value of the land, now owned by the respective governments, would be enough to base financing.

Such planning of the water resources (and the accompanying potential electric power) of the Indus Basin is nothing new; it was for generations largely a function of British-trained Indian engineers of the state of Punjab. They saw the river basin as a unit, as it is in nature. Then partition, a politico-religious instrument, fell like an ax, and colleagues who had worked together all their lives, elbow to elbow, separated because they were Hindu and Sikh, or Moslem. Partition did not repeal engineering or professional principles among these engineers; it merely made them secondary, for a time, to politics and emotion.[28]

28. Ibid.; italics in the original.

Thus the Lilienthal proposal was based on a return to pre-Partition premises for the further development of the Indus Basin irrigation system. The Basin was to be treated as a whole in new construction, in operations, and in maintenance. Dyas' old principle, that "the best line for a canal is that from which the largest extent of country can be irrigated at the smallest cost, irrespective of the name or nature of the existing Government of the country in question," was to be embodied in a supranational agency modeled on the T.V.A. (We have seen on page 70 the inherent contradiction in the Dyas principle.)

To forestall any technical objections that the Indus Basin is not the Tennessee Valley, that the T.V.A. provides no irrigation, and that although it may be a comparatively simple matter to locate dams for maximum flood control and hydroelectric generation, and then to transmit the power where it is needed, the distribution of irrigation water is not so simple (as experience with the Missouri Valley Interagency Committee amply demonstrated), Lilienthal asserted that there was plenty of water in the Indus system (in the western rivers to be sure) and that two-thirds of it was running waste to the sea. He was quite correct in asserting that an integrated system could be designed—we have seen that most of its parts were on the drafting boards before Partition—and a century of experience, including *most* of the four years since Partition, indicated that it could be operated.

But in retrospect the basic flaw in Lilienthal's argument was that, by 1951, neither India nor Pakistan wanted an integrated system, even if the World Bank could be persuaded to *lend* much of the cost. India did not want it because she could go ahead, at considerably less ultimate cost to herself, with the Bhakra-Beas-Rajasthan Project. Nor did many Indians want to accept Partition "as a final and permanent thing" (Lilienthal's proposition A). Pakistan did not want it because her entire experience from the Cabinet Mission and Mountbatten-Menon negotiations, through the Partition holocaust, to Kashmir and the canal closures of April 1948, had indicated that she could not trust control of her life's supply of irrigation water to India. No integrated system could be designed, especially if India remained in possession of southern Kashmir, that would not leave Pakistan vulnerable to an Indian change of heart. Lilienthal's proposition B was not valid. By 1951, India and Pakistan *had* come to

"accept an armed truce as the natural relation" and had no desire
to "integrate their economic and cultural life, and become dependent
on each other as neighbors." Lilienthal had cited U.S.-Canadian
experience, overlooking the early years of that history when (especially in 1812–15) Canada stood in fear of her stronger neighbor to
the south. He had forgotten "Fifty-four forty or fight." Lilienthal
cited the Schuman Plan, overlooking the eighty years of conflict,
and the utter exhaustion of the nations involved, which preceded
the Franco-German rapprochement of 1950–51. He cited the Port
of New York Authority, although the only serious territorial dispute
between New York and New Jersey had been over the possession of
Staten Island. In 1951, India and Pakistan were where the United
States and Canada stood in 1783 or 1815, where France and Germany stood in 1871, and where New York and New Jersey stood
before the Articles of Confederation.

But however weak these analogies may have been, the Lilienthal
proposal had two profound advantages. First, it provided a new
avenue of negotiations, negotiations that could be based, in part at
least, on engineering data and opinions rather than on threats and
tenuous legal arguments. Second, it introduced a new party and a
new potential source of financial assistance. When Eugene R. Black,
President of the International Bank for Reconstruction and Development (called the World Bank for short), and a close friend of
Lilienthal's, read the *Collier's* article he called Lilienthal, expressed
great enthusiasm, and asked for Lilienthal's suggestions for getting
India and Pakistan to accept the proposals. Lilienthal had already
shown an advance copy of the article to the Pakistan Ambassador to
the United States, and had received an enthusiastic endorsement
from John Laylin of the legal firm of Covington and Burling, which
represented Pakistan's interests in the United States. So Lilienthal
told Black that he thought Pakistan would accept his proposals and
that the problem was to make sure India understood the advantages
of discussions and then to bring the nations together for conversations.[29]

At a meeting on August 8, 1951, Lilienthal discussed the matter
with Black, Davidson Sommers (general counsel for the World
Bank), and William Iliff (Black's assistant who had already been

29. Lilienthal, *Journals, 3*, pp. 198–200, 205.

briefed by Laylin). It was pointed out that both India and Pakistan seemed to be agreed on one key point, that the waters dispute be considered separately from the dispute over Kashmir. When the question of how to approach India and Pakistan came up, Lilienthal recommended that Black write directly to Nehru and Liaquat Ali Khan. This Black did, early in September.[30]

President Black informed the two Prime Ministers of the World Bank's interest in the Lilienthal proposals and tentatively offered the Bank's good offices for discussion of the dispute and negotiation of a settlement. Pakistan accepted almost immediately, and India by the end of September. Meanwhile, Lilienthal had been urged by Laylin, and by Chester Bowles (recently nominated as United States Ambassador to India), to serve as mediator, but Lilienthal felt that the first step was to secure an agreement by India and Pakistan on the propositions contained in his article. At a meeting with Robert Garner (Vice President of the World Bank), Davidson Sommers, and General Raymond A. Wheeler (chief engineering adviser of the Bank) in New York on October 8, 1951, Lilienthal again urged against turning the discussions over to engineers before there was a clear political agreement by the Prime Ministers on the principles set forth in his article and especially on treating the Indus Basin as a unit and on guaranteeing Pakistan at least her existing uses of water (though not necessarily from the same sources). Lilienthal also recommended against the Bank representatives assuming the position of an arbitrator who would decide the issues, and suggested that the Bank select an engineer who was not an American and a locale for the discussions which was not in the United States, the United Kingdom, India, or Pakistan.[31] As matters turned out, all but the first of these recommendations were ignored.

The assassination of Liaquat Ali Khan on October 16, 1951 delayed further action on the Lilienthal proposals, and when, on November 8, President Black of the World Bank wrote identical letters to Nehru and Khwaja Nazimuddin, Pakistan's new Prime Minister, he unfortunately was not as explicit about guaranteeing Pakistan's existing uses as Lilienthal had urged. Black asked the Prime Ministers to agree only to the following premises before he

30. Ibid., pp. 210, 223–24.
31. Ibid., pp. 233–36, 269.

formally submitted the matter to the Executive Directors of the Bank:

a. Indus waters are sufficient for present and future needs.

b. Water resources of the Indus Basin should be cooperatively developed and used in such manner as most effectively to promote the economic development of the Indus Basin viewed as a unit.

c. The problem of development and use of the Indus Basin water resources should be solved on a functional and not a political plane, without relation to past negotiations and past claims and independently of political issues.[32]

As Lilienthal points out, the specification that "Indus waters are sufficient for present and future needs" was not the same as a clear understanding that Pakistan was entitled to no less than her existing uses of water in the Indus Basin.[33] It might also be pointed out that "future needs" covers a great deal, and that the entire experience of the Sind-Punjab disputes indicated that no solution involving allocation of water could be solved purely on a functional plane. It was one thing to exclude the Kashmir dispute from the Indus waters negotiations; it was another thing entirely to expect engineers to achieve a functional solution to a problem which, even within an integrated system, would ipso facto involve allocations of water in certain quantities and at certain periods between two sovereign nations and among various political entities within those nations.

It is not surprising, therefore, that the replies received by President Black to his identical letters were apparently equivocal, with the reply from Pakistan apparently expressing concern over the lack of a guarantee of her existing uses. In December, Lilienthal wrote to A. N. Khosla, Nehru's chief engineering adviser, then serving as Chairman of India's Central Water and Power Commission. (Khosla, the gifted engineer who had designed the Trimmu Barrage, described in Chapter 4, had subsequently become Chief Engineer in the pre-Partition Punjab. In 1947, he had gone to India where he had worked on the Bhakra and other engineering projects.) Lilienthal had met Khosla on his visit to India and again in October 1951, and the two had a great respect for each other. Now Lilienthal urged

32. Letter dated November 8, 1951 from Eugene R. Black, President of the International Bank for Reconstruction and Development, to Khwaja Nazimuddin, Prime Minister of Pakistan.

33. Lilienthal, *Journals, 3,* pp. 262–63, 269.

him to get Nehru to make the desired guarantee to Pakistan.[34] But when Nehru replied to Black in January 1952 his letter insisted on considering the May 1948 Inter-Dominion Agreement as a treaty recognizing Indian rights to the waters of the Sutlej, Beas, and Ravi. Rather than engage in any further correspondence, Lilienthal now recommended that Black take up the matter directly with the two Prime Ministers when he visited India and Pakistan later that month.[35]

As a result of President Black's discussions with Nehru and Nazimuddin in January and February 1952, both parties accepted the good offices of the Bank and India promised at least that Pakistan would continue to receive her present uses of water so long as the discussions continued:

> on March 10, 1952, President Black was able to confirm that one of the bases of common understanding was "that [the] ultimate objective is to carry out specific engineering measures by which supplies effectively available to each country will be increased substantially." He also recorded agreement of the parties that "so long as the cooperative work continues with the participation of the Bank neither side will take any action to diminish the supplies available to the other side with the existing uses." [36]

Thus, when the delegations from India, Pakistan, and the World Bank finally convened in Washington in May 1952 for the first round of negotiations, there had still been no public statement to the effect that the Lilienthal proposals had been accepted in their entirety as the basis for discussion or that Pakistan's rights in perpetuity to the amount and timing of the water supplies she had received at the time of Partition would be guaranteed. Lilienthal, who went to Washington for the brief opening ceremony on May 6, still saw the solution of the problem in the creation of a surplus of water over and above Pakistan's existing uses by the construction of storage facilities within India (where the best dam sites were located) with Pakistan contributing to the cost of these facilities

34. Ibid., pp. 235–36, 281.
35. Ibid., pp. 290–91.
36. Ahmad, "Canal Water Problem," p. 36.

and with both countries agreeing on the design and operation of an integrated system.[37] It took some time for the Bank's negotiators to realize that neither Pakistan nor India was concerned only with preserving existing uses or with a moderate expansion of irrigation after such a surplus had been created, but rather that each nation had far-reaching plans for enlarging its own irrigation system and that there was not enough water in all of the Indus Rivers to satisfy these ambitions.

In contrast to what Lilienthal had recommended, the World Bank was bringing together, in the United States, two teams of Indian and Pakistani engineers with a Bank team consisting solely of Americans, all of whom lacked an adequate set of agreed-upon ground rules. Their terms of reference were technical, not political: "to prepare an outline of program and lists of studies for possible technical measures to increase the supplies of water available from the Indus system of rivers for purposes of economic development."[38] Without a previous political decision regarding the shares or ultimate uses of the increased supplies of water, the engineers could hardly be expected to settle questions that were largely beyond their competence and that should have been settled previously (as they had to be ultimately, though much later) at a heads of state level.

On the technical level, however, no finer set of negotiators could be desired. If the Governments of India and Pakistan were not fundamentally anxious to agree on an integrated development and operation of the Indus Basin system, at least each was determined that its interests be represented by a highly qualified team of engineers. Heading the Indian team was A. N. Khosla, assisted by N. D. Gulhati, Chief of the Natural Resources Division of India's Planning Commission and Deputy Secretary to the Ministry of Natural Resources and Scientific Research, and Dr. J. K. Malhotra, Officer on Special Duty in that Ministry. (The Central Ministry of Irrigation and Power was formed shortly afterward; see Chapter 8.) Leading the Pakistani delegation was M. A. Hamid, who had served as Chief Engineer, Irrigation, of the West Punjab from 1947 to 1952. He was assisted by Pir Muhammad Ibrahim, Irrigation Adviser to the

37. Lilienthal, *Journals*, 3, pp. 311–13.
38. International Bank for Reconstruction and Development (IBRD or World Bank henceforth), Press Release, June 26, 1952.

Government of Pakistan; Ahmad Hassan, Chief Engineer of Baha-walpur; A. Rahman, Irrigation Adviser to the Public Works Department of the North West Frontier Province; and M. S. Quraishy, Superintending Engineer from Sind. (The complete regional representation from the Pakistani portions of the Indus Basin should be noted as an indication of the need to keep all regional political interests satisfied at this period.)

The World Bank team was headed by its Engineering Adviser, General Raymond A. Wheeler, formerly Chief of the Corps of Engineers, U.S. Army, a man with intimate knowledge of the engineering problems of the Missouri Basin. General Wheeler was assisted by Dr. Harry W. Bashore, an irrigation engineer and former U.S. Commissioner of Reclamation, and by Neil Bass of the World Bank Staff, formerly with T.V.A.[39] The "Working Party" consisted of Khosla, Hamid, and Wheeler, but the advisers participated in almost all of the meetings. The first session, which lasted until June 18, 1952, was stormy and gave indication of troubles to come. Apparently very little agreement could be reached about anything. Much time was devoted to compiling and enchanging "detailed lists of studies and forms for studies that are needed for the preparation of the comprehensive plan," and the only tangible result was that the parties agreed to conduct further, but separate, studies in their respective countries and "to meet again at Karachi on November 1, 1952, for the purpose of exchanging completed studies and forms, visiting sites and determining further action."[40]

When the Working Party with its advisers reassembled in Karachi, it proceeded on a 9,000-mile field trip throughout the Indus Basin. In some respects, this trip recalled the tour of the Indian Irrigation Commission forty-nine years before (see Chapter 3, page 83). Both groups chose the proper season of the year. But while the I.I.C. never went below Sukkur, the Working Party began at the lower end of the system, where work on the Ghulam Mohammad

39. Volume 3 of the Lilienthal *Journals* contains a number of insights into the relationships that existed among the various negotiators and in particular those between General Wheeler and Dr. Bashore. It may be noted that Wheeler, Bashore, Bass (and Lilienthal) represented the three major United States agencies that had been concerned with integrated river basin development in the country over the preceding twenty years.

40. IBRD Press Release, June 26, 1952.

Barrage was in full swing, and ended at Bhakra, where the first storage dam in the Basin was about to rise. In between, it saw Sukkur, the beginnings of Taunsa, the rapidly expanding Thal Project, and the whole of the Triple Canals and Sutlej Valley projects which had caused such concern to the I.I.C. It saw Harike and the link canals that were then the physical evidence of the division of the Basin. It gathered a mass of data, including the twenty-five-year records of discharge at the rim stations, collection of which had begun in October 1921 at the instigation of Sir Thomas Ward (to settle the disputes growing out of the Sutlej Valley and Sukkur projects) and had been maintained systematically through 1946. Although there was some disagreement about measurements after 1946, the twenty-five-year record was at least an indisputable basis for discussions. Much additional unquestioned data were collected, but the teams, which held another session in New Delhi in January 1953, were not able to agree on a common approach to a plan for integrated development. The Bank representatives therefore suggested that each designee (India and Pakistan) prepare and submit a comprehensive plan.

The respective plans were submitted in Washington on October 6, 1953. The Pakistani plan was confined to the Pakistani part of the Indus Basin, whereas the Indian plan encompassed the entire system. In effect, the Pakistani plan would have allocated all water beyond India's actual uses in the past to the Pakistan portion of the Basin. Under the Indian Plan, all the water of the Sutlej, Beas, and Ravi (henceforth referred to as the "Eastern Rivers") would go to India along with 7 per cent of the water of the Chenab, Jhelum, and the Indus itself (henceforth the "Western Rivers"); in other words, India would proceed with the Bhakra-Beas-Rajasthan Project and in addition make some withdrawals via the Marhu Tunnel from the Chenab to the Ravi (see Map 3). Pakistan's plan envisaged retention of all of the Western Rivers plus use of 70 per cent of the water in the Eastern Rivers. Put into quantitative terms, the two plans called for the division of Indus Basin waters shown in Table 8.

A comparison of the figures in Table 8 indicates that India and Pakistan were not far apart on their estimates of the total amount of water usable for irrigation in the Indus Basin (see also Chapter 2, Table 1). But the question was how it should be divided. This came

230

Table 8. Indian and Pakistani Plans for Use of the Waters of the Indus Rivers as Submitted to the World Bank in 1953 (in millions of acre feet of water)[a]

	Total Uses Excluding Losses and Unusable Supplies		
Plan	*For India*	*For Pakistan*	*Total Usable*
Indian	29	90	119
Pakistani	15.5	102.5	118

a. Source: IBRD Press Release No. 380, December 10, 1954, Appendix I, February 5, 1954, p. 2.

down to a dispute over the term "existing uses." India had modified its previous stand on upper riparian proprietary rights to the extent of admitting that Pakistan had a right by prior allocation to the "existing use" of water in the Basin. But India insisted that "existing uses" meant only actual historic withdrawals, whereas Pakistan maintained that "existing uses" meant not only the withdrawals actually accomplished in the past, but all those contemplated by the Anderson Committee, the Indus (Rau) Commission, and the Sind-Punjab Chief Engineers' Agreement of 1945. Furthermore, India maintained that Pakistan's rights were only to a quantity of water within the Basin—water that could be obtained from the Western Rivers only rather than from both the Western and the Eastern.

Pakistan insisted that its right was to the actual historic and sanctioned (prior to Partition) withdrawals from the specific rivers previously considered. Pakistan argued that to the extent that water would be distributed by India to new areas in Rajasthan, this water would be removed from the Indus Basin, and that this had never been contemplated prior to Partition.[41] Pakistan was thus arguing part of Punjab's (and all of Bahawalpur's) old case, i.e. that the Sutlej Valley Project must be made to function properly by the allocation of sufficient water *from the Beas-Sutlej,* as well as all of Sind's (and Khairpur's) old case, i.e. that withdrawals for the S.V.P. and Punjab's other projects must not be allowed to prejudice

41. IBRD Press Release No. 380, December 10, 1954, Appendix I, dated February 5, 1954, "Proposal by the International Bank Representative for a Plan for the Development and Use of the Indus Basin Waters," pp. 3–4. "There has been discussion about the location of the easterly boundary of the Indus Basin, a question which is difficult to settle since the area is a desert with no discernible watershed." (Ibid., p. 11; see above, p. 217, n. 22.)

supplies at Sukkur. Furthermore, Sind had consented to the Bhakra Project only on the understanding that she be allowed (and assisted) to proceed with what became the Ghulam Mohammad and Gudu projects. So, in the Pakistani view, India could not proceed with Bhakra, even minus the allocations to Rajasthan, without assurances and compensation to West Pakistan.

But India held to the position that none of the pre-Partition arrangements later than those envisaged by the Anderson Committee (Trimmu-Haveli and Thal) had been formalized, and so were not binding. Bhakra water could be used anywhere, and she had a perfect right to proceed with storage dams on the Beas and Ravi and with a diversion from the Chenab. (It should be noted, however, that in both plans the figures on "usable supplies" reflected only one storage reservoir, Bhakra on the Sutlej, and that the figures represented not average annual flows but dependable flows.[42])

It was essentially on the definition of "existing uses" that the plans put forward by India and Pakistan foundered. But there were two other basic difficulties, as pointed out by the World Bank early in 1954:

> a. Water supplies and storage potentialities are inadequate to the needs of the basin. . . . even after full development, there will not be enough water to supply all the needs of the area.
>
> This means that there can be no ideal plan which will fully satisfy both sides. Any plan must involve a large element of compromise under which each country will have to forego some of the irrigation uses that it would wish to develop if adequate supplies and storage were available.
>
> b. Although the Working Party are planning on the basis of the development of the Indus Basin as an economic unit, two sovereign states are involved. This greatly limits the practical potentialities of planning. A comprehensive plan can achieve maximum efficiency, economy and usefulness when it is developed and administered by a single authority. Under such an authority, decisions can be made promptly, plans can be readily changed to meet new circumstances and accommodations made to meet emergencies.

42. Ibid., Appendix I, pp. 2, 9.

232

When two sovereign authorities are concerned, it is difficult to use resources to the greatest advantage. Problems must be solved by negotiation and agreement rather than by decision. Minor questions of planning and operational detail must be referred to high authority and dealt with, perhaps, through diplomatic channels. Moreover the two countries may follow different development policies, or may have unequal resources available for development. They may also (as has been evident in the present discussions) be reluctant to have works regulating water supplies on which they depend constructed in territory controlled by another country.[43]

A comparison of the preceding statement with propositions set forth by Lilienthal (above, page 221) and the premises that President Black had attempted to get India and Pakistan to accept (above, pages 225–26) indicates how far two years of negotiations had brought the parties. Not only was it apparent that the two countries would not be able to run an integrated system without exasperating and costly delays, but it had become clear that, left to themselves, they would not be able to agree on designing such a system. Even Lilienthal's basic assumption that there was plenty of water in the system for the needs of both countries had been vitiated by the plans each country put forth. Accordingly, the World Bank concluded, on February 5, 1954:

The present status is that it has not yet been possible to reach agreement and that, in the absence of some new development, there is no prospect of further progress in the Working Party.[44]

One fundamental cause of the impasse reached by early 1954 may be assigned to the lack of a preliminary political agreement between India and Pakistan regarding sharing of the waters, costs of development, and operation of an integrated irrigation system. We have seen that Lilienthal had repeatedly urged that such an agreement be reached, at the highest political level, before the technical arrangements were referred to the teams of engineers. But the other fundamental cause—and this had not been foreseen by Lilienthal—

43. Ibid., Appendix I, pp. 3–4.
44. Ibid., Appendix I, p. 2.

was the physical inability of the Indus Rivers system, no matter what engineering measures were adopted, to supply the amount of water required to fulfill the hopes and plans of the two nations. Toward the end of January 1954 President Black met with Lilienthal and informed him that the Working Party could not reach an agreement. Black was now prepared to move the discussions to a political plane, perhaps involving Nehru and Nasir Ahmed, Pakistan's Secretary of Resources. He also wanted to consult with Lilienthal about the next moves, but Lilienthal told him he preferred to leave matters to the Bank (though not to the engineers) unless the discussions came to a breaking point.[45] They almost did.

On February 3, 1954, Bank Vice President Garner, General Wheeler, and Neil Bass met with Lilienthal and showed him a memorandum outlining the reasons for the impasse. (This was presumably the draft of the memorandum quoted above and dated February 5, 1954, though not made public at that time.) This memorandum proceeded to outline the Bank's own plan for settling the Indus waters dispute by assigning the waters of the three Western Rivers to Pakistan and those of the three Eastern Rivers to India. When the Bank plan was released, it included the following statement:

> In the circumstances, the Bank Representative feels that he has the responsibility to put forward a proposal for the consideration of both sides to serve as the basis of a comprehensive plan. The proposal has the concurrence of the engineering consultants to the Bank Representative and is put forward with the full support of the management of the Bank.[46]

Actually, there are good reasons for believing that the parties asked General Wheeler to make a proposal as a means of breaking the deadlock. But neither he nor the Bank was in the position of mediator or arbitrator. The Bank had merely offered its good offices and though its representative was "free to express his views on any aspect of the matter," the Bank was not about to express any opinion as to the rights of the parties nor to make any suggestion that might be construed as an award.[47]

45. Lilienthal, *Journals*, 3, p. 464.
46. IBRD Press Release No. 380, Appendix I, February 5, 1954, p. 5.
47. Ibid.

When they showed the Bank plan to Lilienthal, Garner, Wheeler, and Bass said that it was designed to preserve the principles of his *Collier's* proposal by protecting the existing uses. But as Lilienthal points out in his *Journals*, a partition of the rivers, giving each nation an independent and separate supply, was very different from his proposal that the Indus system be operated jointly and as a unit. Nevertheless, Lilienthal suggested that Black present the plan not only to the Indian and Pakistani teams but directly to the Prime Ministers as the best possible solution under the circumstances.[48] The Bank proposal was accordingly submitted to the delegations on February 5 and simultaneously transmitted to Prime Ministers Nehru and Mohammad Ali (who had replaced Nazimuddin). The Bank summarized its plan as follows:

> The entire flow of the Western rivers (Indus, Jhelum and Chenab) would be available for the exclusive use and benefit of Pakistan, and for development by Pakistan, except for the insignificant volume of Jhelum flow presently used in Kashmir.
>
> The entire flow of the Eastern rivers (Ravi, Beas and Sutlej) would be available for the exclusive use and benefit of India, and for development by India, except that for a specified transition period India would continue to supply from these rivers, in accordance with an agreed schedule, the historic withdrawals from these rivers in Pakistan.
>
> The transition period would be calculated on the basis of the time estimated to be required to complete the link canals needed in Pakistan to make transfers for the purpose of replacing supplies from India. A temporary cooperative administration would be needed to supervise the carrying out of the transitional arrangements.
>
> Each country would construct the works located on its own territories which are planned for the development of the supplies. The costs of such works would be borne by the country to be benefited thereby. Although no works are planned for joint construction by the two countries, certain link canals in Pakistan will, as stated above, be needed to replace supplies from India. India would bear the costs of such works to the

48. Lilienthal, *Journals*, 3, pp. 469–70.

extent of the benefits to be received by her therefrom. An appropriate procedure would be established for adjudicating or arbitrating disputes concerning the allocation of costs under this principle.[49]

In expanding upon the advantages of its plan, the Bank pointed out that a partition of the Indus Rivers would, at least after the transition period, eliminate those disputes which, as experience had shown, were sure to arise from any attempt to construct and operate an integrated system embracing portions of two sovereign nations. There would be no need to determine the eastern boundary of the Indus Basin (or to become involved in the Kashmir Dispute) for the settlement would deal only with water and not with land. India would, of course, have to guarantee Pakistan her historic withdrawals from the Eastern Rivers during the transition period (estimated at five years) as well as unhindered use of the Western Rivers (except for minor uses from the Jhelum and Chenab in Kashmir). Because the link canals, when completed, would render Pakistan independent of supplies from the Eastern Rivers, the main cause of the Indus Waters Dispute would be eliminated. The Bank stated that its proposal embodied

> the principle that historic withdrawals of water must be continued, but not necessarily from existing sources. This principle allows water resources to be used so as most effectively to promote development. . . .
>
> The Bank proposal also embodies the principle that, in view of existing circumstances, allocation of supplies to the two countries should be such as to afford the greatest possible freedom of action by each country in the operation, maintenance and future development of its irrigation facilities.[50]

But as far as Pakistan was concerned, the key feature of the Bank's plan as presented on February 5, 1954, was that

> no reservoir storage (aside from the Bhakra dam which should be completed by the end of the transition period) will be re-

49. IBRD Press Release No. 380, Appendix I, February 5, 1954, p. 7.
50. Ibid., p. 6.

236

quired to supplement flow water in continuing the historic withdrawals. The inter-connected system which the link canals would
provide could be so operated as to meet the existing requirements of the Sutlej Valley lands except, perhaps, in small
amounts in a few canals in exceptional years.

Even without further storage construction, . . . after the transition period, Pakistan could supply her historic withdrawals and
could bring most of the Sutlej Valley Canals up to allocation.
She could also meet the requirements of projects in progress
on the Indus.[51]

Thus the Bank's engineers, on the basis of the data collected and
of their field inspection of sites and works, felt that they could guarantee, without providing storage facilities in West Pakistan, as much
water as her canals had actually enjoyed prior to Partition, and in
addition could give more water to the S.V.P. canals, bringing them
up to allocation "except, perhaps, in small amounts in a few canals
in exceptional years." This question of bringing the S.V.P. canals
up to allocation lay at the root of Pakistan's insistence that "historic
uses" did not mean just actual uses at the time of Partition (whether
or not "actual" meant minimum, maximum, or average) but the full,
sanctioned uses mentioned in the pre-Partition agreements, even
though these sanctioned uses had never been attained in practice.
And even if the Bank's engineers proposed to guarantee the full,
sanctioned uses, they would run afoul of the 1923 Sind-Punjab dispute, for guaranteeing the S.V.P. might, depending on when and
how the "surplus" flow of the Western Rivers was used, injure Sukkur and of course Gudu (construction of which had not yet begun).
When pressed on the point, the Bank's engineers said they felt they
could guarantee Ghulam Mohammad (Kotri), which was almost
finished, as well as Thal.[52] (Nothing was said of Taunsa.)

Such guarantees might go a long way toward satisfying West
Punjab, but they would not satisfy Sind. The core of the problem, as
Pakistan saw it, was not the *quantity* of water in the Western Rivers
but the *timing* of the runoff. Pakistan's engineers and consultants

51. Ibid., p. 9.
52. IBRD Press Release No. 380, December 10, 1954, Appendix II, no date,
"Terms of Reference and Procedure for Resumption of Cooperative Work on
Basis of Bank Proposal," p. 1.

maintained that unless the timing could be controlled, and that meant storage by dams, there would still be shortages in the critical rabi-maturing–kharif-sowing and kharif-maturing–rabi-sowing phases (see Chapter 4, pages 114–17) even after the link canals envisaged for replacement purposes were in operation. Conceding that the average annual flow of the Western Rivers might be more than sufficient for replacement needs, Pakistan maintained that what was needed was provision of storage so that water could be held over from one kharif to the start of the next. Even the Bank plan admitted that reservoir storage would be necessary for full development of the system,[53] but it denied that storage was necessary for replacement purposes or that, accordingly, India should be required to pay for it. For these reasons, when Pakistan replied to the Bank on May 14, 1954, she asked for a reexamination of the proposals to determine whether her calculations, or those of the Bank's engineers, were correct.

As for India, which accepted the Bank plan on March 25, 1954, she would get what she wanted, with two exceptions. The Bank plan would give her unfettered use (after a transition period) of the three Eastern Rivers. She would have to relinquish her claim to the Chenab with its Marhu Tunnel diversion possibility, and might accordingly have to slow the Rajasthan Project until additional storage on the Beas (at Pong) and Ravi (at Thein) was available to supplement Bhakra. But this delay, and continued supplies to Pakistan over a transition period of perhaps five years, were a small price to pay for the three rivers, especially since her contributions to the link canals would be limited to her benefits. If Pakistan chose to enlarge their capacities over and above "replacement," or to incorporate any storage dams in the project, India would make no contribution to these extras. The Bank plan as published acknowledged that reservoir storage would be essential for the full development of the system and to reduce the possibility of shortages, but could not estimate costs or capacities beyond saying that the potential storage capacities on each set of rivers would be roughly equal. Again, no storage capacity except Bhakra's was included in the estimate of quantities the Bank plan would provide each country (see Table 9). When the Bank finally made public its proposal, it took pains to explain that its

53. IBRD Press Release No. 380, Appendix I, February 5, 1954, p. 9.

Table 9. Comparison of the Bank Proposal for Division of the Indus Rivers
(February 1954) with the Plans Submitted by India and Pakistan (October 1953)
(in millions of acre feet of water)[a]

| Plan | *Total Uses Excluding Losses and Unusable Supplies* | | |
	For India	*For Pakistan*	*Total Usable*
World Bank	22	97	119
Indian	29	90	119
Pakistani	15.5	102.5	118

a. Source: IBRD Press Release No. 380, December 10, 1954, Appendix I,
February 5, 1954, p. 10.

formula for sharing the waters was no mere averaging of the demands
of each party, but rather resulted from the Bank's engineers' analysis
of the usable supplies on each of the six Indus Rivers.

Simplicity of concept and execution was the great merit of the
Bank plan. Once the transition period was over, the two countries
could go their separate ways; no further agreements and no continual
consensus on operation was essential. Of course, Pakistan would have
to take India's word that she would not interfere with the Chenab or
Jhelum supplies. (India argued for, and eventually obtained, the right
to make minor uses of these waters in the Himalayas and even in—
though without any recognition of her claim to—Jammu and Kashmir.) But since, in 1954 as in 1948, recourse to war seemed to be the
only way to change that, it would be preferable to have India committed by a treaty and by the sanction of the World Bank to leaving
the Chenab and Jhelum flows alone. Besides, India would have her
hands full utilizing the Eastern Rivers for some time to come.

Of course, one admitted shortcoming in the Bank plan was that,
as long as southern Jammu-Kashmir remained in Indian hands,
Pakistan could make no use of the Dhiangarh dam site on the Chenab
nor of the Wular Lake site on the Jhelum. But, as General Wheeler
has pointed out, the net cost of the Dhiangarh site to Pakistan is only
about 2.5 million acre feet per year [54] and the advantage of the
Wular Lake site is restricted by the danger of flooding the Vale and
Srinagar. Pakistan did not oppose the Bank plan because it would
not have given her any dam sites in Indian-held Jammu-Kashmir;
she opposed it mainly because it did not include provisions for con-

54. In an interview with the author, Washington, D.C., June 12, 1963.

structing and paying for storage dams at sites in Pakistan or Azad Kashmir. We have seen that the Bank's engineers were aware of this need, and acknowledged it in their statement, but Pakistan wanted the dams included in the plan and in the financial arrangements.

It is also relevant to point out that, by the late spring of 1954, Pakistan's relative bargaining position had improved considerably. Despite the domestic political turmoil that ensued after the assassination of Liaquat Ali Khan in October 1951, and that continued almost unabated up to the revolution of October 1958, Pakistan's economic position was stronger. The economic recovery of Europe and even the Korean war, both of which increased demand for Pakistan's raw materials, notably jute and cotton, had strengthened her financial position. Under the guidance of Ghulam Mohammad, a civil servant experienced in fiscal affairs and Finance Minister until he became an unusually active Governor-General at the death of Liaquat, Pakistan began to put its economic house in order. (Ghulam Mohammad intervened in April 1953 to replace Nazimuddin with Mohammad Ali, and again in October 1954, when he shook up Mohammad Ali's Cabinet and made General Ayub Khan Defense Minister. But he was forced by illness to retire in 1955, and died later that year.[55] The Kotri Barrage completed in 1955 was named in his honor.) New jute mills and cotton factories, cement and fertilizer plants, foundries and shipyards were established in both Wings.

In the early 1950s, American technical and economic assistance began in a small way, to be greatly increased after 1954. With the enactment by the United States of Public Law 480 in that year, Pakistan, like so many other famine-prone nations, including India, had a reliable source of food supplies in years of shortage or natural disaster. But the real significance of 1954 for Pakistan was that in May of that year she agreed to accept American military aid and with it considerable "defense support" assistance. Membership in SEATO and CENTO soon followed, with concomitant benefits. Despite American and British assurances to India, it was obvious that India's strategic superiority in the Indus Basin and in Bengal was slated for diminution. One result was a toughening of the Indian attitude on Kashmir and the gradual repudiation of the pledge to hold a plebiscite there.

55. Stephens, *Pakistan*, pp. 240–44.

Had Pakistan felt as weak in May 1954 as she had in May 1948 or even in May 1952 when the Indus Waters Treaty negotiations began, she might well have been tempted to accept the Bank's plan as quickly as India had. But perhaps for the first time in her young experience Pakistan began to feel that time might be on her side. Indeed, the prompt Indian acceptance may have suggested to Pakistan that she should hold out for further concessions, either from India or from the Bank, on the storage issue. Also contributing to Pakistan's recalcitrance was the fact that on April 2, 1954, she had opened the Balloki-Suleimanke Link (see above, p. 210), thus alleviating though certainly not solving the problem of kharif supplies for the Sutlej Valley canals. The actual timing of Pakistan's reply to the Bank plan may have been triggered by India's announcement, to Pakistan and to the World Bank, on May 10, 1954, that she would open the Bhakra Main Line Canal (served by the new headworks at Nangal, see Map 7) to make use of the kharif supplies on the Sutlej in June.

In accepting the Bank's plan on March 25, India had urged the necessity of reaching some ad hoc agreement about the Sutlej supplies since both the B-S Link and the Bhakra Main Canal were nearing completion. India apparently felt that Pakistan's failure to negotiate such an agreement, or to accept the Bank's plan, combined with her one-sided opening of the link, fully justified India in proceeding to make withdrawals at Nangal.[56] The difference, of course, was that the B-S Link, which transferred water from the Chenab to the Sutlej, could not diminish any supplies available to India, whereas the Nangal Barrage could diminish supplies available to Pakistan. In actuality, India did not make any use of the Bhakra Main Line Canal until July 8 after alleging that Pakistan had rejected the Bank's plan and broken off negotiations and that accordingly India was released from her pledge not to make any changes that would affect Pakistan while negotiations were continuing.[57]

But what had actually happened was that the omission of any provisions in the Bank's plan with regard to storage facilities, combined with India's announcement concerning opening of the Nangal Barrage, served to convince the Government of Pakistan of what Lilien-

56. Das Gupta, *Indo-Pakistan Relations 1947–1955*, p. 178.
57. Ibid., p. 179.

thal had said all along, that the negotiations could not be left solely to engineers. Accordingly, Pakistan decided to send new personnel to Washington. Arriving in June, the new delegation was headed by Ghulam Mueenuddin, a career civil servant who was then Pakistan's Secretary of Health and Labor (later Establishment Secretary in the Ayub government and Commissioner of Elections in 1964–65) and including Mohammad Shoaib, Pakistan's Executive Director on the Board of the World Bank (later Minister of Finance in the Ayub government). To provide additional engineering advice the new team had the services of S. I. Mahbub and S. S. Kirmani, a young engineer who in the final years of the negotiations worked most closely with Mueenuddin in reshaping the Bank plan to meet Pakistan's needs (and who was later placed in charge of executing the projects he had devised as the director of WAPDA's Indus Basin Projects Division).

But neither the abilities of Pakistan's new team of negotiators, nor her enhanced bargaining position, could produce much progress in the negotiations in June and July of 1954. The Bank was still urging acceptance of its plan in principle by both parties before negotiations resumed. India, eager to clarify the Sutlej situation, was willing to accept a Treaty that would give her full and clear control of the Eastern Rivers, even after a transition period. But she was not willing to pay for the cost of storage projects in Pakistan. And Pakistan was now urging that an outside consultant be brought in to determine whether the Bank plan formula could meet her needs without storage on the Western Rivers. Eventually, the Bank agreed to modify its plan by including a set of "terms of reference" which, it was hoped, would allow negotiations to be resumed on October 1, 1954, with a view to completing a comprehensive plan by September 30, 1955. (Starting with the period April 1 to September 30, 1955, ad hoc agreements were usually, but not always (and sometimes retroactively), worked out to cover Sutlej withdrawals.) The terms of reference took note of Pakistan's position to the extent of stating that the comprehensive plan would aim to supply, from the Western Rivers and after the transition period, the historic (pre-Partition, actual) withdrawals of all canals in Pakistan (and in Jammu-Kashmir) and that it would also attempt to bring most of the Pakistan Sutlej Valley canals up to allocation and to meet the requirements of Thal and Kotri (Ghulam Mohammad). If any surplus flow from the

Western Rivers remained after these needs were met, the comprehensive plan would then "examine the extent to which, and the manner in which . . . the reasonable additional requirements . . . of Sukkur and Gudu" could be met.[58] Thus Pakistan had succeeded in obtaining explicit recognition of the needs of Sind's existing Sukkur and prospective Gudu projects. But the real concession to Pakistan lay in the following provisions:

> In the event that the *flow supplies* [i.e. without storage regulation] of the Western Rivers are found to be inadequate (taking into consideration improved operational methods possible under a system of inter-linked canals) to meet the uses envisaged . . . above, *the plan will outline the feasible means that might be adopted* to meet any deficiencies.
>
> The planning will include consideration of, and recommendations with regard to, the engineering works required, the costs involved and the sharing thereof, the arrangements for the period of transition and all other pertinent matters.[59]

Thus the door was opened for a consideration of storage works and of how they might be financed. Although the terms of reference authorized each party to bring in its consultants, they did not concede Pakistan's demand that the outside consultants hired by the Bank be asked specifically to check on its estimate of the quantities and timing of supplies available from the Western Rivers without storage. These consultants, retained to advise the Bank on all engineering and hydrological issues, included three members of the present New York firm of Tippetts-Abbett-McCarthy-Stratton, or TAMS for short: Gerald T. McCarthy, General James H. Stratton, and John B. Drisko.

Even under the new terms of reference, it was not possible to reconvene the parties in Washington until December 6, 1954. When they met, A. N. Khosla (who had been elected to the Rajya Sabha, or Upper House, of India's Parliament) was replaced by N. D. Gulhati as leader of India's delegation. The Bank team now consisted of Mr. Iliff, General Wheeler, Lars Bengston, a lawyer, and Sir Kenelm Guinness, an engineer. (Guinness started as Secretary of the Bank

58. IBRD Press Release No. 380, Appendix II, p. 1.
59. Ibid., italics supplied.

team, but in late 1956 and early 1957, while General Wheeler was occupied with the Suez Canal clearing operation, Guinness was the only engineer on the team.) During all of 1955, Pakistan continued to press the point that the Western Rivers, *without storage facilities*, would be unable to meet even replacement uses in the critical rabi-maturing–kharif-sowing and kharif-maturing–rabi-sowing phases. At Pakistan's repeated urging, the Bank finally agreed to ask TAMS to appraise the seasonal adequacy of supplies. The TAMS team, led by Drisko, came to the conclusion that Pakistan's engineers indeed were correct. On May 21, 1956, the Bank issued an "Aide Memoire" recognizing that the "flow surplus" in the Western Rivers would not be sufficient to meet even the replacement needs in early and late kharif unless storage was provided.[60] Only after this Aide Memoire was issued did Pakistan accept, in principle, the Bank's plan to divide the waters as modified by the needs set forth in the Aide Memoire. It then became a problem of persuading India to agree to the cost of the storage facilities and enlarged link canals, including an "Upper Indus Link" through the Potwar Plateau, necessary to secure the replacement uses envisaged in the Aide Memoire, at a total cost of $2.3 billion!

When India objected to the increased costs, the Bank asked both parties to search for a less expensive method of meeting Pakistan's requirements. Pakistan was also trying to develop the concept that replacement uses alone were insufficient to compensate her for surrendering all rights to the Eastern Rivers, because she would thereby lose all the *sailab* areas (areas cultivated on the floodplains after the river recedes) and would also have to provide canal irrigation to areas formerly supplied by wells near the rivers after the diversion of their waters by India lowered the groundwater table. Pakistan further asserted that some *development* rather than just *replacement* funding ought to be included in an equitable agreement, because the object was to restore her to her 1947 position, whereas her population had grown and she had been losing cultivated land to waterlogging and salinity throughout the post-Partition period. These

---

60. Personal communication from R. J. Tipton, President, Tipton and Kalmbach, Inc., Denver, Colorado, September 30, 1965. Mr. Tipton served as a consultant to the Pakistan delegation during the Indus Waters Treaty negotiations. See also *Hundred Years of P.W.D.*, p. 63.

arguments obviously did not carry much weight with the Indians.

Even though the regional representation within the Pakistani delegation had been de-emphasized since 1954, and particularly since the adoption of the "One Unit" plan in West Pakistan on October 14, 1955, the Pakistani position was still very much influenced by the interests of Sind. Sind had objected both to the threat to Sukkur and Gudu implicit in the Bank's plan, and to the suggestion that link canals transferring water out of the Indus into the Jhelum and Chenab would be necessary to meet *replacement* uses. The Pakistan Punjab, on the other hand, wanted to reserve any new Jhelum supplies, supplies which could be obtained only by storage, for development purposes rather than for replacement.

When the delegations met in Rome, in May 1958, the Bank team spent most of its time trying to solve an inherent "Sind-Punjab dispute" by convincing the Pakistan delegation that stored Jhelum supplies should be used for replacement and that all Indus water, whether stored or not, should be used for development. In other words, the Bank, having conceded in the Aide Memoire that storage was necessary for replacement, wanted to confine all replacement storage to the Jhelum. The advantage of this arrangement, as the Bank saw it, was that it would greatly reduce the cost of the replacement works, which was the only cost that India was prepared to bear. Pakistan could, of course, build whatever development works she could pay for. Apparently Pakistan then accepted the Bank's suggestion, at least to the extent of conceding the use of Jhelum water for replacement purposes. (As we shall see in Chapter 7, the division of the Indus Basin Project into a Jhelum-Chenab Zone and an Indus Zone recapitulated the work of the Rome meeting.)

India apparently did not contribute much at the Rome meeting, but she kept her Marhu plan (see below) in abeyance. The delegations next convened at London, in July 1958, where Pakistan submitted her "less expensive" alternative to the scheme of works envisaged in the Aide Memoire plan. The Pakistan London plan eliminated the costly Upper Indus Link through the Potwar Plateau. It proposed instead a dam on the Jhelum at Mangla to store water for replacement and a dam on the Indus at Tarbela to be used for development in Sind and, via two trans-Thal links (Kalabagh-Jhelum and Taunsa-Panjnad), for replacement in the lower Punjab and Bahawalpur. The plan also included three smaller storages on Indus and Jhelum tributaries and a series of link canals for bringing Jhelum water to the upper Punjab and upper Bahawalpur. The total cost of Pakistan's London alternative plan was about $1.12 billion.

Now India objected to the cost of such "replacement" works, and in turn submitted her alternative plan in November 1958. This new Indian plan, which embodied certain features of the original Indian plan of 1953, would authorize India to make use of several sites on the Chenab in Jammu-Kashmir and in Himachal Pradesh, sites which she pointed out were useless to Pakistan in any case. By building a diversion tunnel from the Chenab to a tributary of the Ravi at Marhu, another from the Chandra tributary of the Chenab to the Beas near Palchar (see Maps 3 and 7), and if necessary also constructing a storage dam on the Chenab at Dhiangarh, India could make use of Chenab water that would otherwise go to waste. The replacement requirements of Pakistan were estimated at 10 million acre feet. If Pakistan would authorize her to make use of the Chenab sites, India would guarantee to deliver to Pakistan at Ferozepore, on the Central Bari Doab "Channels," and (if Dhiangarh were built) at Marala, a total of some 5 million acre feet, or half Pakistan's replacement needs. The other half would come from the three link canals (BRBD, M-R, and B-S links) which Pakistan was now completing. Thus Pakistan would be dependent on India for only half her replacement needs instead of all of them as under the Inter-Dominion and ad hoc agreements; the cost of the Indian projects was much lower than those proposed by Pakistan; and India could tie them into her own system. Finally, India would guarantee the supplies and the time schedule in the treaty.[61]

Pakistan's rejoinder could have been anticipated. The 5 million acre feet in her three links was not "replacement" but just diversion of water which she had enjoyed before Partition from one part of her irrigation system to another. "Replacement" meant tapping new supplies, and that meant storage works. And Pakistan was not going to allow those works to be built on Indian soil, nor was she going to accept the Dhiangarh site (in Jammu-Kashmir) as forever lost to her. And she certainly was not going to remain dependent upon

61. A. N. Khosla, "Development of the Indus River System: An Engineering Approach," *India Quarterly, 14* (1958), 249–52.

India for any part of her irrigation needs beyond the transition period, treaty or no treaty, and no matter what the cost of an all-Pakistan replacement-and-development system.

Although, from the Bank's standpoint, the Marhu plan had the great advantage of economy, it was obvious that it would never be acceptable to Pakistan. The only way out of the impasse was to divorce the two basic issues, the scheme of works necessary for replacement (or replacement plus development as the Pakistanis saw it) and the cost of such a scheme. All India was really concerned about was getting unrestricted use of the Eastern Rivers after a reasonable transition period (plus certain minor uses on the upper reaches of the Western Rivers) and having a limit placed on her contribution to replacement works. As far as Pakistan was concerned, replacement and development had become inextricably interwoven, but if the Bank could find a way to agree on a set of works and to pay for them, then Pakistan would be satisfied. With this in mind, early in 1959, the Bank began sounding out some of its members with a view to underwriting an Indus Basin settlement scheme. These members were to form a consortium of "friendly Governments," as the Bank termed them (not to be confused with the "Aid to Pakistan Consortium" formed later to assist the Five Year Plans).

In May 1959 Bank President Black again visited India and Pakistan. He suggested to Mr. Nehru that India's contribution be set at a fixed amount, regardless of the cost of the "replacement" works. In exchange for this and the promise of a loan toward the Beas Dam at the Pong site, he obtained Nehru's acquiescence in a ten-year transition period during which India would continue to supply water to Pakistan. Then President Black met with President Mohammad Ayub Khan, members of his cabinet, and representatives of the West Pakistan Irrigation Department and of the year-old WAPDA organization (see above, page 216) which would be entrusted with carrying out the replacement works. Although they had brought with them a Bank-prepared scheme of replacement works, Black and his advisers were forced to admit that this scheme, which omitted the dam on the Indus because the Bank considered it a development work, might still involve small shortages on some canals in exceptional years. President Black found that Pakistani thinking had indeed crystallized around the storage facilities. WAPDA was about to start preparatory work on the Mangla site (access roads, bridges, etc.), and the investigations along the Indus had become focused on the Tarbela site (see Chapter 7). Pakistan was willing to assume some of the other costs of replacement works, and offered to delete off-channel storage at Rohtas below Mangla if Tarbela were included in the plan. This the Bank agreed to do (as long as the cost did not exceed a certain amount), and President Black suggested that Pakistan proceed to draw up a realistic plan for replacement works, including storage dams on the Jhelum and Indus, and a certain amount of development. He told the press:

> I think I can now say that we have succeeded in establishing certain general principles acceptable to both governments, that afford a firm basis for negotiating a final settlement.
>
> I am now returning to firm up with the friendly Governments the amount of financial aid they will be prepared to extend; and I am hopeful that within the next two months it will be possible for the Bank to invite representatives of India and Pakistan to meet with the Bank for the purpose of working out Heads of Agreement for an International Water Treaty.[62]

By August 1959 President Black had succeeded in persuading the "friendly Governments"—the United States, Canada, the United Kingdom, West Germany, Australia, and New Zealand—to underwrite a waters settlement that would advance the cause of peace in the Indus Basin at a total cost of about one billion dollars. This rough estimate included the cost of works in both India and Pakistan, but the contributions of the consortium, in the form of *grants* totaling over half a billion dollars, would go to Pakistan. The United States and the World Bank would, in addition, make *loans* to both Pakistan and India totaling another $200 million. India would make a contribution toward the cost of the works in Pakistan, and the remainder of the costs would be borne by the country concerned. (In the Indus Basin Development Fund Agreement, concluded in September 1960, the total cost of the works *in Pakistan* was set at $893.5 million, of which the consortium provided $541 million in grants, India contributed $174 million, and Pakistan received loans totaling $150 million. But in April 1964 a Supplemental Agreement

62. Statement to the press by Eugene R. Black, President of the World Bank, Karachi, May 18, 1959.

came into effect under which the consortium provided an additional $315 million in foreign exchange for the projects. The Indian contribution, of course, remained fixed at $173.8 million, or 19.5 per cent of the original Fund Agreement figure.[63])

Accordingly, W. A. B. Iliff, now Vice President of the World Bank, was able to announce at the end of meetings of the parties held in London in August that some aspects of the "Heads of Agreement" or outline for a treaty had been settled.[64] Discussions continued in London in September, when Pakistan presented new figures, and in Washington in October. Actually, it was not until September 19, 1960, that the Treaty and Development Fund Agreement could be signed. But in the year between Iliff's announcement and the signature of the treaty, the main dispute over what facilities would be included in an Indus Basin settlement scheme was one between Pakistan and the Bank. Except for a few details, the Indian position had been settled. In exchange for a fixed commitment to the cost of replacement works, she would get the Eastern Rivers at the end of a ten-year Transition Period. In the meantime she could proceed at will with the Bhakra-Beas-Rajasthan Project, hampered only by the need to continue supplies from Ferozepore and Madhopur. All major Chenab projects were abandoned, and it no longer mattered to India what Pakistan and the Bank arranged. To paraphrase an earlier sentiment, "What Pakistan did with Pakistan's rivers was Pakistan's (and the Bank's) affair."

What Pakistan proposed to do with her rivers became clear in the autumn of 1959 when the Pakistan delegation presented (as the Bank had requested in May) its "realistic" plan for replacement cum development works. The new Pakistani plan was the work of the Indus Basin Advisory Board (IBAB) which had been established to coordinate planning among WAPDA, the Irrigation Department, other agencies concerned, and the treaty delegation with its consultants. The IBAB first convened in Lahore in June 1959, and met again in London toward the end of September. It had divided its work among subcommittees, eight of which presented reports at London

---

63. IBRD, *Indus Basin Development Fund Agreement*, dated September 19, 1960; Lt. Gen. Emerson C. Itschner, "Indus Basin Plan," *Military Engineer, 55*, No. 364 (1963), 109; IBRD Press Release No. 64/10, April 8, 1964, p. 1.

64. IBRD Press Release, London, August 26, 1959.

where the IBAB participants were joined by associates from WAPDA, the Irrigation Department, and the World Bank. Although we shall, for convenience, refer to the "IBAB plan," what emerged from the London meetings was not an integrated report but rather a series of memoranda with a covering "Memorandum of Final Meeting of Indus Basin Advisory Board—18 September 1959" prepared by G. Mueenuddin (chairman of both the IBAB and the Pakistani Treaty Delegation) and his assistants.[65] From the engineering side, the guiding spirit in developing the IBAB Plan was S. S. Kirmani, who, most fittingly, was entrusted with carrying out the Indus Basin Project after the Treaty and the Development Fund Agreement went into effect one year later.

The IBAB estimated the total cost of its plan, including the Mangla and Tarbela dams, new link canals and barrages, improvement of existing links, and some provision for tubewells and drainages, at $936 million, or almost as much as the combined estimated costs of projects in India and Pakistan. Furthermore, in deriving this figure, IBAB had included a sum of $94.7 million for land acquisition, most of which resulted from the greatly increased developmental aspects of the IBAB scheme and thus, according to the Bank, could not properly be chargeable to the financing envisaged by Black and Ayub in May. Accordingly, the Bank, in January 1960, summoned representatives of the various engineering firms WAPDA had already selected to serve as consultants for the various components of the replacement works (see Chapter 8) to a meeting with *its* engineers and consultants in Washington, D.C. The Bank requested WAPDA's consultants to revise their estimates downward "on a realistic and the best available basis."

65. Personal communication from R. J. Tipton, October 8, 1965. The members of the IBAB who participated in the London meetings were: G. Mueenuddin, Chairman; M. A. Hamid, Engineering Adviser to the Government of Pakistan; R. J. Tipton, Consultant to WAPDA; F. F. Haigh, Consultant to WAPDA; John B. Drisko, Consultant to the World Bank; Khalil-ur-Rahman, seconded (i.e. temporarily assigned) from the Irrigation Department to the Treaty Delegation; and S. S. Kirmani, chief WAPDA representative on the Treaty Delegation. Also participating as associates were Sir K. Guinness of the World Bank; O. Kalmbach, WAPDA Consultant; S. M. Niaz, WAPDA representative on the Treaty Delegation; Altaf Hussain, seconded from the Irrigation Department to the Treaty Delegation; and S. I. Mahbub of the West Pakistan Irrigation Department. (Personal communication from John B. Drisko, September 21, 1965.)

To urge them on, in February, the Bank's consultants submitted their own estimates for the projects in Pakistan, totaling $838 million (or approximately the figure discussed by Black and Ayub in May). Half of the $98 million difference was accounted for in the estimates for the dams and new link canals, but the other half lay in the land acquisition costs which the Bank would not accept. On March 1, 1960, the Bank made public the figures pledged by the "friendly Governments," perhaps in an effort to induce the Pakistanis to restrict the size of the scheme of works and thus lower the costs since, presumably, no more than the amounts indicated in Table 10 would be forthcoming.

Table 10. Pledges by the "Friendly Governments" and Loans
Promised by the U.S.A. and World Bank to Pakistan and India
Toward the Costs of a Waters Settlement in the Indus Basin[a]

Contributor	Amount Pledged		*U.S. $ Equivalent (Millions)*	Type	Recipient
Australia	£A	6,964,286	15.54	Grant	Pakistan
Canada	U.S. $	22,100,000	22.19	"	"
West Germany	DM	126,000,000	30.21	"	"
New Zealand	£NZ	1,000,000	2.78	"	"
United Kingdom	£	20,860,000	58.48	"	"
United States	$	177,000,000	177.00	"	"
United States	$	235,000,000 in Pak. Rs.	235.00	"	"
		Total	541.20	"	"
United States	$	70,000,000	70.00	Loan	Pakistan
United States	$	33,000,000	33.00	"	India
World Bank	$	80,000,000	80.00	"	Pakistan
World Bank	$	23,000,000	23.00	"	India
	Total Grants and loans to Pakistan		691.20		
	Total loans to India		56.00		
	Total aid to Pakistan and India		747.20		

a. Source: IBRD Press Release No. 626, March 1, 1960, Washington, D.C. The pledges made in other currencies have been converted into United States dollars at the selling, or mid-point, rates for 1960 as reported by the International Monetary Fund.

WAPDA's consultants did not submit their new "realistic and best available" estimates until June 1960. These were *higher* by $361 million over the IBAB estimates and by $459.3 million over the Bank's estimates (see Table 11).

Table 11. Comparison of Estimates by Indus Basin Advisory Board,
World Bank Consultants, and WAPDA Consultants for the Indus Basin
Project, West Pakistan, by Components, in Millions of Dollars[a]

Component	I B A B (Sept. 1959)	Bank Consultants (Feb. 1960)	WAPDA Consultants (June 1960)
Jhelum Dam	326.0	277.0	492.8
Indus Dam	210.0	194.0	374.8
New Links	235.1	202.5	255.2
Barrages	86.9	86.9	96.5
Existing Links	28.0	28.0	28.0
Tubewells and Drainages	50.00	50.0	50.0
Totals	936.0	838.0	1,297.3

a. Source: West Pakistan WAPDA, *Indus Basin Settlement Plan, Report on the Consultants' Cost Estimates*, Part I, Summary (July, 1960), Annexures A, B, C. The report uses "Mangla Dam" instead of "Jhelum Dam" and "Tarbela Dam" instead of "Indus Dam." But although preliminary work at Mangla was begun in the summer of 1959, the site of the Indus Dam was still under discussion. For reasons explained later in the text, the Indus Basin Deveolpment Fund Agreement refers only to "Jhelum" and "Indus" dams, and it seems more appropriate to substitute these designations here.

At this, the Bank was upset, feeling that Pakistan was upping the ante at the last moment in the hope of getting the Bank and the "friendly Governments" to go along with it rather than lose the prospect of a treaty. The Bank was particularly incensed at the timing of the consultants' estimates, which were not formally transmitted to it until September 2, 1960! To which WAPDA and the Pakistan delegation replied that even these estimates were still preliminary, and that not enough detailed investigations had yet been carried out on the projects to allow firm determinations of costs. Actually, the consultants' estimates were the first to be based essentially upon local investigations and determinations of costs in Pakistan rather than upon interpolations and assumptions made in London or Washington. They were also the first estimates prepared on the Pakistan side by agents who were more or less immune from the traditional departmental attitude (not unknown in the U.S.A. or U.K.) that once "Government" was committed to a project it would have to follow through, no matter how the cost escalated.

Furthermore, WAPDA and its consultants had now taken the

"development" bit firmly in their teeth and had redesigned the Jhelum and Indus dams to allow for future raising of the dams to provide additional storage. They had also improved the quality of the dams, for safety and other technical reasons, and included two new barrages. They had corrected certain "omissions" in the IBAB plan. And, significantly, because the Bank and the "friendly Governments" wanted the Settlement Plan carried out on the basis of international contractors' bid rather than by the traditional departmental methods on which the IBAB estimates were based, WAPDA and its consultants had increased the engineering and construction costs of the works by $60.3 million in the total costs and $72.9 million in foreign exchange. They had increased the estimates for Mangla and Tarbela by $75.9 million in order to incorporate provisions in the initial dams for their ultimate raising. And the consultants had included $90.4 million for customs duties and sales taxes to be paid to the Government of Pakistan! Actually, of the $361.3 million increase over the IBAB estimates, $309.1 million were to be in foreign exchange costs, and of the $459.3 million increase over the Bank's estimates, $325.3 million were to reflect foreign exchange costs.[66]

Thus Pakistan was asking the Bank and the "friendly Governments" to pay for a scheme of works going far beyond replacement needs. Not only was a considerable amount of development included in the Indus dam, but the incorporation of costly provisions for raising both dams represented additional future development. But what really upset the Bank was the incorporation of $99.5 million for land acquisition and $90.4 million for customs duties and sales taxes on materials procured for the project and even income taxes on contractors' profits. (The $90.4 million would thus have ended up in Pakistan's treasury as a general subsidy to the economy.) It was a strong effort, but it did not work. Pakistan had to back down from this position and accept, temporarily at least, the figure of $893.5 million in the Development Fund Agreement. But, as we shall see, although the Indus Waters Treaty settled the Indus Waters Dispute between India and Pakistan, the accompanying Fund Agreement prolonged what had now become a new dispute between Pakistan and the Bank.

66. West Pakistan WAPDA, *Indus Basin Settlement Plan, Report on the Consultants' Cost Estimates,* Part I, "Summary" (July 1960), pp. 1-7.

The Indus Waters Treaty and the Development Fund Agreement

It is perhaps significant of the circumstances under which an Indus Basin Settlement was reached that the Treaty of September 19, 1960 was published as an Annexure to the Development Fund Agreement, rather than vice versa. Although this is explainable on the grounds that India would have nothing to do with the Fund Agreement and also that the Governments of India and Pakistan would themselves publish the Treaty and deposit it with the United Nations, it may be taken as an indication that the Bank and the "friendly Governments," chiefly the United States, had actually purchased an agreement. Certainly after President Black's talk with Prime Minister Nehru in May 1959, this was true of India, for the Indian contribution had been set at a fixed amount that was considerably less than what the Pakistani negotiators had in mind.[67] It was also true of Pakistan, for even though the sum of $893.5 million was far less than her ultimate demand, it represented a *grant* to Pakistan of $305.9 million in hard currencies from the "friendly Governments" of the consortium, plus a contribution of $173.8 million (payable in pounds sterling) from India, and an additional grant of $235 million worth of Pakistani rupees "owed" to the United States under the Public Law 480 and similar programs. Discounting this last item, the net gain to Pakistan in foreign exchange which she could use for the project came to $479.7, or over half of the Development Fund.[68]

In addition, Pakistan received a total of $150 million in loans from the World Bank and the United States. Her own contribution

67. India also was promised offsetting loans of $33 million from the United States and $23 million from the World Bank, to be used for the Beas Dam at Pong (IBRD Press Release No. 650, September 19, 1960, p. 10). This was not part of the Indus Basin Development Fund. Both loans were finally made in 1966.

68. These figures differ slightly from those in Table 10 because the Australian contribution was rounded off to £A 6,965,000 in the Development Fund Agreement. Other contributions remained as indicated in Table 10. But since the six parties pay their shares in half-yearly installments, any conversions into U.S. dollars are subject to periodic readjustments. For example, the value of the West German pledge has appreciated and that of the Canadian has depreciated with respect to the U.S. dollar since the Treaty was signed. The World Bank, as Administrator of the Fund, may make disbursements in any currencies, and determines their respective values by its usual procedures.

to the Fund was only the equivalent of $28.8 million, of which about $1.2 million was made in pounds sterling and the remainder in rupees (at, of course, the official rather than the free market rate). Although some of the "friendly Governments" would recover something if their nationals and firms were hired as consultants or contractors for the design and execution of the Indus Basin Project, and to the extent that they could sell materials and equipment for it to Pakistan, there was no requirement tying Pakistan's choice other than that of competitive bidding for the supply of materials and that all goods and services be procured from a member of the *Bank* (not necessarily of the "friendly Governments") or from New Zealand (not a member of the IBRD in 1960) or Switzerland.

Furthermore, Pakistan proceeded to levy import duties on materials and equipment brought in for the Project, to collect sales taxes on materials procured in Pakistan, and to levy income taxes on the contractors. (In May 1961 the Bank as Administrator of the Fund managed to circumvent this procedure by requiring that all such amounts be repaid into the Fund.) Since it is hardly conceivable that Pakistan could have executed works of such magnitude within the Transition Period without foreign contractors and consultants, one might conclude that she was indeed getting a bargain for her money. The Pakistanis did not regard matters in this light, however, and as more detailed surveys, designs, and estimates of the projects were made—and as the unprecedented local expenditures for land acquisition, labor, building materials, etc., produced an inevitable inflation—she has found the Development Fund less and less adequate. By the time it is completed, the Indus Basin Project (which, as we shall see, has been greatly elaborated) will probably cost at least the equivalent of $1.5 billion over and above the $893.5 million in the Fund.

But more of this in Chapter 7. Having dealt at such length with the disputes and negotiations leading up to the Indus Waters Treaty, we must now examine its main provisions. The ten articles of the Treaty itself (which was signed at Karachi on September 19, 1960, retroactive to April 1, 1960, by Prime Minister Nehru and President Ayub and for certain specified purposes by Mr. Iliff for the World Bank) are short, a mere eighteen pages in the published text. But its eight Annexures (A through H, with their appendixes) occupy an additional 114 pages. (The ten articles are reprinted in the Appendix to this book.)

The Treaty of course awards the Eastern Rivers (Sutlej, Ravi, and Beas) to India and the Western Rivers (Chenab, Jhelum, and Indus) to Pakistan. But there are certain exceptions. The most important of these is the establishment of a ten-year Transition Period during which India will continue to supply Pakistan with water in the "Central Bari Doab Channels" (the Lahore and Main branches of the UBDC in Pakistan; see Map 5) and in the Pakistan Sutlej Valley system. The Transition Period was agreed to have begun on April 1, 1960, and it will end on March 31, 1970 unless Pakistan requests extension by one, two, or three years, but in no case beyond March 31, 1973. During the Transition Period, Pakistan will pay to India only a proportional share of the *working expenses* of the Madhopur and Ferozepore headworks and of the carrier channels within India. But if she requests extension, Pakistan will have to pay graduated charges for the water itself (Article V) out of the Development Fund.

In the incredibly detailed Annexure H, which is three times as long as the Treaty proper, arrangements for the Transition Period are spelled out. Every conceivable safeguard which Pakistan's engineers and lawyers could suggest was included to prevent India from altering the amount or the timing of her water supplies to Pakistan during the Transition Period. The portions of the "distributable supply" which India shall furnish to the Central Bari Doab Channels are specified not only for rabi and kharif, but for six intervals within these periods, and provision is made for India to reduce supplies if the "distributable supply" falls below certain levels, if closures are necessary for safety, operations, or maintenance, or if Pakistan has completed the highest links (Rasul-Qadirabad and Qadirabad-Balloki; see Map 6). As regards the Pakistan Sutlej Valley canals, the Transition Period is divided into two phases (Phase I up to a point between March 31, 1965 and March 31, 1966, depending on completion of the Trimmu-Sidhnai-Islam [now the Trimmu-Sidhnai-Mailsi-Bahawal] Link, and Phase II from the end of Phase I to the end of the Transition Period). Indian commitments to supply water to the Sutlej system are adjusted by phases and by subperiods within both rabi and kharif—subperiods reflecting the intricate operations of the Triple Canals Project (because of the Montgomery-Pakpattan Link) and of the new Indus Basin Project links. If Annexure H is any example, the proverbial mills of the gods can hardly grind any finer than engineers and lawyers, who in this case negotiated for eight years, with each minute detail becoming a major issue.

Other exceptions to the division of the waters are contained in Article II and Annexure B of the Treaty, which detail the uses Pakistan may make of the waters of the Ravi and Sutlej (and of their tributaries) where, because the old district lines form the border, the rivers flow through Pakistan before they *finally* flow *into* Pakistan (at points specified as about 1.5 miles upstream of the BRBD siphon on the Ravi and near the Hasta Bund upstream of Suleimanke on the Sutlej). Pakistan may make "Domestic and Non-Consumptive" uses (see Article I, "Definitions") above these points and may also make "Agricultural Use" of the waters *if available* for the irrigation of a total of 45,400 acres on four tributaries of the Ravi, but without thereby incurring any prescriptive claim or right to such withdrawals. This provision was inserted to allow Pakistan to replace *sailab* irrigation to the extent that it is rendered impossible by storage or withdrawals upstream in India.

Of more significance are the provisions in Article III and Annexures C and D which provide for continued withdrawals up to specified limits by India from the Western Rivers. These provisions relate to areas in Jammu irrigated by the Ranbir and Pratap inundation canals offtaking from the Chenab above Marala, and they even allow India to build a barrage (but not a dam) to control them. In addition, India may continue to irrigate from the Western Rivers all other areas that were irrigated on the effective date of the Treaty (April 1, 1960), and may even enlarge the irrigated cropped *acreage* (counted twice if cropped twice a year) by 70,000 acres in the Indus Valley, 400,000 in the Jhelum Valley, and 225,000 (of which not more than 100,000 may be in Jammu District) in the Chenab Valley, plus 6,000 acres from the Chenab but outside its basin. To do so, India may construct storage capacities of up to 250,000 acre feet on the upper Indus, 500,000 a.f. on the Jhelum above Verinag (actually very high on the stream where it enters the Vale of Kashmir), and 500,000 a.f. on the Bhaga and Chandra tributaries of the Chenab, plus some additional capacity for power generation and (on the Jhelum only) flood control, all subject to elaborate restrictions and regulations (Annexures D and E). In effect, India can continue to operate specified hydroelectric plants that were in operation on the effective date, can complete specified plants that were under construction on that date, and can, with the acquiescence of Pakistan and subject to the Treaty provision (Article IX) for settlement of disputes, build new *run of the river* (i.e. no significant pondage) hydroelectric plants. But any large storage or diversion works (such as those contemplated in the Marhu Tunnel plan of November 1958) on the Western Rivers in India were ruled out.

Article IV contains provisions relating to both Eastern and Western Rivers and includes the first mention of the "replacement" works, stating in paragraph (1) that:

> Pakistan shall use its best endeavours to construct and bring into operation, with due regard to expedition and economy, *that part of a system of works which will accomplish the replacement,* from the Western Rivers and other sources, of water supplies for irrigation canals in Pakistan which, on 15th August 1947, were dependent on water supplies from the Eastern Rivers [italics added].

It should be noted that here and elsewhere the Treaty recognizes that the "system of works," i.e. the Indus Basin Project, is not exclusively or entirely for "replacement" purposes. Article IV also requires Pakistan to maintain, or even to enlarge at India's cost, certain drains that serve territory on both sides of the border. It prohibits either party (actually only Pakistan might have contemplated this; see above, page 205) from diverting the Ravi between Madhopur and Lahore or the Sutlej between Harike and Suleimanke, a prohibition that finally vitiates the effect of Radcliffe's specification that the district boundaries, rather than the actual course of the rivers, should form the border.

Paragraphs (8) through (10) of Article IV provide that the "use of the natural channels of the Rivers for the discharge of flood *or other excess waters* shall be free and not subject to limitation by either Party"; that:

> Each Party declares its intention to operate its storage dams, barrages and irrigation canals in such manner, *consistent with the normal operations of its hydraulic systems,* so as to avoid, as far as feasible, material damage to the other Party. . . .

Indus Waters Treaty

and that "Each Party declares its intention to prevent, *as far as practicable, undue pollution* of the waters of the Rivers" (see the Appendix for full text; all italics were added). Since these provisions may have a bearing on the use of the Eastern Rivers as drains for India's surface and groundwater irrigation effluents, they will be discussed further in Chapter 9.

Article V deals with financial provisions between the parties. Paragraph (1) states:

> In consideration of the fact that the purpose of *part* of the system of works referred to in Article IV(1) is the *replacement*, from the Western Rivers and other sources, of water supplies for irrigation canals in Pakistan which, on 15th August 1947, were dependent on water supplies from the Eastern Rivers, India agrees to make a fixed contribution of Pounds Sterling 62,060,000 towards the costs of these works. *The amount in Pounds Sterling of this contribution shall remain unchanged* irrespective of any alteration in the par value of any currency. [Italics added.]

The article further provides that India shall pay the sum in ten equal annual installments to the World Bank for the credit of the Indus Basin Development Fund. And it provides for the payment to India by the Bank out of the Fund a graduated scale of sums if Pakistan extends the Transition Period:

Period of Aggregate Extension of Transition Period	*Payment to. India*
One year	£ Stg. 3,125,000
Two years	£ Stg. 6,406,250
Three years	£ Stg. 9,850,000

Article V contains the only mentions of the Development Fund in the Treaty itself, and it further specifies that, aside from the payments by India into the Fund and the possible payments by the Fund to India if the Transition Period is extended,

> neither Party shall be entitled to claim any payment for observance of the provisions of this Treaty or to make any charge for water received from it by the other Party.

259

Thus the legalistic dispute discussed at the beginning of this chapter is settled by inference in the Treaty: proprietary rights to the waters in the Eastern and Western rivers, with the specified exceptions, are vested in India and Pakistan, respectively, but India's proprietary rights to the supplies for the Central Bari Doab Channels and the Pakistan Sutlej Valley canals do not begin until April 1, 1970, after which Pakistan would have to pay for the water itself.

Article V also states that nothing in its first paragraph (quoted above) or in the first paragraph of Article IV (quoted on page 258) shall be construed to confer upon India any right to participate in the decisions as to the systems of works which Pakistan constructs or to constitute an assumption of any responsibility by India or an agreement by India in regard to such works. This clearly leaves the Indus Basin Project as a matter solely between the Bank and the Governments on the one hand and Pakistan on the other. In fact, the "system of works" is nowhere described in the Treaty *or* its Annexures, but is left to the Development Fund Agreement (perhaps another reason for publishing the Treaty as an Annexure to the Agreement rather than vice versa). This procedure and the above provision in Article V serve to avoid any commitment by India with respect to one of the key elements of the Indus Basin Project, the Mangla Dam, whose left abutments and auxiliary works lie in Azad Kashmir (see also Article XI).

Articles VI and VII deal with regular exchanges of data on discharges, withdrawals, deliveries, etc., between the parties in perpetuity, and provide for establishment of hydrological and meteorological observation stations, and even new drainage works, in the territory of one party at the behest of the other (to the extent that the requested party considers them practicable, and on agreement by the requesting party to pay the costs involved). Article VII also provides for exchange of data on new irrigation works, voluntarily or upon request.

Although the original intent of the Bank's plan was to avoid the establishment of any continuing joint administration of the Indus Basin irrigation system, it was felt desirable to create a Permanent Indus Commission to oversee the implementation of the Treaty (but not of the Development Fund Agreement or of the Indus Basin Project) and to settle any questions that might arise thereunder.

Accordingly, Article VIII provides that India and Pakistan should each appoint a Commissioner for Indus Waters, ordinarily a high-ranking engineer, and that he be given appropriate status by his own Government and accorded the privileges and immunities of a representative to the United Nations by the other Government. The duties of the two Commissioners are to serve as regular channels of communication for the exchange of information and data and the giving of notices and responses as provided by the Treaty. Together the two Commissioners form the Permanent Indus Commission which can study any problem referred to it by the Governments, make initial attempts to settle any difference or dispute, undertake general tours of inspection every five years and special tours at any time upon the request of either Commissioner, and oversee the implementation of Annexure H. The Commission is to meet regularly at least once a year, alternately in India and Pakistan, and to submit at least a yearly report to the two Governments. Of course, the Governments may supersede the Commission and deal directly with each other if they so desire.

In the event that the Commission cannot decide any question of interpretation, application, or alleged breach of the Treaty, Article IX and Annexure F provide for reference to a Neutral Expert. Failing resolution of any dispute by a Neutral Expert, Article IX and Annexure G provide for the selection of a Court of Arbitration.

Article X is an Emergency Provision inserted at the behest of Pakistan. It was designed to provide for the reopening of negotiations and modification of the Treaty if, prior to March 31, 1965, Pakistan should be prevented by the outbreak of "large-scale international hostilities arising out of causes beyond the control of Pakistan" from completing the "replacement element" of the scheme of works by March 31, 1973. Since the operative date had passed even before the September 1965 war, Article X has no further bearing.

Article XI (see the Appendix) is, however, still pregnant with meaning. It specifically confines the application of the Treaty to "the use of the waters of the Rivers and matters incidental thereto" and excludes any construction of the Treaty "whether tacit, by implication or otherwise" as affecting any other rights or claims whatsoever of the parties. It also states that the execution of the Development Fund Agreement (to which India is not a party) shall have no effect on the rights and obligations of the parties to the Treaty. In other words, despite the sentiments of goodwill and friendship expressed in the Preamble, neither India nor Pakistan intended the Treaty to alter by one iota its position with respect to Jammu-Kashmir or regarding any residual border disputes or property claims stemming from Partition. Although, as we have seen, the Treaty mentions the "replacement" works, it does not mention any specific works, and even the Annexures mention specifically only some of the link canals. India would not countenance mention of Mangla by name, or even of a "dam on the Jhelum" for fear that Pakistan would claim that this was tacit recognition of Pakistan's position in Azad Kashmir or of Pakistan's claim to all of Kashmir. Similarly, although the Treaty and its Annexures contemplate certain uses of water and even certain construction projects to be carried out by India on the Western Rivers in Jammu-Kashmir, Article XI precludes any claim by her that Pakistan tacitly recognized her position in southern Kashmir. Thus, though the Treaty settled the Waters Dispute, it accomplished nothing toward a Kashmir solution. It may be noted, however, that after Mr. Nehru and Field Marshal Ayub signed the Treaty in Karachi on September 19, 1960, they did meet again at Rawalpindi for further discussions, but without much result.[69]

Coincident with the signing of the Treaty, the Indus Basin Development Fund Agreement and the Loan Agreement (Indus Basin Project) between Pakistan and the Bank were signed at Karachi. We have already noted the basic terms of the Development Fund Agreement, which was signed by Mr. Iliff, the Vice President of the Bank (President Black was ill), by Mohammed Shoaib, Finance Minister of Pakistan, and by the Ambassadors of the "friendly Governments" contributing to the Fund. India did not sign, her contribution being covered in Article V of the Treaty. In designating the Bank as Administrator, the Fund Agreement placed that organization in a special relation to Pakistan. Not only would the Bank make disbursements from the Fund, setting aside out of the Indian payments a Special Reserve of $28 million to cover payments to India under Article V if

69. Stephens, p. 253. An agreement on border demarcation had been reached in 1959 after the first Ayub-Nehru meeting in New Delhi. But as the events of the spring and summer of 1965 indicated, there are still boundary disputes in the Rann of Cutch and elsewhere, although the Kashmir dispute is far more than a quarrel over the demarcation of a border.

Pakistan had to extend the Transition Period, but the Bank would act as a sort of overseer and auditor for the Fund and for the Indus Basin Project.

Pakistan undertook to carry out the Project with "due diligence and efficiency and in conformity with sound engineering and financial practices" and to "accord appropriate priority, satisfactory to the Administrator, to that part of the Project whose purpose is replacement."[70] Pakistan would procure all "goods" (defined to include "equipment, supplies, other property and services") for the Project on the basis of international competition, unless the Administrator approved an exception on grounds of efficiency or economy, and would furnish all plans and specifications, cost estimates, and construction schedules for the Project to the Administrator in such detail as the Bank requested. Pakistan would maintain records and accounts, make them available to the Administrator, and enable the Administrator to inspect the Project, goods acquired for the Project, and any relevant records or documents.[71] To receive disbursements from the Fund, Pakistan would make application to the Administrator, supported by such documents and other evidence "as the Administrator shall reasonably request in accordance with the Bank's usual procedures, whether before or after the Administrator shall have permitted any withdrawal requested in the application.[72] In turn, the Bank would report to all the "friendly Governments," and would consult with them and with Pakistan from time to time.

Pakistan had two degrees of freedom under the Fund Agreement: she could designate a government agency or agencies (WAPDA) to carry out the duties of the Central Government under the Agreement; and, although all goods and services to be reimbursed from the Fund had to be procured from members *of the Bank* (not the "friendly Governments" alone), this gave her a wide choice of suppliers, contractors, and consultants. (The Bank in 1960 had 66 members; by 1964 the number had risen to 101.)

There is nothing unusual in the Loan Agreement signed by Mr. Iliff for the Bank and by Mr. Shoaib for Pakistan on September 19, 1960, in Karachi. The actual amount of the loan is $90 million,

70. IBRD, *Indus Basin Development Fund Agreement*, p. 11.
71. Ibid., pp. 11–12.
72. Ibid., p. 10.

of which $10 million are set aside for the interest and commitment charges. The loan proceeds of $80 million are paid into the Fund in such installments as the Bank, in its capacity as Administrator of the Fund, determines. Once paid into the Fund, the installments become subject to all of its disbursement provisions. Interest is charged only on these installments: Pakistan's Ministry of Finance issues tax-free bonds in the amount of each installment, and interest on the bonds is offset against the interest on the installment. The Bank may sell the bonds, though no purchaser acquires any right with respect to the administration of the Fund or of the Project. There are provisions for accounting, exchange of information, visitation and inspection, and arbitration of disputes similar to those of the Fund Agreement.[73]

The relations between Pakistan and the Bank under the Fund and Loan Agreements have been detailed because those relating to the Fund at least have contributed to Pakistan's feeling that she was placed under undue restrictions with regard to the execution of the Indus Basin Project. The Pakistani position, right or wrong, is that she "sold" the water of the Eastern Rivers to India, and that to the extent that the Bank and the consortium nations contributed toward the cost of the "replacement" works (and Pakistan defines "replacement" as including some "development" to offset her population growth and loss of irrigable lands since 1947) they were bailing India out of her obligations. Thus Pakistan felt that she had a "right" to much of the Fund, and the continual accounting to the Fund Administrator and visits and inspections by the Bank's representatives have not facilitated easy relations between Pakistan and the Bank, especially in view of the dispute that grew up around the Tarbela Dam and the underlying question of whether the Fund Agreement guaranteed Pakistan a fixed sum of money only or a complete set of works in exchange for the Eastern Rivers.

As is so often apparent after the fact, more precise wording of the Fund Agreement could have eliminated the long and costly argument which lasted until March 1964 and culminated in the signing of a Supplemental Agreement to the Indus Basin Development Fund Agreement (see below, pages 311–13). The Supplemental Agreement

73. *Loan Agreement (Indus Basin Project) between Republic of Pakistan and IBRD, September 19, 1960.*

provided an additional sum of $310 million in foreign exchange for the Indus Basin Project, but, as a lesson learned from four years of experience, it makes abundantly clear (a) that the $310 million is in full and final settlement of any and all claims by Pakistan arising out of the underwriting of the Indus waters settlement by the World Bank and the "friendly Governments," and (b) that whatever may have been their intent in the original Development Fund Agreement, the "friendly Governments" were not committed to pay the entire foreign exchange cost of Tarbela Dam after the signing of the Supplemental Agreement.

The complicated questions of Tarbela Dam and of the evolving relations between Pakistan, WAPDA, and its consultants, on the one hand, and the "friendly Governments," the Bank, and its consultants, on the other, will be dealt with further in Chapters 7 and 8.

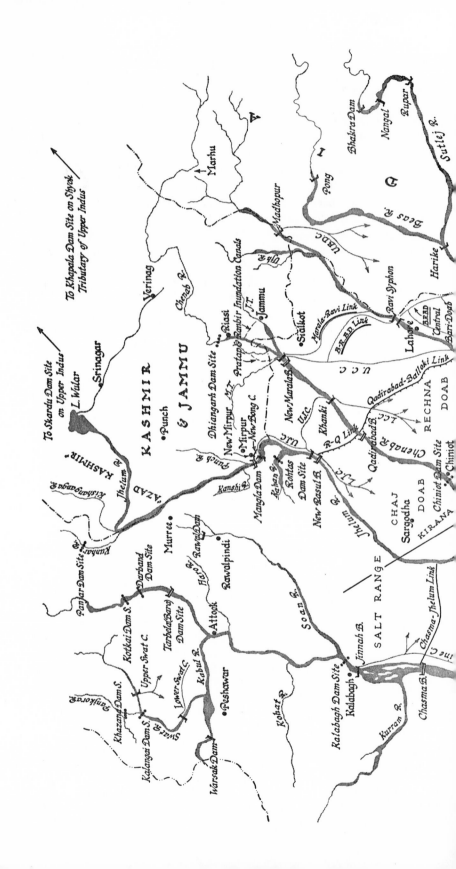

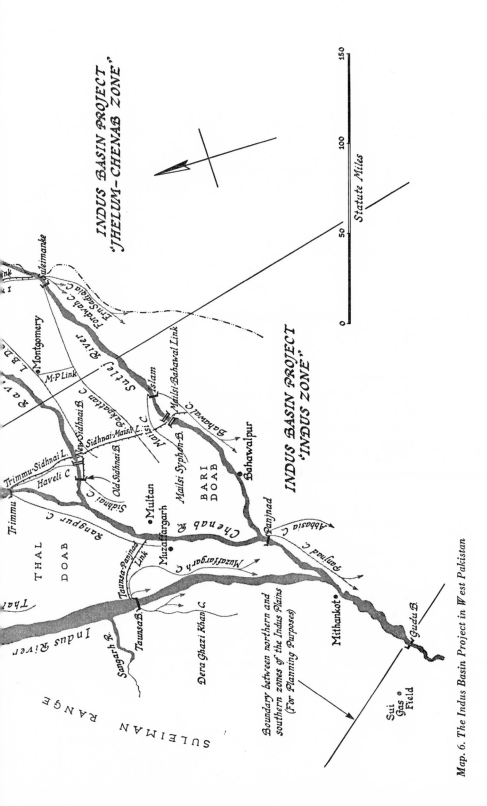

Map. 6. The Indus Basin Project in West Pakistan

7. Implementing the Treaty

The Indus Basin Project (West Pakistan)

The system of works that made an Indus Waters settlement possible was not, for the reasons given in Chapter 6, described in the Treaty. The works in India were described in the loan agreements between India and the World Bank and the United States. The works in West Pakistan, properly referred to as the Indus Basin Project,[1] were set forth as Annexure D to the Indus Basin Development Fund Agreement:

Project Description

1. The Project consists of a system of works to be constructed by Pakistan which will:

---

1. The term "Indus Basin Settlement Plan" has frequently been used by Pakistanis, and occasionally by the World Bank, as a synonym for the Indus Basin Project. Legally, however, "Settlement Plan" has no meaning, and logically it should include both the Indus Basin Project, which is entirely in West Pakistan and is financed by the Indus Basin Development Fund, and the Beas component of the Bhakra-Beas-Rajasthan scheme in India, no part of which is financed from the Fund but to which the proceeds of the U.S. $33-million loan and the World Bank's $23-million loan are to be devoted. (See IBRD Press Release No. 650, September 19, 1960, Washington, D.C., p. 10 and attached map.) The Indian works will be discussed in the last section of this chapter, but we shall avoid using the term "Settlement Plan" because of its ambiguity.

(a) transfer water from the three Western Rivers of the Indus system (Indus, Jhelum and Chenab), *to meet existing irrigation uses in Pakistan* which have hitherto depended upon the waters of the three Eastern Rivers (Ravi, Beas and Sutlej), thereby releasing the whole flow of the three Eastern Rivers for irrigation developments in India;

(b) *provide substantial additional irrigation development in West Pakistan;*

(c) develop 300,000 kw of hydro-electric potential for West Pakistan;

(d) make an important contribution to soil reclamation and drainage in West Pakistan by lowering ground water levels in water-logged and saline areas; and

(e) afford a measure of flood protection in West Pakistan.

2. The system of works includes:

	Location	*Capacity*
A. Dams and Related Works	(1) Jhelum River	Live storage of 4.75 million acre feet
	(a) hydro-electric generating facilities	300,000 kw.
	(2) Indus River	Live storage of 4.2 million acre feet
B. Link Canals (Construction and remodeling)	Rasul-Qadirabad	19,000 cusecs
	Qadirabad-Balloki	18,600 "
	Balloki-Suleimanki	18,500 "
	Marala-Ravi	22,000 "
	Bambanwala-Ravi-Bedian-Dipalpur	5,000 "
	Trimmu-Islam	11,000 "
	Kalabagh-Jhelum	22,000 "
	Taunsa-Panjnad	12,000 "
C. Barrages	Qadirabad	
	Ravi River	
	Sutlej River	
D. Tubewells and Drainage Works		

     (1) About 2,500 tubewells to contribute to a lowering of the water-table, some of which will yield additional water supplies for irrigation use; and

     (2) A system of open drains to lower the water-table in about 2.5 million acres of land now under cultivation but seriously threatened by water-logging and salinity.

E. Other Works

Ancillary irrigation works directly related to the foregoing, including remodeling of existing works.[2]

Analysis of the "Project Description" indicates that the Pakistani negotiators had indeed succeeded in getting storage facilities and both developmental and reclamation aspects included in the project, rather than merely the large link canals for "replacement" of supplies from the Eastern Rivers as the Bank originally had suggested (see Chapter 6, pages 235–38 and 244). In fact, once President Black had succeeded, in May 1959, in securing agreement that India's contribution to the Fund would be a fixed amount, the Pakistani negotiators (and the engineers and consultants supporting them) had a free hand from the engineering, though not from the financial, standpoint in designing the system of works they wanted. Thus, the project described in the Fund Agreement is essentially a modified Indus Basin Advisory Board plan (see Chapter 6, page 249) at least in its inherent logic and basic assumptions. The logic is simple, the assumptions uncomplicated, but the execution and operation of the Indus Basin Project (IBP, henceforth) are such as to stagger the imagination. (A rough parallel might be drawn to the problems involved in the design of a modern superhighway system that must be imposed on the existing urban and rural road pattern. The IBP includes 400 miles of major link canals with a total discharge capacity of 150,000 cusecs, or about two-thirds that of the entire preexisting system in West Pakistan. The IBP is the largest single irrigation project in history.)

The logic of the IBP, of course, is to gain enough water by means of storage and new link transfers from the formerly unused flows of the Western Rivers to meet the needs of the areas formerly supplied

2. IBRD, *Indus Basin Development Fund Agreement,* dated September 19, 1960, Annexure D. Italics added.

from the Eastern Rivers. The "needs" or "uses" are variously defined as actual pre-Partition historic withdrawals plus reclamation
supplies (for the Triple Canals Project and the CBDC); adjusted
allocations, including some reclamation supplies for the upper
Pakistan Sutlej Valley canals (Dipalpur Canal plus Suleimanke system); allocations for the lower Pakistan Sutlej Valley canals (Islam
system); historic withdrawals for Taunsa; and adjusted allocations
for Haveli, Panjnad, and all the Indus projects except Taunsa from
Thal (Kalabagh) to Ghulam Mohammad (Kotri). For operating
purposes, the Pakistan portion of the Indus Basin was divided into
two zones: the Jhelum-Chenab Zone, including the five linked canals
of the TCP, the post-Partition Links (M-R, B-S, and BRBD), the
CBDC, and the upper Sutlej Valley canals (Dipalpur and the Suleimanke system); and the Indus Zone, which included all the rest (as
above; see Map 6).

Although the Indus, with its average runoff of 93 million acre
feet, is to supply Haveli and Panjnad (via link canals across the
Thal Doab), and the Islam system (via the links from Trimmu to
Mailsi), priority is to go to the main-stem projects (which means
that Sind is to be satisfied first). If there are shortages at Panjnad,
i.e. if the Indus flows cannot meet the requirements of the trans-
Thal links in addition to the main-stem needs, these shortages are to
be met from the Jhelum-Chenab flow at Trimmu before diversion
into the Haveli and Trimmu-Mailsi links. Thus, if the Indus cannot
supply the non-main-stem projects in the "Indus Zone," their burden
is to be transferred to the "Jhelum-Chenab Zone" and ultimately to
the Jhelum storage dam at Mangla.[3]

In other words, the logic and underlying assumptions of the IBP
(as of the IBAB plan) are a reversion to the status quo ante Partition between Punjab and Sind. The waters of the Indus are to be
used according to the allocations worked out by the Anderson Committee for the main-stem projects including Thal and Taunsa, but
with priority for the projects in Sind. Three Punjab projects (Haveli,
Panjnad, Islam) may draw on Indus waters through the link canals,

3. West Pakistan WAPDA, Indus Basin Projects (IBP, henceforth) Division,
IBP Publication No. 81, *Effects of Substituting Raised Mangla Dam for Tarbela
Dam on the Uses of Various Projects (Revised)* (Lahore, WAPDA, April 1963),
Appendix I.

but never to the detriment of the main-stem projects. The remaining Punjab projects (TCP, CBDC, Dipalpur, and Suleimanke) will benefit from the Mangla storage and are relieved of the burden of Haveli, Panjnad, and Islam except when the Indus cannot supply them. Thus, it is conceivable that, in a really bad year in both zones, the Jhelum-Chenab Zone would have an additional burden put upon it just when it was least able to accept it. Of course such an eventuality is unlikely, and the provision of storage dams on both the Jhelum and the Indus makes it remote. But the assumptions of the IBP make it clear that, despite Independence, Partition, and the One Unit Plan, Sind still is protecting its interests with respect to Punjab.

A further indication that the IBP cannot possibly solve all of the irrigation needs of West Pakistan may be found in some calculations that S. S. Kirmani, Chief Engineer, IBP, and principal author of the IBAB plan, worked out in the summer of 1962. By 1975, Kirmani estimated that only 39 million irrigated, cropped acres will be available in the Pakistan Indus Plains (including presently used acreage, new acreage, and possibilities of double-cropping on both).[4] To irrigate these 39 million acres will require a total of 133 million acre feet (m.a.f.) of water, 85 m.a.f. in Punjab and 48 m.a.f. in Sind. Sind will have the canal capacities and the surface water supplies to meet its goal (groundwater potential in Sind is apparently quite limited). But Punjab's canal system, unless remodeled at great expense, would be able to handle only 59 m.a.f. annually, and the remainder would have to come from the groundwater reservoir. It was estimated that, because of reduced evaporation and seepage losses, 18 m.a.f. of groundwater could do the job of 26 m.a.f. of surface water (the point of measurement of groundwater is at the heads of the watercourses, of surface water at the heads of the main

4. IBP Publication No. 53, *Settlement Plan without Tarbela, An Appraisal* (Lahore, WAPDA, July 1962), pp. 1–2. The 39 million acres represent: 19 million acres in the Punjab, cropped at 150 per cent intensity; 5.4 million acres of rice land in Sind, cropped at 80 per cent intensity; and 4.6 million acres of perennial lands in Sind, cropped at 135 per cent intensity. Adding an estimated 10 million acres cropped by dry farming (*barani* cultivation) or in minor irrigation systems outside the Indus Plains, Kirmani found that West Pakistan would still fall short by 6 million cropped acres of the 55 million needed to support the projected 1975 population at a minimum average daily intake of 2,300 calories. The only way to make up this deficit is by increasing yields, a matter to be discussed in Chaps. 9 and 10.

canals). Taking, then, a total of 107 m.a.f. of surface water required by West Pakistan in 1975, Kirmani pointed out that even if a Tarbela dam with a live storage capacity of 6.6 m.a.f. (2.4 m.a.f. more than indicated in the "Project Description" of the Development Fund Agreement) were in existence on the Indus at that time, there would still be a shortage of 11 m.a.f. on the basis of average annual flows. Thus, he argued that the completion of the IBP, including a 6.6 m.a.f. Tarbela storage, by 1975 would still not fulfill West Pakistan's needs, and that the situation would grow progressively worse thereafter unless other means were taken. (What these means might be will be discussed below in this chapter and in Chapters 9 and 10.)

It is possible that Kirmani's estimates, published in the summer of 1962, may have been on the conservative side for bargaining purposes (see below, pages 295–300). If some good quality groundwater is "mined," i.e. withdrawn without replenishment, and if the aquifer is developed as a balancing reservoir for surface flows as the groundwater advocates recommend, it is likely that at least 119 m.a.f. and *possibly* more than 133 m.a.f. of surface and groundwater can be diverted into canals or pumped into watercourses by 1975 (see Chapter 10, Table 24). But the basic shortcoming as far as surface water development alone is concerned is that West Pakistan does not contain or control enough good storage sites on the Western Rivers to do the job. The best storage sites, from the topographical standpoint, are inaccessible; conversely, most of the accessible sites are small. As we have seen, the Chenab, within West Pakistan, offers only the Chiniot site, well out on the plains where 1.4 m.a.f. of live storage could be developed only at the cost of building enormous bunds to enclose the reservoir, thereby inundating much arable land and requiring the resettlement of the farmers (see Map 6). The Dhiangarh site on the Chenab in Jammu-Kashmir could provide another 2.5 m.a.f. of live storage, but it is of no use to Pakistan under present political conditions. Nor is the site below Wular Lake in Kashmir where, even if it should one day come to Pakistan, a dam of any size would flood much of the Vale, including Srinagar. West Pakistan does include the Panjar site on the Kunhar tributary of the Jhelum, where 2.5 m.a.f. of live storage might be developed. And the Rohtas site on the Jhelum's Kahan tributary below Mangla could be used to supplement Mangla's live storage by about 1.8 m.a.f. But at Mangla itself, topography precludes raising the dam to store more than about 7.75 m.a.f. Thus, Mangla plus Rohtas plus Panjar would furnish a total of only 12 m.a.f. of live storage, whereas 16 m.a.f. are necessary for complete regulation of the Jhelum's 23 m.a.f. annual flow.[5]

The best sites, on the Indus at Skardu (15 m.a.f. live storage) and at Khapalu on the Indus' Shyok tributary (10 m.a.f. live), are inaccessible in the extreme. Lower down on the Indus, a high dam at Kalabagh would flood the valuable Peshawar Vale, while the Chasma site resembles that at Chiniot in that full utilization (for 9 m.a.f. of live storage) would involve enormous bunds, the flooding of lands already developed, and resettling the farmers. Although there are three sites with a total of 11 m.a.f. of live storage on the Swat River which flows via the Kabul into the Indus at Attock, present interest centers on the Tarbela site on the Indus itself, which offers around 9.3 m.a.f. of live storage. Silting would reduce this to 1 m.a.f. within fifty years unless a dam were built upstream, but there are off-channel storage possibilities totaling about 30 m.a.f. which could be developed during this period and operated almost indefinitely thereafter. More will be said of these possibilities later in this chapter.

As already noted, the "Project Description" included in the Development Fund Agreement does not refer to either Mangla or Tarbela by name. "Jhelum River" was used for the former in order to avoid giving umbrage to India because the left-hand abutments and various auxiliary works of the Mangla Dam (as indeed the intake and upper reaches of the old UJC) lie in Jammu-Kashmir, albeit in Pakistan-occupied Azad Kashmir. "Indus River" was used for the latter not because of any dispute with India but to be consistent, and possibly also because final selection of a site had not been made (although most Pakistani engineers were arguing strongly for Tarbela which, as envisaged at that time, corresponded with the figure of 4.2 m.a.f. live storage). Since then, as we shall see, a lively debate has raged over whether Tarbela should be built at all; at the moment

5. IBP Publication No. 97, *Mangla Dam Project* (Lahore, WAPDA, October 1963), p. 2; and letter from John B. Drisko, August 19, 1965. Mr. Drisko notes that the small sites on the Jammu Tavi and Monawar Tavi rivers would also be useful for regulatory structures to provide timely releases in the Jhelum-Chenab Zone.

of writing it seems most likely that it will be included in the IBP, although it can hardly be completed before 1975.

The IBP has undergone other changes since the Fund Agreement was signed. Because little engineering design had gone into the original "Project Description," further investigations showed that various modifications were essential or at least highly desirable. These have all been gradually worked out between WAPDA (as the agent of the Government of Pakistan) and its consultants, on the one hand, and the Bank (as Administrator of the Fund) and its consultants, on the other.

Two major changes in the project occurred on the Indus below Kalabagh and on the Sutlej at Mailsi. On the Indus, it was originally planned to use a remodeled Kalabagh (Jinnah) Barrage to feed a 22,000-cusec link across the upper Thal Doab into the Jhelum above Trimmu. But more careful investigation showed that the Kalabagh Barrage, even if remodeled, could not efficiently perform this function in addition to serving the Thal canals. It was therefore decided to build a new barrage downstream at Chasma (below the confluence of the Kurram River with the Indus) and to construct a shorter link canal of 21,700-cusec capacity from there to the Chenab. Thus, the Kalabagh-Jhelum Link of the "Project Description" became the Chasma-Jhelum Link, and a fourth barrage was added to the IBP.

On the Sutlej, however, the problem was to bring water from the "Trimmu-Islam" Link across to feed the Bahawal Canal south of the river and thus relieve the Islam headworks of a duty it has never been able to perform adequately. The original plan was to bring water from the Chenab into the Sutlej upstream of Islam, but investigations of the slopes involved indicated that a gradient of only 1 in 22,000 was available on this alignment whereas a minimum of 1 in 10,500 was necessary for proper operation.[6] Then it was proposed to build a new barrage near Mailsi, about 30 miles below Islam, and to pass the water across the river as was done at Balloki (Triple Canals Project) and Sidhnai (Haveli Project). But on closer investigation it was found that, in order to achieve command of the lower Bahawal Canal, such a new barrage would have to be so high that it would pond water back far upstream, increasing waterlogging and evapo-

6. IBP Publication No. 100, *Sidhnai-Mailsi Link* (Lahore, WAPDA, October 1963), p. 1.

ration. Furthermore, such a barrage would produce a pond level 5.5 feet higher than the estimated flood level, thus creating serious and perhaps dangerous problems in flood time.[7] Consideration of possible alternatives led to the selection of a new species of structure, a siphon topped with gates. Water from the link would pass under the river in the siphon; gates would maintain a lower pond level and allow safe regulation in times of flood. Thus, the "Trimmu-Islam" Link became the "Trimmu-Sidhnai-Mailsi-Bahawal" (TSMB) Link, and the Sutlej River Barrage became the Mailsi Siphon-Barrage which also carries a road bridge.

The Ravi River Barrage called for in the "Project Description" was a new barrage at Sidhnai, designed to pass the flows in the Trimmu-Sidhnai portion of the link to the Sidhnai-Mailsi portion while continuing to serve the Sidhnai Canal system. It underwent several metamorphoses in the attempt to perform all of these functions. The site for the Qadirabad Barrage, on the Chenab below Khanki, was fixed by the time the Treaty was signed, although there had been an earlier proposal to build a Mangla-Khanki-Balloki-Suleimanke link. Such a link might have eliminated construction of a new headworks, but its alignment would have been tortuous and costly (as was that of the UJC), and it would not have permitted water from the proposed Rohtas storage to be used in the Jhelum-Chenab Zone. So it was decided to drop the link offtake down to Rasul, which meant that Khanki would be too high to pass flows across the Chenab, and to build a new barrage at Qadirabad. Under this scheme, it was originally hoped to use the old Rasul Barrage (remodeled), but it turned out it would cost more to remodel Rasul than to build a new barrage *there* (about 2 miles downstream of the existing one). Finally, in 1964, it was found that it would be cheaper to replace the Marala Barrage on the Chenab (with all or most of its siltation problems) with a new one to serve both the UCC and the remodeled Marala-Ravi (M-R) Link.

Thus, as the IBP has evolved to date, it has been found necessary to build six new barrages (counting the Mailsi Siphon-Barrage as one) rather than the three originally proposed: Chasma on the Indus, Rasul on the Jhelum, Marala and Qadirabad on the Chenab, Sidhnai

---

7. IBP Publication No. 101, *Mailsi Syphon* (Lahore, WAPDA, October 1963), pp. 1–2.

on the Ravi, and Mailsi on the Sutlej. Taunsa (Indus), Trimmu (Jhelum-Chenab), and Balloki (Ravi) are all being remodeled, and of course the Mangla Dam provides a new intake for the "no barrage" UJC headworks. Kalabagh (Indus), Khanki (Chenab), Suleimanke (Sutlej), and Islam (Sutlej) are the only barrages in the Punjab that are neither being replaced nor remodeled under the Indus Basin Project.

All of these changes, and many others too numerous to discuss, had to be worked out between WAPDA and the World Bank, with the assistance of the consultants, over the early years of the IBP. By May 1963, spurred on by inflationary factors of which the IBP itself was the major cause, estimates had reached $1.9 billion, or more than twice the original estimate for the IBP.[8] The net effect was to leave nothing in the Development Fund for the Indus Dam, a critical element from the standpoint of West Pakistan and Sind in particular. This "Tarbela Crisis" led to renewed negotiations with the Bank and with the "friendly Governments," and ultimately to an increase of $315 million in the Fund. But we shall come to that part of the story later. To understand how the Indus Dam ties into the IBP, and how the IBP is designed to reintegrate the irrigation system in the Pakistani portion of the Indus Basin, we must first examine the components of the scheme.

It will be recalled from our analysis of the Indus Waters Treaty (see Chapter 6, page 256) that India's commitment to supply water for the Pakistan Sutlej Valley canals under Annexure H is divided into two phases, Phase I to end between March 31, 1965, and March 31, 1966, whenever the Trimmu-Sidhnai-Islam (actually TSMB) Link went into operation. The Treaty also obliges Pakistan to proceed expeditiously with those portions of the IBP which have replacement as their goal. Accordingly, the TSMB works received high priority in the IBP and, along with Mangla Dam which continues into Phase II, were incorporated into Phase I of the Project. The other barrages and links, and the Indus Dam, were placed in Phase II. As Table 12 indicates, the TSMB projects all had contract target dates in March or April of 1965, and all were finished ahead of

8. WAPDA, *WAPDA Miscellany, 1964* (An Annual Review of the Activities of the West Pakistan Water and Power Development Authority) (Lahore, WAPDA, June 1964), p. 37.

schedule, although WAPDA announced that it would use the "extra" year for testing and the elimination of any deficiencies.[9]

The bonus provisions included in the contracts as shown in Table 12 were an indication of WAPDA's earnest desire to push on with the Phase I works. But it is only realistic to note that it is to any contractor's advantage to finish such a project ahead of time, quite aside from bonus or penalty provisions. By doing so, he frees his men and equipment for other jobs, and limits the length of time his working capital is tied up. Furthermore, in a continuing project such as the IBP, the contractor who is already established in the country finds himself in a superior position to bid on new projects. He eliminates or reduces further transportation costs and import duties. Ordinarily, much of his equipment and many of his personnel can be used in the new project. Of equal importance, he has learned how to do business in the host country, and he has established contacts and channels of supply that can serve for the new project. Taking all of this into consideration, he can usually underbid a newcomer. If he does not bid, or loses the bid, he is faced with the problems of disposing of his equipment (in many cases at a loss) or of transporting it out of the country. Thus, it is not surprising that the Mailsiphon consortium was successful in obtaining the Phase II contract for the Qadirabad Barrage, or that Cogefar-Astaldi (actually a partnership of the Italian firms of Costruzioni Farsura and Impresa Astaldi) obtained the contracts for both the Rasul-Qadirabad Link and the new Rasul Barrage.

At the end of Phase I, the newly completed TSMB system was neither fish nor fowl. It could, and did, divert Jhelum-Chenab water for the ultimate use of the Islam system, delivering 4,200 cusecs to the lower portion of the Mailsi Canal (see Map 6), 700 cusecs to its Karam Branch, and another 4,000 cusecs (via the Mailsi Siphon and M-B Link) to the lower Bahawal Canal. This immediately raised irrigation intensities in the Islam command and brought them up to allocation for the first time since the barrage was built. Some relief

9. WAPDA, *WAPDA Weekly* (Lahore, WAPDA Press), February 5, 1965; March 5, 1965; June 25, 1965. India was notified that, beginning with the kharif of 1965, she could reduce supplies to the Pakistan Sutlej Valley Canals to the levels specified in Annexure H for Phase II. In May 1966 WAPDA announced that the TSMB links would be turned over to the Irrigation Department for operation from June 30, 1966. (*WAPDA Weekly*, May 25, 1966, p. 1.)

Table 12. Phase I of the Indus Basin Project: Trimmu-Sidhnai-Mailsi-Bahawal Links and Barrages[a]

Project	Length, Capacity, and Lining (Links Only)	Contractor (Nationality)	Date Contract Signed	Completion Dates		Cost (million rupees)	Bonus Provision (rupees)
				Contract Target	Actual		
Trimmu-Sidhnai Link	44 miles 11,000 cusecs (unlined)	Kaiser Engineers, Inc. (U.S.A.)	2/13/62	4/14/65	1/15/65	120	10,000/day for up to 180 days
Sidhnai Barrage	710 feet 167,000 cusecs	Societé Dumez (France)	3/24/62	3/31/65	1/28/65	119	12,000/day for up to 100 days
Sidhnai-Mailsi Link	62 miles 10,100 cusecs (last 47 miles lined)	Cogefar-Astaldi (Italy)	4/20/62	4/30/65	2/65	200	10,000/day for up to 180 days
Mailsi Siphon-Barrage	1,600 feet 429,000 cusecs	Mailsiphon (Denmark, France, Pakistan)	5/18/62	3/31/65	8/64	108	12,000/day for up to 100 days
Mailsi-Bahawal Link	13 miles 4,000 cusecs (lined)	Mir Aslam Khan Hastam Khan & Sons (Pakistan)	8/30/62	3/31/65	2/65	30	

a. Sources: IBP Publications Nos. 98–101; *WAPDA Miscellany, 1964*; and various issues of *WAPDA Weekly* gazette (all Lahore, WAPDA).

Note: Part of the remodeling of Trimmu headworks (the new link intake) was included in the T-S Link contract, as was realignment of the last 6 miles of the Haveli Canal. Other portions of the Trimmu remodeling were later awarded to two Pakistani contractors at a total cost of 1.17 million rupees. Since it was impracticable to exclude or carry through all the silt in the T-S Link, it was designed with a settling basin just below the intake. Two hydraulic dredges, one for this basin and another for the Qadirabad-Balloki Link (to be used meanwhile in clearing some of the 252 million cubic feet accumulated in the M-R Link) were purchased from the Australian firm of C. H. & J. A. Watson, Ltd., for a total cost of 5.6 million rupees (*WAPDA Weekly*, March 6, 1964).

The tender for the Sidhnai-Mailsi-Bahawal Link was divided into two contracts in order to allow Pakistani firms to bid on the smaller portion south of the Sutlej. The successful bidder, Mir A. Khan H. Khan & Sons, found himself at a disadvantage vis-à-vis foreign firms in that he had to apply for foreign exchange allocations from the State Bank of Pakistan for purchasing materials and equipment and had considerable difficulty in getting them. But, using donkeys, baskets, and a great deal of hand labor, he also managed to complete his portion ahead of time.

was also furnished to the Suleimanke system, inasmuch as the S-M Link diverts 1,200 cusecs to the lower Pakpattan Canal and one of its distributaries, thus making possible higher intensities up-doab. (The T-S Link, running as it does on the up-doab side of the Haveli Canal, provides no irrigation in the Rechna Doab.) But all 10,100 cusecs represent Jhelum-Chenab water whereas, as we have seen, the TSMB system is supposed to be supplied (except in short years) by the Indus via the trans-Thal links. The situation at Panjnad has not improved; in fact it may have deteriorated. For the TSMB system extracts an additional 11,000 cusecs at Trimmu, and little of this water finds its way back above Panjnad (and what does is substantially higher in salt content). So although the TSMB Links represent a net gain, both from the standpoint of more water for the lower Bari Doab and Bahawalpur and from the standpoint of lower payments to India for Ferozepore operations and maintenance costs, they cannot yet operate according to the IBP plan.

Hence the urgency of the Phase II works, and especially of the trans-Thal links and Tarbela Dam. Phase I is of little use in rabi without Phase II, which will be of limited value even if completed by the target date, March 31, 1970, mentioned in Annexure H to the Treaty, unless Tarbela—or some equivalent source of storage and regulation, which *might* include a larger groundwater program —follows quickly. Like the comparable Aswan Project in Egypt, the IBP is really a race against time, each year meaning more mouths to feed, cropped acres foregone for lack of sufficient water at the right time, and crops foregone on unreclaimed saline and water-logged lands. But Tarbela Dam has already been so delayed by disputes over size, design, cost, and alternatives that it cannot possibly be finished even by the end of the extended Transition Period, March 31, 1973. In fact, WAPDA is now talking in terms of a "third phase" to include Chasma Barrage and the trans-Thal links (Group B in Table 13), and Tarbela might even become a "fourth phase" if it is delayed much longer. But we shall retain the Treaty terminology for the present.

Judging by the progress made in Phase I, there is every reason to believe that by the spring of 1968 all of the Phase II, Group A projects (with the exception of the new Marala Barrage; see Table 13) will be ready for operation. By this time, the Mangla Dam, on which the entire Jhelum-Chenab Zone depends, should be complete in its first stage and capable of providing the live storage of 4.75 m.a.f. called for in the "Project Description." Diversion of the Jhelum was accomplished in September 1965, and by July 1, 1966, a 225-foot closure dam was completed to absorb the 1966 kharif floods while work proceeds on the 380-foot high main dam.[10] Now that the most critical period has safely passed, the main dam should be finished in time to store enough of the 1967 flood to bring the reservoir to its initial capacity (there is no plan for holdover storage at Mangla because, in contrast to Bhakra, the capacity of the reservoir is small in relation to the 23 million acre feet of runoff in an average year). So there is every indication that as early as the kharif-maturing–rabi-sowing period of 1967, the Jhelum-Chenab Zone can come into operation—though not as planned, since it will have to carry part of the burden of the TSMB, Haveli, and Panjnad projects until the trans-Thal links can be used (hopefully, starting with the rise of the Indus in the kharif-sowing period of 1970) and some of it until Tarbela, or its equivalent, is completed. Still, with the termination of the Phase II, Group A works and of Mangla Dam, the IBP will have moved a long way toward accomplishing its purposes.

IBP: Mangla and Tarbela

The critical roles to be played by the storage dams, Mangla and Tarbela, as well as their unique design and construction features, warrant a more detailed analysis of each of these components.

The idea for a *dam* at Mangla does not antedate Partition, although there were earlier suggestions for storage facilities on the affluents of the Jhelum above and below the Mangla site. It is an interesting commentary on West Pakistan's position before and after the Treaty to note that the pre-Partition planning included only the Wular Lake scheme on the Jhelum (no significant storage for fear of inundating

10. The closure dam *had* to be completed in this period because it had to be capable of storing enough water to reduce a flood as great as that of 1929, or 1,100,000 cusecs, to the 300,000 cusecs that can be passed through the diversion tunnels. Even then, there was a certain "statistical gamble" that the flood of 1966 would not exceed that of 1929. (IBP Publication No. 97, *Mangla Dam Project*, p. 3.)

Table 13. Phase II of the Indus Basin Project: Upper Punjab and Trans-Thal Link Canals and Barrages[a]

GROUP A: Projects designed to convey Jhelum and Chenab waters to the Ravi and Sutlej

Project	Length, Capacity, and Lining (Links Only)	Stage of Design, Contracting or Construction	Contractor or Lowest Bidder (if bids opened)	Completion Target Date	Cost (million rupees)
New Rasul Barrage	3,209 feet 850,000 cusecs	Contract awarded 1/12/65; under construction	Cogefar-Astaldi (Italy)	3/31/68	140
Rasul-Qadirabad Link	30 miles 19,000 cusecs (unlined)	Contract awarded 12/15/64; under construction	Cogefar-Astaldi (Italy)	3/31/68	118
Qadirabad Barrage	3,510 feet 912,000 cusecs	Contract awarded 11/6/64; under construction	Mailsiphon (Denmark, France, Pakistan)	3/31/68	181
Qadirabad-Balloki Link[b]	83 miles 18,600 cusecs (unlined)	Contract awarded 3/10/64; under construction	Canal Constructors Corporation (Pakistan, U.S.A.)	1967	240
Remodeling Balloki Barrage[c]	(raising the crest and other changes)	Contract awarded 9/16/64; works completed	M. A. Rashid Said Alam Khan (Pakistan) and Remodelling Org. (I.D.-WAPDA)		15.5
Remodeling Balloki-Suleimanke Link I[c]	15 miles 18,500 cusecs (unlined)	Contract awarded 2/1/65; under construction	Machinery Pool Organization (WAPDA)		12.0
Balloki-Suleimanke Link II[c]	39 miles 6,500 cusecs (unlined)	Contract awarded 7/22/65; under construction	M. A. Rashid Said Alam (Pakistan)	3/31/68	67.3
New Marala Barrage[d]		Contract awarded 1/30/65; under construction	Zublin GMBH (West Germany)	12/31/68	183
Remodeling Marala-Ravi Link	63 miles 22,000 cusecs (unlined)	Completed	Remodelling Organization (I.D.-WAPDA)		
Remodeling BRBD Link[e]	102 miles 5,000 cusecs (miles 52 to	Completed	Remodelling Organization (I.D.-WAPDA)		

Project	Length, Capacity, and Lining (Links Only)	Stage of Design, Contracting, or Construction	Contractor or Lowest Bidder (if bids opened)	Completion Target Date	Cost (million rupees)
Chasma Barrage[e]	4,200 feet 1 million cusecs	Contract to be awarded in 8/66; work to begin in 10/66		1970	
Chasma-Jhelum Link	63 miles 21,700 cusecs (unlined)	Tenders to be issued in 7/66; contract to be awarded in 11/66		1970	
Taunsa-Panjnad Link	38 miles 12,000 cusecs (unlined)	Contract for excavation awarded 5/30/66; under construction	Messrs. T. P. Link Task Force (Pakistan)	3/31/70	75.4 (for excavation work only)

a. Source: Various issues of *WAPDA Weekly*.

b. The contract includes construction of the LCC Feeder, offtaking the Q-B Link after 18 miles, with a capacity of 4,100 cusecs to permit higher intensities and to provide additional water for reclamation purposes in the LCC command (central Rechna Doab).

c. In 1961, the Remodelling Organization of the Irrigation Department was temporarily transferred ("seconded") to WAPDA for various tasks in the IBP. Before the Remodelling Organization was returned to the I.D. in July of 1965, it had completed remodelling of the Marala-Ravi (M-R) and Bambanwala-Ravi-Dipalpur-Bedian (BRBD) links. The Remodelling Organization had begun work on the Balloki Barrage when, in September 1964, this project was taken over by WAPDA's Links Construction Directorate, which proceeded to contract some of it to M. A. Rashid Said Alam, the same firm that was awarded the contract for the new B-S II Link in July 1965. B-S I is being remodeled by WAPDA'S Machinery Pool Organization to accommodate 18,500 cusecs for the first 15 miles. At this point, B-S II begins and will carry 6,500 cusecs to Suleimanke, while B-S I continues to carry the remaining 12,000 cusecs to the same point.

d. By agreement with the Administrator, WAPDA left the decision as to whether to remodel the existing Marala Barrage or to construct a new one to be decided by the bids. When these were received, it was found that a new barrage could be constructed 1,000 feet downstream more cheaply than the old one could be remodeled. (The same situation prevailed at Rasul. Both the old Marala and Rasul barrages will be demolished.) There is no change in capacity of the M-R Link, which will be tied into the new Marala Barrage.

e. The BRBD Link will continue to function as before, offtaking the UCC below the new Marala headworks. Some remodeling below the Ravi siphon will enable it to deliver 2,700 cusecs to the CBDC and 2,000 cusecs to the Dipalpur Canal, which has also been slightly changed to accommodate its distribution system to the remodeled links.

f. The Chasma Barrage is to be raised 7 feet above the height originally approved by the World Bank in order to increase its pond storage capacity from 400,000 to 720,000 acre feet. This will increase rabi supplies downstream. The cost of raising the barrage is to be paid by Pakistan out of her own funds and the original cost out of the Development Fund.

the Vale, including Srinagar) and no schemes at all on the Indus. In both cases, the heavy sedimentation rate must be blamed:[11] on the Indus any dam will have a short life unless another one is built upstream; on the Jhelum, Wular Lake provides a natural sedimentation basin, but the heavy sediment loads of the tributaries between it and Mangla (notably the Kishanganga and the Kunhar, both joining near Muzaffarabad) militated against the latter site.

With Partition and the Kashmir situation, the alternatives inherited by Pakistan were seriously reduced, and sites previously ignored had to be investigated. In 1951, S. S. Kirmani (who was then Director of Central Designs in the Punjab Irrigation Department) brought in a report of investigations on the Jhelum and its tributaries. This was his first exposition of a concept that has come to play an increasingly important role (as has Mr. Kirmani) in Pakistan's plans for its portion of the Indus Basin. The concept is that of off-channel storage. In other words, even though a dam on the main stem of a river may be doomed to short life by sedimentation, it can still perform a useful function as long as some substantial live storage can be maintained at the top of the reservoir, since clear water can be diverted from there to be stored elsewhere (if suitable sites are available) and re-released for irrigation and power. The main stem structure starts life as a dam but gradually becomes a sort of barrage (though one with a sizable "pond"), the main function of which is to divert water to other storages. The scheme works for three reasons: (1) most of the volume of any reservoir is in its upper portions, i.e. it widens upward; (2) as flood waters enter a long reservoir, they rapidly lose velocity and hence deposit most of their coarse materials at the upstream end; and (3) a large reservoir cannot silt up completely so long as some water can be discharged over, through, or around the dam, carrying silt with it and scouring the top of the reservoir to some degree.

11. Most of this sediment is contributed by the Siwaliks via the tributaries that rise in them. Thus the pre-Partition proposals for dams were all in the inner Siwaliks or above them: Bhakra, Larji or Dhawala (Beas), Thein, Dhiangarh, and the Wular Lake scheme which, as we saw in Chap. 3, was suggested to the Indian Irrigation Commission of 1901–03. Outer Siwalik sites, such as Mangla or Pong (which will depend in part on Larji) came into consideration only after Partition. See IBP Publication No. 97, *Mangla Dam Project*, p. 1; S. S. Kirmani, "Sediment Problems in the Indus Basin, Part I"; and Chap. 2.

In Kirmani's 1951 proposal, two dams were to be built on the Jhelum, at Kamalpur (2.4 m.a.f.) and Mangla (2.7 m.a.f.), and one off-channel storage on the Kanshi at Kanshi (3.9 m.a.f.), another on the Kahan at Rohtas (3.8 m.a.f.). Though Kamalpur and Mangla would silt up, they would still be able to supply silt-free water to Kanshi and Rohtas, respectively. In 1952, at the behest of the Pakistan Central Government, the Punjab Irrigation Department established the Dams Investigations Circle, headed by Mr. Kirmani, and also hired the firm of Tipton and Hill to serve as consultants for investigating the sites. In 1954, Tipton and Hill endorsed a higher dam at Mangla, with a gross capacity of 4.1 m.a.f., which would submerge the Kamalpur site and thus obviate the off-channel storage at Kanshi (unless lift pumps were employed) but which could feed a 2 m.a.f. off-channel storage at Rohtas.[12]

By this time, Kirmani was serving as engineering adviser on the Pakistan Treaty delegation, and the negotiations were bogged down over Pakistan's insistence on the need for storage and India's refusal to pay for it. The Government of Pakistan nevertheless went ahead with Mangla planning and hired the London partners, Binnie, Deacon and Gourley as consulting engineers. This firm, in 1959, recommended a 366-foot high Mangla Dam with a gross capacity of 5.35 m.a.f. but with no immediate provision for the off-channel storage at Rohtas. After Eugene Black, President of the World Bank, had secured Nehru's and Ayub's agreement to the "Indus Settlement" arrangements, Kirmani and the other members of the IBAB (see Chapter 6) substantially incorporated this Mangla scheme in their plan, submitted at the end of 1959. The IBAB plan called for raising the height to 380 feet to provide a gross storage of 5.75 m.a.f. of which 4.75 would be the initial live storage, destined to be reduced in about 120 years to 1 m.a.f. unless the Mangla Dam were raised. But neither the raising of Mangla nor the Rohtas scheme for off-channel storage was mentioned in the Development Fund "Project Description."

Preliminary work on access roads, a railway spur, and bridges was actually started at Mangla in 1959, but it was not until early 1962 that the contractor arrived on the scene. In the intervening

12. IBP Publication No. 97, *Mangla Dam Project*, p. 1.

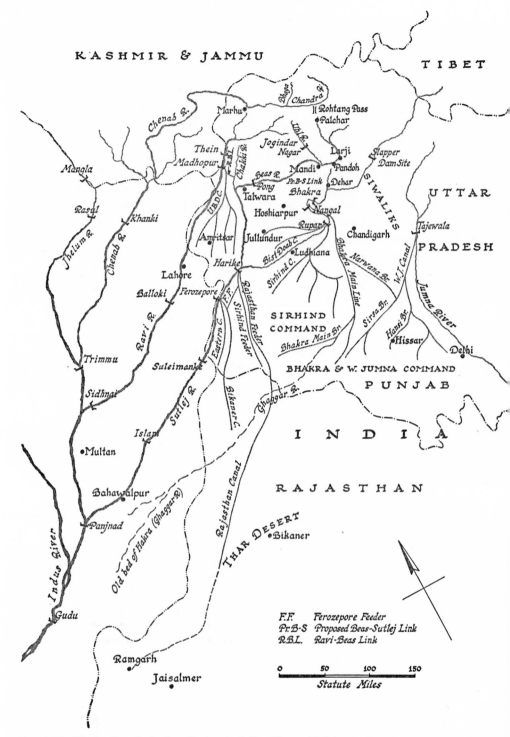

Map 7. The Bhakra-Beas-Rajasthan Project in India. (Note added in proof: The boundaries shown for the Indian Punjab are those which prevailed before November 1, 1966, when its territory was divided among Punjabi Suba, Haryana Pant, and Himachal Pradesh.)

period, the design of the dam was elaborated by WAPDA's consultants (the firm had become Binnie and Partners), and tenders had been prepared and issued. The project was broken down into no fewer than fourteen contracts, of which Contract No. 2, "Mangla Dam Civil Engineering Works," amounted to Rs. 1,685,500,000, or about $355 million. This contract was awarded to an American consortium of eight firms, led by Guy F. Atkinson Company of San Francisco. It represented the largest single contract awarded in the history of civil engineering. Even taking the 1965 revised estimated cost of Mangla, Rs 2,500 million or about $540 million (which represents over half of the original estimated cost of the entire IBP, and over one-fourth of the revised estimate of $1.9 million), Contract No. 2 amounts to about two-thirds of the total cost of the dam.

The Mangla project merits other superlatives as well. Although the main dam is surpassed in volume by other rolled-earth structures on the Missouri and Volga rivers, the total amount of fill in the project, including subsidiary dikes and dams, comes to over 120 million cubic yards, or more than in any similar project to date. The length of the main dam, 11,000 feet; its height, 380 feet (which will be raised to 420); the size of the reservoir, 100 square miles (gross storage 5.75 m.a.f. initially and 8.75 m.a.f. when raised); the capacity of the main spillway, 900,000 cusecs; and the ultimate hydroelectric potential, 1,000,000 kw, also compare well with similar structures on the Missouri, though not with those on the Volga. Mangla Dam cannot be compared directly with Bhakra, which is a gravity, concrete structure over twice as high, but the specifications are of the same order of magnitude as those of the Pong Dam, being built by India at a geologically similar site on the Beas as part of her Indus Basin development envisaged by the Treaty arrangements (see Table 14). The Tarbela Dam, if built as now designed, would be an earth- and rock-fill structure and would dwarf both Mangla and Pong in most respects.

To provide a sufficiently large reservoir at Mangla, it became necessary to build three side or "saddle" dams east of the Jhelum (in Azad Kashmir). The longest of these, the Sukian Dike, 17,000 feet long and 80 feet high, is also the simplest in design and construction. But the Jari Dam, which cuts off the Jari Nala and which will form part of the southern rim of the reservoir, is 5,700 feet

Table 14. Comparison of the Major Dams in the Indus Basin (West Pakistan and India) [a]

	Mangla	Raised Mangla	Pong	Tabela	Bhakra
Location:	Jhelum River		Beas River	Indus River	Sutlej River
Type:	Rolled earth fill		Rolled earth fill	Earth and rock fill	Concrete, gravity
Height above river bed:	380 feet	420 feet	330 feet	485 feet	620 feet
above foundation:			380 feet		740 feet
Length:	11,000 feet	11,000 feet	5,750 feet	9,000 feet	250 feet at base to 1,700 feet at top
Volume:	75 million cubic yards		35 million cubic yards	159 million cubic yards	5.4 million cubic yards
Length of Reservoir:	40 miles		23 miles	50 miles	55 miles
Area of Reservoir:	100 square miles			92 square miles	64 square miles
Volume of Reservoir:	5.75 million acre feet	8.75 million acre feet	6.55 million acre feet	11.1 million acre feet	8 million acre feet
Volume of Live Storage:	4.75 million acre feet	7.75 million acre feet	5.50 million acre feet	9.3 million acre feet	6.3 million acre feet
Hydroelectric Potential:	1 million kw	1 million kw	.36 million kw	2.1 million kw	1.05 million kw
Estimated Cost:	Rs. 2,500 million ($540 million)		Rs. 1,108 million ($243 million)	?	Rs. 824 million ($173 million)

a. Sources: IBP Publication No. 97, *Mangla Dam Project*; various issues of *WAPDA Weekly*; Bureau of Reclamation, United States Department of the Interior, *Beas and Rajasthan Projects*; Public Relations Officer, Bhakra-Nangal Project, *Facts and Figures, Bhakra-Nangal* and *Bhakra-Nangal Project* (Nangal, Punjab, March 1957 and July 1961 respectively).

long and 234 feet high and required 23 million cubic yards of fill. The Jari Dam construction was almost as complicated as that of the main dam since it, too, involved excavation down to bedrock, cementing of weak zones in this rock, inclusion of a rolled clay core to prevent seepage, and provision for raising when the main dam is raised. The Jari Dam even has its own discharge facility to provide water for irrigation along the Jari Nala. The Kakra Dam, 750 feet long and 125 feet high, is merely an eastward extension of the Jari Dam and posed no special problems.

The submergence of 65,100 acres by the Mangla reservoir has displaced over 80,000 persons in Pakistan and Azad Kashmir, including some 9,000 inhabitants of the old town of Mirpur, which will lie under 80 feet of water. Most of these "Mangla affected persons" have been resettled, on fairly generous terms, in the Lyallpur, Sargodha, and Multan districts where they are learning the irrigation agriculture that submergence of their homes is to enhance. On the hills overlooking the reservoir from the south, a New Mirpur town has been built with provision for an eventual population of some 30,000. The total cost of resettlement and the building of New Mirpur is about RS 180 million, or 7 per cent of the total cost of the Mangla project.

In operation, at least until it is raised, the normal maximum level of the Mangla reservoir will be 1,202 feet above sea level or 32 feet below the initial crest of the dam. This 32 feet of "freeboard," combined with the 900,000-cusec capacity of the main spillway and the 212,000-cusec capacity of the emergency spillway (elevation 1,206), are considered sufficient to store or pass a flood of 2.6 million cusecs. (The historic flood of record at Mangla occurred in 1929, the year of the Islam disaster on the Sutlej, and amounted to 1.1 million cusecs.)

The main and emergency spillways are located on the right or western flank of the main dam. The emergency spillway, which will discharge back into the Jhelum via the Bara Kas Nala, is merely a concrete-lined, unregulated open cut in the hills. But the main spillway is a remarkable piece of engineering. Because it must pass up to 900,000 cusecs of flow down a drop of over 500 feet, the energy created by this falling water at maximum discharge will amount to some 40 million horsepower. Most of this must be dissipated before it returns to the Jhelum, lest it erode the bed. To perform the dissipating function, two "stilling basins" are provided. The upper stilling basin does two-thirds of the work. Water released through the nine submerged gates of the spillway strikes the floor of the upper stilling basin with a velocity of 100 miles per hour. "The stilling basin will contain an hydraulic jump (standing wave in the English usage), an extremely turbulent and efficient phenomenon which dissipates the energy principally as heat. A series of steel-clad and reinforced concrete pillars serves to aggravate the turbulence, enhance the energy dissipation, and make it possible for a smaller basin than otherwise would be required to contain the jump." The lower stilling basin completes the task. The entire main spillway section requires 26.7 million cubic yards of excavation and contains 1.2 million cubic yards of concrete. Upper and lower stilling basins and the connecting chute include 40 acres of concrete and cost Rs 296 million ($62 million).[13]

Until one realizes that water will flow over the main spillway only for short and unpredictable periods, the loss of this energy seems a pity. But the Jhelum will be made to do as much work as is feasible. On the left flank of Mangla, five diversion tunnels, each 30 feet in diameter and 1,950 feet long, each with a capacity of 9,000 cusecs, will continuously draw off water for power generation and irrigation uses. These five tunnels were drilled through the semicompacted rock and earth materials underlying Mangla Hill. Use of a specially designed "mole" with rotating cutters on its face made possible completion of the tunnels in an average time of six weeks apiece. But in excavating the tunnels, so much unconsolidated material was encountered that it was decided to line them throughout with steel tubes encased in concrete. (The final decision to line the tunnels was reached after a sizable "hydraulic jump" or "standing wave," which would be dangerous in an enclosed space, showed up in hydraulic model studies representing conditions that could be expected during the diversion period, after closure of the dam, and with the entire river flow passing through the tunnels.)

The power-cum-irrigation tunnels, originally used for diverting the river, terminate at the powerhouse below Mangla Hill. Here

13. Ibid., pp. 4, 5, 8. The quotation is from a letter of August 19, 1965 from John B. Drisko.

each one bifurcates, so as eventually to supply ten turbogenerator units, each of 100,000 kw capacity. (Six units will be installed by 1970 and probably all ten by 1975.) Each of the ten penstocks will have a bypass valve which can be used to release supplies for irrigation if turbine releases are insufficient. As much as 35,000 cusecs discharged from the powerhouse will pass through another stilling basin into the new Bong Canal which runs parallel to and just above the head reach of the old UJC. After three canal miles (15,000 feet) the Bong Canal passes 11,500 cusecs into the old UJC and discharges the remainder back into the bed of the Jhelum for abstraction at Rasul (LJC and R-Q Link).

Thus, despite all of the modifications to the Punjab irrigation system introduced by the IBP, Mangla will remain in a preeminent position for control of the Chaj, Rechna, and Bari doabs (see Chapter 3). From the new Mangla Dam, the entire Jhelum-Chenab Zone will be controlled, including all five old canals linked together by the Triple Canals Project (UJC, LJC, UCC, LCC, LBDC); the new RQBS Links; the old BRBD and M-R links; and the upper Pakistan Sutlej Valley canals (Dipalpur plus those offtaking at Suleimanke). Until the trans-Thal links and the Tarbela Dam (or alternative) are ready, and in years of short supply thereafter, Mangla Dam will also control the Trimmu-based canals and links and thus supply areas to and including Panjnad that have been designated part of the Indus Zone.

But the ultimate operation of the IBP requires the construction of a storage dam on the Indus as well as Mangla on the Jhelum. Even when Mangla is raised to the full potential of its site, its live capacity will be only 7.75 m.a.f. This is 1.2 m.a.f. less than the combined live capacities of the Jhelum and Indus dams envisaged in the "Project Description" attached to the Development Fund Agreement. Without a dam on the Indus, even raised Mangla could not carry the burden of the Jhelum-Chenab Zone plus the non-main-stem projects of the Indus Zone. Instead of the occasional and rather unlikely shortages envisaged in the IBAB-IBP plans, shortages would be chronic. Mangla has no holdover storage from one kharif to the next. The Jhelum-Chenab Zone and the non-main-stem Indus Zone would be shorn of extra water for development and reclamation, and might not even obtain their "replacement" needs. The position of Sind would be worse than it was in 1947, for the combined effect of the Treaty and of the incomplete IBP would be to deprive her of any increment from Panjnad and force her to rely entirely upon the unregulated Indus. In fact, in the years from mid-1962 to early 1965, when it appeared that the Indus dam might be dropped from the IBP, Sind was prepared to scrap not only the IBAB-IBP plan but the Treaty itself. For Sind, with its late start in perennial irrigation and its relatively more serious waterlogging and salinity problems, sees all three of its vast, main-stem projects (Gudu, Sukkur, and Ghulam Mohammad) menaced if there is no way to control the great river itself.

The fact that the Indus contributes 93 of the 176 m.a.f. available at the rim stations in an average year (see Table I) must never be lost sight of. Under the Treaty provisions, the contribution becomes even more significant, for West Pakistan is left with a total average annual runoff of 142 m.a.f., of which over 65 per cent is represented by the Indus at Attock (including 23.1 m.a.f. from the Kabul River). In terms of storage potentials, since there are no easily developable storage sites on the Chenab within West Pakistan's present territory, and since the full development of the Mangla site can yield only 7.75 m.a.f. plus possibly 2.5 m.a.f. in off-channel storage at Rohtas, the potential of the Indus, offering 9.3 m.a.f. at Tarbela plus about 30 m.a.f. in off-channel storages fed from Tarbela, represents about 80 per cent of the easily developable storage potential on the Western Rivers.[14] Thus, quite aside from questions of power generation

14. It should be noted that the ability of a reservoir to control a river for irrigation or power purposes is not measured only by the reservoir's capacity but by the river's seasonal regime. Thus, initial Mangla Dam, with a live storage capacity of 4.75 m.a.f., can actually make use of about 8 m.a.f. of the Jhelum's 23 m.a.f. average annual flow by means of a well-designed schedule of releases and impoundings. Since over 10 m.a.f. of the Jhelum's flow are already being used for irrigation, the total useful regulation on the Jhelum (whether by diversion or storage) now amounts to about 18 m.a.f., or over three-fourths of the total flow.

It should also be noted that because of the immensity of the Indus' flow, the Tarbela Dam would not have to provide any holdover storage from one monsoon to the next. It would only impound and prolong the use of one season's runoff, though there might be some holdover storage in the off-channel reservoirs. Despite the great disparity in size, in operation the Tarbela Dam would resemble the nearby Warsak facility, which does not really "store" the Kabul's waters (its capacity is only 26,000 a.f. compared to an average annual flow there of

or flood control, a regulating dam on the Indus seemed to offer the only means of allowing both Sind and Punjab to maintain their existing systems, bring them up to allocation, reclaim salinized lands, and provide for reasonable development to keep pace with the rising population after the loss of the Eastern Rivers to India.

As we have seen, serious investigation of storage sites on the Indus did not begin until after Partition. In the mid-1950s Tipton and Hill were called upon to aid the Dams Investigation Circle on the Indus as they had on the Jhelum. Seven or eight sites were considered, and some preliminary estimates of storage capacities and sedimentation problems were made. The highest of these sites, at Skardu (see Map 2) where the Indus first widens out, was found ideal in that the river, down to that point, has mainly cut through the hard rocks of the Himalayas themselves and thus has little sediment load. But the difficulties of getting men and equipment into the area, and its remoteness from the irrigated areas of the Plains (which would necessitate further diversions and an elaborate distribution system downstream, after the clear waters released at Skardu had picked up even more sediment than they do now), ruled it out as a first-priority project. The next site, at Kotkai where the Indus, after cutting through the northwestern end of the Pir Panjal Range leaves its 300-mile Himalayan gorge, was found both difficult of access and too limited in storage capacity—only 2.65 m.a.f. for a 600-foot high dam.

Below Kotkai, the Indus cuts through the friable Siwaliks where tributaries further increase its transported load and the depth of alluvium in its bed. Thus, at Darband and Tarbela, the next sites considered, the depth to bedrock was estimated by seismographic refraction to be between 200 to 400 feet. But the Tarbela site—or rather three possible sites in the vicinity of Tarbela—was found to offer a sizable reservoir capacity developable with a moderately high earth- and rock-fill dam. At Attock, where the narrow bedrock gorge below the historic fort was chosen for the bridge serving the North Western Railway and the Grand Trunk Road, geological conditions for a

---

17.4 m.a.f.) but just "re-regulates" them, primarily for power-generation purposes. As Tarbela's storage capacity is reduced by siltation, its function will come to resemble that of a gigantic barrage, diverting water into the off-channel storages.

dam are quite favorable. But although a reservoir here would have a theoretical capacity of 16 m.a.f., only 1 m.a.f. could be used before parts of the fertile and populous Peshawar and Mardan vales were flooded. Similarly, near Kalabagh (about 12 miles above the Jinnah Barrage), a narrow rock gorge would allow the construction of a 250-foot dam with a capacity of 8 m.a.f., but anything higher (up to 325 feet and 30 m.a.f. is theoretically possible) would flood rich upstream lands.

Finally, a site well out on the Indus Plains was considered at Chasma (where a new barrage is being built to serve the upper trans-Thal link). Here it would be necessary, in order to create a sizable artificial reservoir, to construct an earth-fill dam 8 miles long and 120 feet high, with marginal dikes on either side of up to 30 miles in length. And even this would submerge 350,000 acres, of which half is under cultivation, although after completion it would presumably be possible to increase the irrigated acreage by several times that amount.

Thus, the choice was limited to Kalabagh or to one of the three Tarbela sites, and estimates were made of the sedimentation rates at both places. At first it was estimated (on the basis of samples taken since 1954) that a dam at Kalabagh would impound about 230,000 acre feet of silt per year, while one at Tarbela (above the Kabul confluence) would impound only 90,000. But later it developed that the deposition at Tarbela would be 129,000 acre feet or more per year. The best of the Tarbela sites seemed to be the one farthest downstream, at Bara, where some 11 m.a.f. of gross storage could be obtained compared to only 8 m.a.f. (without destructive flooding) at Kalabagh. Kalabagh offered the better foundations (only 60 feet to bedrock as compared to 400 or more at Bara) but was less easily accessible and would require a larger and more costly spillway. The topography of the Tarbela-Bara site, with hills close to the river on both banks and a convenient gap for a spillway on the left flank, made the design of the dam somewhat simpler than that at Mangla.

But perhaps the decisive factors, as far as WAPDA was concerned, were that the sediment problems at Kalabagh were more serious than those at Tarbela and that, while Kalabagh would last only thirty-five years and could not be raised, Tarbela's first stage would last forty-seven years, and this could be prolonged to eighty-five by raising the dam to full height. Tarbela also offered more hydroelectric potential and possibilities of off-channel storages up to 32 m.a.f., while Kalabagh offered none. Thus, WAPDA's Chief Engineer concluded, although neither site is attractive, Tarbela is less unattractive than Kalabagh. Furthermore, while either would satisfy the Development Fund Agreement's requirements (a storage dam on the Indus with a live storage capacity of 4.2 m.a.f.), the two were not competitive but complimentary, i.e. both should be built. The question was one of priority, and by building Tarbela first, Pakistan would secure more water and more power. Kalabagh, when built, would have a longer life because Tarbela would absorb much of the sediment.[15]

IBP: The Tarbela Crisis

Such was the position maintained by WAPDA as agent of the Government of Pakistan one year after the Treaty was signed. But the position of the Bank, as Administrator of the Development Fund Agreement, was quite different. Confronted with the cumulative changes in the barrages and link canals and in the design of Mangla Dam, the Bank was beginning to suspect that WAPDA was proceeding with the IBP as though its consultants' estimates of June 1960 (formally submitted to the Bank only on September 2, 1960; see Chapter 6) had been accepted rather than rejected by the Bank and the "friendly Governments." It will be recalled that these consultants' estimates put the cost of the IBP at $1,297.3 million, of which $745.4 million was in foreign exchange. (The estimated cost of the Tarbela Dam had been given as $374.8 million, of which $239.6 million constituted foreign exchange.) Although Pakistan had to back down from this position and to accept a figure of $893.5 million for the Development Fund, of which total foreign exchange in grants

15. The foregoing discussion of dam sites on the Indus is based on a report written by A. Rashid Kazi when he was Chief Engineer, West Pakistan WAPDA and entitled *Factors Affecting the Selection of a Dam Site—Selection of the First Storage Dam on the Indus* (Lahore, WAPDA, September 1961, mimeographed). More recent estimates of Tarbela's life would give the initial dam about forty-five years and raised Tarbela about sixty. But the last million acre feet or so of storage could be maintained almost indefinitely and used to feed the off-channel storages which are now estimated at 30 m.a.f. of live capacity.

and loans amounted to $632 million, she could of course increase the amount of her own expenditure on the IBP over and above the Fund figure.

But Pakistan, and WAPDA as her agent, still had to submit *all* plans, specifications, estimates, and schedules for the IBP to the Bank as Administrator, and the Bank had the power to refuse to make disbursements—or to delay them—if it did not approve of the manner in which Pakistan was executing the IBP (see Chapter 6). In other words, Pakistan's first duty (under the Treaty to India and under the Fund Agreement to the Bank and the "friendly Governments") was to complete with "due diligence and efficiency and in conformity with sound engineering and financial practices . . . that part of the Project whose purpose is replacement"[16] (see also Chapter 6, page 258). After the replacement portion of the works (to the limited extent that it could be separated out) had been completed, Pakistan could go ahead with the rest of the "Project Description" and could add to the IBP anything she could pay for. But if the elaboration of projects and the escalation of costs became so great in the initial stages as to threaten the eventual completion of even the replacement portion, then the Bank felt a duty with respect to the "friendly Governments" to intervene in Pakistan's management of the IBP. Even aside from the specific provisions of the Fund Agreement regarding the Administrator's role, the Bank itself was lending Pakistan $80 million and had an obligation to all of its members to see that the project as originally described was completed at a cost that would not imperil Pakistan's ability to repay the loan portions of the Fund (including the $70 million loan from the U.S.A., though that could be repaid in rupees whereas the Bank loan could not) and to meet her other international obligations.

It is also relevant to point out that four of the six "friendly Governments" contributing to the Development Fund were also members of the "Aid to Pakistan Consortium" organized by the World Bank to supply financial assistance to Pakistan's Second Five Year Plan (1960–65). As of January 1962 the participants in the Consortium were the World Bank, the United States, the United Kingdom, Canada, West Germany, France, and Japan. Before Pakistan had signed the Indus Waters Treaty and the Development Fund Agreement, she

16. IBRD, *Indus Basin Development Fund Agreement,* p. 11.

had elicited assurances from the "friendly Governments" and the Bank that their contributions to the Fund would not be written off against their contributions to her general development under the Plans but would be considered as additions to such aid. Thus, any elaborations of the IBP, even if included under the Five Year Plans, affect the "friendly Governments," the other members of the "Aid to Pakistan Consortium," and Pakistan's general economic health, especially if they contribute to the inflationary spiral. The "friendly Governments" had legitimate reason to be concerned about the escalation in the IBP estimates.

The basic difficulty between the Bank and WAPDA lay in the fact that even though about 40 per cent of the difference between the WAPDA consultants' estimates of June 1960 and those of the Bank's consultants submitted in February 1960 lay in such items as land acquisition costs, import duties, and sales and income taxes—items which the Bank insisted should not be charged to the Fund—the elaboration of the IBP components and the escalation of costs had reached a point where the absolute amount of the WAPDA consultants' estimates, irrespective of how they were derived or presented, came quite by coincidence to seem more "realistic" than the Bank's own estimates or the amount of $893.5 million agreed upon in the Development Fund Agreement. Even in presenting the June 1960 estimates, WAPDA and its consultants had warned that *they* were still preliminary and subject to revision. And revision of course means revision upward, especially when a project is spread over ten or fifteen years and represents such a sizable impact upon an economy that it is bound to produce inflation.

At any rate, there is no evidence that WAPDA ever abandoned its consultants' cost estimates of June 1960.[17] From *its* point of view, *downward* revisions would have been both professionally dishonest and unpatriotic. Instead, as planning, investigation, design, the letting of tenders and receipt of bids, and domestic and world inflation proceeded, the estimated costs of the IBP steadily mounted. By March 1962 they had reached $1,795 million, of which $960 million represented foreign exchange. Although the almost exact doubling of the original Development Fund amount is only a coincidence, the

17. WAPDA, *Indus Basin Settlement Plan, Construction and Expenditure Schedules* (Lahore, WAPDA, October 1960). Note month.

increase was of such proportions as to alarm the Bank. For Pakistan could not hope to provide the extra funds herself without wrecking her economic development in other sectors. Yet for the Bank to recommend to its directors and to the "friendly Governments" additional loans or contributions on the order of $330 million for the completion of the IBP was, in the light of the Bank's earlier estimates and statements, awkward to say the least.

The alternative was to restrict the scope of the works, if necessary by eliminating certain components. And since the Tarbela Dam, which had now displaced Mangla as the single most costly component (estimated in March 1962 at $552.4 million), and since its estimated foreign exchange cost was nearly $300 million, the Bank suggested that it be deleted from the IBP. In Tarbela's place, the Bank suggested that the Mangla Dam be built to its ultimate height of 420 feet to provide a total of 7.75 m.a.f. rather than the 4.75 m.a.f. of live storage indicated in the Development Fund Agreement's "Project Description." Although "Raised Mangla" would fall short by 1.20 m.a.f. of the 8.95 m.a.f. of live storage visualized in the "Project Description," it could be completed by 1970 with no change in design and with little loss at Tarbela, where only preliminary investigations and designs had been carried out (about $11 million had been spent on Tarbela by mid-1962). The role to be played by the Indus Zone would have to be redesigned, as would the operation of the entire IBP, but the Bank and the "friendly Governments" would be much more willing to make a reasonable contribution toward an IBP shorn of Tarbela than toward one costing twice the Development Fund Agreement figure.

Pakistan's reaction to the Bank's proposal might have been anticipated, since her basic position had not changed since the summer of 1960. Pakistan felt that she was selling three rivers to India in exchange for a system of works. This system of works had to replace the irrigation uses from the Eastern Rivers, including the loss of *sailab* uses and the lowering of adjacent water tables beyond the reach of wells (both of which would necessitate new canal or distributary construction). It had to provide excess water supplies for reclamation purposes, and it had to have an element of development in it to compensate for the losses to waterlogging and salinity and the growth of population since 1947.

Furthermore, Pakistan maintained, the IBP as described in the

Development Fund Agreement did not satisfy her legitimate claims but merely provided the foundation from which she herself could satisfy them at a later date. The "Project Description," with its total of 8.95 m.a.f. of live storage, would fall short by some 5 to 7 m.a.f. of the uses embodied in the IBAB Plan, which themselves were *lower* than the pre-Partition sanctioned allocations (see above, page 271). To bring Pakistan back to the relative position she had enjoyed in 1947 would require not only the building of Raised Mangla, but the building and raising of Tarbela too. By 1974, when all of this could be completed, only the IBAB uses would be met, and Pakistan would have "lost" some twenty-six years of development. After 1974, the development of off-channel storages would have to be undertaken to make up for the loss of storage capacity due to silting in Mangla and Tarbela reservoirs, to bring the old irrigation projects up to pre-Partition sanctioned allocations, and to permit intensification of irrigation in accordance with modern American (Blaney-Criddle) standards rather than the traditional British practice of spreading the water thin (see Chapter 3).[18]

The "Project Description" called for a dam on the Indus. Investigations had shown that the Tarbela site at Bara was best suited, although new estimates of siltation rates indicated that the initial dam there would have to have a live storage capacity of 6.6 m.a.f. rather than the 4.2 originally specified "in order to achieve storage benefits commensurate with those contemplated in the Treaty."[19] The cost was immaterial. Pakistan had warned, on the eve of signing the Treaty, that her consultants' estimates were substantially higher than either the IBAB estimates or those of the Bank's consultants. She had signed the Treaty and the Development Fund Agreement only in the belief that she was getting a *system of works,* not just a fixed sum of money, and that system included "a dam on the Indus."

The danger of rising costs was there and recognized long before the Treaty and the Fund Agreement were signed but Pakistan was assured that what was sacrosanct from the point

18. IBP Publication No. 49, *Settlement Plan without Tarbela, An Appraisal* (Lahore, WAPDA, July 1962), pp. 3–4. This publication was subsequently revised and reissued as IBP Publication No. 53 but bearing the same date (July 1962). The reference should be to the Development Fund Agreement rather than to the Treaty.

19. Ibid., footnote to p. 5.

of view of Bank and friendly countries was the system of works and not the price tag on it. It was in view of these assurances that Pakistan gave up many of its legitimate financial claims and accepting the Bank as the Administrator of the Fund, embarked, despite the inadequate phraseology of the Fund Agreement, on the implementation of the Treaty Works. Any attempt on the part of the Bank or the friendly countries to treat the price tag on the works and not the works themselves as sacrosanct . . . after Pakistan signed away its rights on the three rivers to India, can be rightly construed at least as a breach of faith if not a breach of a treaty in the legal sense.

The Bank had a critical role to play in Water Dispute. It was the chief architect of the Settlement Plan and also the party primarily responsible for making Pakistan agree on the basis of it to part with its resource heritage. The so called solution now offered by the Bank alters, as the foregoing analysis indicates, the very basis of the Plan. Apart from negation of a pledged word and solemn assurances it takes away from the Plan all those elements in consideration of which Pakistan signed the Treaty. This is a solution with which Pakistan cannot just afford to live and must be rejected.[20]

Whether or not Pakistan would actually have denounced the Treaty if Tarbela had been excluded from the IBP, there had developed between her and the Bank by the summer of 1962 a situation not unlike the one that existed between Egypt and the World Bank (plus the U.S. and U.K.) in the summer of 1956 over the Aswan Dam. Perhaps bearing that precedent in mind, Sir William Iliff, Vice President of the Bank (he had been knighted after the signing of the Treaty), flew to Pakistan in July 1962 for discussions with President Ayub, other members of the Government of Pakistan, and WAPDA representatives at Murree.[21] Iliff still urged eliminating Tarbela and raising the height of Mangla, but WAPDA had come up with an alternative suggestion. Although the position with respect to the dam

20. Ibid., p. 12.
21. The hill station that serves Rawalpindi as Simla serves Delhi. Rawalpindi had been designated the interim capital of Pakistan in 1959, pending the completion of the new city of Islamabad at the foot of the Siwaliks between Rawalpindi and Murree.

on the Indus had not changed since the summer of 1960, a new development had created some room for maneuver on another component of the "Project Description"—the $50 million set aside for tubewells and drainages.

In April 1961 Dr. Abdus Salam, a distinguished Pakistani physicist and science adviser to President Ayub, had visited the United States in connection with the Centennial of the Massachusetts Institute of Technology. Speaking at the convocation, he mentioned his distress that the tools of modern science had not yet been brought to bear on the problems of waterlogging and salinity illustrated in the Indus Basin. In the audience was Dr. Jerome B. Wiesner, Special Assistant for Science and Technology to President John F. Kennedy. Weisner spoke to Dr. Salam and informally offered the services of his office in solving the problem, indicating that the initiative ought to come from Pakistan. On his return home, Dr. Salam mentioned the proposal to President Ayub, who responded most favorably.[22] When Ayub visited Washington, in July 1961, he raised the matter with Kennedy, who had been briefed by Wiesner. Thus arose the White House–Interior Panel on Waterlogging and Salinity in West Pakistan, headed by Dr. Roger Revelle, then science adviser to the U. S. Secretary of the Interior. The panel, whose work will be discussed at length in Chapter 9, included earth scientists and economists from Harvard, M.I.T., the universities of California and Chicago, the U.S.G.S., the U. S. Department of Agriculture, other government agencies, and several private firms. It was what the Pakistanis call a "high-powered panel." In September and October 1961, the panel paid its first visit to Pakistan, where the records and services of

22. Interview with Dr. Abdus Salam, Professor of Theoretical Physics, Imperial College of Science and Technology, London, July 31, 1963. It should be mentioned that the United States had furnished, under its technical assistance program, a team of hydrologists from the U. S. Geological Survey to Pakistan as early as 1954. These experts worked with the Ground Water Development Organization of the Punjab Irrigation Department in assaying the groundwater resources and in laying the foundation for the first Salinity Control and Reclamation Project (SCARP I in the Rechna Doab) which was undertaken by WAPDA in 1960 with assistance from the U.S. International Cooperation Administration. In 1960, the Ground Water Development Organization was transferred to WAPDA, where it became WASID (Water and Soils Investigation Division), and shortly thereafter WAPDA established its Groundwater and Reclamation Division (see Chapter 8) to plan and execute additional SCARPs.

WAPDA's Water and Soils Investigation Division (WASID) were immediately placed at its disposal. Thus, by early 1962, WAPDA had a pretty clear indication that the Americans were going to do something about the waterlogging problem in the entire Pakistan portion of the Indus Basin. So, when the World Bank reacted to the March 1962 estimates by suggesting that Tarbela be eliminated, WAPDA responded by proposing that the $50 million set aside for the Tubewells and Drainage Works component of the IBP be transferred instead to the cost of the Tarbela Dam.

Both alternatives were discussed at the Murree meetings in July 1962, but as the above quotation indicates, Iliff found the Pakistanis firmly opposed to the deletion of Tarbela. They would transfer the $50 million from the Tubewells and Drainages component, and would also assume the entire rupees cost, equivalent to $807 million, of the IBP. But they insisted that the Bank and the "friendly Governments" were morally bound to provide the additional foreign exchange needed to complete the "scheme of works" specified in the "Project Description." Finally, Iliff said that he was willing to recommend to the Bank and the "friendly Governments" that they make an additional contribution of $310 million in foreign exchange to the Fund. But this contribution was to be the last, and Pakistan was to agree that it represented the discharge of all obligations, explicit or implied, regarding the financing of the IBP.

This was a reasonable proposal inasmuch as, by eliminating the $50 million Tubewells and Drainages component, the March 1962 estimates could be reduced to $1,745 million and the foreign exchange portion from $960 million to $938 million. Pakistan would receive a total of $942 million ($632 million in grants and loans under the original Development Fund Agreement, plus $310 million under a supplementary agreement). Of course, Pakistan would have had to contribute $108 million in foreign exchange to the Fund to offset the $80-million worth of rupees originally scheduled to be bought with foreign exchange plus the $28 million which had gone into the Special Reserve out of India's contribution in pounds sterling. (Pakistan, it will be remembered, would have these Special Reserve funds turned over to her in the event that she did not extend the Transition Period.) Thus Pakistan would have incurred a net obligation of $104 million in foreign exchange, to be met out of her Five Year Plan allocations. But the Murree proposal also envisaged that Pakistan would devote to the IBP (with the approval of the governments concerned) all the rupee counterpart funds arising from sales of United States agricultural products under the "Food for Peace" program (less amounts reserved for U.S. uses in Pakistan) or from sales of commodities supplied by other countries (notably West Germany) under similar programs. This meant that the net burden on Pakistan was limited to $104 million in foreign exchange plus any amounts in rupees not covered by counterpart funds (impossible to estimate accurately).

On the whole, it seemed to be another good bargain for Pakistan, and Iliff believed that his proposal had been accepted.[23] But no agreement was signed, inasmuch as Iliff was in no position to sign one until he had consulted with the directors of the Bank and with the "friendly Governments." This took some time and met with some reluctance. Meanwhile, two new factors, one basic and one seemingly extraneous, were injected into the situation. The basic factor was the submission, in November 1962, of the design studies and new estimates for the Tarbela Dam by the New York firm of Tippetts-Abbett-McCarthy-Stratton (TAMS), now serving as WAPDA's consultants for the project. Including a $20-million contingency allowance suggested by WAPDA's general consultants, Harza Engineering Company International of Chicago (see Chapter 8 for the roles played by the various consultants), these raised the cost of Tarbela to $702.8 million, or $150.4 million above the March 1962 estimate.

The seemingly extraneous factor was injected in October 1962 when Chinese forces attacked Indian outposts in eastern Kashmir (Ladakh) and in the North East Frontier Agency (N. E. F. A.). The Indian Army withdrew and was in full retreat when the Chinese halted and pulled back. Whether the Chinese withdrawal was due to the prompt supply of American and British weapons and military advisers to India or, as many Indians seem to believe, to action by the Soviet Union in cutting off petroleum shipments to China, or whether the Chinese themselves decided that they had secured their immediate objectives, Indian foreign policy and Pakistan-Western

23. The reader may note certain analogies between the Iliff Mission and the Cabinet Mission which left the subcontinent just sixteen years previously after hill-station conferences and in the belief that its plan had been accepted.

relations had undergone an unprecedented shift. Pakistan had stood aside, contemplating with a certain satisfaction the humiliation of her proud neighbor. Whether or not the United States and United Kingdom asked their SEATO/CENTO ally Pakistan to come to India's aid is not known. What is known is that Pakistan continued to make any rapprochement with India contingent upon a Kashmir settlement (discussions were resumed, at U.S.-U.K. urging, in the spring of 1963 but came to naught) and also continued negotiating a border treaty, cultural exchange, and air transit agreement with China. Although Pakistan's position is perfectly understandable from her premises (including the conviction that India had been unjustly occupying Jammu-Kashmir for fifteen years and the fact that India's Defence Minister, V. K. Krishna Menon, had been calling Pakistan "India's Number One Enemy" for most of this time), her attitude toward the Chinese-Indian fighting and her denunciation of "massive Western arms assistance to India" were not appreciated by the State Department or Foreign Office.

Returning from these political heights to the more practical level of the IBP, it is hardly necessary to point out that the U.S. and the U.K. are the main contributors to the Fund as well as the mainstays of the World Bank. Thus, Pakistan's bargaining position with respect to "massive Western financial assistance for the IBP" (if one may adapt a phrase) was somewhat impaired by her foreign policy in late 1962 and early 1963. Furthermore, on purely technical grounds, WAPDA's willingness to exclude the Tubewells and Drainages component from the IBP, and the activities of the Revelle Mission on which this concession was apparently based, had opened up an entirely new approach to replacement and development of water supplies in the Indus Basin. For now the "groundwater advocates" in and out of Pakistan came to the fore to challenge the need for Tarbela and the Indus Zone works in the "surface water" IBP scheme. They spoke in terms of a groundwater reservoir of at least two *billion* acre feet (14 times the average annual runoff of the Western Rivers and almost 50 times the maximum storage capacity at Tarbela *including* off-channel storages) underlying the "Northern Zone" of the Indus Plains ("Northern Zone" being defined as the area above the Gudu Barrage; see page 41 and Map 6) in West Pakistan. With such a reservoir of generally low-salinity groundwater underlying the very works of the IBP and developable at reasonable cost through tubewells, which would also serve to lower the water table and thus to reclaim land, why put $703 million or more into a dam with an expected life of less than fifty years?

The interchangeability of surface water and groundwater in meeting the irrigation needs of the Indus Plains is an extremely complex problem, which we shall discuss in detail in Chapters 9 and 10. It is possible that, as far as the Northern Zone is concerned, and in terms of water actually reaching the crops after allowances for all losses, groundwater may come to play a role as great as that of surface water today. But meanwhile the role of surface water, even in the Northern Zone, will have to be practically doubled. In the Southern Zone, i.e. Sind and Khairpur, the groundwater reservoir appears to be substantially smaller and, with certain localized exceptions, much higher in salt content. Thus, as far as Sind is concerned—and this point can hardly be overemphasized—ground water is *not* an alternative to surface water even in the early stages of development. Ultimately, West Pakistan will have to develop both surface water and groundwater resources to their respective points of diminishing return in relation to each other and to other agricultural inputs. Furthermore, tubewells and processing industries require cheap electric power, and until Pakistan's network of thermal power plants (based increasingly on the natural gas at Sui, northwest of Gudu, and other fields) are much further developed, hydroelectricity from Tarbela will be cheaper. Finally, in many areas even in the Northern Zone, groundwater is too high in salt content to be applied to crops without dilution with surface water, and that means reservoir storage.

So although it is true that if one could somehow have suspended the entire IBP operation in the summer of 1963, while the groundwater investigations were continued, one *might* have concluded, after several years, that Pakistan would be better advised to use the remainder of the Development Fund for a groundwater program with incidental modifications to the surface water system, human affairs are not, and probably cannot be, conducted in such a scientific fashion. By the summer of 1963, Tarbela had become (like Aswan in 1956) a burning public issue in Pakistan. It was grouped with Kashmir, Gurdaspur, other issues along the Indian border, refugee grievances and claims, new reports of persecutions of Muslims in

West Bengal, and fear over Western (and Soviet) arms aid to India as another example of injustice to Pakistan. Pakistan had signed away her birthright rivers to the "enemy." Was she now to be denied her mess of pottage by a combination of former colonialists and neo-imperialists represented by the "friendly Governments" and the World Bank?

This may be putting matters too harshly, but they certainly were seen in this light by many literate Pakistanis.[24] Tarbela had become a symbol, an idée fixe in the public mind. And the odd thing about it was that even those Pakistani engineers and planners, and their conscientious and loyal foreign consultants, who honestly believed that the groundwater program provided the fundamental, long-range answer, had to conceal their enthusiasm and word their reports cau-

24. Pakistan, which has received over $4 billion in Western economic and military assistance, has proved to be increasingly sensitive on this matter in recent years as she has tried to reorient her foreign policy toward the non-aligned position of most Afro-Asian states. She has been vociferous both in demanding "aid without strings" and in asserting her determination to reduce her dependence upon foreign aid for development. When in the summer of 1965 the meeting of the "Aid to Pakistan Consortium," which was to discuss underwriting of her Third Five Year Plan, was postponed at U.S. instigation, Pakistan's Foreign Minister, Zulfikar Ali Bhutto, "declared that Pakistan values its independence more than economic development and emphasised that she is opposed to all forms of colonialism, domination and dictation no matter from which quarter they came. . . . Mr. Bhutto said that Pakistan was an aggrieved country. It was betrayed, he said, before it came into existence and then again after its independence. India was made stronger at Pakistan's expense and all the Muslim majority areas were not given to Pakistan and they had to meet one challenge after another." (Government of Pakistan, Ministry of Information and Broadcasting, Press Information Department, *Pakistan News Digest* [Karachi, The Times Press], July 15, 1965, pp. 1, 9.) The September War brought further curtailments of U.S. and U.K. assistance to both Pakistan and India, and by early November the Ministry of Planning in Karachi announced that development expenditures in the Third Five Year Plan would have to be reduced both because of restricted foreign assistance and because of increased defense allocations. In December 1965 President Ayub visited Washington for discussions with President Johnson, and in January 1966 at Tashkent Ayub and Prime Minister Shastri of India agreed to restore the status quo ante in Kashmir and along the Indo-Pakistan border. When U.S. Vice President Humphrey visited New Delhi and Karachi in February 1966 he announced a limited resumption of American aid to each country. On June 15, 1966, the United States announced simultaneous full-scale resumption of aid to India and Pakistan. Coincidentally, President Ayub relieved Foreign Minister Bhutto of his duties and assumed them himself. (In July Pirzada Sharifuddin was appointed Foreign Minister.)

tiously lest they seem to imply that something was wrong with Tarbela. The "groundwater" and "surface water" schools of thought cut across departmental and ministerial lines. WAPDA, the Irrigation and Power Department with its Irrigation Research Institute, the provincial Department of Agriculture, the central Ministry of Agriculture, the provincial Soils Reclamation Board, and the central Planning Commission all had their advocates of each approach, and of both in varying combinations.

Nor could one even assume that an "old-timer," an engineer who had spent most of his life in the Irrigation Department and subsequently, perhaps, had been transferred to WAPDA, was necessarily a "surface water man" while a "newcomer," an engineer fresh out of the university or recently returned from graduate work abroad and assigned to WAPDA, was necessarily a "groundwater man." For there had been groundwater advocates in the Irrigation Department as early as the 1920s and there were young men in WAPDA who saw more problems than potential in it. Even S. S. Kirmani, Chief Engineer of the IBP and Tarbela's staunchest advocate, saw a necessary and increasing role for groundwater (18 m.a.f. in the Northern Zone; see above, page 272), though he stressed the need for Tarbela as an immediate measure, as a source of supplementary fresh surface water for diluting saline groundwater, and as a source of cheap hydroelectricity to operate the tubewells. And nobody, not even the staunchest groundwater advocate and Tarbela opponent, had figured out what to do with the effluent of massive groundwater irrigation in the Northern Zone except to send it down the Indus to further poison Sind's fields or perhaps to transport it at exorbitant cost to a point where it can be dumped directly into the sea or into the desert along the Indian border.

Nevertheless, by early 1963 the Bank's engineers and economists appeared to be sufficiently impressed with the possibilities of groundwater development as an alternative to Tarbela that they were more reluctant than ever to proceed with the dam, especially on the basis of the November 1962 estimates. The "friendly Governments," on both political and technical grounds, were ill-disposed toward putting any more money into completing the surface water system of the IBP. Rather, like India in the spring of 1959, they were now mainly interested in putting a ceiling on their own contributions. From the standpoint of *Realpolitik* they no longer saw either the need or the likelihood of purchasing Pakistan's goodwill. On the one hand, they did not appreciate Pakistan's attitude in the Sino-Indian conflict. On the other, they saw a chance (perhaps ephemeral) to replace her with a much stronger "ally" in South Asia. So why pay for Tarbela? At the behest of the "friendly Governments" the Bank again suggested that WAPDA eliminate Tarbela, substitute Raised Mangla, and finish the job as close to the original cost estimates as possible.

Faced with this combination of political, financial, and technical objections to Tarbela, and realizing that Pakistan's bargaining position had deteriorated since the Murree meetings, WAPDA began to give way in a somewhat oblique fashion. In May 1963 it published new estimates for the IBP, revised to reflect the November 1962 Tarbela figures and all other changes occurring since March 1962. The new total cost of the IBP including Tarbela but excluding the $50 million for tubewells and drainages came to $1,900.5 million, or $1,802.6 million after excluding the customs duties and sales taxes on materials procured for the project which Pakistan had been required to refund to the Development Fund. If Tarbela were excluded, and Raised Mangla substituted (the Bank's plan), then Pakistan would insist on keeping the $50 million component for tubewells and drainages. The total cost would then amount to $1,373.5 million, or $1,299.1 million after reimbursement of customs and taxes. Thus, the net cost of keeping Tarbela in the project was "only" $503.5 million.

But the real point in WAPDA's May 1963 submission was that Pakistan would pay a larger portion of the foreign exchange costs of Tarbela. She would make foreign exchange contributions of $160.2 million via her Five Year Plans, plus another $15.4 million through the Development Fund, for a total of $175.6 million as compared with the $104 million in the Murree proposals. According to WAPDA's new estimates, these contributions would amount to *more* than the added cost *in foreign exchange* ($143.7 million) of keeping Tarbela in the project, while eliminating Tubewells and Drainages, as compared to completing the original "Project Description." The additional cost of Tarbela in rupees would be $359.8 million, but here too Pakistan would make concessions. She would assume all but $80 million of the $154.6 million originally set aside in the Fund for rupee purchases, and would increase her own rupee contributions to the Fund by $14.3 million. If the United States would allow her to devote all of the accumulated and prospective Public Law 480 and Food for Peace counterpart rupees (excluding amounts reserved for United States uses) to the IBP, Pakistan would promise to make up any shortfall, though it hoped there would be none.

What all this meant was that Pakistan was asking the United States for an additional $454.3 million in counterpart rupees over and above the $231.8 million included in the original Fund Agreement. Coupled with the original U.S. dollar contributions in grants and loans, the WAPDA proposal would have raised the total U.S. share in the Fund to about $1,105 million. Even granting that Food for Peace is a "giveaway" program, inasmuch as the United States can never begin to use the counterpart funds generated by its commodity shipments but instead devotes them to projects suggested by the recipient nation, total *dollar grants* to Pakistan would come to about $298 million and total *dollar loans* to $121 million under this plan (and World Bank loans to almost $140 million). So despite Pakistan's willingness to make foreign exchange allocations from her Five Year Plans (which are also supported by the "friendly Governments" contributing to the Indus Basin Development Fund), she was still asking for considerable assistance from the United States, the other "friendly Governments," and the Bank at a time when there was little disposition to accede to her requests.

Indeed, for some strange reason, WAPDA's May 1963 submission entitled *Financing the Indus Project on the Basis of Sir William Iliff's Financial Plan of July, 1962*,[25] which states that it "does not present a proposal but only indicates the requirements of funds from the various Contributing Governments and the Bank under the two alternatives," consistently employs figures based on an assumption that the *entire* additional foreign exchange costs of the IBP, including Tarbela, would be divided among the "friendly Governments" in the proportions used in the original Development Fund. This is true despite the fact that the report notes that Iliff's proposal limited their additional contribution to $310 million, points out that Pakistan will have to assume the added foreign exchange burden of $160.2

25. IBP Publication No. 87 (Lahore, WAPDA, May 1963).

million by allocations from her Five Year Plans, and mentions as an additional "concession" by Pakistan her "limiting the maximum liability of the contributors to the Fund specified in the Agreement" if Tarbela is included. Perhaps the reason for this rather oblique approach lies in this statement:

> If, however, Tarbela is excluded from the Plan and Raised Mangla substituted instead, as now suggested by the Contributing Governments and the World Bank, the concessions given by the Pakistan Government would not apply and the financing of a Plan excluding Tarbela and substituting [raised] Mangla instead would have to be strictly in accordance with the principles laid down in the Fund Agreement.[26]

At any rate, WAPDA's use of figures that the Murree proposals had rendered purely hypothetical seems to contradict WAPDA's effort to demonstrate how much the contributing governments would "save" by adopting its suggestion rather than that of the Bank. There was no real possibility, by the summer of 1963, that the "friendly Governments" would increase their contributions over the amount suggested at Murree. There was even a very real question whether they would be willing to do as much, considering the events of the intervening year. WAPDA's May 1963 submission assumes that they would, and suggests that they might do more, but there were anxious hours in Lahore and Rawalpindi that summer and fall. Indeed, it was not until the end of the year that Pakistan could relax in the assurance that the $310 million would be forthcoming.

In November 1963 Bank President George D. Woods, who had succeeded Eugene Black in January 1963, met with President Ayub and agreed to recommend the supplementary contribution to the "friendly Governments" provided that Pakistan would allow the Bank to conduct a fundamental study of water and power resources of the Indus Basin, including both the surface water and groundwater aspects. The two presidents agreed in principle, and the following month a WAPDA team visited Washington where details of the accord were worked out. The Bank and "friendly Governments" would make the contribution of $310 million foreseen at Murree, plus an allocation of $5 million for the Indus Resources Study. The "tech-

26. Ibid., p. 6.

nical feasibility" and "economic viability" of a dam on the Indus
were to form the first portion of the study, which was to be completed within a year, and the entire study was to be available in 1966.

To formalize these arrangements, a Supplemental Agreement to the
Indus Basin Development Fund Agreement was signed at Washington
on March 31, 1964, by representatives of the Bank and the U.S.A.,
and one week later by the representatives of the other "friendly Governments" and Pakistan. Its salient features are as follows:

1. All parties accept the Supplemental Agreement as "a full and
   complete discharge of all obligations, whether legal or moral, expressed or implied" under the 1960 Agreement.
2. The parties will make the following supplemental contributions
   to the Development Fund:

		Grants	*Loans*
Australia	£A	4,669,643	
Canada	Can. $	16,810,794	
West Germany	DM	80,400,000	
New Zealand	£NZ	503,434	
United Kingdom	£	13,978,571	
United States		U.S. $118,590,000	U.S. $ 51,220,000
World Bank International Development Association			U.S. $ 58,540,000 (in various currencies)

3. No further rupee purchases shall be made from the Fund.
4. Pakistan shall pay all additional rupee costs of the project, using
   for this purpose either U.S. counterpart rupees (by agreement
   with the U.S.A.) or her own rupee resources.
5. Priority of disbursements from the Fund shall be accorded to:
   a. Materials costs of Mangla Dam and related works
   b. Materials costs of the "Links Canals, Barrages and Other
      Works" set forth in the "Project Description" appended to the
      1960 Agreement, as already modified by agreement between
      Pakistan and the Administrator with the approval of the
      "friendly Governments," but excluding the Tubewells and
      Drainage Works Component

c. Overhead and engineering costs related to (a) and (b)

d. Expenses incurred by the Administrator for his services

e. The costs of the Study described in (7) below

6. After all of the above expenses have been met, any non-rupee assets remaining in the Fund will be disbursed to meet the non-rupee costs of the Tarbela project *if Pakistan and the Bank agree that Tarbela is justified on the basis of the Study* described in (7) below; if they do not so agree, then these funds will be allocated *to some other development project* or projects *in the water and power sector* in West Pakistan as agreed between Pakistan and the Bank.

7. The Administrator shall organize and administer a study of the water and power resources of West Pakistan which would provide the Government of Pakistan with a basis for development planning under the Five Year Plans; the study will be completed within two years of its commencement; and the first objective of the Study will be a report on the technical feasibility, construction cost, and economic return of a dam on the Indus at Tarbela, this portion to be completed if possibly by the end of 1964.

8. There is no commitment by the parties to participate in any project arising out of the Study except as provided in (6) above.[27]

With this Supplemental Agreement, the Bank and the "friendly Governments" had achieved a number of objectives. Their total liability toward the IBP had been fixed. Their contributions would be used to complete the project as originally described and subsequently modified, but *not* including Tarbela unless the Bank and Pakistan agreed that it was justified, and then *only* if any foreign exchange remained in the Fund (a highly unlikely contingency). And if, by some chance, some foreign exchange did remain in the fund, it could be used for any water or power development project in West Pakistan acceptable to both the Bank and WAPDA, such as groundwater development. Of course, even if the Bank study ruled out Tarbela, Pakistan theoretically remained free to finance it out of her own

27. IBRD, *The Indus Basin Development Fund (Supplemental) Agreement, 1964,* and IBRD Press Release No. 64/10, "Indus Supplemental Agreement" (Washington, D.C., April 8, 1964). This summary is a paraphrase; italics are the author's.

resources, but the Supplemental Agreement required her first to meet any foreign exchange requirements of the project minus Tarbela, plus all of its remaining rupee requirements to the extent that they were not met by U.S. or other counterpart rupees. The Bank had also secured two more of its aims, though not quite in the order it wanted to achieve them. Tarbela would be subjected to a technical and economic reappraisal, and a fundamental investigation of all water (including groundwater) and power resources of the Pakistan portion of the Indus Basin would be carried out under the Bank's direction.

From an ideal point of view there was one flaw in the Supplemental Agreement arrangements. The Tarbela investigation was to be completed a year ahead of the general study. Thus feasibility and viability of Tarbela would have to be decided in the absence of full data on the groundwater alternative, if any existed. In the view of an impartial observer, this would seem to be putting the cart before the horse.

In the event, the Tarbela study largely revisited old ground which had been covered since 1952 by the Irrigation Department's Dams Investigation Circle, by the consulting firms of Tipton and Hill and TAMS, and by WAPDA itself. The section of the World Bank team concerned with the Tarbela report was divided into three groups to investigate each of the following aspects:

A. Dam sites and side valley storage sites, rates of silting and costs including those of building a dam further up the Indus to prolong Tarbela's life
B. Power aspects
C. Economic aspects

Group A investigated eight possible sites on the Indus, eliminated all but Kalabagh and Tarbela, and finally came up with an opinion not much different from that expressed by WAPDA's Chief Engineer (A. R. Kazi) in 1961, i.e. that Tarbela was not attractive, but less unattractive than Kalabagh (see above, page 295).

The Tarbela section of the report would have been ready by November 1964, but was delayed at WAPDA's own request to allow the submission of new benefit analyses. It was finally presented to the Bank in February 1965, and by the Bank to Pakistan in March. On March 18, 1965, the Ministry of Finance announced:

The report finds the construction of a dam on the Indus at Tarbela technically feasible and economically justifiable.

In view of the size of the Tarbela project and the magnitude of its cost in terms of both foreign exchange and domestic expenditure, the financial implications require further discussions by the Government of Pakistan with others, amongst them the World Bank as Administrator of the Indus Basin Development Fund and as the leading international agency in economic development financing.

It is likely that the discussions will take some time.[28]

One reason why the discussions would "take some time" apparently lay in the need to coordinate the funding of Tarbela with other development expenditures included in Pakistan's Third Five Year Plan, due to begin on July 1, 1965. Excessive spending on capital works that do not increase the production of consumable goods until many years have passed is, of course, a frequent and serious contributor to inflation in developing nations. Although, as we have seen, Pakistan proposed to finance most of the domestic costs of Tarbela out of counterpart funds generated by the U. S. Food for Peace and similar programs, such a procedure might well give pause to an economist. For these "accumulated" rupees exist only as accounting balances. The only way Pakistan can use them is to print them and issue them in exchange for domestic goods and services—a sure path to self-defeating inflation. Thus, for all practical purposes, the only counterpart funds Pakistan could devote to the Tarbela project would be those accruing *in the future* from the sale of American (and other) surplus commodities. But in the spring of 1965, the U.S.A. was starting to reappraise not only its Food for Peace program but its entire foreign aid operation in both economic and political terms. In June, the United States Government refused to renew the annual Food for Peace agreements with India, announcing that it would continue such shipments only on a month-by-month basis pending a thorough review of India's programs for agricultural development. (The Food for Peace agreement with Pakistan did not expire until December.) In September, after the outbreak of the Kashmir War, the U.S.A.

28. Embassy of Pakistan, Washington, D.C., *Pakistan Affairs*, April 16, 1965, p. 5.

suspended all aid to both countries except what was "in the pipeline," and it was not until early 1966 that aid, on a limited scale, was resumed. We shall discuss the implications of the events of 1965 for the IBP in more detail in Chapter 10.

Meanwhile, late in 1964, WAPDA had requested its Tarbela consultants (TAMS) to prepare final designs for a raised dam with 9.3 m.a.f. of live storage. Early in 1965, WAPDA announced its intention, if the Bank approved, to invite tenders for the dam in June 1965, to award the contract in March 1966, and to complete the dam by March 1973.[29] WAPDA also announced plans to proceed with raising Mangla by 40 feet, completing it by June 30, 1970, the end of the Third Five Year Plan. Although the outline of the Third Five Year Plan does not specifically include allocations for Mangla, Tarbela, or any of the IBP works, it estimates that IBP requirements would absorb 2.2 billion rupees ($463 million) of the expected Food for Peace counterpart funds accruing over fiscal 1965–70.[30] Making allowances for United States uses and contingencies, this would leave about one billion rupees for items specifically included in the Plan. And it was indicated that Tarbela would be specifically included in the Fourth Plan.

June 1965 passed without any invitations of tenders for Tarbela, and it soon became apparent that the dam's status was again in jeopardy as a result of the uncertainty over future Food for Peace shipments and because of the U.S.-initiated postponement of "Aid to Pakistan Consortium" discussions on the whole Third Plan. But in the spring of 1966, after the Ayub-Shastri meeting at Tashkent and the withdrawal of Indian and Pakistani forces to the positions occupied in August 1965, the World Bank began to release payments from the Development Fund to cover the cost of the railway spur and power line which WAPDA was building to the Tarbela site. This would seem to be a firm indication that the Bank was prepared to proceed with Tarbela as long as there was no new deterioration in the political situation. At the beginning of June 1966, S. S. Kirmani, Chief Engineer, IBP, said he expected that the Consortium meeting scheduled for July would give final approval to the dam, and that

29. *WAPDA Weekly*, January 29, 1965 and February 19, 1965.
30. Government of Pakistan, Planning Commission, *Outline of the Third Five-Year Plan (1965–70)* (Karachi, August 1964), p. 62.

the Bank had already released Rs 120 million ($25.4 million) for the preliminary works.[31] But since actual construction of the dam cannot begin until a bridge has been placed across the Indus at the site, it does not seem possible to begin work before early 1968 or to finish Tarbela before late 1974 or early 1975, about two years after the end of the Transition Period outlined in the Treaty.

Also in 1965, WAPDA's regional consultants for the Lower Indus Basin or "Southern Zone," Hunting Technical Services, Ltd., and Sir M. MacDonald and Partners, both of London, had completed a 56-volume, 28,000-page investigation report as a basis for planning. But as of mid 1966 this report has not been released. Meanwhile, the regional consultants for the "Northern Zone," Tipton and Kalmbach of Denver (the successor firm to Tipton and Hill), were continuing their work not only on a project-by-project basis but on a regional plan for the Zone, due for completion, though probably not for release, in September 1966.

As for the World Bank's comprehensive study of water and power resources in West Pakistan, its completion was delayed from the end of 1965 to May 1966 and then to early in 1967. The second portion of the Harza Appraisal Report, which is to carry the report released in March 1964 up to 1985 or 1990, was postponed from the end of 1965 to mid 1967 in order to allow the general consultants to incorporate the results of the Hunting-MacDonald, Tipton and Kalmbach, and World Bank studies. Thus WAPDA's Master Plan for Water and Power Development in West Pakistan can hardly be completed much before 1969 or even 1970.

The Bhakra-Beas-Rajasthan Project (India)

If India's position in the Indus Basin was good in 1947, it was even better in 1960. On the one hand, the Indus Waters Treaty had conferred upon her, in exchange for the sum of $174 million (offset by loans totaling $56 million from the United States and the World Bank), undisputed ownership of the three Eastern Rivers. On the

31. *WAPDA Weekly*, June 8, 1966, p. 3. Added in proof: The World Bank finally authorized WAPDA to issue Tarbela tender invitations in March 1967, with tenders due in September 1967. Hopefully, this marks the end of the Tarbela crisis.

other hand, in the period between Partition and the signing of the Treaty, India had completed the Harike and Nangal barrages on the Sutlej, the Bhakra Main Line and Bist Doab canals and their distribution systems, and had made substantial progress on the Rajasthan Feeder Canal and on the single most important component of her Indus Basin works, Bhakra Dam.[32]

But over this period, the Bhakra Project had come to mean something quite different from what it conveyed in 1947. Partition meant, from the Indian standpoint, that Bhakra storage need no longer be used for bringing the Pakistan Sutlej Valley canals up to allocation while assuring Sind of her historic and "sanctioned "allocations. Instead, Bhakra water could be used first to increase supplies for some 3.5 million acres, most of them in the Sirhind command, and then to add 6.5 million acres of newly irrigated lands in East Punjab and Rajasthan. About 3.85 million acres of these new lands lay in the Jullundur District and in the cis-Sutlej Punjab (see Table 15). The rest lay in Bikaner, at the lower end of the Bhakra Main system, or further west under the projected Rajasthan Canal.

We have described in Chapter 6 how, almost immediately after Partition, India built the Harike Barrage below the Sutlej-Beas confluence to replace Ferozepore as the intake for the Eastern and Bikaner canals and to serve, eventually, a Rajasthan Canal extending far to the southwest, into the Thar Desert. We have also mentioned the modifications made at Madhopur to bring Ravi waters into the Beas via a short link, and at Rupar to bring Sutlej water for the first time to the southern Bist-Jullundur Doab via the 1,600-cusec Bist Doab Canal. We have indicated how, as early as 1954, the Nangal Barrage stood complete on the Sutlej below Bhakra to divert

32. Work on the diversion tunnels for the Bhakra Dam was begun in 1948. Although the Sutlej was fully diverted only after the 1954 monsoon, excavations for the foundations had begun in November 1953. Concreting began in November 1955, and was sufficiently advanced to allow storage to begin with the monsoon runoff of 1958. At that point, completion by March of 1960 was anticipated, but changes in design and technical difficulties forced postponement first to the summer of 1961 and then until mid 1962. In August 1959 the collapse in the right-hand diversion tunnel occurred (see Chapter 8, pp. 378–79), which delayed power installation more than completion of the dam itself. Bhakra Dam reached its full height late in 1961. Civil engineering work was substantially completed by mid 1962, and initial power installations in 1963. The dam was officially dedicated by Prime Minister Nehru on October 22, 1963. (See also Chapter 6, pp. 206–07.)

Table 15. New Irrigation in East Punjab Made Possible by the Bhakra Canal
System (includes Bhakra Main Line Canal and Bist Doab Canal)[a, b]

	Culturable Commanded Area (Million Acres)			
District	Restricted Perennial[c]	Nonperennial	Perennial	Total
Jullundur	.450	0	0	.450
Ferozepur	0	.3825	.174	.556
Ludhiana	.1395	.1105	0	.250
Karnal	.4096	0	.2646	.674
Hissar	0	0	1.824	1.824
Ambala	.099	0	0	.099
Total	1.098	.493	2.2625	3.854[d]

a. Source: Director, Public Relations, Punjab, "Index Plan, showing Area to be Irrigated from Bhakra Canals," 1952.

b. The Bhakra Main Line begins at the lower end of the Nangal Hydel Channel near Rupar with an initial capacity of 12,455 cusecs, and runs for 108 miles south and west through Patiala and Hissar to the Rajasthan border. Its branches, which total 545 miles in length, include the Narwana Branch, which intercepts the old Sirsa Branch of the Western Jumna Canal, and the Barwala Branch, which takes over some command from the old Hansi Branch of the WJC. Thus, the Bhakra Canal releases 1,844 cusecs from these two branches of the WJC making possible increased intensities and the irrigation of 300,000 new acres under that command. The Bist Doab Canal offtakes Rupar headworks with an initial capacity of 1,601 cusecs and a length of 29 miles. With its 58 miles of branches, it irrigates the 450,000 culturable commanded area in the Jullundur district.

c. "Restricted Perennial" means rabi irrigation plus early kharif irrigation in foothill districts that draw their main kharif supplies from rainfall and wells.

d. Slight discrepancies in source.

water into the Bhakra Main Line Canal to serve areas in Hissar and Bikaner.

But at least until the Treaty negotiations had reached the stage of the Bank's proposal for dividing the rivers (see Chapter 6, page 235), which India accepted in March 1954, India had not irrevocably committed herself to use of Sutlej, Beas, or Ravi water beyond the Indus Basin.[33] Thereafter, apparently on the basis that she had

33. We come back to the interesting question of what constitutes the Indus Basin. In Table 3 we saw that the Indian Irrigation Commission of 1901–03 joined the Luni Basin to that of the Indus and drew a distinction between them and that of the Jumna-Ganges. The difficulty in deciding the question is that there are no perennial streams in the Thar Desert, and the watershed between the Sutlej and the Jumna in southernmost Punjab is so flat as to be virtually indistinguishable. A small amount of Bhakra water is indeed being used to

indicated acceptance of the Bank's proposal in principle and was willing to sign a treaty to that effect whenever Pakistan came around with "reasonable" estimates for the cost of the "replacement" works, India went ahead with planning the use of "Indus water" in the Thar Desert. The first indication of this was the tripartite Interstate Agreement signed among the recently integrated states of Punjab and Rajasthan and the Indian-administered State of Kashmir in 1955. (In view of the repartition of the Indian Punjab in November 1966, the division will have to be revised between Punjab and Haryana.) The next formal indication was in 1956 when India renounced the Barcelona Convention on international rivers (see Chapter 6, page 197).

The interesting aspect of the 1955 Interstate Agreement is not only that it allocated somewhat more water to Rajasthan (8.0 m.a.f.) than to Punjab (7.2 m.a.f.) and Kashmir (0.65 m.a.f.) combined, but that the total supply of 15.85 m.a.f. over and above the pre-Partition allocations of about 9 m.a.f. in these states was more than the average annual flow of the Sutlej (14 m.a.f.) and far more than the total which Bhakra Dam, despite its live storage capacity of 6.3 m.a.f., could make available on a sustained annual basis including hold-over storage. To fulfill the goals of the 1955 Interstate Agreement and provide 8 m.a.f. to Rajasthan would require the construction at Pong on the Beas, which has an average annual flow of 13 m.a.f. or almost as much as the Sutlej, of a dam with a live-storage capacity (5.5 m.a.f.) almost as great as Bhakra's, and would eventually require the provision of additional storage capacities above Pong on the Beas, above Bhakra on the Sutlej, and at Thein on the Ravi. In other words, the 1955 Interstate Agreement envisioned not only the use of Sutlej water stored by Bhakra but the allocation of the waters of all three Eastern Rivers under an integrated program of development. As this Indian program took shape over the ensuing years, and the Bhakra Project became inseparably interwoven with

---

supplement the irrigation of the Western Jumna Canal. Eastern Rajasthan, including Jaipur, is definitely in the Jumna-Ganges Basin. But whether or not the rest of Rajasthan belongs to the Indus Basin, the point to be made here is that it was not until 1955 that India began firmly to plan for use of water which, but for the intervention of man, would unquestionably find its way into the Indus in regions where it unquestionably now will not.

the projects for the Beas and in Rajasthan, it came to resemble the IBAB-IBP program in the Pakistani portion of the Basin. Therefore, it is more logical to refer to them as a single project, the Bhakra-Beas-Rajasthan Project (BBRP henceforth).

What the BBRP entails in construction and operation may be summarized as follows:

1. The three Eastern Rivers will be developed as an integrated unit, and in addition will be integrated to a degree with the Jumna insofar as the Sutlej-Jumna link (the Narwana Branch of the Bhakra Main Line Canal; see Map 7) allows Sutlej waters to be used in Western Jumna Canal areas in the Indian Punjab.

2. Sutlej waters (13.329 m.a.f. in the average year at Bhakra) will be stored at Bhakra and used first to meet the needs of the Punjab via diversions at Nangal, Rupar, and Harike, with a small portion going to Rajasthan via Harike. Ultimately, a reservoir of 1 to 2 m.a.f. may be provided above Bhakra at the Slapper site both to reduce sedimentation and to increase storage (cf. Skardu and Kotkai on the Indus above Tarbela).

3. Meanwhile, in order to help fill the Bhakra reservoir in view of the heavy demands upon it from Indian Punjab and Rajasthan, 3.823 m.a.f. of Beas water will be diverted into the Sutlej via a high-level canal and two tunnels between the Beas at Pandoh and the Bhakra reservoir (Beas-Sutlej Link). Ultimately, a reservoir of 1 to 2 m.a.f. may be provided on the Beas at Larji above Pandoh to regulate flow and reduce sedimentation.

4. Meanwhile, the remainder of Beas water (9.185 m.a.f. in the average year) will continue to flow into the Pong reservoir where 5.5 m.a.f. can be impounded to be released as required at Harike. Thus, the main burden of the Rajasthan Canal component would be carried by the Pong reservoir on the Beas.

5. Harike also benefits from the Ravi-Beas Link Canal built with a capacity of 10,000 cusecs in 1952–54 from the Madhopur head-works to the Chakki tributary of the Beas. Ultimately, if the Thein Dam with a storage capacity of 1 m.a.f. is built upstream of Madhopur on the Ravi, 1.946 m.a.f. per year can be made available to Harike via this link.[34]

34. Bureau of Reclamation, United States Department of the Interior, *Beas and Rajasthan Projects*, p. 22.

Not that the BBRP plan sprang full grown into existence in 1955. Rather, like the IBAB-IBP plan, it grew component by component. Between 1955 and the signing of the Treaty, India (as far as Indus Basin development was concerned) had her hands full with Bhakra Dam. Nevertheless, in full realization that the Sutlej waters stored at Bhakra would be inadequate for the Rajasthan Project, investigations were started on the Beas, both at the Pong dam site and at the Pandoh diversion site, as early as 1955. By 1958, preliminary design studies of the Pong Dam were undertaken by the Bhakra Designs Directorate, which shortly became the Bhakra-Beas Designs Directorate, keeping the same offices in Delhi, the same engineers, draftsmen, drawing boards, and pencils. In other words, India was starting to realize some economies of mass production where dams were concerned, even though Pong is quite dissimilar to Bhakra. By the time the Treaty was signed, equipment and personnel were already being transferred from Bhakra to Pong, and the new administrative town of Talwara, with its offices, housing facilities, warehouses, and workshops, was beginning to rise 4 miles downstream, just as Nangal had been "created" to support the Bhakra operations.[35] At first, only enough men and equipment could be spared to work on the local infrastructure of access roads, bridges, and buildings. But by 1962, actual excavation work for the diversion tunnels had been started at Pong. Although Pong Dam is not scheduled for completion before 1971, it furnishes many interesting points of comparison and contrast with Mangla Dam, construction of which also began in 1962 after three years of "local infrastructure" preparation.

Table 14 presents a statistical comparison of Mangla (in its initial and raised form) and Pong, both earth-fill dams of roughly comparable design (at least to the layman). It indicates that initial Mangla will be 50 feet higher than Pong, almost twice as long, and (even excluding the Sukian dike and Jari and Kakra dams) more than twice as massive. Mangla has three times the hydroelectric potential of Pong.

Since the $540-million figure for initial Mangla includes all of the auxiliary works as well as the cost of building New Mirpur town

35. Visit to Pong and Talwara and interview with O. P. Mehta, Under Secretary to Government Punjab, Beas Project Administration, at Talwara, March 19, 1964.

and resettling the 80,000 "Mangla Affected Persons," and the $243-million figure for Pong also includes the costs of Talwara and of resettling some 60,000 "Pong Affected Persons," a better comparison would be between a figure of approximately $290 million for the Mangla Dam proper, including spillways and power installations, and a comparable figure of about $133 million for Pong. Because initial Mangla is nearing completion and the estimates for it are now pretty firm, whereas Pong's final design is not yet complete, even this comparison is far from accurate, but it does begin to point up two significant contrasts between the projects: (1) Mangla is the first large dam to be built in the Pakistan portion of the Indus Basin (it literally dwarfs both the Warsak and Rawal dams) whereas Pong takes full advantage of the experience, men, and equipment transferred from Bhakra (and the experience with other earth-fill dams constructed since Independence in other parts of India); and (2) Pakistan, under great pressure to complete the IBP, is trading money (most of it in grants from the "friendly Governments") for time by using foreign contractors and consultants on a scale unprecedented in engineering history, whereas India, with less of a stake in the Indus Basin and less foreign aid for her projects there, is trading time for money and building her projects by departmental or "superdepartmental" methods (which will be analyzed in Chapter 8) using no foreign contractors and a minimum of foreign advice. India does have $56 million in loans forthcoming from the United States and the World Bank for the Pong Project, and may ask for more, and she is receiving some technical assistance from the U.S. Bureau of Reclamation on the Pong Dam, Beas-Sutlej Diversion, and Rajasthan Projects (see Chapter 8), but her approach is fundamentally different from Pakistan's.

Yet there are inescapable similarities between the two projects. Like Mangla, Pong is an "outer Siwalik" site where the Beas finally leaves the mountains and debouches onto the plains. Although the bedrock geology of the Pong site seems superior to Mangla in that the early Pleistocene sandstones, siltstones, and claystones are more highly compacted, and the diversion tunnels have not yet encountered zones of unconsolidated materials,[36] the sedimentation problems are very similar to Mangla's. Just as the Jhelum, after losing most of its

36. Bureau of Reclamation, p. 59, and visit of March 19, 1964.

silt in Lake Wular, is joined above Mangla by the Kishanganga, Kunhar, and Punch rivers (see Map 6) with their heavy loads of Siwalik sediments, so the Beas is joined above Pong by the Neogal, Buner, Gaj, and Dehar streams which contribute almost all of its sediment load at the dam site.[37] But whereas Mangla's initial live storage capacity of 4.75 m.a.f. would be reduced to 1 m.a.f. within 120 years, Pong will lose only 35 per cent of its gross capacity in a century.[38] In neither case can much be done upstream: the Mangla reservoir will inundate the Kamalpur site and other main stem sites lying in Indian-occupied Kashmir, whereas on the Beas there is no site upstream until one reaches Larji which (like Skardu on the Indus) is above the zone of greatest sedimentation. In both cases, the remedy is similar: raising the initial dam to provide a larger capacity for silt absorption. At Mangla, the raising is apparently going to be done between 1967 and 1970. At Pong, if the recommendations of the Bureau of Reclamation team are followed, it is likely to be included in the final design.[39]

Because both dams are located just below the foothills where the monsoons strike hardest, rather than in the inner Himalayas, both must go through critical periods in construction when the whole project will be threatened by abnormal runoff. At Mangla the period came in the kharif of 1966 when the 225-foot closure dam and the diversion tunnels had to be ready to store and pass a flood of up to 1.1 million cusecs, the flood of record. At Pong, there will be two critical periods, the first occurring in the winter of 1966–67 when the Beas is diverted by a temporary cofferdam to allow work on the foundation up to riverbed level, and the second from the following winter through the summer of 1968 when the river will again be diverted and the dam raised to a height that should be sufficient to absorb the monsoon runoff. The difference between the projects is that the Pong foundations will be laid in one "cool season" while the Beas is entirely diverted through the tunnels, whereas most of the Mangla foundation has been prepared behind cofferdams over three years, with the Jhelum confined but not diverted.

A significant reason for this difference is that the Jhelum, even in

37. Bureau of Reclamation, p. 153.
38. Ibid., p. 58.
39. Ibid., pp. 83–85.

winter, has about twice the flow of the Beas and begins to rise in February, whereas the Beas does not show any significant rise until the end of April and does not fill its banks until the end of June.[40] Since the flood of record at Pong (600,000 cusecs in September 1947) happens to have almost the same ratio to that at Mangla (1.1 million cusecs in August 1929) as the average annual flow of the Beas (13 m.a.f.) has to that of the Jhelum (23 m.a.f.), it will be possible to design a proportionally smaller spillway of 475,000-cusec capacity at Pong as compared to 900,000 cusecs at Mangla. The Indian design for Pong called for only 250,000 cusecs, but this was revised upward after consultation with the Bureau of Reclamation team,[41] and the Pong spillway, in the left abutment, will require only one stilling basin. Both dams will make use of five 30-foot-diameter diversion tunnels, but where all five of the Mangla tunnels will be used for both irrigation and power purposes, only three of those at Pong will be harnessed for power, the other two outlets being used for irrigation releases as required over and above the power outflow.

A further contrast between the two projects is that Mangla will immediately serve the irrigation needs of the UJC via the new Bong Feeder, whereas even after Pong is built there will be no irrigation directly from the Beas. The upper portion of the Bist-Jullundur Doab consists of the "dry" district of Hoshiarpur, up against and including some of the foothills, which relies on rainfall and wells, and the southern portion of the doab, in the Jullundur District, is now irrigated from Rupar via the Bist Doab Canal. So the releases from Pong will actually not be used until they reach Rajasthan, via Harike headworks and the Rajasthan Feeder Canal. In this respect, the function of Pong in the BBRP is more akin to that of Tarbela in the IBP, which is upstream storage designed *primarily* for downstream diversion and the irrigation of new lands (as Gudu and Ghulam Mohammad are brought up to allocation) in the "Southern Zone." Similarly, the function of Bhakra may be compared to that of Mangla since most of its water is being used in the long-established irrigated area of the southern Punjab and very little finds its way to Rajasthan. Table 16 clarifies the relation between Pong and Bhakra in the operation of the BBRP.

40. Khosla, "Development of the Indus River System," 236–37. See also Bureau of Reclamation, p. 55.
41. Bureau of Reclamation, pp. 29, 83–85, 156.

Table 16. Projected Releases from Pong and Bhakra Reservoirs to Meet
the Needs of Punjab and Rajasthan at Harike Barrage[a]

	Mean Year (m.a.f.)	*Dependable Year (m.a.f.)*
From Pong Reservoir via Beas	9.027	6.220
Gain in Beas from Pong to Mandi Plain[b]	.582	.428
Gain from Ravi via Madhopur-Beas Link	1.946	1.446
From Bhakra Reservoir via Sutlej	.926	1.331
Total receipts at Harike	12.481	9.420[c]
Distribution from Harike		
To Punjab Canals (via Sirhind and		
Ferozepore Feeders)	3.663	2.914
To Rajasthan Feeder and Canal	8.818[d]	6.506[d]

a. Source: Bureau of Reclamation, United States Department of the Interior,
Beas and Rajasthan Projects, p. 56.

b. Mandi Plain, west of Kapurthala, is the historic gauging station for the
Beas. It is not the rim station, and it should not be confused with Mandi or
"Mandi Hill" (the center of the former Mandi State) in the mountains near
Pandoh. (See Map 2.)

c. Total does not add exactly.

d. Rajasthan's *requirements* at Harike are 8.858 m.a.f.

Table 16 makes clear that Bhakra alone could never supply the
12.5 m.a.f. needed at Harike or the 8.8 m.a.f. needed in Rajasthan.
This burden must be met primarily from Pong. Ultimately, with the
provision of upstream storages at Slapper on the Sutlej and Larji on
the Beas, and with the construction of the Thein Dam on the Ravi
above Madhopur, the BBRP system will be in much better shape. But
experience at Bhakra, where impounding began with the kharif of
1958, has already demonstrated that, due to heavy withdrawals for
power generation and irrigation, it will be hard to fill that reservoir
in most years, and the mean-year operation study for Pong indicates
that that reservoir will have to be emptied and refilled each year.[42]

To provide some immediate relief for Bhakra itself, the Indians
have decided to proceed, simultaneously with Pong's construction,
with a scheme for diverting Beas water above Pong into the upper
reaches of the Bhakra reservoir. This project, although designated
"Unit I" of the Beas-Rajasthan scheme, is less advanced than "Unit
II," Pong Dam. What the Indians propose in Unit I, the Beas-Sutlej
Link, is to build a small dam at Pandoh, where the Beas comes

42. Ibid., p. 56.

closest to the Sutlej, and to transfer some 3.8 m.a.f. per year into Bhakra reservoir. To do this will entail the drilling of two long tunnels, 8 and 8.5 miles respectively, through the pre-Himalayas (not the friable Siwaliks), each of them longer than the new 7.25-mile Mont Blanc vehicular tunnel or the 7.8-mile railway Cascade Tunnel in the state of Washington. Of course, these tunnels are going to be only 30 and 28 feet, respectively, in diameter, but only two adits are possible for building the first and only three for the second.[43] So it will not be an easy job, and it will require at least ten years and cost at least $210 million, including a power station at the Sutlej end (Dehar) tying into the Bhakra grid at Nangal.

The Beas-Sutlej Link was never seriously proposed prior to Partition. Even during the long negotiations for the Treaty, it will be recalled, India was suggesting only the easier tunnel links from the Chenab at Marhu to the Ravi and from the Chandra tributary of the Chenab to the Beas at Palchar (see page 246 and Map 7). But in signing away any significant development of the Chenab, India had to focus her attention on the more difficult possibilities of upstream diversions from the Beas to the Sutlej. It is also correct to say that as the Rajasthan Canal Project grew to a total length of 426 miles, commanding 4.5 million cultivable acres of which 3.5 million would be irrigated in any given year, Indian planners had to find additional sources of regulated supplies, and it is probably true that the initial hopes for filling the Bhakra reservoir from the Sutlej alone were more sanguine than experience has warranted.

Tentative plans for the Beas-Sutlej Link include a 140-foot high, gravity concrete dam on the Beas at Pandoh, which would provide a reservoir with a gross capacity of 14,400 acre feet and a live capacity of 8,400 acre feet. From this reservoir, at an elevation of about 2,800 feet, a 9,000-cusec tunnel would be drilled for 8 miles, 6 of which are in granite and 2 in phyllites. This Pandoh-Baggi tunnel would discharge into a 7.2-mile canal, the Sundarnagar Hydel Channel, across the Suketi Valley leading to a 13,000-acre-foot balancing reservoir formed by a 100-foot high, 3,000-foot long earth-fill dam. From the balancing reservoir, the second tunnel, Sundarnagar-Sutlej, would be drilled for 8.5 miles through the dolomite, limestone, phyllite, slate, and quartzite to a valve chamber above the Dehar

43. Ibid., pp. 27–28, 37–39.

power plant. Three penstocks dividing into six would provide a head of about 1,000 feet for operating six 106,000-kilowatt turbogenerators in the Dehar plant on the shore of the Bhakra reservoir. A short, 1,700-foot, 7,500-cusec tunnel would bypass the power plant for direct diversion of irrigation supplies into the reservoir. It is estimated that the Beas-Sutlej Link, by diverting 3.8 m.a.f. per year on a run-of-the-river basis, would increase the *regulated supply available for irrigation* from Bhakra from 6.3 m.a.f. at present to 8.3 m.a.f. (see page 292, footnote 14), and would increase Bhakra's power output by 30 per cent in addition to the 2 billion kilowatt-hours per year generated at Dehar. Ultimately, with Larji Dam built upstream, both water supply and power generation would be further enhanced.[44]

But these are merely estimates, and the Bureau of Reclamation team recommended that final decisions on capacities await more thorough investigation of the project, especially of the problems involved in building such long tunnels under difficult geological conditions. In fact, the team pointed out that under the Indian estimates the small Pandoh reservoir would be filled by sediment in thirty-three years unless Larji is built in the meantime, and suggested that the entire Beas-Sutlej diversion *might* be made from the Larji, eliminating the Pandoh Dam and the Pandoh-Baggi tunnel.[45] The team was particularly concerned about the abrasive effects of sediment on the tunnel and suggested that a means be found for sediment exclusion before water enters the tunnel rather than extraction en route (use of 1,500 cusecs for sediment exclusion before entering the second tunnel accounts for the decrease in capacity between the two tunnels). And the team recommended that India first bring in expert geologists and tunnel engineers to further evaluate the problems, including possible effects of earthquakes, and to retain a highly qualified tunnel superintendent if it is decided to proceed with Unit I as planned.[46] The tunnels alone would cost $56.8 million (tentative estimate), an amount equal to the estimated foreign exchange component of the entire $210-million project with no allowance for inflation. India herself is clearly capable of doing everything except the tunnels, but prudence dictates that she proceed on Unit I only after careful inves-

44. Ibid., pp. 2, 28–30.
45. Ibid., p. 38.
46. Ibid., pp. 3, 50–51.

tigation and with adequate advice—and even then, tunnel building in the geologically complex Siwaliks and Himalayas is an uncertain affair, as was demonstrated both at Bhakra and at Mangla.

What is termed "Unit III" of the BBRP, the Rajasthan Canal Project, is actually the farthest advanced. Work on the 134-mile Rajasthan Feeder, offtaking Harike Barrage with an initial capacity of 18,500 cusecs, was actually started in 1958. By the summer of 1966, the feeder and approximately 100 miles of the 292-mile Rajasthan Canal had been finished. After unblocking the intake at Harike and installing gates, water was admitted and irrigation began in the kharif of 1964. The ultimate development will take until 1988 according to the schedule given in Table 17.

Progress on the Rajasthan Canal continues at a rate of about 16 miles per year. Most of the work is done in the "cool season" when conditions in the Thar Desert are more bearable and when more labor, including that of the Rajasthani nomads (men and women), is available. About half the work is done using machinery, the other half using shovels, baskets, donkeys, and mules. Apparently, the cost of either method is roughly the same on this project, but India obviously saves on foreign exchange for earthmoving equipment and fuel, and contributes to local employment by using some 12,000 people and 5,000 animals on the Rajasthan Project. The Rajasthan Feeder and Canal will be entirely lined, using two crisscrossed layers of kiln-baked tiles (really 12x6x2-inch bricks) set in concrete-sand mortar. Fuel for baking the tiles is scarce in Rajasthan, but local clays are available. A concrete lining would be far more expensive, as the cement would have to be transported for hundreds of miles. But despite these economies of labor and materials, the cost of the Rajasthan Feeder and Canal, originally estimated at only $100 million, has now risen to three times that amount.[47] In Pakistan, the only really comparable project, employing a maximum of hand labor and local materials and a minimum of equipment, is the 13-mile tile-lined Mailsi-Bahawal Link, which cost only $500,000 per mile.

47. Ibid., p. 98. For a thorough analysis of the relative advantages of hand labor and machines in earthwork, see United Nations Economic Commission for Asia and the Far East, *Proceedings of the Third Regional Technical Conference on Water Resources Development in Asia and the Far East*, Flood Control Series No. 13 (Bangkok, UNECAFE, 1958), pp. 33–40 and 89–104.

(Hand labor was used on the lined portion of the Sidhnai-Mailsi Link only for setting tiles after earthmoving equipment had done the excavating, filling, rolling, and grading.)

The Bureau of Reclamation team, which had been requested at the last minute to look at the Rajasthan and Beas-Sutlej Link schemes in addition to that for the Pong Dam, did not express an opinion on the economic feasibility of the Rajasthan Project per se but only as it related to the use of water from Pong and its ability to meet its allotted share (about $12 million) of the Pong costs. The team report states:

> The Team had time for only a brief inspection of the Rajasthan Project while in India. In a project of this magnitude, the procedure for settlement and operation obviously has no parallel in the United States. . . .
>
> In order to make a comprehensive study of a project calling for the irrigation of $4\frac{1}{2}$ million acres of land, it would be necessary for the Bureau of Reclamation to devote years of time in making land classification, agricultural economics and settlement studies, and plans for development of the project. The Government of India and the State of Rajasthan have made studies which they feel are adequate to indicate strong enough justification for them to commence construction of the Rajasthan Project. The Team is of the opinion that further investigations would have been highly desirable prior to initiation of construction. However, the Team fully appreciates the fact that because of the pressing need for a substantial increase in the production of food, it probably became necessary to shortcut desired or approved procedures in formulating plans for development. Based upon the available data, inspection of the area, and a comparison with somewhat similar developments in the United States, the Team is of the opinion that a cost benefit ratio for the proposed Project development would exceed 1:1.[48]

Despite this rather general and diplomatically phrased appraisal of a project it had no time to inspect thoroughly, the team added:

48. Bureau of Reclamation, p. 98.

> If the time comes when a formal request is made for financial assistance, it is the opinion of the Team that considerable engineering, cost, economics, soils, and other data not now available would have to be compiled.[49]

Viewed realistically, and perhaps undiplomatically, the Rajasthan Project in its ultimate form is a dubious one. India has yielded to the same sort of temptation that induced Pakistan to construct the Ghulam Mohammad Project on the lower Indus. The idea of extending the Rajasthan Canal parallel to the Indo-Pakistan border in the northern portion of the Thar Desert down to a point about opposite the Sukkur Barrage was a seductive one: 7.9 million acres could be brought under command, and 6.7 million of these are potentially cultivable, although the project in its present form is limited to supplying water to only 4.5 million acres, of which only 3.5 million would be cultivated in a given year. Even then, these lands will receive only 1 cusec of water for each 250 to 300 acres, an intensity even lower than what has prevailed in the Punjab since British times (1 cusec for 200 acres) and less than one-third of what prevails in the United States.[50]

Cut off by Partition from most of the Punjab irrigated tracts which the British had designed to be the granary of the United Provinces (although the population growth even in the pre-Partition period had eliminated any overall surplus within the united Punjab), India quite naturally turned to the desert margins to replace the lost acreage and crops. Assured by her geographical position and later by the Treaty of the full use of the Eastern Rivers, India naturally sought an area to irrigate, an area in which to demonstrate that Free India could do as much as the British in bringing new lands under cultivation. Forgotten or overlooked were the fundamental differences between the Punjab, with its convergent, perennial streams, tapering doabs, and silty soils, and the Thar Desert, hundreds of miles from the Sutlej, with its sands and sand dunes. Of course, the domestic political factor played its part here, as it did in Pakistan. Rajasthan, like Sind, wanted its share of development, and Bikaner had even been promised Sutlej water under the original Bhakra project of 1923 (see Chapter 4).

49. Ibid., p. 99.
50. Ibid., p. 185.

The cumulative irrigation experience of India, Iraq, Egypt, the United States, and the Soviet Union indicates that more food and fiber can be obtained by increasing the water allowance to existing cultivated lands than by spreading the water thin over new tracts. But the idea of making the desert bloom as the rose is one of the oldest (and most pernicious) in irrigation history, and in India it was compounded with the legend of the Sarasvati (see Chapter 2) which once flowed through Rajasthan before the Jumna (or the Sutlej) took it away. Combined with the political pressures from Rajasthan, the idea of sending Sutlej-Beas water some 426 miles into the desert proved as compelling in India as the Ghulam Mohammad scheme had in Pakistan.

Irrigation agriculture is one of the most expensive systems known to man. It can be employed to advantage on new or old alluvial soils close to perennial streams, and sometimes it can, with proper rotations and generous use of legumes and green manures, be employed to build up sandy desert soils. It can even be employed to make the desert bloom at a considerable distance from the rivers in a country such as the United States or the U.S.S.R. where the food and fiber needs, especially for seasonal or exotic crops, of the bulk of the country are such, and the standard of living is such, as to provide direct or indirect subsidization. It may be employed in the Negev because Israel has no other choice and can subsidize it. But to introduce it into the Thar Desert (and the same may be true for parts of the Thal Desert between the Indus and the Chenab) is economically unjustifiable. The 8.8 m.a.f. of Beas-Sutlej-Ravi water that are to be diverted from Harike for the Rajasthan Canal (when available; see Table 17) could be put to much better use in the East Punjab (i.e. the Indian Punjab as it existed prior to November 1, 1966), north and south of the Sutlej, and in the eastern margins of Rajasthan served by the Bikaner Canal and Sirhind Feeder. Combined with concentrated application of the limited fertilizer at India's disposal,[51]

51. The Fertilizer Corporation of India (owned by the Government of India) produces 388,000 tons of 20.5 per cent nitro-limestone fertilizer per year at a plant opened in Naya Nangal in February 1961. This plant takes 164,000 kw of Bhakra's power, and uses 80 million gallons of Sutlej water per day. The Naya Nangal production is pooled with that from Trombay, near Bombay, and from Rourkela, Orissa, and with imported fertilizer. Distribution throughout India is controlled by a Central Board under the Ministry of Oil and Gas. (Visit to

Table 17. Projected Irrigation under the Rajasthan Canal[a]

Period Ending[b]	Expected Annual Irrigation in Acres
Third Five Year Plan, 1965–66	228,000
Fourth Five Year Plan, 1970–71	779,770
Fifth Five Year Plan, 1975–76	1,717,530
Sixth Five Year Plan, 1980–81	2,772,180
Seventh Five Year Plan, 1985–86	3,468,980
Completion, 1987–88	3,533,100

a. Source: Bureau of Reclamation, p. 97.

b. The Indian fiscal year runs from April 1 through March 31; that in Pakistan from July 1 through June 30. Thus, the Indian fiscal year coincides with the traditional irrigation year whereas that in Pakistan cuts across it.

yields in the established areas could be doubled or trebled at a saving in cost and pain in Rajasthan. The very experience with the Bhakra Project itself, which increased water supplies to 3.3 million acres south of the Sutlej, demonstrates this. Yet even here, out of every 182 cusecs run into a canal, 112 are lost by seepage, evaporation, and nonbeneficial transpiration of plants. On the Rajasthan system, although the lining will reduce seepage *in the main canal* to a minimum, evaporation alone may reduce supplies by 50 per cent. And the seepage losses in the unlined branch canals, distributaries, minors, subminors, watercourses, and *on the bunded fields themselves* will further reduce the share of water that can be used beneficially by plants of economic value. In fact, in order to get any significant return from the Rajasthan Project, India has decided to substitute row-irrigation for such crops as cotton and sugarcane, thereby reducing though certainly not eliminating the seepage losses in these sandy soils and also facilitating weed control and mechanization.[52]

Of course, science and technology may come to India's rescue in Rajasthan as they seem to be doing in Pakistan's groundwater and reclamation projects. The Irrigation and Power Research Institute at Amritsar, an Indian Punjab State organization which does work

Naya Nangal plant on March 18, 1964, and interview with P. Tribhuwan, Public Relations Officer.) Starting in 1966, and at U.S. urging, private foreign investment in fertilizer plants and private fertilizer imports were to be encouraged.

52. Interview with Dr. H. L. Uppal, Director, Irrigation and Power Research Institute, Amritsar, March 16, 1964. Row irrigation allows the use of tractor-drawn cultivators to keep the topsoil porous and free of weeds.

for other states as well, is actively experimenting with polyethylene and other sheets which can be imbedded in canals and distributaries to reduce seepage losses, at least until the thin sheet is broken.[53] Although this Institute has not had much success with monomolecular films, spread on tanks and reservoirs to retard evaporation but easily broken by wind-blown sand or wave action, this line of research is being actively pursued in other countries and the benefits could be extended to India. The Irrigation Research Institute at Lahore is experimenting with kerosene-based compounds which can be spread on ponded sections of canals during the annual closure for maintenance and allowed to sink to the bottom where they provide a temporary seepage retardant. But, by the same logic employed above, the effects of such technological advances would be greater if applied in areas with denser soils and lower summer temperatures than in Rajasthan. (In petroleum-rich areas of the United States, North Africa, and the Middle East, oil has been sprayed on the fields both to retard evaporation and to help stabilize the shifting sands, but the cost of this process seems far beyond the reach of either India or Pakistan.)

The Bureau of Reclamation team also noted a lack of planning for development of the Rajasthan Project. About the only thing that is known of the soils in the project area is that they are, like all desert soils, highly porous and deficient in organic matter. (The two features are, of course, intimately related.) The only soil survey carried out in the project covered 9.6 million acres in two cool seasons of work, taking 500 samples which may represent from 150 to 300 soil "profiles," i.e. distinctive soil types, subtypes, or phases. This would represent one imperfectly analyzed profile for each 30,000 to 60,000 acres of the project![54] Yet on this basis, which is utterly inadequate for any land classification even remotely resembling that done in the United States prior to development and settlement, it is proposed to

53. Ibid., and tour of the Institute, same day. The Amritsar Institute was set up after Partition to replace the one at Lahore, and includes many former members of the latter's staff, such as Dr. Uppal. There are now twelve such irrigation, power, hydraulic, and soils research institutions in India, owing their inception to the Central Board of Irrigation and Power which was established on a cooperative basis by the Government of India in 1927. (See UNECAFE, *Multiple-Purpose River Basin Development*, p. 70.)

54. Bureau of Reclamation, p. 97.

provide irrigation for up to 4.5 million acres, and to settle two million people where perhaps 71,000 now live by 1988. Up to 50 per cent of this land in some areas is occupied by sand dunes, some of them partially anchored by coarse vegetation and some of them shifting in the almost daily sandstorms. Each family will receive a maximum of 32 acres of such land and will be expected to level it, to build the field watercourses, and to start farming in the hopes of being able to pay the water charges which will reflect the amortization of the construction costs plus the operations and maintenance costs of the canals and distributaries.[55] Yet, although settlement has begun along the upper reaches of the Rajasthan Canal, there is no program of farmer training for this most difficult type of agriculture, irrigation in the desert.

It is true that the British, in their spectacularly successful program of settling the Crown Waste Lands of the West Punjab (and, technically, the Rajasthan Project lands are exactly the same thing—state-owned wastelands purchased by the project for development), did not provide a farmer education and training program. But they did most deliberately recruit competent farmers from the crowded "dry districts" of the foothills in the expectation that these men would adapt to the irrigation conditions of the Canal Colonies and turn them into productive lands. Overwhelmingly, they did adapt, though a few found the *bar* uplands and the *jungli* bandits too much for them and returned to their home districts (see Chapter 3). But the adjustment that will be demanded of farmers coming from dry districts, or even from the canal-irrigated districts of East Punjab, to the deserts of Rajasthan will be far more difficult, primarily because of the difference in soils but also because evaporation rates in the Thar are significantly higher. British recognition of the difficulties of desert soils and shifting sands led to the postponement of the Thal Project for at least thirty years, until all the *bar* uplands had been settled. And even the Thal Project, settled mainly by refugee farmers from India, has not yet been pushed from the northern foothill region (along the Muhajir Branch; see Chapter 6) or the western margins (along the Thal Main Line) into the dead heart of the desert with its shifting rows of sand dunes. And Thal is already in trouble along its inner margins where the soils are too

55. Ibid., p. 30.

light to hold water and too quickly salinized by evaporation. The
Central Thal Canal remains under study while WASID and Pakistan's
foreign consultants, notably Tipton and Kalmbach, carry out intensive soil surveys and land classification studies with a view, primarily,
to *reclaiming* lands ruined by salinization.

Both the author and the Bureau of Reclamation have had experience with another project comparable to Thal and to Rajasthan.
This is the Helmand Valley Project in southwestern Afghanistan,
where up to two million acres were to be provided with water and
used for the settlement of former nomads and destitute farmers.
Like Rajasthan, the Helmand Project was undertaken and settlement
begun before adequate soils surveys and land classification had been
carried out. The result was frustration and land abandonment,
negating the political as well as the economic values Afghanistan
had hoped to derive from the project. In 1960, the Bureau of Reclamation was called in to bail out the Helmand—literally, for the
irrigation water, applied in exuberant quantities by untrained hands
unaccustomed to such a water supply, had built up to a point where
soils became waterlogged and salt and alkali were poisoning the
upper horizon. So far, the Bureau's Helmand team has directed the
reclamation of about 100,000 acres with open and tile drains, but
it will be another twenty years or more before the Helmand Project
begins to live up to its promise.[56]

The Rajasthan Project is unlikely to become quickly waterlogged,
both because of the low water allowance and because, from the little
that is known of subsurface conditions, the water table seems to be
200 or 300 feet deep, rather than the 20 to 30 feet in the Helmand,
where it was held up by a layer of impervious conglomerate. But
very little *is* known of the drainage conditions in Rajasthan, and
there may be localized problems of waterlogging just as there are in
the Thal, despite its sandy soils and deep well line. And salinity,
which can result just from the repeated evaporation of irrigation
water which never has time to seep down into the water table, carrying salts with it, may be a severe problem in Rajasthan, for desert
soils by definition have a natural accumulation of salts near the
surface. And the Rajasthan scheme, with its meager allocation of

56. See Michel, *The Kabul, Kunduz, and Helmand Valleys.*

water for cropping, allows no surplus at all for flushing these salts downward.

The Bureau team in India was unable to obtain any hard data on the drainage aspects of the Rajasthan Project, although they were assured that these had been considered.[57] What this apparently means is that, with most of the laterals or distributaries pointing toward the Bahawalpur (Pakistan) border, the Indians assume that the subsoil water will drain in that direction. And this is logical because the old and dry Hakra riverbed (see Chapter 2 and Map 2) bisects Bahawalpur, running parallel to the Sutlej until it apparently turns south through the Nara bed (now occupied by one of the Sukkur canals) toward the Rann of Cutch. So it seems safe to assume that whatever natural subsoil drainage exists in northwestern Rajasthan collects into the Hakra, just as the much more recently abandoned channel of the Sukh Beas in the Bari Doab collected much of the subsoil drainage from nearby irrigated tracts. In fact, the upper reaches of the Hakra (called the Ghaggar) in the cis-Sutlej (Indian) Punjab have begun to carry water since the Bhakra Project went into operation, and it is bad water, the effluent of the irrigation system and of some drainage schemes carried out by India.

So, in the absence of any well-planned drainage system in the Rajasthan Project, it may be assumed that Bahawalpur and Sind may have to bear the burden of India's effluent along with that of the West Punjab. This is exactly the sort of problem that the Indus Waters Treaty (see Chapter 6 and the Appendix) should have solved. It does indeed deal with it, but in somewhat equivocal fashion. Paragraph (3) of Article IV provides:

> (c) except as provided in Paragraph (5) and Article VII(1) (b), India shall not take any action to increase the catchment area, beyond the area on the Effective Date, of any natural or artificial drainage or drain which crosses into Pakistan, and shall not undertake such construction or remodeling of any drainage or drain which so crosses or falls into a drainage or drain which so crosses as might cause material damage in Pakistan or entail the construction of a new drain or enlargement of an existing drainage or drain in Pakistan.

57. Bureau of Reclamation, p. 95.

Paragraph (5) proceeds to modify this by excluding four drains, one of which (Fazilka) serves the Bikaner Canal system, which Pakistan agreed to deepen or widen within its territory "as a work of public interest, provided India agrees to pay the cost of the deepening or widening." And Article VII(1)(b) provides that:

> (b) Each Party, to the extent it considers practicable and on agreement by the other Party to pay the costs to be incurred, will, at the request of the other Party, carry out such new drainage works as may be required in connection with new drainage works of the other Party.

Shorn of legalistic doubletalk, the net effect of these provisions would seem to be that Pakistan is required to enlarge the Fazilka Drain if India pays for it, but can object to carrying out any new drainage works farther down on the grounds that they are "impracticable" even though India would pay the costs. And it would seem, with these exceptions, that paragraph (3)(c) of Article IV prohibits India from enlarging the *catchment area,* beyond the area on the effective date, of any natural drainage which crosses into Pakistan, e.g. the Hakra bed. It may be noted that by the effective date of the Treaty (April 1, 1960), India had considerably increased the catchment area of the Hakra by executing the Bhakra scheme and certain reclamation projects in the cis-Sutlej Punjab. Now, with the Rajasthan scheme coming into being, the effective catchment area of the Hakra is being further enlarged, but this is occurring in the subsoil rather than on the surface. So the whole issue will ultimately turn on the definition of "catchment area" (which is not defined in the Treaty). If "catchment area" includes subsurface flows, then Pakistan is secure, provided India adheres to the Treaty. But if "catchment area" includes only surface flows, and this seems the more likely interpretation, then India cannot be prevented from draining the Rajasthan Project into the Hakra bed and thus eventually interfering with the operation of the Eastern Nara Canal. (Of course, it might be pointed out that Pakistan could return the favor by dumping the effluent of her groundwater schemes into the Thar Desert along the Indian border, as has been suggested. But presumably this would drain into India only in some of the westernmost portions of Rajasthan, beyond the command of the Rajasthan Canal, where it would do little "material damage.")

Should Pakistan find that she cannot secure redress on the basis that subsoil drainage forms part of the "catchment area" of the Hakra, the Treaty provides another tenuous line of argument. Paragraphs (8), (9), and (10) of Article IV state in part:

> (8) The use of the natural channels of the Rivers for the discharge of flood *or other excess waters* [italics supplied] shall be free and not subject to limitation by either Party, and neither Party shall have any claim against the other in respect of any damage caused by such use. . . .
>
> (9) Each Party declares its intention to operate its storage dams, barrages and irrigation canals in such manner, consistent with the normal operations of its hydraulic systems, as to avoid, as far as feasible, material damage to the other Party.
>
> (10) Each Party declares its intention to prevent, as far as practicable, undue pollution of the waters of the Rivers which might affect adversely uses similar in nature to those to which the waters were put on the Effective Date . . . Provided that the criterion of reasonableness shall be the customary practice in similar situations on the Rivers.

Here Pakistan would have to argue, first, that the Hakra and Nara are either "tributaries" of the Indus or "channels or creeks of the main stem" of the Indus (see Article I, "Definitions," in the Appendix). If this could be established, then Pakistan could argue that discharge of saline effluent from the Rajasthan Project constitutes either "material damage" to Pakistan or "undue pollution of the waters." But this argument is vitiated by the permissive language of paragraph (8), by the fact that paragraphs (9) and (10) constitute only "declarations of intention," and by the fact that "pollution" (not defined in the Treaty) is generally taken to mean only the introduction of municipal or industrial waste rather than the return of irrigation waters, however saline.

That the foregoing analysis is not merely an academic exercise may be understood if one recalls the recent U.S.-Mexican disputes over the quality of the water delivered to Mexico in the lower Colorado and Rio Grande rivers as well as by noting the first conclusion of the Bureau of Reclamation team study on the Rajasthan Project:

> On the Rajasthan Project, plans for trunk drains have apparently not been firmed up. Inasmuch as the Project lies close to West Pakistan, and main laterals point westward toward the border, it is felt that an overall drainage plan would allay any concern for future international difficulties that might arise.[58]

A comprehensive plan for drainage of the Rajasthan Project would also allay *some* of the fears for its economic feasibility, and might even lead to a realization that the scheme, if carried out as now projected, will be overextended. A smaller Rajasthan Project, concentrated, say, under command of the upper 150 miles of the canal, would not only permit raising water intensities to more adequate levels for crops and provision of a surplus for continuously leaching the salts downward, but would reduce both the costs of canal and of drain construction. Then, even if saline subsurface water found its way into the Hakra bed, it would probably be dissipated long before it could reach the Nara. Pakistan would undoubtedly object to this, but she would presumably be unable to demonstrate "material damage." By increasing intensities and preventing salinization in upper Rajasthan as well as in East Punjab, India would be able to satisfy her legitimate desires for more food and fiber in a more efficient fashion than by spreading the water thin over 4.5 million acres. She might even be able to settle the projected two million persons by providing them with 16-acre plots which could, with adequate fertilizers, be double-cropped each year, rather than allotting 32 acres per family of which at most 25 can be farmed in a two-season year.

But such logic is not likely to prevail. The political lure of acreage figures is virulent and most difficult to offset by citing examples from the U.S.A., the U.S.S.R., the Helmand Valley of Afghanistan, or the Ghulam Mohammad and Thal projects in Pakistan. Although every irrigation engineer worth his salt now admits, at least in theory, that no irrigation project is complete without an adequate drainage system, there is always the tendency to postpone

58. Ibid., p. 98.

the latter expense until conditions force the undertaking of reclamation operations. As we shall see in Chapter 9, Indian engineers have been slow to come to grips with the groundwater problem even in East Punjab. And engineers no longer carry the weight they did prior to 1947 in making developmental decisions in the Indus Basin.

8. Reorganizing to Develop
the Indus Basin

*"The Water and Power Development Authority has been created . . .
because the country could not tolerate the slow tempo of traditional
government departments."*
—Pakistan Food and Agriculture Commission, 1960

Effects of Independence

The reader may recall that Chapter 3 was subtitled "Engineers and
Administrators," and that at the end of Chapter 4 we remarked,
"engineers and administrators deferred to statesmen and politicians."
We were referring there to the situation on the eve of Partition, but
the comment is really applicable to the whole of the last two decades
and in both the Indian and Pakistani portions of the Indus Basin.
Engineers and administrators have continued to play vital roles,
of course, in advisory and operational capacities, but the basic
decisions from the disposition of the Ferozepore and Madhopur
headworks to the fate of Tarbela Dam have been made by political
leaders, lawyers, bankers, and economists. The elevation of India
and Pakistan into independent nations, and the creation of an international border bisecting the Indus Basin, meant in effect that, just
as wars have today become too important to be left to generals,

irrigation matters were too important to be left to engineers. Thus we have seen that although both countries and the World Bank were represented by engineers at the start of the Indus Waters Treaty negotiations, Pakistan sent in a senior civil servant to head her team as early as 1954, and the final negotiations were conducted at a heads-of-state and President of the World Bank level.

What was true on the international plane was no less true domestically. As far as the engineers were concerned, Partition destroyed their frame of reference, a functionally integrated system which had been built over a century. The September 1945 agreement between the Chief Engineers of Sind and Punjab, encompassing irrigation allocations and operations in virtually the entire Basin, represented the culmination of an autonomy that had grown since the establishment of the respective public works departments. With Partition, the role of the engineers was restricted in both territorial extent and authority. In West Pakistan, it became at first one of piecing together Pakistan's portions of the system with link canals and then (after negotiations based on the Lilienthal plan of integrated operation and development had failed) of devising and executing a plan under which the Western Rivers could supply the whole region. In India, it became a task of redesigning the Bhakra scheme to serve only areas in India, giving to Rajasthan what had been intended for the Sutlej Valley Project and Sind. Because the Partition Line had become an international boundary, and because both India and Pakistan proceeded (though at different rates and to different degrees) to integrate the administration of their portions of the Basin and to enhance the role of central development planning, engineers became staff advisers and implementers of decisions rather than decision makers.

The same was true of engineers at and below the provincial or state level. The Government of India Act of 1935 (taking effect in 1937, when Sind also became a separate province) represented the culmination of provincial autonomy not only in irrigation matters but in most areas of economic planning and development. With Partition, and with the establishment of the federal system in India, departments of irrigation and power at the state level found themselves in an entirely new relation to their counterparts in adjoining states and to the Central Government. By 1952 there had emerged, in response to Nehru's desire for a centrally planned economy, both a Central Planning Commission and a Central Ministry of Irrigation and Power, as well as a series of interstate project agencies on which the Central Government was represented. Although, as we shall see shortly, it can be argued that the States, as represented by their Governors or Chief Ministers, had more influence in these agencies than the Central Government, there is little doubt that the engineers were relegated to an advisory and implementation role. For example, in November 1950 the Bhakra Project was entrusted to a Control Board with representatives of the Central Ministry of Finance, of the predecessors of the Central Water and Power Commission and the Central Ministry of Irrigation and Power, and of the states involved, with the stipulation that "the Chief Engineer concerned with any part of the project will be invited to attend *as Adviser* when matters relating to his part of the project are under consideration of the Control Board."[1]

The role of administrators at and below the provincial or state level was also modified by post-Independence constitutional changes. In India, where the early trend was toward consolidation, the role of the upper-level administrators who survived was accordingly enhanced. India's former provinces and Princely States were gradually merged until by November 1, 1956, P.E.P.S.U. (Patiala and East Punjab States Union) had been merged into Punjab, the Punjab Hill States had been formed into Himachal Pradesh, and (in three stages) all the states of Rajasthan were unified.

In West Pakistan, provinces, states, and states unions (e.g. Baluchistan States Union) continued to exist side by side until One Unit rule was established on October 14, 1955. By that time, although the writ of the newly formed Department of Irrigation, Communications, and Works ran throughout the now-integrated province of West Pakistan, its authority was already circumscribed by the provincial departments of Finance and of Planning and Development as well as by the central ministries of Finance, of Fuel, Power, and

---

1. "Constitution and Functions of the Bhakra Control Board and Bhakra Advisory Board, India," reprinted as Appendix B to the *Proceedings of the Third Regional Technical Conference*, Flood Control Series No. 13 (Bangkok, UNECAFE, 1958). Italics added. Rajasthan's Chief Engineer was a member of the Control Board.

Natural Resources, and the central Planning Commission. (The former Electricity Branch of the Punjab Public Works Department was similarly included in a separate provincial department and was similarly circumscribed). In addition, the establishment of the Soil Reclamation Board (for the Punjab in 1952 but extended to the province of West Pakistan in 1957), although it operated under the Irrigation Department, had begun to abstract from the latter's authority in groundwater development and reclamation operations. But the real blow to the Irrigation Department came in 1958 with the establishment of WAPDA, a public corporation set up by West Pakistan "for development of water and power resources." The Department was shorn of its surface and groundwater development functions in the Indus Plains. It was left with canal operations and maintenance, assessment of water rates (see pages 390–95 for a discussion of this function), enforcement of irrigation ordinances, irrigation and hydrological research, various aspects of flood control, and a few small projects outside the Indus Plains. WAPDA even took over the work on the Gudu Barrage.

In May 1962 the Department of Irrigation, Communications, and Works was subdivided into a Communications and Works Department and an Irrigation and Power Department, each organized as a secretariat, and the latter under the Minister of Food, Agriculture, Irrigation, and Power.[2] This change was accompanied by a return to the traditional practice of having an engineer rather than a civil servant as head (secretary) of the Department, but the minister of course remained a political appointee.[3]

2. "Power" may appear to be a misnomer inasmuch as after 1955 the Irrigation, Communications, and Works Department had nothing to do with power, and by 1962 the Electricity Department had been incorporated into WAPDA. However, as will be explained below in the text, WAPDA must submit its water and power development projects to the West Pakistan Government through the Irrigation and Power Department and the Minister of Food, Agriculture, Irrigation, and Power, so in that sense the title is correct. The Food and Agriculture departments are separate, each having its own secretary.

3. It should be pointed out that in both the provincial governments and the Central Government of Pakistan, the secretariat system, inherited from the British, is employed. The secretary is a career officer and an expert in his field. He may be an engineer, a member of the Revenue Service, a member of the Provincial Civil Service, or a member of that elite body, the Civil Service of Pakistan. A few C.S.P. officers serve in the provincial departments, but none of them serve as provincial ministers. The logic is that the minister, who is a political

344

There was nothing untoward or unnatural in these developments. The high degree of provincial autonomy established by the Government of India Act of 1935 and envisaged in the Cabinet Mission Plan (even with its grouping provisions) was found unsuitable both in India, where the substitution of linguistic states now appears worse than the disease of provincialism, and in Pakistan, which since 1955 has tried to ignore regionalism in the West Wing and has concentrated on holding the two provinces, East and West, together. Like other developing nations, India and Pakistan have found it necessary to introduce central controls on economic life, including development projects, public and private spending, and the allocation of vital foreign exchange. To somewhat different degrees, both have found it necessary to arrive at basic developmental decisions through central planning and to enforce them from the center. This does not mean that "regionalism" or "provincialism" has disappeared, or that "logrolling" in budget making is unknown. Far from it. But it does mean that the former provincial administrator, who now finds himself Chief Commissioner of a division, has no more to say in policy-making than he did when he was just Deputy Commissioner of a district. In the realm of irrigation, where there were three Chief Engineers for all of West Pakistan (Punjab, Sind,

---

appointee, makes or transmits the policy decisions, which are executed by the secretary, thus providing continuity and expertise in implementation. The secretariat system has come under criticism because it divorces policy making from policy implementation. Also under attack has been the system of "notations" or endorsements under which no matter may come to a secretary's attention until a congeries of subordinate officials have affixed their remarks and signatures to the file. The burdensome and time-consuming nature of the "notation" system has been partly relieved by the institution of "section officers" who are empowered to act for the secretaries on certain matters and within well-defined limits. But the burden on the secretaries is still a crushing one.

The author remembers well being ushered into the office of A. Rashid Kazi, the West Pakistan Secretary of Irrigation and Power, early on a Monday morning. As we were talking, a "peon" appeared (how the word "peon" came into Indo-Pakistani usage is a mystery, but it described the man's function perfectly) bearing the Secretary's work for the week. He looked like a khaki-clad Santa Claus, bearing not one but two huge bundles of files wrapped in sheets. Each of these files had to be inspected by the Secretary, previous notations read, and his own endorsement added before any further action could be taken.

For a penetrating analysis of Pakistan's administrative organization, see Henry F. Goodnow, *The Civil Service of Pakistan: Bureaucracy in a New Nation* (New Haven and London, Yale University Press, 1964).

North West Frontier Province) in 1947, there are now fourteen (six in the Irrigation and Power Department and eight in WAPDA). As numbers have proliferated, responsibility, at least in regional terms, has declined. And in both India and Pakistan the provincial or state irrigation departments have lost much or all of their development responsibilities for the larger projects and have come to serve primarily as operations, maintenance, and advisory services.

Both India and Pakistan have found it necessary to create new agencies for the execution of their water and power development projects in the Indus Basin. Both WAPDA and the Bhakra Control Board (with its adjuncts) bear certain resemblances to the United States Tennessee Valley Authority or Columbia Basin Inter-Agency Committee but there are significant differences between and among them, as we shall see. Especially as so few large dams had been built in either country, and as experience with tubewells was limited, both India and Pakistan have had to call on foreign nations for technical and financial assistance to supplement domestic talent and resources. But their manner of doing so is significantly different, and also worthy of some analysis.

As in other respects, Pakistan was less well endowed with economic resources and talent than India at Independence. In part, this is a reflection of the differences in size and population. It may also be said with perfect justice that India had bigger problems to solve and more development projects to build. But partly because higher education for Muslims was limited and partly because, between the Mutiny and the inception of Gandhi's civil disobedience campaigns around 1920, Muslims were apparently less trusted than Hindus or Sikhs in administrative positions, Pakistan in 1947 found herself critically short of personnel for the public and technical services. Even on a relative basis, there were far fewer Muslims with training abroad or experience at senior levels in the civil service and technical branches (though this was not as true of the army or the judiciary). And although Pakistan received an influx of many professional persons and skilled workers from India, the exodus of professional, commercial, and administrative Hindus and Sikhs left her comparatively shorthanded. This was one reason why Jinnah, who refused to accept Mountbatten as Governor-General of Pakistan, actively encouraged Englishmen to remain in Pakistan's armed forces, civil and technical services, and commercial organizations. In many instances, in the early years, Pakistanis had to be promoted to positions for which neither their training nor their experience suited them, with the result that even with the best motivation they served as a drag on her development. Even today, while India is hard pressed to give employment to thousands of college graduates, Pakistan feels the need for capable persons in the lower echelons.

On the other hand, it probably is no exaggeration to say that Pakistan, from the start, was less xenophobic than India. Remembering the Mogul rule as well as the British, the Congress Party felt that the retention of foreigners on a significant scale would be a confession of inability (predicted for years by some Englishmen) to rule alone. Furthermore, the concept of central planning was established earlier and more firmly in India than in Pakistan, and it would hardly seem logical that a nation so recently emerged from colonial status would entrust such vital functions to foreigners. So although it is true that both nations have made use of "expatriate" personnel as well as of technical assistance from the United Nations, the U.S.A., the U.S.S.R., and the Colombo Plan countries over the past twenty years, India has generally been more sensitive than Pakistan to any suggestion of foreign influence or control. Considering only the field of water resource development, only a handful of foreign technicians have served, on temporary assignments, with the central Indian Ministry of Irrigation and Power. As far as the Bhakra-Beas-Rajasthan Project is concerned, the International Engineering Company of San Francisco did some preliminary design work for the Bhakra Dam in the late 1940s. But from 1950 on, the Bhakra Designs Directorate, centered in Delhi, was increasingly an all-Indian operation. In all, some sixty foreigners (including the American engineer Harvey Slocum and his assistants) were associated, at one time or another, with the Bhakra Project, but all had been phased out by 1960 and none were carried over on a continuing basis with the Beas designs and construction operation. In Pakistan, on the other hand, both Mangla and Tarbela have been designed and revised by foreigners; the former is being built by an American engineering consortium; and from 1961 to 1964 the entire IBP organization had the services of an American Chief Technical Adviser, General Emerson C. Itschner, retired Chief of the Corps of Engineers. Nor are there any plans to build Tarbela without foreign engineers.

Thus, it may be said that, from Independence, India had a philosophy both of development and of the role foreigners might be allowed to play in it. Pakistan, at least until after the 1958 "Revolution," had neither, and her approach was purely empirical. On the whole, it has been no less effective, and in some areas considerably more so, than India's.

West Pakistan: WAPDA and Its Associates

At Independence, both India and Pakistan could choose among several basically different approaches in the construction of development projects. Both nations had inherited from the British a framework of provincial and central departments concerned with irrigation, power, roads, bridges, railways, public buildings, etc. Some of these departments possessed their own engineering construction facilities, including the workshops of the irrigation departments and the locomotive and wagon-building facilities of the railways. In both nations rudimentary private construction firms had also developed, as well as some private firms making simple engineering equipment. But in India neither the traditional departments nor the existing private firms were equipped to handle projects on the order of Bhakra. Hence India proceeded to establish, within the existing framework, the Bhakra Directorate which both utilized the skills and equipment of the old departments and supplemented them as a "superdepartment."

West Pakistan, on the other hand, was not immediately faced with any single task of such magnitude, although foreign consultants were called in for the Warsak Project, the first *dam* built in West Pakistan, late in 1948. The Indus barrages at Taunsa and Kotri were entrusted to the traditional methods of the Irrigation Department, with private firms used incidentally. But Pakistan found herself faced with a need for strengthening a whole series of basic industries, many of which had relied upon processing facilities now located in India. Thus, shortly after Independence, the Pakistan Industrial Development Corporation (PIDC) was established to plan, build, and initially operate jute, paper, fertilizer, cement, and sugar factories. It was felt that only a concentrated application of the resources of the Central Government could bring these new and badly needed industries into operation quickly enough to provide new employment, markets for the raw materials concerned, and the key products needed by farmers,

348

builders, and consumers. Significantly, "the more lucrative field of textiles, where the knowhow was comparatively easier to obtain and profits better, was left for the private entrepreneur."[4] Also significantly, PIDC, which in 1962 was divided into separate corporations for West and East Pakistan, has now begun to divest itself of the factories by selling them to private entrepreneurs.

The PIDC was Pakistan's first venture with a public corporation, a venture justified not in terms of national philosophy but national need and the inability of private enterprise to meet it with sufficient speed. The next experiment, and one that has proven conspicuously successful, was the establishment of Pakistan International Airlines (PIA) "in the wake of the virtual collapse of the private aviation companies."[5] Again, the justification was pragmatic, not philosophical, and Pakistan was following the example of virtually every nation in the world, developed or underdeveloped, outside North America.

In the realm of water resources development, there was at first no felt need to go beyond traditional departmental methods. When Canada offered to help Pakistan with the construction of a power-cum-irrigation project at Warsak, on the Kabul River above Peshawar, a public corporation was set up by the Central Government to do the job. But the Warsak Dam Corporation was involved only with construction, and no provision was made for building the transmission system. When that problem was faced, in 1955, it was decided that the only organization that could build the transmission system in time was the PIDC. Thus this task was assigned, on a purely ad hoc basic, to that organization rather than to the West Pakistan Electricity Department, which had come into being with the integration of October 1955, and which would in turn take over the power operations after generation and transmission began.

Realization that West Pakistan lacked an organization capable of dealing with the unified and planned development of her water and power resources was a major factor in the inception of WAPDA. Another was the realization of the magnitude of the waterlogging and

4. N .H. Jafarey, "Public Corporation as a Device for Economic Development," *Indus*, 5 (March 1964), 9.

5. Ghulam Ishaq, "WAPDA as a Public Corporation," *Indus*, 4 (August 1963), 12.

salinity problem that grew out of the Irrigation Department-USGS investigations begun in 1954. Despite the existence since 1952 of the Soil Reclamation Board, its role was limited by its subordination to the Irrigation Department. The scope of the groundwater and reclamation operations in the Northern Zone of West Pakistan alone was one to give pause to the planners in Lahore and Karachi. And as the Treaty negotiations progressed to a point where the scope of the replacement works became visible, it was apparent that neither the methods nor the resources of the Irrigation Department (then concentrated on the Gudu Barrage) would be sufficient *or would be impressive enough to attract foreign aid.* To carry out the groundwater and reclamation projects and the Indus Basin Project, and to develop an integrated water and power development program, Pakistan clearly had to step beyond the traditional methods and the timeworn system of dividing responsibility among a number of departments to the point where it became blurred and where one department or official could always shift the blame for delay and shortcomings to another. And Pakistan had to find a method for cutting through the bureaucratic red tape involved in designing, approving, budgeting, and executing projects and in recruiting personnel and hiring contractors and consultants.

The answer was WAPDA, established in the spring of 1958 by the West Pakistan Government as a public corporation, first by a simple ordinance, then, to lend it more authority, by an Act of the Provincial Legislature. (A similar WAPDA was established in East Pakistan.) WAPDA was to be owned by the provincial government, and its revenues allotted as part of the annual provincial budget. WAPDA's projects would also be approved by the provincial planning and finance departments, and, to the extent that they formed part of the Five Year Plans, by the Central Planning Commission and the National Economic Council. After approval, they would be fitted into the Annual Development Programme for West Pakistan and submitted to the Provincial Legislature in the annual budget.[6]

But from the point of budget approval onward, WAPDA has sole responsibility for executing projects. Its procurements and disbursements, though subject to scrutiny and fiscal verification, need no

6. Ibid., p. 7.

further approval. Its contracts must be awarded on the basis of competitive tenders, but the contractor deals only with WAPDA, and WAPDA may for good cause refuse to accept the lowest bid. WAPDA may hire and fire without reference to the Public Service Commission of West Pakistan. Although WAPDA has evolved its own systems and procedures, it is not bound by the mass of regulations and precedents of the regular departments. When WAPDA wants to change its procedures it may do so by action of its three-man board without reference to the provincial governor, the Legislative Assembly, or the Law Department. WAPDA's table of organization is flexible, and no outside approval is needed for changes. Perhaps most important of all, WAPDA has a sufficiently broad field of operations, regionally and functionally, to enable it to operate without hindrance or delay in most water and power matters in West Pakistan. Specifically, the enabling act empowers WAPDA to perform the following activities:

1. The development of irrigation water supply, drainage, and the recreational use of water
2. The generation, transmission, and distribution of power; and the construction, maintenance and operation of power houses and grids
3. Flood control
4. The prevention of waterlogging and salinity; and the reclamation of waterlogged and saline lands
5. Inland navigation[7]

In establishing WAPDA, the West Pakistan Government disestablished the Electricity Department. Thus WAPDA has full control of electric power development and operations throughout West Pakistan, whether the generation is thermal or hydroelectric and whether the distribution is urban or rural. WAPDA's Power Wing operates on a strictly commercial basis, although it is not self-sufficient. Revenue from sales of electricity has to be ploughed back into development or placed at the disposal of the provincial government. On the other hand, WAPDA receives allocations from the provincial budget for capital expenditures in power, irrigation, groundwater development, and reclamation operations. As far as the IBP is concerned, WAPDA is acting as the agent of the Central Government of Pakistan. The

7. Ibid., p. 5.

project is being executed by the IBP Division of WAPDA's Water Wing, and WAPDA deals directly with the World Bank as Administrator of the Development Fund.

Since its establishment in 1958, WAPDA has controlled both power development and operations in West Pakistan, and, with a few minor exceptions, all *water development* (the Gudu Project was transferred from the Irrigation Department to WAPDA, but the Irrigation Department retains a few small development schemes, as does the Agricultural Development Corporation, most of which are located outside the Indus Plains). *Surface water operations* are still controlled by the Irrigation Department which still assesses and collects the water dues. *Groundwater operations,* however, are neither WAPDA's nor the Irrigation Department's responsibility. Instead, since 1964, these schemes are transferred, upon completion by WAPDA, to the new Land and Water Management Board (see Chapter 9, page 500) of which both WAPDA's Chairman and the Secretary of Irrigation and Power are members but which is most closely tied to the provincial Board of Revenue.

The creation of the West Pakistan Agricultural Development Corporation (ADC henceforth) in September 1961 on the recommendation of the Central Government's Food and Agriculture Commission confused the situation to the extent that the ADC, whose primary responsibilities relate to the provision of seed, fertilizers, plant protection equipment, pesticides, and agricultural machinery and implements throughout the province, also was assigned the tasks of completing the distribution systems (i.e. land leveling and construction of distributaries and laterals) and colonization of the Ghulam Mohammad and Gudu commands. In 1963 the ADC also subsumed the Thal Development Authority (T.D.A.). The ADC also has a Small Dams Organization which carries out minor development projects in the foothill areas of West Pakistan. More will be said of its role in the last section of this chapter and in Chapters 9 and 10.

As things stand, WAPDA, even excluding the IBP Division, is still the largest organization in West Pakistan in terms of budget and employment. And although it has been estimated that the completion of the IBP will enable the IBP Division to relinquish about 20 per cent of the floor space of WAPDA House (completed in 1966 to replace the old estate of Maharaja of Kashmir plus the thirty-odd buildings rented by WAPDA throughout Lahore), there is little doubt that by this time WAPDA's other operations will have grown to fill the vacuum.

It might also be noted that WAPDA's growth has both been criticized and resisted. Much resistance has understandably come from the Irrigation Department, whose proud tradition was somewhat slighted by the creation of the Authority and the transfer to it of all significant water development projects including Gudu. WAPDA has of course also absorbed many personnel from the Irrigation Department, including WAPDA's first Chief Engineer, A. Rashid Kazi, who had been in charge of Gudu's designs and construction, and most of the higher-ranking engineering personnel in the Water Wing. In 1962, when it was decided to return the secretaryship of Irrigation and Power to an engineer, A. Rashid Kazi was chosen to fill the role. Since WAPDA schemes must be submitted to the Government of West Pakistan *through* the Secretariat of Irrigation and Power (and then through the Minister of Food, Agriculture, Irrigation, and Power), the Secretary is in a position to advance or retard such projects. Because the Department's venerable Irrigation Research Institute carries out hydraulic model studies for WAPDA and has an active tubewell research section (see Chapter 9), there are frequent differences of opinion, especially with the Groundwater and Reclamation and Water and Soils Investigation (WASID) divisions of the Authority.

On the other hand, WAPDA has grown so large, and its schemes are so vitally and visibly connected with the public interest, that despite this technical subordination on project approval the Authority usually gets its way, although there may be agonizing delays en route. The positions on the WAPDA Board, which consists of a chairman and two members, one for Finance and one for Administration, have thus far been filled with civil servants of such seniority, prestige, and influence (the chairmen have all been members of the C.S.P.) that a way around the Secretariat can always be found if necessary. As has been noted, upper echelon engineers in Pakistan now serve mainly in staff capacity. M. A. Hamid, for example, was Chief Engineering Adviser to the Government of Pakistan as well as Pakistan's first Indus Waters Commissioner. It is also worth noting that WAPDA's second chairman, Ghulam Faruque, is now the Central

Minister of Commerce, a position from which he can and does continue to foster the development of the Authority.

Within WAPDA, engineers and civil servants seem to get along remarkably well, both because they are much too busy for bickering and because they are highly motivated by the importance of the projects and the degree of control which they have, thanks to the Authority's nature, in executing them. Over its short life, WAPDA has built up considerable esprit de corps. This is true despite the fact that many of the engineers, including nearly all of those in the "ad hoc" IBP Division, are delegated on extended temporary duty from the Irrigation Department and presumably will return there when the projects are completed. Should this occur, such personnel would presumably preserve the seniority they have built up during the temporary delegation. S. S. Kirmani, for example, is both WAPDA's Chief Engineer, IBP, and Chief Engineer of the Irrigation Department's Water Treaty Implementation Cell, and acts in the latter capacity as adviser to the Pakistan Commissioner on the Indus Waters Commission. In the long run it seems far more likely that the Irrigation Department will be merged into a new superorganization, perhaps under the Land and Water Management Board, concerned with all surface and groundwater operations in West Pakistan, and that engineers from both the Department and WAPDA's IBP Division will find themselves merged in such an organization.

The Irrigation Department has farmed out other engineers to the Soil Reclamation Board (1952), the Thal Development Authority (1949), the Agricultural Development Corporation (1961), and the new Land and Water Management Board (1964), in addition to having its secretary serving as a member of several of these. If only because of its impressive record and prestige, the Irrigation Department cannot be ignored by WAPDA or any other agency. Perhaps its present role in development can be compared to that of the House of Lords, having power to recommend changes and to delay action, but not to overrule a basic scheme. For example, the Irrigation Department was able to force changes in the design of the new Sidhnai Barrage so that two old, small canals would continue to be gravity fed via the feeders and aqueduct rather than pump fed. On another plane, the Irrigation Department in the course of its long history has built up a fine system of canal inspection roads and of inspection

354

rest houses. No one travels on these unpaved but beautifully maintained roads, or stays in the rest houses, complete with resident managers and cooks, without permission of the Irrigation Department. Even WAPDA must apply for this permission, which is not automatically or invariably given.[8] In the field of groundwater and reclamation, the Department's Irrigation Research Institute has provided ammunition for criticisms, in the Provincial Assembly and in the press, of WAPDA's tubewell program. The gist of these criticisms is that WAPDA's tubewells cost up to three times those built by the Irrigation Department using "traditional methods" or by private contractors for private owners. WAPDA's reply is that its tubewells have up to three times the capacity of the others and will last up to ten times as long. (We shall discuss this further in Chapter 9; WAPDA might also add that its tubewells are largely financed by foreign assistance whereas those built by the Department or by private owners use only domestic resources.)

Disagreements of this sort are not a major deterrent to WAPDA's operations, and may even serve a healthy purpose. They resemble in some measure the disagreements between the Corps of Engineers and the Bureau of Reclamation in United States' water and power development projects. The valid objections to such disagreements are that they may cause costly delays and that, when publicly aired, they provide arguments for critics of WAPDA (politicians, large landholders, etc.) who may have ulterior motives. WAPDA, like T.V.A., provides a socio-economic leveling influence since the ultimate effect of its water development programs will benefit the small and medium farmers who can afford to do nothing for themselves more than the large landowners who can. But the criticism directed by vested interests and others at WAPDA's water programs is nothing compared to that incurred by the power program.

From the start, WAPDA gave priority to increasing the number of connections rather than the amount and dependability of service to existing customers, though the latter was certainly not neglected. This leveling approach brought attacks from factory owners, businessmen, and those members of the gentry who could afford air-

8. The author traveled thousands of miles on these roads in 1963–64, stayed in many of the rest houses, and was extremely appreciative both of their existence and for permission to use them.

conditioners, refrigerators, and other heavy duty appliances. As the load on WAPDA's grids increased, so did the frequency of breakdowns, especially in summer. Repairs and improvements to the system also brought interruptions of service inasmuch as—as WAPDA's Public Relations Director once pointed out—repairing the system is like trying to repair a jet plane in flight. But WAPDA has struck back at its critics, repeatedly emphasizing that the power situation will not basically improve until the new thermal plants near Hyderabad, Lahore, and Lyallpur are ready to supplement those at Multan, Sukkur, and Quetta, and, above all, until Mangla and Tarbela dams are in operation. To underscore its socio-economic philosophy, WAPDA announced a substantial reduction in rates effective August 1, 1965, with the main savings going to domestic and general consumers rather than to industry or farmers (i.e. private tubewell owners). But substantial concessions were made to small industries and to industrial and commercial users of air-conditioners.[9]

To meet public criticism, but more importantly to help fill the need for public information, WAPDA maintains an efficient Public Relations Office, publishing the *WAPDA Weekly* (which also serves as an official gazette for the publication of tender notices and announcements concerning bids and contract awards), the monthly journal *Indus,* and the annual *WAPDA Miscellany.* The Public Relations Office also produces informational films and helps prepare the frequent broadcasts made by WAPDA officials and their speeches to professional and business groups and visiting delegations. But the audience for these publications (all in English), broadcasts, and speeches necessarily is limited, although it may be influential. The public is often ready to believe the worst of WAPDA, just as any public corporation or "public" utility of comparable size in any country which stands in creditor relationship to so many consumers is prone to attack. In any event, WAPDA cannot be "nationalized," and its public image is bound to improve as its electricity service improves and as the effect of the surface and groundwater programs becomes more widely felt. WAPDA has already secured notable successes, with the completion of the Gudu Barrage, the Rawal Dam (municipal water supply for Rawalpindi-Islamabad and a small amount of irrigation), and SCARP I (Salinity Control and Reclama-

9. *WAPDA Weekly,* July 18, 1965.

tion Project I in the Rechna Doab between Sheikhupura and Lyall-pur), as well as with the Sukkur, Multan, and Quetta thermal power stations. Its *prestige* (a function of political power as well as of performance) is already high, and its *image* (a function of perform-ance and public relations activity) is steadily improving.

Thus one may conclude that the device of a public corporation has served West Pakistan well in its water and power development pro-gram. Bureaucratic red tape, buck-passing, and congenital inefficiency have been reduced significantly, though of course not eliminated, and it seems clear that through WAPDA West Pakistan is saving *time*. And time is the key ingredient. Faced every five minutes with a popu-lation increase of ten persons and a loss of one acre to waterlogging and salinity, West Pakistan has no other choice than to ignore tra-ditional public and vested private interests in the attempt to secure a massive breakthrough on the irrigation and power fronts. That WAPDA is filling this function in an admirable fashion cannot be denied, and the outsider can only hope that whatever administrative arrangements are worked out for land and water *operations*, WAPDA's *development* work will not be hamstrung in the process. One can also hope that just as so many of the Irrigation Depart-ment's personnel have been transferred to WAPDA, temporarily or permanently, much of the historic prestige of the Department will come to be shared by the two agencies and both will advance together in service to the public.

The emphasis upon saving time brings us to another aspect of WAPDA's operations which has elicited much criticism, mostly from the uninformed or misinformed. This is the practice of employing foreign contractors and consultants. The need for using foreign con-tractors for the IBP was explored in Chapter 7 where we saw that there is just no other way to complete the projects in time—time measured by the growth in population and food requirements as well as by the Transition Period. The justification for employing foreign contractors for the groundwater and power programs, and foreign consultants for all aspects of WAPDA's activity including the IBP, is essentially similar. But because WAPDA's use of consultants is new for Pakistan, contrasts strongly with India's approach, and in-volves additional "public relations" problems, it merits further con-sideration here.

Actually, the employment of foreign engineering talent in the design and construction of what became the IBP goes back to 1953–54 when the Irrigation Department's Dams Investigations Circle employed Tipton and Hill (the predecessors of Tipton and Kalmbach) to examine sites on the Jhelum and Indus (see Chapter 7). In 1958, the Government of Pakistan hired Binnie, Deacon and Gourley (now Binnie and Partners) of London to design Mangla Dam. In August 1959, WAPDA established its Tarbela Dam Organization, and in February 1960 retained Tippetts-Abbett-McCarthy-Stratton (TAMS for short) of New York, formerly consultants to the World Bank on the Treaty negotiations, to design the dam.

WAPDA's connection with the Harza Engineering Company International of Chicago dates almost from the Authority's inception in 1958. Harza serves as general consultant for both water and power development, including the IBP. But its most important duty has been in the preparation of a master plan for development (the forerunner of the World Bank's survey) of which the first stage, the "Appraisal Report," was released in March 1964.

Even before the Treaty was signed, WAPDA had hired consultants for the barrages (Coode and Partners, London) and link canals (Tipton and Kalmbach, Denver).[10] Tipton and Kalmbach has had a triple role to play since 1961 when WAPDA named it as consultant also for groundwater and reclamation projects and for regional planning in what has become the "Northern Zone" of the Indus Plains (above the Gudu Barrage—see Map 6). Similar responsibility in the "Southern Zone" went to Hunting Technical Services of London as early as August 1959, and has since been expanded into the Lower Indus Project (primarily drainage and salinity control but including some groundwater development) in which Hunting is assisted by Sir M. MacDonald and Partners, also of London. Independently, Sir M. MacDonald and Partners serve as consultants for the Sibi-Jhatpat

10. In fact, WAPDA's proclivity to employ foreign consultants may have helped persuade the World Bank that the Authority could effectively serve as Pakistan's agent for the IBP as permitted by the Loan and Development Fund agreements. See the text of Ghulam Faruque's radio address, "A New Approach," made early in 1961 when he was still Chairman of WAPDA and reprinted in *A New Approach* (Texts of Broadcasts on Radio Pakistan, Lahore) (Lahore, WAPDA, n.d.), p. 4. See also the article by a member of the Planning Commission, which also makes use of many foreign consultants provided by foundations or technical assistance programs: I. A. Zafar, "Role of Consultants in Development," *Indus, 3* (January 1963), 24–28.

Project southeast of Quetta. Other surface water projects outside the Indus Plains have been entrusted to Energoprojekt of Yugoslavia (the Gomal River and Dera Ismail Khan projects) and to the Associated Consulting Engineers, WAPDA's only Pakistani consultants to date (Rawal Dam, completed in 1962, and ongoing projects on the Hub, Siran, Haro, and Soan rivers and in Gilgit).

In addition, WAPDA has half a dozen foreign consultants for various phases of its power program, including the new thermal stations and improvements to the grid, and an overall accounting consultant, A. F. Ferguson, Ltd., of Lahore. The World Bank has its engineering consultants, Sir Alexander Gibb and Partners of London, and its accounting consultants, Cooper and Lybrand of London. Up to 1964 the Bank and its consultants were concerned only with the IBP, and therefore directly only with WAPDA, Harza, and Ferguson, and indirectly only with Binnie and Partners (Mangla), TAMS (Tarbela), T and K (links), and Coode and Partners (barrages). Under the Supplementary Agreement to the Development Fund Agreement, however, and even though the tubewells and drainages component of the Fund has been dropped, the Bank is undertaking its own survey of water and power resources in all of West Pakistan. This survey not only brings the Bank into an indirect relationship with all of WAPDA's consultants, including those for the power and non-Indus Plains projects, but the Bank has employed no less than five additional consulting firms from the U.K., U.S.A., and Canada to carry out the survey. One might be tempted to say that never before have so many consulted so much on so little.[11]

Ultimately, with the completion of the Bank's survey and of the IBP, the number of consultants *ought* to decrease (unless new ones are hired to advise on new projects foreseen in the survey). Then there will remain, for water and reclamation projects in the Indus Plains, T and K, Hunting-MacDonald, and Harza. But the greatest of these is Harza, for in its role as general consultant it has to review the work of the others before it is submitted to WAPDA, the Government of West Pakistan, or the Central Government.

11. In the sense that, as has been mentioned, the survey consultants must rely heavily on the earlier work of WAPDA's consultants, Harza in particular, in order to complete their work within the allotted time. The projects of course are enormous, as is their cost.

Such a proliferation of consultants may appear to be a fine example of the application of Parkinson's Laws. To the extent that their activities overlap, as in review by the World Bank consultants of work done by WAPDA's consultants, or in review by Harza of work done by the others, the justification must be sought in the number of significant errors discovered and the number of superior alternatives suggested. Disagreements among consultants, like those between WAPDA and the Irrigation Department, though costly in time, may prove to be beneficial and economical in the long run. There is obviously no way to assess the value of such services to the Bank as representative of the "friendly Governments" or to WAPDA as representative of the Government of Pakistan. Undoubtedly there is much duplication, but the price of leaving errors undetected or alternatives unexplored might be much more costly. Pakistan is certainly getting an expensive water and power development and land reclamation system. She may also be getting the best in the world.

Nevertheless, the issues of "consultantship" on such a scale are worthy of further analysis, inconclusive though it must be. Could not Pakistan secure *most* of the benefits of the Indus Basin Project and the reclamation and power schemes if she proceeded without foreign consultants, utilizing just her own talent to design and supervise the execution of the works? Quite obviously she could not, for the same reasons that she cannot rely on domestic talent and equipment alone to execute them. As has been seen, Pakistan is not yet equipped with sufficient skills, in numbers of qualified engineers, to design and build works of this magnitude within the time limits imposed by the Treaty for the IBP and by her rapidly growing population with its need for all of the irrigation, power, and reclamation works. Pakistan has to run just to keep her place on the population treadmill. By using foreign contractors and foreign consultants, she has a chance to gain a march, though obviously at considerable cost. *Pakistan is trading money for time.* Fortunately, much of it is not her own money, and the logic of the IBP and other schemes is that they will return enough to the economy, in more and better crops, in cheap electricity and all it can be converted into, and in land saved from deterioration to enable her to repay the loan components and still to increase per capita national income.

Yet another alternative exists. Could not the costs of "consultantship" be reduced? Are the large "establishments" of the consultants excessive, and could not the same return be achieved at lower cost? Is it not strange that WAPDA's foreign consultants for the IBP are all drawn from the U.S. or the U.K., the two main contributors to the Fund, and that American and British personnel dominate the non-IBP consulting arrangements as well? Is it necessary to support these personnel, and their dependents, in Pakistan at or near (and in some cases above) the standards to which they are accustomed at home? There has been some complaining, especially in Lahore, about the size of the "foreign colony," its comparative affluence, the various concessions made to its members, and the "fact" that Pakistanis doing the "same" work as foreigners may receive only one-fifth the compensation.

But these criticisms, inevitable in a society that is modernizing rapidly but that still has enormous extremes of wealth and poverty, do not stand up to vigorous logical analysis. First of all, there is nothing in the Treaty or the loan agreements requiring Pakistan to hire consultants (though the hiring of an independent and reliable accounting firm is implied). WAPDA has done so in its own calculated interest, first to obtain foreign assistance and then to get the job done quickly and well and to make sure that its *contractors* perform according to international standards. (In contrast to some other developing nations, Pakistan did not make the mistake of trying to economize by allowing a contractor to provide his own consulting services. Quite the contrary, for by employing Harza as a "superconsultant" WAPDA gets a double check: consultants on contractors, Harza on consultants.) Secondly, WAPDA has a free hand in the choice and retention of consultants. Although the Fund Agreement specifies that Pakistan must procure all *services* for the *IBP* from members of the *Bank*, this now gives her over a hundred possibilities, and there is of course no restriction whatever on where she gets her consultants for other projects. Thus, if WAPDA finds that Yugoslavia, Italy, Egypt, Nigeria, or Peru can provide consultants more cheaply than the United States, the United Kingdom, or Canada, she can—indeed, she should—hire them. The fact that she has done so only in the cases of Montecatini of Italy (for the primary power grid) and the state-supported Geostratizvanija and Energoprojekt of Yugoslavia is an indication of the scarcity of such talent.

Thirdly, the supply of consultants' services, and the compensation (including concessions) offered to individual consultants, is strictly a matter of supply and demand. With comparatively few exceptions, the individual consultants working in Pakistan are men who could command nearly the same total compensation back home. The additional pay and "concessions" (including payment by the firm of the Pakistan income tax, which the firm promptly passes along to WAPDA in its consulting fees—as it does the customs duties and transportation costs of consultants' private cars and its own corporate tax) represent, in most cases, the "opportunity cost" necessary to persuade the individual to work in Pakistan rather than at home. So the "privileges" accorded to the consultants (which do not include any sort of legal or diplomatic privileges) must realistically be reckoned as part of the cost to Pakistan of gaining time in her development program. And on the whole these privileges have not been abused.

Fourthly, it is not irrelevant to point out that Pakistan is also benefiting, and has already benefited more than any other nation except South Korea, from the foreign aid programs of the United States, Canada, and the Commonwealth (Colombo Plan). To a large extent these programs, including the counterpart Food for Peace plan so vital to Tarbela financing, are free. Technical assistance, including that of A.I.D. and the Peace Corps, costs Pakistan nothing: even the local costs are paid in counterpart rupees. While it is true that some loans and grants from the United States, West Germany, and Japan are tied to purchases from the lending country, the United States Development Loan Fund loans for the IBP are not, and are repayable in rupees at the official rate of exchange. So although Pakistan is paying her U.S., U.K., and Canadian consultants in dollars, these dollars and many others are virtual gifts to her, and she is also benefiting from sizable, free programs of technical assistance from these very nations. Now that Pakistan has apparently entered into a new era in foreign relations, she may accept further offers of technical assistance from the U.S.S.R. and from China, and she may even "employ" or utilize consultants from these nations in the belief that their services will be "cheaper" than those of the West. But unless there is a mammoth shift in the source of foreign assistance to Pakistan, it is hard to see how they can be cheaper in the long run.

The argument that foreigners are paid five times as much as Pakistanis for performing the same services applies only in the upper echelons. Pakistan does have some engineers and administrators who could hold the jobs of foreign consultants. Indeed, a few have been offered jobs by the consultants at several times their present pay, and some have accepted with alacrity. And therein is the fallacy in the argument; for a foreign consulting firm would generally be happy to reduce its own wage and fringe-benefit costs by hiring Pakistanis if they were available. But they are not, at least not in significant numbers. Those who perform services equivalent to the foreigners' are already working for WAPDA or the Irrigation Department or private Pakistani firms at reasonably commensurate total compensations (including considerations of seniority, which will continue to accumulate long after the consultants have left Pakistan). Aside from patriotism, which acts in not a few cases, there is nothing prohibiting such men from taking employment with the consultants (though the consulting firms would soon find themselves unpopular with WAPDA and with the Irrigation Department).

At lower echelons, one might think that the consultants hire away good men from WAPDA by offering them better salaries. That is not what happens. WAPDA supplies such technicians, junior engineers, clerks, accountants, bookkeepers, secretaries, drivers, etc., to the consultants but keeps them on its own payroll. Many of these Pakistanis are being trained as "counterparts" who will one day replace the foreigner. A check of the May 1963 edition of the WAPDA telephone directory indicated that the consultant firms alone (excluding the contractors) had 149 Pakistanis of sufficient rank to be listed opposite a telephone number as compared with 197 foreigners. (WAPDA itself, incidentally, listed only one foreigner directly employed: General Itschner, Chief Technical Adviser.) This is hardly a ratio to be deplored, and it will probably improve with time.

In summation, one can conclude that whatever the criticisms and complaints directed at foreign consultants hired by WAPDA or other Pakistan governmental agencies, the foreigners must be worth it or Pakistan would get rid of them. Unless one assumes a broad conspiracy, tying further foreign aid—direct or through the World Bank —to the employment by Pakistan of foreign consultants, and particularly of consultants from the nations contributing to the aid programs and to the development fund administered by the Bank, the numbers and compensation of such consultants seem to be a function of supply and demand. Even if such a conspiracy did exist, would not Pakistan seek to make only token compliance, or, now that she has apparently received all the aid she can expect for the IBP, seek to diminish the role of foreign consultants for the IBP? Would she not, in particular, try to replace American, Canadian, and British consultants with less costly firms from other member nations of the World Bank? Would she not transfer consulting arrangements for the non-IBP (hence, completely unrestricted) portions of her water and power development programs to firms other than those from the U.S., Canada, and the U.K., and possibly even invite technical assistants from the U.S.S.R. and China to take their place? Here, of course, we enter the political arena, and one could argue that Pakistan does not do so for fear of losing other forms of assistance from the West. But even that ultimate argument seems self-defeating, for it implies that the total contribution Pakistan receives, even minus the additional costs of using Western consultants, is greater than she could hope to obtain if she tried to replace them. Which conclusion, no matter on what plane it is reached, is undoubtedly correct.

Returning from these political summits to the plane of WAPDA operations, one still has a lingering doubt that all of the three-tiered consultant operations (consultants, superconsultant, World Bank consultants) are really necessary. As has been said, it seems impossible to arrive at any conclusive answer, especially as the World Bank consultants for the survey of water, land, and power resources in West Pakistan are presumably of short tenure. Perhaps what is needed is a consultant on consultants to make a survey of consultantship in West Pakistan and to determine where one reaches the point of diminishing returns.

India: The Center and the States

It is one of the many paradoxes of political development in the subcontinent since Partition that India, theoretically committed from Independence to centralized administration and planning, has evolved in many ways into a looser confederation than was proposed by the Cabinet Mission, while Pakistan, which delayed integration until 1955 and her first Constitution until 1956, has evolved a system of two highly centralized provinces, or Wings, under a national government whose main role often seems to be that of keeping them together by performing the functions the Cabinet Mission Plan would have left with the Center (see Chapter 5), and by allocating resources for development in such a manner as to keep both provinces more or less content. This ebb and flow of centralized administration has been characteristic of other large states in the modern period, notably of the U.S.S.R. It is a continuing problem in Indonesia and, one suspects, in China. But in India it acquires a more acute form, both because India is trying to achieve democratic rule and because of her cultural geography. India consists of many "countries." The British Raj united them to a greater degree than Asoka or the Moguls, but even the British had to (or, in the eyes of most Indians, chose to) recognize the distinctiveness of the different provinces and of the many Princely States.

Up to 1919, British rule worked generally toward integration. Like most things British, it worked by fits and starts, by trial and error. In the eighteenth and nineteenth centuries, the development of Bengal, Bihar, Orissa, Madras, and Bombay, and particularly of the United Provinces and Central Provinces, was generally a matter of annexing and integrating the Princely States. In the Punjab, where Ranjit Singh had already laid the foundations, further integration under the British made less progress. Some of the cis-Sutlej and trans-Sutlej states were integrated with the Sikh state in 1846–49, but others, notably Patiala, Kapurthala, Bahawalpur, Nabha, Jind, and the congeries of Hill States, remained outside. Rajputana was integrated only in name, and the North West Frontier Province, the frontier tribal districts and states (such as Swat and Chitral), and Baluchistan remained as disunited as their equivalents in the northeast of India.

By the end of Victoria's reign, integration in the Indian Empire had gone as far as it was to go under the British Raj. In 1905 an attempt was made to divide Bengal into two provinces, but this was reversed in 1911. In response to the demands for self-rule, however, the Government of India Act of 1919 delegated some authority from the Central Government to the provinces. The trend was continued in the Government of India Act of 1935, which provided for the election of provincial legislatures and ministries and gave them more authority than they ever had known. As we saw in Chapter 5, the Cabinet Mission wanted to build Free India's constitution on the

1935 model, though providing for grouping and for the adherence of Princely States. But Nehru would have none of it, fearing that it would leave the Center too weak to rule and especially to plan for economic development. Jinnah did not care, for he was intent only on obtaining his six provinces, and the facts of economic geography made it clear that Bengal, with or without Assam, would have to function as one unit while Punjab, N.W.F.P., Sind, Baluchistan, and Kashmir would function as another, with or without the adherence of Bahawalpur, Khairpur, Kalat, etc. The problem of holding East and West Pakistan together was so overwhelming that it dwarfed the problems within the West Wing, and though these last should never be underestimated, they were overridden in peremptory fashion when One Unit Rule was established in October 1955. Long before the administrative reform, West Pakistan had been fused not only by internal economic factors but by the external pressures of India and Afghanistan.

But in India the situation was far different, compounded by manifold linguistic differences as well as by the political heritage from the British. V. P. Menon, the architect of the final partition plan, and his successors in the States Ministry, spent the next eight years fusing the Princely States into States Unions (Rajasthan, P.E.P.S.U., etc.), and the 1950 Constitution was amended half a dozen times to accommodate the changes. Since Independence, Free India has gone through the same experience as British India: first integration and then decentralization. In 1950, there were eight Part A states, corresponding to the governors' provinces of British India; seven part B states, corresponding to the larger Princely States or States Unions; and ten Part C states, corresponding to the chief commissioners' provinces. By 1956, with the passage of the States Reorganization Act which replaced all of these with fourteen states, and six centrally administered territories, the tide of integration had ebbed. True, P.E.P.S.U. had been incorporated in Punjab and Bilaspur in Himachal Pradesh, but in 1953 Andhra Pradesh had been separated from Madras on linguistic grounds, starting a trend that led to the 1960 division of Bombay into Gujarat and Maharashtra.[12] The Nagas on

12. *The Statesman's Yearbook, 1964–65*, S. H. Steinberg, ed. (New York, St. Martin's Press, 1964), pp. 412–13; and V. P. Menon, *The Integration of the Indian States* (Calcutta, Orient Longmans, 1956).

the Burmese border got a state in 1962 but are agitating for complete autonomy. In the spring of 1966 it was announced that, to satisfy the Sikhs, a Punjab state would be created by dividing the Punjab into Punjabi- and Hindi-speaking areas to be known as Punjabi Suba and Haryana, with the Chandigarh area to become a union territory and serve, at least temporarily, as the capital for both states. Thus, by 1967 the Indian Union will consist of seventeen states and ten union territories. Where this trend will lead is anyone's guess, and some see it as India's greatest problem.[13]

In the field of water-resources development, Free India inherited a cumbersome administrative system. Each step toward decentralization had created more problems for the Center. The Act of 1919 made irrigation a provincial but reserved matter: projects affecting more than one province or costing more than Rs 5 million had to be referred to the Government of India and ultimately to the Secretary of State for sanction.[14] Although the post of Inspector-General of Irrigation, created in 1906, was abolished in 1923, a Central Board of Irrigation (later Irrigation and Power) had to be established in January 1927 to advise the Government of India on technical points involved in disputes among the provinces and states (which were represented on the Board by their Chief Engineers) and to advise on irrigation, hydroelectric, and flood-control projects referred to it.[15] It was also responsible for fostering and coordinating research work. Clearly, decentralization in irrigation matters could only go so far. The Government of India Act of 1935 probably took it too far. Each province acquired complete control of internal irrigation and power development. Interprovincial matters could be settled by interprovincial agreements, such as the stillborn 1945 agreement between the Chief Engineers of Sind and Punjab (see Chapter 4). Only if one province formally complained against another would the Governor-General step in, as he had on Sind's complaint over Bhakra, by ap-

13. See for example Selig S. Harrison, *India: The Most Dangerous Decades* (Princeton, N.J., Princeton University Press, 1960).

14. UNECAFE, *Multiple-Purpose River Basin Development*, p. 70.

15. Government of India, Ministry of Home Affairs, Secretariat Training School, *Organisational Set-up and Functions of the Ministries/Departments of the Government of India* (2nd ed., New Delhi, 1962), p. 149; and Government of India, Ministry of Information and Broadcasting, Publications Division, *India: A Reference Annual, 1954* (New Delhi, April 1954), p. 187.

pointing a commission such as the Rau Commission to investigate and make recommendations. The Governor-General could act on these recommendations, subject to appeal by the provinces to the King in Council.[16]

Although the delays inherent in the provisions of the Act of 1935 had redounded to India's benefit in the Indus Basin (see Chapter 4), the procedure was repugnant to Nehru and the Congress leaders. Free India had too many interstate, multipurpose water-resource development projects to tackle, and too little time to accomplish them, to allow the states to delay them through an appeals procedure. Yet even the demands of the post-Independence Central Government to streamline this procedure met with resistance from the states. The legislation proposed in 1950 still embodied a time-consuming appeals procedure. It would have enabled the Government of India

(a) to assume adequate power for co-ordinating and regulating all developments in respect of interstate rivers and river valleys, for purposes of irrigation, navigation, flood control, ground water drainage, water conservation, water-power and prevention of pollution;
(b) to set up regional boards for such purposes and in such areas as may be necessary for the full development of any interstate river and river valley; [and]
(c) to set up a Central Water and Power Authority to adjudicate on disputes relating to the development of interstate rivers and river valleys which may be referred to it by the Central Government or any state government or regional board.

But it also called for the Central Government

(d) to make provision for a final appeal against any decision of the Central Water and Power Authority along the lines of sections 130 to 134 of the Government of India Act, 1935.[17]

Yet even these proposals, which were circulated to the state governments in June 1950, and discussed at an interstate conference in May 1951, proved too strong for the states. Ultimately, after much further

16. UNECAFE, *Multiple-Purpose River Basin Development*, p. 70.
17. Ibid.

discussion and modification, two bills were passed by the Indian Parliament in 1956:

1. The River Boards Bill empowering the Central Government to set up, in consultation with the state concerned, river boards in respect of interstate rivers. The boards, which include representatives of the states, are to advise the state governments with regard to development of the rivers, to prepare new schemes and recommend them to the states, to allocate costs, and to try to secure agreement on the schemes among the states. If any state does not accept the recommendations, the matter is referred to arbitration by arbitrators appointed by the Chief Justice of India, whose decision is binding on the states. The bill also empowers the Central Government to frame rules and regulations concerning the functions which a board may perform, the terms and conditions of service of its members, budgets and accounting procedures, and the annual report and other information to be supplied by the board to the Central Government.

2. The Interstate Water Disputes Bill which provides for the establishment of ad hoc tribunals when necessary for adjudication of disputes on use, distribution, and control of interstate rivers. Only disputes submitted by a state government, not those of individuals, and only disputes which do not arise from refusal of a state to accept or implement the advice of a river board, will be handled by such tribunals, which consist of judges of the Supreme Court or of high courts of noninvolved states, plus assessors where necessary.[18]

It is to be noted that neither of these bills confers upon the Central Government the desired authority to coordinate and regulate all developments concerning interstate rivers or to establish a Central Water and Power Authority to adjudicate disputes relating to such development. Rather, the bills only provide a general authority for the establishment of river boards, something the Central Government had been doing on an ad hoc basis anyway, and they emphasize an arbitration and appeals procedure only slightly less awkward than that under the Government of India Act of 1935.

But even under that Act, it had been found necessary to establish a Central Waterways, Irrigation, and Navigation Commission in April 1945 "to act as a Central fact-finding, planning and co-ordi-

18. Ibid., pp. 70–71.

nating organisation with authority to undertake construction work."[19]
After Independence, this Commission was first changed to "Water-
Power, Irrigation and Navigation" and then in June 1951 amalgamated with the Central Electricity Commission to form the Central
Water and Power Commission with authority to design and plan
multipurpose river development projects, but not to carry them out
except in conjunction with the states. As the Commissions' plans
came off the drafting table in the late 1940s and early 1950s, ad hoc
arrangements were made to carry them out. The Damodar Valley
Project, which concerns both West Bengal and Bihar, was entrusted
to a Damodar Valley Corporation, modeled largely on the T.V.A.,
established by the Central Government in July 1948 in agreement
with the two states. Like WAPDA, the D.V.C. is a corporate body
with a chairman and two members, appointed by the Central Government in consultation with the state concerned. The Hirakud Project,
which involves only the state of Orissa, was executed by the Central
Government as agent of the state and under the supervision of a
Control Board on which both were represented. The Bhakra Project,
involving Punjab, P.E.P.S.U., and Rajasthan and also affecting
Bilaspur, was entrusted to a Control Board and an Advisory Board
on which the Central Government and the states were represented by
a special act passed in 1950 and amended subsequently to conform
to the constitutional changes involving Punjab and Himachal Pradesh.
The Interstate Agreement of 1955 among Punjab, Rajasthan, and
Kashmir worked out the allocations of water from Bhakra and any
further development schemes on all three Eastern Rivers. It will now
have to be amended to take cognizance of the November 1, 1966,
partition of the Indian Punjab into Punjabi Suba and Haryana Pant
with the hilly areas going to Himachal Pradesh.

The role of the Central Government was enhanced as central planning got under way. As early as April 1948 an Industrial Policy Resolution had "defined the objectives of policy and the fields of
operation of government and private enterprises, [and] envisaged
the establishment of a national planning commission to formulate
programmes of development and to secure their achievement."[20] The
Central Planning Commission was established in March 1950, and

19. *India: A Reference Annual*, 1954, pp. 187–88.
20. UNECAFE, *Multiple-Purpose River Basin Development*, p. 65.

by July 1951 had prepared, in consultation with central ministries and state governments, India's first Five Year Plan which included seventeen major river development schemes, among them Bhakra, Damodar, and Hirakud, and no less than two hundred minor schemes. In October 1953 the Planning Commission set up an Advisory Committee on Irrigation and Power Projects to examine projects proposed by the states and to advise on their technical and economic feasibility. To work with this Committee and to expedite decisions on its recommendations, a Co-Ordination Board of Ministers for River Valley Projects, including the Central Minister of Irrigation and Power (as chairman) and the Ministers for Irrigation and Power of the Punjab, Rajasthan, Uttar Pradesh, and six other states was established in 1954.[21]

Thus India, by the time the Indus Treaty negotiations got under way, was well along not only with the Bhakra Project but with a host of others throughout her vast territory. But she still had no central ministry of irrigation for the simple reason that in August 1947, when the departments of the central government of British India were redesignated as the ministries of the government of Free India, there was no central department of irrigation but only, as we have seen, a Central Board of Irrigation (later of Irrigation and Power) and a Central Waterways, Irrigation and Navigation Commission (which later was merged with the Central Electricity Commission to become the Central Water and Power Commission). For convenience, by 1951 these two commissions had been attached to the Ministry of National Resources and Scientific Research (headed by Maulana Abul Kalam Azad, the most prominent Muslim member of the Congress Party, who was also Minister of Education). But on May 13, 1952, a week after the negotiations got under way in Washington, the Government of India announced the formation of a separate Central Ministry of Irrigation and Power which began to function on August 1, 1952 (under Gulzarilal Nanda who was also, and significantly, Minister for Planning). The primary functions of the new Ministry of Irrigation and Power were as follows:

1. Regulation and development of inter-State rivers and river valleys.

21. Ibid., pp. 65–67; and Indian Institute of Public Administration, *The Organisation of the Government of India* (Bombay, Asia Publishing House, 1958), pp. 246, 353.

2. General policy and technical assistance in the field of irrigation, power, flood control, anti-water-logging, drainage and anti-sea erosion.
3. Basic, fundamental and applied research on river valley projects and flood control works.[22]

The Ministry was made responsible for irrigation and power schemes in the union territories but, with the exception of the Damodar Valley Corporation, not in or among the states. The Central Water and Power Commission, the Central Board of Irrigation and Power, and the Damodar Valley Corporation (but not the Bhakra or Hirakud organizations) were attached to the new Ministry, which later took over administration of the River Boards and Interstate Water Disputes Acts of 1956. From 1960, the Ministry has included the office of the Indian Commissioner for Indus Waters, established pursuant to the Treaty.

The fact that, for India, water-resource development in the Indus Basin was only one of several schemes of comparable magnitude, whereas for West Pakistan it was practically the entire basis of development, contributed not only to the nature of India's representations and representatives in the Treaty negotiations (see Chapter 6) but to her whole attitude toward Indus Basin Development. For the Bhakra Project, and the emerging BBRP (Bhakra-Beas-Rajasthan Project), could be viewed in long-range perspective. The Central Water and Power Commission, whose chairman was represented both on the Bhakra Control Board and the Advisory Board (the only other common members of both boards were the representative of the Central Ministry of Finance and the Bhakra general manager), could afford to take a long-range view and to relate India's position in the Basin, geographically and politically superior to that of Pakistan, to alternatives in other river valleys. West Pakistan, obviously, had no such alternatives, and in both the Treaty negotiations and in carrying out the project had had to act under urgent pressures of time, due to both population pressure and the waterlogging-salinity menace.

In addition, geographical size and the number of major river development schemes available enabled India to experiment with

22. *Organisational Set-up and Functions of the Ministries/Departments of the Government of India*, p. 145.

different types of organization for development. Damodar, Hirakud, and Bhakra were three of the possible alternatives, and she could compare their relative progress and make changes accordingly (the D.V.C. underwent fundamental changes in the mid-fifties, and the Beas Control Board and Standing Committee represent some differences in approach as compared to the Bhakra boards). Aside from earlier experience with the Pakistan Industrial Development Corporation (for the Warsak power distribution system), the Thal Development Corporation, and the Soil Reclamation Board (under the Irrigation Department), Pakistan had to guess right the first time in establishing WAPDA and entrusting virtually all responsibility for water and power development in the Indus Basin, including the IBP, to this public corporation. In brief, Pakistan had less time and less room for experimentation than India.

Time and experiment restrictions were key factors, along with the absence of a well-developed philosophy of central planning, in Pakistan's and WAPDA's reliance on foreign contractors and consultants for Indus Basin development. Furthermore, the need to convince foreign governments and the World Bank of her ability to execute the works rapidly and efficiently played a much larger role in Pakistan than in India, where *direct* foreign assistance for Bhakra was nil and indirect assistance through the Five Year Plans was diluted over many projects of comparable magnitude. Ostensibly, India financed the Bhakra Project by extending loans from the Central Government to the states (a carry-over from British procedure even after 1919) and suggesting that the states recover the costs by levying betterment taxes on the enhanced values of affected lands and by increasing the water rates which, hand-in-hand with the British system of spreading the water thin, had remained ridiculously low especially in view of the general inflation of the farmer's other costs and of the prices he received.

Bearing in mind these considerations of Bhakra's role in total Indian development, as well as the considerations of available engineering talent, limitations of private construction firms, and India's attitude toward the economic and political aspects of employing foreign consultants and contractors, it is not surprising that, after preliminary design work by the International Engineering Company of San Francisco, India chose to redesign and build the Bhakra

Project with a minimum of foreign talent (a total of perhaps sixty foreign engineers, all of whom were phased out before Bhakra personnel were transferred to the Beas projects), and no foreign contractors except those setting up foreign-supplied equipment. The Bhakra Project was designed and built by fusing the available talents of the state and Central governments; hiring a few foreign engineers (notably Harvey Slocum) on an individual contract basis for services that could not be so handled; hiring one firm (International Engineering) for preliminary designing; letting contracts on a bid basis to Indian firms for some work (such as the building of housing, office, and warehouse facilities) and for supplying some materials and equipment; and procuring necessary foreign equipment and materials on the basis of competitive bids and on the account of the states involved.[23]

By the terms of the Bhakra enabling act, the states of Punjab and Rajasthan agreed to delegate to their respective Chief Engineers the power to contract for works, supplies, and services at the direction of the Bhakra Control Board, the contracts to be executed as on behalf of the state governments and the movable equipment to remain the property of these states. The Chief Engineer of Punjab, who became general manager of the Bhakra Dam Organization, was empowered to act for both P.E.P.S.U. and Bilaspur (ultimately Himachal Pradesh).[24] But the policy decisions, including overall

23. The Indian Central Planning Commission has actively encouraged the private sector to manufacture the simpler types of earthmoving equipment and such items as pipes, pumps, valves, cables, and even some of the structural and reinforcing steel needed in enormous quantities not only at Bhakra Dam but in other parts of the project and in other projects throughout the country. Foreign firms supplied heavy earthmoving equipment, trucks, jeeps, cranes, and concrete mixing, moving, and pouring equipment, most of which could be moved to other projects within East Punjab, as well as turbines (from Japan), generators (from the U.K.), transformers, switching gear, etc., which have been permanently installed at Bhakra or at the two powerhouses along the power canal below the Nangal Barrage. Foreign firms supplying equipment did send technicians to supervise its installation or to train Indians in its use. Perhaps the most noteworthy of such arrangements was that made with an Italian firm to train technicians and workmen of the Bhakra Aggregate Processing Division in the preparation of pozzolana, a cement made largely from fly ash or volcanic ash, which was used in enormous quantities in building the dam.

24. "Constitution and Functions of the Bhakra Control Board and Bhakra Advisory Board," in UNECAFE, *Proceedings of the Third Regional Technical Conference*, p. 121.

technical and financial aspects in Punjab, Himachal Pradesh, and Rajasthan, were entrusted to the Control and Advisory boards. The Control Board located in New Delhi passed on the estimates and recommended modifications before submitting them to the states. It examined and approved the delegation of technical and financial powers to the Chief Engineers, and it approved all subestimates and contracts beyond the level left to the Chief Engineers' discretion. It received monthly progress reports on works and expenditures from the Chief Engineers, and reviewed the progress and recommended ways of expediting it. Thus, although considerable executive responsibility was delegated to the Chief Engineers of Punjab and Rajasthan, their work was scrutinized at least once a month at meetings of the Control Board. But though the Control Board had considerable prestige and authority, it could only recommend expenditures to the states, just as WAPDA must submit its projects for incorporation into the West Pakistan budget and national Five Year Plans.

The Advisory Board, which met every three months, was established to coordinate the views and interests of the state and Central governments, to resolve technical differences, to phase the program including the rate of installation of hydroelectric capacity and withdrawals of water for irrigation during construction, and, at the request of the state governments, to advise on the allocation of supplies from Bhakra (a matter eventually settled by the 1955 Interstate Agreement). The membership of both boards is given in Table 18 to facilitate comparison.

Although the control board device, originating with Bhakra in 1950, had been extended by the Government of India to no less than fourteen river development projects by 1962, the Bhakra Board remained unique in including no Central or state minister. On all but one of the boards, however, either the Governor or the Chief Minister of a state served as chairman.[25] Thus, although the control boards are not statutory authorities but just administrative agencies created by executive power, the high-level state representation means that the state governments almost invariably go along with the boards' recommendations, and in some instances even review the

25. S. S. Khera, *Government in Business* (Bombay, Asia Publishing House, Issued Under the Auspices of the Indian Institute of Public Administration, 1963), pp. 106, 110–11.

Table 18. Composition of Supervisory Boards, Bhakra Project
(Bhakra Dam, Bhakra Canal System, Rajasthan Canal)ᵃ

Bhakra Control Board	*Both Boards*	*Bhakra Advisory Board*
Chairman: Governor of the Punjab (in his personal capacity)		
Vice-Chairman: Secretary to the Government of India, Ministry of Irrigation and Power		
	Chairman, Central Water and Power Commission	
	Joint Secretary or Representative, Ministry of Finance, Government of India	
	General Manager, Bhakra Dam (Chief Engineer, Punjab)	
	Chief Engineer, Irrigation, Rajasthan	
	Chief Secretary, Himachal Pradesh	
		Member for Hydroelectricity, Central Water and Power Commission
		Chief Engineer, Electricity, Punjab
		Chief Engineer, Bhakra Canals, Punjab
		Finance Secretary, Punjab
		Finance Secretary, Rajasthan

a. Source: "Constitution and Functions of the Bhakra Control Board and Bhakra Advisory Board," in UNECAFE, *Proceedings of the Third Regional Technical Conference,* pp. 121–22. A common secretariat for both boards was maintained in New Delhi, headed by a Superintending Engineer and with a Deputy Secretary drawn from the Finance Department.

proposals of the engineers before they are submitted to the boards. S. S. Khera, writing in 1962, found this situation dubious since the boards, being merely advisory and not statutory, are not legally accountable for their actions and because there is no Central accounting procedure for the large amounts of money lent by the Central Government to the states for the projects.[26]

But the Central Ministry of Finance did at least have representation on both Bhakra Boards. The three other members common to both boards represented the interests of the three states involved,

26. Ibid., pp. 111–12.

and two of them, the Chief Engineers of Punjab and Rajasthan, were the individuals directly responsible for executing the works (along with the Chief Engineer, Bhakra Canals, Punjab, who was concerned with bringing Bhakra water from the Nangal Hydel Canal down to the south Punjab and integrating it there with the Sirhind and Western Jumna systems). It is worth noting that Kashmir, though a party to the 1955 Interstate Agreement on future water allocations from the Eastern Rivers, had no say on the Bhakra Project.

Below the position of the general manager, the Bhakra Dam Organization offers further contrasts with the system adopted for the IBP. The General Manager, Bhakra Dam, supervised three directorates:

1. Bhakra Dam Designs, housed primarily in New Delhi where it could maintain close liaison with the Central Water and Power Commission, the Central Ministry of Irrigation and Power, the Central Ministry of Finance, and the Planning Commission

2. Construction and Plant Design, located at Nangal,[27] with divisions for excavation, exploration drilling and grouting, aggregate processing, aggregate transportation, forms construction, forms assembly, rigging, mechanical engineering, powerhouse construction, communications and materials, and shops

3. Inspection and Control, also at Nangal, with three divisions for concrete inspection, one for grouting control, one for electrical and mechanical control, a research officer, a deputy commissioner for resettlement from Bilaspur, and a general dam inspector.

The general manager, Bhakra Dam, was thus responsible for design, construction, quality control, and inspection. Aside from the foreign engineers hired on contract principally in the early stages of the project, he had no "consultants," nor was there a separate general consultant (such as Harza for WAPDA including the IBP) to check on his work and to counsel the Control and Advisory boards. In other words, the Bhakra Dam Organization, and the Bhakra Project Organization as a whole, included their own consultants and inspectors. This approach was an economical one, since

27. There was no room for office facilities in the Bhakra gorge, so Nangal and Naya Nangal, on opposite sides of the Sutlej about seven miles below the dam, were developed to house these organizations and also for storage of materials and equipment.

377

it used a minimum of foreign advice and foreign exchange, but it was also a risky one, since there was an inevitable tendency for one division below the general manager to collaborate with another, and particularly for the Inspection and Control Directorate to look more leniently upon the work of the Construction and Plant Design Directorate than a totally disinterested inspector or consultant might have done. The general manager had to check on both of these directorates as well as on the Designs Directorate back in New Delhi. This was quite a burden for one man, even though he was provided with some foreign expertise and was overseen by the Control and Advisory boards. The other members of these boards, of course, had other responsibilities, and this was especially true of the representatives of the Central Water and Power Commission and the Central Ministry of Irrigation and Power whose work embraced all of India and included operation and maintenance of existing systems as well as initiation of new projects comparable to Bhakra.

Only one serious error occurred during Bhakra's construction, responsibility for which seems to lie more in the manner in which the plans were (or were not) executed than in the design itself. In drilling the 2,700-foot-long, 50-foot-diameter right diversion tunnel, between 1948 and 1954, extremely weak rock was encountered. The engineering solution to such a problem is to "grout" the rock, i.e. to force a mixture of cement and fine sand into the interstices of the rock to impregnate it. But, apparently for reasons of economy, the grouting was stopped halfway, leaving the tunnel and its gate and hoist chambers inadequately protected. These chambers were incorporated and provided with steel gates in order to shut off the flow of water and allow the diversion tunnel to be permanently sealed after it had served its purpose.

In August 1959, only one month before the right diversion tunnel was to be sealed (and during the temporary absence of Harvey Slocum, the chief construction engineer) the inadequately grouted tunnel and chambers began to collapse, probably because the reservoir had been raised above the level Slocum considered safe from the standpoint of pressure on the tunnel. Faced with this emergency, the engineers on the scene tried to close the gates in the rupturing chamber, only to have them stick partly open. Water quickly rose through the chambers into an adit connecting them to the galleries of the dam. Through the galleries it flowed across the dam to the left side, drowning ten workmen. Here the lower portion of the left diversion tunnel had already been sealed, and the upper portion had been connected to the powerhouse where two of its five 90,000-kw generators had already been installed. The pressure of the water flowing under a 190-foot head into the right diversion tunnel made it impossible to reach the gate chamber from the lower end to seal it, and it was necessary to punch holes in a lower gallery wall in order to dewater the dam itself.

The eventual solution to this catastrophe, proposed by Slocum and tested on the Bhakra model at the East Punjab Irrigation and Power Research Institute near Madhopur, was to drop over half a million tons of clay, rock, and sand in layers, and of concrete and pozzolana in crates, from barges onto the tunnel intake until it was sufficiently sealed for a new adit to be driven to the gate and hoist chamber, which was finally sealed with concrete by mid 1960. Meanwhile, the reservoir had to be drawn down 100 feet to reduce pressure in the tunnel, representing a considerable loss of irrigation supplies as well as of the power that could have been generated during the early part of 1960.[28]

Although some Indians connected with the Bhakra administration have suggested that the fault lay in designing the gates of the diversion tunnel to fall diagonally rather than vertically, on the assumption that vertical gates could have been closed even against a 190-foot head of water in a collapsing chamber, it seems far more likely that the error was not one of design but (a) of inadequate grouting in the first place, and (b) of the decision to try to close the gates in a rupturing chamber rather than leave them open in order to draw down the reservoir below the intake of the tunnel so that it could have been sealed more easily. For these reasons, it seems unlikely that a more independent check on the work of the Bhakra Designs Directorate could have avoided the disaster of August 1959.

Any comparison of the methods adopted by the Central Government and the states in constructing the Bhakra Project with those adopted by West Pakistan for the IBP really raises two separate issues. One of these relates to the use of foreign consultants, and

28. *Engineering News Record, 163*, September 3, 1959, p. 23; October 15, 1959, pp. 23–24; and *164*, February 25, 1960, pp. 50–52.

the other to the use of foreign contractors. By doing the actual work herself, India has saved sizable amounts of foreign exchange. In using departmental or "superdepartmental" methods, including the "seconding" (or temporary assignment) of some three hundred engineers to the Bhakra Organization, India has given her own technical personnel the opportunity to take responsibility and has literally forced them to come up to standard. In using the "force account" or "daily labor" system under which the Bhakra Organization hired some 12,000 manual laborers, India greatly increased the pool of trained manpower which could be transferred to the Beas projects. By purchasing on the account of the Punjab Government a sizable machinery pool, which can be used on other projects as long as it can be kept running and provided with spare parts, India probably secured economies over paying a contractor to bring in the equipment, charging her for its transportation, depreciation, and use, and later removing or selling it. (WAPDA's Machinery Pool Organization represents an attempt to secure this sort of economy by purchasing many of the jeeps, trucks, bulldozers, etc., directly on WAPDA account.) By eliminating all but a handful of foreign engineers, India avoided the problems of housing them and their dependents and providing the "fringe benefits" and "privileges" that may be necessary to induce them to take up such jobs but that produce, rightly or wrongly, resentment from the local technicians and populace. There was no such thing as a Bhakra consortium of contractors with their "Little America" as there is at Mangla; the few foreign experts at Nangal or in Delhi fitted in rather inconspicuously.

On the other hand, had India let out substantial portions of the Bhakra project to international contract, she would undoubtedly have finished the dam earlier. As it was, Bhakra took fourteen years and ran at least three years behind schedule (it was supposed to be finished in 1959). No international contractor could afford to tie up his men and equipment for so long a period (see Chapter 7, page 278). The delay was reflected in the inability to make full use of Sutlej water in the remodeled Sirhind command and in the new Bhakra main command, and although the Rajasthan Project is phased out from 1964–65 to 1987–88 (see Chapter 7, Table 17), the rate of development there will depend largely upon progress with the Pong Dam, which in turn could not be started until men and equipment were released from Bhakra. But India, as has been said, had other water development projects in hand, and other resources (notably coal and iron ore) to develop with the foreign aid that came her way, whereas West Pakistan is almost totally involved with developing the water and power resources of the Indus Basin.

Again, it is urged that by proceeding on the "force account" system, India was able to begin work before designs had been finalized and to make changes (such as the spillway changes after model studies were completed at the Irrigation Research Station at Malakpur near Madhopur and the decision to raise the maximum storage level of the reservoir and thus increase its capacity to 8 m.a.f.) as it progressed. Under the contract system, unless the contractor is paid on a "unit price" or "cost plus" basis, it is obviously impossible to obtain bids until the design has been finalized, and it is very difficult to make subsequent changes. But the flexibility of the "force account" system has its perils too, in that decisions may be postponed until it is too late to make necessary changes without incurring exorbitant costs. (This could happen at Pong.) In theory, and often in practice, it is far better to have a thorough and completely-thought-out design before work begins on any major component of a project. On the other hand, there are advantages in not having to adhere to a fixed schedule where any delay by one contractor may hold up the work of another who is ready to proceed and who must charge for his "dead time."[29]

So one cannot make any categorical judgment that Pakistan's

29. For an excellent discussion and analysis of the pros and cons of the government agency "force account" system versus the private contract system, see UNECAFE, *Proceedings of the Third Regional Technical Conference*, pp. 40–47 and pp. 105–19. The alternative of a national construction corporation, government subsidized at first but eventually forced to bid in the open market, is also discussed, as are the various types of contract that may be employed. In UNECAFE, *Multiple-Purpose River Basin Development*, pp. 73–74, India's "crash program" to train engineers, which was spurred by the Planning Commission, is discussed. In contrast, Pakistan has done relatively little to increase the number of qualified engineers trained at home or abroad. When General Itschner left WAPDA in 1964, he devoted part of his "farewell address" to urging that vigorous steps be taken to remedy this situation. For even if the IBP is completed by 1975, the demand for engineers for the off-channel and up-Indus storages, as well as in the groundwater and power programs, is certain to increase.

method of construction is right and India's wrong, or vice versa. India has gained a fund of experience and cadres of trained engineers, technicians, and skilled workmen while saving foreign exchange but "losing" time. Pakistan is spending money (most of it from foreign sources) at an unprecedented rate in the IBP and the groundwater program, but she should have, by 1975 or so, the biggest, best-designed, and best-integrated irrigation system in the world.

But the question of foreign consultants is somewhat different, and here even the Indians seem somewhat disenchanted with their previous methods. For the Beas and Rajasthan projects, they have finally made use of the General Agreement for Technical Cooperation signed with the United States Government in 1950 and the more specific Agreement for Scientific and Technical Engineering Services by the U.S. Bureau of Reclamation to the Central Water and Power Commission, signed in 1951. In 1962 and in early 1963, India obtained two consultants from the Bureau to advise on foundation, materials exploration, design, and alternative layouts for the Pong Dam, and in April 1963 she obtained the aid of an entire Bureau team (see Chapter 7, page 324) to review the overall project, including geological and hydrological data, construction schedule, costs, methods, procedures, and qualifications of the local organization to complete the Pong Dam. At the last minute, as has been indicated, India requested that the team's survey include the Beas-Sutlej Link and Rajasthan Canal components as well as Pong Dam.[30]

It should be pointed out, of course, that a review of the plans for the Pong Dam by a U.S. agency was required for India to obtain the $33-million loan set aside by the Development Loan Fund under the agreement that accompanied the signing of the Indus Waters Treaty, and that a similar review of plans for the Beas-Sutlej Link and the Rajasthan Project will be required if India requests further U.S. assistance for these components of the BBRP. But the Bureau team's report conveys the impression that the Indians desire advice—at the nominal rates charged by the Bureau if they can get it—for at least the Beas components if not for the Rajasthan Canal and drainage system. The Bureau team, of course, countered with recommendations that India hire eminently qualified geologists and tunnel experts for

30. Bureau of Reclamation, United States Department of the Interior, *Beas and Rajasthan Projects*, pp. 1, 9–10.

the Beas-Sutlej Link and drainage experts for Rajasthan. Whether India will do so remains to be seen. But the organizational arrangements for the Beas Project do not indicate any provision for a stricter control over design by a domestic authority completely divorced from that performing the actual work. On the executive levels of the Beas Project Organization, a single general manager (R. S. Gill who served most ably as Director of Inspection and Control of the Bhakra Project) is still responsible for project planning and designs, for administration, and for both Units I and II.[31] And Units I and II (Beas-Sutlej Link and Pong Dam) each include their own directorates of Inspection as well as Plant Design and Construction under *their* respective Chief Engineers. These latter features apparently continue what may have been the principal flaw in the Bhakra organization: lack of an impartial review and inspection of both the project designs and the execution. (For the higher levels of supervision in the Beas organization, see Table 19.)

So the best way to sum up this comparison between the perils of too many consultants in Pakistan and the dangers of no consultants in India might be to suggest that Pakistan lend some of her surplus consultants to India for the future benefit of the entire Indus Basin. Since such an event is unlikely, to say the least, the next best arrangement to be hoped for is that India will indeed take the advice of the Bureau of Reclamation team (she may have to if she is to receive any United States aid for the Beas-Sutlej Link and Rajasthan Project) and hire some foreign consultants for investigation and design of tunnels and drainage systems and hopefully for a continuing review, inspection, and control of her plans, including their economic feasibility. In engineering as in medicine, good consultants are expensive, and one can certainly have too many of them. But in both realms there is also danger in refusing to spend any money for an occasional checkup.

Bringing Development to the Farmers

In this chapter, and indeed throughout most of this study, our attention has been focused on the engineers and administrators who make the broad decisions and designs for supplying water from the

31. The Chief Design Engineer for the entire Beas Project is P. S. Bhatnagar, who served as Director of Bhakra Dams Design.

Table 19. Composition of Supervisory Organizations, Beas Project
(Unit I, Beas-Sutlej Link; and Unit II, Pong Dam)[a]

Beas Control Board	*Both*	*Beas Standing Committee*
Chairman: Governor of the Punjab (in his personal capacity)		
Lieutenant Governor, Himachal Pradesh		
Chief Minister, Punjab		
Chief Minister, Rajasthan		
Minister of Irrigation and Power, Punjab		
Minister of Irrigation and Power, Rajasthan		
		Secretary to Government of India, Ministry of Irrigation and Power (Chairman, Standing Committee)
		Chairman, Central Water and Power Commission
		Joint Secretary, Ministry of Finance, Government of India
		General Manager, Beas Project
		Secretary of Irrigation and Power, Punjab
		Secretary of Irrigation and Power, Rajasthan
		Secretary, Finance Department, Punjab
		Secretary, Finance Department, Rajasthan
		Chief Secretary, Himachal Pradesh

a. Source: Bureau of Reclamation, United States Department of the Interior, *Beas and Rajasthan Projects*, pp. 141–42.

Indus Rivers to the farms of the Basin. We have not said very much about the impact of the irrigation projects upon the rural population as a whole, the farm village or family as a community, or the farmer as an entrepreneur. This seeming neglect is partially justified because the excellent studies mentioned in Chapter 1 cover much of this material, at least for the earlier periods. But the real justification lies in the fact that a detailed analysis of rural population adjustments in response to the situation created by Partition, and especially to the changes in the irrigation system after Partition and under the Indus Waters Treaty, will form a more coherent whole if left to the next study in this series.

Nevertheless, we cannot understand the full significance of the Indus Basin Project and the Bhakra-Beas-Rajasthan Project in bringing more surface water to the fields of the Indus Basin, or proceed to a meaningful analysis of West Pakistan's massive groundwater and reclamation program—which aims at the integration of both surface water and groundwater into a multifactor approach to the problems of agriculture—unless we pause to ask ourselves how successfully the engineers and administrators have bridged the gap between their projects, plans, and procedures and the farmer in the fields. For just as land without water is practically worthless in most of the Indus Basin, so dams and barrages, canals and tubewells, authorities and control boards, five-year plans and development fund agreements, tables of organization and manuals of procedure are of no value without seeds, implements, bullocks, and the labor, skills, and initiative of the farmers who till the plains. Development must embrace all of these factors, and any project, program, or study that neglects them falls short of a realistic appraisal of the situation.

Perhaps the most realistic way to examine the extent to which modern agricultural development based upon irrigation has been and is being brought to the farmers of the Indus Basin is to review the effects which the efforts of some of the agencies just discussed, and of others which supplement them, have had upon the farmers, how well they have fulfilled their assigned roles from his standpoint, and what shortcomings or omissions have been detected by analysts of the agricultural problem. In the old Punjab, as we saw in Chapter 3, the impact of the Irrigation Branch of the Public Works Department was felt by the farmer almost as early, and often more directly, than the impact of the administrative officer. Nor was this impact limited to the areas of the Canal Colonies, for the colonists were largely recruited from the "dry districts" (those served by wells but not canals) at the foot of the Siwaliks with a view both to relieving congestion there and to selecting good farmers who knew each other and who would cooperate in bringing the *bar* or *jangal* lands under cultivation. As Paustian pointed out in his 1930 study, the UBDC and the Sirhind Canals were built through fairly populous lands, and the first real canal colony to include a substantial amount of Crown Waste Land (the Lower Sohag and Para inundation scheme; see page 74) was settled, starting in 1882, from the immediate vicinity.[32]

32. Paustian, *Canal Irrigation in the Punjab*, p. 85.

But after the first group of colonists for the Sidhnai project, who had been drawn from many scattered areas, gave up in face of the arduous conditions, the Government hit upon the scheme of sending out a second group, drawn from the densely settled Amritsar district, which prospered and remained.

The Sidhnai success was duplicated, although not without initial frustrations, in the much larger LCC Colony, almost all of which was located on Crown Waste Land, by settlers drawn mainly from the Sialkot, Amritsar, Jullundur, Gurdaspur, Hoshiarpur, Lahore, Ludhiana, and Gujrat districts. Although Paustian cites the Chunian Colony, developed between 1894 and 1904 at the lower end of the UBDC, as "the first colony to be settled under the policy of lessening population pressure in a specific area" (almost all of the colonists were drawn from the Lahore District), by the turn of the century the twin policies of relieving pressure on the land in the Eastern Punjab and of sending out compact groups of efficient farmers who were accustomed to working with each other was firmly established.[33]

Thus, during most of the period of British administration in the Punjab, the farmer in an irrigated district found himself in direct relations with both the Irrigation Branch and the Civil Administration. Because the district officer combined the functions of revenue collector, police magistrate, and civil judge (see page 58), the farmer dealt ultimately with one and the same man on the administrative side:

> The Deputy Commissioner and his staff in a district are members of the revenue service . . . and occupy a paramount position quite different from that of any other department. They are a part of the concept of an exceptional cadre of men in administrative control of the country and their main business has been the collection of land revenue, maintenance of land records and preservation of law and order. With the power

33. Ibid., pp. 48–58 and 85–89. In an interview with the present author, one distinguished retired member of the I.C.S. who had served as Deputy Commissioner of a dry district in the 1920s recalled the dilemma of whether to send only superior farmers to the T.C.P. and S.V.P. colonies, thereby depriving the home district of some of its more efficient revenue-producers, or to include some of those who were regarded as a burden on the land. Of course, there never was any question of compulsory migration. But after 1900 the success of the Canal Colonies was so generally known, and the terms of the grants considered so generous, that the applicants greatly exceeded the quotas.

associated with taxation, magistracy and police, their prestige has naturally been the highest in the land and they have been expected to operate as the senior service representing the government itself, maintaining contact between government and people, dealing with every emergency, and, in general, supervising anything affecting government in the district.[34]

Although ultimate appeal from decisions of the Deputy Commissioner could be made to the Board of Revenue or to the civil and criminal courts (and although civil litigation has long been one of the most popular forms of entertainment for those who are able to afford it), the peasant of the Indus Basin seldom goes beyond the Deputy Commissioner (universally known as the "D.C.") in matters of revenue, rent, tenure, or inheritance disputes. On the administrative side, then, the D.C., or his assistants, the Sub-Divisional and Circle Officers, represented the provincial government to the farmer of the Indus Basin up to the time of Partition. Nor was there much change after 1947, for the evolution of States in India and the introduction of One Unit rule in West Pakistan left undisturbed the relations between the D.C. and the farmer. After 1959, the establishment of the Basic Democracies system in West Pakistan modified the administrative power structure to a certain extent (see Table 20). But the Basic Democrat, who is elected by about 1,000 adult voters to a Union Council in the rural areas, really provides an additional channel for airing grievances and urging claims rather than replacing the old apparatus. The D.C. remains an ex-officio member and chairman of the District Council, and the *tahsildar*, who has traditionally been the D.C.'s chief assistant for revenue matters at the tahsil level, is ex officio the chairman of the Tahsil Council, intermediate between the District Council and the Union Council. (The *tahsils* are administrative subdivisions of districts, established by the British throughout the portions of the Indus Basin they controlled, for purposes of making the land revenue assessments known as "settlements" and for the collection of the revenue.[35])

Both West Pakistan and India have retained the tahsil unit and

34. Government of Pakistan, Ministry of Food and Agriculture, *Report of the Food and Agriculture Commission* (Karachi, Manager of Publications, November 1960), pp. 192–93. Cited hereafter as *Report of the F.A.C.*

35. Robert D. Campbell, *Pakistan: Emerging Democracy* (Princeton, N.J., D. Van Nostrand Company [Searchlight Books], 1963), pp. 53–55.

Table 20. Parallel Organizations in the Government of West Pakistan[a]

Administrative Divisions	Basic Democracies	Governor, West Pakistan, and Ministers	Main Secretariat / Secretaries / Irrigation	Irrigation staff	Irrigation Divisions
Province	Basic Democracies Advisory Council (Chairman is the Governor, ex. off.)	Board of Revenue (Five Members, each of whom is also a Secretary to Government, West Pakistan: Judicial, Land Reforms, Land Utilization, Colonies (& Transport), Revenue	Main Secretariat (Services and General Administration Department) in charge of Chief Secretary — Other Secretaries — Secretary, Irrigation & Power		Province
				Chief Engineer (CE)	Region or Zone
Division	Basic Democracies Divisional Council (Chairman is the Commissioner, ex. off.)	Commissioner		Superintending Engineer (SE)	Circle
District	Basic Democracies District Council (Chairman is the Deputy Commissioner, ex. off.)	Deputy Commissioner (acts as Revenue Collector, Magistrate, and Civil Judge)		Executive Engineer (XEN) — REVENUE SIDE / SUPPLY SIDE	Division
Tahsil	Basic Democracies Tahsil Council (Chairman is the Tahsildar, ex.off.)	Tahsildar		Deputy Collector = Subdivisional Officer (SDO)	Subdivision
				Zilladar	
Circle	Basic Democracies Union Council	Qanungo		Overseer (one per 20 miles of canal)	
Village	Basic Democrat (one per 1,000 to 1,500 voters)	Civil Patwari (one per 2 to 4 villages)		Canal Patwari (one per 3,000 to 5,000 acres)	
				Gauge Reader	

a. Sources: Robert D. Campbell, *Pakistan: Emerging Democracy* (Princeton, Van Nostrand, 1963), pp. 53–55; *Report of the Food and Agriculture Commission* (Karachi, Manager of Publications, November 1960), pp. 172, 190–93; *Functional and Operational Flow Chart of the Irrigation and Power Department* (Lahore, C. M. Division, n.d.); and *Telephone Directory of the West Pakistan Secretariat*, Lahore, October 1963 (Lahore, Superintendent, Government Printing, West Pakistan, 1963).

introduced it into those former Princely States which did not already have it, in the process of bringing them into the Indian States or into the single province of West Pakistan. For revenue administration purposes, the tahsil is subdivided into circles, each in charge of a *qanungo*, and the circles into groups of two to four villages, each group in charge of a civil *patwari* or accountant who keeps the records and who collects the annual land revenue from the registered owner or, if such is the agreement, from the tenant. It is not necessary to examine the assessment procedures in detail, but it should be noted that by the time the British administration was extended to the Punjab, the rulers had become sufficiently impressed with the defects of Permanent Settlement (introduced by Lord Cornwallis in Bengal in 1793, when it conferred proprietary rights upon the revenue collectors or "tax farmers" making them *zamindars* or, to all intents and purposes, owners of the land) that they substituted the Temporary Settlement under which the assessments are revised every thirty or forty years.

In Sind, under the Bombay Government, the *ryotwari* system common to south and west India was introduced. Here the *ryot* is regarded as the tenant of the Government, but he is secure in his tenure and in the right to transfer it or pass it to his heirs as long as the land revenue or "rent" is paid. Since the *ryot* of Sind is generally a large landowner rather than a peasant, however, for all practical purposes the *zamindari* system under Temporary Settlement and the *ryotwari* system as practiced in Sind are practically identical.[36] In India, since Independence, tenurial matters have been the responsibility of the States, and the *ryotwari* system has virtually displaced the *zamindari* system. The Indian Punjab, P.E.P.S.U., and Rajasthan undertook revised settlements in 1955–56. But few tahsils in the Pakistani portion of the Indus Basin have had a revised settlement since Partition, with most of those in the area of the West Punjab still operating under a pre-Partition assessment. It

36. S. M. Akhtar, *Economics of Pakistan* (Lahore, Publishers United Ltd., 1963), pp. 148–52. Prof. Akhtar's is one of the fullest and clearest accounts of the extremely complicated subjects of land tenure and land reform in West Pakistan. Heavy reliance is placed upon it later in this section. But see also the earlier treatment in J. Russell Andrus and Azizali F. Mohammed, *The Economy of Pakistan* (Stanford, Calif., Stanford University Press, 1958).

should also be noted that the land revenue is not technically considered to be a tax but rather the State's share in the rent, profit, or produce of an estate or holding, and that proprietorship of land is not technically considered "ownership" in fee simple as it would be in the U.K. or the U.S.A., but rather a recognition by the State of a "permanent right to occupy and till it [the land] or arrange for its tillage [i.e. by rental or sharecropping]" so long as the revenue is paid.[37]

As far as irrigated land is concerned, the land revenue is but one of three rates the owner must pay to the Government. A water rate, most significantly assessed in relation to the *area and type* of the *matured* crop, must be paid to the Irrigation Department, which maintains its own *separate* revenue staff (*patwaris, zilladars* and subdivisional officers or deputy collectors, reporting to the executive engineers) for this purpose. In addition, what was originally called a "water advantage rate" and what is now known as the "portion of land revenue due to irrigation" is levied by the *civil patwari* and paid to the Revenue Department along with the regular land revenue. As Paustian remarked:

> It is difficult to discover the basis for this third rate, since it would appear to fall naturally under one of the other two assessments against the land, namely the water rate proper or the land revenue. Nor is it easy to discover the mode of assessing this additional rate on land. Since the revenue assessments are paid to the Government regardless of the name applied to the particular assessment it would seem as though the British have in this case merely added to their bookkeeping task an additional item. It could be quite logically included in the water rate since it applies only to lands irrigated by canals. It might equally well be added to the land revenue proper, although in that case the flat-rate policy would apparently need to be discarded. In any case, this item, "water advantage revenue" or "advantage due to irrigation" adds to the Government's income from irrigation projects in operation."[38]

37. Douie, *Punjab Settlement Manual*, p. 1.
38. Paustian, pp. 126–27. The authority of the canal *zilladar* to recommend a reduction in the water rate in the event of crop failure may account for the separate existence of the water advantage rate, which was remitted only if canal supplies had to be curtailed.

What Paustian wrote in 1930 is still true today in the irrigated areas of both West Pakistan and northern India. On the other hand, the relative significance of the rates has changed greatly. When Paustian did his research in the undivided Punjab of the 1920s, the water rate per acre of matured crop amounted to about 5.25 rupees for wheat, 12 rupees for sugarcane, and from 5.5 to 7.5 rupees for cotton (there was considerable variation among canal commands for cotton, but far less for wheat or sugarcane) as compared with a land revenue rate of only 1.5 rupees per acre and a "water advantage rate" of only .7 rupees per acre. Paustian felt that the cost of irrigation was somewhat excessive with respect to the return realized from the crops, but not if one took into consideration the capital investment made by the Government in new irrigation facilities, buildings, roads, research, and other agricultural, industrial, and social improvements.[39]

Land and water rates in what is now West Pakistan remained substantially what they were from the time Paustian wrote up to the inception of the Second Five Year Plan of 1960–65. During the period of enthusiasm, reforms, and Martial Law government which followed the "Revolution" of October 1958, the Ayub administration not only promulgated the West Pakistan Land Reforms Regulation (Martial Law Regulation No. 64 of February 7, 1959), of which more will be said shortly, but drastically altered the allocation of revenues between the Central Government and the provinces in favor of the latter, and saw to it that the provinces revised the antiquated rate structure on land and water. The following quotations from the text of the Second Five Year Plan indicate both the necessity and the direction of these reforms:

> Gross land revenue collections (including water rates) in both East and West Pakistan are estimated at about Rs 300 million at present [1959–60]. This is more than twice as much as was being collected in 1949–50. The increase has been made possible, however, by the collection of accumulated arrears [one of the major early achievements of the "Revolution"] and by the acquisition of rental interests in East Pakistan [where the old Permanent Settlement and the subfeudatories were eliminated]. . . . Actually, land revenue rates have not changed much. Land

39. Ibid., pp. 150–60.

revenue still constitutes only 2 per cent of the total agricultural income in the country, and contributes a mere 16 per cent of the total tax revenues of the Government although agricultural incomes are about 55 per cent of the total national income.

The low yield from land revenue in West Pakistan is explained mainly by two factors: (i) a long period of settlement [i.e. no change in assessments] in most cases, varying between 30 to 40 years, and (ii) maximum ceiling of 25 per cent on the enhancement of land revenue at the time of settlement. The Taxation Enquiry Committee has suggested the reduction of the period of settlement to 15 years, and the abolition of the legal bar on the enhancement of land revenue. As an interim measure, a 25 per cent flat increase was proposed. . . .

Water rates have remained fixed in most cases for the last 30 years. In West Pakistan, the Irrigation Department has been running a substantial deficit which is made up by indirect credits from the Land Revenue Department. *A large subsidy has been implicit in the provision of water.* There may be some justification for a subsidy for specific purposes and for a specific period of time, but the continuation of such a large concealed subsidy is not justified. In general, water rates need to be raised sufficiently to cover the full cost of providing water. The price of water will still be much less than the improved agricultural productivity made possible by its provision. The West Pakistan Government has already revised water rates so as to make up a part of the deficit incurred by the Irrigation Department. The rates should be increased sufficiently to run the department as nearly on commercial lines as possible. Additional revenue from agriculture can also be raised through betterment levies and the extension of estate duty to agricultural property. The First Plan recommended that a betterment tax should be levied on lands which have received improved irrigation as a result of the construction of new barrages, but very little to this effect has been done.[40]

As a result of the increase of water rates, the share of irrigation dues in the total revenue of West Pakistan increased from 8.6 per

40. Government of Pakistan, Planning Commission, *The Second Five Year Plan (1960–65)*, pp. 53–54. Italics added.

cent in 1959–60 to about 20 per cent in both 1960–61 and 1961–62. But in 1961 the land revenue assessments were actually reduced by 25 per cent in Sind (i.e. the Hyderabad and Khairpur divisions), with the result that the contribution from this source *fell* from 20 per cent in 1959–60 to 7 per cent in the two ensuing fiscal years. Thus, the share of the West Pakistan provincial revenues contributed by the Irrigation Department in recent years has been even higher in proportion to that from land revenues than it was in Paustian's day (30 per cent from irrigation rates and 18 per cent from land revenues in 1928–29) [41] despite the vast new areas brought under cultivation in the Sukkur, Thal, and Ghulam Mohammad commands and despite the considerable inflation of agricultural prices and land values that has occurred since around 1939.

But whatever the discrepancy between the land revenue and water rates, it cannot be said that the latter now serve as any constraint to the use of water. On the contrary, it has often been suggested that still higher rates, and especially a shift to a volumetric basis for charging, rather than by the area of the matured crop (as calculated by the *zilladar*, who may recommend a remission if the yield appears to be more than 25 per cent below the norm for the area), would force farmers to economize in the use of irrigation water and at the same time encourage them to adopt higher-yielding crops. [42] The problems in the way of volumetric assessment, however, would lie in the design, installation, maintenance, and reading of thousands, perhaps millions, of small gauges. The simplest gauge now available is the concrete module installed at a determined height where the watercourse feeds a given field. Knowing the height and cross section of the module, and assuming that the watercourse has been full throughout the period during which the module has been left open, the volume of water passed can be calculated. But farmers have been known to move or bypass the modules, and to bribe the *patwaris* and *zilladars* (who can determine the turns, known as *warabandi*, of the water users, or levy special charges for unauthorized irrigation).

Nor will the situation be eased by the advent of Government-owned tubewells in the groundwater schemes, since these discharge into the

41. Economic Adviser to the Government of Pakistan, Ministry of Finance, *Economic Survey of Pakistan, 1961–62*, Rawalpindi, 1962, Table No. 76, pp. 138–39.

42. *Report of the F.A.C.*, p. 174.

watercourses rather than into the individual fields. However, the fact that the chairman of the new Land and Water Management Board of West Pakistan, which is taking over operation of the groundwater project areas upon completion by WAPDA, is the Member for Land Reforms of the Board of Revenue (a highly significant arrangement which will be commented upon further in Chapter 9) is an indication that the seriousness of the whole problem of land and water revenue is well understood in West Pakistan. The Indian States of the Indus Basin have also increased both land and water rates, but the matured-crop-area and *patwari* system have been preserved and there is neither a basinwide policy for India nor, in the absence of a real groundwater program in the East Punjab and Rajasthan, a Land and Water Management Board that might produce one.

Administrative policy in the Indus Basin has also had an enormous, although intermittent, influence upon the size and quality of the holding at the disposal of the farmer. Since 1850, almost 50 million acres of cultivable lands have been placed under command of canals fed by the Indus Rivers, and over 40 million acres are now provided with complete distribution systems (i.e. can receive surface or ground water). But even in the perennial commands, the same acre does not generally support two crops per year. As we saw in Chapters 3 and 4, the aim of the Canal Colony schemes in the Punjab, and of the Sukkur scheme in Sind, was to increase the total area of land under cultivation and particularly the amount sown to winter or rabi crops. Because land has always been more abundant than water, because cotton, sugarcane, and rice have long growing periods, and because, in the absence of natural and artificial fertilizers, fallowing was and still is necessary to allow the soil to recoup some of its nitrates, perennial irrigation did not, in most areas, mean that the same field was sown twice in any one agricultural year. What it did mean was that the farmer could sow about 25 per cent of his land to a kharif crop (usually a cash crop such as cotton or sugarcane but in recent decades with increasing need for food and on lands which were becoming waterlogged, more often rice), about 50 per cent of his land to a rabi crop (usually wheat, which would provide food for the summer and, in earlier decades, a surplus for export to other regions), and leave the remaining 25 per cent fallow. Most nonperennial canals were designed to permit a 70 per cent cropping intensity in kharif, but none in rabi, unless of course the farmer could supplement canal supplies from wells. Canal capacities were designed to provide only these intensities and, in the Canal Colonies, the standard holdings (usually 12.5 acres in the Punjab but larger if the farmer performed certain services such as horse or mule breeding, and larger in Sind) were designed to support the farm family and to produce a moderate income from the cash crops.[43]

But even though the original grant may have been adequate, the rapid rise in population in the Canal Colonies (induced in large measure by the improved sanitary and dietary conditions to be found there) combined with alienation of land for debt (somewhat restricted after 1901 by the Punjab Land Alienation Act), and especially with the division of land among heirs, quickly conspired to reduce the size of the holdings. By 1927–28, according to Paustian, the average size of a holding in the Canal Colonies had shrunk to 9.8 acres, high in comparison with the average of 6.7 acres for the entire Punjab, but well below the size of the original allotments.[44] By 1959, the average agricultural holding (irrigated and nonirrigated) in the twenty-two districts comprising the Pakistani Punjab (which, as we have seen, included all of the major Canal Colonies of the old Punjab) had shrunk to 3 acres. It ranged from a low of .97 acres in the Rawalpindi District, a "dry district" where canal irrigation accounted for only half of 1 per cent of the cultivated land, to 8.7 acres in the Multan District where canal irrigation accounted for 93 per cent of the cultivated land.[45] In the Lyallpur District, also typical of the older Canal Colonies, with over 93 per cent of the land canal-irrigated, the average holding was 8.5 acres, and in the Sukkur District, typical of the newer projects with almost 89 per cent of the cultivated land canal-irrigated, the average holding was 8.2 acres. For all of West Pakistan, the average canal-irrigated holding was just under 7 acres in size.[46]

Thus, although the introduction of modern irrigation did serve to

43. Ibid., pp. 40, 43–44.
44. Paustian, p. 102.
45. *Report of the F.A.C.*, p. 87.
46. Government of Pakistan, Ministry of Agriculture and Works, Agricultural Census Organization, *1960 Pakistan Census of Agriculture*, Karachi, October 1963, 2, *West Pakistan, Report 2*, Table 17, p. 152.

increase greatly the total amount of land under cultivation in the Indus Plains, the increases in the size of the irrigated holding that followed introduction of new schemes have been quickly offset by subdivision and by the increase of population. Dealing with the undivided Punjab, Paustian reported that the amount of agricultural land had increased from 20.2 million acres in 1868 to 30 million acres in 1921 while the amount of cultivated land per capita increased from 1.25 to 1.41 acres over this period.[47] The 1921 Census, of course, predated both the S.V.P. and the Sukkur Project in Sind. By the 1961 censuses, there had been added to the Indus Rivers the Bhakra Project in India and the Thal, Taunsa, and Ghulam Mohammad projects in West Pakistan (though colonization of new lands in Thal and Ghulam Mohammad was still far from complete and had not begun in Gudu). Yet these huge projects were insufficient to offset the growth of population and the net effects of the migrations following Partition. By 1961, when the canal irrigated area in the Indian Punjab had reached 6.6 million acres, the amount of cultivated area per capita was slightly less than one acre.[48] For all of West Pakistan, where 21.7 million acres were canal-irrigated by 1961, the total cultivated acreage (37.25 million acres, including 14 per cent current fallow) represented .9 acre per capital. In the nine districts of the former Pakistani Punjab which included all of the old and new (Thal, Taunsa) Canal Colonies, the average gross sown area (including both fallow and double cropping) over the period 1949–50 to 1958–59 was 12.84 million acres. But the population of these districts increased from 12.7 million to 15.9 million over this period, or 2.51 per cent (compounded) per year, while the average yearly increase in gross sown area was only 1.64 per cent per year. For Sind, where the Sukkur Project was still being colonized and where the Ghulam Mohammad Project was inaugurated in 1955, the average yearly increase over the period was only .84 per cent in gross sown area, while the population rose from 5.0 million to 6.4 million or 2.5 per cent (compounded) per year.[49] Thus, what Paustian foresaw forty years ago has come to

47. Paustian, pp. 80–81.
48. Government of India, Ministry of Information and Broadcasting, Publications Division, New Delhi, *India, A Reference Annual*, 1963, p. 247.
49. White House–Department of Interior Panel on Waterlogging and Salinity

pass: "the development of irrigation schemes making possible the cultivation of otherwise arid waste lands is not a permanent solution of the problem of population pressure on the means of subsistence."[50]

As far as the individual farmer is concerned, however, the efforts of the engineer in providing more land under canal command, and, by means of surface water storage and tubewell programs, more water to apply, may be less significant than the efforts of the administrator to confer and preserve an economic holding. Just as the farmer's propagative instinct and desire for what may be termed the social security of sons have nullified the overall increases in irrigated acreages, so do his traditional inheritance laws and need or propensity to go into debt nullify the efforts to maintain the size of the holdings. Paustian, Darling, and Calvert have all emphasized "the point that the Punjab peasant made the interesting discovery that land which he owned provided a basis for credit and that with the increasing utilization of land as security for loans, the peasant naturally fell into the clutches of the money lender."[51] Calvert really got to the heart of the matter when he wrote:

> The assumption, frequently made, that debt is due to poverty, cannot be entertained. Debt is due to credit and credit depends upon prosperity and not poverty. Without someone to lend there can be no borrowers and without the wherewithal to lend there can be no borrowing. There must be men with money to lend before a peasantry can become involved in debt. If it be said that the agriculturists are thriftless and improvident, it may be urged in reply that thriftlessness may be encouraged by excessive facilities for borrowing and that improvident borrowing is only another aspect of improvident lending.

in West Pakistan, *Report on Land and Water Development in the Indus Plain* (Washington, D.C., The White House, January 1964), Tables 1.4 and 1.13, pp. 71, 84. As this report pointed out, although an increase of 500,000 acres of gross sown area occurred in the Mianwali and Muzaffargarh Districts of the old Punjab as a result of the introduction of the Thal and Taunsa commands, almost all of the rest was the result of spreading a given amount of irrigation water even further than was customary in the past. (Ibid., p. 45.)

50. Paustian, p. 102.

51. Ibid., pp. 103–04, referring to Darling, *The Punjab Peasant in Prosperity and Debt;* see also Hubert Calvert, I.C.S., *The Wealth and Welfare of the Punjab* (Lahore, Civil and Military Gazette Press, 1922), pp. 132–34.

The indebtedness of the Punjab peasantry may thus be ascribed (1) to the sudden enhancement of credit due to new conditions introduced by the British Government, (2) to the abuse of this credit by clever usurers who encouraged borrowing in order to secure control of the produce, (3) to the famines . . . and heavy mortality amongst cattle which drove the cultivators to borrow and so involved them in the moneylenders clutches, (4) to the rigidity of land-revenue collection accentuated by the tactics of the usurer who seized the whole produce and so compelled the cultivator to borrow afresh for the State demand and (5) to a system of civil law which was unsuitable inasmuch as it favoured the clever money-lender against the ignorant peasant.[52]

Not only does prosperity breed debt, but it attracts a host of parasites:

The Punjab is dominated by the money-lender to an extent unknown in any other province. In the whole of India, excluding this province, the proportion of money-lenders to total population is 1:367; here it is 1:100. Although the population of the Punjab is only one-eleventh of the whole, one-fourth of all money-lenders found in British India reside and work here.[53]

On the basis of loans made by the Punjab Co-operative Societies, Calvert estimated that, in the first two decades of this century, the major causes of borrowing were to pay the land revenues and to purchase (or replace) cattle. But Darling, who was skeptical that the reported object of debt was the true object, found that the purpose of the largest category of new loans was simply to repay old ones, and estimated that around 1930, when the land revenue charges in the Punjab averaged only Rs 2 per cultivated acre, the average debt per cultivated acre was Rs 46. Darling thus suggested that the major causes of agricultural debt were the fantastic interest charges of the moneylenders and the propensity or social need to provide elaborate weddings and funerals—all factors that are common to most of Asia.[54] Inasmuch as, for the reasons given above, land

52. Calvert, p. 132.
53. Ibid., p. 130; the data apparently refer to the Census of 1911.
54. Darling, p. 20 and n. 1.

revenues in the Punjab have not been enhanced by much more than
25 per cent since 1920 or 1930 (the maximum increase permitted in
a new settlement), while agricultural prices have more than doubled
since 1939, the main causes of borrowing today would appear to be
to repay old debts, to buy or replace cattle, or to pay the rent to
the *zamindars* (who frequently are the moneylenders as well). Although the collateral offered for a debt may have little or no relation
to the object for which the debt is incurred, it is interesting to note
that the 1960 Census of Agriculture for West Pakistan reported that
only 16 per cent of the nonofficial loans were raised through mort-
gage of land (63 per cent of which, however, were debts of Rs 500
or more) and only 2 per cent of such loans represented crop mortgages (but 93 per cent of these loans were of Rs 100 or more).[55]
Thus, the inference is that most collateral for debt today is in the
form of cattle or movable chattels.

Undoubtedly, one reason why relatively little land is mortgaged
is the old restriction placed upon the alienation of land to non-
agriculturalists in satisfaction of debt. The Punjab Land Alienation
Act of 1901 forbade the sale of agricultural land in execution of a
decree and made illegal all existing and future conditional sale
clauses in mortgages. It also required special governmental sanction
for sales of land by a member of an agricultural tribe to one who
was not a member, and to prevent evasion forbade leases for a period
of over five years.[56] But because so many moneylenders were themselves agriculturalists, the 1901 Act, designed primarily to prevent
reductions in the size of holdings in the Canal Colonies, fell far
short of preventing sales to or foreclosures by lenders who were also
farmers. And, of course, it did nothing to prevent fragmentation by
inheritance, even in the Canal Colonies.

Further acts in the Punjab and Bombay Province (i.e. Sind)

55. *1960 Pakistan Census of Agriculture, A Summary of West Pakistan Data,*
Karachi, October 1963, p. 35. The Census also indicated that only 29 per cent
of the farms in West Pakistan reported debt (undoubtedly low, due to reluctance to report debt or failure to report debt to relatives and friends) but that
96 per cent of those reporting debt said that the loans came from unofficial
sources whereas only 14 per cent reported loans from official sources (where
interest rates are controlled). Of these farms, 10 per cent reported unofficial
debt as well.
56. Calvert, p. 136.

required moneylenders to be registered and licensed and in the Punjab to keep accounts and inform the debtors periodically of their position. Some attempts at fixing maximum rates of interest were also made, as were moratoria, liquidations, and compulsory scalings down of debt during the Depression years. But none of these measures produced as much of an impact as did the rise of prices due to the Second World War or the "cancellations" of debt that resulted from the exodus of Hindu and Sikh moneylenders from Pakistan after Partition. Professor Akhtar of the University of the Panjab, Lahore, reports that although no comprehensive study of rural debt has been made since Partition, relatives and friends, landlords and cooperatives, have largely replaced the professional moneylender (who, in any case, operates at somewhat of a disadvantage in an Islamic society) in West Pakistan, although he maintains his preeminent position in India where he supplies about 70 per cent of all credit.[57]

Data collated by Professor Akhtar indicate that, at the most, cooperatives supply only 14 per cent of the rural credit in West Pakistan. This is somewhat surprising in view of the long history of the cooperative credit movement in the subcontinent. The establishment of private credit societies in British India was encouraged by the Co-operative Credit Societies Act of 1904 and expanded by the Co-operative Societies Act of 1912. Under the Government of India Act of 1919, cooperation became a provincial subject and the Punjab and Bombay (including Sind) set up Co-operative Departments. But the Depression dealt the societies a severe blow, especially as virtually all of the rural credit societies were of unlimited liability, and the Second World War, by inflating agricultural prices, reduced the need for credit. By 1945–46, the 172,000 societies in all of British India had only 9.16 million primary members. Bombay led the provinces in terms of membership and capital resources, with the Punjab second in the former and Sind second (Punjab third) in the latter respect.[58] In 1947–48, there were some 9,071 agricultural credit cooperatives in West Pakistan, with a membership of 246,000. Ten years later, the number of societies had increased to 11,244 and the membership to 375,000. Although later figures

57. Akhtar, pp. 230–36.
58. Ibid., pp. 262–66.

400

were not available, Professor Akhtar, writing in 1963, termed the progress "very moderate" and indicated that the unlimited liability type of society (and over 99 per cent were of this type) was in a "stagnant condition."[59] The Pakistan Food and Agriculture Commission in its 1960 report said of the cooperative movement:

> It owes its origin rather to the individual enthusiasm of certain government officers in former days [among them Hubert Calvert, who served as Registrar of Co-operative Societies, Punjab, when he wrote his classic *Wealth and Welfare*] who wished to encourage people in rural areas to emancipate themselves from middlemen and moneylenders. From this beginning it has grown into a combination of a movement with a vertical structure (ranging from primary societies in the villages to Central Co-operative Banks, representing a union of such societies, and to an Apex Bank at the provincial level) and a department headed by a Registrar and staff supervising the movement. . . . Its main concern has been access to cheap credit so that small men by combining together could help themselves to improve their incomes and establish a better bargaining position. Unfortunately, this extremely important objective has so far had only a modicum of success in West Pakistan and none at all in East Pakistan.
>
> There are a variety of reasons, historical and otherwise, for this comparative failure. In early days one of the strong tenets of the cooperative movement was the principle of unlimited liability. When prices were depressed, those with assets found that they had to pay the debts of other members who had none and the movement lost favour. After Independence, when the banking system hitherto managed by Hindus collapsed, the cooperatives were called in to help fill the gap. They performed a good service for the country in that respect but, in the process, the Cooperative Central Banks who financed the primary so-

59. Ibid., pp. 273–75. In 1958–59, the Indian Punjab had 17,107 agricultural credit societies (excluding grain banks) with a membership of 1,126,000; Rajasthan had 9,281 societies with 513,000 members. (Government of India, Central Statistical Organisation, Department of Statistics, *Statistical Abstract, India, 1961* [New Series, No. 10] [Delhi, The Manager of Publications, 1961], Table 80, p. 209.)

cieties switched their interest to commercial loans to individuals.
. . . the effect has been to turn the upper tier of the cooperative
movement into ordinary banking, financing the very merchants
against whom it was designed to protect the small man and
neglecting the primary societies. . . .

In these circumstances it is not surprising that, with the
exception of parts of the Punjab, in our tours of the country
we found the state of the co-operative movement generally
moribund.[60]

Direct governmental credit assistance to farmers in West Pakistan
includes the time-honored but relatively insignificant *taccavi* loans
made by the Revenue Department (under the Land Improvement
Loans Act of 1883 and the Agriculturists' Loan Act of 1884 superseded by the West Pakistan Agriculturists' Loan Act of 1958) for
minor irrigation, drainage, or reclamation improvements, for emergency relief, or for purchase of seed, cattle, or implements. The
loans must be secured by land or chattels, but the interest rate of 5.5
per cent is relatively low. However, the total amounts available have
been small and the procedure arduous. The Pakistan Agricultural
Development Bank, established in 1961, represented a merger of the
Agricultural Development Finance Corporation of 1952 and the Agricultural Bank of Pakistan of 1956. So widely scattered are its
offices and so ponderous its procedures (mortgages are made only
on sound business terms, must be based on *patwaris'* certificates
of title and registered with *tahsildars,* witnesses procured, etc.) that
the Bank's clientele is almost entirely restricted to large landowners.[61]

Despite these efforts of the Government to improve the credit situation in West Pakistan, the fact that only 9 per cent of the rural debt
recorded in the 1960 Census of Agriculture is from official sources
(and one suspects that the unofficial debt is much higher than reported) would seem to be an indication that the farmer has merely
exchanged the old Hindu or Sikh *bania* (moneylender) for one of
his own faith, or has gone into debt to a relative or friend, or,
most likely, to the middleman who buys his crops and who extends
credit on the understanding (glossing over the traditional Muslim

60. *Report of the F.A.C.,* pp. 178–79.
61. Akhtar, pp. 237–39; *Report of the F.A.C.,* p. 183.

prohibition on usury) that he will pay less than the going market rate for the harvest.

Hand in hand with the debt problem is that of sharecropping, which is after all only a different form of debt. According to the 1960 Census, only 41 per cent of West Pakistan's farms, comprising 51 per cent of the farm area (48.9 million acres of which 37 million are cultivated) are owner-operated; 42 per cent of the farms (comprising 39 per cent of the farm area) are tenant-operated, and 17 per cent (with 23 per cent of the area) are operated by farmers who own some of the land and rent the rest.[62] Although the Punjab Tenancy (Amendment) Act of 1952 limits the landlord's share of the produce to 40 per cent, and the Sind Tenancy Act of 1950 to 50 per cent (33 or 40 per cent where the tenant provides and maintains the implements), evasion of these limits is common especially where the landlord is also the moneylender, the purchaser of the crop, or both.[63]

Because of the virtual impossibility of closing all the loopholes to exploitation of the small farmer by his landlord, his creditor, and the middleman who buys his crop, much of the recent effort to improve the lot of the peasant in the Indus Basin has taken the form of efforts both to increase the total size of the holding and to reverse the process, known as fragmentation, in which alienation for debt and inheritance have combined to destroy the unity of that holding. Our discussion thus far has dealt only with changes in the aggregate size of the average individual holding: increases as large new tracts are brought under canal command and cultivation; decreases as popu-

---

62. *1960 Pakistan Census of Agriculture, A Summary of West Pakistan Data*, pp. 13, 22. The propensity of the Punjab farmer to rent some of his land is due both to the inconvenience of tilling the many scattered plots that make up the "average" holding (which leads farmers to lease distant fields and to rent nearby fields from other owners) and to the prestige of being a landlord, however small. Calvert had this to say: "the Punjab is not singular in the small size of its holdings. Where it seems to be peculiar is that the owners prefer to cultivate smaller parcels of land than they need. It is probably correct to say that every owner of more than 25 acres lets part of it to a tenant. There is no effort to achieve large scale farming, even by those who can do it on their own land. Similarly tenants seldom attempt to cultivate more than 25 acres, although more may be available. If anyone obtains a lease for a greater area he sublets a portion." (Calvert, p. 75.)

63. Akhtar, pp. 170, 173.

lation growth and inheritance produce subdivision of the original holding. Now we must take into account the effects of fragmentation as well. Although in theory sale for debt could result in the aggregation and consolidation of larger and larger holdings in the hands of fewer and fewer owners, it would seem that population growth and inheritance have more than offset any such tendencies, i.e. that the middle-sized holding has lost out both to the very large and the very small, and that both large and small holdings tend to be in several scattered parcels (see Table 21). A basic reason for this development was neatly expressed by Calvert forty-five years ago:

> Progressive sub-division of holdings, consequent on the custom of inheritance whereby each son has a right to succeed to a share, has led to the land being cut up into small parcels that, in the vast majority of cases, are less than the owner could cultivate with his existing resources. These holdings can only be increased by snapping up any plots that happen to be for sale. So that the majority of owners are prospective purchasers of any field that may be offered. The small holdings, and the fact that each is scattered over the village area in ten or a dozen places, facilitates sale. . . . Here, the small fields, and the fact that already fields cultivated by the same person are not contiguous, render sale easy. The average area sold in one transaction is very small, and accordingly the price is not beyond the means or the credit of many in the village, nearly all of whom, as has been remarked, are anxious to add to their own possessions. . . . Thus the plots are not only small, but are steadily becoming smaller.[64]

To which Paustian had this to add:

> Mention has been made of the limited size of the average holding in the Punjab. The average size of the cultivated holding has been given as 6.7 acres for the whole province. This however does not mean that the tenant is able to cultivate a plot as large as 6.7 acres. Because most of these holdings are fragmented in successive generations in accordance with the operation of the Hindu law of inheritance, these holdings are greatly reduced in

64. Calvert, p. 109.

404

Table 21. Size Distribution and Fragmentation of Farms in West Pakistan According to the 1960 Census of Agriculture[a]

Total Number of Farms	4,859,983
Total Number of Farms Not Fragmented	1,915,160 (39 per cent)
Total Farm Area (acres)	48,929,583
Total Number of Fragmented Farms	2,944,823 (61 per cent)

Degree of Fragmentation of the 2,944,823 Farms

In 2 or 3 parcels	54 per cent
In 4 or 5 parcels	20 per cent
In 6 to 9 parcels	15 per cent
In 10 or more parcels	11 per cent

Size Distribution of Farms as a Per Cent

	of the Total No. of Farms	of the Total Farm Area
under 1.0 acre	15	1
" 2.5 acres	33	3
" 5.0 "	49	9
" 7.5 "	61	17
" 12.5 "	77	32
" 25.0 "	92	57
" 50.0 "	98	77
" 150.0 "	100	90
over 150.0 "	100	100

a. Source: 1960 Pakistan Census of Agriculture, A Summary of West Pakistan Data, pp. 12, 19.

size. Even though the total holdings cultivated by tenant or
owner may be equal to 6.7 acres on the average, many of the
plots cultivated are less than 1/20 of an acre in size. In addition to this hindrance due to size, the fragments lie within the
village plot of land and many small fragments and individual
plots are not enclosed. Hence, the total village land area must
be cultivated according to custom and not in accordance with
the abilities and desires of the individual owners. It is still necessary in the Punjab village to consider the inconvenience of
crossing the many fields of one's neighbors in order to gain
access to the particular small plot to be worked upon on a given
day. But, while the plots are not enclosed they are carefully
marked by boundary limits in the form of stakes or blocks of
stone. Thus, while the plots are necessarily cultivated according
to the custom of the village peasants, the village land is not
worked as a unit. Each individual peasant tends his own plots.
He necessarily wastes much time and energy going from one of
his scattered plots to another. The obvious solution to the problem of excessive fragmentation is consolidation of holdings.
But in the successful carrying to fruition of a plan to consolidate
holdings among these Indian peasants the would-be-reformer
meets with all the inertia founded on long traditional practice.
Land ownership as such, regardless of its profitable or uneconomic nature, is a matter of social prestige in the Punjab. The
desire on the part of the people to own land whether in economic units or not has been one of the strongest factors in
forcing the price of land higher in each successive decade. Consolidation of holdings is one of the important goals of the cooperative movement among the peasants of the Punjab sponsored
and supported by the British Government.[65]

But the cooperative consolidation societies were no more successful than the cooperative credit societies. That matters had not
changed for the better in thirty years was shown by the Food and
Agriculture Commission of Pakistan in 1960:

We have also made it clear that, whether large or small, one
of the fatal characteristics of the present holdings is the high

65. Paustian, pp. 106–07.

degree of subdivision and fragmentation to which they are sub-jected. . . . There is a number of causes for this state of affairs and they are extremely difficult to rectify. It is partly the result of the Muslim laws of inheritance, partly of the exercise of an unrestricted right of partition and alienation and partly of the varying productivity and physical situation of land in relation to flooding, homesteads, water points and roads. Sentimental attachment and the lack of alternative occupations and emigra-tion possibilities have further accentuated fragmentation and all of these causes have made it extremely difficult to halt the process.

The small size of the holdings and all these complicating fac-tors sometimes make it seem questionable as to whether it is worthwhile going to all the trouble of consolidation. It must, therefore, be emphatically stated that to let the present process continue is to condemn the country to a future of increasingly insufficient subsistence holdings, increasingly unmanageable for purposes of production and, therefore, liable to decreasing yields. In the present urgent need for production, consolidation and the prohibition of any subsequent uneconomic fragmentation is a change which simply must be faced however great the difficul-ties involved. . . .

An additional virtue of consolidation arises from the sub-sidiary effect it has upon the difficult problem of land tenure. Extensive fragmentation often increases the amount of land which becomes involved in the share cropping system. Owing to the difficulty of managing widely scattered fragments, small holders find it more convenient to rent parcels of land near to their homestead and to lease out parcels which are distant from it so that quite a large number are owners in one place and tenants in another. Although this may even cut some of the burden of inequitable land tenure conditions, it means that larger areas than necessary fall under the system of share crop-ping, with its great disincentive to productive investment. By contrast, consolidation encourages ownership and direct culti-vation by the owner, objectives which the land reform legisla-tion is, particularly, designed to attain.[66]

66. *Report of the F.A.C.*, pp. 88–89.

Before proceeding with a brief review of the post-Independence attempts at land reform and at improving the position of the farmer in the Indus Basin, it must be noted that the goal of such actions is difficult if not impossible to design. In theory, but seldom if ever in practice, the government embarking upon a program of agricultural reform should first decide on the type of society and economy which it aims to produce. Is the goal to move workers out of agriculture and to replace them with machines? (If so, considerable investment will be needed not only for the machines but for the industries that presumably will soak up the workers from the agricultural sector.) Or is the goal to keep the existing share of the labor force on the farm but to increase and more evenly distribute the share of national income which it produces? Or does the goal lie somewhere in between, envisaging a gradual transfer of workers from the agricultural to the industrial and tertiary sectors, while improving the lot of those who remain behind? What should be the lot of the farmer in the emerging society? Should he have a subsistence holding merely or one that will enable him to produce a surplus of grain or of a cash crop? How much of a surplus? Should one aim for the efficiency which can be achieved on a large, commercial, specialized farm? If so, should the government allow or even encourage the *kulaks* to absorb the small and inefficient farmer? Or should the state own and operate all the farms, merely hiring labor?

Obviously, such broad questions of social and economic policy can hardly be treated here, but one must recognize that they exist and that most agricultural reform schemes represent compromises among different, and often conflicting goals. In India and West Pakistan, they not only reflect compromises among various schools of social and economic thought but a compelling urgency to do something about the problems of the rural sector and quite possibly a feeling that until a start has been made there is little need to worry about the goals. But certainly one must recognize that the concepts of "subsistence" or "economic" holdings are relative both according to the standard of living which one wishes the farmer to achieve and to the intensity which has been or can be achieved in a given agricultural system, given certain inputs of land, capital or credit, and technology. Indeed, it is strange that such qualifications are so often lost sight of in present-day discussions of land reform, as is the realization that the size of an "economic" or "subsistence" holding varies from one region of the country to another and may even depend on proximity to an urban market, a road, or a railroad. Back in 1922, Calvert criticized G. F. Keatinge's definition of an economic holding as "a holding which allows a man a chance of producing sufficient to support himself and his family in reasonable comfort after paying his necessary expenses" by saying that

> it is of course impossible to fix accurately the size of such a holding for it is impossible to fix accurately what should be regarded as a reasonable standard of comfort. Situation with regard to markets, fertility and the uses to which the cultivator can put it are determining factors. It may be true that a very large number of holdings in the Punjab are uneconomic now when extensively cultivated that would come well within the economic margin, if the system of cultivation were changed, communications with markets improved, and expenses decreased and income increased by means of Co-operation. It is not area but net product that determines what is an economic holding.
>
> A certain area may constitute an economic holding, if situated close to a large market and intensively cultivated with the help of much manure, which would prove well below the economic limit if situated, say, in the Salt Range or in the middle of the Sind Sagar Doab. Proximity to market may be as important as fertility and even more important if facilities for transport are not susceptible of improvement. Fertility is nowadays largely a matter of intelligence, industry and the correct application of capital. Similarly a given area may provide a decent living if irrigated from a well under the cultivator's control, while it might prove inadequate if irrigated from a canal working on a rotation. For it is not only the amount of water available, but also its availability at the time best suited to the requirements of the particular plant, that determines the use to which the land can most profitably be put.[67]

Bearing these important qualifications in mind, let us briefly review the progress that has been made in "land reform" in West Pakistan and India since Independence.

67. Calvert, p. 81.

If we define the term "land reform" in the narrow sense of efforts directed to enlarging and unifying the average holding, it really began in the Indus Basin only after 1950. For while the British efforts to confer and maintain adequate holdings in the Canal Colonies and to consolidate holdings on a voluntary basis through cooperative societies might be considered indirect types of land reform in this restricted sense, the British never achieved even a provincewide redistribution of holdings to bring about enlargement of the small at the expense of the large. This fundamental type of land reform got under way in the Indian Punjab around 1950, but did not begin in West Pakistan until 1959. Thus, Pakistan and India came to grips with land reform well after the Soviet, Mexican, East European, and even Japanese examples could be observed. But the delay cannot be assigned to British policy alone, and especially not in Pakistan where over a decade passed from Independence to the land reforms of the Ayub administration. Rather, much of the delay and most of the half-hearted measures dealing with less fundamental aspects of the tenurial problem must be assigned to a more complex and bewildering array of rights in land and to its produce than any of the above-mentioned nations had to contend with.

Independent India and Pakistan not only had to face the contrasts among the *zamindari* systems, with either Permanent or Temporary Settlements, and the *ryotwari* system (see above, page 389), but an incredibly confused system of subinfeudation in which as many as fifty intermediate interests might exist between the peasant and the landlord.[68] Further complications had been introduced by the granting—under Moguls, Mahrattas, Sikhs, and British—of *jagirs,* or the right to receive part of the land revenue, to persons (*jagirdars*) who had performed some outstanding military or political service for the ruler. Other feudal features included allocations of income or produce from land to religious and charitable institutions (the *auqaf* system of the Muslims, often employed as a subterfuge for a family endowment) and shrines and the persistence, in the face of prohibiting legislation, of taxes in kind and personal services due to the landlords. Thus, if the political map of the subcontinent in 1946 re-

68. Akhtar, pp. 149–50; Carl C. Taylor, Douglas Ensminger, Helen W. Johnson, and Jean Joyce, *India's Roots of Democracy* (Calcutta, Orient Longmans, 1965), pp. 130–31.

sembled that of the Holy Roman Empire in 1800, the feudal pattern of rents, cesses, and services resembled that of France in 1789.

Independence offered an opportunity to sweep clean, but radical changes were slow in coming. In India, the problem became one for each state to solve, and we shall discuss the measures taken in the East Punjab and Rajasthan shortly. As far as Pakistan was concerned, the first major change did not come in the Indus Basin at all but in East Bengal, where the passage of the State Acquisition and Tenancy Act of 1951 allowed the government to acquire, with compensation, all rent-receiving interests between the peasant and the state and which placed a ceiling of 33 acres, or 3.3 acres per family member, whichever was larger, on holdings. The excess land was acquired, with compensation, by the government for distribution among small holders or landless peasants. In effect, the East Bengal Act of 1951 substituted *ryotwari* tenancy for the *zamindari* system instituted by the Permanent Settlement of 1793 (considerably modified by the Tenancy Act of 1885 and the Bengal Acts of 1907 and 1938) but with the difference that the *ryots* of East Pakistan became the direct tenants of the state whereas *ryotwari* under the British usually meant that the *ryots* were large landowners virtually indistinguishable from *zamindars. Ryots* in East Bengal gained permanent, heritable, and transferable rights in the land, rents were fixed for a period of thirty years, and there were some restrictions on subdivision and some provisions for consolidation. But the sharecroppers were not even recognized as tenants, and endless surveys and litigation slowed the acquisition of large estates.[69]

In West Pakistan, up to the introduction of One Unit rule in October 1955, each Province acted separately on land reforms, though both Sind and Punjab abolished personal, but not military service or religious and charitable, *jagirs* in the early 1950s. Due in large measure to the late introduction of barrage-controlled irrigation, Sind had remained a region of large landowners (though they were considered *ryots* or direct tenants of the government rather than *zamindars* or proprietors, see page 389). Spurred by the Sukkur Project, in which the *new* lands brought under canal command were allocated as they were in the Punjab Canal Colonies and by the

69. Akhtar, pp. 161–65.

creation of a separate province in 1937, tenancy law committees were appointed in 1942 and again in 1947 to look into the problem of granting permanent rights to the tenants-at-will. But no action was taken until after Independence.

The Sind Tenancy Act of 1950 abolished free services and feudal cesses and conferred permanent rights on the tenant if he had culti-vated at least 4 acres for the same landlord for at least three con-tinuous years (though not necessarily the same area each year be-cause the need to fallow the land meant that continuous rotation was necessary; see above, page 394). As a result, many landlords in Sind refused to allow tenants to cultivate land for more than two years lest they acquire permanent rights, and harassed those who had until they abandoned the land and lost the rights which the Act conferred upon them. Thus most Sind tenants remained tenants-at-will, and no limits were placed on the size of holdings, nor was any attempt made to further consolidation of the plots.[70]

In the Punjab, with its much larger share of Canal Colonies, no security existed for the tenant-at-will who, under the Punjab Ten-ancy Act of 1887, could become an occupancy tenant only after twenty or thirty years of continuous cultivation, and then only if he met certain conditions would his tenure be protected. In 1950, all personal services and feudal cesses were abolished, and in 1952 the Punjab Tenancy (Amendment) Act made all occupancy tenants own-ers of the land, with a compensation of twenty times the annual rent to the landlord. This Act also made a feeble first attempt to limit the amount of land which a landowner could reserve for personal use to 50 acres of irrigated land or 100 acres of nonirrigated. But the deadline for selecting the reserved area was repeatedly postponed, and there was no attempt to sequester or redistribute the remainder. As we have seen, the 1952 Act set the maximum rental for share croppers at 40 per cent, but it required them to pay 60 per cent of the land rental and water rates, burdens previously assumed by the owners, and thus left them little improvement over their previous economic position.[71]

This, in general, was the unsatisfactory land tenure situation pre-vailing in the Pakistani portions of the Indus Plains when the

70. Ibid., pp. 168–71.
71. Ibid., pp. 171–75.

"Revolution" of October 1958 brought Martial Law government and the first serious attempt to deal with the size and distribution of holdings. With the political power of the landowners (traditionally exercised through the provincial legislatures) temporarily suspended, the Ayub administration appointed a Land Reforms Commission to consider the problems of inequitable ownership and tenancy. Noting that 0.1 per cent of the owners had 15 per cent of the land whereas 65 per cent of the owners had holdings of less than 5 acres apiece, the Commission recommended:

1. Ceiling on individual ownership in order to break concentration of landed wealth and to encourage a more intensive land use and productive investment;
2. acquisition of the land in excess of the ceiling for distribution to landless tenants and holders of uneconomic holdings on payment of a fair price, along with an active programme of resettlement of this class on newly reclaimed Government land with a view to improving their energies for greater production;
3. conversion of occupancy tenancies [which remained only in Sind as far as the Indus Plains were concerned] into full ownership;
4. abolition of jagirs and elimination of other intermediary interests, in order to simplify the tenure system and to relieve the present crowding of interests in land;
5. security of tenure to the tenants, fixation of a fair rent, elimination of illegal exactions, and compensation for improvements;
6. encouragement of the creation of a strong middle class and laying the foundation for owner-operated farms on holdings of economic size through consolidation of existing holdings, prevention of fragmentation by making holdings below a certain size impartible and elimination of small indifferently managed farms;
7. expansion of co-operatives and strengthening of credit and marketing facilities with a view to increasing production, and
8. improvement of the conditions of employment of agricultural labourers.[72]

72. *Pakistan News Digest*, February 15, 1966, p. 6; Akhtar, pp. 179–80.

Thus the Commission not only came to grips directly with the problems of maldistribution, fragmentation, and intermediary interests, but in recommendation 6 made an attempt to set forth a socio-economic policy for the agricultural sector in Pakistan.

The redistribution recommendations of the Land Reforms Commission led to the promulgation in West Pakistan of Martial Law Regulation No. 64 of February 7, 1959. This regulation prohibited the ownership by a single person of more than 500 acres of irrigated land or 1,000 acres of unirrigated land. These rather indiscriminate limitations, however, were modified by the incorporation of an index of comparative productivity—the Produce Index Unit (P.I.U.)— which had been developed over the preceding decade for the purpose of satisfying claims of refugees from India. Based on the annual gross produce value of an acre of land, separately calculated according to the various classes of soil and other conditions,[73] the P.I.U. device was intended to give the refugee a piece of land which would produce the same average income as the one he had lost, though the area and cropping pattern might be different. The P.I.U. device represented the first attempt to take geographical variations into consideration, though not in as comprehensive a form as had been suggested long before by Calvert (see above). If the 500 or 1,000 acres would not yield 36,000 Produce Index Units, the landowner was allowed to retain an area that would. He could also keep an additional 150 acres of orchards as long as they were used for that purpose. And he could alienate by gift up to 24,000 P.I.U.s to his heirs and female dependents. In fact, in many instances, nominal subdivisions within the landowner's family allowed him to evade the reform altogether.[74]

Martial Law Regulation No. 64 also abolished all remaining *jagirs* without compensation, though it did recognize the right of approved charitable and religious institutions to retain larger holdings than the above ceilings allowed (i.e. they could own and manage land but not remain as *jagirdars* or assignees of the land revenue from lands they did not own; the government assumed the cost of replac-

73. Government of Pakistan, Planning Commission, *The Second Five Year Plan*, note 1 to p. 185. One acre of the best irrigated land in Lyallpur District would represent 80 P.I.U.s (Akhtar, pp. 183–84).

74. Akhtar, pp. 181–82.

ing such revenues, for approved institutions, out of its annual budget). And recognized educational and private research institutions, model farms, and livestock breeding farms could retain lands in excess of the ceilings as long as they continued to use them for these purposes. In line with the announced socio-economic policy of the Commission, and to prevent future fragmentation, the Regulation defined both "economic" and "subsistence" holdings and made them impartible except for genuine building purposes (generally around municipalities). In former Khairpur and Sind (Hyderabad and Karachi divisions), a subsistence holding consists of 16 acres and an economic holding of 64 acres, the assumption being that the former would yield an annual income of about Rs 1,200, or enough for a family of four adults, while the latter would further the creation of a class of middle-income farmers able to avail themselves of technological improvements. Elsewhere in West Pakistan, including the former Punjab and Bahawalpur, the subsistence holding was defined as 12.5 acres and the economic holding as 50 acres. As Professor Akhtar points out, these definitions are rather rigid and do not take into consideration whether or not the land is irrigated, the type of soil, the crops to which it is sown, or its location with respect to transportation or markets.[75] Why the P.I.U. device was not applied to these definitions is not clear. Subsistence and economic holdings cannot be alienated by sale or inheritance except in total, and no part of a less-than-subsistence holding can be alienated except to a farmer of the same village.

To implement the redistribution provisions of Regulation No. 64, a West Pakistan Land Commission was constituted and all owners of land in excess of 500 acres were asked to submit declarations to it. About 5,900 declarations were received (which would correspond to 0.1 per cent of the total number of holdings reported in the 1960 Census of Agriculture), of which over 25 per cent came from the Hyderabad Division.[76] The total area declared was 7,750,000 acres, of which 4,803,000 acres were retained by the declarants. Excluding the additional area transferred by gifts, only 2,345,000 acres were left for resumption by the government. On the basis of the 1960 Census of Agriculture, the resumed land amounted to only

75. Ibid., pp. 187–88.
76. Ibid., p. 183.

4.8 per cent of the total farm area of the province. But since only 700,000 of the resumed acres were cultivated land, it would appear that the government netted less than 1.8 per cent of the cultivated area (including current fallow) of the province for redistribution! This low yield was partly offset by the fact that 1.2 million of the resumed acres were classified as culturable waste, meaning that they could be developed if capital was provided. The remaining 400,000 acres which were not culturable may be presumed to lie mostly in Baluchistan (Kalat Division) since the Land Commission reported only 1.9 million acres resumed in the "settled areas," i.e. areas which had been subjected to cadastral surveys and revenue assessments. Implementation of Regulation No. 64 in Baluchistan required the extension of settlement operations to the unsettled areas, but the yield in terms of culturable land was very low.[77]

Thus it might be said that as far as land redistribution is concerned, the West Pakistan Land Commission operated from the start with a net of large mesh and a number of holes through which many of the landowners swam unscathed. Those who were caught were of course compensated, but on a diminishing scale in proportion to the number of P.I.U.s resumed: from Rs 5 for the first 18,000 P.I.U.s down to Rs 1 for each unit over 150,000. Because the landowners were allowed to select the lands they retained as well as those they "gave" to their relations, the Commission netted only the poorest lands in most cases, only 128,000 acres of which were being cultivated by the landowners and only 545,000 by tenants!

The resumed lands were offered in the first instance to the tenants who were actually cultivating them, and thereafter to tenants displaced from the lands retained by the owners or to other tenants, small holders, or deserving migrants. These new owners were charged Rs 8 per P.I.U., which meant, for example, that the purchaser of one acre of the best irrigated land in the Lyallpur District, representing 80 P.I.U.s, paid Rs 640, a price which Professor Akhtar finds high in relation to those paid under similar land reforms in other countries but not excessive in relation to the prices of agricultural land and agricultural produce in West Pakistan.[78] The land-

77. Ibid., and *The Second Five Year Plan* (Pakistan), p. 185; *Pakistan News Digest*, February 15, 1966, pp. 7, 10.
78. Akhtar, p. 184

owners were compensated in the form of twenty-five-year bonds bearing simple interest at 4 per cent a year, and the purchasers have twenty-five years in which to make their payments. But so many of the purchasers paid cash (bearing out Calvert's remarks, see page 404) over the first six years of the program, that Rs 44.7 million of the Rs 92.5 million worth of bonds issued have already been redeemed.[79]

> After the implementation of the Sale Scheme [Martial Law Regulation No. 64] the Commission also prescribed the Upgrading Scheme according to which the tenants who had purchased resumed land, could upgrade their holdings to the economic level, if they had the means to purchase additional areas and were also willing to purchase it.
>
> Besides the tenants, the Commission also allowed the small landowners in a village to upgrade their holdings to the subsistence level.
>
> They were also, like tenants, required to pay the price of land in 50 half yearly equated easy instalments.
>
> The holdings of about 5,000 small landowners have been upgraded. Thereafter the Commission prescribed the Auction Scheme, according to which the untenanted uncultivated surplus area was put to auction.
>
> Under this Scheme, the Commission has so far sold about 2,000,000 acres of land.
>
> There is still a large area of inferior lands available for disposal and with a view to disposing of it the Commission has permitted its sale even at a price below the reserve price.[80]

In all, it appears that slightly more than half of the resumed land had been disposed of by the end of 1965, and that only 150,000 tenants (of the two million in the province) have become proprietors.[81] This can hardly be considered very impressive. Moreover, many of these new owners do not have a "subsistence" holding, let alone an "economic" one. On the other hand, the land reform in West Pakistan has given a much greater security to the nonoccupancy

79. *Pakistan News Digest*, February 15, 1966, p. 7.
80. Ibid., p. 10.
81. Ibid., pp. 7, 10.

tenant who cannot now be ejected except for failure to pay the rent or to cultivate the land, or for misuse or subletting of the land, and any of these grounds must now be established in a Revenue Court. Thus it may be said that West Pakistan's land reform has eliminated both the occupancy tenant (converting those who remained into small holders where land was available and where they could raise the money to buy it) and the tenant-at-will (giving him security of tenure except as indicated above).

Although it prohibited future subdivisions of economic and subsistence holdings, Martial Law Regulation No. 64 did not deal directly with the problem of existing fragmentation but instead left consolidation to the Land Commission and provincial government. During the entire British period and up to March 1959, only 2.3 million out of the 24 million acres of cultivated land in the former Pakistan Punjab and North West Frontier Province had been consolidated (including 500,000 under Pakistan's First Five Year Plan, 1955–60).[82] At the urging of the Land Commission, the Governor of West Pakistan promulgated the Consolidation of Holdings Ordinance of 1960 under which compulsory consolidations were to be carried out throughout the province during the Second Five Year Plan, but implementation has fallen far short of the goal. At the instance of the Credit Enquiry Commission, appointed by the Central Government in 1959, the government of West Pakistan has also taken steps to increase the amounts which are made available for *taccavi* loans to ease the position of the small farmer,[83] but the procedures are still cumbersome and not much use appears to have been made of this device.

But although implementation of land reforms in West Pakistan seems, at the time of writing, to have remained far short of the goals enunciated by the Pakistan Land Reforms Commission of 1959, the work of that Commission does not represent the only contribution made by the Ayub administration toward solving the agricultural problems of the country. The Central Credit Enquiry Commission, just mentioned, had some further recommendations which will be treated below. But the most salient contribution was the appointment of the Food and Agriculture Commission on July 16, 1959. The

82. *The Second Five Year Plan* (Pakistan), p. 188.
83. Akhtar, p. 193.

terms of reference of the F.A.C. authorized it to undertake the broadest possible inquiry into agricultural practices and performance, to fix goals for production (in cooperation with the Planning Commission), and to recommend methods of achieving them not only on the farms but through administrative changes redefining, if necessary, the respective roles of the Central and provincial governments. The membership of the Commission, including the Governor of West Pakistan, was such as to ensure respect for its recommendations. In addition, two agricultural economists provided by the World Bank were regular members, and half a dozen others from the Bank, the F.A.O., and I.C.A. (now A.I.D.) served as full- or part-time advisers. The report of the F.A.C., published in November 1960, is a lucid and hard-hitting document, typical of the early Martial Law period when Pakistan shook off the traditional ways of doing things long enough to face up to, though unfortunately not to solve, the fundamental problems facing her.

The Pakistan F.A.C. went to work just after the Land Reforms Commission had finished its task and attempted to adopt its recommendations to the tenurial pattern envisaged by the latter Commission and partly promulgated in Martial Law Regulation No. 64. More significantly, the F.A.C. really tried to bridge the usual gap between the files and the fields, i.e. between the various commission reports which clutter the administrative offices and the farmer who is the subject of all that verbiage. We have already quoted some of the findings of the F.A.C. relating to the problem of bringing development to the farmer and taking cognizance of his abilities and needs. But the single most important conclusion of the Commission was that none of the agencies in existence was in a position to give the farmer, in an integrated fashion, the most basic requirements other than land and water for improving his position and thereby the agricultural position of Pakistan.

After a careful review of the situation of the peasant in each of the major geographical regions of the country, the F.A.C. identified his most pressing needs as the "five firsts"—better seed, fertilizer, plant protection, better cultivation techniques, and short- and medium-term credit.[84] After explaining the importance of each of these

84. *Report of the F.A.C.*, p. 64. In identifying the "five firsts" the F.A.C. added, "It may be thought that irrigation should be included among the "firsts"

inputs, the Commission proceeded to demonstrate that none of the eight departments or agencies connected with agricultural development was in a position to give the farmer the timely and responsive "front line" service he requires and deserves. Briefly, the Commission found the following shortcomings in each of these agencies:

1. Provincial Department of Agriculture, including Research

> Operating under all of the handicaps of a minor provincial service starved of funds and low in public esteem, its original purpose was that of a very attenuated advisory service confined mostly to demonstration to rural leaders and larger landowners. In no sense was it an action department equipped to account urgently for something being done.

Research

> Although useful work has been done in individual cases, un-fortunately, in its present general state research is full of deficiencies which make it totally unsuited to meet the immense and urgent challenge it is now required to face. In the first place, no adequate funds are provided for it. With the low status accorded to agriculture this is not surprising, particularly, as one of the characteristics of research is its continual greed for money with often only very rare and uncertain returns. . . . A second weakness is in the absence of any planned approach to the problem just outlined. Research is now the concurrent responsibility of the Central and Provincial Governments.

2. Animal Husbandry Department

> The department is really incorrectly named. No department is concerned yet with the interaction of crops and livestock or has an extension service advising farmers on this subject. The Animal Husbandry Department is really a veterinary department and operates quite out of contact with Agriculture. It has two

---

because of its immense importance to production. We have not included it at this point because its proper and economical use almost invariably involves changes in existing land use patterns and it will be discussed under that heading."

main jobs, disease control and supply of stud animals. The farmer's need of these is less continuous than that of improving his crop yields, but when the veterinarian is needed he is badly needed. Unfortunately, the department's resources to assist him are very meagre and their effectiveness is confined to those parts in a district where they happen to be located.

3. Irrigation Department and Water and Power Development Authority

The Irrigation Department has always been in a different category from the Departments of Agriculture and Animal Husbandry. Responsible for the magnificent barrages and canals of West Pakistan, it has been associated with the prestige of engineers rather than with the "illiterate person" of agriculture. As far as farmers are concerned, it is a department with power actively to help or harm. It is not an advisory service. It supplies the water and collects the charges for it. This places it in importance second only to the revenue service. Government recognises this importance by pay scales, facilities and provision of staff analogous to the revenue service. Its position illustrates one of the curious anomalies from the past, namely that government has provided far more lavishly for the services collecting revenue from agriculture than for the services needed to increase the farmer's agricultural production.

Irrigation, of course, does increase agricultural production but one of the first points to note about the Irrigation Department is that it is essentially an engineer's affair, supplying water at a field outlet point and leaving the farmer to distribute and use it as he likes. The best agricultural usage of water is not the department's business. Its staff are purely there to supply the water in the canals, see what crops are grown and collect the water charges. . . . The engineers are not agriculturists and the agriculturists have not applied themselves sufficiently to the problems of irrigated agriculture. Very little research has been done on the interrelation between crops and irrigation in the different parts of the country and no extension service is provided to advise farmers on the subject. . . .

The Water and Power Development Authority has already

been created in each wing of the country because the country could not tolerate the slow tempo of traditional government departments in curing the problem of salinity and extending the vital infrastructure of water and power supply. WAPDA's sphere of operations is essentially in such infrastructure but, ... the very investment which WAPDA is making in tube-wells and which may be necessary in future in major drainage will be dependent for its efficacy on the way farmers use the water and possibly, in places, on field drainage on their lands.

It is too early to know yet what particular method of combating salinity will be most appropriate in any particular area but it is already certain that, unless farmers follow the right procedures and rotations needed to reclaim their land, salinity will not be cured. No organisation yet exists to tell farmers what to do, to finance, where necessary, their field drains and to see that they do it. WAPDA itself has an immense job on the engineering infrastructure side and is unsuited for the agricultural follow-up. The Soil Reclamation Board whose scientists have devised and will continue to be needed to watch over the necessary procedures has no extension arm to see that they are carried out. The most logical arrangement would be for a new agricultural extension arm, already carrying the "five firsts" to the farmer and advising him on irrigated agriculture, to take on this duty in the areas affected, in close cooperation with the scientists of the Soil Reclamation Board. (The F.A.C.'s comments in this paragraph are of utmost significance to the questions which will be discussed in Chapter 9.)

4. Cooperative Department—See above, pages 400–02.

5. Agricultural Credit Institutions

Apart from cooperatives, institutional rural credit is handled by the Agricultural Bank and the Agricultural Development Finance Corporation, about to be merged, and the *taccavi* loan system by the Revenue Department. All of them together, including the cooperatives, are thought to handle only a fraction of the rural credit used, the bulk being provided by friends and relations or by merchants who purchase the crops. Unscrupulous and greedy as these latter classes may be, they are much more convenient than government institutions. . . . The bank's clients are, therefore, largely confined to important land-owners. The *taccavi* system . . . has until now been usually operated as a somewhat indiscriminate handout of small amounts by Revenue Department officials to meet disasters or to assist in some cases men of influence and has had an even worse reputation for repayment than the cooperatives.

Fully conscious of these shortcomings and pressed with the urgent need for development, each of these institutions is anxious to expand its credit services, particularly, to the smaller man. There is some danger that this may result not only in some confusion but in excessive indebtedness. None of these institutions is in a position to ensure that its loans are actually used for increased agricultural production or to supervise such use and farmers may be tempted to borrow what they can from government, while continuing to borrow from their other sources.

6. Village Agricultural and Industrial Development (Village-AID, the commuity development organization established in Pakistan after 1953 with considerable assistance from the United States' foreign assistance program, which ran afoul of the older departments and of the traditional power structure in many villages and which, even as the F.A.C. was discussing it, was nearing its end).

Village-AID is unique among the departments mainly concerned with agriculture. It actually has a reasonably satisfactory establishment in the front line specialising in village work. At present, its operations are confined to certain selected parts of different districts covering in all about a fifth of the country's cultivated area but where it operates it concentrates. . . . The main reason for these much more adequate facilities and staff is that, while the former departments are dependent on provincial finance and attitudes, Village-AID has been largely financed through Central Government and from foreign aid funds. There are particular reasons for this differential treatment and it is important to appreciate them.

Village-AID springs from the concept of progress through

community development which has become popular in so many parts of the world since the war. This concept has a very strong appeal both philosophically and politically to believers in democracy because of the emphasis it places on participation by people in their own affairs. The arguments used in favour of cooperatives on this account apply all the more strongly to community development because it covers all aspects of progress and not just the economic emancipation of the small man. In the conflict of ideologies in today's world, progress by participation, as opposed to massive coercion by a small clique through a state machine, has values for civilisation which foundations and governments in the Western world have been very ready to support with financial aid. . . .

There is, however, one aspect of Village-AID which is causing a great deal of controversy. . . . Village-AID claims to be the sole extension service for all departments. This claim is based, partly, on the argument that the country cannot afford separate extension services down to village level and that a multitude of different advisers would anyway confuse the villagers and, partly, on the argument that Village-AID alone uses the right method for mass communication and motivation.

This policy has not been accepted as suitable in all cases, particularly by the Department of Agriculture, and Village-AID is criticised for boosting its value by claiming credit for all rural progress.

This controversy is very relevant to the problem of assessing what should be the relationship between Village-AID and the new organisation in agriculture which is needed to supply the many techniques and services required for increasing the farmer's production. Excellent as its values are in their own field, it is apparent that Village-AID is in no position to execute the functions which have led us to feel the need for such an organisation. Certainly a principal activity of Village-AID has been demonstration but its field is motivation not organisation and supply. It is in no position to operate even a package deal project of the "five firsts" for farmers. It cannot produce better seed. It has no stores or supply line. It cannot manage loans. Yet these are the simplest services to farmers which an agricultural front line ought to provide and in a manner which makes it all available through one office near the farm. Still less can Village-AID be contemplated as the front extension line as the problem passes over to more complicated needs like the right preparation for irrigation, the introduction of machinery, or the management of farm blocks, marketing and processing.

7. National Development Organisation (N.D.O.) and Basic Democracies. (The N.D.O. represented the Ayub administration's first attempt to bring Village-AID under closer political control. By 1961, with the division of Village-AID functions between the Basic Democracies and the newly created Agricultural Development Corporation [ADC], N.D.O. ceased its operations. The structure of the system of Basic Democracies has been explained above, see pages 387–88.)

The basic democracies are also clearly an expression of the principle of participation by people in their own affairs and they have been specifically charged with the duty of development. We found a number of different views in the course of our tours as to how they were to carry out this duty which has yet to be defined. Some Union Council Chairman thought that they should issue instructions to agricultural staff. Others thought that the Council itself should manage a union store and issue seeds and fertilizers. Yet others thought that cooperatives should handle these supplies . . . with the Chairman of the Union Council as Chairman of cooperatives. This would, obviously, identify the elected head of local government with the provision of economic aids, a system which might well have serious drawbacks. Among government officials two main differences of approach were evident. Some thought that the Basic Democracy Councils should have executive responsibility for development using technical officers as their aids. . . . Others thought that the councils would be overtaxed, if they were expected to handle the day-to-day needs of development and to see that timely and effective decisions were made and implemented and for this reason felt that their chief role should be to formulate policy.

It is not our business to suggest how local government should evolve. . . . We mention these various views because it is against a background of some uncertainty that we have to assess what should be the relationship of a new organisational arm in agriculture to the basic democracies. We are convinced . . . that the techniques and services which we have elaborated are urgently needed on a national plane. . . . We have also suggested that they should be tackled project-wise so that the relevant aspects can be dovetailed together under a project leader in a team manner. Naturally, we would consider it disastrous if plans of this kind were to be imperilled by the whims of local councils.

8. The Revenue and General Administration Services (these have been described above, see pages 386–92.)

The Deputy Commissioner and his staff have often been embarrassed by the fact that, although they are responsible for the general effectiveness of any programme, members of the technical departments are not under their direct control but take their orders from the head of their department. . . . In these circumstances, the Deputy Commissioner is often exasperated by the poor quality of the results while the staff of the technical departments who are frequently older and more experienced in their own profession tend to feel treated more as inferiors than technicians and blamed for circumstances beyond their control. These feelings are accentuated when the Deputy Commissioner can really do little to put right the long-term deficiencies and, above all, has little time to listen because he is already overburdened with work.[85]

In view of the overburdening of the revenue and general administration service, of the specialized concerns of the Basic Democracies system, the Irrigation Department, and WAPDA, and of the demonstrated inadequacies of the other departments, the F.A.C. recommended the creation, in each Wing of the country, of a new organization to be known as the Agricultural Development Corporation (ADC henceforth), which would have many of the advantages

85. *Report of the F.A.C.*, pp. 153–94, *passim.*

of the Water and Power Development Authorities. The East and West Pakistan ADCs would be semiautonomous bodies with their own budgets, exempted from the need to recruit through the Public Service Commission but able to borrow technicians "on extended temporary duty" from the older departments. Their primary responsibility would be the provision of the "five-firsts" (i.e. better seed, fertilizers, plant protection, better cultivation techniques, and short- and medium-term credit), and they would attempt to provide these in an integrated fashion and on a project basis, i.e. concentrating the integrated applications in certain specified areas, but eventually covering the whole of the country.

As the F.A.C. foresaw it, the Agriculture Department would cede extension and supply work to the ADC but would retain basic research. The Animal Husbandry Department would become in name what it was in effect, a Veterinary Department concentrating on disease control and letting ADC handle the breeding and distribution of superior stock and measures to ensure the provision of superior forage and fodder. The Cooperative Department "would be relieved of the hopeless prospect of trying to run the whole country's supply and marketing with inadequate resources" and would concentrate on organizing cooperative societies and enlisting the farmer's enthusiasm for the cooperative approach. As a further impetus, ADC would be instructed to make use of cooperative organizations wherever feasible in its work. As for the cooperative banks, the F.A.C. did not find it necessary to go as far as had the Credit Enquiry Commission, which recommended that they withdraw entirely from commercial loans; but the F.A.C. suggested that the cooperative banks be permitted to finance "outside" transactions only when these involved the purchase of agricultural commodities and only if the deposits they attracted were used to finance agricultural development.[86]

The Agricultural Development Bank would be permitted to continue financing "men of property" but would be encouraged to underwrite cooperatives as well. But ADC would provide, in cooperation with these institutions and with an expanded program of *taccavi* loans, "supervised credit" to the small farmer especially in

---

86. Akhtar, p. 271; *Report of the F.A.C.*, p. 305.

the form of loans in kind which could not so easily be diverted from their original purposes.[87] Village-AID would abandon its claim to be the exclusive extension service and concentrate on the work of arousing enthusiasm and correct motivation for development among the farmers, while "superfluous staff of the N.D.O., who felt more interested in active agriculture, might join the new arm.[88] The Basic Democracies system would also play a key role in arousing enthusiasm for development, but would be left free to evolve as a primarily political organization designed to give expression to the wishes of the whole population though divorced from the provision of goods and services.

> To subordinate agricultural development entirely to local councils would be to disparage its enormous national importance and to deny the farmers the help that they could get from a corporation run on businesslike lines. We envisage rather that the basic democracies will be concerned with development as a whole and as it affects a locality and that the corporation will accordingly work with the local councils and particularly invoke their assistance in getting the cooperation of the local farmers.[89]

One would surmise that, in view of the "high-powered" nature of the Food and Agriculture Commission, its recommendations would have been adopted swiftly and without change, especially as Martial Law government was still in force throughout the country. Even under Martial Law, however, the old departmental interests retained much influence, and as the years passed the military administrators found themselves less and less able to cope with the multitude of problems and of conflicting recommendations without calling upon the "old hands" in the technical and administrative services. These

87. *Report of the F.A.C.*, pp. 221, 254–55.
88. Ibid., pp. 199, 260–61.
89. Ibid., p. 208. It should be noted that the F.A.C., while striving to prevent conflicts between the proposed Agricultural Development Corporations and the Basic Democracies system, sidestepped the issue of a conflict between the Basic Democracies and Village-AID, a conflict which was, of course, beyond its competence. At the same time, it should be emphasized that nothing in the report of the F.A.C. advocated the termination of the Village-AID program, although the government used the creation of the Agricultural Development Corporations in each Wing as an excuse to accomplish this result.

428

"old hands" apparently decided that delay and imprecision would eventually work to their advantage, and that as far as the ADCs were concerned it would be best to give token endorsement to the recommendations of the F.A.C. and to work out the details later (indeed, something of the same procedure was followed with respect to the recommendations of the Land Reform Commission, as we have seen). Thus, when the West Pakistan ADC was established by Governor's Ordinance on September 20, 1961, its duties were spelled out in only general terms, and in particular the crucial matter of establishing the "project areas" was left to be handled on an ad hoc basis. The Ordinance requires the West Pakistan ADC

> 1. To deal with all matters pertaining to agricultural development including land reclamation, organization of agriculture in new colonies, planning of crop rotation, farming, marketing, organization of co-operative and block-farming, in any area of the Province to be declared a "Project Area" by the Government. In Project Areas, the Corporation is also required to encourage intensive and co-ordinated use of improved seed, fertilizers, plant protection material and introduce better cultivation techniques and a sound credit system; and
>
> 2. To make suitable arrangements throughout the Province on a commercial basis for the procurement, transport, storage and distribution to agriculturists of essential supplies such as seed, fertilizers, plant protection equipment, pesticides and agricultural machinery and implements.[90]

Like WAPDA, ADC is a semiautonomous corporation with its own budget and personnel-recruitment program. It is administered by a Board and divided into wings. The Board consists of the Chairman, who directly supervises the Administrative Wing, and includes three member-directors each of whom supervises an additional wing: Supply, Field, and Finance. The Provincial Commissioner of Co-operatives is an ex-officio member of the Board, and ADC is directed to make use of cooperatives wherever possible in its supply operations. The Irrigation Department has provided ADC with a Chief

90. West Pakistan Agricultural Development Corporation, *Anniversary Souvenir*, October 1, 1962 (Lahore, Public Relations Division, West Pakistan Agricultural Development Corporation, 1962), p. 6.

Engineer and Adviser for Irrigation, and the Agriculture Department has furnished an Agricultural Adviser. F.A.O. has provided a special Adviser for Seed.

The ADC (henceforth, unless specifically indicated, "ADC" will refer only to the West Pakistan corporation) reaches the farmer through its Supply and Field Wings. The Supply Wing has province-wide responsibility, exercised through six regional offices, "for all operations concerning the planning, procurement, storage, movement and distribution of fertilizers, improved varieties of seed, implements, pesticides, plant protection equipment, and other agricultural supplies."[91] Although ADC has taken over government-owned seed multiplication and livestock breeding farms and fruit nurseries, it does not manufacture machinery, implements, pesticides, insecticides or other plant protection material but can encourage private firms to engage in their manufacture. Fertilizers are procured from the PIDC factories or imported on ADC account. Basic research has been left to the Agriculture Department.

The Field Wing operates only within the project areas entrusted to the ADC by the provincial government for development operations. Development includes "colonization, settlement, resumption of lands, irrigation, extension and augmentation of agricultural produce, buildings and roads. Each Project is placed under the Project Director who has the necessary departments to deal with various aspects of the project."[92] For its work in the designated project areas, the Field Wing is divided into a Project Division for physical operations (such as the clearing and leveling of fields and the construction of distributaries, watercourses, and drains), a Farms Division concerned only with livestock improvement, and a Training Division which provides extension and educational services to the farmers. It is to be noted that this Training Division of ADC has taken over the "front line" personnel of the former Village-AID organization (as well as a few of the personnel of the defunct N.D.O.) and that accordingly almost all of the extension and farmer education work now being done in West Pakistan is restricted to the ADC project areas (the exception being the inadequate extension services still provided by the Agriculture Department outside these areas).

91. Ibid., p. 7.
92. Ibid., p. 11.

It should also be noted that ADC does not deal in provincewide credit operations, and even within its project areas can only attempt to "facilitate" credit availability to the farmers from the Agricultural Development Bank and the cooperative banks.[93] The provision of loans in kind, strongly advocated by the F.A.C., has not materialized to any extent.

Thus, although the report of the F.A.C. stressed the interdependence of the "five firsts" (better seed, fertilizer, plant protection, better cultivation techniques, and short- and medium-term credit), and the "need to bring them as a package deal within easy reach of the farmer,"[94] the ADC Ordinance authorizes the corporation to do this only within its project areas. Even there, ADC has no direct control over credit availability. Although ADC has provincewide responsibility for seed and fertilizer distribution, it must depend upon outside sources to manufacture the fertilizers as well as for insecticides, pesticides, implements, and farm machinery. But most crucial of all, the extension services and farmer education which are absolutely essential to enable the farmer to make proper use of these inputs and to develop "better cultivation techniques" can only be provided within the designated project areas.

Of course, it would be impossible to offer the "five firsts" in an integrated program all over the province of West Pakistan from the start. The F.A.C. clearly recognized this, but they also clearly anticipated that the ADC would be entrusted with one project area after another until the entire province was covered. The F.A.C. suggested that initial project areas be scattered around the province to provide experience with the varying types of representative problem areas. The Commission suggested choosing a district of high production with comparatively progressive farmers and a variety of crops (such as Montgomery, Rahimyar Khan, or Nawabshah) or a similar district where the emphasis was on one or two crops; special problem areas such as a new colonization project (Ghulam Mohammad command), an area of high population pressure where reorganization of farming is critical (Sialkot), an area badly affected by salinity (Rechna Doab), a soil conservation area (Rawalpindi), and a hill catchment area where re-afforestation and seed

93. Ibid., p. 10.
94. Ibid., p. 5.

farming could be applied; plus areas where special programs might be tried on an experimental basis such as an area of hill range in Baluchistan, a desert range area (Cholistan in Bahawalpur), a cooperative farming village in Multan, a potato seed and fruit development area in Quetta, a riverine area between the Kalabagh and Sukkur barrages on the Indus floodplain, and a flood irrigation area in the Sibi plains.[95]

But instead of assigning to ADC a phased program of representative project areas, in which experience from successful experiments could be applied to analogous areas as techniques and personnel were accumulated, the policy of the Government of West Pakistan has been to entrust to the ADC only large colonization projects which will absorb all of its resources and talent in the rather repetitious and rather mundane operations common to such projects. From the start, ADC was handed the development work in the Ghulam Mohammad command, subsuming the Colonization Directorate which had been established for that purpose. When WAPDA finished work on the Gudu Project in 1961, ADC was ordered to take over its development. And, after lengthy negotiations, ADC took over the Thal Development Authority in December 1962. Of course, each of these projects is essential and valuable, but the F.A.C. did not intend that ADC become merely a super colonization directorate or a super development authority. Yet, aside from its Small Dams Organization, established within the Field Wing in 1961 and designed to bring irrigation to small areas outside the Indus Plains, that is exactly what ADC has become (aside from its direct provincewide responsibilities for seed and the indirect responsibilities for the other "firsts" as explained above). So involved had ADC become with these colonization-development schemes that, as we shall see in Chapter 9, the West Pakistan Government had to set up a separate organization, the Land and Water Management Board, to handle the problem of bringing the "five firsts" to the groundwater development and reclamation project areas as they are constructed by WAPDA. In theory, and as envisaged by the F.A.C.,[96] there is no reason why ADC could not have handled this vital task. But in practice, ADC has not been allowed to grow into a provincewide organization

95. *Report of the F.A.C.*, pp. 245–47.
96. Ibid., p. 224.

capable of bringing the "five firsts" to all of the farmers of West Pakistan. There is no question that the ADC recognized its high responsibility.

> While each of the items included among "five firsts" can alone effect some limited increase in production, it is their combined application which really brings substantial results and benefits. In point of fact the basic concept of the "five firsts" and the need to bring them as a package deal to the farmer's door represents a revolution in ideas which is being given a tangible shape through the agency of the Agricultural Development Corporation.[97]

But, as with Village-AID before it, the ADC has been circumscribed and circumvented by the very departments and vested interests whose shortcomings and narrow vision it was designed to overcome.

We have analyzed the work of Pakistan's Food and Agriculture Commission and the role of the West Pakistan ADC at great length because of their direct bearing on the groundwater and reclamation programs to be discussed in the next chapter. Although much of what the Food and Agriculture Commission had to say concerning the shortcomings of the traditional agencies would be applicable to India as well, we can only briefly summarize the post-Partition administrative developments in the Indian Punjab and Rajasthan. As far as revenue collection is concerned, the theory that the land belongs to the state and that the land revenue, as evidence of this ultimate claim, is the state's share of the produce of the land is no different in the Indian portions of the Basin. Nor are the parallel administrative structures for collecting the land revenue, the "water advantage rate," and the water rate. But the Indian Punjab and Rajasthan, at the urging of the Central Government, have made a concerted effort to recover more of the costs of the post-Partition irrigation projects by means of betterment taxes (reflecting the enhanced values of affected lands) and by raising the water rates. Nevertheless, in the 1963–64 budget estimates, the land revenue contributed only 5.1 per cent and the revenue from irrigation, navigation,

97. West Pakistan Agricultural Development Corporation, *Anniversary Souvenir*, October 1, 1962, p. 5.

embankment, and drainage works only 5.7 per cent of the estimated receipts for the Indian Punjab (excluding net contributions from the Central Government) and only 1.7 and 1.8 per cent, respectively, for Rajasthan.[98]

As in Pakistan, post-Independence land reforms in India aimed primarily at the abolition of intermediate rights and the substitution of *ryotwari* tenures, with the state receiving the land revenue directly and as a rent, for *zamindari* tenures. Land reform matters were left to the states, and both the Indian Punjab and Rajasthan acted in the early 1950s, as did P.E.P.S.U., to abolish *zamindari* tenures with compensation and *jagirs*, so common in P.E.P.S.U. and Rajasthan, without compensation. But although India's First Five Year Plan endorsed the concept of an upper limit on individual holdings, both the actual limits and the degree of implementation remained up to the states. In the area that formed P.E.P.S.U. up to 1956, where large landholdings and *jagirs* had been so common, a ceiling of thirty standard acres (calculated in roughly similar fashion to Pakistan's P.I.U.s) was established. By 1962, the Punjab Government had declared 36,000 standard acres in former P.E.P.S.U. to be surplus and had redistributed 11,000 of these. But in the former British Punjab, no ceiling on holdings has been imposed. Instead, the government merely asserted its right to settle tenants on lands in excess of the declared limits even if these were being personally farmed by the owners. Since the former British areas were, for the most part, either long crowded "dry districts" (Hoshiarpur, Gurdaspur, Jullundur, etc.) or long settled Canal Colonies (Amritsar, Ludhiana, Ferozepore, etc.) very few holdings in excess of 30 standard acres existed and the policy of requiring large landlords to accept more tenants is probably sufficient if fairly and universally enforced. By 1962 in the former British Punjab 347,000 standard acres had been declared surplus and 34,000 tenant farmers had been settled on 62,000 of these.[99]

All tenants in the Indian Punjab have been granted permanent tenure and the right to purchase lands which they have cultivated for six years or more. A landlord may, however, resume up to 30 standard acres for his own use so long as no tenant is thereby left

98. *India, A Reference Annual, 1963,* pp. 380, 382.
99. Ibid., p. 222.

with less than 5 acres. Rents may not exceed one-third of the gross produce or its value. In Rajasthan, where the limit on holdings is 30 standard acres, rents may not exceed one-sixth of the gross produce or twice the annual land revenue. Here about 100,000 tenants have acquired proprietorship rights to 600,000 acres. According to the official figures, the Indian Punjab has made surprising progress with consolidation; over 90 per cent of the net sown area had been consolidated by early 1962, as compared with only 8 per cent in Rajasthan. To prevent further fragmentation, both states have enacted legislation regulating transfers, partitions, and leases.[100]

But both the Indian Punjab and Rajasthan have encountered the same problem as has West Pakistan in evasions of land reform regulations by nominal divisions among members of the same family, illegal eviction of tenants, and also in the formation of bogus co-operatives to make it appear that interests have been pooled.[101] As in Pakistan, the lack of accurate data on tenure was a handicap to the implementation of land reforms in India, especially in states such as P.E.P.S.U. and Rajasthan where large holdings were common. As a basis for reform, special censuses of landholding and cultivation were undertaken in conjunction with the Census of 1951 and under the First Five Year Plan. But the official interpretation of the results, and especially the definition of anyone who makes the responsible decisions regarding cultivation as a farmer or owner-operator, has been severely criticized.[102]

100. Ibid., pp. 221–23.
101. Government of India, Planning Commission, *Second Five Year Plan, a Draft Outline* (New Delhi, February 1956), pp. 78–79; and K. N. Bhattacharyya, *Indian Plans: A Generalist Approach* (New York, Asia Publishing House, 1963), p. 117. In March 1964 the present author was traveling in the Ferozepore District of the Indian Punjab when he passed a tubewell being operated by means of a belt connected to a tractor. Somewhat surprised to see a tubewell in this area (under command of the Sirhind Feeder offtaking Harike Barrage) he stopped to ask who owned the tubewell. On being told that it was private, he asked how many acres were in the holding. He was told 400. The next question was how the 400 acres had been kept within the one holding rather than being forcibly tenanted down to the 30 standard acre allowance. "Oh," came the reply, "the *zamindar* merely called in all his relatives when the limit was imposed."
102. See Chapter 10, "Agrarian Revolution by Census Redefinition," in Daniel and Alice Thorner, *Land and Labour in India* (Bombay, Asia Publishing House, 1962), pp. 131–50, especially pp. 131–36. In the first chapter of the book, the authors, who spent ten years studying the agrarian problems of India, conclude

India's most ambitious attempt to come to grips with her agrarian problems took the form of the community development program which was inaugurated in October 1952. The Indian program has many similarities to Pakistan's Village-AID program, though it should be acknowledged that the latter probably owed more to the former than vice versa. But both had their antecedents in the British period. F. L. Brayne, District Commissioner of the Gurgaon District in the southernmost Punjab, started rural development work there on an experimental scale as early as 1928, with the emphasis on manure collection, composting, improved agricultural implements, and female education. But Brayne's work came to a halt when he was transferred from the district. After the election of a popular government in the United Provinces in 1937, a Development Minister was appointed and an attempt was made to substitute a single "Village Level Worker" for the many, uncoordinated officials of the traditional departments concerned with the farmer. But the U.P. scheme never rose above the district level, and it petered out with the coming of the Second World War and the attendant political crises described in Chapter 5. On the other hand, the first "Grow More Food Campaign" was inaugurated in 1942 and helped to focus attention on the basic needs of the farmer, while Gandhi's continued insistence on the role of the village in Indian society kept alive the idea of trying to enlist the farmer in development.[103]

After Independence, these precedents and the experience in working with refugees in the Nilokheri and Faridabad rehabilitation projects attracted the attention of the Ford Foundation. A pilot project was started at Etawah in the U.P. (now Uttar Pradesh), and by 1952 the Foundation was supporting fifteen such projects plus thirty-four training centers for multipurpose village-level workers. In May

---

that, if measured by their announced aims, the post-Partition land reforms in India have failed, that tenancy continues to be rampant even in the Punjab, and that the larger owners still hold a great deal of land but manage to get it cultivated by others. (Ibid., p. 3.) See also B. C. Tandon, ed., *The Third Five Year Plan and India's Economic Growth* (Allahabad, Chaitanya Publishing House, 1962), pp. 167–68.

103. M. S. Randhawa, I.C.S., Development Commissioner, Punjab, *National Extension Service and Community Projects in Punjab* (Chandigarh, Punjab Government, Community Projects Administration, 1955), pp. 3, 4; and Taylor et al., *India's Roots of Democracy*, pp. 169–74.

1952 the United States Point Four program entered into an agreement with the Government of India for a vast community development program, and in October of that year it was announced that
within ten years the whole country would be covered with a series
of 5,000 Community Development Blocks. Each block would include
approximately one hundred villages and 75,000 people. But again
the Central Government left implementation to the states, suggesting
that each state establish a development board or commission with
the state's Chief Minister as chairman and a Development Commissioner as secretary. At the district level would be a district development committee, with the D.C. as chairman and with representation
from such departments as Agriculture, Education, Health, and Public Works. A district development officer would be in charge of the
actual work, subject to the D.C. Below the district level came the
blocks, each with an administrative officer and a staff including
specialists from the traditional departments, "seconded" for development work to the administrative officer. Each block officer would
have ten or twenty village-level workers, each responsible for five
villages if the program was to be "intensive" or for ten in an "extensive" program. After a period of training in the various technical
fields, but emphasizing agriculture, the village-level worker would
take up residence in one of his villages. His primary responsibility
was to arouse the enthusiasm of the villagers, get them to identify
their most pressing needs and to find ways of meeting them. In help-
ing them to identify and solve their problems, the village-level worker
could call on the technicians at the block level. But the emphasis was
to be on cooperative "self-help."[104]

India's community development and extension program was
launched with a great deal of enthusiasm. Punjab, Rajasthan, and
all of the other states adopted the mechanism more or less as suggested by the Center. During the mid 1950s, a great many villages
were cleaned up, refuse was collected and composted, sanitary wells
driven and covered, decent village access roads built, new schools,
clinics, and assembly halls constructed. The use of fertilizers, green
manures, improved seed varieties, new crops and rotations, pesticides

104. Ibid., pp. 174–77; and Walter C. Neale, *India: The Search for Unity,
Democracy and Progress* (Princeton, N.J., D. Van Nostrand Company [Search-
light Books], 1965), pp. 32, 33, 37–39.

and insecticides was taught. But even by 1957 it had become apparent that all was not going well.[105] Part of the trouble was that, despite the emphasis on the intimate village-level approach, with the community development workers supposed to evoke the needs and enthusiasm of the villagers, the program was becoming a top-down or superimposed affair. Too many village-level workers were assuming the role of managers or even petty dictators. And they were coming into conflict not only with the *patwaris* and village headmen but with the traditional power structure in the villages as represented by the *panchayats* or councils of the various castes. At a higher level, the block and district development officers were running afoul of the *tahsildars*, the D.C.s, and the traditional departments.

By 1960, it looked as though India's community development program (which had by then been extended to about three-fourths of the villages in the nation) would suffer the fate that was impending for Pakistan's Village-AID. But then the Central Government hit upon a new idea: since the community development apparatus lacked a political base, it should be provided with one. The idea of *panchayat*, or village council decision making, is an old one in most of India, and it is particularly strong among the Hindu agricultural castes and the Sikhs of northwestern India. So the Central Government set out, again through the states, to implement a system of truly democratic council rule, known as *Panchayati Raj*, paralleling the community development organization. Beginning with the village

105. Hugh Tinker, a careful analyst of administrative developments in the subcontinent, writes: "A hint that there was a divergence between the 'image' of a utopian society where all were striving harmoniously together for the public good, and the reality of an imperfect democracy, with clashes of interests and the pursuit of self-gain, came with the publication of the 'Balvantray Report' on community development in November 1957. This report provided an indictment of the theoretical, formalistic approach of the Planning Commission and the Community Development agencies in the States. The programme had begun by assuming that the village people could be rapidly persuaded to take over responsibility for the new development projects; instead, the officials, high and low, had directed and controlled everything. As a 'people's programme,' community development was an illusion." (Hugh Tinker, *India and Pakistan: A Political Analysis* [New York, Frederick A. Praeger, 1962], p. 61, citing the *Report of the Team for the Study of Community Projects and National Extension Service*, Committee on Plan Projects [New Delhi, November, 1957].)

For a detailed analysis of India's community development program see Taylor et al., Chapter 25, pp. 610–37.

panchayat, elected on the basis of one man, one vote, *Panchayati Raj* ascends through the block council or *Panchayat Samiti* to the district council or *Zila Parishad* representing perhaps 2,000 villages and a million people. But the new *panchayat* organization does not go above district level, its responsibilities are confined to social and economic development, and it is not yet strong enough to "buck" the D.C. Most of the states, including Punjab and Rajasthan where all rural areas had been included in the system by 1963, have attempted to exclude party politics from *Panchayati Raj.* According to Professor Walter C. Neale, the main influence of the system occurs at the block or *Samiti* level where the councils have been granted a large share of financial resources.[106]

As it has developed so far, *Panchayati Raj* would not appear to be directly comparable to Pakistan's Basic Democracies system, which begins only above the village level (with the Union Council; see Table 20) and which continues up to the provincial level, and which is frankly political. *Panchayati Raj* still has to contend with the old caste *panchayats* and appears less able to influence or circumvent the D.C. On the other hand, *Panchayati Raj* is designed to implement the existing community development program whereas the Basic Democracies system, in fact though not in theory and whatever its political advantages, destroyed the Village-AID organization in Pakistan. While it is too soon to say whether *Panchayati Raj* will succeed in bringing democracy to India's villages or in mobilizing the villages for development, it can be said that, prior to the institution of the new system, the community development program was certainly not fulfilling its role. Thus India, like Pakistan, is still groping with the mechanics of the problem of bridging the gap between the technicians and administrators, on the one hand, and the farmers on the other.

It is the cruelest and most ironic paradox of the many-faceted problem of making genuine improvements in the agricultural sectors of developing nations that precisely those "outputs" which are least expensive in terms of measurable "inputs" are the ones that continue to elude us. We have already seen something of the tremendous cost

106. Neale, p. 34. The description of *Panchayati Raj* in this and the following paragraphs is based on Neale, pp. 32–34.

of the dams, barrages, link canals, and distribution systems necessary to bring water to the fields of the Indus Basin. In Chapter 9, we
shall see something of the cost of tubewells and fertilizers. But these
are all tangible inputs which can be measured in prices. The insight,
motivation, and experience on which a community development program must be based are intangibles, and no one—least of all a foreigner, no matter how well-intentioned—can guarantee that for a
certain sum of money such a program can be developed, much less
that it will succeed. Such a program can develop and succeed only
if there is a felt need for it among the people themselves, and patient
enthusiasm among both the leaders and the followers. Unfortunately,
in both India and Pakistan, much of the enthusiasm which was generated by Independence and which emerged with the first community
development programs has been dissipated by the relative failure of
those programs. It will be much harder to arouse such enthusiasm a
second or third time, but without it, as we said at the start of this
chapter, the tangible inputs are ultimately useless.

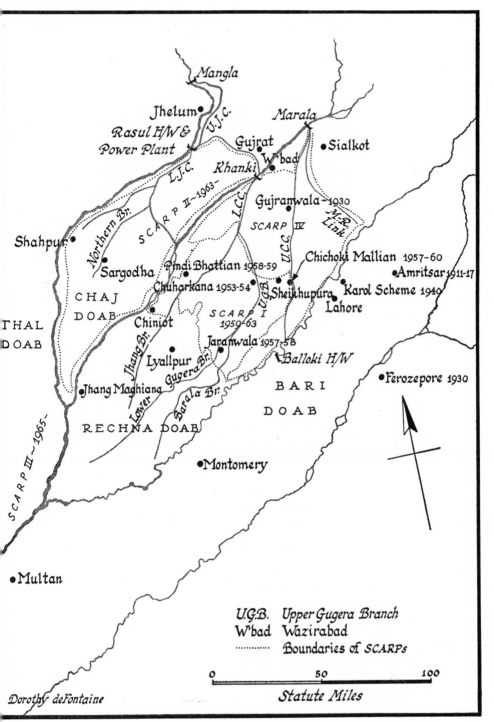

THAL
DOAB

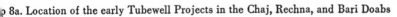

8a. Location of the early Tubewell Projects in the Chaj, Rechna, and Bari Doabs

KEY TO MAP 8b—Tentative Priority Assigned to Groundwater and Reclamation Proj‹ by the Harza Report[a]

Priority Number	Project	Canal Command(s)
NORTHERN ZONE		
RECHNA DOAB		
1	SCARP I (Central Rechna)	LCC
4	SCARP IV (Upper Rechna)	M-R Link, UCC, LCC
7	Lower Rechna	LCC and Haveli-Sidhnai
CHAJ DOAB		
2	SCARP II	UJC; LJC
THAL DOAB		
3	SCARP III (Lower Thal)	Muzaffargarh, Rangpur
10	Upper Thal	Thal
BARI DOAB		
6	Eastern Bari Doab	LBDC, Dipalpur, Pakpatt‹
8	Western Bari Doab	Sidhnai, Mailsi
9	Northern Bari Doab	Central Bari Doab Canals
BAHAWALPUR PLAIN		
5	Lower Bahawalpur	Abbasia, Panjnad
11	Central Bahawalpur	Qaimpur, Bahawal, Fordv‹
12	Upper Bahawalpur	Eastern Sadiqia
SOUTHERN ZONE		
CENTRAL SIND PLAIN		
1	Khairpur I	Sukkur
8	Rohri Perennial	Sukkur
11	Khairpur II	Sukkur
13	Rohri South and Eastern Nara	Sukkur
LOWER SIND PLAIN		
2	Gaja	Ghulam Mohammad
P G	Pinyari-Guni (Priority Not Determined)	Ghulam Mohammad
UPPER SIND PLAIN		
3	Larkana-Shikarpur	Gudu, Sukkur
6	Western Nara Valley, Gaj Dam, Hamal and Manchhar Lakes	Sukkur
7	Sukkur Right Bank (Nonperennial)	Sukkur
9	Kashmor-Jacobabad (Nonperennial)	Gudu
10	Sukkur Right Bank (Perennial)	Sukkur
12a	Kashmor-Jacobabad (Perennial)	Gudu
INDUS CORRIDOR		
5	Ghotki (Perennial)	Gudu, Sukkur
12b	Ghotki (Nonperennial)	Gudu, Sukkur
INDUS DELTA		
4	Miscellaneous Nonperennial Areas	Ghulam Mohammad

Abbreviations: S—Sukkur Barrage
ND—Priority Not Determined
a. Source: Harza Report, Exhibit II–4.

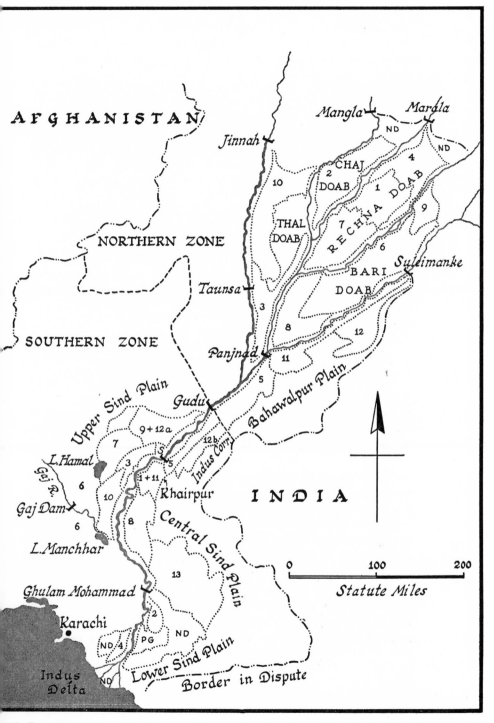

AFGHANISTAN

Mangla

Marala

ND

Jinnah

ND

CHAJ
DOAB

2

4

RECHNA DOAB

NORTHERN ZONE

10

THAL
DOAB

7

1

9

6

Taunsa

BARI

Suleimanke

SOUTHERN ZONE

3

DOAB

8

12

Panjnad

11

Bahawalpur Plain

5

Upper Sind Plain

Gudu

9 + 12a

7

12b

Indus Conn.

L. Hamal

3

5

Gaj R.

6

1 + 11

Khairpur

INDIA

Gaj Dam

10

6

8

L. Manchhar

Central Sind Plain

13

Ghulam Mohammad

Karachi

2

ND. 4

PG

ND

Indus
Delta

ND

Lower Sind Plain

Border in Dispute

N

0   100   200

Statute Miles

ₚ 8b. Tentative priority assigned to groundwater and reclamation projects by the Harza Report

9. The Groundwater Programs

"Heroic measures are essential if the Punjab is not to be destroyed."
—A. M. R. Montagu, 1946

"Such an ambitious program will require heroic efforts by the Government and people of West Pakistan."
—Revelle Panel Report, 1964

Precursors

Most of what has been written in the eight preceding chapters relates to the development of surface water irrigation in the Indus Basin. The historical evolution from the projects of the Mogul engineer, Ali Mardan Khan (see Chapter 3), to those of the IBP and BBRP might be represented by a logarithmic curve. There would be certain discontinuities along this curve, indicating the points where new technology was introduced or where projects such as Sukkur or Bhakra, each representing a new order of magnitude, were commissioned. But the layman can appreciate that what occurred in the Indus Basin after 1849 was essentially an attempt to apply advances in civil and hydraulic engineering, developed in the coal mines, barge canals, and railways of Great Britain, to the problems of surface water irrigation in a subhumid region. The initial efforts were not always successful (on the Sirhind Canal for example), changes in design theory had to be made, and eventually

444

the new science of the stable-regime canal was developed (see Chapter 3).

But even the dramatic advances exemplified by the imaginative Triple Canals Project were really changes in degree rather than in kind. As late as 1933, when the Sukkur Barrage and the Sutlej Valley Project were completed, methods of construction and of harnessing surface water flows had not radically changed from those employed at Rupar, Sidhnai, or Madhopur (see Map 3). True, the introduction of the gated weir or barrage, first used at Balloki in 1913, represented a major advance made possible by improvements in the design and manufacture of gates, mechanical winches, and counterbalances. True also, the work of Gerald Lacey and others was beginning to yield sophisticated formulas for canal design. But even Sukkur was a masonry structure, not essentially different from the Grand Anicut barrage, built on the Coleroon distributary of the Cauvery River in Madras 1,700 years previously, except that mortar was used at Sukkur.[1] All of the Sutlej Valley barrages were masonry structures, and it was not until the Haveli Project of 1937–39 that the Indus Basin could boast a single reinforced concrete barrage, that at Trimmu.

Reinforced concrete apparently was invented in France around 1868, and by the turn of the century Portland cement had been improved to the point where concrete could be used in sufficient masses for large dams. The first high dam built of Portland cement in India was the 214-foot Mettur Dam built on the Cauvery in the late 1920s and early 1930s. But the problems of developing cements that will set rapidly, not react with soil chemicals, and not generate more heat in hardening than can be dissipated by a cooling network of waterpipes embedded in the structure were not finally solved in a massive application until Boulder (Hoover) Dam was completed on the Colorado in 1936.[2] Both the Mettur and the Boulder dams

1. Buckley, *The Irrigation Works of India,* p. 110. For a long time it was believed that mortar had been used in the Grand Anicut, but when the British engineers remodeled it in 1830 they discovered that the stones had been set only in clay. The mortar used in the Sukkur Barrage, of course, was the best hydraulic cement available at the time.

2. Edward A. Ackerman and George O. G. Löf, *Technology in American Water Resource Development* (Washington, D.C., Resources for the Future, 1959), pp. 227–29; and John C. Page, "Dams," in *Technological Trends and*

provided analogies for the pre- and post-Partition designs of Bhakra. West Pakistan's Warsak and Rawal dams, both reinforced concrete structures though much lower than Bhakra, were completed before Bhakra. The post-Partition barrages in both countries (Harike, Nangal, Taunsa, Ghulam Mohammad, and Gudu) were also reinforced concrete structures.

Hand in hand with new materials had come new equipment. Even before the development of the internal combustion engine, steam power had been applied to tractors, steamrollers, and steam shovels. But as far as canal and barrage construction in the Indus Basin was concerned, manual and animal labor was generally so plentiful and cheap, and coal so distant and expensive, that steam powered equipment could not compete. Some steam driven excavation machinery was tried on the Lower Bari Doab Canal in the Triple Canals Project, but it proved a failure. But during the decade 1910–20, the gasoline or diesel powered farm tractor had largely replaced the heavy and inefficient steam tractors on American farms, while the British development of the first tanks in World War I produced a fruitful combination of an internal combustion engine with an endless link tread. Blades were soon attached to the front of these machines, and by the 1930s the modern bulldozers, scrapers, and graders

---

National Policy (Report of the Subcommittee on Technology to the National Resources Committee) (Washington, D.C., U.S. Government Printing Office, 1937), pp. 380–82. The rapid-hardening, low-heat, sulphate-resistant cements now employed in dam construction are either modified Portland-alumina cements or Portland-pozzolana cements containing fly ash or, where available, natural volcanic ash. The term "pozzolana" comes from the town of Pozzuoli near Naples which, like Pompeii, was partly obliterated in the eruption of Vesuvius in A.D. 79. Volcanic ash from Pozzuoli was long used in various mortars, but it was only in this century that its particular value was recognized for dam construction, where cracking and lowering of moisture resistance will result from the reaction of alkali in ordinary cement with sulphates in the soil or in the rock aggregate used to make concrete.

Norris Dam on the Clinch River, the first to be built entirely by the T.V.A., was also nearing completion in 1936. Henry F. Hart has pointed out that the Mettur Dam, built five year earlier, has many similarities to Norris and that taken together with the Krishnaraja Sagar hydroelectric station, completed in 1931 above Mettur on the Cauvery, anticipated many of the multipurpose features for which T.V.A. is usually cited as the prototype. (Henry C. Hart, *New India's Rivers* [Calcutta, Orient Longmans, 1956], pp. 38–39, 236–37, and 252.) As we have seen, however, T.V.A. had a great influence on the Bhakra and other post-Independence Indian projects.

were making their appearance. Dump trucks and self-loaders kept pace. As far as Indus Basin irrigation developments were concerned, A. M. R. Montagu notes that although the first machines employed (due to shortage of labor and time) on the S.V.P. were steam operated, "towards the end of this project we were using diesel-electric machines of vastly greater efficiency and greatly lowered unit costs."[3] In the Haveli Project, modern earthmoving equipment of all sorts was used with great success.

Thus, by the 1930s, man had machines to replace the shovel, the hoe, the basket, the wheelbarrow, and the donkey. The availability of modern earthmoving equipment wrought a revolution in dam building. True, hydraulic-fill dams, in which directed streams of water were used to place and compact earth (placer mining in reverse) had been built since 1868, but they were hazardous and limited in size and location. With the new equipment, it became possible to build an earth-fill or rock-fill dam almost anywhere that the equipment could be assembled and quarry or borrow pits located. The costs of such dams were a fraction of those of concrete structures, and the only limitations on size were the calculations of benefit-cost ratios. The first large-scale applications of the earth-fill and rock-fill dam techniques were in the Missouri Basin projects, although the first of these dams was in large measure a modern hydraulic-fill structure.

> At Fort Peck the four electrically operated dredges, each having a 28-inch discharge, place from 3½ to 4 million cubic yards of material each month at an average cost of approximately 25 cents per cubic yard. The cost of placing concrete in dams is approximately $4.75 per cubic yard. [These are 1937 estimates.]
>
> It would have been impracticable from an economical standpoint, and almost impossible from a physical standpoint to have erected these structures without the aid of modern machinery, due primarily to the inaccessibility of site and the large volume of water flow. Presenting a concrete example, Boulder Dam and the Great Pyramid have practically identical volumes. According to historians, 100,000 men labored 20 years in the con-

3. Personal communication, September 6, 1965.

struction of the pyramid, while 1,200 men in less than 2 years built Boulder Dam. The pyramid thus required 2,000,000 man-years of direct labor and the dam, 2,400.[4]

Again, a world war led to further improvements in the design and capacity of the equipment, influencing further developments in the Missouri Basin and in the Volga Basin of the Soviet Union. In the subcontinent, massive earth-fill dams made their appearance in the 1950s, in the Panchet Hill Dam of the Damodar Valley Project, the composite earth-fill and concrete Hirakud Dam, and the designs for the Mangla Dam of the IBP and the Pong Dam of the BBRP.

Thus, surface water engineering and construction methods may be said to have come of age and to have opened broad new vistas for storing and distributing runoff. But along with the new techniques came new problems. The very size of the reservoirs and of the main canals, link canals, and distributaries which earthmoving equipment rendered possible brought in their wake unheard-of losses in evaporation and seepage. So engineers and designers turned increasingly to the groundwater alternative, where nature provides the reservoir, where seepage may be an advantage, and where evaporation is inherently restricted or impossible.

Groundwater irrigation engineering had to await modern technology in two respects. First, the extent of the resource was not realized until deep drilling and other prospecting techniques were available. Second, until around 1937 the maximum lift of a pump was limited to about 25 feet, although 50 feet could be realized by installing the pump at the bottom of a shaft. Then the vertical turbine pump was introduced, making possible the tapping of groundwater to depths of 500 or 1,000 feet, and in 1948 the submersible pump, used previously in the petroleum industry, became commercially available for raising water from as deep as 5,000 feet if the value warranted the cost.[5]

Well irrigation is as old, if not older, than canal irrigation. Just as canals were no doubt suggested to man by the action of rivers in breaching their natural levees, so wells must have been suggested by springs and by the receding waters on floodplains. When the spring

4. Page, p. 381.
5. Ackerman and Löf, pp. 281–83.

went dry, or the flood level dropped, men began to dig for water, and in some areas of the arid zone well depths up to 200 feet have been found. But the limit to a dug well is usually less than 100 feet, and its construction and repair are arduous, dangerous tasks. So is raising water from the well. Early man soon devised the balanced beam method (known as the *lat* in northern India, *piccotah* in southern India, and *shaduf* in the Arabic-speaking lands) for shallow lifts: a pot or skin is slung from one end of a pole, the pole is balanced on a fulcrum, and by "pumping" the free end water can be raised from the well to the fields. But the height of lift is limited by the height of the fulcrum and the length of the pole, and the *lat* is seldom used where the depth to water is more than about 10 feet.

Man soon learned to use draft animals for water raising by placing the fulcrum, in the form of a pulley, at the top of an inclined plane (*mote* in the subcontinent), and driving the beasts up and down to lower and raise the bucket. But this technique did not significantly increase the depth attainable. The Persian wheel (*saqia* in Arabic) was a great advance, both allowing the use of animal power and greatly increasing the height of lift. Here an endless chain of pots or buckets is worked by a gear-and-shaft mechanism, translating the horizontal rotary effort of yoked beasts walking in an endless circle into a vertical rotation of the buckets which automatically spill, though usually with a considerable loss, into a trough leading to the fields. Using strong ropes (and later chains) and light pots (later empty kerosene cans) the Persian wheels in the subcontinent sometimes tap water as deep as 80 or 100 feet, though generally no more than 50 or 60 feet.[6]

But well irrigation, even with Persian wheels, is slow and costly

6. Around 1900, the Indian Irrigation Commission estimated that 79,200 Persian wheels, 57,600 *lats* or *piccotahs,* and 33,000 *doons* (oscillating troughs worked like *picottahs* but limited to a lift of 4 feet) were in use in British India, where 13 million acres were irrigated from wells, over half of them in Punjab and the United Provinces (i.e. close to the Western Himalayan foothills where water tables are high but rainfall inadequate, especially in winter). At this time, a total of 44 million acres were under irrigation in British India, 17 million from canals, 13 million from wells, 8 million from tanks (small reservoirs dug to conserve rainfall but often intersecting the water table), and 6 million from springs, *karezes* (lines of wells connected by a tunnel that both intersects the water table and acts as an infiltration gallery), and other sources. (Buckley, pp. 3–4.) The permanent wells in the Punjab irrigated an average of 12 acres apiece.

since the beasts require some supervision and much feed and cannot be used for other purposes while they are drawing water. Where perennial canals were introduced they quickly put many deep wells out of operation. But well irrigation continued in the foothill districts and floodplain areas with high water tables, and even in the perennial areas where the seepage from the canals had the beneficial effect of raising the water table and making some shallow wells more productive. In the nonperennial areas, the use of wells continues on a substantial basis to this day, but obviously is inferior for rabi irrigation when the water table drops as the rivers fall and infiltration from the canals ceases.

Although it is worth recalling that the reciprocating steam engine was originally developed *to pump water* out of British coal mines and was only subsequently applied to drive textile machinery and locomotives, this seminal invention of the Industrial Revolution was of little use for irrigation. The steam engine required coal as a fuel, and the installation was both too massive and too expensive to be applied to the pumping of water for agricultural use. It was only with the development of the internal combustion engine, and particularly of the diesel engine with its cheap fuel and easy maintenance, that small units could be designed for farm use. Where regions of irrigated agriculture coincided with regions of petroleum or natural gas extraction, as in Texas or southern California, several factors combined to produce rapid expansion of pumped well irrigation: power costs were low, oil and gas prospecting uncovered unsuspected bodies of groundwater to depths of hundreds or thousands of feet, and the technology developed for petroleum or natural gas could quickly be applied to water.

It is sometimes said that the modern science of groundwater utilization developed as an offshoot of petroleum engineering. This is not true. Certainly there was considerable interaction between them, and considerable areal coincidence, especially in the United States. But petroleum exploration probably owes as much to water development as the other way around. For example, rotary drilling methods (both "direct" and "reverse" circulation) which substituted a rotating bit for a percussion bit operated by a steam hammer, were used in water drilling before they were applied to petroleum.[7] But it is correct to

7. Ackerman and Löf, p. 272.

say that it took a more valuable resource than water, even in arid regions, to persuade men to probe deep enough to uncover the full dimensions of the groundwater reservoir and to develop the vertical turbine pumps with which to raise it to the surface.

By the 1930s, the costs of diesel engines and centrifugal vacuum pumps had been lowered sufficiently so that northern India began to be dotted with tubewells. Their incidence was largely limited to the "dry districts" where canal water was unavailable and where ground-water lay within 25 feet or so of the surface. At first only rich *zamindars* could afford them, although the Government soon stepped in (the famous United Provinces scheme of the 1930s will be discussed below) and although gradually some villages, especially in the Sikh areas, began to construct communal tubewells for domestic supplies and irrigation. A facilitating factor lay in the use of a single diesel engine for several purposes: it could be harnessed to a pump during the irrigation periods, then switched to drive a cotton gin, a sugarcane mill, or a flour mill after the crop was harvested. Just as the kerosene lamp (and the kerosene container) represented the first real impact of the fuel and power revolution on village life, the diesel engine represented the second. Soon the traveler along the Grand Trunk Road could recognize the more prosperous villages by the steady "pong, pong, pong" of the diesel exhaust (usually covered with an earthenware pot, which reverberates), and if he stopped to investigate the source of the sound, would find that it led him to the well or the mill.

After the Second World War, some of these villages began to grow quiet again. But the silence represented still another advance: the substitution of electric motors for diesel engines. Rural electrification came late to the Punjab. Local diesel or steam plants were established as early as 1910, but their power was meant only for the government services, cantonments, urban areas, or hill stations (Simla was one of the first towns to be electrified, in 1913).[8] Lahore and Amritsar had some electric power by 1929, and in 1933 the Mandi State hydroelectric scheme was inaugurated (see Map 3). Tapping the Uhl tributary of the Beas, the Jogindar Nagar powerhouse provided 48,000 kilowatts for distribution via Kangra, Pathankot, and Dhariwal to Amritsar and Lahore, and beyond to Ferozepore, Jaranwala,

8. *Hundred Years of P.W.D.*, p. 187.

and Lyallpur. Although Jogindar Nagar had a surplus capacity up to 1941 or 1942, the distribution was not extended to the rural areas. In 1938, the fall in the Upper Swat Canal was harnessed by the 9,600-kilowatt Malakand Hydroelectric Scheme with distribution to Mardan, Charsadda, Peshawar, and Nowshera, again only urban and cantonment areas. Aside from a few coal and diesel based thermal plants, these were the only electrical developments in the Indus Basin prior to Independence.[9] Cost of power, distribution, and appliances were still the inhibiting factors, retarding rural electrification and the substitution of electric motors for diesel engines to drive tubewells.

Tubewells in the Punjab

The use of tubewells by public agencies as distinct from private owners in the Punjab was not originally tied to irrigation. Its inception, rather, was linked to the needs for pure water supplies in the cities and at the railway stations (for both passengers and steam engines). The Centennial Publication, *Hundred Years of P.W.D.*, lists thirty-six tubewells installed in and around Lahore in the first twenty-five years of this century which are still in operation. Simultaneously, research on tubewell design, especially on the design of the "strainer" or "screen" which keeps sand and gravel out of the well, was being conducted at the central workshop at Amritsar. The first tubewells installed for any purpose directly connected with agriculture were the fifteen drilled near Amritsar between 1911 and 1917. Electric power was provided by harnessing a fall in the UBDC Main Branch. This experiment proved unsatisfactory as an antiwaterlogging measure and was abandoned in 1936. Smaller attempts at Gujranwala and Ferozepore were abandoned in 1930–31.[10]

The reasons for the failure of these early attempts in using tubewells to combat waterlogging are now evident, though they were not at the time. Basically, one cannot expect any significant effect from a small number of scattered, low-capacity (1 to 2 cusecs) tubewells. Infiltration from the outside will more than compensate for the amount of water pumped and negate any temporary lowering of the water table, especially as the capacity of the tubewells declines with age due to clogging of the strainers. These early tubewells, more-

9. Ibid., pp. 187–88.
10. Ibid., pp. 101–02.

over, were all shallow and all employed centrifugal pumps driven by diesel motors.

The influence of foreign experience with tubewell *irrigation*, however, was beginning to be felt in the Punjab. Between 1926 and 1930, the Agriculture Department had a Lift Irrigation Division to investigate possibilities and to design schemes. The Division, headed by an engineer borrowed from the Irrigation Branch of the Public Works Department, proposed six schemes, three of them in central Rechna Doab (where SCARP I was located thirty years later), and one each in Jhang, Gurdaspur, and Amritsar districts (see Map 4). But none of these was implemented.[11]

One can understand why the Punjab, and its Irrigation Branch in particular, was not particularly interested in tubewell irrigation. The province had the S.V.P. in hand, and was busy designing the Bhakra, Haveli, and Thal projects (see Chapter 4). Surface water technology, design, and construction methods were coming into their prime, and there was no foreseeable need for using groundwater, especially as only the top 25 to 50 feet of the aquifer could be tapped with the equipment then available, and no one knew what lay beneath. Nevertheless, around 1930 an example too close to be ignored presented itself. Under the leadership of Sir William Stamp, Chief Engineer, the Irrigation Branch of the United Provinces, where the possibilities of canal irrigation without storage seemed nearly exhausted, had begun installing tubewells the primary purpose of which was to increase irrigation supplies. To provide power for these tubewells, the U. P. Irrigation Branch remodeled the Ganges Canal between Hardwar and Allahabad, combining thirteen low falls into seven higher ones and providing, in conjunction with the Electricity Branch, turbogenerators at each of the new falls. A combined capacity of 19,900 kilowatts was installed over the period 1928–37, and this was supplemented by an equal capacity in thermal electric generation by the time of Partition. The steam generation was to supplement the hydroelectric, particularly during the months when the nonperennial Ganges Canal was closed. The U. P. tubewells were owned and managed by the province, and costs were recovered from the farmers just as were the costs of surface canal water. Between 1936 and 1946, the number of government-owned tubewells in the U. P. increased from 800 to 1,800, and each one served from 250 to 500 acres. But

11. Ibid., p. 102.

these were all centrifugal pumps, drawing water from relatively shallow depths, and fitted with 12-horsepower motors, providing no more than 2 cusecs from each well.[12] Their purpose was to provide additional irrigation supplies, not to lower water tables in the effort to reclaim waterlogged or salinized lands.

The success of the U. P. scheme, along with the delays encountered on the Bhakra and Thal projects (see Chapter 4), led to the appointment of A. M. R. Montagu as Officer on Special Duty to investigate the potential of tubewell irrigation in the Punjab.[13] From Montagu's work developed the first significant tubewell *irrigation* scheme in the Punjab, twenty wells installed on an experimental basis in the Karol area (near the Shalimar Gardens outside Lahore) in 1940. As each Karol well was bored, some of them to a depth of 350 feet, a careful record was kept of the type of formation encountered. The cores were analyzed with respect to sand, silt, and clay content. When the casing was installed, it was constructed so that the strainer sections would lie opposite the coarse and medium sand formations that would give the highest yields of water with the least danger of blockage. Brass strainer with .0016 inch slits, designed to exclude the sand, was used, and an average of 120 to 130 feet of strainer was inserted into each well, the rest of the casing consisting of "blind" pipe. The strainer diameter varied from 4 to 6 inches in the lower sections up to 10 inches above. Only centrifugal pumps were available, and these were set 7 to 10 feet below the water table and run by shafts from an electric motor at the surface. The initial capacity of each well was 1.5 cusecs, and the early performance was good enough to inspire the Rasul scheme which we shall discuss shortly. It is worth noting, however, that despite the proximity of the Karol scheme to the Ravi River, deterioration set in fairly early. Between 1947 and 1950, yields were already considered unsatisfactory, and by October 1960, twelve of the tubewells had either been abandoned, damaged, or replaced, three of them were yielding 20 per cent below the designed discharge, and the remaining five were yielding 50 per cent below design. Four wells deteriorated even after replacement of the strainers.[14]

12. Hart, *New India's Rivers*, pp. 240–42.
13. *Hundred Years of P.W.D.*, p. 102.
14. Nazir Ahmad, "Control of Water-Logging and Salinity by Tube-Well Pumping," *Pakistan Journal of Science, 14* (March 1962), p. 50.

Waterlogging

Previous to the Karol scheme, the Punjab Irrigation Department was more concerned with decreasing waterlogging than with increasing the supplies of water for irrigation. Waterlogging had been a problem associated with Punjab irrigation since the very beginning. Indeed, even before 1859 when the Western Jumna command (see Map 3) became part of the Punjab Province, the problem of waterlogging and salinity was evident. The *General Report on the Administration of the Punjab and its Dependencies for 1859–60* contains the following revealing passage on the Western Jumna Canal:

> Fiscally, nothing can be more satisfactory: unhappily there is another side to the picture. Unscientifically constructed, the canal bed is in many places above the level of the country and interferes with its drainage. Swamps are formed: the soil is deteriorated: worst of all, with the excess of water up comes from below a coating of salts, which has for several years gone on spreading, and has unquestionably not only injured the productive powers of the land, but impaired the physical condition of the people. The Lieutenant-Governor has reduced the land revenue wherever deterioration of the soil has been proved, and doubtless much relief has thus been afforded; but a permanent remedy will probably be found only in an extensive system of drainage, which Captain Trumbull is now devising.[15]

In January 1865, John Lawrence, then Governor-General and Viceroy of India, wrote from Fort William (Calcutta) to the Secretary of State in London to announce the dispatch by steamer of three boxes containing specimens of soil from *Reh* (i.e. waterlogged) lands on the Western Jumna Canal, and samples of canal and well water, and to request

> that measures may be taken for their careful analysis by an agricultural chemist, whose attention should be directed to the discussions that have taken place on the subject.

15. Government of India, *Administration Reports* (1859–60), *General Report on the Administration of the Punjab and its Dependencies for 1859–60* (Calcutta, Savielle & Cranenburgh, 1861), Section IV, "Public Works," Part II, "Canals," para. 93, p. 23.

The object in view is to determine, as far as may be practicable in this manner, whether the opinion which has been generally adopted in this country as to the origin of the salt in question seems to be borne out by the facts as ascertained from an analysis of the constituent elements of the soil.

If the efflorescence of the salt and its general determination to the surface of the soil are due to continued surface evaporation, and if the salts are supplied from the sub-soil itself, and are not introduced from the canal water, it may be anticipated that the analysis will show that the sub-soil contains the salts in a sensible proportion, a result which could not be attributed to the action of the canal.[16]

Unfortunately, we do not know the results of the tests or the conclusions drawn from them. In April 1865 the Government of India forwarded to London further papers received from the Government of Punjab on the *Reh* lands along the Western Jumna Canal, but action was postponed in view of plans to remodel and realign the canal in order to avoid the worst low-lying and waterlogged areas.[17] In 1867 the Government sanctioned the drainage of a portion of the lands on the right bank of the Delhi Branch of the Western Jumna Canal.[18] Eighty years later, A. M. R. Montagu commented:

The remedy was very soon recognised and applied. The entire alignment of the irrigation channels was re-designed and the natural drainages cleared between 1870 and 1880. It is on record that these measures resulted in lowering the water-table between the years 1892 and 1905 from 5 to 15 feet.

The costly lesson learnt on the Western Jumna Canal has never been forgotten and the fact that the water-table continues to rise in other irrigated areas in the Punjab, is an indication that the correct alignment of irrigation channels and the opening up of drainage are, by themselves, insufficient to cure water-

16. Government of India, Public Works Department, "Public Works Letter No. 4 of 1865 (Civil Works/Agricultural) to the Secretary of State for India," Fort William, dated 10 January 1865, in "India, Public Works Department, Letters Received, 1865" (London, India Office Library).

17. Ibid., "Public Works Letter No. 48," 12 April 1865.

18. Government of India, Public Works Department (Irrigation), "Public Works Letter No. 150 to the Secretary of State for India," dated 10 September 1867, in "India, Public Works Department, Letters Received, 1867" (London, India Office Library).

logging and solve the problem which is now [1946] so pronounced in the Chaj and Rechna doabs.

In the year 1908, serious complaints of waterlogging were
heard in the Lower Chenab Canal [inaugurated sixteen years
before, in 1892] area. The remedial measures suggested were:

        (a) restriction of supplies
        (b) excavation of drains
        (c) lining of canals
        (d) pumping from the subsoil.[19]

Restriction of supplies, of course, played havoc with the whole basis
of irrigation operations and agriculture, and had to be abandoned.
Little success was obtained with lining materials, although opening
up the natural drainages blocked by roads, railway embankments,
and the canals themselves helped in some areas. Yet Montagu indicates that as late as the early 1920s there was a

> violent division of opinion which existed amongst all officers
> whose attention had been directed to this problem. Even in the
> Irrigation Branch itself, officers were found who flatly denied
> the increase of the trouble. But the abnormal rains of 1925
> brought conviction to Government and led to the appointment
> of a Waterlogging Enquiry Committee. . . . This Committee
> initiated the invaluable statistical investigations and also ex-
> perimental work in connection both with waterlogging and with
> the growth of the areas affected by thur [salinity]. In 1928,
> the Waterlogging Enquiry Committee was extended and re-
> modelled under the title of a Waterlogging Board consisting of
> Financial Commissioner, Financial Secretary, Directors of Ag-
> riculture and Public Health and Chief Engineers. . . . In 1932,
> the Rural Sanitary Board was taken over by the Irrigation
> Branch which thus became responsible for all drainage and
> pumping works in the Province, exclusive of purely sanitary
> works.[20]

Thus one must conclude that although the Irrigation Department of
the Punjab was not much interested in the possibilities of expanding
irrigation with groundwater, they were well aware of the waterlogging
and salinity problems and of the possibilities of using tubewells to

19. A. M. R. Montagu, "Presidential Address," pp. xii-xiii.
20. Ibid., p. xiii.

combat the latter if not to provide the former. Montagu also comments on the establishment of the Irrigation Research Institute at Lahore in 1930 (an Irrigation Laboratory was set up in 1922) and on its success with leaching experiments (applying excess water to wash down the salts) where water tables were low, but not where they were high (leaching attempts compounded the problem). Montagu remarks that after forty years of intermittent attempts to solve the waterlogging problem in Punjab, the Chief Engineers were right back to the 1908 recommendations.[21]

Part of Montagu's chagrin was due to repeated postponements of the Rasul scheme, which would *combine tubewell irrigation with tubewell drainage.* The scheme was originally suggested as early as 1927 by H. W. Nicholson (of the Nicholson-Trench Committee). Nicholson had visited the United States and inspected antiwaterlogging measures there. He saw some promise in canal linings, but decided it would take too long and cost too much to employ them in the Punjab except on new projects (e.g. Haveli and Thal). Therefore he recommended installing some 1,700 tubewells of 1-cusec capacity apiece in the waterlogged areas of Rechna and Chaj doabs. To operate these tubewells, Nicholson proposed installing a hydroelectric plant utilizing the 80-foot difference in elevation between the UJC where it comes closest to the LJC in the Pabbi Hills near Rasul. The tubewells would be installed along the LJC, UCC, and LCC canals and some of their branches. Had the scheme been carried out in 1930, as proposed, it would have cost Rs 26 million.[22]

But the Rasul scheme was repeatedly postponed, first because of a jurisdictional dispute over who would supply the power;[23] second because other measures, including open drains,[24] small amounts of

21. Ibid., p. xiv.
22. Ibid., p. xv.
23. The Chief Engineer of the Electricity Department wanted to supply the Rasul tubewells from the Mandi (Jogindar Nagar) scheme because he felt there would be surplus capacity available from Mandi for a number of years (experience up to World War II demonstrated that he was right). By incorporating the Rasul scheme, he could increase his demand-load and thus make possible a more economic operation. In the event, Jogindar Nagar was both overburdened and awarded to India before the Rasul scheme got under way.
24. Between 1933 and 1947, 2,263 miles of drains were constructed in the Punjab. (Mian Muzaffar Ahmad, "A Study of Waterlogging & Thur Problems of West Pakistan" [Lahore, Superintendent, Government Printing, 1958], p. 1.)

pumping, and periodical canal closures, were showing some initial success; and third because of the financial stringencies of the Depression period. Then came World War II, and by the time the Rasul scheme was finally sanctioned in 1944, the estimated cost had risen to Rs 80 million.[25]

Work was actually begun on the Rasul power plant and on some of the tubewells in 1945. The partition chaos brought a cessation of activity in 1947, and it was not until July 1952 that the power plant was commissioned. An intake channel of 4,000-cusec capacity was built from the UJC to a settling and regulating basin above the penstocks. But even by running the upper reach of the UJC, between Mangla headworks and Rasul, above its capacity of 9,500 cusecs, sufficient water could not be provided for more than two 5,500 kw turbogenerators. (Provision had been made for adding a third.) Even then, to keep the power plant in constant operation, not only for the tubewells but for other demands placed upon it in the early post-Partition years (Mandi Hydroelectric scheme supplies to Pakistan ceased in April 1948), the canal had to be run without closure for maintenance or repairs from July 1952 to July 11 1960, when extraordinary rains of 21 inches in two days produced a flood overtopping the settling basin and nearly wrecking the power plant.[26]

Nor did the Rasul tubewells function successfully, but here the reasons were quite different and not early understood. One reason lay in the location of many of the 495 wells installed in the Chaj Doab at a distance of only 65 feet from the LJC and its branches (see Map 8a). Such wells were intended to recover canal seepage and return it directly to the canal. But because they were so close to the canal bank, they apparently served mainly to accelerate seepage and thus recycled the water with no appreciable lowering of the adjacent water table. The distance from one well to the next was also too short for optimum performance, although it could be argued conversely that had there been even more of them they would have "dominated the drainage" and produced the desired lowering of water

25. Montagu, p. xv.
26. Flood waters rose inside the powerhouse and breaches occurred in both the UJC and LJC canal banks. But the worst effect was that the coarse sands brought down through the penstocks ruined the blades of one turbine, which had to be replaced, and severely damaged those of the other. (Visit of January 24, 1964, and discussions with the superintending engineers.)

459

tables. At any rate, the "Rasul" approach to the waterlogging problem in the Chaj Doab, though greater in scope than anything that preceded it, must be reckoned a failure, especially along the Northern Branch of the LJC near Sargodha where of the 200 wells installed, 130 were located within 65 feet of the canal bank. Of the 200, only 82 were working by 1961, almost all of these being the ones placed 600 feet from the canal. Of the 495 "Rasul" tubewells in the Chaj Doab, 313 were working in 1961, but only 36 were still yielding their designed discharge of 2 cusecs; 109 were yielding 30 per cent below design, and 95 were yielding 10 per cent below design.[27]

Most of the 762 "Rasul" tubewells installed in the Rechna Doab were set back 600 feet from the canals. The Irrigation Research Institute reported on 624 "Rasul" tubewells in the Rechna Doab in 1961 and indicated that 489 (including seventeen replacements) were still in operation, although 185 were giving yields of 40 to 50 per cent below design and another 79 of 20 per cent below design. The "Rasul" wells in Rechna apparently were far enough from the canals to avoid accelerating seepage, but they were too close to each other (installed in groups of three or five wells with only 500 feet between wells and 2,000 feet between groups) and thus interfered with each other. Like the wells in the Karol pilot project, most of the "Rasul" wells were fitted with a total of around 140 feet of brass strainer, set opposite the medium and coarse sand formations, the rest of the lining consisting of blind iron pipe. Some of the wells were as deep as 400 or 450 feet, but they employed only centrifugal pumps, with lift capacities of about 45 feet, set deep in pits and connected to a 15- or 20-horsepower motor by shafts. All "Rasul" wells had an initial capacity of 2 cusecs. As an experiment, 214 of the "Rasul" wells used wooden instead of brass strainers. The wooden strainers were made of sheesham, 8 or 10 inches in diameter, and these wells had no blind sections.[28]

As "Rasul" tubewells in the Rechna Doab failed, or declined in yield to the point where they had to be replaced, some of the strainers were pulled for examination. It then became apparent that the main cause of declining yields was the blockage of the strainer. It is now understood that such blockage can result from either or both of two basic causes. If the slits in the strainers are very fine (and the brass

27. Nazir Ahmad, "Control," pp. 54–57.
28. Ibid., pp. 53–59.

strainers in the Rasul scheme had slits ranging from .0012 to .0018 inch, as compared with .0016 inch in the Karol wells) and if the strainers are not surrounded with a carefully graded gravel pack, sands will be carried to the strainer until they block the slits and the interstices in the formation material. This is purely a physical problem, and can be overcome by careful design of slit size and by providing a gravel pack, or "shroud," surrounding each strainer. The newer technique of "developing" a tubewell by high-pressure surging of water back and forth through the strainer and shroud until the formation material is redistributed according to size also contributes to initial efficiency and longevity, and can often be employed to reactivate a tubewell that has declined in yield due to physical blockage of the strainer.

Groundwater technicians have also come to understand more about the process of chemical blockage known as "incrustation." It has long been known that deposits of carbonates build up on well strainers. The usual explanation given for this phenomenon is that the deposition occurs at the slits where the pressure suddenly drops, allowing most of the dissolved carbon dioxide to escape. As long as the groundwater contains a reasonable amount of carbon dioxide, and therefore of weak carbonic acid $(CO_2 + H_2O > H_2CO_3)$, the carbonates remain dissolved. But when the carbon dioxide suddenly escapes at the screen, due to the decrease in pressure as the water enters the well, the solubility of the carbonates immediately falls, and they are precipitated out just as they are when water is evaporated in a steam boiler or teapot.

But this simple theory has been challenged in recent years. It has been pointed out that it would apply only when the carbon dioxide concentration is very close to saturation, and when the change in pressure ("loss of head") at the screen is considerable. Neither of these conditions seems to apply in the Punjab. Furthermore, analysts of the Rasul scheme pointed to the fact that incrustation generally was greatest on the wells that had stood idle for a number of years before power could be brought to them. Due to the early difficulties with the Rasul power plant and the other demands placed upon it, as well as to shortage of materials for the transmission system, only 36 "Rasul" tubewells were energized in 1946; all the rest had to wait until 1954, although most of them had been drilled and cased by 1950.

Furthermore, incrustation was notably less in the wells fitted with wooden strainers. These considerations pointed to another cause, which by 1964 seemed to have been identified as the action of sulphate-reducing bacteria present in the groundwater or introduced in drilling the wells. Incrustation due to bacterial action is a well-established phenomenon in the petroleum industry. It would account for the rapid deterioration of wells in the Punjab, and especially for the high mortality of wells that were not energized immediately in the Rasul Project or in the later SCARP I. Bacterial incrustation, too, can be overcome by proper selection of screen materials or, if not too expensive, by treating affected wells with acids to dissolve the crust, providing that the strainer material can withstand the treatment. More will be said of this later, for it represents one of the most critical factors affecting tubewell longevity, and hence amortization of groundwater projects, in the Indus Basin.[29]

Before proceeding to a discussion of SCARP I, it should be mentioned that the Irrigation Department also began work on two additional reclamation-irrigation projects in the Rechna Doab in the late 1950s: the Pindi Bhattian scheme with twenty-one tubewells begun in 1958 and energized in 1959, and the Chichoki-Mallian scheme with only eleven tubewells, begun in 1957 and energized in 1960 (see Map 8a). The latter is of interest because it was the first *irrigation*

29. Much of the preceding analysis of the technological problems of tubewells is based on conversations and correspondence with David W. Greenman, a geologist and groundwater hydrologist presently with the firm of Tipton and Kalmbach and formerly chief of the USGS team (U.S.A.I.D., Engineering Division, Water Resources Branch), Lahore. In both capacities, Mr. Greenman has been intimately associated with the evolution of groundwater planning and operations in WAPDA's Groundwater and Reclamation Division and in WASID. Mr. Greenman has also contributed the benefit of his experience to the historical account of the groundwater programs that follows, but as the text makes clear, this is one aspect of recent engineering and policy development in West Pakistan that is subject to many differing interpretations. All opinions expressed, unless otherwise attributed, are those of the author, including some that would be disputed by Mr. Greenman, and others that would be disputed by other highly competent persons associated with the groundwater program.

In commenting on the role of the sulphate-reducing bacteria in incrustation, Mr. Greenman noted that their primary function is "as depolarizing agents, thus sustaining the activity of corrosion cells that occur on the steel. The corrosion products, in turn, have 5 to 30 times the volume of the steel which accounts for the sealing of the slots. Also, the corrosion mechanism apparently promotes deposition of iron and calcium carbonates from solution." (Personal communication, October 14, 1965.)

scheme to employ deep-lift turbine pumps. Both schemes were incorporated into SCARP I, as were two Food and Agriculture Organization–Irrigation Department schemes, Chuharkana and Jaranwala, which are described below.

The Modern, Massive Approach in West Pakistan

Like the surface water program of the IBP, the groundwater program in West Pakistan has been greatly influenced by foreign technical and financial assistance. In the late 1940s, Pakistan (which was admitted to United Nations membership on September 30, 1947) requested and received technical assistance from the United Nations Food and Agriculture Organization (the F.A.O.). Thus it was the Central Ministry of Agriculture that first brought foreign technical assistance to bear on the waterlogging and salinity problem in the Indus Basin, although the provincial Irrigation Department and (after its establishment in 1952) the Soil Reclamation Board quickly came into the picture. After several years of investigation, the F.A.O. team recommended a trial project that would combine reclamation and irrigation through the use of tubewells. The pilot project area selected was near Chuharkana in the salinized portion of the central Rechna Doab (just west of Sheikhupura under command of the Upper Gugera Branch, LCC). Twenty-four wells, fitted with brass strainers and with 2-cusec centrifugal pumps, were installed by the Irrigation Department over a gross area of 11,000 acres and went into operation in 1953–54. Like the Rasul-scheme wells, those at Chuharkana were not provided with suitable gravel packs, nor were they "developed" by surging. By 1961, of the twenty-four Chuharkana wells, three were yielding only 50 per cent of capacity, and six more were down by 30 per cent.[30] By October 1962, after eight years of operation, the *net* decline in the fluctuating water table amounted to only 3 inches,[31] indicating that the scale of approach—including

30. Nazir Ahmad, "Control," p. 58.
31. White House–Department of Interior Panel on Waterlogging and Salinity in West Pakistan, *Report on Land and Water Development in the Indus Plain* (Washington, D.C., The White House, January 1964), p. 334, Table 7.3. This is the final version of the report prepared by the panel headed by Dr. Roger Revelle, and will henceforth be cited as "Revelle II." The preliminary version, which will be cited as "Revelle I," has the following official designation: Presi-

463

the number and capacity of tubewells and the size of the area—was too small.

In 1957–58 F.A.O. sponsored another pilot project near Jaranwala, midway between Sheikhupura and Lyallpur in the central Rechna Doab. Here, of the forty-one 2-cusec wells in operation, only twenty-three were working at capacity by November 1961.[32] The Jaranwala scheme was taken over into SCARP I (as were Chuharkana and the Irrigation Department's Pindi Bhattian and Chichoki Mallian reclamation schemes) and expanded to 91,000 acres with 145 tubewells.[33]

It was also at the instigation of the Central Ministry of Agriculture that the Government of Pakistan in 1954, through the Colombo Plan Organization (of which Pakistan had become a charter member in 1951), requested the Government of Canada to undertake an aerial photo reconnaissance and mapping survey of West Pakistan. This survey, which was carried out by the Canadian Department of Mines and Technical Surveys with the contracted services of the Canadian affiliate of Hunting Technical Services, Ltd., resulted among other things in the preparation of maps (on a scale of 1:253,440, or 4 miles to the inch) of landforms, soils, and land use in the Indus Plains, and a textual commentary on them, published in 1958.[34] Although circulation of these maps was restricted, for security reasons, they became available for use within Pakistan by qualified personnel, including foreign technical assistants and advisers such as the F.A.O. teams which continued to work with the Central Ministry of Agriculture and the Soil Conservation Project of West Pakistan in the preparation of an overall soils survey, classification, and conservation program.

The Colombo Survey maps and report have also been of considerable value to WAPDA and its consultants in project and regional

dent's Science Advisory Committee, *White House–Interior Panel on Waterlogging and Salinity in West Pakistan, First Draft* (Washington, D.C., The White House, September 1962).

32. Nazir Ahmad, "Control," p. 58.

33. Revelle II, p. 334, Table 7.3.

34. Canada, Department of Mines and Technical Surveys, maps on landforms, land use, and soils of West Pakistan, published by the Government of Canada for the Government of Pakistan (Ottawa, 1956); *Landforms, Soils and Land Use of the Indus Plains, West Pakistan*, published for the Government of Pakistan by the Government of Canada, a Colombo Plan Cooperative Project (Ottawa, February 1958).

planning. But perhaps the outstanding contribution of this survey was that it provided a "scientific" and external confirmation of what the Irrigation Department's Soil Reclamation Board and Ground Water Development Organization (see page 301, fn. 22, and below) had been saying for some time: that the magnitude of the reclamation problem in the Indus Plains was enormous, and that only a massive attack upon it had any chance of success. Actually, due to the inherent limitations on aerial photographic interpretation, the estimates of the Colombo Survey—that the Indus Plains, with a total area of about 51 million acres in West Pakistan, contained 11 million acres that were poorly drained or waterlogged and another 16 million acres affected by salinity (of which 5 million were severely salinized)— were much too high, although similar to previous estimates by the Soil Reclamation Board. They were reduced by more than half in the preliminary version of the White House–Interior Panel Report on Waterlogging and Salinity in West Pakistan which was transmitted by President Kennedy to President Ayub in September 1962. But coming when they did, and directed as they were to the Central Government of Pakistan, they served to persuade even the most skeptical that A. M. R. Montagu was right when he said, back in 1946, "Heroic measures are essential if the Punjab is not to be destroyed [by waterlogging and salinity]."[35]

The Colombo Survey–Soil Reclamation Board estimates were also embodied in WAPDA's May 1961, "Program for Waterlogging and Salinity Control in the Irrigated Areas of West Pakistan." But the credit for that program, and for its first embodiment in a massive project area, the Salinity Control and Reclamation Project in Central Rechna (which came to be known at SCARP I), can more correctly be given to two small groups of dedicated men whose cooperative efforts since 1954 represent one of the finest examples of the counterpart approach in the U. S. Point Four program. We have mentioned above that one of the early American technical assistance projects in Pakistan consisted of furnishing U. S. Geological Survey (USGS henceforth) experts to assist the Punjab Irrigation Department in its survey and analysis of waterlogged and saline areas. Under the technical assistance agreement, the United States supplied technicians and equipment, and Pakistan furnished local facilities

35. Montagu, p. xiv.

465

and a team of counterpart engineers, soil scientists, laboratory tech-nicians, and field assistants. The organizational arrangements placed the American technicians under the United States technical operations mission (successively the Foreign Operations Administration, the International Cooperation Administration, and the Agency for International Development) and the Pakistanis under the Ground Water Development Organization (GWDO henceforth) of the Irrigation Department, which was established for this purpose in 1954.

The initial investigations were confined to three of the Punjab doabs, Rechna, Chaj, and Thal. Following the administrative integration of October 1955, GWDO extended its operations to parts of Bahalwalpur and even into Khairpur, but by 1959 WAPDA had hired Hunting Technical Services, and later Sir M. MacDonald and Partners in cooperation with Hunting, for investigations in Khairpur and Sind. Thus, when GWDO was transferred to WAPDA in 1960 (becoming WASID), its operations were confined to the "Northern Zone" (Punjab, Bahawalpur) of the Indus Plains above Kashmor, and the British consultants took over investigations in the "Southern Zone" (Khairpur and Sind).

The USGS team and the Irrigation Department's GWDO did on and below the ground what the Colombo Survey had attempted to do from the air. Detailed soil surveying in the field is perhaps the most arduous task in agronomic-irrigation engineering. It is one thing to sit in an office, preferably air-conditioned, in Lahore and to lay out irrigation and reclamation projects on generalized land-form and soils maps. It is another thing to travel around the doabs, or the deserts of Thal and Bahawalpur, in summer (i.e. April to June, before the monsoon arrives) with temperatures of 110 or 120 degrees Fahrenheit, taking soil samples with augurs or digging pits to measure water infiltration rates. Even the laboratory analysis of hundreds of soil and water samples is a tedious, repetitive operation, particularly when the standards set by the Pakistani supervisors and American advisers are as tough as any in the world. Small wonder that GWDO and WASID had the highest turnover rates for lower echelon employees of any branches of the Irrigation Department or WAPDA. But this is exactly the sort of work that must be done *before* reclamation and development operations are started. This is exactly what was not done in the Helmand Valley Project or the

Thal Project, and what India has not yet done in the Rajasthan Project (see Chapter 8).

As early as 1956, the GWDO director, Sayyid Hamid, and the USGS team leader, George La Rocque, had come to the conclusion that such efforts as the Rasul scheme were bound to fail partly because the techniques were faulty (no gravel packs and no "development" of the wells) but mainly because the number and capacity of the wells was insufficient. In other words, quite aside from the magnitude of the reclamation problem in relation to West Pakistan's irrigated area, there were technical reasons for a massive approach: scale was essential to success; small, isolated schemes with low-capacity, shallow tubewells could never "dominate the drainage"; and in the economic sense there was a minimum level of operations below which no returns could be expected. At that stage, however, neither the provincial nor the central governments, nor the I.C.A., could be persuaded of the necessity for a massive attack, and Sayyid Hamid found himself at odds with many of his seniors in the Irrigation Department, which continued with such piecemeal, small-scale schemes as Pindi-Bhattian, Chichoki Mallian, Chuharkana, and Jaranwala. Quite possible, too, I.C.A. felt that there was no agency in West Pakistan capable of making the coordinated effort, free from traditional red tape, necessary to achieve a breakthrough in reclamation.

With the inception of WAPDA in 1958, things began to change. It will be recalled that WAPDA's enabling act specifically entrusted the Authority with "the prevention of waterlogging and salinity, and reclamation of waterlogged and saline lands." By September 1958, Sayyid Hamid had persuaded Ghulam Faruque (who became WAPDA's second chairman, and who is now Central Minister of Commerce) that a massive assault was the only hope, and had enlisted his enthusiastic support. Meanwhile, I.C.A. had been impressed with the potential of the WAPDA organization and the arguments of the USGS team. Furthermore, the Development Loan Fund (D.L.F.), with its less rigid cost-benefit and repayment criteria, had come into being. Under these circumstances, the final SCARP I scheme was designed between September 1958 and January 1959, submitted to the D.L.F. in February, and a loan of $15.2 million approved almost immediately.

467

SCARP I was entrusted to WAPDA as one of its first projects on March 1, 1959, "in anticipation of sanction" by the Government of West Pakistan, which was forthcoming in April. WAPDA proceeded to hire the American firm of Harold T. Smith, Inc., which installed 1,074 tubewells in SCARP I between January 1960 and July 1961. WAPDA itself installed another 722 tubewells using equipment supplied by Australia under the Colombo Plan. And 200-odd wells were taken over from the various Irrigation Department schemes in Central Rechna. Thus, SCARP I embodies nearly 2,000 tubewells, of which over half were installed in eighteen months and a total of 1,796 within a three-year period. As in the Rasul scheme, however, SCARP I encountered delays in electrification, and some wells stood idle for up to two years before power could be brought to them over nearly 1,500 miles of new transmission lines. But by March 1963, when the scheme was formally dedicated, all of the wells drilled into fresh groundwater were in operation (about 100 hit saline groundwater and were not activated).[36]

> The project as constructed covers an area of 1.2 million acres in the central part of Rechna Doab. This area originally comprised some of the best canal colony lands [LCC command in the Gujranwala, Sheikhupura, and Lyallpur districts; see Map 8a] but by 1958 about 15 per cent of the area had completely gone out of production and another 20 per cent was in varying degrees of deterioration because of salinization. The groundwater was within 3 to 6 feet from the land surface in most of the area, and the incidence of malaria was one of the highest in the country.[37]

In all, the new tubewells and the electrification of SCARP I cost Rs 166 million, or about $35 million, or $30 per acre. After the first year of operation, 38,000 acres had been restored to cultivation, cropping intensities had been raised as much as 40 per cent in some areas, the value of crops produced had increased by about 20 per cent, and water tables had been lowered up to 4 feet in some areas.[38]

36. WAPDA *Inauguration Souvenir, Central Rechna Project*, March 29, 1963, p. 3. Harza Report, p. II–12.
37. WAPDA *Inauguration Souvenir, Central Rechna Project*, p. 3.
38. Harza Report, p. II–12.

At full development, after five years, WAPDA estimated that the annual increase in food production in SCARP I would reach 500,000 tons and that the annual increase in income per acre would be Rs 130, or $29, even after subtracting water charges and the additional farm improvement costs incurred by the farmers.[39] SCARP I has made available to its farmers more than as much groundwater as they receive from the surface water supplies of the LCC.

So one might conclude that all of the problems of irrigation, waterlogging, and salinity in the Indus Plains are now on the verge of solution. Unfortunately, the problem is not quite that simple. SCARP I does represent a technological, and probably an economic, breakthrough. By employing vertical turbine pumps, with capacities of up to 5 cusecs apiece, and by drawing water from depths of 30 to 70 feet (in wells 225 to 300 feet deep), and especially by concentrating some 2,000 such tubewells in an area of 1.2 million acres, WAPDA has demonstrated that the secret of success in reclamation lies in a massive application of modern tubewell technology over an area sufficiently large that the tubewells neither interfere with one another nor draw water directly out of the canals.[40]

39. WAPDA *Inauguration Souvenir, Central Rechna Project*, p. 3.
40. For the final version of its report, the Revelle Panel was able to analyze the effects of tubewell operations in SCARP I on the basis of the performance of 1,727 of the wells in the irrigation year 1961–62. Although the report pointed out that one year's data may not be representative of long-run conditions, the panel felt that it certainly bore out the computer analysis made in conjunction with its preliminary report, which indicated that large fields would be more successful than smaller areas in which excessive lateral infiltration occurs. With respect to the use of larger capacity deep-lift wells fited with 3- to 5-cusec turbine pumps, the analysis was less conclusive. The older fields, inherited from the Irrigation Department-F.A.O. programs, were analyzed as "Group I" tubewells. Two of these fields were very small (Chuharkana had 24 wells and Chichoki Mallian only 11) although they were fitted with deep-lift turbine pumps. Chuharkana showed a net reduction in water table of only .25 feet; Chichoki Mallian of .80 feet. The Pindi Bhattian field with 21 centrifugal pumps of 2-cusec capacity showed a reduction of 2.75 feet. But the Jaranwala field, where 22 of the wells were Irrigation Department-F.A.O. wells fitted with 2-cusec centrifugal pumps and 123 wells were WAPDA wells installed since 1959 and fitted with deep-lift turbine pumps, showed a reduction in the water table of only .60 feet in 1961–62 as compared to 1.5 feet in each of the two preceding years (Revelle II, pp. 317, 334, and Table 7.3).
The "Group II" tubewells, 1,014 wells installed by the Smith Company and WAPDA after 1959, fitted with 3- to 5-cusec capacity deep-lift turbine pumps and in operation from 1961, showed reductions in the water table ranging from

On the other hand, the cost of the SCARP I wells and pumps is high: about $2,500 for the motor and turbine pump as compared to $700 for a motor and 2-cusec centrifugal pump; and about $6 per foot for the 10-inch diameter mild (low carbon) steel casing of the well itself, thus amounting to from $1,200 to $1,400 per well plus another $360 to $840 for the 30 to 70 feet of the well which must be provided with 14- or 16-inch diameter pipe to house the pump and bowl assembly; to which must be added the costs of drilling and of inserting the gravel pack or "shroud." Thus, the average cost of a SCARP I tubewell, excluding electrification, which has to be provided regardless of the design of the pump and casing, amounted to about $11,000 as compared to the $6,000 or so average cost of a "Rasul" tubewell with a brass strainer (at $16 per foot for the 10-inch diameter pipe) or the $2,500 to $3,000 cost of the ½- to 1 cusec well fitted with a centrifugal pump installed by some private landowners in the Punjab.[41]

We have noted in Chapter 8 that the high relative cost of WAPDA's large-capacity, turbine-pump, deep-lift, properly shrouded tubewells has brought criticism from the Irrigation Research Institute, notably from Dr. Nazir Ahmad, the Institute's physicist, who advocates the use of multiple-bore shallow wells fitted with centrifugal pumps and cheap strainers that can be replaced when they become blocked. Marshaling data from the Karol, Rasul, and other schemes, Dr. Nazir maintains that early tubewell obsolescence is a fact of life that must be lived with in the Indus Plains. He suggests that reclamation and groundwater irrigation planning be based on

---

2.48 to 5.06 feet and averaging 3.72 feet for the first year of operation. The period of operation of the "Group III" tubewells, which were installed and energized in 1962, was too short for any conclusions to be drawn. However, the panel pointed out that the rate of decline of the water table in the Group II areas was nearly three times that in the Group I areas, indicating a far more effective operation. (Ibid., p. 318.) The panel also stated, "A matter of concern is the fact that the yield of tubewells in the Chuharkana Unit has decreased 26 percent in eight years, while wells in the Pindi Bhattian Unit lost 28 percent of their capacity in three years. Presumably these losses resulted from well designs and construction which did not adequately provide for deposition, incrustation, and corrosion occurring in and around the tubewell screens." (Ibid., pp. 317–18.)

41. Nazir Ahmad, "Exploitation of Ground Water: A Review of Technique Developed in Pakistan," *Engineering News,* 7 (March 1962), p. 6; and WAPDA *Inauguration Souvenir, Central Rechna Project,* p. 4.

the expectation that most tubewells will become hopelessly blocked or incrusted within fifteen or twenty years, depending upon the quality of the subsoil water in the area where they are sunk. Yet they can still be amortized within this period providing that initial costs are held to a minimum. To do this, Dr. Nazir suggests that only shallow tubewells, fitted with centrifugal pumps (which are now being manufactured in Pakistan) be used. The capacity of such wells can be increased, despite their shallow depth, if multiple bores are provided, i.e. if a single centrifugal pump of, say, 3-cusec capacity is connected to three separate bores. These can be worked simultaneously, in which case the suction will be distributed and the tendency to pump fine material reduced, or alternately, concentrating on each bore in turn. Dr. Nazir has tested such multiple-bore tubewells both near Lahore and in the Lower Indus.[42]

To further reduce initial costs, and thereby offset the short life expectancy, Dr. Nazir suggests using coir string strainers, which cost between $1 and $3 per foot. The coir strainer is made by wrapping string tightly around a cage made of iron bars, or even around wood or bamboo strips appropriately supported. The fiber is unaffected by highly saline water, and thus, although the initial opening is much greater than that of a mild steel strainer, it will not be increased by corrosion. On the other hand, even the coir strainers are eventually affected by blockage, and must be replaced, but Dr. Nazir suggested that in a multiple-bore tubewell a new well could be sunk as an old one became blocked, and the new bores could be staggered in time and location so as to keep the central pump, and its associated local distribution system, operating without interruption.

Although Dr. Nazir's suggestions were warmly greeted by chauvinistic members of the Provincial Assembly who objected to spending so much on foreign materials and services, as well as by large landowners who could install their own tubewells and who objected to the economic leveling inherent in WAPDA's schemes, they seem to have little technical validity. While West Pakistan's Minister of Food, Agriculture, Irrigation and Power and WAPDA's Chairman and members were busy defending the SCARP projects and Author-

42. Nazir Ahmad, "Exploitation," p. 43.

ity policies,[43] WAPDA's talented Ground Water and Reclamation Division (formed in 1960 and placed, most fittingly, under the direction of Sayyid Hamid) and WASID were collecting data more convincing than Dr. Nazir's to demonstrate that the massive approach is not only technically sound but far more economical in the long run. Aside from the inherent inability of small-capacity, shallow wells to "dominate the drainage" and the "mine" water by pumping from depth in excess of recharge, the justification of the SCARP type of tubewell lies in its greater efficiency, lower consumption of power per cusec, and longevity.

Of these considerations, longevity is most critical from the economic standpoint. Dr. Nazir's estimates are based on a life of fifteen or twenty years for each bore, but WAPDA's investigations of private wells in the Rechna Doab indicated that their average life was less than five years! At times WAPDA has used a figure of only fifteen years for its own wells, but this was apparently merely a conservative bookkeeping device designed to meet the A.I.D.-Development Loan Fund requirement that SCARP I be amortized over a fifteen-year period. For SCARP III, in the Lower Thal, much of which is being underwritten by West German aid, a figure of forty years was adopted for the irrigation tubewells and a life of twenty years for the pumps, motors, controls, and drainage tubewells.[44]

It is true that in late 1963 and early 1964 there was an alarming incidence of rapid tubewell deterioration in some of the areas of SCARP I as well as in some of the pilot projects (e.g. the Mona area) incorporated into SCARP II in the Chaj Doab. At WASID's Mogulpura Laboratory, outside Lahore, records are kept of all the tubewells installed by WAPDA. Green symbols indicate wells functioning at or near designed capacity; yellow is used for those showing some deterioration; and red indicates wells that have ceased to function. In September 1963 there were only a dozen red symbols

43. See Chap. 8, p. 355; similar criticisms were of course directed at T.V.A. when it began selling power at cheap rates to consumers' cooperatives.

44. Tipton and Kalmbach, Inc., *Feasibility Report on Salintiy Control and Reclamation Project No. 3, Lower Thal Doab, West Pakistan*, prepared by Tipton and Kalmbach, Inc., and the Projects Planning and Preparation Circle of the Ground Water and Reclamation Division, WAPDA (Lahore, WAPDA, April 1963), p. 50, Table 21.

on the charts. By the late spring of 1964, the number had increased to over fifty, and WAPDA's reclamation (and regional) consultants for the Northern Zone (Tipton and Kalmbach) found it necessary to advise that operations in SCARP II be suspended until the trouble could be diagnosed.

Several of the deteriorated wells were pulled, analyses were made, and consultations with American specialists took place both in Lahore and in the United States. Examination of the pulled well screens showed that severe incrustation and corrosion had either blacked the strainer slits or else enlarged them to the point where, despite the gravel packs or shrouds enclosing the strainers, they were passing sands that damaged the pumps and ultimately blocked the well. It appeared that several forces were at work. Corrosion of the mild (low carbon) steel by saline water was one cause which could be corrected by employing brass, stainless steel, plastic, or fiber-glass strainers.

A more serious cause, however, appeared to be the incrustation of the strainers resulting primarily from the action of the sulphate-reducing bacteria previously mentioned. In order to eliminate this problem, it would be necessary to sterilize the wells by acid treatment, and this in turn means that the strainer material must be acid-resistant: stainless steel, plastic, or fiber glass. The most promising of these appears to be fiber glass, the material advocated by Tipton and Kalmbach and finally adopted by WAPDA. Whereas the cost of a stainless-steel strainer is around $32 per foot, as compared to $6 per foot for mild steel, the cost of fiber-glass screen has fallen rapidly as more manufacturers have come into the field. Contractors have also acquired more experience in installing fiber-glass wells, and now find it easier to handle than steel. The total cost of material and installation may well turn out to be lower than that of mild steel in the very near future. So, at the time of writing, it seems likely that the principal technological threat to the SCARPs has disappeared.

At any rate, by the end of 1964 the incidence of seriously deteriorated wells *from all causes* in SCARP I had fallen off, and by mid 1965 it appeared that no more than 100 wells, or 5 per cent of the total, would have to be written off or replaced. As with any comparable enterprise, representing a pioneer approach, one can expect that most of the defects would show up in the early stages.

In comparison with municipal tubewell fields in the United States, the SCARP I "mortality" appears entirely acceptable, although one must realize that such comparisons are not entirely valid because of the difficulty Pakistan has in raising domestic capital for development projects. Until such a point as the reclamation program becomes self-sustaining, either through the increased production of food and fiber for export or through the substitution of domestically produced food grains for imports that actually cost Pakistan foreign exchange (and Food for Peace grain imports do not), continued and substantial injections of foreign aid will be required.

On the other hand, it should become increasingly possible for Pakistan to manufacture the equipment, including fiber-glass strainers and turbine pumps, needed in the SCARP programs. If she can do so, and if the use of such equipment validates the assumptions concerning the longevity of the SCARP-type tubewells, then there is little doubt that the modern, massive approach will demonstrate its validity even to its severest critics.

Meanwhile, the planners have been running ahead of the engineers. Between the completion of the SCARP I plan in January 1959 and the inception of the Wiesner Mission in the summer of 1961, WAPDA had produced a master plan for reclamation (not to be confused with the master plan for long-range water and power development, which is due for completion in 1969 or 1970 and of which the Harza Appraisal Report, due in mid 1967, represents a preliminary study). WAPDA's master plan for reclamation was drafted in conjunction with its regional planning consultants for the Northern Zone (Tipton and Kalmbach) and Southern Zone (Hunting Technical Services and Sir M. MacDonald and Partners) and, through WASID, in cooperation with the USGS team and I.C.A. It called for the reclamation of the 27.3 million acres identified in 1954 plus those areas that had become affected in the meantime—a total of 29 million acres. The SCARP I model was to be applied to nine additional projects in the Northern Zone and to sixteen projects in the Southern Zone. Because of the apparent paucity of good groundwater in Sind, the Southern Zone reclamation projects were to consist primarily of open drains supplemented where necessary by tubewells for drainage purposes alone. The Northern Zone projects were to combine tubewell drainage with tubewell irrigation, making

474

use of fresh groundwater where possible, but the emphasis was definitely upon the reclamation aspect. In all, 31,500 tubewells, 7,500 miles of major drainage channels, and 25,000 miles of supplemental drains were to be provided over a ten-year period. The total capital cost, including power facilities, was estimated at about $1.25 billion, and it was proposed to seek financial assistance from the "Aid to Pakistan Consortium" which was underwriting the Five Year Plans as well as directly from the U.S. and possibly from the U.S.S.R.[45]

Although WAPDA would have no responsibility for operating the project areas after the facilities were installed, the master plan for reclamation recognized that success would be dependent upon improved irrigation practices, soil management, and farming methods, as well as upon increased inputs of fertilizer, seed, equipment, and labor. Taking these into consideration, it was estimated that agricultural production could be increased by at least 15 per cent per year in the initial stages, and that an overall benefit-to-cost ratio of 2.25:1 (2.1:1 in the Northern Zone and 2.6:1 in the Southern) could be achieved even with allowances for amortization and operation expenses.[46]

WAPDA's reclamation plan was embodied in a program prepared by WAPDA in the six weeks between the convening of a conference on the problem in Lahore on April 3, 1961, and the visit of U. S. Vice President Lyndon B. Johnson to West Pakistan in late May when he was briefed on the program by President Ayub and the WAPDA Chairman. Thus, the submission of the WAPDA plan (which we shall refer to as the May 1961 master plan) more or less coincided with Dr. Abdus Salam's visit to the M.I.T. Centennial (see Chapter 7, page 301) and his discussion with Jerome B. Wiesner, President Kennedy's Science Adviser. By the time President Ayub visited Kennedy in July 1961, foundations had been laid both in Pakistan and in Washington for a high-level scientific investigation of the waterlogging and salinity problem, as well as of the economic and administrative aspects of a solution.

45. WAPDA, *Visit of the U.S. Scientific Mission on Waterlogging and Salinity in West Pakistan, September–October, 1961"* (Lahore, WAPDA, n.d.), pp. 11–13.
46. Ibid., pp. 12–15.

The Revelle Approach

In response to President Ayub's request, President Kennedy directed Wiesner to assemble a panel of experts from the physical and social sciences, including specialists from the Bureau of Reclamation, the U. S. Department of Agriculture, Harvard, M.I.T., the University of California, and from private research and engineering firms.[47] It is noteworthy that some of the experts selected were conversant neither with irrigation-reclamation problems nor with the specifics of economic development and administration in West Pakistan. Rather, the intention was to bring to bear upon the problems of the Indus Plains a broad variety of skills and experience *both* with analogous problems elsewhere and with problems resembling those of West Pakistan only in that they might be susceptible to computer-age analysis and the application of sophisticated technology. In other words, the panel was so constituted as to be able to look both at the forest and at the trees.

The Wiesner Mission was divided into two groups, each of which

47. Included in the original mission, besides Wiesner and Revelle, were: Mr. John B. Blandford, I.C.A. Consultant; Dr. Claude A. Bower, Director of the U. S. Salinity Laboratory, Riverside, Calif.; Prof. Ayers Brinser now with the University of Michigan; Prof. Robert Dorfman, Harvard; Prof. John D. Isaacs of the University of California Scripps Institution; Dr. Leonhard Katz, President, Astro-Dynamics, Inc.; Dr. George D. Lukes of the Office of the Special Assistant to the President for Science and Technology; Mr. Thomas Maddock of the USGS; Mr. R. C. Reeve of the U. S. Salinity Laboratory; Prof. Harold A. Thomas, Jr., Harvard; and Prof. David K. Todd, University of California, Berkeley. Subsequent members of the panel included Dr. Robert P. Burden, Harvard; Mr. Rollin Eckis, President, Richfield Oil Corp.; Prof. Walter P. Falcon, Harvard; Prof. Robert Gomer, University of Chicago; Dr. Walter Langbein, USGS; Dr. R. A. Laudise, Bell Telephone Laboratories; Prof. A. S. Michaels, M.I.T.; Mr. Herbert Skibitske, USGS; and Dr. C. A. Wadleigh, Director, Soil and Water Conservation Research, Agricultural Research Service. Among those who accompanied the Revelle Mission on its tour were Mr. Kenneth Vernon, I.C.A., Karachi; Mr. David Greenman, I.C.A. Adviser (USGS team); Mr. Olin Kalmbach, WAPDA Consultant; Mr. Sayyid Hamid, Project Director, WAPDA Ground Water and Reclamation Division; Mr. S. M. Said, Project Director, WAPDA WASID; Mr. Shamim Ahmad, Project Director, SCARP I; Ch. Muhammad Nazir of WAPDA's Reclamation Division; Khan Sarwar Jan Khan, Additional Chief Engineer (Development), Irrigation Department; and Dr. A. G. Asghar, Director, Land Reclamation, Irrigation Department or his deputy, Ch. Muhammad Hussain. (Ibid., p. 5, and Revelle II, opposite Preface.)

spent about ten days in West Pakistan in late September and early October 1961. Dr. Wiesner acted as leader of the mission and of one of the groups. The second group was led by Dr. Roger Revelle, who in July had left the University of California to become science adviser to the Secretary of the Interior. Because Dr. Revelle subsequently assumed direction of the entire operation, which included many visits to Pakistan by members of the panel and its staff, we shall refer to the panel as the "Revelle Panel" and to its two reports as "Revelle I" (preliminary report of September 1962) and "Revelle II" (final report of January 1964). The objectives of the Wiesner Mission–Revelle Panel were set forth in a letter addressed by President Kennedy to President Ayub in August 1961:

1. A comprehensive and, to the extent possible, detailed analysis of the probable effects of different proposed systems for combating waterlogging and salt accumulation in the soil, and at the same time increasing the supply of irrigation water, with the objective of identifying the best and most practical system.

2. An examination of applicable irrigation techniques and management plans for the Rechna Doab area in which wells are now being installed. [SCARP I] in Rechna Doab will provide a means of checking the analytical studies as well as the efficacy of the tubewell approach. . . . Since the West Pakistan Water and Power Development Authority's responsibility for construction will shortly be completed, you may wish to consider as soon as practicable the kind of management organization and procedures which the new irrigation practices required by the tube-well system in Rechna Doab will demand, if they are to be effective.

3. Maintaining and increasing the harvest from irrigated lands, having in mind the fact that agricultural conditions may be improved by availability of more water than heretofore.

4. To examine the extent to which the equipment and materials needed in these enterprises could be supplied by your industry, either from existing or new plants.[48]

48. WAPDA, "Visit," pp. 6–7.

Although the anniversary passed unnoticed, the Wiesner Mission assembled in Lahore exactly sixty years after the Indian Irrigation Commission, whose work did so much to determine the course of irrigation development in the Indus Basin during the first half of this century. Although its areal scope was far more restricted, and although the Revelle Panel had no authority whatever (beyond the influence which their report was bound to carry with the principal aid-giving government), in theory the panel's recommendations could play as significant a role in Pakistan's portion of the Basin over the next half-century as did those of the 1901–03 Commission. A comparison of the panel's objectives with those of the Commission (see Chapter 3, page 82) indicates that the panel's functional mandate was even broader. Not only could the members offer the latest expertise in groundwater engineering, agronomy, saline soil and water research, and computer analysis, but they could recommend a coordinated, multifactor approach to the problems of reclamation, an approach that could include administrative and fiscal modifications. Their recommendations would be transmitted at the highest level, and could deal not only with the construction of facilities but with their subsequent operation and management, with long-range agricultural policy, and even with the question of domestic versus foreign procurement of materials and equipment.

On the other hand, it is most important to note that the Wiesner Mission or Revelle Panel was by no means operating in a vacuum. Upon their arrival in Pakistan, the experts were joined by local I.C.A. and USGS personnel, by the directors of WAPDA's Groundwater and Reclamation Division and WASID, by some of WAPDA's consultants, by the SCARP I project director, and by representatives of the Irrigation Department. Most of the panel's basic information, on the first and on subsequent visits, came from these individuals and agencies, or from the Soil Reclamation Board, the provincial Department of Agriculture, and the newly formed West Pakistan Agricultural Development Corporation. Most of these agencies had their own programs. Some of them, as we have seen, had been dealing with the reclamation problems for seven to ten years. The GWDO-USGS program had evolved into SCARP I, which the panel was to evaluate, and into WAPDA's May 1961 master plan for reclamation of 29 million acres over a ten-year period. By the time the panel's

478

computer analyses provided theoretical justification for the approach, SCARP I was already demonstrating in practice that only extensive fields with large-capacity, deep-draft wells could effectively lower water tables.

On the administrative side, the ordinance creating the West Pakistan Agricultural Development Corporation (ADC) had been passed only a few days before the Wiesner Mission arrived in Pakistan (see Chapter 8, page 429). But it was already apparent that ADC's integrated approach would be reasonably comprehensive only in the large colonization areas, such as the 2.8 million acre Ghulam Mohammad Command, entrusted to it and that even in such project areas it would lack direct control of fertilizer production and credit facilities. Although the Food and Agriculture Commission had specifically recommended that ADC take charge of reclamation operations in a salinized area such as the Rechna Doab and proceed in a phased program from one such area to another, we have seen that the Government of West Pakistan had failed to implement this recommendation. In their visits and discussions, as well as from the F.A.C. Report, the Revelle Panel quickly learned the shortcomings of the other provincial agencies charged with agricultural development and found that the Village-AID program, so promising in its inception, had run into insuperable obstacles and was about to be superseded. Thus, most of the elements were there. But what was lacking was an integrated approach that could bring all of the elements to bear simultaneously in a limited area so that their beneficial effects could reinforce each other to the degree that the net gain would not be merely the sum of the different inputs but their geometrical product, due to the multiplier effect or what the panel termed "the principle of interaction."

On the average, the yield from present crops could be increased 5 to 10 per cent simply by providing enough water to equal the amount of evapotranspiration during the growing season; additional water to meet the leaching requirement would give a further 5 to 10 per cent increase. Fallow land, which now makes up 7 to 15 per cent of the cultivated area, could be virtually eliminated with water plus fertilizer; the intensity of cropping could be raised by 30 to 40 per cent; and the cropping pattern could be modified in the direction of more valuable but more water-demanding crops, giving an increase in average value per acre of about 5 per cent. Moderate application of nitrogen fertilizer would result in an average yield increase of 25 to 30 per cent, not only for the present cropping pattern, but in the increased gross sown area and for the more valuable crops. For these given percentages, the minimum increase is 103 per cent: (1.10) (1.07) (1.30) (1.05) (1.25)−1.00=1.03, and the maximum increase is 164 per cent: (1.20) (1.15) (1.40) (1.05) (1.30)−1.00=1.64. Much larger increases could be obtained, given adequate water, by larger investments in fertilizer, including both nitrogen and phosphate, use of better seeds and pesticides, and improvement in agricultural techniques. In accordance with the principle of interaction . . . , the yield increase should be more than the cumulative one computed [above]. When all the factors of production are used in the proper combination, the yield response is much larger than the sum of the responses to each separately.[49]

Also lacking, aside from the ADC project areas, was an administrative arrangement that would allow a specific agency to take over the management of each project area as (or even before) it was completed and stay with it indefinitely, so that there would be no internal bickering or "jurisdictional disputes" and so that the benefit of experience with early project areas could be passed along cumulatively and directly to later areas. The preliminary report of the Revelle Panel recommended that West Pakistan "shift from an administrative structure based on function to one based on area"[50] and concentrate the efforts on each area in turn rather than dispersing them throughout the province:

> Our plan consists of, and depends on, an interweaving of the physical means of increasing agricultural production with the necessary economic, political and social factors. Integration of application is required, not only within the project areas of concentration; effective support by Provincial agencies is essen-

49. Revelle II, pp. 139–40. The calculations apply to a proposed project area in the Punjab.
50. Revelle I, p. 54; Revelle II, p. 130.

tial. Such an ambitious program will require heroic efforts by the Government and people of West Pakistan. Major administrative changes and major expansion in certain areas will be required. . . . We believe we should not make specific and detailed recommendation for the establishment of an administrative apparatus to carry out the program. At the same time, so many of the technical, educational, supply, operational, and coordination functions impinge on administrative matters that the question cannot be begged.[51]

Despite item 2 in President Kennedy's letter to President Ayub, the panel in September 1962 did not feel that it should include any specific recommendation for an administrative apparatus. Nevertheless, such a recommendation was already in existence. John B. Blandford, consultant with I.C.A. in Karachi and later with A.I.D. in Washington, who had joined the panel in Pakistan, had prepared a section dealing specifically with administrative aspects and recommending the establishment of a Land and Water Development Board to administer the project areas (after construction by WAPDA).[52] But this material was omitted from the preliminary report so as to avoid any appearance of interfering in Pakistan's domestic affairs or in the "jurisdictional disputes" among WAPDA, the Irrigation Department, the Soil Reclamation Board, the ADC, or the provincial ministries. When Pakistan subsequently requested specific administrative recommendations, however (possibly as a means of transferring to foreigners the onus of stepping on anyone's toes) an entire chapter was devoted to the subject in the final version of the Revelle Report.

As Revelle II envisages it, within each project area a single project director would assume responsibility for all functional aspects, using personnel delegated or "seconded" to him by the appropriate agencies. During the first three or four years, while WAPDA was locating, drilling, and electrifying the wells, and PIDC was constructing the associated fertilizer plant (one plant would serve several areas and would preferably be located in the nearest city receiving natural gas by pipeline), the project director would have

51. Revelle I, pp. 56–57.
52. Interview with Paul W. Bedard, Coordinator for Indus Plains Projects, U.S.A.I.D., Lahore, September 18, 1963.

an opportunity to organize his staff, establish an experiment station and statistical service, and set up extension, training, and credit facilities for the farmers. Demonstration plots and seed farms would be established, and field agents would help introduce innovations on some of the farms, using credit as an inducement to farmers both to undertake improvements and to grow superior seed for sale. Thus, by the time the tubewell field and its associated fertilizer plant was completed in one project area, and WAPDA and PIDC moved on to the next area or areas, the administrative and extension infrastructure would be well established under the project director who would remain with it.[53] Such a concentrated approach in project areas averaging 1 million acres in size represented an innovation over the WAPDA May 1961 program as well as over the program of the ADC, which was addressed specifically to areas of entire barrage commands and generally to seed testing, and seed, fertilizer, and implement supply over all of West Pakistan.[54]

Two additional contributions of the Revelle approach should be mentioned. Although the panel agreed with the Soil Reclamation Board, the Colombo Survey, and WAPDA's May 1961 program that the waterlogging and salinity menace was indeed a most serious problem, it took issue with their estimates of the areas affected and of those severely damaged. Pointing to the limitations of aerial photographic analysis (which the Colombo Survey itself acknowledged and which were more serious in a survey flown and interpreted with 1954 equipment than they would be today), the Revelle Panel attempted to substitute estimates of crop damage from salinization or measurements of water levels and soil salt content.[55]

For estimates of crop damage, the panel turned to the Bureau of Statistics of the West Pakistan Department of Power, Irrigation, and Development, which in November 1958 had published *Statistics of West Pakistan, Agricultural Data by Division and District, 1947–48 through 1956–57* (on the basis of the agricultural-irrigation year running from April 1 through March 31). This report had

53. Revelle II, pp. 157–58.
54. West Pakistan Agricultural Development Corporation, *Agricultural Development in West Pakistan: the Role and Functions of the West Pakistan ADC* (Lahore, Public Relations Division, WPADC, November 1963), pp. 4–5.
55. Revelle I, p. 16.

defined "salinity damage" as "areas in which white effervescence is apparent on the natural surface during the months of December, January, or February, causing ⅕ or more damage to the crop of the area" and "waterlogging damage" as "the fields rendered unfit for cultivation to the extent of ⅕ or more of the area by their sub-soil moisture," but concluded that about 97 per cent of the damage was due to salinity.[56]

Using these definitions, the Revelle Panel concluded that less than one-fourth of the areas given in the Colombo Survey and in WAPDA's May 1961 program were seriously affected, a total of between 5 and 6.5 million acres in all of the Indus Plains and Potwar Upland (Attock, Jhelum, and Rawalpindi districts below the Siwaliks—areas also included in the Colombo Survey). Of the total area seriously affected, perhaps 2.41 million acres lay in the Punjab and N.W.F.P., another 500,000 acres in Bahawalpur, and between 2.1 and 3.6 million acres in Khairpur and Sind. The total represented between 14 and 19 per cent of the 34.6 million acres of cultivated lands (irrigated and nonirrigated) in these portions of West Pakistan, and between 22 and 28 per cent of the 23 million acres in West Pakistan which are *annually canal-irrigated and sown to at least one crop.*[57]

In addition to reducing the estimates of seriously affected lands, the Revelle Report dismissed the threat that all of West Pakistan's cultivated area would become severely waterlogged or salinized. It pointed out that, although the area of severe affectation was increasing by 50,000 to 100,000 acres, or .2 to .4 per cent per year, a dynamic equilibrium would be reached "when the acreage from which underground evaporation is occurring, times the average rate of evaporation, in feet per year, equals the quantity of water, in acre feet per year, which leaks downward to the aquifer from canals, distributaries, and water courses."[58] In other words, natural evapo-transpiration in the Indus Plains would eventually balance out the waterlogging when sufficient surface area was affected. But this might not occur until, in the Punjab at least, about twice the present acreage (2.41 million acres, or 11.9 per cent of the cultivated area)

56. Ibid., n. 14; Revelle II, p. 57, n. 29.
57. Revelle I, p. 18 and Table I–12.
58. Ibid., p. 18.

became waterlogged, and the degree of salinity within the water-logged areas would slowly increase as evaporation left additional salt deposits behind.

At the same time, the Revelle Report conceded that, "There is little question that in several million additional acres the soil salt contents are too high to allow optimum crop production."[59] Ultimately, if left uncorrected, some 20 to 25 per cent of West Pakistan's irrigated lands could be removed from production.

Partly to offset this menace, but mainly to lift all of West Pakistan's irrigated agriculture to a level where it could support the rapidly increasing population at a reasonable standard, the Revelle Panel suggested a program almost as great as WAPDA's in geographical scope at its initial level (around 26 million acres), longer in duration (from fifteen to twenty years), and considerably more expensive in initial capital costs (about $2.3 billion, or approximately as much as the IBP, including Tarbela, for this first level of development). The program would proceed, initially, at the rate of one project area of about 1 million acres per year, but would accelerate in later years as experience, staff, and equipment were accumulated, until it had encompassed 16.4 million acres in the Northern Zone and 9 or 10 million acres in the Southern Zone.[60] The initial phase of the Revelle program would entail capital costs of $81 per acre in the Northern Zone and $100 to $110 in Sind, as compared to the $30 per acre in SCARP I or the $31 per acre estimated in WAPDA's master plan.

But in making comparisons between the Revelle program and WAPDA's May 1961 program, it must be emphasized that although the former calls for fewer tubewells[61] and less surface drainage, at

59. Ibid.
60. Revelle II, p. 11.
61. Although the Revelle Report did not make a specific recommendation, one computer analysis of optimum spacing of wells in the northern doabs indicated one well per 1,600 acres, or 625 wells per million-acre project area. (See Revelle II, pp. 319–25 and Table 7.5, p. 336.) Assuming that this rate were applied in Sind as well as in Punjab, although it probably would not be, the Revelle Program would involve a maximum of 15,725 tubewells or just about half the 31,500 envisaged in the WAPDA May 1961 master plan. The computer calculation, however, did not take into account the very practical consideration that tubewells should be located at the heads of existing watercourses, wherever possible, in order to minimize costs of conveyance channels and to reduce con-

least in the initial stages, it includes a far greater emphasis on improving agricultural practices, better seeds, pest and disease control, and introducing a nitrogen fertilizer program which alone would cost around $250 million for the initial production and distribution facilities.[62] Ultimately, as the research, extension, and education services envisaged by Revelle were developed, and as phosphate fertilizer facilities were added, the capital as well as the operating costs of the program would increase. But this is the key to the whole Revelle approach—a concentrated and simultaneous attack upon all aspects of the agricultural problem in each project area: more water, less salt, better drainage, more fertilizers, better seeds, bullocks, and tools, control of pests and diseases, and an integrated effort to train farmers in the application of these factors.

---

veyance losses. Taking this into consideration, the Harza Appraisal Report (to be discussed later) came up with a figure of 34,000 tubewells (averaging a capacity of 4 cusecs in the Northern Zone and 3 cusecs in Sind) for the first phase of its program (by 1975). (Harza Report, p. II–37, Table II–16.) Obviously, there is a great variation possible in the size and spacing of the tubewells, and, as the Revelle Report notes, any computer analysis must be highly theoretical.

62. Granting the assumptions made by the Revelle Panel concerning surface and groundwater supplies (which will be discussed in Chapter 10), the success of the recommended program would depend very heavily upon achieving much greater fertilizer inputs—at least 30 pounds of nitrogen per crop per acre and 30 to 40 pounds of P_2O_5 per acre every second or third year, as there is some carry-over of phosphate in the soil from year to year. Fairly reliable data on wheat responses to phosphate and nitrogen are available, but not much on responses of other crops to phosphate. Revelle uses the Planning Commission's estimates of other crops' responses to nitrogen. The Revelle Panel also examined the economics of producing fertilizers in Pakistan as compared to importing them. The raw material and fuel base for nitrogen fertilizer plants is available in West Pakistan's natural gas fields at Sui, west of Gudu, and at Mari and Uch, with total reserves certainly in excess of 15 trillion cubic feet. Since much exploration remains to be done, and since the Revelle Report estimates that a natural gas production of 60 billion cubic feet per year could supply 1.25 billion pounds of nitrogen in addition to generating *all* the power necessary for West Pakistan's tubewells, there is little doubt that such an allocation would be economical in the long run. But the capital costs of nitrogen fertilizer plants sufficient to supply the 25-million-acre project areas envisaged at Revelle's first level of development would be about $200 million, distribution facilities might cost an additional $50 million, and the annual production and distribution costs would be about $125 million. Because Pakistan must import the raw materials for phosphate fertilizer production (phosphate rock and sulfur), the respective figures would be around $33 and $29 million, but this would represent a substantial saving over importing the prepared fertilizer. (Revelle II, pp. 100–06 and 415–16.)

With respect to concentration of effort and coincidence of timing within limited project areas, most of the differences between the Revelle approach and the WAPDA and ADC programs (and those of other agencies) are quantitative rather than qualitative. But one basic qualitative innovation suggested by Revelle, and directly related to the revised estimates of the type and extent of the problem, was starting with the *best* lands, rather than with the worst. The reasons for this were physical as well as economic and sociopolitical. From the physical standpoint, the panel emphasized that "bad land protects good land," i.e. that the lower-lying waterlogged areas act as sumps, collecting the natural drainage with some of the salts from surrounding higher areas. As these higher areas are provided with tubewells and *their* water tables lowered, the area of waterlogging would automatically be decreased.

From the economic standpoint, it would be much cheaper and quicker to achieve results from the multifactor approach if one started with good lands rather than at an initial handicap with bad lands. Thus, the program would slowly begin to pay for itself as crop yields rose. In fact, it was hoped that by choosing only good lands to begin with, and by applying all of the above-mentioned factors, a 15 per cent annual increase in crop yields could be achieved for each year from the fourth through the eighth in each project area, followed by an increase of 7.5 per cent per year for an indefinite period. Finally, on the sociopolitical level, demonstrated success in project areas located in good soil and groundwater areas would generate enthusiasm for the program as a whole and would see it through to completion over a generation or more.[63]

On the logic of starting with the best areas, the Revelle Report recommended early projects in the Lyallpur, Multan, or Montgomery districts where yields are already high, and in the northernmost sector of the Indus Plains where rainfall is relatively high, evapotranspiration relatively low, and thus where less investment in facilities for additional water supplies would be necessary. In Sind, the panel thought, on the basis of investigations conducted by Hunting-MacDonald, that the 600,000 acres examined in the Khairpur area might serve as the initial project.[64] Of course SCARP I, which was

63. Revelle II, pp. 131–32 and 139–42.
64. Revelle II, pp. 141–42; specific suggestions of areas for the early projects were not included in Revelle I.

in an advanced stage of development, and SCARP II, in the Chaj Doab, which was then in advanced planning with some pilot schemes installed, should be continued. But neither of these SCARPs meets the Revelle desiderata with respect to quality of soils and groundwater, and SCARP III, which was undertaken in 1965 in the Lower Thal area, is even less desirable as a demonstration project. SCARP IV, in the upper Rechna Doab, adjoining SCARP I, meets some of the requirements of a project where water needs are relatively low, but projects in the Lyallpur, Multan, and Montgomery districts were tentatively scheduled only by WAPDA after a project in lower Bahawalpur (see Map 8b).[65]

The logic of starting with the "best," i.e. saline but not waterlogged, lands has been challenged by some of WAPDA's engineers and consultants who point out that a more significant distinction would be that between soils that are merely salinized (i.e. have an excessive content of all salts, but the salts are soluble because the exchangeable-sodium percentage is less than 15 and soil structure is not seriously impaired) and those that are alkaline or "sodium-damaged" as well (i.e. the exchangeable-sodium percentage is greater than 15, and ordinary leaching produces sodium hydroxide or sodium carbonate, which further impairs soil structure and renders the soil impermeable to water or air).[66] The merely saline soils can be reclaimed quickly by excess applications of good water, over and above crop requirements, once drains or tubewells are installed. But reclamation of "sodium-damaged" soils requires more lengthy and careful treatment, perhaps including complex soil amendments such as the addition of gypsum and cultivation with alkali-tolerant crops that remove the sodium and serve to restore soil structure, after which more economic crops may be introduced into the rotation pattern. The Revelle Report indicates that at least 6 million acres of culturable commanded land in the Indus Plains are sodium-damaged, most of them in Sind. Even in SCARP I, perhaps 25 per cent of the land is "sodium-damaged," and half of this may require special

65. Harza Report, Exhibit II-4. As of mid 1966 it appeared that SCARP V would be the Lower Rechna project including Lyallpur (area 7, Northern Zone, on Map 8b), followed by the Panjnad or Lower Bahawalpur project (area 5) and the Eastern Bari Doab project, including Montgomery (area 6).

66. U. S. Salinity Laboratory Staff, *Diagnosis and Improvement of Saline and Alkali Soils* (Agriculture Handbook No. 60) (Washington, D.C., U. S. Department of Agriculture, February 1954), pp. 4–5.

leaching, soil amendments, and careful cropping patterns for a number of years.[67]

As more detailed analyses are made, and as more experience with reclamation practices is accumulated, it should not be particularly difficult for WAPDA, working with its consultants for the Northern and Southern zones and its general consultants, to determine the proper economic priority for reclamation projects. On the other hand, it would be unrealistic to expect that WAPDA, despite its semiautonomous status, can be completely immune from domestic political influences which will demand some rough regional equality in assigning priorities for reclamation and development.

Because the Revelle Panel was immune from domestic politics in West Pakistan, it was able to recommend a program that would not only deal with the best lands first but one that would, at its "first level of development," presumably around 1980, reclaim only 16.4 million acres in the Northern Zone and between 7.3 and 11 million (depending upon quality of groundwater) in the Southern Zone.[68] Even at the second, or ultimate, level of development, to be reached around the year 2000, the Revelle Panel would reclaim and/or irrigate only 29.7 million acres in all of the Indus Plains of West Pakistan (18.3 million acres in the Northern Zone and 11.4 million in the Southern Zone).[69] This ultimate figure is less than the 32.8 million acres now under canal command and implies that it will neither be necessary nor economical for Pakistan to extend irrigation to the full culturable commanded area (13.3 million acres) encompassed by the Sukkur, Ghulam Mohammad, and Gudu commands. (Development of the Sukkur command is now at a standstill, but development in Ghulam Mohammad and Gudu has been proceeding

67. Revelle II, pp. 111–12, 132–33. Where the exchangeable-sodium percentage is high, and has destroyed soil structure and hence permeability, the use of waters that have a high ratio of calcium and magnesium rather than sodium, and a relatively low carbonate content, can actually reduce the amount of exchangeable sodium and prepare the way for further reclamation and normal cropping patterns. Thus, the sodium, residual sodium carbonate, and boron (which is toxic to some plants and animals) content of the groundwater may be of far greater significance than just the total dissolved salt content. See Harza Report, pp. II-12, II-13, and C. A. Bower and M. Maasland, "Sodium Hazard of Punjab Ground Waters," *Symposium on Waterlogging and Salinity* (Lahore, West Pakistan Engineering Congress, October 1963), pp. 49–61.

68. Revelle II, pp. 283–85.

69. Ibid., p. 288.

steadily since the ADC assumed responsibility for these areas in 1961.) Instead, the Revelle approach envisages such a concentration of surface and groundwater development combined with reclamation, drainage, fertilizer, and improved seed and management practices as to allow virtual double-cropping (200 per cent intensity) of these areas, thus producing around 50 million acres of crops per year at the first level and almost 60 million at the ultimate level of development.[70] The Revelle approach suggests that West Pakistan can produce more than sufficient food and fiber for her projected population in the year 2000 at a *lower* cost by concentrating all of the inputs on a limited area than if she spreads them over the full culturable area now under canal command or embarks on added significant irrigation projects.

Evaluation and Alternatives

There is no doubt that the principal recommendations of the Revelle Panel, although they are not and perhaps never will be the official policy of West Pakistan, represent a significant contribution toward solution of the technological, economic, and administrative problems of the irrigation-based agriculture in Pakistan's Indus Plains. Precedents can be found for most of the elements in the Revelle approach, but the combination and emphasis were novel. The Revelle Panel analyzed and endorsed the massive approach embodied in WAPDA's SCARP I, suggested modifications in the scope and phasing of WAPDA's master plan of May 1961, endorsed ADC's multifactor approach but asked for a much more concentrated application, and, at the urging of Pakistan, made specific recommendations for long-range administrative arrangements. Of all the panel's recommendations, substitution of an administrative structure based on a limited area rather than function, initial and ultimate concentration on the better lands, heavy emphasis upon fertilizer inputs, and the stress upon the principle of interaction represent the major contributions. Whether or not they are adopted remains to be seen, but, thanks to the Revelle Panel, West Pakistan has received a highly competent diagnosis of her irrigation-reclamation problem and some imaginative suggestions for solution.

Indeed, the reactions generated by the Revelle reports may ulti-

70. Ibid.

mately prove far more significant than any of the specific estimates, priorities, rates of development, or assumed responses included, for all of these are clearly subject to revision and modification. But both the preliminary and the final version of the Revelle Report represented interjections from the highest political level into an arena already fully occupied by central and provincial ministries, departments, planning agencies, semiautonomous public corporations, consultants, and international aid organizations. Most of these agencies were already formulating or even executing their own projects. WAPDA not only had its May 1961 master plan for reclamation, but was working through its general consultants, Harza, on the Master Plan for Water and Power resource development in the Indus Plains, a preliminary version of which appeared as the Harza Appraisal Report of September 1963, to be discussed shortly. WAPDA's regional consultants, Tipton and Kalmbach and Hunting-MacDonald were hard at work on long-range plans for the Northern and Southern zones, respectively, as well as on plans for individual projects within each zone. And, beginning in January 1964, WAPDA and its consultants were assisting the World Bank consultants in their survey of water and power resources in all of West Pakistan, to be completed in 1967 (see Chapter 8, page 359).

In addition, although we have not mentioned them before, Pakistan has two resident teams of economic experts who deal with questions of planning and investment allocation for resource development. The Harvard Advisory Group has been assisting the Central Planning Commission since April 1954, when the first members arrived to help that new organization (then called the Planning Board) to prepare the first Five Year Plan by April 1955.[71] Thus, the Harvard Group was in a position, both in Karachi and in Cambridge, to provide information and guidance to the Revelle Panel. In fact there

71. The Harvard Advisory Group originally functioned under Harvard University's Graduate School of Public Administration. In 1962, its headquarters were transferred to the new Development Advisory Service of the Harvard Center for International Studies, also in Cambridge. See *Design for Pakistan: A Report on Assistance to the Pakistan Planning Commission by the Ford Foundation and Harvard University* (New York, The Ford Foundation, February 1965). The initial support for the Harvard Group came entirely from the Ford Foundation; later it was shared by Ford and I.C.A.-A.I.D.; and by 1965 it had been assumed by the Development Advisory Service of the World Bank.

was some overlap in membership between the two, especially in the period from the first draft of September 1962 to the final report of January 1964. The final version was worked out by a subcommittee of the panel, consisting of Dr. Revelle and four members of the Harvard faculty. And the Appendix Report, including most of the cost-benefit analyses, was prepared with the aid of computers by the Harvard Water Resources Group, which has produced a number of theoretical studies of multipurpose river basin development.[72] The contributions, controls, and criticisms of the Revelle Report by the Harvard experts in Karachi and Cambridge were thus largely internal and were embodied in the final version.

The other resident team of economists was that of the Institute of Development Economics, a research and training organization originally established as an autonomous agency under a contract arrangement between the Government of Pakistan and Stanford University, underwritten by the Ford Foundation. The role of the I.D.E. was both to conduct independent research and to train, in Pakistan and abroad, members of its own staff and of Pakistan Government agencies including the Planning Commission. The I.D.E. has now become a statutory body of the Central Government, and new contractual arrangements have been made with Yale University. But especially in the earlier context, members of the Institute were in a position both to make informal contributions to the Revelle Panel and to voice independent criticism of its suggestions (and of any other recommendations for development projects in Pakistan).[73] In the Summer 1963 issue of the Quarterly Journal of the I.D.E., two of its members, Ghulam Mohammad and Christoph Beringer, reviewed the preliminary version of the Revelle Report.[74]

With respect to general investment policy, Mohammad and Beringer found that the Revelle program should be well within the water and power parameters of Pakistan's Third Five Year Plan

72. E.g. Arthur Maass et al., *Design of Water-Resource Systems* (Cambridge, Mass., Harvard University Press, 1962). The authors of this study included Profs. Dorfman and Thomas, who were members of the Revelle Panel.

73. The Institute of Development Economics, *Annual Report, 1962–63* (Karachi, I.D.E., 1963).

74. Ghulam Mohammad and Christoph Beringer, "Waterlogging and Salinity in West Pakistan: An Analysis of the Revelle Report," *Pakistan Development Review* (Quarterly Journal of the Institute of Development Economics, Karachi, Pakistan) *3* (1963), 249–79.

and succeeding ones. Because the best lands in West Pakistan (from the standpoint of location, gradient, and soil quality) have already been developed for irrigation agriculture, and costs of irrigation projects have steadily risen in relation to benefits over the past century (both because the more rewarding projects were generally undertaken first and since the costs of labor, compensation for owned land, machinery, and equipment are rising) Mohammad and Beringer agreed that it would be far more economical to reclaim the deteriorated portions of the existing irrigated areas than to try to replace them with "virgin" lands. The critics recognized the value of the concentrated, multifactor approach recommended by Revelle and of substituting an areal for a functional administration (though they noted the lack of detailed recommendations in Revelle I).

But Mohammad and Beringer questioned some of the key technical assumptions made by the panel, in particular those relating to the amount and quality of groundwater underlying the irrigated areas of the Indus Plains. On the basis of early experience in SCARP I and of previous studies by the above-mentioned agencies and by C. R. Maierhofer (a U. S. Bureau of Reclamation expert who made a reconnaissance report as early as 1952), they felt that the panel was unrealistic both in assuming that good quality groundwater underlies 19 million acres of the Northern Zone to a depth of 400 feet and that the recharge over this entire area could be recovered without construction of costly new conduits, since only 13.6 million acres lie within existing canal commands. But a more fundamental question was whether or not the panel had adopted too high a *storage coefficient* in estimating the amount of water contained in the aquifer. Here the experts were in disagreement. Tipton and Kalmbach, WAPDA's consultants for reclamation and regional planning in the Northern Zone, in reviewing SCARP I and in designing SCARP II, had assumed a storage coefficient of 25 per cent (i.e. that each cubic foot of aquifer contained .25 cubic feet of water that could be extracted by pumping—also termed "specific yield"). But Hunting-MacDonald, working in Sind, and some of the earlier GWDO-USGS and WAPDA reports from the Northern Zone, employed a storage coefficient of only 10 per cent. Revelle I had adopted 25 per cent without explaining why. Mohammad and Beringer questioned this, although they indicated that even a 10 per cent figure might not vitiate the feasibility of the Revelle program.[75]

In the final version of the Revelle Report, the use of coefficients of from 20 to 30 per cent is justified "in predicting the drawdown by pumping from deep mining wells" on the basis of studies performed in the Rechna Doab, new theoretical models devised by the USGS in the United States, and comparisons of the deep subsoil of the Punjab with that of southern California.[76] Tipton and Kalmbach reduced the storage coefficient to 20 per cent for their feasibility report on SCARP III.[77] In a comprehensive study of the ground-water hydrology of the Punjab, summarizing the results of over twenty preliminary reports prepared under USGS-GWDO-WASID auspices since 1954, three USGS advisers to WASID estimated the specific yield of the aquifer at about 20 per cent in 1963.[78] One of these USGS experts, W. V. Swarzenski, and WASID's superintending geologist, Zamir-uddin Kidwai, adopted the 20 per cent coefficient in their presentation to the October 1963 Symposium on Waterlogging and Salinity in Lahore.[79]

Actually, the storage coefficient or specific yield of the aquifer is important only in determining the economics of mining groundwater, i.e. in the initial stages of operations in those areas where the groundwater is of good quality and can be used for crops. In such areas, a higher storage coefficient means a greater yield and hence a lower relative cost of mining down to a given depth. Thereafter, when mining has ceased, it is the rate of recharge (i.e. the rate of infiltra-

75. Ibid., p. 268.
76. Revelle II, p. 268.
77. WAPDA, *Feasibility Report on Salinity Control and Reclamation Project No. 3*, p. 28.
78. Greenman, Swarzenski, and Bennett, "The Ground Water Hydrology of the Punjab, West Pakistan" (WASID Bulletin No. 6), pp. 19, 29.
79. Kidwai and Swarzenski, "Results of Geologic and Ground-water Investigations in the Punjab Plain, West Pakistan," *Symposium on Waterlogging and Salinity* (October 1963), pp. 64–68. The authors, assuming only the present canal diversions of 45 m.a.f. per year, suggest a potential recharge to the aquifer of 1 foot per year or 30 m.a.f. per year over the entire Northern Zone of the Indus Plains. They estimate that the water under 21 of the 30 million acres contains less than 1,000 parts per million of total dissolved salts, and that this nonsaline reserve alone amounts to some 2 billion acre feet to a depth of 450 feet.

tion of fresh water from rainfall, stream flow, canal and distributary leakage, and field seepage) that becomes critical. (Both specific yield and recharge rate have a direct bearing on the size, depth, design, and spacing of tubewells and thus on their cost.) Estimates of the magnitude of these inputs to the groundwater table vary considerably according to assumptions concerning future operation of the irrigation system, including its deliberate manipulation to increase recharge (especially from the link canals, which cut across the grain of the subsoil and seep copiously if not lined). The Revelle Panel assumed a recharge rate of .67 feet per year in the Northern Zone, and, despite the criticism of Mohammad and Beringer, retained it in Revelle II although they inserted a caveat, based on initial experience in SCARP I, indicating that it might be only .5 feet per year.[80]

No one yet knows what the recharge rate will prove to be over the fairly well-explored Northern Zone, let alone in Sind where groundwater investigations are just getting started. More recent data from SCARP I seem to indicate that the long-range recharge rate, even without manipulation of the irrigation system, will be even greater than .67 feet per year. If this proves to be the case, then a combination of properly designed wells (which can be varied in capacity and depth to suit aquifer conditions from area to area), well spacings within the fields, and manipulated operation of the surface water system (which will require computer programing anyhow, once the IBP is finished) can more than offset the effects of a lower noninduced recharge rate.

For the initial stage of development in the Northern Zone, Revelle proposes to mine the groundwater in the nonsaline portions of the aquifer so as to lower the watertable by 100 feet in thirty years, eliminating waterlogging and breaking the capillary contact that brings salts to the surface. In the saline groundwater areas of the Northern Zone and in most of the Southern Zone where there is little fresh groundwater, facilities to remove the mined water or to

80. Revelle II, p. 318. This was the 1961–62 experience with the Group II tubewells (see n. 40 above). But the panel thought that the difference might be due to the fact that the water table was still high, with direct capillary contact to the surface and therefore high evapotranspiration, and with limited canal seepage due to the low water-table gradient. They also suggested that less-than-average rainfall might have contributed. At any rate, they retained the figure of .67 feet per year.

dilute it with fresh water will have to be provided, and mining will proceed at only half the above rate. Most of the wells installed in Sind will be merely drainage wells. No one yet knows how much of the Southern Zone is underlain by good quality groundwater. Apparently a zone 10 to 15 miles wide on either side of the Indus, extending from Gudu to at least 100 miles below Sukkur (a total distance of 250 miles) is underlain by groundwater with less than 1,500 parts per million (ppm, henceforth) of salts to depths of at least 250 feet. From this area of 4 million acres, which is apparently fed by the Indus itself and 30 per cent of which lies inside the river bunds where tubewell installation and operation would be difficult, and final version of the Revelle Report assumes that possibly as much as 12 m.a.f. per year of usable groundwater could be developed.[81]

Not only does no one yet know exactly how the quality of groundwater varies from one part of the Indus Plains to another, but the exact affects of various types of salts on particular crops anywhere in the world are still largely to be determined and explained. In Revelle I, 28 million acres of the Northern Zone were divided into 19 million acres overlying groundwater with "less than 1,000 milligrams per liter [same as 1,000 ppm] of dissolved salts" and 9 million acres overlying "saline water with an average of 4,000 milligrams per liter of salinity."[82] These assumptions were challenged by Mohammad and Beringer on the basis of the earlier reports and the indication that in over 200,000 acres, or 17 per cent of the area of SCARP I the groundwater was unfit for irrigation use even when mixed with canal water.[83] In Revelle II, the quality issue is sidestepped by describing 23 million acres in the Northern Zone as overlying groundwater "containing an average of 700 milligrams per liter of dissolved salts" and 7 million acres as overlying "saline water with an average of 6,000 milligrams per liter of salinity."[84]

What apparently disturbed Mohammad and Beringer was not just the question of the quality of groundwater in the Northern Zone but

81. Revelle II, p. 284, and T. N. Jewitt, "Salinity and Ground-water Conditions in the Lower Indus Plains," *Symposium on Waterlogging and Salinity* (Lahore, West Pakistan Engineering Congress, October 1963), pp. 15–25.
82. Revelle I, p. 104.
83. Mohammad and Beringer, p. 269.
84. Revelle II, p. 272.

the possible effects in Sind if any significant amount of saline groundwater were sent downstream.

> The Panel suggests that to maintain the salt balance at a satisfactory level for agriculture, about 10 per cent of the water will eventually have to be exported from the region. For the next 10 or 20 years the annual amount does not need to be more than one million acre feet. The "export" of saline groundwater from the Northern Zone will cause a 42 per cent increase in the average salinity of Indus River water in the former Sind. Ultimately, when 10 per cent of the water pumped is exported, the salinity of Indus water entering Sind will be raised to about 835 parts per million or 280 per cent of what it is at present.
>
> Water containing 835 parts of salts per million can be used for agriculture if the quantity of water applied for irrigation is in excess of the consumptive use by crops by about 15–20 per cent. However, according to the calculations of the Panel, Sind would get only 1.77 acre feet of water per acre per year if the 13 million acres commanded by canals were to be irrigated. This is obviously much less than the consumptive use requirements of crops; and the Panel, therefore, rightly suggests that the irrigated area in former Sind would have to be much smaller than 13 million acres. If the area is not reduced, water applied at this rate would make the former Sind soils highly saline with disastrous results for agriculture in the area. There is, therefore, a direct relationship between the depth to which water is pumped in the Northern Zone and the amount of water which has to be exported. As the quantity of saline water which has to be exported increases the area which can be profitably cropped in former Sind automatically decreases. This statement holds *a fortiori* if the groundwater salinity in the Northern Zone is a positive function of depth.[85]

To quiet such fears, Revelle II added the following comment: "There is uncertainty as to the degree of salinity in the ground water in many areas, and it is not possible to predict accurately the amount of saline water that can be diluted with surface water and used in irrigation, and the amount that must be exported. Our analysis of the cost of salt-export wells and conveyance channels is

85. Mohammad and Beringer, p. 270.

based upon predications made in the Water Budget in which ⅔ of mined water in the saline area is used for crops and ⅓ exported to waste lagoons or desert areas."[86] But if the use of waste lagoons or desert areas will solve the problem as far as Sind is concerned, it may create a problem with India, as noted in Chapter 7.

In actual practice, since it is possible to dilute saline water with fresh water from canals (averaging 250 ppm in the Northern Zone and only 260 ppm in the Southern Zone according to Revelle and under present conditions) and since water with up to 2,000 ppm is generally accepted for irrigation use, there is considerable operational flexibility in the use of groundwater either mixed or alternated with surface water. The Harza Appraisal Report suggests that "normal cropping patterns can be developed for irrigation with water containing up to 3,000 ppm of salts."[87] As we have seen, the critical

86. Revelle II, p. 321. The summary volume of the Harza Appraisal Report, released in March 1964, was somewhat less encouraging: "Highly saline outflows from canal areas in the Northern Zone can be discharged into the river channels during seasons when flows are sufficient for the necessary dilution. In other seasons, the saline outflows must be withheld in ponds or reservoirs for later discharge into the rivers or for disposal by evaporation. Preliminary studies indicate that *at least half* of the saline drainage water can be emptied into the rivers. Reclamation projects must include facilities for disposal of these drainage waters without detriment to downstream irrigation. Part of the drainage waters from the Southern Zone can be discharged directly to the Arabian Sea." (Harza Report, p. 52.) Beyond the added statement that, "Disposal of saline water by evaporation may be accomplished in numerous small ponds created in unproductive areas [which] would minimize expenditures for systems of collector drains" (ibid., p. 58), the general consultants were not specific as to the regional or international implications of saline water disposal. It would seem that if the "unproductive areas" were not carefully chosen, the concentration of highly saline water in ponds awaiting evaporation might have deleterious effects upon the quality of groundwater in the adjacent areas.

87. Harza Report, pp. II-12, II-13. Use of water with more than 2,000 ppm of course implies dilution or alternate use. In the summary volume, the Harza Report (p. 37) gives the following *estimates* of groundwater salinity in the Northern Zone:

Total salts, ppm	Per cent of total area, Northern Zone
Below 500	31
500–1,000	28
1,000–2,000	16
2,000–3,000	4
3,000–5,000	4
Above 5,000	11
Unknown	6

factor may not be the total dissolved salt content but rather the exchangeable sodium percentage (see above, page 487). In a paper submitted to the October 1963 Lahore Symposium, C. A. Bower, Director of the U. S. Salinity Laboratory at Riverside, California, and a member of the Revelle Panel, and Marinus Maasland, one of Harza's outstanding groundwater experts, stated:

> If the 74 tubewell waters considered in this study are repre-
> sentative of a substantial fraction of Punjab ground waters,
> then . . . a potential sodium hazard is involved in the use of
> many of these waters for irrigation. It seems evident that if some
> of the ground waters are used as the sole source of water for
> irrigation, the soil will accumulate injurious amounts of ex-
> changeable Na with time. On the other hand, if hazardous
> ground water is used to supplement surface water for irrigation
> by dilution or by alternate use, no excessive accumulation of
> exchangeable Na may occur. . . . It is evident that the Na
> hazard of Punjab ground waters needs further study with par-
> ticular attention being given as to how surface waters, ground
> waters, and soils can be managed so as to prevent harmful
> accumulations of exchangeable Na.[88]

With this and other studies in mind, the Harza Appraisal Report states, referring to the Northern Zone, "it would seem prudent to assume that conditions encountered in the SCARP I project in Rechna Doab may exist elsewhere. Accordingly, it is unrealistic to assume that more than 60 per cent of the low-salinity (so-called "fresh") ground water can be used safely for irrigation without dilution or mixed use."[89]

But these are only estimates of total salt content, and the 80 per cent of the area of the Northern Zone that has less than 3,000 ppm may not be coincident with canal commands where tubewells can economically be integrated into the surface water system. Furthermore, as explained in n. 67 above, even such areas of low total salt content may have a sodium or boron hazard. Too little is known of the quantity or quality of groundwater in Sind for even such estimates to be made.

88. Bower and Maasland, "Sodium Hazard," p. 60.
89. Harza Report, pp. II-12, II-13. This may be overly conservative. Others would put it as high as 80 per cent. But until detailed knowledge of quality of groundwater in the Northern Zone is available, conservatism seems justified.

Most of Mohammad and Beringer's other criticisms of the preliminary version of the Revelle Report seem to have been met in
the final version, especially when one bears in mind that the panel
was attempting more to lay down guidelines and stimulate thinking
than to suggest a rigid program with specific numerical quantities
and goals. That neither Revelle I nor Revelle II could be as specific
with respect to the Southern Zone as they were for the Northern
Zone was due to the lack of basic information, which is only now
becoming available.[90] Although Revelle II did go into more detail
on suggested cropping patterns (also requested by Mohammad and
Beringer) it stresses, using Khairpur as an example, that "a number of crops have water requirements and prices that are approximately equal," that the solutions offered are only some of "several
possible ways to use scarce resources efficiently," and that "it is very
unlikely that there can be 'one' best cropping pattern for all farms
of the region."[91] Revelle II also devotes an entire chapter to possible
economic advantages to be derived from agricultural diversification,
especially in the direction of increased livestock and poultry production in Sind.

Mohammad and Beringer pointed out the need for a careful analysis of the effects of extremely low water rates traditionally levied
on a per-acre basis in allowing farmers to stay with antiquated and
wasteful agricultural practices. But Revelle II continued to justify
its program essentially on the basis of increased production of food
and fiber rather than on increased revenues from the supply of
water. In the aforementioned Blandford chapter on administrative
recommendations, Revelle II does suggest that each project area
have a "Water Distribution and Assessments Service," and it does
elsewhere recommend that *land revenues* "should be increased to
recapture a portion of the productivity increases achieved by the
development program."[92] But apparently the Revelle approach pre-

90. In November 1965 WASID completed a program of 144 exploratory drill-
ings and installation of 44 test tubewells over 8,000 square miles in the Sukkur
and Ghulam Mohammad commands. (*WAPDA Weekly*, January 7, 1966, p. 1.)
Information from such investigations will be of considerable help to Hunting-
MacDonald in refining their regional plan for the lower Indus (see p. 316
above).

91. Revelle II, p. 209.

92. Ibid., pp. 183, 158.

fers to employ the "carrot" of tying credit facilities to adoption of better practices rather than the "stick" of higher water rates which might make it more difficult for farmers to buy fertilizers, pesticides, improved seeds, and better implements. In adopting this approach, the panel may have had in mind certain post-Partition projects in India where peasants refused to use irrigation water because they felt that the charges were excessive and hoped to bring them down (or have them canceled altogether) by the boycott.

At any rate, it is interesting to speculate on the extent to which the establishment of the West Pakistan Land and Water *Management* Board, early in 1964, represents the adoption of Revelle II's administrative recommendations relating to the program in general and to its fiscal aspects in particular. Revelle II suggested that a Land and Water *Development* Board be formed around the old Soil Reclamation Board, that its chairman be an additional Chief Secretary reporting to the Minister of Food, Agriculture, Irrigation, and Power, and that it have a "Finance Member." Instead, although the Management Board does include all of the other representatives suggested by Revelle II, its chairman is the Member for Land Reforms of the West Pakistan Board of Revenue, and it is not subordinated to the Ministry of Agriculture but directly to the Government of West Pakistan.[93]

The enhanced role of a member of the Board of Revenue *may* indicate that higher assessments may be adopted and that, especially if less foreign assistance is forthcoming for the reclamation program, first priority will be placed on obtaining revenues from the SCARPs rather than on expediting the program through the concentrated approach recommended by the panel. It is somewhat disturbing that the Board has not yet moved in the direction of appointing project managers and allowing them to organize the administrative, farmer-training, credit, and experimental services over the initial three or

93. The membership of the West Pakistan Land and Water Management Board is as follows: Member for Land Reforms, Board of Revenue (Chairman of the Management Board); Chairman, WAPDA; Chairman, West Pakistan A.D.C.; Secretary to Government of West Pakistan for Finance; Secretary for Agriculture; Secretary for Irrigation and Power; Secretary for Co-Operation, Labour, and Social Welfare; and Secretary for Basic Democracies and Local Development. All of these except the representative of the Board of Revenue were suggested by Revelle II, p. 180.

four years of each project area as recommended by the panel. For the early administrative start, embodying both a concentrated localized application and the cumulative development of a cadre of specialists, represents not only an essential feature of the Revelle approach but undoubtedly one of the most difficult to achieve in the intertwined context of traditional farming attitudes and bureaucratic inertia in West Pakistan. As Mohammad and Beringer recognized:

> The brief experience with the Village AID Programme in Pakistan and the Intensive Agricultural Districts Development Programme in India suggests that the road from experiment station research results to village application under our conditions is long and tedious. In most cases it involves further on-the-spot research . . . It also involves adult education and extensive vocational training for young people.
>
> We believe that the main hurdle to the implementation of the Revelle Plan is likely to be the difficult problem of administration, education and extension and not the cost of pumps and fertilizer which, on balance, have received most of the emphasis in the Report. [Despite the additions indicated, this is still true of Revelle II.]
>
> The Panel's suggestion to concentrate all efforts on limited-project areas is certainly sound as a development strategy for agriculture. Spreading limited "administrative and planning inputs" over too wide an area, as has been done in the past, is just as unprofitable as to spread other scarce physical inputs over an unlimited area.[94]

Still, one must question how far a panel of foreign experts can go in suggesting changes in the administrative structure of a host nation. In response to requests from Pakistan, Revelle II did spell out administrative recommendations that cut across both jurisdictional lines and district boundaries. In view of the fact that even the requested recommendations have not yet been fully implemented, one might conclude that the panel's discretion was well justified.

Paradoxically, the administrative suggestions of a panel of foreign

94. Mohammad and Beringer, pp. 275–76.

experts might be easier to implement in a nation less developed than Pakistan. Bureaucratic inertia (which may mean momentum in an undesirable direction as well as stagnation) is fearful to behold in fully "developed" nations, and as this entire study indicates, Pakistan is highly "developed" with respect to irrigation facilities and related fiscal and administrative procedures. The crucial task of modifying those facilities and procedures is one that can only be undertaken by Pakistanis. Foreign advice, even when expressly invited, starts with an initial handicap. In 1963, Mohammad and Beringer, as members of the I.D.E., may have been in a somewhat better position than the panel in suggesting such changes. It is to be hoped that their successors in the Institute, as well as the members of the central and provincial planning departments, can continue to press as vigorously for meaningful and effective administrative reform. Such forums as the I.D.E. and the Development Advisory Service of the World Bank (which now includes the "Harvard Advisory Group") have a unique advantage (though a delicate one to preserve) in being able to develop and present suggestions for administrative reforms hand in hand with their Pakistani counterparts.

Criticisms of Revelle I by members of the central and provincial civil and technical services were less privileged. They had to be muted to conform to the inherent restraints of the secretariat system (see Chapter 8), especially in view of the tenuous negotiations in progress with the World Bank over the IBP and its Tarbela component. But many "off the record" criticisms came out indirectly, voiced by members of the Provincial Assembly (as were Dr. Nazir's reservations concerning expensive tubewells) or in unattributed articles in the press. Professional papers and conferences (notably the Symposium on Waterlogging and Salinity in West Pakistan held in conjunction with the Golden Jubilee Session of the West Pakistan Engineering Congress in Lahore in October 1963) provided other channels for indirect criticism or the suggestion of alternatives. As a semiautonomous agency with its own press and publications program (see Chapter 8), WAPDA could be somewhat more direct in its comments or could manage to insert its views in the reports of its consultants, letting them carry the responsibility. Because the Revelle Report, despite its estimable credentials, had not been adopted as official West Pakistan policy, the suggestion of alternative programs by officials of WAPDA or the ADC can hardly be considered "out of line."[95]

Thus, the singular value of the Revelle Report in our discussion of the prospects of irrigation development in the Pakistani portion of the Indus Plains lies not only in the fact that the panel had access to the cumulative work of so many agencies (without which it could hardly have prepared even a preliminary report in the short space of one year), but that between the preliminary and final versions the report was subjected to a considerable amount of "feedback" from these agencies. Although it has not been, and probably never will be, adopted in toto as an official policy or program by West Pakistan, it remains as a frame of reference with which to compare the programs of WAPDA, ADC, the new Land and Water Management Board, other agencies in Pakistan, and even the proposals of the consultants to the World Bank and WAPDA.

At the same time, we have seen that even WAPDA includes proponents of both the surface water and groundwater schools of thought, as do WAPDA's consultants. So even the Harza Appraisal Report, released in March 1964, as was Revelle II, reflects the contributions of both schools. The Harza Report, though in the form of a submission from the general consultants to the Authority, comes closer than any other single document in stating WAPDA's reaction to the Revelle approach. Indeed, there was a mutual influence, for the preliminary version of the Harza Report was available to the Revelle Panel's subcommittee from at least as early as September 1963.[96]

95. Ahmad Hassan, Adviser for Irrigation of the West Pakistan ADC, has published in the Lahore press some fundamental criticisms both of the priorities and of the costs envisaged by the Revelle Report. In effect, he suggests that the *worst areas* (waterlogged, with saline groundwater) be tackled first, before they are damaged beyond reclamation.

96. Apparently there was far less revision between the September 1963 Harza Appraisal Report and the version released in March 1964 than between the initial and final versions of the Revelle Report. The bulk of the Harza Report, consisting of the "Supporting Studies—An Appraisal of Resources and Potential Development," was released with very few changes. The summary volume, however, which bore the subtitle, "Master Plan—Initial Phase," and the date, January 1964, may be assumed to have been reworked in some detail before it was released. Both volumes bore the title "Program for Water and Power Development in West Pakistan through 1975," and both are cited here simply as "Harza Report." All page references including a roman numeral or a letter (for

We must devote some attention to the program outlined in the Harza Appraisal Report both because it reflects the initial impact of the Revelle approach and because it represents a sort of "halfway house" to the long-range master plan which WAPDA is to present to the West Pakistan Government in 1969 or 1970. Until this master plan is presented, there will be no "official" policy or program other than that prepared by WAPDA in May 1961 and accepted by the Government prior to the inception of the Wiesner Mission and Revelle Panel. WAPDA is still more or less following the priority of projects in that 1961 program, and the tentative priority given in the Harza Appraisal Report is derived from it. In contrast to the Revelle approach, there would not be in Harza's program an initial concentration on areas of good land and good groundwater but rather a staggered program in which waterlogged and badly salinized areas are included, perhaps for reasons of domestic politics. However, the Harza Report covered only the period through 1975, and a second report, extending the program to 1990, will be submitted well before the master plan is finalized. By 1968, also, WAPDA, Harza, and the Government of Pakistan should have the benefit of the World Bank's study (see pages 313–16), and of the regional studies prepared by the consultants for the Northern and Southern zones. So there is little to be gained by a detailed analysis of the Harza program beyond comparing its general approach with the preexisting programs and the Revelle recommendations.

The most basic difference between the Harza and Revelle approaches stems from the fact that WAPDA's general consultants cannot plan an attack on the problems of reclamation and development on as broad a front as could the Revelle Panel. For although WAPDA is entrusted with reclamation and water and power development throughout the province, its role is limited to construction of irrigation and drainage facilities which—in contrast to power facilities—must be turned over to another agency for operation. Thus, neither WAPDA nor its general consultants can really make any administrative recommendations, and the Harza Report restricts itself to the rather vague notice that

---

the appendixes) are from the "Supporting Studies." Those with only an arabic numeral are from the summary volume.

504

undoubtedly, organizational changes will be required, in addition to the changes in technical data and procedures, to cope efficiently with the operational requirements of the more complex water and power systems. Thought must be given soon to the framework under which these changes will be effected. . . . if WAPDA is to participate in the operation of completed water developments, personnel must be hired or trained, procedures established, and the necessary operating departments created.[97]

Furthermore, although WAPDA and its general consultants recognize and endorse the value of the multifactor approach and the principle of interaction, WAPDA has no control over the supply of elements other than water and power. Thus the Harza Report, like WAPDA's May 1961 program (see page 475) notes that its assumed responses "are predicated on fully adequate irrigation water supplies and progressive improvements in farm operation and management, including use of improved seeds, fertilizers, pesticides and insecticides,"[98] but also notes that "the agricultural development program is beyond the scope of this report."[99]

Partly because Harza realizes that WAPDA will have no control over the other inputs, particularly the fertilizer supplies on which Revelle relies so heavily, but also because it prefers more conservative estimates until more experience is available, the estimated benefits from its program are less sanguine than Revelle's. Harza agrees that a compounded 15 per cent per annum increase could be achieved, largely by the application of more water for crop use and for leaching salts, over the first five years. But it does not go along with the 7.5 per cent per annum increase compounded indefinitely thereafter. A comparison of the crop responses assumed by Revelle with those assumed by Harza, in a typical project area, is provided in Table 22. Similarly, a comparison of the total and per acre costs under the two plans is presented in Table 23. Obviously, neither should be taken as a *direct* comparison, because the Revelle estimates are based upon much higher inputs of factors other than water, and also because each estimate is based upon different assumptions regarding cropping patterns and, more significantly, cropping intensities and

97. Harza Report, pp. 73, 72.
98. Ibid., p. 29.
99. Ibid., p. 2.

Table 22. Assumed Crop Responses in Project Areas under the
Revelle and Harza-WAPDA Programs[a]

	Crop Yield in Per Cent of Base Yield	
Years after Reclamation	*Revelle*	*Harza*
1	115	115
5	201	201
10	282	276
15	394	310
20	551	335

a. Source: Harza Report, p. II-44, and calculated for Revelle.

Table 23. Comparisons of Areas and Costs for the Initial Stages
of the Revelle and Harza Programs[a]

	Revelle—First Level (1980?)	Harza 1975
Area Included in Projects		
Northern Zone (million acres)	16.4	12.9
Southern Zone (million acres)	9 or 10	6.0
Total Capital Cost of Program (billions)	$2.3	$1.1
Per Acre Capital Cost		
Northern Zone	$81	$46
Southern Zone	$100–$110	$79

a. Source: Revelle II, p. 11; Harza Report, Table II-16, p. II-37 and Table VI-3, p. VI-30.

the rate of reclamation. Although Harza's rate of reclamation is initially more ambitious (1.5 million acres per year from the start, rather than the average of 1 million acres proposed by Revelle), the built-in acceleration in the Revelle program would apparently bring both to a total of around 26.4 million reclaimed acres by 1980.[100]

100. Revelle suggests proceeding at a rate of about 1 million acres per year for the first five or six years, and then accelerating so that by the first level of development—presumably around 1980—16.4 million acres would be reclaimed in the Northern Zone and between 7.3 and 11 million in the Southern Zone, depending upon what is discovered with respect to drainage and groundwater conditions. Harza would proceed at the more ambitious rate of 1 million acres per year in the Northern Zone plus 500,000 acres per year in the Southern Zone, so as to reclaim a total of 18.8 million acres by 1975—a figure which, if it can be directly extrapolated, would represent around 26.4 million acres by 1980. On p. 288, Revelle II uses exactly the same figure, 26.4 million acres (of which 16.4 would be in the Northern Zone) for the area to be included in the program at the first level of development. (See Revelle II, pp. 283–85, and Harza Report, p. II-35.)

But Revelle would provide sufficient water and fertilizer to allow double-cropping of virtually the entire area, whereas Harza assumes that the available quantities of both elements would permit only an average cropping intensity of 150 per cent in the perennial areas of each zone (12.9 million acres in the Northern Zone and 3 million in the Southern Zone by *1975*) and of 90 per cent on the nonperennial areas of the Southern Zone (3 million acres by *1975*).[101]

Thus the Revelle project areas alone would provide a *cropped acreage* of around 50 million acres at the first level of development, whereas Harza's plan would provide only 26.55 million cropped acres *in project areas* by 1975 and perhaps 37 or 38 million by 1980. At the ultimate level of development, around the year 2000, Harza assumes that the *equivalent* of 32.8 million acres of culturable lands now under canal command in the Indus Plains (which includes the full extent of the Sukkur, Ghulam Mohammad, and Gudu culturable commanded areas) would be under cultivation at the above intensities. But the report added:

> This is an optimistic assumption, since it is known that some of the soils in both of the zones are severely affected by salinity and alkalinity and may not be reclaimable, that water-quality considerations and economics may preclude or limit development in some areas underlain by unusable ground water, and that the water supply which can be developed economically may be a limiting factor. It is *logical and equitable,* however, to assume for appraisal purposes that commanded land found unsuitable for use would be replaced by other suitable land which could be served by canals, if sufficient water were available.[102]

The Harza Report takes issue with the 1959 program prepared by the Irrigation Department for the development of the Ghulam Mohammad and Gudu commands (now being executed by the ADC, but also under review by WAPDA's consultants for the Southern Zone as part of their regional planning). The implication is that expansion of development in these commands to the full culturable commanded area

---

101. Harza Report, p. II-45, and Table II-18, p. II-40.

102. Ibid., p. II-16. Italics added. Tipton and Kalmbach regard all soils in the Northern Zone as physically and ultimately reclaimable, but the question of relative economic cost remains.

is probably not the best use that can be made of the surface water provided by the barrages and by the IBP dams. Harza also points out that "10 to 20 percent more water is required to obtain the same yield of crop on an acre in the Southern Zone than in the Northern Zone."[103] But they concluded, "The determination of the locations and areas of lands to be irrigated and the cropping intensities to be applied thereto are functions of regional and master planning."[104] (They might append, "and of domestic political bargaining.")

It is highly significant that both the Revelle approach, by suggesting that the irrigated area of the Indus Plains at the second level of development by limited to 29.7 million acres (of which only 11.4 million will be in the Southern Zone where the Sukkur, Ghulam Mohammad, and Gudu commands embrace 13.3 million culturable acres), and the Harza Report, by assuming only the *equivalent* of 32.8 million acres and including the above caveats,[105] have apparently reached the same conclusion: that full development of the Sind commands would be a mistake. In 1960–61, only about 7.6 million acres were irrigated in all three commands, and only 500,000 acres were double-cropped.[106] In the light of both the Revelle and Harza reports, it would seem logical to cease this development, or at least to slow it down, so that only about 10 million acres would be irrigated in all three commands by 1980 and at most 11.5 million by the year 2000 (always allowing for unprecedented discoveries of good quality groundwater in Sind). The only justification for proceeding with development in the Sind commands is the political-prestige value associated with large irrigation projects, a justification weak in theory but strong in practice. If West Pakistan could bring herself to face the ultimate reality suggested by both Revelle and Harza—that 30 million acres within the existing culturable commanded area, or at most the *equivalent* of the present culturable commanded area of 32.8 million acres, can, with proper inputs of water, seed, fertilizer, and

103. Harza Report, p. II-34.
104. Ibid., p. II-33.
105. It might also be added that apparently Harza is thinking in terms of perpetuity, i.e. that it has already made allowances for losses of irrigated lands as urban and industrial development occurs, whereas under the Revelle program such losses would be compensated by increased efficiency on the remaining irrigated area.
106. Harza Report, p. II-15.

management, produce more than sufficient food and fiber at a *lower* cost than if the inputs are spread over a larger area—then she could save any additional developmental expenses in these Sind commands and devote them instead to reclamation and intensification. The likelihood of this occurring is, unfortunately, about as great as that of India's curtailing the Rajasthan Project some 200 miles to the east.

In contrast to India, West Pakistan had at present only minor plans to *extend* her culturable commanded area. Most of these are small projects, and most of them lie outside the Indus Plains in Baluchistan or the old N.W.F.P. The Revelle Report cautions against putting additional large areas under irrigation in new canal systems because the returns are distant and uncertain, and "in view of the ultimate deficiency of water."[107]

By implication and for the latter reason, the Harza Report rejects any substantial expansion of the culturable commanded area.[108]

The Indian Experience in East Punjab

If we now turn from the groundwater program and experience in West Pakistan to that in the Indian portion of the Indus Basin, we are at once confronted with two fundamental contrasts. First of all, the Hindu and Sikh members of the Irrigation Branch of the pre-Partition Punjab Public Works Department, who moved in 1947 to Amritsar and Ludhiana (and later to Chandigarh), did not take with them any Rasul-scheme experience. In other words, the first program in the Punjab that combined the reclamation and irrigation uses of tubewells had barely been inaugurated prior to Partition. Secondly, and perhaps of greater importance, the key personnel who left the Irrigation Research Institute at Lahore and founded the new Irrigation and Power Research Institute (now the Land Reclamation, Irrigation, and Power Research Institute) at Amritsar, happened to be adherents of the "natural causation" theory of waterlogging and salinity.

Despite all the evidence of the rise of water tables (taken mostly from well measurements) in the areas under command of the irrigation canals, the Amritsar people believed that the fundamental

107. Revelle II, p. 96.
108. Harza Report, p. II-31.

cause lay in a cycle of increased rainfall that began around 1928. Artificial impediments to the natural drainage (road and railway embankments, and the canals themselves) contributed to waterlogging, but the fundamental solution to the problem, they thought, lay in "opening up the natural drainage of the country" and in waiting for a cycle of drier years to set in. The Amritsar people, led by Dr. H. L. Uppal, Director of the Institute,[109] do not question that large-capacity, deep-drawing turbine pumps installed in large numbers can effectively lower water tables at least in the initial stages. But they do not believe that the long-range effectiveness of the tubewells justifies the cost. Thus, there is an interesting measure of agreement between Dr. Uppal and his old colleague at Lahore, Dr. Nazir Ahmad. Dr. Nazir's efforts are aimed at reducing the cost of the tubewell installations and writing them off after ten or fifteen years. He is not interested in mining the deep aquifer of low-salinity water underlying the Punjab Plains so much as in producing local alleviation of waterlogging and some increased supplies of irrigation water for crop use and for the leaching of salts. Dr. Uppal simply does not believe in the economic efficacy of tuewells *for reclamation* in the East Punjab. And he does not feel that there is a need for developing a program of tubewell irrigation combined with reclamation in any of the areas served by the canal system.

In other words, in West Pakistan where surface water supplies will be limited in relation to canal commanded area even after completion of the IBP (see Chapter 7), one can justify a tubewell program partly on the need to develop the groundwater reserve for additional irrigation and leaching supplies. As we have seen, even S. S. Kirmani is a "groundwater" advocate to this extent. But in the East Punjab, Dr. Uppal feels, there will be sufficient surface water available after the completion of Pong and Thein dams, the Beas-Sutlej Link, and perhaps the upper storages on the Sutlej and Beas. So one does not need groundwater for irrigation, and one cannot justify the cost of the tubewell fields on the twin basis of irrigation-reclamation. Furthermore, Dr. Uppal fully shares Dr. Nazir's skepticism about the longevity of tubewells anywhere in the Punjab, and here he has his own experience as a guide.

109. Interview of March 16, 1964.

For the East Punjab does have tubewells. Over 1,500 of them have been constructed in the course of India's three Five Year Plans, some in connection with the "Grow More Food Program" of the early 1950s and others in areas provided with canal water. And that is the fundamental difference between the tubewells of the Indian Punjab and those of West Pakistan.

For the post-Partition Indian tubewell program was a logical outgrowth of Sir William Stamp's United Provinces scheme of the 1930s. Stamp's tubewells were designed to provide irrigation water in areas out of canal commands or in areas receiving insufficient canal supplies. As taken up in the postwar and post-Partition Indian planning, tubewells were used only for irrigation, not for reclamation. In brief, India—and particularly the Indian Punjab—has never had a Rasul scheme. (Perhaps it is just as well, for as we have seen, the Rasul experience was a shaky basis on which to embark on programs of the order of SCARP I or WAPDA's master plan or the Revelle program.) Instead, as hydroelectric power became available from the post-Partition multipurpose schemes, and from new thermal plants built under the Five Year Plans, part of it was diverted to tubewell installations, especially in the United Provinces. But there was never a tubewell program as such in the U. P. or in the East Punjab. Instead, tubewells were incorporated in the much broader community development program or in the overall agricultural "Grow More Food Program."

Looked at from a different angle, it may fairly be said that India adopted a "grass-roots" approach, building from the village level upward with a coordinated program of agricultural, cottage industry, rural roads, sanitation, and educational development (see Chapter 8). The community development program brought tubewells with it into the "dry districts" of the Punjab, but they were just one element, as was the fertilizer distribution element, the composting element, and the introduction of hybrid corn.

Thus one might say that although India has not had a Wiesner Mission or a Revelle Panel (though Dr. Revelle is currently serving as a member of India's new Commission on National Education), it has tried the Revelle approach, in a much more diluted form, toward agricultural development. The community development projects in India never put the emphasis upon additional water supplies, especially from tubewells, or upon fertilizers, which the Revelle Panel recommended for the 1-million acre project areas. No state in India, especially the East Punjab with its heavy commitments to the Bhakra and Pong projects, ever had the resources to undertake such a program—and it remains to be seen whether Pakistan will be able to marshal them. Thus, one cannot really speak of a "groundwater program" in the Indian Punjab unless one confines the term to the small-scale tubewell operations scattered throughout the "dry districts." And it is not likely that the East Punjab will adopt a broad irrigation-reclamation groundwater program until that distant day when so much water is needed by the Rajasthan Project that it becomes necessary to revise the 1955 Interstate Agreement that gives Punjab over 45 per cent of all additional supplies developed on the Eastern Rivers. Probably that day will never come, especially if India, at the urging of the U. S. Bureau of Reclamation and others, undertakes a thorough analysis of the incremental yield of surface water in Rajasthan compared with what it could produce in Punjab.

On the other hand, one can and must speak of a *reclamation* program in East Punjab, even though tubewells play no significant role in it. Waterlogging and salinity is a serious problem in the irrigated districts of the Indian Punjab, even in those areas of the cis-Sutlej Punjab where the Bhakra Canal provided increased allowances or brought irrigation for the first time barely ten years ago. We have indicated in Chapter 7 that the Hakra river bed has again begun to flow in certain seasons due to seepage from the canals. More exact information is provided in the annual report of the Irrigation and Power Research Institute (Amritsar) for 1959, which indicated that the total area of land in East Punjab damaged by waterlogging and salinity rose from 412,509 acres in 1956–57 to 520,245 acres in 1959–60.[110]

Compared with a total cropped area (including double-cropping) of some 24,450,040 acres in 1956–57, the damaged area seems small (less than 2 per cent), but the rate of increase (over 3.5 per cent per year) over this period is alarming. It is all the more alarming when one considers that it was just in this period that India succeeded in

110. Irrigation and Power Research Institute, Amritsar (India), *Report for the Year Ending November, 1959* (Amritsar, Irrigation Research Institute, November 1960), p. 93.

doing what the Bhakra Project was designed to do—introducing perennial or "restricted perennial" irrigation into areas of the East Punjab that had had either no irrigation or only nonperennial before; in other words, she created the precise conditions that led to the rapid rise of water tables in the perennial irrigated areas of the doabs in West Pakistan. Furthermore, since the foothill districts of the East Punjab receive significant amounts of effective rainfall, the combined seepage from the up-doab areas and the canal system into the aquifer may well produce a more rapid rise of the water table than historically occurred in the down-doab areas of the West Punjab with little rainfall and high rates of evapotranspiration.

It is interesting to note that the Indians are in accord with the Pakistanis in that they also attribute 97 per cent of the damage to salinity and only 3 per cent to waterlogging.[111] But as we have seen, the only way to reduce salinity is to provide good drainage and then apply excess water to leach down the salts, keeping the water table sufficiently low so that capillary rise cannot bring water back to the surface where it evaporates, leaving the salts behind. In a reclamation program of this sort, the Indians would have the advantage of the abundant surface water from the Bhakra and Pong dams, and the Beas-Sutlej Link, plus the added advantage of a higher natural rainfall over much of the East Punjab. Presumably, they would not need additional water supplies from the groundwater reservoir, although on the basis of West Pakistan's investigations, the aquifer of the East Punjab must be abundantly charged with water of good quality. But even without the expense of tubewells, drainage has to be provided. And the Indians in the East Punjab, let alone in Rajasthan, are not seriously engaged in providing a drainage system to complement the surface water irrigation system (see Chapter 7).

Instead, reclamation operations in East Punjab consist largely of "opening up the natural drainage," experimenting with canal linings (see Chapter 7), and designing crop rotations suitable for waterlogged, saline, or alkaline lands.[112] Much can be done with crop rotations, emphasizing rice or sugarcane culture on waterlogged lands or on saline lands that still have some natural drainage. Green manuring or fodder crops such as *jantar* or *guara* are useful on water-

111. Ibid.
112. Ibid., pp. 86–92.

logged lands, and will increase the yields of wheat or cotton sown subsequently in rotation patterns. But this is temporizing with the problem, not solving it. On the basis of the experience of the Indus Basin as a whole, the sooner a solution is found, the cheaper it will be. For the East Punjab (and for Rajasthan) the solution undoubtedly lies in open or tile drains. For even if one proposes to "write off" waterlogged and salinized areas in Punjab and replace them with new lands in Rajasthan, our discussion has indicated that the cost of developing the new lands, combined with the marginal costs of providing them with water that could be used more efficiently in the Punjab and of maintaining an overextended surface water system, would be far higher than the cost of draining the Punjab lands today. And what will India do when the Rajasthan lands, in turn, become salinized or even waterlogged?

10. Prospects for Future Development

"Only God knows the future; only a Prophet foretells it; and only a fool predicts it."

—Punjabi Proverb

A Brief Retrospect

Although the wise geographer avoids any suggestion of physical determinism, just as the wise historian shuns prediction, no student of the Indus Basin can escape the conclusion that its location and topography, combined with its endowments in water, soils, and climate, have made it one of the more frequented and continuously inhabited regions of this earth. The middle and lower Indus, its Punjab, Kabul-Swat, Kurram, and Gomal tributaries, and the piedmont route now marked by the Grand Trunk Road have served as thoroughfares during all of recorded time. The generally accepted route of Alexander the Great was no accident, but followed the path where food, forage, and plunder were available.[1] For in this climate

1. Although part of Alexander's army apparently moved down the Kabul Valley to Charsadda (opposite Peshawar), Alexander himself went up the Kunar (called the Chitral in Pakistan), crossed into Dir and Swat, and rejoined the rest of his forces at a point some distance above Attock for the Indus crossing. Then he proceeded to Taxila, near modern Rawalpindi, where he was well received. He crossed the Jhelum near the present city of that name and, after defeating Porus, crossed the Chenab near Marala and the Ravi above Lahore. When he reached the Beas, his army refused to continue. Alexander returned to

man cannot travel far from water, and the pattern of the rivers on the Indus Plains has served to channel movement not only between the delta and the foothills but across the piedmont, where the rivers and the floodplain agriculture they supported served as convenient resting and provisioning places. When one considers the high natural water tables of the foothill districts, including those below the Salt and Suleiman ranges and around the Kirana Hills, one can make a persuasive explanation for the ancient caravan routes that led from river to river and from well to well.

As man learned the techniques of inundation- and well-irrigation, the climate and soils of the Indus Plains began to nurture civilizations comparable to those of Mesopotamia and the Nile. But the very value of these irrigated lands has, time and again, proved to be an attraction fatal to the inhabitants of the Basin. From the time of the great massacre, attested by the skeletons unearthed at Mohenjo Daro, to the Punjab massacres of 1947, the value of water and irrigated land in the Indus Basin has been one of the prime factors in its turbulent history. Although British rule brought peace to the Indus Plains (though not to the hill districts of the North West Frontier) for a century, during which British engineering and administrative skill brought unheard-of prosperity to the doabs, the British Raj proved incapable of transferring power without a return to violence, which was motivated by economic as well as by political and communal factors.

But whatever improvements can be suggested, with the inestimable advantage of hindsight and time for analysis, in Lord Radcliffe's Partition Line (not affecting Kashmir) it is a boundary that has been lived with for nineteen years. Granting that political partition had become inevitable by the summer of 1947, and granting also that *both* Pakistan and India are the permanent legatees of the British in the Basin (unless a third power comes to control all or most of it), one can conclude that the inequities of the Partition Line were set right—within the limits of human dealings and patience—by the Indus Waters Treaty and the Development Fund Agreement. To ask

---

the Jhelum, where a fleet of boats was prepared, and the army then moved both on boats and on shore down the Jhelum and then down the Chenab and Panjnad to the Indus, reaching the delta in the summer of 325 B.C. (Encyclopaedia Britannica, 1959 edition, vol. I, "Alexander the Great," p. 569.)

that a finer adjustment be made is to find fault with eight years of painstaking work by some of the best-qualified engineers and negotiators of both nations, of the World Bank, and of the consultants associated with them. On a purely theoretical plane, one could say that the post-Partition development—physical, political, and economic —of the Indus Basin would have been facilitated had the Treaty negotiations preceded Independence and had provisions somewhat similar to those of the Treaty been made a part of the Indian Independence Act. But in practice that would have been impossible under the conditions of 1947. Again in theory it is possible to find fault with the Treaty itself, but in practice it would be hard to justify any further delay in the projects for the sake of a few more acre feet of water or a few more dollars.

Certainly, with the signing of the Supplemental Agreement of March 1964 Pakistan had gained as much as can reasonably be expected in a world that is less than young Candide was taught to believe. And if India was unhappy over the assignment of the Chenab to Pakistan (see pages 256–58), she had secured the undisputed right to do as she pleased with the Eastern Rivers after 1970 or 1973. Her contribution to the cost of the "replacement" works, when offset by the loans from the World Bank and the United States Government, amounted to only $118 million, or about 13 per cent of the original Development Fund. It is well worth noting both that India continued to make her payments to the Fund during and after the "September War" crisis, and that neither side took this occasion to denounce the Treaty. Although some of the irrigation works, notably the section of the BRBD Link that extends from the Ravi siphon across the Grand Trunk Road to Bedian near Kasur, figured in the fighting, neither side went so far as to bomb a major barrage or dam (possibly out of fear of retaliation, but hopefully also because of a realization of what such destruction would mean to the people dependent upon it). Although the Indo-Pakistan border was crossed in many places (notably around the Marala, Ferozepore, and Suleimanke headworks), the Ayub-Shastri agreement signed in Tashkent on January 10, 1966, has resulted in its restoration to where Lord Radcliffe and the Indian Independence Act put it: from the Ujh tributary of the Ravi to (but not necessarily including) the Rann of Cutch. With the restoration of the boundary and continued observance of the Treaty, it seems fair to say that, as far as the surface flows of the Indus Rivers are concerned, the issues created in 1947 were settled in 1960.

Would this were true of Kashmir! But as this is written that problem seems as insoluble as ever. In many ways, it is the antithesis of the Indus Waters Dispute. For the Kashmir problem is not *essentially* a question of land or water, but of people and prestige. As the partition and the Indus Waters Treaty demonstrate, questions of land and water rights can be solved, however imperfectly, by awards made by impartial referees in the secrecy of their chambers, or though painstaking negotiations conducted in confidence and with the benefit of expert technical advice and financial compensation. But the Kashmir Dispute has dragged on through two hot wars and eighteen years of unsteady truce along the cease-fire line. It has been the subject of innumerable Security Council debates and resolutions, conducted in the full glare of publicity and complicated by official statements of "unalterable" positions. The fixed positions of India and Pakistan have become so well known that it is hard to envisage negotiations, much less an acceptable solution. Prediction would be foolhardy, but it is relevant to point out that the negotiations that led to the Indus Waters Treaty can hardly be cited as a precedent for a Kashmir solution. Far different issues, and far deeper feelings, are involved. Water, money, even land can be the subjects of give-and-take negotiations. Peaceful exchanges of population have occasionally been worked out, notably among Greece, Turkey, and Bulgaria. But there is no precedent for the peaceful transfer of 3.5 million people from one sovereignty to another.

As long as the Kashmir problem remains confined to the territory of Kashmir, and the Indus Waters Treaty is observed, even a change in political alignment would not drastically affect the programs considered in this study. As was indicated in Chapter 6, the Treaty was carefully worded so as to cover most contingencies in Kashmir. Only in the extreme, but extremely unlikely, case of either nation acquiring control of all of Jammu-Kashmir would a revision of the Treaty be necessary, and such a revision would affect land, not water. Indian control of Azad Kashmir would bring the left abutments of the Mangla Dam (including the diversion tunnels, powerhouse, and the intake and upper reach of the UJC with its new Bong Canal alignment) into her hands. India would also gain some of the upper storage sites on the Indus, such as Skardu, which would be of no use to her for irrigation and which are so inaccessible as to preclude their use even by Pakistan in the foreseeable future. Pakistani control of Jammu and southern Kashmir would give her the Dhiangarh storage site on the Chenab, the possibility of constructing smaller reservoirs on its Monawar and Jammu Tavi affluents, and the right abutments of the Madhopur headworks (including the short "Kashmir" Canal) and of the proposed Ravi dam at Thein. But in either of these highly unlikely events, there would be no need to change the water allocations of the Treaty (except for India's rights to make small uses of water in the Western Rivers; see page 257). In the somewhat less unlikely event of a partition of Kashmir more or less along communal lines, it might be possible to draw the boundary not just on the basis of district or tahsil majority lines, but so as to place the border along the Chenab in the Dhiangarh reach. Under these conditions, the Treaty might be amended to allow construction of a dam, with India and Pakistan sharing the costs, and sharing, in equitable proportions, the water and power, as a token of cooperation and as an incentive to abide by the partition agreement. It is even conceivable that such an understanding could be extended to the upper Chenab, allowing development of the Marhu and Palchar reaches with costs and benefits equitably shared. But for the present and foreseeable future, one can ask only that the Treaty as signed continues to be observed.

Indeed, as viewed from the vantage point of mid 1966, the signing of the Indus Waters Treaty in September 1960 represents the high point in nineteen years of Indo-Pakistan relations. Due to causes that are largely beyond the scope of this study, relations between the two nations deteriorated almost steadily from September 1960 to September 1965. Landmarks in the decline were Pakistan's attitude during the Chinese-Indian conflict in the autumn of 1962, Pakistan's strenuous objections to "massive Western arms aid" to India, Pakistan's border agreement with China, the failure of the series of discussions held (at the urging of the U.S. and U.K.) on Kashmir early in 1963, India's progressive constitutional integration of Kashmir State, the failure of Sheikh Abdullah, the former Prime Minister of Indian Kashmir, to secure any meeting of the minds on the problem during his brief period of free travel, the Rann of Cutch fighting in the spring of 1965 (literally and figuratively a dry run for what came later), and of course the "September War." The death of Nehru during the period when Sheikh Abdullah was trying to arrange a Nehru-Ayub meeting on Kashmir, and the death of Shastri immediately after signing the Tashkent agreement, have further prejudiced chances of negotiation. On the other hand, it may be that the "September War" has had a salutary effect in convincing both parties that a violent solution is out of the question. Militarily, the war was a standoff; economically, a disaster. Aside from a few extremists on either side, apparently both parties were glad to see hostilities terminated. Neither country really wanted, nor could either afford, a longer and larger war. The fact that, as far as is known, both armies conducted themselves according to the "rules of war" represents an uncommon courtesy these days. The fact that the war did not spread to East Pakistan indicates that the objectives of both sides were limited. Above all the fact that, as far as is known, fears of communal retaliations against Muslims in India and Hindus in East Pakistan proved unfounded provides an encouraging contrast to 1947. So there may be some hope that, even if the Kashmir impasse persists, India and Pakistan can devote most of their resources to domestic problems which, especially in India, are serious enough to warrant full attention.

Economic and Political Outlook: India and Pakistan

The "September War" with Pakistan climaxed three lean years for India. The confrontation with China starting in October 1962 and the growing animosity of Pakistan coincided with a series of poor harvests, hoarding and maldistribution of food supplies, continued demands for regional autonomy (notably by the Nagas and the Akali Sikhs),[2] and the political uncertainty following the death of Nehru

2. The Nagas in Assam and Manipur want full independence; the Akali Sikhs wish to divide the (East) Punjab into two states, one of which would have a Sikh majority, and will apparently achieve their goal by the end of 1966. This demand may be viewed as part of the continuing search for an area that will be dominantly Sikh in religion and Punjabi in language. As was shown in Chapter 5, even the influx of Sikh refugees from Pakistan at the time of Partition failed to give them a majority in the East Punjab as that state was delineated. But Chapter 5 also indicates that the Sikhs are far from united, and in fact many "Congress Sikhs" were opposed to the Akali demands for a separate Sikh-Punjabi state.

520

on May 27, 1964. As is well known, Prime Minister Shastri devoted most of his short tenure to efforts to solve India's agricultural crisis. But the increased defense allocations necessitated by the Chinese and Pakistani threats have made it impossible for India to concentrate on her developmental projects in recent years. In April 1965, coincident with the fighting in the Rann of Cutch but for reasons not fully understood even in the United States, President Lyndon Johnson requested both Prime Minister Shastri and President Ayub to postpone their visits scheduled for the following May and June. When Shastri reacted by canceling his visit entirely, the United States quickly announced that it was joining with the nine other member nations of the "Aid to India Consortium" organized by the World Bank in pledging a total of $1.027 billion for the final year of India's Third Five Year Plan (the American pledge amounted to $435 million, or the same amount as she had contributed to the third and fourth years of the plan).

But India had come to regard such aid as a continuing commitment, and the pledge did little to mollify feelings in New Delhi.[3] (We shall shortly examine the situation in Rawalpindi.) In June, the United States refused to renew the annual Food for Peace agreement with India, and announced instead that grain shipments would be continued on a month-by-month basis until India demonstrated that she was doing everything in her power to close her own agricultural gap. With the onset of the "September War" the United States canceled all military aid to both India and Pakistan, and said that it would make no new commitments for economic aid beyond what was in the "pipeline." Even after India and Pakistan accepted the United Nations truce proposal, Food for Peace shipments to India remained on a month-by-month basis (and went on such a basis for Pakistan in December when the annual agreement expired), giving rise to charges that food was being used as a political weapon. Although late in December 1965 President Johnson announced that the United States would send up to 15 million tons of wheat to India in 1966, if it was needed to prevent starvation, there was no new commitment on economic aid. Instead, it was made clear that India's agricultural policy would be high on the agenda when Prime Minister Shastri

3. *New York Times*, April 21, 1965, pp. 1, 5; and April 23, 1965, pp. 1, 5.

came (in response to a new invitation) to Washington in February 1966.[4]

Shastri's death in Tashkent on January 10, 1966, again postponed a heads-of-government meeting, and although Prime Minister Indira Gandhi came to Washington at the end of March, India was forced to enter her Fourth Five Year Plan period on April 1, 1966 (an interim one year plan was substituted for the first year) without a firm commitment that America would continue its massive underwriting. Any lingering doubts that the United States had embarked on a new foreign aid course were dispelled by President Johnson's 1966 State of the Union Message, in which he called upon Congress "to give a new and daring direction to our foreign aid program, designed to make a maximum attack on hunger, disease and ignorance in those countries determined to help themselves—and to help those nations trying to control population growth."[5] That India, which received 6 million tons, or half of the Indian and one-fifth of the American wheat crop in 1964–65, would be a prime example of the new policy was hardly in doubt. Indeed, many Indians agreed that a thorough review of agricultural policy was called for, including both the expansion of the irrigated area and intensification of production through the use of fertilizers, plant-protection chemicals, and better techniques and incentives.

Late in April 1966, Asoka Mehta, the Indian Minister of Planning, came to Washington for discussions with U.S. and World Bank officials. Mehta asked that the Consortium increase its annual aid from the $1.1 billion per year of the Third Five Year Plan to about $1.7 billion per year during the Fourth, with the American contribution rising to $700 or $750 million per year.[6] Mehta apparently was told that any increase in assistance would depend on liberalization of India's import restrictions on raw materials, spare parts, and components and of India's policy toward foreign private investment, especially in fertilizer production facilities. Stress was also laid upon a more effective birth-control program and on devaluation of the

4. Ibid., November 30, 1965, pp. 1, 7; January 24, 1966, pp. 37, 48; *India Briefing* (New York, The India Council of the Asia Society), November 1965, p. 2.

5. *New York Times*, January 13, 1966, p. 13.

6. Ibid., April 17, 1966, p. 2.

rupee. Only after India had undertaken or promised all of these measures, despite severe criticism from Krishna Menon and others, was full-scale resumption of U. S. aid announced on June 15, 1966. At the same time it was reported that the Consortium would lend India $900 million in nonproject aid, designed to pay for the above-mentioned imports up to March 31, 1967. Indications were that project assistance agreements, for dams, factories, etc., might total $400 million, but that they would be negotiated on a bilateral basis with Consortium members at least until April 1, 1967 when India's revised Fourth Five Year Plan will go into effect after further revision by India and appraisal by the Consortium.[7]

How the revision and appraisal would affect India's projects in the Indus Basin is hard to say. On the one hand, projections are simpler than for the Pakistani portion, because in India at the present time only surface water development is significant. The Pong Dam component of the BBRP is not only under construction, but is as essential to surface water operations in that program as Tarbela is in the IBP. Furthermore, the United States was morally committed, under the terms of the Indus Waters agreement, to lend India $33 million for Pong as soon as India satisfied the requirements of the Development Loan Fund (see page 254, n. 67), and the World Bank provided another $23 million. Although India will have to raise at least another $187 million for Pong, it seems reasonable to expect that the dam will be completed more or less on schedule (around 1971). And it is likely that a Beas-Sutlej Link of some sort (not necessarily involving the Pandoh Tunnel) will follow Pong. The Larji Dam may be included both as part of the Beas-Sutlej diversion and to increase regulated supplies on the Beas. But Thein on the Ravi and Slapper on the upper Sutlej may not be undertaken until near the end of this century unless India's economic prospects radically improve.

For it must be remembered that, although the East Punjab and Rajasthan account for almost 20 per cent of the total irrigated area of India, about 25 per cent of the canal-irrigated area, and almost 16 per cent of the cropped area (including double-cropping), that great

7. Ibid., June 16, 1966, pp. 1, 4. The membership of both the "Aid to India" and the "Aid to Pakistan" consortiums now includes the World Bank and the following nations: United States, United Kingdom, Canada, France, West Germany, Belgium, Netherlands, Austria, Italy, and Japan.

nation has many other irrigation schemes under construction or in the planning stages. Thus, while the contribution of the BBRP can be a significant one, in itself it cannot solve India's agricultural crisis. (In West Pakistan, on the other hand, the irrigated agriculture of the Indus Plains contributes 75 per cent of all food and fiber. Although there is some exchange of agricultural products between the East and West Wings, East Pakistan is twice as dependent upon food imports from West Pakistan as the other way around. So the success or failure of the IBP and the groundwater programs in West Pakistan is far more critical for the country as a whole than the success or failure of the BBRP is for India.)

Indeed, what India apparently needs is a Revelle-type approach for the entire nation. Such an approach would not necessarily emphasize tubewells, though groundwater and reclamation will undoubtedly play a major role in certain areas, but would incorporate the concentrated application of inputs on those areas that show the most promise of achieving a multiplier effect. Within the Indus Basin, the review made by the Bureau of Reclamation team (see Chapters 7 and 8) already suggests that India should substitute more intensive use of surface water and fertilizers on the existing commands, especially in the Punjab, rather than continue to extend the Rajasthan Canal into the Thar Desert. If our discussion of what little is known of relative soil and drainage conditions in Rajasthan and the East Punjab is even an approximation of true conditions, then India would be well served by such a redirection of development expenditures. If the present crisis, in which the failure of agriculture to keep pace with population growth has played a far more fundamental role than hostilities with China or Pakistan, ultimately produces a shift from a policy of adding new lands of dubious productivity to one of concentrating irrigation supplies and other inputs on the best of existing lands, then India should be far better off in the long run. For it must be realized that harsh winters, like that of 1963–64, and failures of the monsoon, such as occurred in 1965, are not just occasional disasters but endemic factors in the climate of the subcontinent. The only sure safeguard against them is an agricultural-population policy that is based on maximizing yields and minimizing demands.

Before proceeding to analyze the effect of 1965 developments upon the prospects for irrigation agriculture in West Pakistan, therefore, we must take note of another aspect of United States policy that underwent rapid evolution during that year. Although the United States had indicated a willingness to help developing nations with research and information on population control during the Kennedy Administration, notably when Sweden asked the United Nations General Assembly to debate population policy in December 1962, it was the Johnson Administration, beginning with the 1965 State of the Union Message, that moved toward giving preference in economic aid to those nations that are actively striving to curb population growth.[8] The White House Conference on International Cooperation, held in Washington at the end of November 1965, went a step further by suggesting that "a new emphasis upon food production and population planning in United States assistance programs" be combined with a recognition of the rights to birth-control information and freedom of choice in making use of such information both in developing nations and in the United States itself.[9] As noted above, the first of these suggestions was formally incorporated in the 1966 State of the Union Message. Adoption of the second suggestion through a publicity or incentive program for smaller families in the United States would not only serve to expedite achievement of the "Great Society" but would counteract any implication that we were asking the peoples of Latin America, Africa, and Asia to curb their burgeoning populations while doing nothing about our own.

There is no need to go into either a moral or an economic justification for population control in this study. The facts of life—too much life—on this planet are becoming increasingly obvious. Anyone familiar with the urban depravity of New York or New Delhi, Chicago or Karachi, Cairo or Calcutta, Rome or Rio de Janeiro, Mexico City or Manila, Djakarta or Bombay, or with the rural squalor of Appalachia, the Brazilian northeast, the Italian Mezzogiorno, and most of Africa and Asia, including the Indo-Pakistan subcontinent, needs little convincing that all of the benefits projected by the various plans for development could be greatly enhanced (or, realistically

8. Ibid., December 26, 1965, p. E4; and Arthur M. Schlesinger, Jr., *A Thousand Days* (Boston, Houghton Mifflin Co., 1965), pp. 602–03.
9. *New York Times*, November 29, 1965, pp. 1, 13; November 30, 1965, pp. 1, 20.

speaking, rendered possible) by decreasing the denominator of the resource-to-man fraction.

To mention only the programs with which we have dealt most extensively, the Harza approach is calculated to provide a diet of 2,522 calories per day to an estimated 1975 population of 65 million West Pakistanis, as compared with the estimated 2,000 calories per day (including 1 million tons of food imports per year) available to the 1961 population of 43 million. The 1975 population estimate was based on the probability that the 1951–61 rate of growth, 2.4 per cent per annum, would reach 3.0 per cent by 1975. The 1975 average intake is above the 2,300 calories per day *minimum* set by F.A.O., but does not meet F.A.O. minimum requirements for protein and fat intake.[10] Despite the 3.5 per cent per annum increase in agricultural output achieved during Pakistan's Second Five Year Plan, it seems questionable whether Harza's 1975 goal, which involves increasing the domestic agricultural output in West Pakistan from the 11 million tons produced in 1961 to 25 million tons, will be achieved.

The Revelle program aims at doubling the per capita yields after twenty-five years even with a population increase of 3 per cent per annum, but as we have seen, it depends upon higher rates of inputs and more concentrated administrative attention than it is likely to receive. Perhaps because United States policy on population control assistance had not advanced so far by 1962, or even by early 1964— although Pakistan had officially endorsed population planning in the mid 1950s—neither Revelle I nor Revelle II suggests the increase in per capita benefits to be achieved if the population of West Pakistan does *not* reach the "probable" figure of 67.4 million by 1981 or 78.3 million by 1986.[11]

Through March 1965 one might have said that there was a reasonable chance for Pakistan to meet the goals set by either the Revelle or the Harza program. On March 18, as we have noted, the World Bank survey team announced that the Tarbela scheme, on which both the Revelle and Harza programs rely, was technically feasible and

10. Harza Report, pp. 25, 30, 32.
11. Revelle II, p. 70, Table 1, 3, derived from United Nations, Department of Economic and Social Affairs, *The Population of Asia and the Far East, 1950–1980* (New York, 1959).

economically justifiable. On the last three days of the month, with the cooperation of the Pakistan Planning Commission, the Harvard Advisory Group held a conference in Cambridge, Massachusetts, to commemorate the tenth anniversary of their work in Pakistan and of the submission of the First Five Year Plan (see page 490). Attending the meeting were distinguished economists from virtually every nation extending assistance to Pakistan, plus representatives of the World Bank, the Organization for Economic Cooperation and Development, the Ford Foundation, and David E. Bell, director of the United States Agency for International Development. Evaluations of recent performance and projections of future development in Pakistan were equally optimistic:

> In the First Plan, the growth of GNP barely exceeded the growth of population. After 1960, in the Second Plan, all the indices began to move sharply upwards and to exceed the expectations of the Plan itself. For instance, GNP increased by nearly 30 per cent, savings rose from 6.8 to 9.5 per cent of GNP, the marginal savings rate rose from a minus quantity to 21.8, exports grew by seven per cent a year and dependence on foreign aid proved to be some six per cent less than had been expected. Moreover, all this rapid expansion took place within a context of almost complete stability of prices. It can be argued that the confident predictions of the Third Plan simply reflect the dynamism already apparent since 1960.
>
> Pakistan's Third Plan has been formulated with a look forward to developments over the next twenty years. During this period, the country hopes to quadruple its Gross National Product and put an end to dependence upon foreign assistance.
>
> The Third Plan proposed through a planned expenditure of $10.9 billion to increase Gross National Product by 37 per cent in the next five years, to provide 6.5 million new jobs, to increase the level of savings from 11.8 per cent to 15.3 per cent, to keep the marginal rate of savings at 22 per cent, to increase exports by nine per cent a year and imports by only seven per cent, thus reducing the country's dependence on foreign resources from 8.1 per cent of GNP to 6.7 per cent.
>
> The economists noted that although such developments were

527

large in the context of contemporary economic achievement, they did not appear to be out of line with the trends of the last five years.[12]

The optimism of the Harvard Group was further reflected in a talk given on May 2 by Professor Gustav V. Papanek, Acting Director of Harvard's Development Advisory Service under which the Group operates, and entitled, "Pakistan: the Development Miracle." Repeating some of the above figures, Professor Papanek made a strong case that Pakistan had made better use of foreign aid than most developing nations. But he concluded with these cautions:

> Pakistan's success has in part been due to a very high rate of foreign aid and remarkable restraint on defense expenditure. It is the only military government that I know, when it was a military government, that did not substantially raise military expenditures.
>
> For another decade anyway, Pakistan's continued growth will depend on a very substantial inflow of foreign resources, and on rather sharp limits on the expenditure for defense. If either of these changes markedly, either because of something that Pakistan does, or something the United States or other aid-givers do, if defense expenditures go up and foreign aid goes down, it could still be disastrous over the next decade. Ten years from now Pakistan ought to be on the way to a declining aid program but this is not the case over the next few years.[13]

Professor Papanek's cautions, delivered on May 2, show a good deal of prescience (the last paragraph quoted is particularly close to the mark). Two factors may have inspired him. During April, a small cloud had grown into a thunderhead over the Rann of Cutch. And, during April, President Johnson had asked President Ayub to postpone his visit until after the United States Congress' annual debate on foreign aid. Although an agreement providing for a cease-fire in the Rann of Cutch to be followed by negotiations and, if necessary,

12. Embassy of Pakistan, Washington, D.C., *Pakistan Affairs*, April 16, 1965, p. 2.
13. Embassy of Pakistan, Information Division, Washington, D.C., "Pakistan: The Development Miracle" (Text of an address by Prof. Gustav F. Papanek given in New York on May 4, 1965, under the joint auspices of the Pakistani-American Chamber of Commerce, Inc., and the Asia Society), p. 12.

by arbitration was signed on June 30, it either came too late or was considered insufficiently relevant to forestall an American request for postponement of the "Aid to Pakistan Consortium" meeting scheduled for July 27. In a footnote to pages 305–06, where we discussed the Aswan-like nature of the Tarbela controversy, we quoted the reaction of Pakistan Foreign Minister Z. A. Bhutto to postponement of the Consortium meeting at the very start of Pakistan's Third Five Year Plan. The reaction of President Ayub was made clear in his customary first-of-the-month broadcast on August 1:

> I received a message from the President of the United States of America indicating that the U.S. Government was asking the World Bank for the postponement of the Consortium meeting scheduled for July 27. The ostensible reason was that certain congressional difficulties and procedures must be got over before the U.S. could pledge its share of economic assistance toward the financing of our Third Five Year Plan.
>
> Interesting enough, neither the mood of the Congress nor the procedural difficulties had prevented the United States from pledging assistance to India well in advance of the authorization by the Congress. The distinction was as obvious as it was invidious.
>
> It was also suggested that the period of postponement could be utilized for discussing "other matters." Enough was mentioned to show that these "other matters" belonged to the realm of politics. My reaction to all this was as simple and straight forward as that of any patriotic Pakistani who values his nation's honor and security more than anything else.
>
> I made it abundantly clear that economic assistance was one thing and political dependence quite another. While countries strive for freedom in order to develop they will not seek development at the cost of freedom. The country's economic progress and prosperity of its people are of the utmost importance, but its security and independence come first. It is our right as an independent nation to normalize our relations with our neighbors however different our ideologies might be and that right we shall not allow to be compromised. It was in this context that I said we are looking for friends not masters.
>
> The situation with which we are faced today involves a prin-

ciple of vital interest to all developing countries of Asia and
Africa. The principle is that economic assistance, which is made
available by affluent countries to those who are struggling for
development, should be governed by purely economic considerations. I have no doubt that opinion in all developing countries
fully endorses this principle.[14]

Whether there was any connection at all between the United States
"foreign aid diplomacy," Pakistan's reaction to it, and the infiltration of Pakistanis into Indian-held Kashmir in August 1965 can only
be conjectured.[15] It is not inconceivable that the coincidence of the
postponement of the Consortium meeting with India's agreement to
submit the Rann of Cutch dispute to negotiation or arbitration led
Pakistan to believe that she had little to lose and possibly much to
gain by bringing the Kashmir issue to the fore. It might also be
suggested that a genuine parallel existed between President Ayub's
sentiments, in July of 1965, and those of President Nasser of Egypt,
in July of 1956 after the United States, the United Kingdom, and
the World Bank had reneged on underwriting the Aswan project.
Pakistan, of course, had no Suez Canal to nationalize. But it did
have, in Kashmir and in the Security Council, an issue that could
prove embarrassing to the Western powers. Perhaps such a comparison is forced, but in the light of the Soviet Union's quick offer
of good offices in September 1965, and of the apparent success of

14. *Pakistan Affairs*, August 2, 1965, p. 1.
15. We place this much stress upon American policy not only because the
U.S. is the generally acknowledged leader of the "Western" alliances and the
principal underwriter of the World Bank, of Pakistan's First and Second Five
Year Plans, and of the Indus Basin Development Fund and Supplementary
Agreement, but because, as has been explained in Chapter 7 (see pp. 308–14),
Pakistan hoped to pay the domestic costs of Tarbela largely with counterpart
rupees generated by the Food for Peace program. Thus, although West Pakistan's agriculture is in a better position than India's, American food shipments
will continue to play a critical role until the IBP and the groundwater program
really show results—presumably, in another ten or fifteen years. At the same
time, it hardly needs to be said that the United States does not control the
foreign policy of its allies, including the members of the "Aid to Pakistan Consortium." At a meeting, finally held in Karachi on November 26, 1965, the
United Kingdom, Canada, France, West Germany, and Italy made bilateral
pledges (i.e. outside the World Bank Consortium) totaling $116.5 million toward
the first year of the Third Plan. The Soviet Union has increased its contribution
from $30 to $50 million. (*Pakistan News Digest*, December 1, 1965, pp. 1, 8–9.)

the Tashkent conference in January 1966, one is tempted to draw the parallel.

From the Soviet point of view, of course, the primary goal of its offer of good offices was to ensure the preservation of India as a counterpoise to China (a goal of Western foreign policy since 1949). In September 1965 this meant sparing India a war on two fronts, and it is even more interesting to speculate on what the Soviet Union would have done, than to speculate on what the West would have done, had China come to Pakistan's aid with more than threats against India. But the Soviet offer was apparently as welcome in Rawalpindi as it was in New Delhi. It is not at all clear that Pakistan really wanted China to move against India. Foreign Minister Bhutto may have desired it; President Ayub most probably did not. For there would have been little glory and little ultimate gain in a joint Pakistan-Chinese victory over India, assuming (and it is a large assumption) that the Big Three permitted one, and Pakistan would have emerged far more beholden to China than she has ever been to the West.

As matters turned out, the Soviet Union at Tashkent managed to replace the United States and Britain as the mediators between India and Pakistan (a role the Western powers were apparently glad to relinquish). By mid 1966, the Tashkent agreements had been carried out, restoring the Partition Line and the Kashmir cease-fire line. The Rann of Cutch dispute was being arbitrated. And Indo-Pakistan relations had returned to "normal," i.e. to a state of armed truce and watchful waiting.

During the months after Tashkent, the Soviet Union made various attempts to capitalize on her new-found popularity in Pakistan. Several new barter and loan agreements under which the Soviet Union would supply Pakistan with pig iron, bulldozers, tractors, and spare parts were signed, followed by an agreement to allow the U.S.S.R. to open consulates in Karachi and Dacca. Similar agreements were reached between Pakistan and East European members of the Soviet Bloc. On Pakistan Day, March 23, 1966 (the anniversary of the 1940 Lahore Resolution), a Pakistan-Soviet Society of Cultural Relations opened in Moscow. The signing of a Pakistan-Soviet Cultural and Scientific Exchange Agreement on April 22 was hailed by Pakistan's Minister for Education, Health, Labour, and Social Welfare who later asserted that Pakistan's ultimate aim was "Islamic Socialism."[16]

Thus one might be tempted to say that in the spring of 1966, as India under Prime Minister Indira Gandhi seemed to be moving to the right and toward the U.S.A., Pakistan seemed to be moving to the left toward the U.S.S.R. But such a generalization would probably be erroneous. The simple dichotomy, too often prevalent in American thinking, is fallacious, especially when applied to Asian nations such as India and Pakistan. A foreign, sovereign nation need not be "either with you or against you"; it may be with you on some matters and against you on others. A more correct assessment of the situation, in the aftermath of the "September War" and the Tashkent Conference, would be that Pakistan is now maturing a more flexible and independent foreign policy. Even the Soviet Union is forced to take note of this fact. For Pakistan's "flirtation" with China, begun in earnest in 1962, continues apparently unabated by Pakistan's new ties with the U.S.S.R. Pakistan entertained Liu Shao-Chi, Chairman of the People's Republic of China, on a prolonged state visit in March and April 1966. The dismissal of Foreign Minister Bhutto on June 18, hailed by some in the West as marking the end of the "flirtation" and the quid for a resumption of full American aid, was put in perspective by President Ayub's assurances of enduring friendship to China's Premier Chou En-Lai when the latter visited Rawalpindi at the end of the month.[17] Even China has managed to extend some limited economic assistance to Pakistan, and President Ayub has reaffirmed his policy of accepting aid from all nations.[18] With the resumption of full U.S. aid, direct and through the Aid to Pakistan Consortium, it would appear, in mid 1966, that this policy is paying off.

Prospects for Irrigation and Reclamation Programs in West Pakistan

The events of 1965 and early 1966 certainly seem to improve Pakistan's chances of obtaining the necessary foreign assistance for completing the IBP and embarking on a major groundwater and reclama-

16. *Pakistan News Digest*, May 1, 1966, p. 10; May 15, 1966, p. 3.
17. *New York Times*, July 1, 1966, p. 4.
18. *Pakistan News Digest*, May 15, 1966, "Chronicle of Events," p. lxxxxv.

tion program in the West Wing. The extent to which the Aswan experience figures in the thinking of U.S., U.K., and World Bank officials in the aftermath of the Tashkent Conference is of course impossible to estimate. But by the end of January 1966 a World Bank team was back in Pakistan to examine projects to be financed by the Consortium, and in February talks were held in Karachi between Bank officials and those of the Government of Pakistan regarding aid for fiscal 1966–67. Shortly thereafter the Bank began to release funds for construction of access works at Tarbela and for paying the consultants designing the dam. In mid-April, coincident with Chinese Chairman Liu's state visit to Pakistan, Finance Minister Shoaib held encouraging discussions in Washington with Bank and U.S. officials. And in June, as we saw in Chapter 7, S. S. Kirmani, Chief Engineer for the IBP, expressed confidence that the Consortium would give final approval to Tarbela's construction.

Thus, after ten years of argument, first over whether storage dams ought to be included in the Indus Waters settlement, then over whether the "friendly Governments" were committed to build a "dam on the Indus" or just to supply a sum of money for the IBP, then over the so-called "groundwater alternative," and finally over the technical and economic feasibility of various sites on the Indus, it seems safe to conclude that Tarbela will indeed be built, one way or another. The World Bank study team has already conceded that Tarbela "is technically feasible and economically justifiable" (see page 314), and the Government of Pakistan has made the dam and all it represents a popular issue, within the country and among other developing nations, in its struggle for the principle (or slogan) that "economic assistance should be governed by purely economic considerations." So it seems fairly likely both that the "Aid to Pakistan Consortium" will continue massive underwriting of Pakistan's Five Year Plans, under which the foreign exchange costs of Tarbela would be subsumed, and that the United States will allow Pakistan to use counterpart funds from a continued Food for Peace program to pay the domestic costs of Tarbela as envisaged in March 1964 (see pages 309, 314). Even if these funds are not forthcoming, or are reduced, Pakistan would still proceed with Tarbela because it represents an integral part of the IBP scheme without which the Jhelum-Chenab Zone would be overloaded and Sind deprived (see pages

291–92) and because it represents a popular political issue. To build Tarbela under these conditions, Pakistan would have to turn to other foreign sources of materials, equipment, and engineering talent. (It would not be inconceivable for the Soviet Union to transfer equipment and engineers as they finish their work on Aswan to Tarbela, though this seems unneeded at the moment.) But Tarbela will be built both because the IBP has now become self-perpetuating and for the same combination of economic and political reasons that Aswan is being built.

On the other hand, a reduction of Consortium and direct American aid would probably result in a curtailment of the groundwater and reclamation program, not only because of the costs involved but because that program is regarded primarily as an American-sponsored program. Such a connotation is of course unfair to the Pakistani groundwater advocates in WAPDA and the former members of the Pakistani GWDO. But because of the work of the A.I.D.-USGS team, the Revelle Panel, and many of the American consultants, the connotation is a political fact of life. A curtailment of American support for the groundwater and reclamation program would not remove all the groundwater advocates, but it would undoubtedly make their task much more difficult. At the moment of writing, however, it does not seem that any serious curtailment will result.

Assuming, then, that Tarbela will be built and that a substantial groundwater and reclamation program will be carried out, let us turn briefly to the long-range question of the roles that will be played by surface water and groundwater in the irrigation of Pakistan's Indus Plains. In the long run, this question will be answered in economic and physical, rather than political, terms. With respect to surface water, the physical limitations are more serious than the economic: that is, even if the funds can be obtained, there is a physical limit to the amount of on- and off-channel storage that can be provided within West Pakistan, and some of this storage capacity has to be allocated for silt. More precisely, it can be said that topographical and hydrological conditions are such that the costs of providing additional surface storage would rise steeply beyond a point which is already in sight, i.e. beyond the off-channel storages that would be associated with Mangla and Tarbela, the 1.5 m.a.f. live storage Munda site on the Swat, and, possibly, the 6.4 m.a.f. live

534

storage site at Kalabagh on the Indus. In addition to these, the Harza Report lists seven major potential sites that are under appraisal or have been the subjects of reconnaissance study, but only three of the seven, with a total of only 12 m.a.f. of live storage, would appear (to this author) to have any likelihood of construction in the foreseeable future.[19]

Even considering the possibilities of using the groundwater reservoir for surface water regulation (i.e. manipulating the operation of the irrigation system so as to cause more water to infiltrate to the groundwater table, from which it will find its way back into the rivers downstream even in the low water season, which has nothing to do with pumping from the groundwater reservoir), the Harza Report concludes, "it is most unlikely that ultimate development of the three rivers by surface storage and artificial recharge of the aquifer will permit the delivery of more than 120 million acre-feet annually to canal heads in the Indus Plains."[20]

Thus the Harza program envisages an ultimate use of only 120 m.a.f. per year in the Indus Plains out of the 138 m.a.f. which would come into Pakistan in an average year after India has made the uses which the Treaty allows in the upper courses of the Western Rivers. By 1975, when Harza assumes that both raised Mangla and raised Tarbela will be in existence, providing a total live storage of 17.4 m.a.f. of which 16.6 m.a.f. would be added to the dry-season flows,

---

19. Harza Report, p. 43. These seven sites and their live storage capacities as listed by Harza are as follows:

River	Site	Live Storage (in m.a.f.)
Shyok	Skardu	10.0
Indus	Chasma	15.0
	Panjar	9.0
Kunhar	Chiniot	2.5
Chenab	Kalangai	1.4
Swat	Khazana	6.5
	Khapalu	3.0

Khapalu, and probably Skardu, may be ruled out because of the inaccessability of Gilgit and Ladakh; Chasma and Chiniot ruled out both because of the enormous bunds that would be necessary to enclose these sites, which lie well out on the Indus Plains, and because of the need to move so many farmers from the area that would be flooded. Only a portion of the water stored on the Swat would be available to the Indus Plains.

20. Harza Report, pp. II-31, II-33.

the amount of surface water diverted into canals would reach 92.1 m.a.f., as compared with 83.5 m.a.f. now.[21]

In order to provide ultimate diversions of 120 m.a.f. per year not only would at least 30 m.a.f. of additional storage capacity have to be built (including the off-channel storages at Mangla and Tarbela), but it would be necessary to enlarge canal capacities to handle such diversions—a costly and technically difficult undertaking, especially in the Jhelum-Chenab Zone where the enlarged canals could be run at capacity for at most two months of the year.[22] But, as the Harza Report points out, interim use of groundwater can defer the need to enlarge canal capacities or to build more reservoirs. They anticipate that 26.9 m.a.f. per year of usable groundwater will be pumped by 1975, and ultimately as much as 40 m.a.f. per year. Making allowances for seepage and nonbeneficial evapotranspiration losses (which amount to 37 per cent of surface water supplies in the canals, distributaries, and watercourses, to 10 per cent of the groundwater supplies in the watercourses, and to a further 25 per cent on the fields themselves), the supplies *available to crops* by 1975 would be about 60 m.a.f. per year (roughly half again as much as at present). The crop supplies would represent approximately a 70 per cent contribution from surface water and a 30 per cent contribution by groundwater. Ultimately, about 82 m.a.f. per year could be supplied to the crops, of which about 68 per cent would represent surface water and 32 per cent groundwater (see Table 24).

Although the Revelle Panel assumes that only initial Mangla and Tarbela will have been built by the end of their first level of development (around 1980), and hence a gain through stored releases of only 11.7 m.a.f. per year, they mention a figure of 92 m.a.f. per year of surface water diversions at the initial stage. Because of uncertainties relating to bank storage and input to the groundwater table, however, they prefer to work with a "firm" diversion of only 89 m.a.f. per year at the first level.[23] At the second level of develop-

21. Ibid., pp. 40, 55, 57.
22. This was pointed out to the author by one of the knowledgeable consultants.
23. The Revelle Panel reasoned that the clearer water discharged from the reservoirs would seep more readily into the banks and into the groundwater reservoir, but stated that they could not accurately predict the magnitude of such seepage (Revelle II, p. 268). Some engineers believe that the desilted water

Table 24. Indus Plains Surface and Groundwater Supplies as Envisaged by the Harza and Revelle Programs[a]

| | Present | Harza | | | | Revelle | | | |
| | | 1975 | | 2000 | | First Level | | Second Level | |
Surface Water	(m.a.f./yr)	(m.a.f./yr)	(%)	(m.a.f./yr)	(%)	(m.a.f./yr)	(%)	(m.a.f./yr)	(%)
Diverted into canals	83.5	92.1	77%	120	75%	89 (92)[d]	59-63%	108	67.5-71 %
Available to crops (after all losses)	39.5	43.5	70%	56.7	68%	51.2	54%	59.1	56 %
Groundwater									
At heads of watercourses[b]	2 ?	26.9	23%	40	25%	53-61	37-41%	44-52	29-32.5%
Available to crops	1.8?	18.2	30%	27	32%	42.8[e]	46%	46.9	44 %
Total Supplies									
Crude total of diversions into canals and pumping into watercourses	85.5?	119.0		160		142-150 (145-153)[d]		152-160	
Available to crops (after all losses)	41.8?	60.2[c]		82.3[c]		94[e]		106	

a. Sources: Harza Report, pp. 54–57; Revelle II, pp. 266–88 and interpolations therefrom.
b. Location of tubewells.
c. Totals are less than the sums of surface and groundwater because of contingency allowances for imperfect coordination of water sources and unexpected increases in needs or conveyance losses (Harza Report, p. 55). Percentages are calculated on the unadjusted sums.
d. See footnote 23 to this chapter.
e. Based on the assumption that 8 m.a.f./yr of usable groundwater are made available in Sind.

ment, around the year 2000, the panel assumes that surface water diversions will rise only to 108 m.a.f. per year, apparently because they do not assume the amount of canal remodeling predicated by Harza to accommodate ultimate diversions of 120 m.a.f. per year. Thus Revelle places a much higher emphasis, absolute and relative, upon groundwater at both levels of development (see Table 24).

At the initial level, Revelle depends heavily upon "mining" groundwater in the Northern Zone, a procedure which, as we saw in Chapter 9, Harza treats with considerable caution due to quality factors. By lowering the water tables in the nonsaline groundwater areas of the Northern Zone by 3.3 feet per year for the first thirty years, and by adding an estimated 4 to 12 m.a.f. per year of good-quality groundwater in Sind, Revelle hopes to provide between 53 and 61 m.a.f. per year of groundwater at the first level of development. Added to the surface water diversions, this would mean a "crude" water supply of 142 to 150 m.a.f. per year around 1980 as compared to Harza's 119 m.a.f. per year by 1975. At Revelle's second level of development, "mining" in the Northern Zone would have to be decreased by 50 per cent in order to avoid pumping costs which increase with depth and to avoid pumping the more saline water which underlies even the good-quality water in the aquifer. But Revelle suggests that this reduction could be offset by more efficient methods of increasing groundwater recharge through manipulation of the irrigation system, of reducing nonbeneficial evapotranspiration, of reducing seepage losses, of desalinizing brackish waters, and of utilizing waters of higher total salt content for crop production if suitable cropping patterns are developed.[24] There would nevertheless be a reduction in the *relative* role of groundwater at Revelle's second level, though it would still remain greater than the share envisaged by Harza around the year 2000. This is especially true if we consider the relative roles in the water made available to crops, rather than in the "crude" supplies, both of which are given in Table

---

leaving the reservoirs will quickly pick up another load of silt, by bank and bed erosion, and that therefore neither bank storage nor throughput (transmission) to the groundwater table will be significantly increased. The experience with the S.V.P. (see Chap. 4) would tend to support these engineers, but for our purposes the difference of 3 m.a.f./yr is not critical.

24. Revelle II, p. 285.

24. At Revelle's second level, the share of groundwater in the supplies reaching the crops would decline from 46 to 44 per cent, whereas in the Harza program it would increase from 30 per cent in 1975 to around 32 per cent in the year 2000.

The estimates given in Table 24 do not provide a definite answer to the question of the relative roles of surface and groundwater in the future irrigation development of West Pakistan's Indus Plains. First of all, they *are* only estimates. They represent different programs envisaging different inputs on different areas and at different intensities. (See Chapter 9 and Tables 22 and 23.) Neither one has been adopted as the policy of West Pakistan, although certainly the Harza program, as the preliminary version of WAPDA's Master Plan for Water and Power Development, has the "inside track."[25] In view both of Pakistan's increasingly stringent foreign exchange situation and of the evident reluctance to "shift from an administrative structure based on function to one based on area" (see pages 500–02), even though it involves less expense and less integration of agencies, Harza's program seems more likely to be implemented than Revelle's—although there may be considerable difficulty in financing even the Harza program. In either program, West Pakistan would get what it paid for, although one could argue that, because of the multiplier effect or the principle of interaction, the returns from the more expensive program would be proportionally greater than from the less costly one. The groundwater program has demonstrated that there is a scale below which it does not pay to operate; the same might be true of the irrigation-reclamation-agriculture program as a whole. The whole logic of the Revelle approach is to secure a breakthrough by a concerted attack on several fronts, of which groundwater is only one. Yet if West Pakistan finds herself simultaneously deprived of massive foreign assistance and of massive American contractors and consultants, she may be forced to place even more emphasis than the Harza Report indicates on sur-

25. In January 1966, WAPDA's Chairman reaffirmed the Authority's intent to reclaim 1.5 million acres per year and to reach the total of 19 million acres embodied in the Harza program by 1975. (*WAPDA Weekly*, January 14, 1966, pp. 1, 3.) The role of the regional planning consultants for the Northern and Southern Zones (Tipton and Kalmbach and Hunting-MacDonald, respectively) in shaping WAPDA's Master Plan should not be underestimated, though Harza will review and presumably revise the work of both regional consultants.

face water both because it is safer (i.e. she has the experience with it and knows what to do and what to expect) and because it may be cheaper in the short run.

But setting aside, temporarily, these political considerations and, permanently, the question of which, if either, program is adopted, a comparison of the Harza and Revelle programs such as it made in Table 24 does permit two fairly definite conclusions leading to a resolution of the surface water, groundwater "controversy." The first conclusion is that, even with an extensive remodeling of the surface water system by the end of this century, there is an upper limit on such development. As noted above, this limit is imposed primarily by factors of physical geography: the runoff of the Western Rivers and the topographical characteristics of the Upper Basin with its paucity of dam sites that are both technically feasible and reasonably accessible. The costs of developing the remote sites at Skardu or Khapalu, or the accessible but physically uncontained sites at Chiniot and Chasma, seem, at the present level of technology, to preclude their use. Thus, within half a century or so, it seems likely that major surface water storage construction in the Pakistani Indus Basin will come to a halt.

The second conclusion is surprisingly similar, for it appears that the groundwater potential also has both physical and economic limitations. The physical limitations will come into play when the good quality groundwater (primarily in the Northern Zone) has been mined, or at least when mining operations have to be cut back (perhaps in thirty years at the rate envisaged by Revelle). Thereafter, the physical factors of recharge rate and specific yield gain in significance. In contrast to surface water storage, there is no visible point at which the cost of providing additional groundwater would skyrocket due to physical conditions alone. Rather, it will be a question of constantly mounting operation and replacement costs, as tubewells must draw from deeper levels to take full advantage of natural or induced recharge. Thus, the Revelle program appears to suggest that, by the turn of the century, the *absolute* contribution of groundwater may have to be cut back, for both physical and economic reasons, to a level not much higher than that envisaged in Harza's program.

Thus it may be suggested that the surface water–groundwater controversy is ultimately an unreal one. Ultimately, West Pakistan will have to develop both her surface water and her groundwater systems. Substitutions of tubewells for Tarbela, or of tubewell fields for remodeled canals, are only a temporary measure. Fundamentally, surface water and groundwater are only two aspects of a single resource, and both will have to be developed hand-in-hand. Manipulation of the surface water system, supported by a properly phased program of surface storage development, will be essential to keep the groundwater system operating after mining ceases. Neither system can be developed to the exclusion of the other, but fortunately both together can make a contribution greater than the sum of the parts. For with a well-designed surface water system, and with water tables lowered beyond the capillary range, the aquifer of the Indus Plains can be employed as an evaporation-free reservoir, soaking up the kharif floods and releasing them via tubewell pumping in rabi. This joint development, it would appear, is the true answer to the surface water–groundwater controversy.

But is it the answer to the irrigation agriculture problems of West Pakistan? Not entirely, and this is where the Revelle approach returns to the fore. Because even if West Pakistan were as successful with a population control program as Japan seems to be, she must be prepared to support a 1975 population of over 60 millions. Water alone cannot do that job. Fertilizers, pest and disease control, better implements, and above all farmer education and credit incentives will represent inputs of equal importance. Moreover, if Pakistan is to achieve either the general goals of her original Third Five Year Plan or the specific industrial goals of the revised plan produced after the "September War,"[26] she will require an agriculture that

26. The revised plan, announced by Finance Minister Shoaib late in November 1965, includes "top priority" for the heavy engineering, heavy electrical, and heavy machine tools complex in East and West Pakistan "to cater to the needs of basic and defense industries." (Economic Division, Embassy of Pakistan, Washington, D.C., *Interim Report Series*, December 1965, p. 2.) The stress on heavy industries and eventual "self-sufficiency" also includes at least one steel mill in each Wing of the country. (Ibid., October 1965, p. 2.) The new industrial investment program "is expected to cost about $740 million—about half in foreign exchange. The Ayub Administration has also announced that in the future Pakistan will accept foreign credits only for the hard-core program, since there is no intention to burden the economy with the repayment of loans for secondary projects." (Ibid., January 1966, p. 1.)

at least is moving toward Japanese standards of efficiency. Fortunately, it is recognized that agriculture along with industry must "receive the highest priority in order to achieve self-sufficiency in food, to provide a maximum surplus of agricultural produce for export and to ensure adequate raw material supplies for industrial production."[27] The original Third Five Year Plan proposed spending nearly $420 million on subsidizing fertilizers, seeds, pesticides, and insecticides:

> The highest priority is being given to boosting fertilizer output. The country hopes to produce 2.5 million tons of nitrogenous fertilizers by the end of 1970. Liberal fertilizer credit is also being given to the agricultural sector for importing tractors, tubewells and other agricultural machinery with a view to increasing farm production.[28]

Apparently, at least the fertilizer program will be continued under the revised Plan, for in January 1966 it was announced that, thanks to the United Nations Special Fund, the foreign exchange underwriting necessary to establish seven plants with a capacity of 800,000 tons of nutrients had been almost completely subscribed. In more general terms, although the development program called for in the first year of the Third Plan has been cut from $936 to $718 million, "the reallocation of financial resources has resulted in an increase in the investment to be made in such productive sectors of the economy as agriculture, which has always received first priority in Pakistani planning."[29]

These adjustments in the Third Five Year Plan reflect the determination on the part of the Planning Commission, and the Government in general, to maintain and even increase the rate of growth of the agricultural sector in the face of political adversity. Whether they can succeed without renewed massive foreign economic assistance is, however, doubtful. If Pakistan-American relations do not return to the old footing, Pakistan may well be able to enlist substantial Soviet assistance (as was noted in relation to prospects for Tarbela), but hardly enough to replace United States contributions

27. Ibid., December 1965, p. 2.
28. Ibid., August 1965, p.1.
29. Ibid., January 1966, p. 1.

542

to the Five Year Plans in Food for Peace counterpart rupees and in dollars through the Consortium. As we have seen, several Commonwealth and West European members of the Consortium have extended bilateral aid to Pakistan since July 1965. France and West Germany, in particular, might be persuaded to make larger contributions or investments. There is even a remote possibility that Pakistan might make use of her RCD (Regional Cooperation for Development) ties with Iran and Turkey to negotiate some sort of economic arrangement with the European Economic Community (of which Turkey is now an associate member). And there is the old Colombo Plan Organization and the new Asian Development Bank in Manila. But none of these, nor all of them taken together, could quite replace Pakistan's very special arrangements with the United States between 1954 and 1965; and certainly the fundamental cause of the mutual disenchantment, Communist China, is in no position to replace Pakistan's old standby.

The historical alternatives to foreign aid for development have been foreign private investment or the marshaling of domestic financial resources. Future large-scale foreign investment in Pakistan may be dismissed briefly, for three reasons: (1) most of what was worth investing in, had been invested in by 1947; (2) natural resources discovered since Independence (i.e. oil and natural gas) are either national monopolies or already fully subscribed; and (3) the companies most likely to invest in new manufacturing facilities are also the most likely to be frightened off by Pakistan's new political posture. Turning then to the question of domestic financial resources, Pakistan might be tempted to follow the example of the Soviet Union or Communist China in nationalizing all businesses and even the land itself. Such a policy, in a country that has prided itself on a pragmatic rather than a doctrinaire approach to economic development, and where, for example, private investment was expected to contribute $4.6 billion of the $10.9 billion in the Third Five Year Plan, would probably ruin the economy entirely. Nor is collectivization the answer, though one or two members of the Planning Commission might like to try it. But the sad performance of Soviet and Chinese agriculture seems unlikely to inspire a country that is underfed to begin with, that derives 80 per cent of its gross national product from the agricultural sector, and that lacks most of the metallic minerals and fuels (other than gas) for heavy industriali-zation. In any event, the elimination of Pakistan's *kulak* class, that small group of farmers who have made a success of agriculture while staying on the land, would surely kill the goose that lays (or may someday lay) the golden egg.

On the other hand, absentee landlordism is still rife in Pakistan, as it is in most of the Middle East and in India. The land reform carried out after February 1960 was so mild, and so generally evaded by anyone who had a nephew or a cousin, that it has barely skimmed the surface. On the other hand the breaking up of large holdings, where they are efficiently run, into parcels too small to be productive, is not the answer. But a tax on rents so designed that it could not be passed on to the tenants would both generate con-siderable revenue and serve as an incentive for landlords to sell land to the medium and larger farmers who know how to make the best use of it. The fact that such a logical measure, even if taken in the name of "national defense," could today hardly be administered is another argument for the substitution of administration based on area rather than on function as reclamation projects are extended over Pakistan's Indus Plains.

But even such a measure, directly tied to agricultural production, would not generate the domestic capital, and could not generate the foreign exchange, needed for West Pakistan's agricultural develop-ment program, much less that needed for the industrial sector as well. (Indeed, if U. S. Food for Peace shipments were curtailed, forcing West Pakistan to grow more wheat and less cotton and East Pakistan to grow more rice and less jute, Pakistan would lose two significant earners of foreign exchange.) Further taxation of luxuries, nonessential imports, and petroleum products has already been in-troduced, and the urban rich (most of whom are absentee landlords though they may be professional persons as well) can probably be squeezed a bit more before the Government's upper-class support evaporates. But to a large extent the Government is drawn from this class and, anyway, the sum total of wealth in the upper classes would not begin to be adequate to the task that now faces Pakistan.

Is the situation then hopeless unless Pakistan returns to close political as well as economic dependence on the United States? We can only presume to give an answer for West Pakistan, and only for the agricultural sector. And there the answer seems to be "No, if . . ." Fortunately, West Pakistan, in the Indus Plains, has a firm foundation upon which to continue to build her agriculture. There is not only the irrigation system inherited at Independence, along with the infrastructure that grew around it, but all of the works added since, including Phase I of the IBP. Phase II is well along, and Mangla Dam will be completed in 1967, a year ahead of schedule, if there is no renewal of the Kashmir fighting. So long as the "friendly Governments" abide by the 1960 Development Fund Agreement and the 1964 Supplementary Agreement, there should be enough foreign exchange for all Phase II works and for the Chasma Barrage and trans-Thal links. Tarbela is the big problem, because the 1964 Agreement makes it the "residuary legatee"—all other works are to be financed first and what is left may be used for Tarbela. Probably little will be left, but as we have explained at some length, Pakistan will undoubtedly complete Tarbela (1) because she has to, (2) because she wants to, and (3) because she will probably obtain most of what she needs from the Consortium and the United States despite (or perhaps because of) her political aloofness.

What may suffer will be the reclamation and groundwater program (1) because "reclamation," like "maintenance," can always be put off a little longer, (2) because foreign-made well screens and turbine pumps are expensive, and (3) because the reclamation-groundwater program, particularly in its Revelle conformations, has acquired American overtones. Yet one of the great advantages inherent in the Revelle multifactor approach is that there is some flexibility among the elements. Granted that the greatest return is to be achieved where land, surface water, groundwater, fertilizer, pest and disease control, cropping patterns and rotations, farmer credit, extension services, and improvements in seeds and techniques are *all* combined in exactly the right proportions (if these can be determined in time to apply them), the principle of interaction applies as soon as two or more are combined. That is to say, if West Pakistan finds that it cannot obtain the foreign exchange necessary for SCARP-type projects at the rate of 1 or 1.5 million acres per year, something can still be gained by combining more surface water with surface drains and fertilizers. Even without more water, it may be that surface drains, fertilizers, better seeds, better practices, and perhaps a different cropping pattern, if employed in combination, will produce cumulative results. Or, if West Germany (which is supporting SCARP III) or Yugoslavia (which is contributing to SCARP II) can be persuaded to continue their efforts on additional project areas, and if half a dozen other nations would undertake a SCARP or two apiece (more than likely the United States would join such a cooperative program, if she did not do even more), headway can still be made against waterlogging and salinity for, as the Revelle Report demonstrates, the problem has its own inherent limitations and, if one starts with the better lands, nature will cooperate. Of course, we are no longer talking about the ideal; we are merely saying that the political events of 1965 have not ruined the work of 115 years in the Indus Basin.

Indeed, the worst mistake West Pakistan could make would be to use a long-range reduction of American aid, if one develops, as an excuse not to get on with the irrigation, reclamation, and agricultural development program, or to revert to the traditional, comfortable, "departmental" procedures. Fortunately, the Pakistanis show no signs of doing so. For the ultimate saviors of West Pakistan are neither the Americans nor the Russians (and certainly not the Chinese) but the Pakistanis. In a way, the foreign aid crises brought on by the events of 1965 could be the most helpful thing that has occurred since the Indus Waters Treaty was signed. For the Government of Pakistan, by its own declarations as well as by the actions of the United States, is now on its own feet. If the experience of 1965 and any long-range stringencies that may develop force the administrators and engineers of Pakistan to cooperate across jurisdictional lines or, better still, if they enable the Government of West Pakistan to put through the sweeping administrative reforms necessary to give the reclamation projects "an administrative structure based on area" (no need to say where the phrase came from), then salvation may really be at hand. Adversity often brings out the best in governments, as in men. For better or for worse, the Indus Basin has never long been a stranger to adversity.

Bibliography

Books and Monographs

ABBOTT, J., I.C.S., *Sind: A Re-Interpretation of the Unhappy Valley*, Bombay and London, Humphrey Milford and Oxford University Press, 1924.

ACKERMAN, EDWARD A., and GEORGE O. G. LÖF, *Technology in American Water Resource Development*, Washington, D.C., Resources for the Future, 1959.

AKHTAR, S. M., *Economics of Pakistan*, Lahore, Publishers United, 1963.

ANDREW, W. P., *The Indus and Its Provinces*, London, Wm. H. Allen, 1857.

ANDRUS, J. RUSSELL, and AZIZALI F. MOHAMMED, *The Economy of Pakistan*, Stanford, Calif., Stanford University Press, 1958.

ARRORA, FAQIR CHAND, *Commerce by River in the Punjab, or a Survey of the Activities of the Marine Department of the Government of the Punjab (1861–62 to 1871–72)*, Lahore, Punjab Government Record Office Publications, Monograph No. 9, 1930.

ATTLEE, C. R., *As It Happened*, London, William Heinemann, 1954.

AZAD, MAULANA ABDUL KALAM, *India Wins Freedom*, New York and London, Longmans Green, 1960.

BHATTACHARYYA, K. N., *Indian Plans: A Generalist Approach*, New York, Asia Publishing House, 1963.

BUCKLEY, ROBERT B., C.S.I., *The Irrigation Works of India*, 2nd ed., London, E. and F. N. Spon, 1905.

CALVERT, HUBERT, I.C.S., *The Wealth and Welfare of the Punjab*, Lahore, Civil and Military Gazette Press, 1922.

The Cambridge History of India, H. H. Dodwell, ed., 6 vols., Vol. 5, "British India, 1497–1858," and Vol. 6, "The Indian Empire, 1858–1918," Cambridge, England, Cambridge University Press, 1929 and 1932.

CAMPBELL, ROBERT D., *Pakistan: Emerging Democracy*, Princeton, N.J., D. Van Nostrand (Searchlight Books), 1963.

CAMPBELL-JOHNSON, ALAN, *Mission with Mountbatten*, London, Robert Hale, 1951.

Conference on World Tensions, University of Bombay, 1961, *Tensions of Economic Development in South-East Asia*, J. C. Daruvala, ed., Bombay, Allied Publishers Private, 1961.

DARLING, SIR MALCOLM L., I.C.S., *The Punjab Peasant in Prosperity and Debt*, 4th ed., London and Bombay, Oxford University Press and Geoffrey Cumberlege, 1947.

DAS GUPTA, J. B., *Indo-Pakistan Relations 1947–1955*, Amsterdam, Djambatan, 1958.

EDWARDES, MICHAEL, *The Necessary Hell: John and Henry Lawrence and the Indian Empire*, London, Cassell, 1958.

EVANS, HUMPHREY, *Thimayya of India: A Soldier's Life*, New York, Harcourt, Brace, 1960.

Ford Foundation, *Design for Pakistan: A Report on Assistance to the Pakistan Planning Commission by the Ford Foundation and Harvard University*, New York, The Ford Foundation, February 1965.

GOODNOW, HENRY F., *The Civil Service of Pakistan: Bureaucracy in a New Nation*, New Haven and London, Yale University Press, 1964.

HAGEN, TONI, *Nepal*, Berne, Kummerly and Frey, 1961.

———, GÜNTER-OSKAR DYHRENFURTH, CHRISTOPH VON FÜRER-HAIMENFORD, and ERWIN SCHNEIDER, *Mount Everest*, London, Oxford University Press, 1963.

HARRISON, SELIG S., *India: The Most Dangerous Decades*, Princeton, N.J., Princeton University Press, 1960.

HART, HENRY C., *Administrative Aspects of River Valley Development*, London, Asia Publishing House for the Indian Institute of Public Administration, New Delhi, 1961.

———, *New India's Rivers*, Calcutta, Orient Longmans, 1956.

Harza Engineering Company International, *A Program for Water and Power Development in West Pakistan, 1963–1975*, Prepared for Water and Power Development Authority of West Pakistan, "Supporting Studies—An Appraisal of Resources and Potential Development," Lahore, September 1963, and "Master Plan—Initial Phase," Lahore, January 1964.

HIRSHLEIFER, JACK, JAMES C. DEHAVEN, and JEROME W. MILLIMAN, *Water Supply: Economics, Technology, and Policy*, Chicago, The University of Chicago Press and the RAND Corporation, 1960.

HOUK, IVAN E., *Irrigation Engineering*, 2 vols. New York, John Wiley & Sons, 1956, 2.

Hundred Years of P.W.D., ed. Mubashir Hasan, Lahore, Publication Committee of P.W.D. [Public Works Department] Centennial, October 1963.

Indian Institute of Public Administration, *The Organisation of the Government Institute of Development Economics, Annual Report, 1962–63*, Karachi, Institute *of India*, Bombay, Asia Publishing House, 1958. of Development Economics, 1963.

Bibliography

ISMAY, General Lord, *The Memoirs of General Lord Ismay*, New York, Viking Press, 1960.

KHERA, S. S., *Government in Business*, Bombay, Asia Publishing House, Issued Under the Auspices of the Indian Institute of Public Administration, 1963.

LILIENTHAL, DAVID E., *The Journals of David E. Lilienthal*, Vol. 3, "Venturesome Years, 1950–55," New York, Evanston, and London, Harper and Row, 1966.

LUMBY, E. W. R., *The Transfer of Power in India 1945–7*, New York, Frederick A. Praeger, 1954.

MAASS, ARTHUR, MAYNARD M. HUFSCHMIDT, ROBERT DORFMAN, HAROLD A. THOMAS, JR., STEPHEN A. MARGLIN, and GORDON MASKEW FAIR, *Design of Water-Resource Systems*, Cambridge, Mass., Harvard University Press, 1962.

MALIK, RASHID A., *Irrigation Development and Land Occupance in the Upper Indus Basin*, Bloomington, Indiana University doctoral dissertation published by the author, August 1963.

MENON, V. P., *The Integration of the Indian States*, Calcutta, Orient Longmans, 1956.

———, *The Transfer of Power in India*, Princeton, Princeton University Press, 1957.

MICHEL, ALOYS ARTHUR, *The Kabul, Kunduz, and Helmand Valleys and the National Economy of Afghanistan*, Washington, D.C., National Academy of Sciences—National Research Council, 1959.

MOLEY, RAYMOND, *What Price Federal Reclamation?*, Washington and New York, American Enterprise Association, National Economic Problems Series, No. 455, 1955.

MOON, PENDEREL, *Divide and Quit*, London, Chatto and Windus, 1961.

MOSLEY, LEONARD, *The Last Days of the British Raj*, New York, Harcourt, Brace & World, and London, Weidenfeld & Nicolson Limited, 1962.

NEALE, WALTER C., *India: The Search for Unity, Democracy and Progress*, Princeton, N.J., D. Van Nostrand (Searchlight Books), 1965.

PAUSTIAN, PAUL W., *Canal Irrigation in the Punjab*, New York, Columbia University Press, 1930.

SCHLESINGER, ARTHUR M., JR., *A Thousand Days*, Boston, Houghton Mifflin, 1965.

SINGH, DEVA, *Colonization in the Rechna Doab, Lahore*, Punjab Government Record Office Publications, Monograph No. 7, 1930.

SINGH, KHUSHWANT, *A History of the Sikhs 1469–1839*, Princeton, Princeton University Press, 1963.

———, *The Sikhs*, London, George Allen and Unwin, 1953.

———, *Train to Pakistan*, London, Chatto and Windus, 1956.

SPATE, O. H. K., *India and Pakistan: A General and Regional Geography*, 2nd ed., London, Methuen, 1957.

The Statesman's Yearbook, 1964–65, S. H. Steinberg, ed., New York, St. Martin's Press, 1964.

STEPHENS, IAN, *Pakistan*, 2nd ed., London, Ernest Benn, 1964.

TAAFFE, ROBERT N., *Rail Transportation and the Economic Development of*

Soviet Central Asia, Chicago, University of Chicago, Department of Geography, Research Paper No. 64, 1960.

TANDON, B. C., ed., *The Third Five Year Plan and India's Economic Growth,* Allahabad, Chaitanya Publishing House, 1962.

TAYLOR, CARL C., DOUGLAS ENSMINGER, HELEN W. JOHNSON, and JEAN JOYCE, *India's Roots of Democracy,* Calcutta, Orient Longmans, 1965.

THORNER, DANIEL and ALICE, *Land and Labour in India,* Bombay, Asia Publishing House, 1962.

TINKER, HUGH, *India and Pakistan: A Political Analysis,* New York, Frederick A. Praeger, 1962.

Tipton and Kalmbach, Inc., *Feasibility Report on Salinity Control and Reclamation Project No. 3, Lower Thal Doab, West Pakistan,* prepared by Tipton and Kalmbach, Inc., and the Projects Planning and Preparation Circle of the Ground Water and Reclamation Division, WAPDA, Lahore, WAPDA, April 1963.

TREVASKIS, HUGH K., *The Land of the Five Rivers,* London, Oxford University Press, 1928.

TUKER, LT.-GEN. SIR FRANCIS, *While Memory Serves,* London, Cassell, 1950.

WEEKES, RICHARD V., *Pakistan: Birth and Growth of a Muslim Nation,* Princeton, N.J., D. Van Nostrand (The Asia Library Series), 1964.

Official Documents and Press Releases

GOVERNMENT OF INDIA, INCLUDING THE PROVINCES, TO 1947

Census of India, 1931, Vol. 17, Punjab, 2 parts, Lahore, Civil & Military Gazette Press, 1933, Part I, "Report"; Part II, "Tables."

Census of India, 1941, Vol. 6, Punjab, Delhi, The Manager of Publications, 1941.

Completion Report with Schedules and Financial Forecast (British Areas Only) of the Sutlej Valley Project, Lahore, Superintendent Government Printing, Punjab, 1935.

FRENCH, L., I.C.S., *The Panjab Colony Manual,* Lahore, Civil & Military Gazette Press, 1907.

Gazette of India, Extraordinary, New Delhi, Sunday, August 17, 1947, Government of India, Legislative Department (Reforms), Notification, No. F. 68/47-R, "Report of the Punjab Boundary Commission to His Excellency the Governor-General."

Gazetteer of the Province of Sind, 2 vols., Vol. A, compiled by E. H. Aitken, Karachi, Printed for Government, 1907.

General Report on the Administration of the Punjab, for the Years 1849–50 and 1850–51, London, Printed for the Court of Directors of the East-India Company by J. and H. Cox (Brothers), 1854.

Government of India, *Administrative Reports (1859–60), General Report on the Administration of the Punjab and its Dependencies for 1859–60,* Calcutta, Savielle & Cranenburgh, 1861.

Bibliography

Government of India, Public Works Department, "Public Works Letter No. 4 of
1865 (Civil Works/Agricultural) to the Secretary of State for India," dated
10 January 1865, and "Public Works Letter No. 48 of 1865 (Civil Works/
Agricultural) to the Secretary of State for India," dated 12 April 1865, in
"India, Public Works Department, Letters Received, 1865" (Vol. 12, London,
India Office Library).

Government of India, Public Works Department (Irrigation), "Public Works
Letter No. 150 to the Secretary of State for India," dated 10 September 1867,
in "India, Public Works Department, Letters Received, 1867" (Vol. 14,
London, India Office Library).

——, "Letter No. 62 (Public Works) to the Secretary of State for India,"
dated April 20, 1868, in "India, Public Works Department, Letters Received,
1868" (Vol. 15, London, India Office Library).

——, "Letter No. 90 (Public Works) to the Secretary of State for India,"
dated 30 June 1870, in "India, Public Works Department, Letters Received,
1870" (Vol. 17, London, India Office Library).

Government of the Punjab, "Proceedings in the Public Works Department during the month of September, 1864, Agricultural Proceeding No. 20," dated
26 September 1864, from the Secretary to Government, Punjab, in the Public
Works Department to the Executive Engineer on Special Duty, Rechna
Doab Canals, London, India Office Library.

Government of the Punjab, "Proceedings in the Public Works Department during the month of December, 1864, Agricultural Proceeding No. 3," dated 16
December 1864, from the Secretary to Government, Punjab, in the Public
Works Department to the Government of India, Public Works Department,
including "Memorandum dated 22 October, 1862, by Captain J. H. Dyas on
Captain Crofton's Preliminary Report of the Sutlej Canal Project," and
"Memorandum dated 26 April 1864 by D. F. McLeod, Financial Commis-
sioner, Punjab, on proposed system of canals to be taken from the Sutlej
near Kirutpore . . . as surveyed and reported on by Captain James Crofton,
Royal Engineers," London, India Office Library.

Government of the Punjab, "Punjab Irrigation Proceedings, March, 1873, Proceeding No. 7," including extract from the "Dispatch from the Secretary of
State for India to the Government of India, No. 114, dated 18 December
1872," London, India Office Library.

The Report of the Indian Irrigation Commission, 1901–03, 4 vols., Calcutta,
Office of the Superintendent of Government Printing, India, 1903.

The Sikh Memorandum to the Punjab Boundary Commission, Harnam Singh,
ed., Lahore, The Mercantile Press, 1947.

GOVERNMENT OF INDIA, INCLUDING THE STATES, AFTER 1947

Census of India, 1941, Vol. 1, India, Delhi, The Manager, Government of India
Publication Branch, 1949.

Government of India, Central Statistical Organisation, Department of Statistics,

Statistical Abstract, India, 1961 (New series, No. 10), Delhi, The Manager of Publications, 1961.

Government of India, Ministry of Home Affairs, Secretariat Training School, *Organisational Set-up and Functions of the Ministries/Departments of the Government of India*, 2nd ed., New Delhi, 1962.

Government of India, Ministry of Information and Broadcasting, Publications Division, *India: A Reference Annual, 1954*, Delhi, April 1954.

————, *India: A Reference Annual, 1963*, Delhi, June 1963.

Government of India, Ministry of Irrigation and Power, *Report, 1962–63*, New Delhi, Ministry of Irrigation and Power, March 1963.

————, *Report, 1963–64*, New Delhi, Ministry of Irrigation and Power, March 1964.

Government of India, Planning Commission, *Second Five Year Plan, a Draft Outline*, New Delhi, February 1956.

Indus Basin Working Party, Draft Outline as Prepared by the Indian Designee, *Comprehensive Long-Range Plan for the Most Effective Utilization of the Water Resources of the Indus Basin*, presented to the Working Party on October 6, 1953, New Delhi, The Manager, Government of India Press, 1954, Annexure I, "Engineering Data."

Irrigation and Power Research Institute, Amritsar (India), *Report for the Year Ending November, 1959*, Amritsar, Irrigation Research Institute, November 1960.

Public Relations Officer, Bhakra-Nangal Project, *Bhakra-Nangal Project*, Nangal, Punjab, July 1961.

————, *Facts and Figures, Bhakra-Nangal*, Punjab, March 1957.

RANDHAWA, M. S., I.C.S., Development Commissioner, Punjab, *National Extension Service and Community Projects in Punjab*, Chandigarh, Punjab Government, Community Projects Administration, 1955.

GOVERNMENT OF PAKISTAN, INCLUDING THE PROVINCES, AFTER 1947

DOUIE, SIR JAMES M., I.C.S., *Punjab Settlement Manual*, 5th ed., issued in 1961, Lahore, Superintendent Government Printing, West Pakistan, 1962.

Economic Adviser to the Government of Pakistan, Ministry of Finance, *Economic Survey of Pakistan, 1961–62*, Rawalpindi, 1962.

Embassy of Pakistan, Washington, D.C., *Pakistan Affairs*, 1963–66.

————, Economic Division, Washington, D.C., *Interim Report Series*, 1964–66.

————, Information Division, Washington, D.C., "Pakistan: The Development Miracle" (Text of an address by Prof. Gustav F. Papanek given in New York on May 4, 1965, under the joint auspices of the Pakistani-American Chamber of Commerce, Inc., and the Asia Society).

FARUQUE, GHULAM, "A New Approach," in *A New Approach* (Texts of Broadcasts on Radio Pakistan, Lahore), Lahore, WAPDA, n.d., pp. 1–8.

Government of Pakistan, Ministry of Agriculture and Works, Agricultural Census Organization, *1960 Pakistan Census of Agriculture*, 2 vols., Vol. 2, *West*

Bibliography

Pakistan, and *A Summary of West Pakistan Data* (to accompany Vol. 2), Karachi, Government of Pakistan, October 1963.

Government of Pakistan, Ministry of Food and Agriculture, *Report of the Food and Agriculture Commission*, Karachi, Manager of Publications, November 1960.

Government of Pakistan, Ministry of Information and Broadcasting, Press Information Department, *Pakistan News Digest*, Karachi, The Times Press, 1963–66.

Government of Pakistan, Planning Commission, *The Second Five Year Plan (1960–65)*, Karachi, June 1960.

Government of Pakistan, *Outline of the Third Five Year Plan (1965–70)*, Karachi, August 1964.

Published for the Government of Pakistan by the Government of Canada, *Landforms, Soils and Land Use of the Indus Plains, West Pakistan* (A Colombo Plan Cooperative Project), Ottawa, February 1958.

Government of West Pakistan, Public Works Department, Irrigation Branch, *Manual of Irrigation Practice*, 1st ed., reprinted 1963, Lahore, Superintendent Government Printing, West Pakistan, 1963.

KAZI, A. RASHID, *Factors Affecting the Selection of a Dam Site—Selection of the First Storage Dam on the Indus*, Lahore, WAPDA, September 1961 (mimeographed).

Report of the Indus Commission, 6 Parts, Part 1, General, *Complaint of Sind and Projects Complained of under Section 130 of the Government of India Act of 1935*, Lahore, reprinted by the Superintendent of Government Printing, Punjab, 1950.

West Pakistan Agricultural Development Corporation, *Anniversary Souvenir*, October 1, 1962, Lahore, Public Relations Division, West Pakistan Agricultural Development Corporation, 1962.

——, *Agricultural Development in West Pakistan: the Role and Functions of the West Pakistan ADC*, Lahore, Public Relations Division, West Pakistan Agricultural Development Corporation, November 1963.

West Pakistan Water and Power Development Authority, *WAPDA Miscellany, 1964* (An Annual Review of the Activities of the West Pakistan Water and Power Development Authority), Lahore, WAPDA, June 1964.

——, *WAPDA Inauguration Souvenir, Central Rechna Project*, Lahore, WAPDA, March 29, 1963.

——, Indus Basin Projects Division, IBP Publications Nos.:

49, *Settlement Plan without Tarbela, An Appraisal*, Lahore, WAPDA, July 1962

53, *Settlement Plan without Tarbela, An Appraisal*, Lahore, WAPDA, July 1962

81, *Effects of Substituting Raised Mangla Dam for Tarbela Dam on the Uses of Various Projects (Revised)*, Lahore, WAPDA, April 1963

87, *Financing the Indus Project on the Basis of Sir William Iliff's Financial Plan of July, 1962*, Lahore, WAPDA, May 1963.

97, *Mangla Dam Project,* Lahore, WAPDA, October 1963

98, *Trimmu-Sidhnai Link,* Lahore, WAPDA, October 1963

99, *Sidhnai Barrage,* Lahore, WAPDA, October 1963

100, *Sidhnai-Mailsi Link,* Lahore, WAPDA, October 1963

101, *Mailsi Syphon,* Lahore, WAPDA, October 1963

——, *Indus Basin Settlement Plan, Report on the Consultants' Cost Estimates,* 2 parts, Part I, Summary, Lahore, WAPDA, July 1960.

——, *Indus Basin Settlement Plan, Construction and Expenditure Schedules,* Lahore, WAPDA, October 1960.

——, *Visit of the U. S. Scientific Mission on Waterlogging and Salinity in West Pakistan, September–October, 1961,* Lahore, WAPDA, n.d.

——, *WAPDA Weekly,* Lahore, WAPDA Press, 1963–66.

INTERNATIONAL BANK FOR RECONSTRUCTION AND DEVELOPMENT

BLACK, EUGENE R., President of the World Bank, *Statement to the Press, Karachi, Pakistan, May 18, 1959.*

Indus Basin Devolopment Fund Agreement, dated September 19, 1960.

The Indus Basin Development Fund (Supplemental) Agreement, 1964.

Loan Agreement (Indus Basin Project) between Republic of Pakistan and IBRD, September 19, 1960.

Press Releases: June 26, 1952; December 10, 1954 (No. 380); August 26, 1959 (London); September 19, 1960 (No. 650); and April 8, 1964 (No. 64/10).

UNITED NATIONS ECONOMIC COMMISSION FOR ASIA AND THE FAR EAST

Multiple-Purpose River Basin Development, Part 2B, "Water Resources Development in Burma, India and Pakistan" (Flood Control Series No. 11), Bangkok, UNECAFE, December 1956.

Proceedings of the Third Regional Technical Conference on Water Resources Development in Asia and the Far East (Flood Control Series No. 13), Bangkok, UNECAFE, 1958.

UNITED STATES OF AMERICA

Bureau of Reclamation, United States Department of the Interior, *Evaluation of Engineering and Economic Feasibility, Beas and Rajasthan Projects, Northern India,* Report Prepared by the United States Department of the Interior, Bureau of Reclamation, for AID, Agency for International Development, Department of State, U.S.A., Washington, D.C., July 1963.

National Resources Committee, Report of the Subcommittee on Technology, *Technological Trends and National Policy,* Washington, U. S. Government Printing Office, 1937.

President's Science Advisory Committee, *White House–Interior Panel on Waterlogging and Salinity in West Pakistan, First Draft,* Washington, D.C., The White House, September 1962.

President's Water Resources Policy Commission, Report, 1950, 2 vols., Vol. 1,

Bibliography

A Water Policy for the American People, Washington, U. S. Government Printing Office, December 1960.

U. S. Salinity Laboratory Staff, Diagnosis and Improvement of Saline and Alkali Soils (Agriculture Handbook No. 60) Washington, D.C., U. S. Department of Agriculture, February 1954.

White House–Department of Interior Panel on Waterlogging and Salinity in West Pakistan, Report on Land and Water Development in the Indus Plain, Washington, D.C., The White House, January 1964.

Articles and Symposia Papers

ABDULLAH, SHEIKH MOHAMMAD, "Kashmir, India and Pakistan," Foreign Affairs, 43 (1965), 528–35.

AHMAD, NAZIR, "Exploitation of Ground Water: A Review of Technique Developed in Pakistan" (Paper read in CENTO Scientific Symposium, Lahore, January 8–13, 1962), Engineering News, 7 (March 1962), 1–10.

———, "Control of Water-Logging and Salinity by Tube-Well Pumping," Pakistan Journal of Science, 14 (March 1962), 49–62.

AHMAD, KAZI S., "Canal Water Problem," Oriental Geographer, 2 (1958), 31–46.

AHMAD, MIAN MUZAFFAR, "A Study of Waterlogging & Thur Problems of West Pakistan" (Paper Read in the 5th Annual Convention of the Institute of Engineers, Pakistan, Dacca, April 27-29, 1958), Lahore, Superintendent Government Printing, West Pakistan, 1958.

BOWER, C. A., and M. MAASLAND, "Sodium Hazard of Punjab Ground Waters," Symposium on Waterlogging and Salinity, Lahore, West Pakistan Engineering Congress, October 1963, 49–61.

DE TERRA, HELMUTH, "Physiographic Results of a Recent Survey in Little Tibet [Ladakh]," Geographical Review, 24 (1934), 12–41.

Engineering News Record, 163, September 3, 1959 and October 15, 1959; 164, February 25, 1960.

FOWLER, F. J., "Some Problems of Water Distribution between East and West Punjab," Geographical Review, 40 (1950), 583–99.

GREENMAN, D. W., W. V. SWARZENSKI, and G. D. BENNETT,"The Ground-Water Hydrology of the Punjab, West Pakistan," West Pakistan Water and Power Development Authority, Water and Soils Investigation Division, Bulletin No. 6, Lahore, WAPDA, 1963.

India Briefing, New York, The India Council of the Asia Society, 1965–66.

ISHAQ, GHULAM, "WAPDA as a Public Corporation," Indus, 4, (August 1963), 4–14.

ITSCHNER, LT. GEN. EMERSON C., "Indus Basin Plan," Military Engineer, 55, No. 364 (1963), 106–109.

JAFAREY, N. H., "Public Corporations as a Device for Economic Development," Indus, 5 (March 1964), 4–11.

JEWETT, T. N., "Salinity and Ground-water Conditions in the Lower Indus

Plains," *Symposium on Waterlogging and Salinity*, Lahore, West Pakistan Engineering Congress, October 1963, 15–25.

KHOSLA, A. N., "Development of the Indus River System: An Engineering Approach," *India Quarterly, 14* (1958), 233–53.

KIDWAI, ZAMIR-UDDIN, "Geology of Rechna and Chaj Doabs, West Pakistan," West Pakistan Water and Power Development Authority, Water and Soils Investigation Division, Bulletin No. 5, Lahore, WAPDA, n.d.

—— and W. V. SWARZENSKI, "Results of Geologic and Ground-water Investigations in the Punjab Plain, West Pakistan," *Symposium on Waterlogging and Salinity*, Lahore, West Pakistan Engineering Congress, October 1963, 63–76.

KIRMANI, S. S., "Design of Silt Stable Canals," *Proceedings of the West Pakistan Engineering Congress*, Lahore, West Pakistan Engineering Congress, 47 (1963, Paper No. 355), 1–68.

——, "Sediment Problems in the Indus Basin, Part I: Sedimentation in Reservoirs," *Proceedings of the West Pakistan Engineering Congress*, Lahore, West Pakistan Engineering Congress, 43 (1959, Paper No. 336).

LILIENTHAL, DAVID E., "Another 'Korea' in the Making?" *Collier's, 128* (August 4, 1951), 23, 56–58.

LOWTHER, LT. W. H., Note "On Cotton" dated 27 August 1851, *Proceedings of the Sixth Meeting of the Agri-Horticultural Society of Lahore, 14 October 1851*, in *Proceedings of the Agri-Horticultural Society of the Punjab from May to 31 December, 1851*, Lahore, Lahore Chronicle Press, 1852.

MOHAMMAD, GHULAM, and CHRISTOPH BERINGER, "Waterlogging and Salinity in West Pakistan: An Analysis of the Revelle Report," *Pakistan Development Review, 3* (1963), 249–79.

MONTAGU, A. M. R., "Presidential Address to the Punjab Engineering Congress, 33rd Session, 1946," in *Proceedings of the Punjab Engineering Congress, 33rd Session*, 1946, i–xvii.

NAYLOR, PETER E., "Economic Investigation as Related to Drainage with Special Reference to Khairpur," *Symposium on Waterlogging and Salinity*, Lahore, West Pakistan Engineering Congress, October 1963.

NEW YORK TIMES, 1965–66.

SPATE, O. H. K., "The Partition of India and the Prospects of Pakistan," *Geographical Review, 38* (1948), 5–29.

ZAFAR, I. A., "Role of Consultants in Development," *Indus, 3* (January 1963), 24–28.

APPENDIX
The Indus Waters Treaty, 1960

PREAMBLE

The Government of India and the Government of Pakistan, being equally desirous of attaining the most complete and satisfactory utilisation of the waters of the Indus system of rivers and recognising the need, therefore, of fixing and delimiting, in a spirit of goodwill and friendship, the rights and obligations of each in relation to the other concerning the use of these waters and of making provision for the settlement, in a cooperative spirit, of all such questions as may hereafter arise in regard to the interpretation or application of the provisions agreed upon herein, have resolved to conclude a Treaty in furtherance of these objectives, and for this purpose have named as their plenipotentiaries:

THE GOVERNMENT OF INDIA:

Shri Jawaharlal Nehru,
Prime Minister of India,

and

THE GOVERNMENT OF PAKISTAN:

Field Marshal Mohammad Ayub Khan, HP., H.J.,
President of Pakistan;

who, having communicated to each other their respective Full Powers and having found them in good and due form, have agreed upon the following Articles and Annexures:—

ARTICLE I

Definitions

As used in this Treaty:

(1) The terms "Article" and "Annexure" mean respectively an Article of, and an Annexure to, this Treaty. Except as otherwise indicated, references to Paragraphs are to the paragraphs in the Article or in the Annexure in which the reference is made.

(2) The term "Tributary" of a river means any surface channel, whether in continuous or intermittent flow and by whatever name called, whose waters in the natural course would fall into that river, e.g. a tributary, a torrent, a natural drainage, an artificial drainage, a *nadi,* a *nallah,* a *nai,* a *khad,* a *cho.* The term also includes any sub-tributary or branch or subsidiary channel, by whatever name called, whose waters, in the natural course, would directly or otherwise flow into that surface channel.

(3) The term "The Indus," "The Jhelum," "The Chenab," "The Ravi," "The

Beas" or "The Sutlej" means the named river (including Connecting Lakes, if any) and all its Tributaries: Provided however that

    (i)   none of the rivers named above shall be deemed to be a Tributary;

    (ii) The Chenab shall be deemed to include the river Panjnad; and

    (iii) the river Chandra and the river Bhaga shall be deemed to be Tributaries of The Chenab.

(4) The term "Main" added after Indus, Jhelum, Chenab, Sutlej, Beas or Ravi means the main stem of the named river excluding its Tributaries, but including all channels and creeks of the main stem of that river and such Connecting Lakes as form part of the main stem itself. The Jhelum Main shall be deemed to extend up to Verinag, and the Chenab Main up to the confluence of the river Chandra and the river Bhaga.

(5) The term "Eastern Rivers" means The Sutlej, The Beas and The Ravi taken together.

(6) The term "Western Rivers" means The Indus, The Jhelum and The Chenab taken together.

(7) The term "the Rivers" means all the rivers, The Sutlej, The Beas, The Ravi, The Indus, The Jhelum and The Chenab.

(8) The term "Connecting Lakes" means any lake which receives water from, or yields water to, any of the Rivers; but any lake which occasionally and irregularly receives only the spill of any of the Rivers and returns only the whole or part of that spill is not a Connecting Lake.

(9) The term "Agricultural Use" means the use of water for irrigation, except for irrigation of household gardens and public recreational gardens.

(10) The term "Domestic Use" means the use of water for:

    (a) drinking, washing, bathing, recreation, sanitation (including the conveyance and dilution of sewage and of industrial and other wastes), stock and poultry, and other like purposes:

    (b) household and municipal purposes (including use for household gardens and public recreational gardens) ; and

    (c) industrial purposes (including mining, milling and other like purposes) ;

but the term does not include Agricultural Use or use for generation of hydro-electric power.

(11) The term "Non-Consumptive Use" means any control or use of water for navigation, floating of timber or other property, flood protection or flood control, fishing or fish culture, wild life or other like beneficial purposes, provided that, exclusive of seepage and evaporation of water incidental to the control or use, the water (undiminished in volume within the practical range of measurement) remains in, or is returned to, the same river or its Tributaries; but the term does not include Agricultural Use or use for the generation of hydro-electric power.

(12) The term "Transition Period" means the period beginning and ending as provided in Article II (6).

(13) The term "Bank" means the International Bank for Reconstruction and Development.

(14) The term "Commissioner" means either of the Commissioners appointed under the provisions of Article VIII (1) and the term "Commission" means the Permanent Indus Commission constituted in accordance with Article VIII (3).

(15) The term "interference with the waters" means:

(a) Any act of withdrawal therefrom; or

(b) Any man-made obstruction to their flow which causes a change in the volume (within the practical range of measurement) of the daily flow of the waters: Provided however that an obstruction which involves only an insignificant and incidental change in the volume of the daily flow, for example, fluctuations due to afflux caused by bridge piers or a temporary by-pass, etc., shall not be deemed to be an interference with the waters.

(16) The term "Effective Date" means the date on which this Treaty takes effect in accordance with the provisions of Article XII, that is, the first of April 1960.

ARTICLE II

Provisions Regarding Eastern Rivers

(1) All the waters of the Eastern Rivers shall be available for the unrestricted use of India, except as otherwise expressly provided in this Article.

(2) Except for Domestic Use and Non-Consumptive Use, Pakistan shall be under an obligation to let flow, and shall not permit any interference with, the waters of the Sutlej Main and the Ravi Main in the reaches where these rivers flow in Pakistan and have not yet finally crossed into Pakistan. The points of final crossing are the following: (a) near the new Hasta Bund upstream of Suleimanke in the case of the Sutlej Main, and (b) about one and a half miles upstream of the syphon for the B-R-B-D Link in the case of the Ravi Main.

(3) Except for Domestic Use, Non-Consumptive Use and Agricultural Use (as specified in Annexure B), Pakistan shall be under an obligation to let flow, and shall not permit any interference with, the waters (while flowing in Pakistan) of any Tributary which in its natural course joins the Sutlej Main or the Ravi Main before these rivers have finally crossed into Pakistan.

(4) All the waters, while flowing in Pakistan, of any Tributary which, in its natural course, joins the Sutlej Main or the Ravi Main after these rivers have finally crossed into Pakistan shall be available for the unrestricted use of Pakistan: Provided however that this provision shall not be construed as giving Pakistan any claim or right to any releases by India in any such Tributary. If Pakistan should deliver any of the waters of any such Tributary, which on the Effective Date joins the Ravi Main after this river has finally crossed into Pakistan, into a reach of the Ravi Main upstream of this crossing, India shall not make use of these waters; each Party agrees to establish such discharge observation stations and make such observations as may be necessary for the determination of the component of water available for the use of Pakistan on account of the aforesaid deliveries by Pakistan, and Pakistan agrees to meet the

cost of establishing the aforesaid discharge observation stations and making the aforesaid observations.

(5) There shall be a Transition Period during which, to the extent specified in Annexure H, India shall
  (i)   limit its withdrawals for Agricultural Use,
  (ii) limit abstractions for storages, and
  (iii) make deliveries to Pakistan from the Eastern Rivers.

(6) The Transition Period shall begin on 1st April 1960 and it shall end on 31st March 1970, or, if extended under the provisions of Part 8 of Annexure H, on the date up to which it has been extended. In any event, whether or not the replacement referred to in Article IV (1) has been accomplished, the Transition Period shall end not later than 31st March 1973.

(7) If the Transition Period is extended beyond 31st March 1970, the provisions of Article V(5) shall apply.

(8) If the Transition Period is extended beyond 31st March 1970, the provisions of Paragraph (5) shall apply during the period of extension beyond 31st March 1970.

(9) During the Transition Period, Pakistan shall receive for unrestricted use the waters of the Eastern Rivers which are to be released by India in accordance with the provisions of Annexure H. After the end of the Transition Period, Pakistan shall have no claim or right to releases by India of any of the waters of the Eastern Rivers. In case there are any releases, Pakistan shall enjoy the unrestricted use of the waters so released after they have finally crossed into Pakistan: Provided that in the event that Pakistan makes any use of these waters, Pakistan shall not acquire any right whatsoever, by prescription or otherwise, to a continuance of such releases or such use.

ARTICLE III

Provisions Regarding Western Rivers

(1) Pakistan shall receive for unrestricted use all those waters of the Western Rivers which India is under obligation to let flow under the provisions of Paragraph (2).

(2) India shall be under an obligation to let flow all the waters of the Western Rivers, and shall not permit any interference with these waters, except for the following uses, restricted (except as provided in item (c) (ii) of Paragraph 5 of Annexure C) in the case of each of the rivers, The Indus, The Jhelum and The Chenab, to the drainage basin thereof:
  (a) Domestic Use;
  (b) Non-Consumptive Use;
  (c) Agricultural Use, as set out in Annexure C; and
  (d) Generation of hydro-electric power, as set out in Annexure D.

(3) Pakistan shall have the unrestricted use of all waters originating from sources other than the Eastern Rivers which are delivered by Pakistan into The

Ravi or The Sutlej, and India shall not make use of these waters. Each Party agrees to establish such discharge observation stations and make such observations as may be considered necessary by the Commission for the determination of the component of water available for the use of Pakistan on account of the aforesaid deliveries by Pakistan.

(4) Except as provided in Annexures D and E, India shall not store any water of, or construct any storage works on, the Western Rivers.

ARTICLE IV

Provisions Regarding Eastern Rivers and Western Rivers

(1) Pakistan shall use its best endeavours to construct and bring into operation, with due regard to expedition and economy, that part of a system of works which will accomplish the replacement, from the Western Rivers and other sources, of water supplies for irrigation canals in Pakistan which, on 15th August 1947, were dependent on water supplies from the Eastern Rivers.

(2) Each Party agrees that any Non-Consumptive Use made by it shall be so made as not to materially change, on account of such use, the flow in any channel to the prejudice of the uses on that channel by the other Party under the provisions of this Treaty. In executing any scheme of flood protection or flood control each Party will avoid, as far as practicable, any material damage to the other Party, and any such scheme carried out by India on the Western Rivers shall not involve any use of water or any storage in addition to that provided under Article III.

(3) Nothing in this Treaty shall be construed as having the effect of preventing either Party from undertaking schemes of drainage, river training, conservation of soil against erosion and dredging, or from removal of stones, gravel or sand from the beds of the Rivers: Provided that

(a) in executing any of the schemes mentioned above, each Party will avoid, as far as practicable, any material damage to the other Party;

(b) any such scheme carried out by India on the Western Rivers shall not involve any use of water or any storage in addition to that provided under Article III;

(c) except as provided in Paragraph (5) and Article VII(1) (b), India shall not take any action to increase the catchment area, beyond the area on the Effective Date, of any natural or artificial drainage or drain which crosses into Pakistan, and shall not undertake such construction or remodelling of any drainage or drain which so crosses or falls into a drainage or drain which so crosses as might cause material damage in Pakistan or entail the construction of a new drain or enlargement of an existing drainage or drain in Pakistan; and

(d) should Pakistan desire to increase the catchment area, beyond the area on the Effective Date, of any natural or artificial drainage or drain, which receives drainage waters from India, or, except in an emergency, to pour any waters into it in excess of the quantities received by it as on the Effective Date, Pakistan shall, before undertaking any work for these purposes, increase the capacity of that drainage or drain to the extent necessary so as not to impair its efficacy for dealing with drainage waters received from India as on the Effective Date.

(4) Pakistan shall maintain in good order its portions of the drainages mentioned below with capacities not less than the capacities as on the Effective Date:—

    (i)   Hudiara Drain

    (ii) Kasur Nala

    (iii) Salimshah Drain

    (iv) Fazilka Drain.

(5) If India finds it necessary that any of the drainages mentioned in Paragraph (4) should be deepened or widened in Pakistan, Pakistan agrees to undertake to do so as a work of public interest, provided India agrees to pay the cost of the deepening or widening.

(6) Each Party will use its best endeavours to maintain the natural channels of the Rivers, as on the Effective Date, in such condition as will avoid, as far as practicable, any obstruction to the flow in these channels likely to cause material damage to the other Party.

(7) Neither Party will take any action which would have the effect of diverting the Ravi Main between Madhopur and Lahore, or the Sutlej Main between Harike and Suleimanke, from its natural channel between high banks.

(8) The use of the natural channels of the Rivers for the discharge of flood or other excess waters shall be free and not subject to limitation by either Party, and neither Party shall have any claim against the other in respect of any damage caused by such use. Each Party agrees to communicate to the other Party, as far in advance as practicable, any information it may have in regard to such extraordinary discharges of water from reservoirs and flood flows as may affect the other Party.

(9) Each Party declares its intention to operate its storage dams, barrages and irrigation canals in such manner, consistent with the normal operations of its hydraulic systems, as to avoid, as far as feasible, material damage to the other Party.

(10) Each Party declares its intention to prevent, as far as practicable, undue pollution of the waters of the Rivers which might affect adversely uses similar in nature to those to which the waters were put on the Effective Date, and agrees to take all reasonable measures to ensure that, before any sewage or industrial waste is allowed to flow into the Rivers, it will be treated, where necessary, in such manner as not materially to affect those uses: Provided that the criterion of reasonableness shall be the customary practice in similar situations on the Rivers.

(11) The Parties agree to adopt, as far as feasible, appropriate measures for the recovery, and restoration to owners, of timber and other property floated or floating down the Rivers, subject to appropriate charges being paid by the owners.

(12) The use of water for industrial purposes under Articles II(2), II(3) and III(2) shall not exceed:

(a) in the case of an industrial process known on the Effective Date, such quantum of use as was customary in that process on the Effective Date;

(b) in the case of an industrial process not known on the Effective Date:

(i) such quantum of use as was customary on the Effective Date in similar or in any way comparable industrial processes; or

(ii) if there was no industrial process on the Effective Date similar or in any way comparable to the new process, such quantum of use as would not have a substantially adverse effect on the other Party.

(13) Such part of any water withdrawn for Domestic Use under the provisions of Articles II(3) and III(2) as is subsequently applied to Agricultural Use shall be accounted for as part of the Agricultural Use specified in Annexure B and Annexure C respectively; each Party will use its best endeavours to return to the same river (directly or through one of its Tributaries) all water withdrawn therefrom for industrial purposes and not consumed either in the industrial processes for which it was withdrawn or in some other Domestic Use.

(14) In the event that either Party should develop a use of the waters of the Rivers which is not in accordance with the provisions of this Treaty, that Party shall not acquire by reason of such use any right, by prescription or otherwise, to a continuance of such use.

(15) Except as otherwise required by the express provisions of this Treaty, nothing in this Treaty shall be construed as affecting existing territorial rights over the waters of any of the Rivers or the beds or banks thereof, or as affecting existing property rights under municipal law over such waters or beds or banks.

ARTICLE V

Financial Provisions

(1) In consideration of the fact that the purpose of part of the system of works referred to in Article IV(1) is the replacement, from the Western Rivers and other sources, of water supplies for irrigation canals in Pakistan which, on 15th August 1947, were dependent on water supplies from the Eastern Rivers, India agrees to make a fixed contribution of Pounds Sterling 62,060,000 towards the costs of these works. The amount in Pounds Sterling of this contribution shall remain unchanged irrespective of any alteration in the par value of any currency.

(2) The sum of Pounds Sterling 62,060,000 specified in Paragraph (1) shall be paid in ten equal annual instalments on the 1st of November of each year. The first of such annual instalments shall be paid on 1st November 1960, or if the Treaty has not entered into force by that date, then within one month after the Treaty enters into force.

(3) Each of the instalments specified in Paragraph (2) shall be paid to the Bank for the credit of the Indus Basin Development Fund to be established and administered by the Bank, and payment shall be made in Pounds Sterling, or

in such other currency or currencies as may from time to time be agreed between India and the Bank.

(4) The payments provided for under the provisions of Paragraph (3) shall be made without deduction or set-off on account of any financial claims of India on Pakistan arising otherwise than under the provisions of this Treaty: Provided that this provision shall in no way absolve Pakistan from the necessity of paying in other ways debts to India which may be outstanding against Pakistan.

(5) If, at the request of Pakistan, the Transition Period is extended in accordance with the provisions of Article II(6) and of Part 8 of Annexure H, the Bank shall thereupon pay to India out of the Indus Basin Development Fund the appropriate amount specified in the Table below:—

Table

Period of Aggregate Extension of Transition Period	*Payment to India*
One year	£Stg. 3,125,000
Two years	£Stg. 6,406,250
Three years	£Stg. 9,850,000

(6) The provisions of Article IV(1) and Article V(1) shall not be construed as conferring upon India any right to participate in the decisions as to the system of works which Pakistan constructs pursuant to Article IV(1) or as constituting an assumption of any responsibility by India or as an agreement by India in regard to such works.

(7) Except for such payments as are specifically provided for in this Treaty, neither Party shall be entitled to claim any payment for observance of the provisions of this Treaty or to make any charge for water received from it by the other Party.

ARTICLE VI

Exchange of Data

(1) The following data with respect to the flow in, and utilisation of the waters of, the Rivers shall be exchanged regularly between the Parties:—

   (a) Daily (or as observed or estimated less frequently) gauge and discharge data relating to flow of the Rivers at all observation sites.

   (b) Daily extractions for or releases from reservoirs.

   (c) Daily withdrawals at the heads of all canals operated by government or by a government agency (hereinafter in this Article called canals), including link canals.

   (d) Daily escapages from all canals, including link canals.

   (e) Daily deliveries from link canals.

These data shall be transmitted monthly by each Party to the other as soon as the data for a calendar month have been collected and tabulated, but not later than three months after the end of the month to which they relate: Provided that such of the data specified above as are considered by either Party to be necessary for operational purposes shall be supplied daily or at less frequent intervals, as may be requested. Should one Party request the supply of any of these data by telegram, telephone, or wireless, it shall reimburse the other Party for the cost of transmission.

(2) If, in addition to the data specified in Paragraph (1) of this Article, either Party requests the supply of any data relating to the hydrology of the Rivers, or to canal or reservoir operation connected with the Rivers, or to any provision of this Treaty, such data shall be supplied by the other Party to the extent that these are available.

ARTICLE VII

Future Co-operation

(1) The two Parties recognize that they have a common interest in the optimum development of the Rivers, and, to that end, they declare their intention to co-operate, by mutual agreement, to the fullest possible extent. In particular:—

(a) Each Party, to the extent it considers practicable and on agreement by the other Party to pay the costs to be incurred, will, at the request of the other Party, set up or install such hydrologic observation stations within the drainage basins of the Rivers, and set up or install such meteorological observation stations relating thereto and carry out such observations thereat, as may be requested, and will supply the data so obtained.

(b) Each Party, to the extent it considers practicable and on agreement by the other Party to pay the costs to be incurred, will, at the request of the other Party, carry out such new drainage works as may be required in connection with new drainage works of the other Party.

(c) At the request of either Party, the two Parties may, by mutual agreement, co-operate in undertaking engineering works on the Rivers.

The formal arrangements, in each case, shall be as agreed upon between the Parties.

(2) If either Party plans to construct any engineering work which would cause interference with the waters of any of the Rivers and which, in its opinion, would affect the other Party materially, it shall notify the other Party of its plans and shall supply such data relating to the work as may be available and as would enable the other Party to inform itself of the nature, magnitude and effect of the work. If a work would cause interference with the waters of any of the Rivers but would not, in the opinion of the Party planning it, affect the other Party materially, nevertheless the Party planning the work shall, on request, supply the other Party with such data regarding the nature, magnitude and effect, if any, of the work as may be available.

ARTICLE VIII

Permanent Indus Commission

(1) India and Pakistan shall each create a permanent post of Commissioner for Indus Waters, and shall appoint to this post, as often as a vacancy occurs, a person who should ordinarily be a high-ranking engineer competent in the field of hydrology and water-use. Unless either Government should decide to take up any particular question directly with the other Government, each Commissioner will be the representative of his Government for all matters arising out of this Treaty, and will serve as the regular channel of communication on all matters relating to the implementation of the Treaty, and, in particular, with respect to

(a) the furnishing or exchange of information or data provided for in the Treaty; and

(b) the giving of any notice or response to any notice provided for in the Treaty.

(2) The status of each Commissioner and his duties and responsibilities towards his Government will be determined by that Government.

(3) The two Commissioners shall together form the Permanent Indus Commission.

(4) The purpose and functions of the Commission shall be to establish and maintain co-operative arrangements for the implementation of this Treaty, to promote co-operation between the Parties in the development of the waters of the Rivers and, in particular,

(a) to study and report to the two Governments on any problem relating to the development of the waters of the Rivers which may be jointly referred to the Commission by the two Governments: in the event that a reference is made by one Government alone, the Commissioner of the other Government shall obtain the authorization of his Government before he procedes to act on the reference;

(b) to make every effort to settle promptly, in accordance with the provisions of Article IX(1), any question arising thereunder;

(c) to undertake, once in every five years, a general tour of inspection of the Rivers for ascertaining the facts connected with various developments and works on the Rivers;

(d) to undertake promptly, at the request of either Commissioner, a tour of inspection of such works or sites on the Rivers as may be considered necessary by him for ascertaining the facts connected with those works

(e) to take, during the Transition Period, such steps as may be necessary or sites; and

for the implementation of the provisions of Annexure H.

(5) The Commission shall meet regularly at least once a year, alternately in India and Pakistan. This regular annual meeting shall be held in November or

in such other month as may be agreed upon between the Commissioners. The Commission shall also meet when requested by either Commissioner.

(6) To enable the Commissioners to perform their functions in the Commission, each Government agrees to accord to the Commissioner of the other Government the same privileges and immunities as are accorded to representatives of member States to the principal and subsidiary organs of the United Nations under Sections 11, 12 and 13 of Article IV of the Convention on the Privileges and Immunities of the United Nations (dated 13th February, 1946) during the periods specified in those Sections. It is understood and agreed that these privileges and immunities are accorded to the Commissioners not for the personal benefit of the individuals themselves but in order to safeguard the independent exercise of their functions in connection with the Commission; consequently, the Government appointing the Commissioner not only has the right but is under a duty to waive the immunity of its Commissioner in any case where, in the opinion of the appointing Government, the immunity would impede the course of justice and can be waived without prejudice to the purpose for which the immunity is accorded.

(7) For the purposes of the inspections specified in Paragraph (4) (c) and (d), each Commissioner may be accompanied by two advisers or assistants to whom appropriate facilities will be accorded.

(8) The Commission shall submit to the Government of India and to the Government of Pakistan, before the first of June of every year, a report on its work for the year ended on the preceding 31st of March, and may submit to the two Governments other reports at such times as it may think desirable.

(9) Each Government shall bear the expenses of its Commissioner and his ordinary staff. The cost of any special staff required in connection with the work mentioned in Article VII (1) shall be borne as provided therein.

(10) The Commission shall determine its own procedures.

ARTICLE IX

Settlement of Differences and Disputes

(1) Any question which arises between the Parties concerning the interpretation or application of this Treaty or the existence of any fact which, if established, might constitute a breach of this Treaty shall first be examined by the Commission, which will endeavour to resolve the question by agreement.

(2) If the Commission does not reach agreement on any of the questions mentioned in Paragraph (1), then a difference will be deemed to have arisen, which shall be dealt with as follows:

    (a) Any difference which, in the opinion of either Commissioner, falls within the provisions of Part 1 of Annexure F shall, at the request of either Commissioner, be dealt with by a Neutral Expert in accordance with the provisions of Part 2 of Annexure F;

    (b) If the difference does not come within the provisions of Paragraph (2) (a), or if a Neutral Expert, in accordance with the provisions of Paragraph 7 of Annexure F, has informed the Commission that, in his opinion, the difference, or a part thereof, should be treated as a dispute, then a dispute will be deemed to have arisen which shall be settled in accordance with the provisions of Paragraphs (3), (4) and (5):

Provided that, at the discretion of the Commission, any difference may either be dealt with by a Neutral Expert in accordance with the provisions of Part 2 of Annexure F or be deemed to be a dispute to be settled in accordance with the provisions of Paragraphs (3), (4) and (5), or may be settled in any other way agreed upon by the Commission.

(3) As soon as a dispute to be settled in accordance with this and the succeeding paragraphs of this Article has arisen, the Commission shall, at the request of either Commissioner, report the fact to the two Governments, as early as practicable, stating in its report the points on which the Commission is in agreement and the issues in dispute, the views of each Commissioner on these issues and his reasons therefor.

(4) Either Government may, following receipt of the report referred to in Paragraph (3), or if it comes to the conclusion that this report is being unduly delayed in the Commission, invite the other Government to resolve the dispute by agreement. In doing so it shall state the names of its negotiators and their readiness to meet with the negotiators to be appointed by the other Government at a time and place to be indicated by the other Government. To assist in these negotiations, the two Governments may agree to enlist the services of one or more mediators acceptable to them.

(5) A Court of Arbitration shall be established to resolve the dispute in the manner provided by Annexure G

(a) upon agreement between the Parties to do so; or

(b) at the request of either Party, if, after negotiations have begun pursuant to Paragraph (4), in its opinion the dispute is not likely to be resolved by negotiation or mediation; or

(c) at the request of either Party, if, after the expiry of one month following receipt by the other Government of the invitation referred to in Paragraph (4), that Party comes to the conclusion that the other Government is unduly delaying the negotiations.

(6) The provisions of Paragraphs (3), (4) and (5) shall not apply to any difference while it is being dealt with by a Neutral Expert.

ARTICLE X

Emergency Provision

If, at any time prior to 31st March 1965, Pakistan should represent to the Bank that, because of the outbreak of large-scale international hostilities arising out of causes beyond the control of Pakistan, it is unable to obtain from abroad the materials and equipment necessary for the completion, by 31st March 1973, of that part of the system of works referred to in Article IV(1) which relates to the replacement referred to therein, (hereinafter referred to as the "replacement element"), and if, after consideration of this representation in consultation with India, the Bank is of the opinion that

(a) these hostilities are on a scale of which the consequence is that Pakistan is unable to obtain in time such materials and equipment as must be procured from abroad for the completion, by 31st March 1973, of the replacement element, and

(b) since the Effective Date, Pakistan has taken all reasonable steps to obtain the said materials and equipment and, with such resources of materials and equipment as have been available to Pakistan both from within Pakistan and from abroad, has carried forward the construction of the replacement element with due diligence and all reasonable expedition,

the Bank shall immediately notify each of the Parties accordingly. The Parties undertake, without prejudice to the provisions of Article XII (3) and (4), that, on being so notified, they will forthwith consult together and enlist the good offices of the Bank in their consultation, with a view to reaching mutual agreement as to whether or not, in the light of all the circumstances then prevailing, any modifications of the provisions of this Treaty are appropriate and advisable and, if so, the nature and the extent of the modifications.

ARTICLE XI

General Provisions

(1) It is expressly understood that

(a) this Treaty governs the rights and obligations of each Party in relation to the other with respect only to the use of the waters of the Rivers and matters incidental thereto; and

(b) nothing contained in this Treaty, and nothing arising out of the execution thereof, shall be construed as constituting a recognition or waiver (whether tacit, by implication or otherwise) of any rights or claims whatsoever of either of the Parties other than those rights or claims which are expressly recognized or waived in this Treaty.

Each of the Parties agrees that it will not invoke this Treaty, anything contained therein, or anything arising out of the execution thereof, in support of any of its own rights or claims whatsoever or in disputing any of the rights or claims whatsoever of the other Party, other than those rights or claims which are expressly recognized or waived in this Treaty.

(2) Nothing in this Treaty shall be construed by the Parties as in any way establishing any general principle of law or any precedent.

(3) The rights and obligations of each Party under this Treaty shall remain unaffected by any provisions contained in, or by anything arising out of the execution of, any agreement establishing the Indus Basin Development Fund.

Appendix

ARTICLE XII

Final Provisions

(1) This Treaty consists of the Preamble, the Articles hereof and Annexures A to H hereto, and may be cited as "The Indus Waters Treaty 1960."

(2) This Treaty shall be ratified and the ratifications thereof shall be exchanged in New Delhi. It shall enter into force upon the exchange of ratifications, and will then take effect retrospectively from the first of April 1960.

(3) The provisions of this Treaty may from time to time be modified by a duly ratified treaty concluded for that purpose between the two Governments.

(4) The provisions of this Treaty, or the provisions of this Treaty as modified under the provisions of Paragraph (3), shall continue in force until terminated by a duly ratified treaty concluded for that purpose between the two Governments.

IN WITNESS WHEREOF the respective Plenipotentiaries have signed this Treaty and have hereunto affixed their seals.

Done in triplicate in English at Karachi on this Nineteenth day of September 1960.

FOR THE GOVERNMENT OF INDIA:
  (Sd) Jawaharlal Nehru ....
FOR THE GOVERNMENT OF PAKISTAN:
  (Sd) Mohammad Ayub Khan ....
    Field Marshal, H.P., H.J.
FOR THE INTERNATIONAL BANK FOR RECONSTRUCTION
  AND DEVELOPMENT
for the purposes specified in Articles V and X and Annexures F, G and H:
  (Sd) W. A. B. Iliff ....

Index

Abbasia Canal (S.V.P.), 95

Abdullah, Sheikh Mohammad, 192, 519–20

Abell, Sir George, 159, 161

Actual uses (withdrawals), 237, 242. *See also* Sanctioned uses

ADC. *See* Agricultural Development Corporation

Administration, 477, 479–82, 489, 499–505, 539, 544, 546

Administrators, 73, 87, 100–01, 110, 343, 346, 363, 375, 383, 386 ff., 394, 397, 419, 428, 433, 437, 439, 476, 516; in Sind, 100–01, 110

Afghanistan, 25 n., 35, 100–01, 335, 339, 366; Government of, 163, 185

Agency for International Development (U.S.A.), 362, 466, 472, 481, 527, 534

Agricultural: cycle, 115; experiment stations, 482, 500–01; extension service, 422, 424, 430–31, 437, 482, 545

Agricultural Development Bank (West Pakistan), 402, 422, 427, 431

Agricultural Development Corporation (West Pakistan), 352, 354, 425–27, 428 n., 429–33, 478–82, 486, 489, 503, 507

Agricultural Development Finance Corporation (West Pakistan), 402, 422

Agriculture Department (Punjab, West Pakistan), 427, 430, 453

Ahmad, Kazi S., quoted 196–97, quoted 227

Ahmad, Nazir, 470–72, 502, 510

A.I.D. *See* Agency for International Development

Aide Memoire, 244–45

"Aid to India" Consortium, 521–23

"Aid to Pakistan" Consortium, 247, 296–97, 306 n., 315, 475, 529–34, 543, 545

Akhtar, S.M., 400, 415–16

Ali Mardan Khan, 49, 444

Ali, Mohammad (Prime Minister, Pakistan), 235, 240

Alienation, land, 395 ff., 403, 407, 414

Alkalinity, soil, 487, 507, 513

Allocation of water supplies, 115, 271, 299

Ambala District, 39, 55–56, 171, 184; Division, 136 n., 137

Amritsar, 38, 50, 175, 179, 183, 186, 189–90, 451–52, 509–10; District, 174, 182 n., 184, 186–92, 386, 434, 453

Anderson Committee (*1935*), 124, 127, 129, 131, 133, 210, 231–32, 271

Animal Husbandry Department (West Pakistan), 421, 427

Aquifer, 453, 494, 510, 513, 535, 538, 541

Aravalli Range, 23, 28, 30

Arbitral Award. *See* Radcliffe Award

Arbitral Tribunal, 5, 8, 195

Assam, 3, 136–37, 156, 158, 163, 366
Assessments, 74 n., 387 ff., 430, 500
Aswan Dam, 280, 300, 305, 529–30, 533–34
Attlee, Clement R., 2, 145–48
Attock, 31, 35, 40, 214, 274, 292–93, 483
Australia, 248, 468
Ayub Khan, Mohammad, 167 n., 240, 247, 250–51, 255, 262, 300, 306 n., 310, 315, 465, 475–77, 481, 517, 520–21, 528, quoted 529–30, 531–32; administration, 391, 410, 413, 418, 541 n.
Azed Kashmir, 5–7, 9, 201, 211, 240, 260, 262, 274, 287, 289, 518
Azed, Maulana Abul Kalam, 138, 140, 146, 371

Bahawal Canal (S.V.P.), 95, 275, 278
Bahawalpur, 6, 39–40, 85, 88, 89 n., 92, 94, 97, 99, 121–24, 136, 175–78, 182 n., 200, 209, 231, 245, 280, 336, 365–66, 415, 432, 442, 466, 483, 486, 488; case in disputes, 117; share in S.V.P., 123
Balloki headworks, 63, 87–91, 176, 210, 275, 277, 445
Balloki-Suleimanki (B-S) Link, 130, 210, 217, 241, 246, 269, 271, 291
Baluchistan, 29, 102, 136, 163, 175, 216, 365–66, 416, 432, 509
Bambanwala-Ravi-Bedian-Dipalpur (BRBD) Link, 181, 209–10, 217, 246, 257, 269, 271, 291, 517; siphon, 209–10, 517. *See also* Ravi siphon
Banihal Pass, 191
Bar, 48 n., 76 n., 85, 334
Bara, 294, 299. *See also* Tarbela
Bari Doab, 6, def. 41, 75, 85, 91, 95, 99, 177, 184, 280, 291, 336, 442; lower, 86–87, 89–90, 121
Barrage, 49, def. 63, 358, 446; controlled irrigation, 81, def. 111, 114
Basic Democracies (Pakistan), 387 ff., 425–26, 428, 439
Bass, Neil, 229, 234–35
Batala tahsil, 187–88, 191
BBRP. *See* Bhakra-Beas-Rajasthan Project
Beas Control Board, 373
Beas Dam. *See* Pong Dam

Beas projects, 325, 374, 383. *See also specific projects*
Beas-Rajasthan component of BBRP, 268 n.; Unit I, *see* Beas-Sutlej Link; Unit II, *see* Pong Dam
Beas River, 7–8, 10, 25, 27–28, 32 ff., 80, 87–88, 92, 131, 180, 182, 184–85, 200–01, 211, 227, 230, 232, 235, 238, 246, 256–57, 269, 317–23, 325–26, 331, 336, 451, 510, 523; course of, 32 ff.; diversion of, 48, 336
Beas Standing Committee, 373
Beas-Sutlej Link, 19, 207, 320, 322, 325–27, 329, 382–83, 510, 513, 523
Beaumont, H. C., 165 n., 169
Bedian, 209, 517
Begari Canal, 104
Bengal, 3, 4, 136–37, 144, 152, 156, 158, 179, 240, 365; East, 158, 196, 411; West, 136 n., 137, 196, 306
Bengal Boundary Commission, 157–58, 163, 168
Bengal Legislative Assembly, 152, 157
Beringer, Christoph, 491–92, 494–95, 499, 502; quoted 496, 501
Betterment taxes, 373, 392, 433
Bhaga River, 35, 257
Bhakra, 32, 88, 214, 317, 327–28, 373, 444; Dam, 10, 15, 63, 114, 200–01, 207 ff., 236, 238, 317, 319–21, 324–25, 347, 378–79, 446, 513; Project, 98 n., 120–22, 128–31, 133, 200–01, 206–08, 210–11, 214–17, 220, 226, 232, 317, 321, 330, 332, 336–37, 342–43, 348, 367, 370–73, 375, 377, 379, 453–54, 512–13
Bhakra Advisory Board, 370, 372, 375
Bhakra-Beas-Rajasthan Project (BBRP), 11, 17, 180, 206–07, 217, 223, 230, 249, 268 n., 316 ff., 320 ff., 347, 372, 382–84, 444, 448, 523–24
Bhakra Control Board, 343, 346, 370, 372, 374
Bhakra Dam Organisation, 374, 377
Bhakra Designs Directorate, 321, 347–48, 377, 379
Bhakra Main Line Canal, 241, 317–18, 320, 380, 512
Bhutto, Z. A., quoted 306 n., 529, 531–32
Bidding, competitive, 255, 278, 374, 381

Bihar, 3, 144, 152, 365
Bikaner, 88, 89 n., 92, 94, 97, 99, 114, 120, 123, 177–79, 317–18, 330; case in disputes, 117, 124, 133; share in S.V.P., 123
Bikaner (Gang) Canal (S.V.P.), 94, 124, 179–80, 206, 217, 317, 331, 337
Bilaspur, 366, 370, 374, 377
Binnie, Deacon, and Gourley (Binnie and Partners), 285, 358–59
Birth control, 522, 525–26
Bist Doab, def. 42, 56, 80 n., 184–86, 317, 324
Bist Doab Canal, 80 n., 208, 317, 324
Bist-Jullundur Doab. *See* Bist Doab
Black, Eugene R., 224–25, 233–35, 247–48, 250–51, 254, 270, 310
Blandford, John B., 481, 499
Board of Administration (Punjab), 54, 57
Board of Control (Punjab), 53, 58
Board of Revenue, 344, 352, 387, 394
Bombay, 52, 102, 365–66
Bombay Government, 67 n., 87, 93, 98–101, 105, 109, 119–20, 129, 211, 389
Bombay Province, 99, 399–400
Bong Feeder Canal, 291, 324, 518
Boundary Awards (Punjab), 4–5, 7, 192–93, 197, 203, 205
Boundary Commission. *See* Punjab Boundary Commission
BRBD Link. *See* Bambanwala-Ravi-Bedian-Dipalpur Link
British Government, 53 ff., 145–48, 155–58, 162–63, 398
British Raj, 51 ff., 330, 334, 347, 365, 386, 389, 516; irrigation policy, 330 ff.
Buckley, R. B., 18, quoted 47–48, 60 n., quoted 79
Bureau of Reclamation (U.S.A.), 322–23, 335, 355, 476, 492, 512; team to India, 324, 327, 329, 333, 336, 339, 382–83, 524
Byrowal, Treaty of (*1846*), 56, 58, 185

Cabinet Mission (*1946*), 2, 136–37, 139, 141, 144–45, 147–48, 154, 160, 169, 223, 364–65
Cabinet Mission Plan, 3, 135 ff., 147, 149, 152, 156, 158, 160, 345, 365

Calcutta, 52, 136 n., 137, 144, 166 n.
California, University of, 476–77
Calvert, Hubert, 17, quoted 397–98, 401, quoted 403 n., quoted 404, quoted 409, 414, 417
Canada, 221, 224, 248, 296, 349, 361, 364, 464; Department of Mines and Technical Services, 464
Canal, contour, 85; link, 85; remodeling, 538, 540–41; stable regime, 61
Canal closures (April *1948*), 205, 223
Canal Colonies, 12–13, 15, 17–18, 39, 165–66, 171, 175, 184, 204, 334, 385, 394–96, 399, 410, 412, 429, 434, 468
Casings, tubewell, 454, 470
Cauvery River, 71, 445, 446 n.
Catchment area, 337–38
CBDC. *See* Central Bari Doab Channels (Canals)
C.C.A. *See* Culturable Commanded Area
Census of Agriculture (Pakistan, *1960*), 399, 403, 415
Census of India: *1931*, 170 ff.; *1941*, 170 ff.; *1951*, 435
CENTO, 240, 304
Central Bari Doab Channels (Canals), 202, 209, 256, 260, 271, 272
Central Board of Irrigation (India), 98 n., 124, 129, 367, 371
Central Board of Irrigation and Power (India), 372
Central Thal Canal, 335
Central Water and Power Authority (India), 368–69
Central Water and Power Commission (India), 226, 343, 369–72, 377–78, 382
Central Waterways, Irrigation, and Navigation Commission (India), 371
Chaj Doab, 41, 79–80, 87, 90, 171, 175, 291, 442, 457–60, 466, 472, 486
Chaks, 39
Chandigarh, 16, 38, 367, 509
Chandra River, 32, 35, 246, 257, 326
Chasma, 274–75, 294, 540; Barrage, 276, 280, 545
Chasma-Jhelum (C-J) Link, 275
Chenab River, 6–10, 25, 28, 34 ff., 74, 77–80, 86, 89–92, 121, 125, 131, 171, 174–76, 183–84, 193, 201, 206, 210,

Chenab River (*continued*)
230, 232, 235, 238–39, 241, 245–46, 249, 256–57, 269, 273, 275–76, 292, 326, 331, 517, 519; course of, 34 ff.
Chichoki-Mallian scheme, 462, 464, 467, 469 n.
Chief Commissioners, 54, 345
Chief Engineer (CE), 95, 345, 374–75, 377, 458
Chief Engineers' (Sind, Punjab) Agreement (*1945*), 13, 132, 200, 216, 342, 367
China, 362, 364, 519–20, 524, 531–32, 543
Chinese, 6, 303, 521, 546
Chiniot, 28, 35, 40, 273–74, 540
Chitral, 163
Chitral River, 29, 35, 41 n.
Christians, 159, 173
Chuharkana scheme, 463–64, 467, 469 n.
Chunian Colony, 386
Cis-Sutlej Punjab, 55, 94, 317, 336–37, 365, 512
Cis-Sutlej States, 184
Civil Service, 346, 354, 386, 502
Civil Service of Pakistan (C.S.P.), 192, 344 n., 353
C-J Link. *See* Chasma-Jhelum Link
Climate, 37–38, 100, 515–16, 524
Coleroon River, 71, 445
Collier's magazine, 219–20, 224, 235
Colombo Plan Organisation, 347, 362, 464, 468, 543
Colombo Survey of West Pakistan, 464–66, 482–83
Colonization, 66 n., 74 n., 396, 429–31, 479
Commissioners, 54
Commissioner for Indus Waters, 261. *See also* Indus Waters Commission
Committee on Distribution of the Waters of the Indus. *See* Anderson Committee
Commonwealth, British, 148, 543
Communal factors, 516; massacres, 144 ff., 149, 168
Communal (religious) majorities, 158, 173, 193, 519
Community development: India, 436–38, 511; Pakistan, 423–24

Computer analysis, 476, 478–79; programming, 494
Concrete, 445–47
Congress (U.S.A.), 522, 528
Congress Party (India), 2–4, 135, 141, 144, 146, 155–56, 158, 170 n., 173 n., 177 n., 347, 368. *See also* Indian National Congress
Consolidation, land, 404 ff., 407, 410, 412–13, 418, 435
Consolidation of Holdings Ordinance (West Pakistan, *1960*), 418
Constituent Assembly: India, *1946–47*, 138, 144–45, 148, 154–55, 157–58, 160, 162–63, 169, 177 n.; Pakistan, 157, 162
Consultants, 243, 250–51, 253, 255, 270, 275, 285, 287, 297, 315, 322, 335, 350, 357–64, 373, 377, 379, 382–83, 464, 473, 478, 487–88, 490, 492, 502–07, 517, 534, 539; estimates, 295, 299. *See also* WAPDA consultants; World Bank consultants
"Consultantship," 360–64, 383
"Contiguous majority" area, 165, 178–79, 193; principle, 183, 186, 188, 193
Contractors, 253, 255, 278, 320, 350, 357, 360–61, 373, 380, 539
Cooperatives, 400 ff., 406, 410, 413, 422–25, 427, 429, 431, 435
Cooperative Department (West Pakistan), 422, 427
Cotton, 66, 67 n., 76, 113, 116–17, 175, 332, 394, 514, 544
Council of India, 55, 58
Counterpart funds, 303, 309, 311, 313–15, 362, 533, 543
Credit, rural, 397, 400 ff., 413, 419, 422–24, 427, 429, 431, 478, 482, 500, 541–42, 545
Cripps, Sir Stafford, 2, 136, 141
Crofton, Capt. James, 67, 68
Cropping intensities, 272 n., 395, 489, 505, 507; patterns, 479–80, 487–88, 497, 499, 505, 538, 545–46
Crop rotations, 412, 422, 429, 437, 513–14, 545
Crown Waste Lands, 14–15, 39, 66, 76, 84, 334, 385
C.S.P. *See* Civil Service of Pakistan

Cultivation techniques, 419, 424, 427, 429, 431, 480, 485, 489, 522, 545–46
Culturable Commanded Areas, 488, 507–511
Cusecs, def. 50 n., 60
Customs duties, 253, 308, 362

Damodar Project, 371, 373, 448
Damodar Valley Corporation (India), 370, 372
"Dam on the Indus." *See* Indus dam
Dams, 49, def. 63, 82, 269, 271, 287 ff., 291, 313, 445 ff., 533
Dam sites, 313, 534–35, 540
Darband, 31, 293
Darling, Sir Malcolm, 18, 74 n., 174 n., 397–98
Debal, 100
Debt, 397 ff., 399 n.
Dehar, 326–27
Delhi, 53, 58. *See also* New Delhi
Department of Agriculture (West Pakistan), 420, 424, 478
Department of Irrigation, Communications, and Works (West Pakistan), 343
Departmental methods (construction), 253, 322, 349
Dependable flows, 232
Deputy Commissioner, 54, 345, 386 ff., 426, 437–39
Dera Ghazi Khan, 41; Canal, 215; District, 214
Derajat, 41, 48, 84, 126, 214
de Terra, Helmuth, 22, 26
"Developing," tubewell, 461, 463, 467
Development, 238, 244–45, 247, 249–50, 253, 270, 304, 330, 357, 360, 385, 504 ff., 543
Development Fund. *See* Indus Basin Development Fund
Development Fund Agreement. *See* Indus Basin Development Fund Agreement
Development Loan Fund (U.S.A.), 362, 382, 467, 472, 523
"Development works," 10, 245
Dhiangarh dam site, 9, 35, 201, 211, 238, 246, 273, 519

Dipalpur Canal, 94, 178–79, 180–81, 183, 189, 193, 196, 202, 209, 271–72
"Direct Action," 141–44, 152
Districts, 437, 501, 519
District Councils: India, 439; Pakistan, 387 ff.
District Gazetteers, 188
District Officer. *See* Deputy Commissioner
Diversion, 47, 81, 536–38
Doabs, def. 12, 42, 47, 76 n., 85, 513, 516. *See also specific doabs*
Dominions, 156, 158, 195, 204
Drainage, 15, 126, 213, 250, 260, 269–70, 301–02, 336–37, 339, 351, 358, 372, 422, 430, 444, 456–59, 465, 467, 472, 474–75, 484–87, 489, 504, 510, 513–14, 545; natural, 509–10, 513; tubewell, 458, 472, 474, 484; works, 302
Drisko, John B., 244, 250 n., 274 n., quoted, 290
"Dry districts," 39, 75, 188, 334, 385, 395, 434, 451, 511–12
Durand Line, 185
Dyas, Capt. J. H., 59, 69, 93, 223

Earth-fill dams, 287, 322, 447
Earthmoving equipment, 125, 446–48
East India Company, 52 ff., 60
East Punjab (India), 8, 41, 117, 137, 163, 165, 180, 190, 200, 208, 212, 317, 331, 334, 339–40, 343, 394, 509–13, 523–24; Government, 202–05, 217
Eastern Canal (S.V.P.), 94, 179–81, 317
Eastern Nara Canal, 104, 106, 109, 337
Eastern Nara riverbed, 28, 105
Eastern Rivers, 202, 230–31, 234–36, 238, 242, 244, 247, 249, 256, 258–60, 264, 269–71, 293, 298, 316, 319, 330, 370, 377, 517
Economic assistance. *See* Foreign aid
"Economic holdings," 408–09, 413, 415, 417–18
Education, farmer, 334, 430–31, 482, 485, 500–01, 511, 541
Effluent, irrigation, 307, 336–38, 496–97
Egypt, 50, 300, 530
Electric power, 305, 313, 351, 451–53,

Electric power (*continued*)
468, 470. *See also* Hydroelectricity
and Thermal power
Electricity Department (West Pakistan), 344 n., 349, 351, 458 n.
Engineers, 341, 353–54, 363, 376, 381 n., 383, 397, 421, 444 ff., 448, 466, 476, 478, 487, 516–17
Equitable distribution, 198–99, 215
Escheat, 55
Evaporation, 332–34, 448, 457, 483–84, 540. *See also* Evapotranspiration
Evapotranspiration, 113, 115, 479, 483, 486, 513, 536, 538
Exchangeable-sodium percentage, 487, 488 n., 498
Executive Engineer (XEN), 95
Existing uses, 225, 228, 231–32
Experiment stations, agricultural, 482, 500–01
Extension services, agricultural, 422, 424, 430–31, 437, 482, 545

F.A.C. *See* Food and Agriculture Commission (Pakistan)
Fallowing, 113, 394, 396, 412, 479
Famine, 66, 74–75, 82, 84
F.A.O. (UN), 419, 430, 463–64, 469 n., 526
Farmers, 384 ff., 419–21, 469, 482, 500, 544; education, *see* Education, farmer
Faruque, Ghulam, 353, 458 n., 467
Ferozepore, 6, 8, 32, 38, 74, 175–76, 178–79, 451–52; District, 56, 94, 174, 177–82, 184, 187–90, 192–93, 434, 435 n.; headworks (S.V.P.), 94, 97, 124, 178, 180–81, 183, 189, 193, 196, 201, 205, 209, 246, 249, 256, 317, 517; tahsil, 179, 183, 187–88
Ferozepore Feeder Canal, 181, 206
Fertilizers, 331, 339, 348, 352, 419, 425, 427, 429–31, 437, 475, 479–82, 485, 489, 500–01, 505, 507–08, 511–12, 522, 524, 541–42, 545–46
Fischer, Louis, quoted 139
"Five Firsts," def. 419, 422, 424, 427, 429–33
Five Year Plans: India, 371, 373, 434–35, 511, 521–23; Pakistan, 247, 296–97, 302, 308–10, 312, 314–15, 350,

375, 391, 418, 475, 490, 526–27, 529, 530 n., 533, 541–43
Flood: of *1929*, 96, 283 n., 289; control, 269, 351, 372; irrigation, 47
Food and Agriculture Commission (Pakistan), 352, quoted 386–87, 401 ff., quoted 401–02, quoted 406–07, 418–19, quoted 420–26, 427, quoted 428, 429–30, 432–33, 479
"Food for Peace" Program (U.S.A.), 303, 309, 314–15, 362, 474, 521, 533, 543–44
Ford Foundation, 436, 491, 527
Fordwah Canal (S.V.P.), 95
Foreign aid, 306 n., 361, 373, 423–24, 474, 478, 500, 521–23, 527–30, 532, 534, 539, 542–43, 546
Foreign exchange, 253, 302, 308–09, 314, 378, 380, 533, 539, 542, 544–45. *See also* Counterpart funds
Fowler, F. J., quoted 198, 204
Foy, T. A. W., 212
Fragmentation of holdings, 399, 403 ff., 407, 413–14, 435, 544
France, 296, 543
"Friendly Governments," 10, 247–48, 252–55, 260, 262–63, 277, 295–98, 300, 302–03, 306–07, 309–312, 322, 360, 533, 545
Fuleli Canal, 49, 104, 106
Fund Agreement. *See* Indus Basin Development Fund Agreement

Gandhi, Indira, 522, 532
Gandhi, Mahatma, 2, 43, 139, 157, 173 n., 346
Gang (Bikaner) Canal (S.V.P.). *See* Bikaner Canal
Ganges: Basin, 84, 319 n.; River, 24–26, 28; Canal, 64, 453
Ganji Bar, 48 n., 84, 91
Garner, Robert, 225, 234–35
Gartang River, 27, 31
Geological Survey (U.S.A.). *See* United States Geological Survey
Germany, West. *See* West Germany
Ghaggar (Hakra) River, 27–28, 336–39, 512
Ghotki Canal, 217
Ghulam Mohammad Barrage, 39, 109, 200, 212–13, 217, 240, 271, 446, *see*

also Hyderabad (Kotri) Barrage; Project, 212 ff., 232, 237, 240, 242, 292, 324, 330–31, 339, 352, 393, 396, 432, 442, 479, 488, 507–08

Gilgit, 7, 26; River, 26, 31

Glancy Barrage. *See* Kalabagh Barrage

Gomal River, 36, 515

"Governments" (Bengal, Bombay, Madras), 52–55

Government of Bombay. *See* Bombay Government

Government of India, 55, 70, 73–75, 89–90, 94, 105, 117, 120, 123–24, 129, 131, 158, 166, 186, 191, 199, 253–54, 329, 342–43, 367–68, 371, 375, 433–34, 437–38, 451, 456

Government of India Act: *1858*, 58; *1919*, 2, 94 n., 98, 110, 365, 367, 400; *1935*, 2, 56, 98 n., 100, 125, 137, 146, 198, 218, 342, 345, 365, 367–69

Government of Pakistan, 117, 212, 241, 253–54, 264, 275, 285, 296, 300, 310–14, 343–52, 358–60, 414–16, 464–65, 504, 533, 542, 544, 546

Government of Punjab (pre-Partition), 70, 73, 75, 77, 89, 94, 119–22, 125–26, 149, 160. *See also* East Punjab; Punjab; India; West Punjab

Government of Sind, 122, 129, 216. *See also* Bombay Government

Government of West Pakistan, 350–51, 353, 359, 392, 432, 468, 479, 500, 502, 504, 510, 539, 546

"Governor" (Bengal, Bombay, Madras), 52–53

Governor-General, 53, 58, 73, 98, 105, 129, 157, 163 n., 343, 346, 367

Grand Anicut (Madras), 49, 445

Grand Trunk Road, 12, 64 n., 451, 515, 517

Greenman, David W., quoted 482 n.

Grey Canals, 94

Groundwater, 16, 30–31, 126, 213, 269, 272–73, 304–05, 307, 310, 313, 340, 350, 352, 358, 385, 432, 444 ff., 453, 462–63, 467–68, 470–71, 475, 478, 486, 488–89, 492, 494–98, 504, 508, 510–13, 524, 534, 536, 538–41, 545; advocates, 503, 534; "alternative," 533; irrigation, 453 ff., 488–89, 495, 498, 510–12, 534; mining, 472, 493;

nonsaline, 494–95, 498, 510, 538, 540; program, 463 ff., 511, 524, 532, 534, 539, 545; projects, 394, 442–43, 454, 475, 480–82, 486; quality, 494 ff., 504, 508, 513, 538, 540; saline, 494–97, 538; supplies, 536–38

Groundwater–surface water controversy, 503, 534, 540–41

Groundwater and Reclamation Division, WAPDA, 301 n., 353, 465–67, 472, 478, 492–93, 534

Group A provinces (Cabinet Mission Plan), 136

Group B provinces, 136–38, 141, 154, 160

Group C provinces, 136–38, 154

"Grow More Food" Campaign (India), 436, 511

Gudu, 132, 201, 245, 305, 442, 488, 495, 507–08; Barrage, 39, 104, 200, 216, 304, 344, 350, 356, 446; Project, 216 ff., 232, 237, 243, 292, 324, 352–53, 432

Guinness, Sir Kenelm, 243, 250 n.

Gujranwala, 452; District, 173, 468

Gujrat, 175; battle (*1849*), 57; District, 39

Gulhati, N. D., 228, 243–44

Gurdaspur award, 190–92, 194; District, 39, 173, 179, 181, 184, 188–93, 305, 434, 453; tahsil, 191

Gurgaon District, 182, 436

GWDO. *See* WASID

Hagen, Toni, 23 ff.

Hajipur, 132

Hakra (Ghaggar) River, 27–28, 336–39, 512

Hamid, M. A., 228–29, 250 n., 353, 467, 472

Harappa, 28, 36, 47

Harike, 27, 32, 88, 258, 320, 325, 331; headworks, 180, 205–09, 217, 317, 320, 324, 328, 446

Harvard: Advisory Group, 490 ff., 502, 527–28; Development Advisory Service, 490 n., 528; Water Resources Group, 491

Haryana Pant, 367, 371

Harza Engineering Company International, 303, 358–61, 490, 498, 504,

Harza Engineering Co. (*continued*)
508, 526, 535, 538; Appraisal Report, 316, 358, 442, 474, 485 n., 490, 497–98, 503 ff., 534–36, 539; approach, 504 ff., 526; program, 504 ff., 526, 535–40

Haveli Canal, 124–25, 271–72, 280; Project, 77, 87, 97, 125, 130–31, 176, 271, 275, 283, 447, 453, 458

Head regulator, 49, 63, 72, 112

Headworks, def. 63

Helmand Valley Project (Afghanistan), 335, 339, 466

Higham, Sir Thomas, 90

Himachal Pradesh, 246, 343, 366, 370, 374–75

Himalayas, 22 ff., 293, 323, 328

Hindu Kush, 26, 29, 31

Hindus, 136–37, 155, 161–62, 165–66, 173, 175, 184, 204, 346, 400, 402, 438, 509, 520

Hirakud Project, 370–71, 373, 448

Hissar District, 49, 57 n., 66 n., 120, 318

Historic uses (withdrawals), 231, 235–37, 242, 271

Holdings, land, 395, 397, 403–04, 407 ff., 413 ff., 434–35, 544. *See also* "Economic holdings"; "Subsistence holdings"

Hoshiarpur District, 39, 56, 184–85, 187, 192, 324, 434

Hunting Technical Services, Ltd., 316, 358, 464, 466, 474, 486, 490, 492

Huslie Canal, 50, 58

Hyderabad (Sind), 12, 37, 40, 100, 105, 212, 214 n., 415

Hyderabad State (India), 5, 213

Hyderabad (Kotri) Barrage, 104, 109, 132, 200, 240. *See also* Ghulam Mohammad Barrage

"Hydraulic jump," 290

Hydroelectric power, 269, 305, 307, 326–27, 453, 458–59

IBAB. *See* Indus Basin Advisory Board

IBP. *See* Indus Basin Project (West Pakistan)

IBRD. *See* World Bank

I.C.A. (U.S.A.), 466–67, 474, 478, 481

I.D.E. *See* Institute of Development Economics

Iliff, Sir William A. B., 224, 243, 249, 255, 262–63, 300, 302–03, 309

Implements, agricultural, 352, 385, 430–31, 436, 475, 482, 485, 500, 541

Import duties, 255, 278, 297

Income taxes, 253, 255, 297, 362

Incrustation (of tubewells), 461–62, 471, 473

India, 117, 303–04, 306, 314, 316, 319, 438, 467, 500, 509 ff., 514, 516–25, 529–32, 535, 544; conflict with China, 303–04; military aid to, 303–04, 306; political organization after Independence, 342–45, 366. *See also* Government of India

India Office, 73

Indian Army, 146, 166, 186, 212, 303

Indian Civil Service, 4, 18, 146–47, 192

Indian Independence Act, 3, 161–62, 163 n., 517

Indian Irrigation Commission (*1901–03*), 82 ff., 88, 90, 92, 98–99, 106, 108–09, 121, 124, 126, 130, 132, 199, 216, 229, 319 n., 449 n., 478

Indian Mutiny (*1857*), 51, 54–55, 58, 67, 186

Indian National Army, 1, 147

Indian National Congress, 2, 137–38, 152, 154, 168. *See also* Congress Party

Indian States, 148–49, 218. *See also* Princely States

Indian Statutory Commission (Simon Commission, *1927–29*), 146

Indo-Pakistan relations, 330, 519, 531

Indus (WAPDA Journal), 356

Indus Basin, 4, 10–11, 16, 18–19, 22 ff., 29 ff., 51, 63, 83, 97, 115, 124, 135–36, 141, 196, 205, 209, 217–21, 226, 230–32, 236, 240, 248, 301–04, 310, 316, 318, 319 n., 342, 346, 372–73, 383–84, 444, 447, 452, 462–63, 478, 509, 514–17, 523–24, 540, 546; British rule in, 55 ff.; irrigation phases, 115; irrigation system, 10, 97, 124, 136, 196, 205, 209, 217–18, 223; law of water use in, 197 ff.; physical geography and geology, 22 ff.; political organization, 135, 141. *See also* Lower

Indus; Middle Indus; Upper Indus
Indus Basin Advisory Board, 249–51,
  285, 320; estimates, 291, 299; Plan,
  250–53, 270–72, 291
Indus Basin Development Fund, 302–
  05, 308–09, 312–15, 352, 364; Special
  Reserve, 302
Indus Basin Development Fund Agreement, 8, 114, 248–50, 253–55, 259–
  62, 264, 268–70, 275–77, 285, 291,
  295–99, 302, 309, 311 ff., 361, 516,
  530 n., 545; Supplemental Agreement, 248, 302, 311 ff., 359, 517,
  530 n., 545
Indus Basin Project (West Pakistan),
  11, 17, 35, 133, 193, 208–11, 216, 245,
  250, 255, 258, 260–64, 268 ff., 275 ff.,
  283, 291–92, 295–98, 300, 302–05,
  307–09, 312, 315, 320, 322, 324, 347,
  350, 357–62, 364, 373, 379, 382, 384,
  448, 463, 484, 494, 502, 507, 510,
  523–24, 532–34, 545; Phase I, 277–
  78, 280, 545; Phase II, 277–78, 280,
  283, 545; Project Description, 268 ff.,
  273–75, 283, 285, 291, 296, 298–302,
  308, 311
Indus Basin Project Division
  (WAPDA), 242, 352, 354
"Indus Basin Settlement Plan," 268 n.;
  "settlement scheme," 247, 249, 253,
  268 n., 300
Indus Basin Special Study, 312, 358–
  59, 364
Indus Basin Working Party, 218, 229
Indus Commission (Rau Commission,
  1941–42), 129–133, 197, 200, 210–11,
  216, 218, 231, 368
Indus Commission, Permanent, 260–61.
  See also Indus Waters Commission
Indus Committee (*1935*), 124. *See also*
  Anderson Committee
Indus dam, 247, 277, 299–300, 311,
  533; "economic viability," 311;
  "technical feasibility," 311. *See also*
  Tarbela Dam
Indus Discharge Committee, 122, 127
Indus Plains, 14, 17, 29 ff., 37 ff., def.
  41, 117, 222, 304–05, 344, 352, 358,
  464–65, 476, 483, 486, 488–90, 492,
  495, 503, 507–09, 516, 524, 534–35,
  541, 545; mapping, 464; Northern

Zone, def. 41, 117; Southern Zone,
  def. 41, 117. *See also* Northern Zone;
  Southern Zone
Indus Resources Study, 311. *See also*
  Indus Basin Special Study
Indus River, 6–8, 10, 22 ff., 31 ff., 84,
  92, 101–03, 106, 118, 123, 131, 212,
  215, 230, 235, 237, 245, 253, 256–57,
  269, 271–75, 277, 280, 284, 291, 293,
  295, 307, 313, 316, 320, 331, 358,
  495–96, 519, 534; course, 31 ff.;
  lower, 40, 106, 118; navigation, 102–
  03; physical characteristics, 22 ff.;
  water supplies, 98 n., 123
Indus Rivers, 8, 41, 46, 64 n., 78, 111,
  164, 193, 234, 239, 384, 518
Indus Waters Commission, 261, 354
Indus Waters Commissioners, 261, 353,
  372
Indus Waters Dispute, 8, 85, 99 ff., 117,
  133, 182, 195 ff., 220 ff., 236, 253,
  262, 300, 518
Indus Waters Settlement, 254, 268. *See
  also* Indus Waters Treaty
Indus Waters Treaty (September
  1960), 8–11, 16–18, 114, 119, 131,
  133, 181, 193, 201, 205, 214, 241,
  249–50, 253–55, 261, 277, 280, 292,
  296, 299–300, 316, 318, 326, 330, 336–
  37, 342, 350, 358, 360–61, 371–72,
  382, 384, 516–19, 535, 546
Indus Zone (IBP), 245, 271, 291, 298,
  304
Infiltration, 452, 493–94, 535
Inheritance, 387 ff., 397, 403–04, 407
Insecticides, 430–31, 437, 505, 542
Institute of Development Economics
  (Karachi), 491, 502
Intensities, irrigation, 94 n., 114, 339,
  395, 539
Interaction, principle of, 479–80, 489,
  505, 539, 545–46
Inter-Dominion Agreement (May
  1948), 202, 205, 209–10, 217, 219,
  227, 246
International Bank for Reconstruction
  and Development. *See* World Bank
International Court of Justice, 219, 221
Interstate Agreement (Indian Punjab,
  Rajasthan, Kashmir, *1955*), 217, 319,
  370, 375, 377, 512

Interstate Water Disputes Act (India, *1956*), 369, 372
Inspector-General of Irrigation (India), 44 n., 367
Interest charges, 398, 400
Interim Government (India), 140–41, 144–45, 149, 159–60
Inundation canals, 47–48; irrigation, 47, def. 111, 516
Irrigation, 46 ff., 425, 433, 488–89, 492, 502–05, 516, 524, 539, 546; barrage, 81; diversion, 47; effects of, 395; experience, 331, 449 n.; flood, 47; groundwater, 451 ff., 469, 474–77; phases, 115; restricted perennial, 513; run-of-the-river, 97; weir-controlled, 81, def. 111; well, 111, 324, 448, 449 n. *See also* Tubewells; Intensities, irrigation; Manipulation; Nonperennial irrigation; Perennial irrigation
Irrigation and Power Department (West Pakistan), 307, 344, 346, 353
Irrigation and Power Research Institute (Amritsar), 332, 379, 509, 512. *See also* Land Reclamation, Irrigation, and Power Research Institute (Amritsar)
Irrigation Branch (Punjab and West Punjab Public Works Department), 64, 90, 93, 95, 127, 182, 215, 385–86, 453, 458, 509
Irrigation Department (West Punjab from *1951*; West Pakistan from *1955*), 247–50, 278 n., 284–85, 307, 348, 350, 352–55, 357, 360, 363, 373, 390, 392, 421, 426, 429, 455, 457, 462–67, 469 n., 478, 481, 503; Dams Investigation Circle, 313, 358
Irrigation Research Institute (Lahore), 307, 333, 353, 355, 458, 460, 470, 509
Islam (Pallah) headworks (S.V.P.), 95–96, 124, 176–77, 209, 210, 271–72, 275, 277–78, 289; "disaster" (*1929*), 96, 289
Itschner, Lt. Gen. Emerson C., 347, 363, 381 n.

Jacob, Col. S. L., 85, quoted 87, 88, 90, 93, 121
Jagirs, 410, 413–14, 434

Jammu, 9, 35, 91, 191, 193, 201, 208, 257, 518–19
Jammu-Kashmir, 6–9, 67–68, 77, 90, 190–91, 239, 242, 246, 262, 273–74, 304, 518
Jammu Tavi, 35 n., 92, 274 n., 519
Japan, 296, 362, 541–42
Jaranwala scheme, 463–64, 467
Jech Doab, def. 42. *See also* Chaj Doab
Jenkins, Sir Evan, 128, 153, 161, 166–67, 168 n., 181 n.
Jhang District, 171–72, 174–75, 185, 453
Jhang Maghiana, 126, 175
Jhelum, 7, 25, 79, 91, 131, 175, 483
Jhelum-Chenab Zone (IBP), 245, 271–72, 276, 283, 291, 533, 536
Jhelum River, 6, 8, 10, 34, 79, 86, 89, 121, 126, 165, 171, 192, 201, 211, 230, 235–36, 239, 245, 248, 253, 256–57, 262, 269, 272–75, 283–87, 289–291, 292 n., 293, 322–23, 358; course of, 34
Jinnah, Mohammad Ali, 135 n., 144, 154–56, 160, 164–67, 176, 186, 191, 346, 366
Jinnah Barrage. *See* Kalabagh Barrage
Jogindar Nagar, 34, 63, 451–54, 458 n.
Johnson, Lyndon B., 306 n., 422, 475, 521, 525, 528
Jullundur District, 56, 182 n., 184–90, 192, 317, 324, 434; Division, 136 n., 137, 174; tahsil, 183, 187–88. *See also* Bist Doab
Jumna River, 27–28, 49, 57 n., 319 n., 320, 331
Junagadh, 5
Junglis, 75 n., 126, 334

Kabul River, 29, 31, 35, 41 n., 56, 124, 274, 292, 294, 349, 515
Kahan River, 273, 285
Kailas Range, 25–28, 31
Kalabagh, 31, 124, 126–27, 176, 201, 274–75, 313; Barrage (Jinnah Barrage), 31, 127, 215, 275, 277, 294, 432; dam site, 294, 535
Kalabagh-Jhelum Link, 245, 269, 275. *See also* Chasma-Jhelum Link
Kamalpur dam site, 285, 323

Index

Kangra District, 56, 185, 451
Kapurthala, 32, 136, 182 n., 186–87, 192, 365
Karachi, 12, 100–03, 128, 212–13, 214 n., 229, 415, 531, 533
Karakorams, 6, 26, 29
Karol scheme, 454–55, 460, 470
Kashmir, 1, 5–8, 10, 16, 89, 191, 193, 201–02, 205, 212, 217–23, 235–36, 262, 272, 284, 303–05, 306 n., 314, 319, 323, 366, 377, 516–20, 530, 545; accession to India, 191; cease fire, 219; cease-fire line, 518, 531; dispute, 6, 8–9, 193, 226, 236, 518; plebiscite, 219, 240; war (September *1965*), 314
Kashmir, Azad. *See* Azad Kashmir
Kashmir Canal, 208, 210, 519
Kashmir, Vale of, 5, 7, 9, 35, 191, 257, 284
Kashmor, 37, 40, 104, 215–16, 466
Kasur, 27, 175, 180, 190, 517
Kasur Branch (UBDC), 188–90
Kazi, A. Rashid, 295 n., 313, 344 n., 353
Kennedy, John F., 301, 465, 475–77, 481; administration, 525
Kennedy, R. C., 62
Khadir, 47, 48 n., 86
Khairpur, 6, 39, 99, 175, 217, 305, 366, 415, 442, 466, 483, 486, 488, 499; case in disputes, 231; Division, 214 n.
"Khalistan," 153, 155
Khanewal, 91, 175
Khanki, 78–79, 87, 89, 91, 121, 276; Barrage, 90, 176, 277
Kharif, 47, 112, 115–16, 118, 210, 256–57, 394, 541; supplies, 123, 241
Kharif-maturing period, 115, 123, 238, 244; -sowing period, 115, 120, 123, 238, 244. *See also* Rabi-sowing period
Khosla, A. N., 125, 226–29, 243
Khyber Pass, 35, 56
Kidwai, Zamir-uddin, 493
Kirana Hills, 28, 30, 35–36, 516
Kirmani, S. S., 242, 250, 272, 284–85, 307, 315, 354, 510, 533
Kishanganga River, 35, 284, 323
Kotkai, 31, 293, 320
Kotri, 102, 107. *See also* Hyderabad (Sind)

Kotri Barrage. *See* Ghulam Mohammad Barrage; Hyderabad Barrage
Kunar River, 29, 35
Kunhar River, 35, 273, 284, 323
Kurram River, 36, 275, 515

Labour Government (U.K.), 1, 132, 146–48
Lacey, Gerald, 62, 445
Ladakh, 6–7, 9, 26, 303
Lahore, 12, 40, 49, 166–68, 175, 179–80, 183, 186, 189, 212, 258, 451, 466, 473, 475, 478; District, 94, 173, 178–81, 183–84, 186, 188–90; Division, 174
Lahore Branch (UBDC), 181, 189, 196, 209, 256
Lahore (Pakistan) Resolution (*1940*), 2, 170 n., 531
Lahore, Treaty of (*1809*), 56, 185
Land: acquisition, 250–51, 253, 255, 297; classification, 329, 333, 335; reform, 408 ff., 414–18, 434–35, 544; revenue, 386–92, 398, 433–35, 499. *See also* Holdings; Revenue assessments; Tenure
Landlords, 400 ff., 412, 434, 544
Landowners, 413–17, 420, 423
Land Reclamation, Irrigation, and Power Research Institute (Amritsar), 509–12
Land Reforms Commission (Pakistan), quoted, 413 ff., 418–19, 429
Land and Water Development Board (West Pakistan), 481, 500. *See also* Land and Water Management Board
Land and Water Management Board (West Pakistan), 352, 354, 394, 432, 500, 503
Larji dam site, 33, 320, 323, 325, 327, 523
Lawrence, John, 57, 455
LBDC. *See* Lower Bari Doab Canal
LCC. *See* Lower Chenab Canal
Leaching, 16, def. 458, 479, 487–88, 505, 510, 513
Legislative Assembly (West Pakistan). *See* Provincial Assembly
Leh, 26, 31
Liaquat Ali Khan, 144, 156–57, 220, 240

583

Lieutenant-Governor, 54, 58, 455

Lilienthal, David E., 10, 219, quoted 220–22, 223–28, 229 n., 233–35, 241–42, 342; journals of, 219, 235

Linings, canal, 333–34, 458, 513

Link canals, 18, 85, def. 125, 235–38, 243–46, 250–51, 270, 358, 448, 494. *See also specific link canals*

LJC. *See* Lower Jhelum Canal

Lloyd Barrage. *See* Sukkur Barrage

Loans: small, 399 ff., 424; in kind, 428, 431

London, 3, 144–47, 156, 160, 245, 249

Lower Bari Doab Canal (LBDC), 63, 89–90, 92 n., 95, 125, 130, 210, 291, 446

Lower Chenab Canal (LCC), 79–80, 92 n., 171, 291, 386, 457–58, 468

Lower Indus, def. 40, 56, 84, 102 n., 103, 107, 175, 200, 330, 499 n., 515

Lower Indus Project, 316, 358

Lower Jhelum Canal (LJC), 80, 83, 92 n., 291, 458–60

Lower Sohag Canals, 94, 385

Ludhiana, 509; District, 56, 171, 174, 184, 434

Luni River, 83–84, 319 n.

Lyall, James, 77

Lyallpur, 12, 452, 464; District, 77, 166, 171, 173–76, 184, 289, 395, 416, 468, 486–87

Maasland, Marinus, quoted 498

MacDonald, Sir M., and Partners, 316, 358, 466, 474, 486, 490, 492

Machinery, earth-moving, 446–47

Madhopur, 8, 32, 34, 59–60, 71, 76, 78, 90, 191, 207, 258, 325; headworks, 71, 176, 181, 188–93, 201–03, 208–10, 217, 249, 256, 317, 320, 519

Madras, 52, 71, 82 n., 365–66, 445

Mailsi Canal (S.V.P.), 95, 271, 275, 278

Mailsi-Bahawal (M-B) Link, 276, 280, 328

Mailsi Siphon-Barrage, 276–78

Main Branch (UBDC), 181, 189, 196, 209, 256

Malik, Rashid Ahmad, 18, 74 n., 214 n.

Mandi, 32; Plain, 32; State hydro-electric scheme, 63, 190, 451, 458 n.

Mandi town, 13

Mangla, 16, 34–35, 80, 87, 89–91, 211, 214, 262, 273–74, 283–85, 291–92, 294, 311, 322–24, 328, 347, 356, 358, 380, 448, 518, 534–36, 545; Dam, 9, 63, 131, 245, 248, 250, 253, 260, 271–73, 277, 280 ff., 285–87, 292 n., 294, 298, 347, 356, 358, 380, 448, 518, 534–36, 545; headworks, 7, 176, 549; Raised Mangla Dam, 298–300, 308, 310, 315

"Mangla affected persons," 289

Mangla-Khanki-Balloki-Suleimanki Link, 276

Manipulation of irrigation system, 535, 538, 541

Manjha, 59, 184, 186

Manures, green, 331, 436–37, 513

Marala, 34, 35 n., 80, 87, 90, 201, 246, 257; headworks, 7, 91–92, 176–77, 210, 276, 280, 517

Marala-Ravi (M-R) Link, 209–10, 217, 246, 269, 271, 276, 291

Mardan, 294, 452

Marhu Tunnel Plan, 201, 230, 238, 245–47, 258, 326, 519

Markets, 13, 415, 425, 429

Martial Law (Pakistan), 391, 428

Martial Law Regulation No. 64 (West Pakistan), 391, 414–19

"Material damage," under Indus Waters Treaty, 338–39

M-B Link. *See* Mailsi-Bahawal Link

Menon, V. K. Krishna, 304, 523

Menon, V. P., 3, 134 n., quoted 135 n., quoted 136 n., quoted 137–38, quoted 138 n., quoted 139 n., 144, quoted 148–49, quoted 152–53, quoted 154–55, 156, quoted 160 n., 163, quoted 168 n., 191, 223, 366

Menon Plan, 3, 156, 160–62

Mettur Dam, 445, 446 n.

Middle Indus, def. 40, 515

Mining, groundwater, 273, 472, 493–97, 510, 538, 540

Minister of Food, Agriculture, Irrigation, and Power (West Pakistan), 344, 353, 500

Minister for Planning (India), 371

Ministry of Agriculture (Pakistan), 463–64

Ministry of Finance: India, 343, 376; Pakistan, 313, 343

Ministry of Irrigation and Power (India), 228, 343, 347, 371, 377–78
Ministry of Natural Resources and Scientific Research (India), 228, 371
Missouri Basin, 229, 447–48
Missouri Valley Interagency Committee, 223
Mithankot, 25, 32, 40, 103, 109, 216
Mithrao Canal, 104
Moguls, 12, 347, 365, 410
Mohammad, Ghulam, 491–92, 494–95, quoted 496, 499, quoted 501, 502
Mohenjo Daro, 28, 36, 47, 516
Monawar Tavi, 35 n., 92, 274 n., 519
Money lenders, 397–400, 402–03
Montagu, A. M. R., quoted 61, quoted 71–73, quoted 92 n., quoted 96 n., quoted 112 n., quoted 447, 454–56, quoted 457, 458, quoted 465
Montgomery, 12, 48 n.; District, 87, 91, 94, 166, 171, 174–79, 184, 431, 486–87
Montgomery-Pakpattan Link, 125, 130, 256
Moon, Penderel, 135 n., 167 n., 177 n.
Mosley, Leonard, 144–46, quoted 161–62, quoted 164, 166, quoted 167, 191, 197, 181 n.
Mountbatten, Lord Louis, 3, 5, 145–49, 152, 153 n., quoted 155, 159–61, 166–67, quoted 168 n., 191, 192, 223, 346
M-R Link. *See* Marala-Ravi Link
Mueenuddin, Ghulam, 242, 250
Muhajir Branch (Thal Canal), 128, 334
Multan, 12, 40, 91, 103, 126, 175; District, 48, 171, 174–75, 185, 289, 395, 432, 486–87; Division, 172, 174; "revolt" (*1848*), 57–58, 185
Multifactor approach, 478–80, 486, 489, 492, 500, 505, 545
Multiplier effect, 479–80, 539. *See also* Principle of interaction
Murree, 300–02, 308, 310; proposals (July *1962*), 300–03, 310
Muslims, 136, 152, 162, 165–66, 170–71, 174–75, 183–84, 305, 346, 410, 520
Muslim League, 3, 135–49, 152, 154–60, 168–69, 170 n., 192
Muslim-majority areas, 153, 158, 162, 165, 173, 178; districts, 157–58, 183,

192–93; tahsils, 179–80, 183, 186–87, 191, 193
Mutiny, Indian (*1857*), 346
Muzaffarabad, 192, 284
Muzaffargarh Canal, 215
Muzaffargarh District, 48, 127, 214

Nagas, 366, 520
Nakodar tahsil, 183, 187–88
Nallas, 76, 90
Nangal, 88, 321, 326, 377, 380; Barrage, 200 n., 206, 208, 217, 241, 317, 320, 446
Nangal Hydel Canal, 377
Nankana Sahib, 162, 166, 183
Napier, Sir Charles, 56, 100
Napier, Col. Robert, 58, 64
Nara River, 336, 338–39. *See also* Eastern Nara riverbed
National Development Organisation (Pakistan), 425, 428, 430
Native States, 53; canals in, 69. *See also* Princely States
Natural gas, 305, 481, 485 n., 543
Natural levees, 36–37, 46
Navigation, 87–88, 351, 433
Nazimuddin, Khwaja, 225, 227, 240
Neale, Walter C., 439
Nehru, Jawaharlal, 3, 137–38, quoted 138 n., 139–40, quoted 140–41, 144, 154–56, 160, 164, 166–67, 176, 197, 219, 225, 227, 234–35, 247, 254–55, 262, 343, 368, 520
Nepal, 25
New Delhi, 57 n., 163, 169, 202, 230, 521, 531
New Mirpur, 289, 321
New Zealand, 248, 255
Nicholson, H. W., 122, 133, 458
Nicholson-Trench Report (*1929*), 128–29, 131, 133
Nile River, 102 n., 516
Nitrates, 394, 480, 485, 542
Nomads, 75, 328, 335
Non-Muslim majority areas, 153, 155–56, 158, 163, 165, 169, 171, 173, 178; districts, 157, 186; tahsils, 179, 184, 186, 193
Nonperennial irrigation, def. 111, 394
North West Frontier, 126, 516
North West Frontier Province (N.W.F.P.), 54, 123, 136, 149, 155,

North West Frontier Province (*cont.*) 163, 175, 185, 346, 365–66, 418, 483, 509
North Western Provinces, 54
North Western Railway, 102, 175
Northern Zone (Indus Plains), def. 41, 117, 304–07, 316, 350, 358, 442, 466, 473–75, 483, 488, 490, 492–95, 498, 504, 507–08, 538, 540

Off-channel storage, 284–85, 292 n., 299, 304, 313, 534
One Unit Rule (West Pakistan, *1955*), 117, 214 n., 245, 272, 343, 366, 387, 411
Orissa, 365, 370
"Other factors" (in Partition), 169, 175, 178–79, 184, 188, 190
Oudh, 53

Pabbi Hills, 79–80, 89, 458
Pack, tubewell, 461, 463, 470, 473. *See also* Shroud, tubewell
Pakistan, 135 n., 136 n., 137 ff., 153, 156, 163, 169, 173, 304, 459, 465, 474–75, 502, 511, 517–21, 524–33, 535, 541, 543–44; bargaining position, 299, 308; economy, 527 ff.; -Western relations, 205, 303, 306 n., 530 n., 542. *See also* East Pakistan; Government of Pakistan; West Pakistan
Pakistan Industrial Development Corporation (PIDC), 348–49, 373, 430, 481–82
Pakistan Sutlej Valley Canals, 256, 260, 271, 277, 291, 317
Pakpattan, 74, 77, 175
Pakpattan Canal, 77, 95, 125, 130, 176, 280
Palchar, 246, 326, 519
Panchayati Raj, 438–39
Pandoh-Baggi tunnel, 207, 326–27, 523
Pandoh dam site, 320–21, 325–27
Panjnad, 25, 27, 97, 121, 206; Canal (S.V.P.), 95, 271–72, 283; headworks, 95–96, 124, 177 n., 271–72, 280, 291–92
Papanek, Gustav, quoted 528
Parliament, 51 ff., 148, 163 n.
Partition, 134 ff., 195, 516, 518

Partition Commission, 3, 5, 163, 169, 195 n.
Partition Council, 3, 5, 195
Partition Line (Radcliffe Line), 6–7, 10, 12, 19, 135, 141, 166, 182–93, 205, 342, 516–17, 531
Patel, Vallabhbhai, 139, 153 n., 156, 166–67
Pathankot, 451; tahsil, 187–88, 190–91, 193
Patiala, 55, 67, 68 n., 70–71, 136, 182 n., 184, 343, 365
Patiala and East Punjab States Union (P.E.P.S.U.), 343, 366, 370, 374, 389, 434–35
Patwaris, 389, 402, 438
Paustian, Paul W., 18, 74 n., 80 n., 385, 386, quoted 390, 393, 395–97, quoted 404, quoted 406
Peasantry, 398, 403. *See also* Farmers
P.E.P.S.U. *See* Patiala and East Punjab States Union
Perennial canals, 49, 450; irrigation, 49–50, def. 111, 114, 394, 513
Permanent Indus Commission, 260–61
Permanent Settlement, 389, 391, 410
Peshawar, 274, 294, 452
Pesticides, 352, 430–31, 437, 480, 484, 500, 505, 541–42, 545
Pethick-Lawrence, Lord, Secretary of State for India, 136, 141, 144, 156
Phosphates, 480, 485
PIDC. *See* Pakistan Industrial Development Corporation
Pindi Bhattian scheme, 462, 464, 467, 469 n.
Pir Panjal Range, 31–34, 191, 293
P.I.U. *See* Produce Index Unit
Planning, 81, 232, 326, 343, 347, 350, 358 ff., 364 ff., 373, 465, 470, 474–75, 490–92, 501–02, 504–08, 511, 526; in India, 326, 342, 364 ff., 511; regional, 81, 358, 374–75, 464–65, 490, 492, 504, 507–08, 539 n.; WAPDA, 358 ff., 508. *See also* Five Year Plans
Planning Commission: India, 140, 228, 343, 370, 377; Pakistan, 307, 344, 419, 438 n., 490 ff., 527, 542–43
Plant protection, 419, 427, 429–31, 522
Point Four Program (U.S.A.), 436, 465

Pollution, water, 338
Pong Dam, 16, 33, 131, 201, 207, 238, 247, 287, 319–25, 329, 381–83, 448, 510, 512–13, 523
Poonch, 5, 323
Population, 244, 384 ff.; control, 525–26, 541; growth, 74, 298, 357, 360, 403–04, 524; pressure, 89, 372, 386, 395–96, 431, 484, 489, 522, 525–26
Potwar Plateau, 11, 41, 80, 175, 244–45, 483
Power: electric, 355, 360, 452, 475, 504–05; hydroelectric, 292, 372, 511, 519; thermal, 356, 511
Presidencies (Bengal, Bombay, Madras), 52–55
Princely States, 5, 14–15, 54–55, 57, 67–70, 88, 136, 178, 343, 365–66, 389
Principle of interaction, 479–80, 489, 505, 539, 545–46
Prior allocation, 199, 215, 231
Prior appropriation, 198–99
Produce Index Unit (P.I.U.), 414, 416, 434
Project areas, groundwater, 429–31, 475, 480–82, 486, 501, 507, 512, 539, 545–46; administration, 431, 480–82, 489, 492, 500; directors, 481–82, 500
Project Description. *See* Indus Basin Project (West Pakistan)
Proprietary rights, 200, 202, 231
Protective works, 78
Province, def. 54–55, 343, 345; Chief Commissioner's, 366; Governor's, 366
Provincial Assembly (Legislative Assembly, West Pakistan), 350, 355, 471, 502
Public Law 480 (U.S.A.), 240, 254, 309. *See also* "Food for Peace" Program
Pumps, tubewell, 448 ff., 472, 501; centrifugal vacuum, 451, 453–54, 460, 463, 469 n., 470–71; vertical turbine, 448, 451, 463, 469–70, 474, 510, 545
Punjab, 3, 7, 11–14, def. 41, 67 n., 83–86, 93, 99, 100, 123, 136–137, 141, 149, 152, 156–57, 159–60, 162–65, 175, 178, 199, 204, 210–11, 214, 231, 245, 330, 345, 365–66, 385, 399–400,

411, 415, 439, 451, 453, 455–58, 461, 465–66, 470, 483, 493, 509; annexation, 58, 185; as granary, 76, 80, 82, 84, 108, 330; British, 57–58, 170, 173–74, 185; irrigation system, 65, 97, 105, 119, 196, *see also* Irrigation; massacres (*1947*), 12, 149, 152, 167, 516; partition of, 162–194, 291
Punjab Board of Administration, 54, 57, 59
Punjab Board of Economic Enquiry, 17
Punjab Boundary Commission, 83, 157, 162–69, 173–74, 179, 196 n.
Punjab Boundary Force, 4, 6–7, 167
Punjab Boundary Line, 135, 182–93. *See also* Partition Line
Punjab Cooperative Societies, 398
Punjab, East. *See* East Punjab; Punjab, Indian
Punjab Government (under British), 70, 73, 75, 77, 89, 94, 119–22, 125–26, 149, 160; case in disputes, 117, 121–24, 130–33
Punjab Hill States, 7, 343, 365
Punjab, Indian, 13, 41, 319–20, 324, 331, 343, 366, 370–71, 374, 377, 380, 389, 396, 410, 433–34, 437, 509–14, 523–24. *See also* East Punjab; Punjabi Suba
Punjab Land Alienation Act, 395, 399
Punjab (Provincial) Legislative Assembly, 152, 155, 157, 162, 168, 170
Punjab (Pakistan), 167, 177, 271–72, 277, 293, 396, 418. *See also* West Punjab
Punjab Partition Order (*1947*), 203
Punjab Public Works Department, 57 n., 64, 344, 385, 453. *See also* Irrigation Branch
Punjab Rivers, def. 41, 81, 92, 120, 515
Punjab States, 159, 171, 182 n., 184
Punjab Tenancy Acts, 403, 412
Punjab, West. *See* West Punjab
Punjabi Suba, 367, 371

Q-B Link. *See* Qadirabad-Balloki Link
Qadirabad-Balloki (Q-B) Link, 256, 269
Qadirabad Barrage, 269, 276, 278
Qaimpur Canal (S.V.P.), 95

Qanungo, 389
Quetta, 56, 215; District, 432; Division, 216

Rabi, 115–16, 118, 256–57, 541; crops, 112, 394; irrigation, 123, 450; -maturing period, 115, 238, 244; -sowing period, 115, 127, 238, 244. *See also* Kharif-maturing period
Radcliffe, Sir (now Viscount) Cyril, 3, 7, 12, 133, 163, 164, quoted 164 n., quoted 165 n., quoted 168, 169 n., 176, quoted 177–78, 178 n., 179, quoted 180, 181–82, quoted 182–83, 186, 188–89, quoted 190, 191 n., 193–94, quoted 194, 195 n., 197, 258
Radcliffe Award, 192–93, 197, 203, 205
Radcliffe Line. *See* Partition Line
Railways, 88, 97, 101 ff., 180–83, 190, 215
Raised Mangla Dam. *See* Mangla
Raised Tarbela Dam. *See* Tarbela
Rajasthan, 6, 13, 38, 120, 200, 206, 217–18, 231–32, 317–20, 324–25, 328–35, 338, 342–43, 366, 370, 374, 377, 383, 389, 394, 433–35, 437, 439, 513–14; case in disputes, 117 ff.
Rajasthan Canal, 19, 206, 317, 320, 326, 328–32, 334, 338, 382, 524
Rajasthan Feeder Canal, 206, 324, 328
Rajasthan Project, 206, 238, 321–22, 328 ff., 333–39, 380, 383, 467, 509, 512, 523. *See also* Bhakra-Beas-Rajasthan Project (BBRP)
Rajputana, 365. *See also* Rajasthan
Ranbir Canal, 257
Rangpur Canal, 125
Ranjit Singh, 55, 170, 185–86, 365
Rann of Cutch, 6, 336, 517, 519, 521, 528, 530–31
Rasul, 79–83, 89, 121, 176, 276, 291, 458–59; new headworks (IBP), 276–78
Rasul-Qadirabad (R-Q) Link, 256, 269, 278, 291
Rasul tubewells scheme, 454, 458–61, 463, 467–70, 509, 511; -type tubewells, 460–61, 463, 470
Rau, B. N., Justice, 129
Rau Commission, 129–33, 197, 368.

See also Indus Commission (*1941–42*)
Ravi-Beas Link (India), 208, 210, 217
Ravi River, 6–8, 25, 28, 32, 34 ff., 59 ff., 71, 74, 76, 80, 85, 87, 90, 125, 131, 182–83, 185, 190, 193, 200, 207, 209–10, 227, 230, 232, 235, 238, 256, 258, 269, 277, 317–20, 325–26, 331, 454, 517, 519, 523; course of, 34; siphon, 209–10, 517
Rawal Dam, 63, 356, 359, 446
Rawalpindi, 16, 175, 179, 262, 356, 483, 521, 531; District, 39, 176, 395, 431; Division, 172
R.C.D. *See* Regional Cooperation for Development
Recharge, groundwater, 472, 493–94, 535, 538, 540
Rechna Doab, def. 42, 58–60, 68 n., 73, 75, 77, 80, 87, 90, 177, 280, 291, 357, 431, 442, 453, 457–60, 462–64, 466, 468, 477, 479, 493, 498; Central, 468; Lower, 121, 124–25; Upper, 486
Rechna Doab Canal, 68, 91. *See also* Lower Chenab Canal
Reclamation, 269–71, 298, 335, 337, 350–51, 358, 360, 385, 429, 442–43, 463–67, 469–70, 473–79, 488–92, 504, 507–13, 524, 532–34, 539, 544–46; rate of, 506
Redistribution, land, 413 ff.
Refugees, 4, 214, 305, 414
Regenerated supplies, 76
Regime (canal), 61
Region, def. 14
Regional Cooperation for Development, 543
Regional planning. *See* Planning, regional
Regulating Act (*1773*), 51–52
Reh, 455–56. *See also* Waterlogging
Remodeling, 270 ff.
Rent, 387 ff., 412, 418, 434–35, 544
Replacement, 209–11, 238, 244–49, 253, 258–61, 264, 270; supplies, 235, 304
"Replacement works," 10, 245–46, 258, 264, 296, 319, 517
Research, agricultural, 420–21, 476–78
Reservoir, groundwater, 448, 451, 513, 535, 536 n., 541. *See also* Storage
Residents, British, 53, 185

Resumption of land, 415–16, 430
Revelle Panel, 301, 304, 469 n., 477–82, 485 n., 488–92, 494, 496, 498, 500–04, 511–12, 534, 536; approach, 476 ff., 483–89, 499–504, 508, 511, 524, 539–41, 545
Revelle Program, 484–85, 488, 491–94, 501, 504–06, 511, 523, 526, 536–40, 545; first level of development, 488–89, 494, 536–39; second level of development, 488–89, 508, 536–39
Revelle Report, 476 ff., 484 n., 485 n., 490–91, 499, 502–03, 508–09; Revelle I (September *1962*), 463 n., 476, 480–81, 491–92, 495, 499, 502–03, 526; Revelle II (January *1964*), 463 n., 476, 479–81, 486–87, 491, 493–96, 499–503, 526
Revelle, Roger, 301, 304, 476 ff., 491, 511
Revenue, 74 n., 75, 387 ff., 544; assessments, 74 n., 387 ff., 392, 430, 500; service, 386, 421, 426
Revenue Department (Punjab, West Pakistan), 390, 402, 422–23, 426
Rice, 113, 116–17, 394, 513
Rim station, 41, 64, 71, 210, 292; headworks, 64, 71
Riparian rights, 198, 200, 231
River Boards (India), 369 n., 372
Rock-fill dams, 287, 447
Rohri, 103–06; Barrage, *see* Sukkur Barrage; Canal Project, 105, 109. *See also* Sukkur Project
Rohtas dam site, 35 n., 248, 273, 276, 285, 292
Rolled-earth dams, 287
Rotation, crop, 412, 422, 429, 437, 513–14, 545
Round Table Conferences (*1931*), 2
R-Q Link. *See* Rasul-Qadirabad Link
Runoff, 115, 540
Run-of-the-river irrigation, 97, 111, 211
Rupar, 32, 55, 71, 78, 88, 120; headworks, 176, 206, 208, 217, 317, 320, 324
Russians. *See* U.S.S.R.
Ryotwari system 389, 410–11, 434

Sabraon, 56, 180
Sabraon Branch (UBDC), 188–90

Sailab, def., 111, 244, 257, 298
Sailaba, def. 111
Salam, Abdus, 301, 475
Sales taxes, 253, 255, 297, 308
Salinity, 15, 79, 126, 213, 244, 269–70, 298, 301, 304–05, 335, 339, 350–51, 358, 372, 422, 431, 452, 454–57, 463, 465, 467–70, 475–79, 482–87, 494–97, 504–07, 512–14, 546
Salinity Control and Reclamation Projects. *See* SCARPs
Salinization. *See* Salinity
Salt content, 498, 538. *See also* Groundwater quality
Salt Range, 31, 35, 79, 126, 128, 409, 516
Sanctioned uses (withdrawals), 199 ff., 231, 237, 317
Sarasvati, 27, 331
Sargodha, 12, 175, 460; District, 289
SCARPs (Salinity Control and Reclamation Projects), 442, 453, 462, 464 ff., 471, 474, 486, 500, 545. *See also particular SCARP*
SCARP I, 301 n., 356, 442, 453, 462, 464–70, 472–74, 477–79, 484, 486–89, 492–95, 498, 511
SCARP II, 442, 472–73, 486, 492, 546
SCARP III, 442, 473, 486, 493, 546
SCARP IV, 442, 486
"Scheme of works," 302. *See also* "System of works"
Scouring, 62, 96
Screens, tubewell, 452, 461, 473, 545. *See also* Strainers, tubewell
SEATO, 240, 304
Secretariat system, 344 n., 502
Secretary, Irrigation and Power (West Pakistan), 352
Secretary of State for India, 55, 67, 70, 73, 94 n., 110, 118–19, 122, 135 n., 367, 455
Security Council (UN), 518, 530
Sedimentation, 284, 293, 320, 322, 327. *See also* Siltation
Seeds, 352, 385, 419, 424–25, 427, 429–32, 437, 475, 480, 482, 485, 489, 500, 505, 508, 542, 545–46
Seepage, 332–33, 448, 450, 459, 494, 513, 536, 538

"September War" (*1965*), 10, 19, 314, 517, 520–21, 532, 541
Settlements, 74 n. *See also* Assessments
"Settlement Plan," 253, 268 n., 300. *See also* "Indus Basin Settlement Plan"
Shah Jahan, 49–50
Shakargarh tahsil, 187–88, 190
Shalimar Gardens, 50, 454
Share capacity, 114
Sharecropping, 403, 407, 412
Shares program, 92 n., 199
Shastri, Lal Bahadur, 306 n., 315, 517, 520–22
Sheikhupura, 12, 49, 167 n., 175, 463–64; District, 162, 166, 173, 183, 468
Shikarpur, 101–02, 104
Shoaib, Mohammed, 262–63, 541 n.
Shroud, tubewell, 461, 470, 473. *See also* Pack
Shutters (on weirs), 61, 78, 79
Shyok River, 6, 31, 274
Sialkot, 38, 175; District, 39, 173, 431
Sibi, 36, 432
Sidhnai, 77–78, 275; Canal, 276; new barrage (IBP), 276, 354; Project, 74, 76 ff., 80, 85, 125, 171, 176, 386
Sidhnai-Mailsi (S-M) Link, 276, 280, 329
Sikhs, 3, 5, 7, 12, 56–58, 66, 136–38, 149, 152, 159, 161–62, 165–71, 174–76, 184–86, 204, 346, 365, 367, 400, 402, 410, 438, 451, 509, 520; Akali, 159, 161, 520; policies, 149, 159 ff., 169 ff., 185; proposals, 169, 176, 185
Sikh Army, 66
Sikh Communists, 159
Sikh Durbar, 56, 58, 185
Sikh Legislators, 170, 185
Sikh Memorandum, 169 ff.
Sikh Panthic Board, 160
Sikh Wars, 56–57
Siltation, 62, 78, 210, 284, 313, 534. *See also* Sedimentation
Simla, 155, 451; District, 173
Simon Commission (Indian Statutory Commission, *1927–29*), 2, 146
Sind, 6, 11, 13–14, 16, 18, 39, 56, 67 n., 84, 87, 93, 98 ff., 106, 116, 118 ff., 123, 136, 199, 201, 211–13, 215, 237,

245, 271–72, 292–93, 305, 307, 330, 336, 342, 345, 366–67, 389, 393, 396, 399–400, 411, 413, 415, 466, 474, 483–84, 486–87, 492, 494–96, 499, 508–09, 533, 538; agriculture in, 106, 116; annexation, 56; geography, 99 ff.; history, 99 ff.; irrigation in, 104 ff.; transportation in, 101 ff.
Sind Gazetteer (*1907*), 101
Sind Government. *See* Government of Sind; Bombay Government
Sind Legislative Assembly, 163
Sind-Punjab Chief Engineers' Agreement, 216, 218, 231
Sind-Punjab Disputes, 16, 18, 98 n., 117 ff., 122 ff., 128 ff., 197, 226, 237, 245
Sind Tenancy Act (*1950*), 403, 412
Sind Sagar Doab, def. 41, 84, 86, 88, 92, 98, 121, 126, 409. *See also* Thal Doab
Sind Sagar Doab Colonization Act, 126
Sindhu, 42
Singh, Baldev, 144, 154, 156, 159–60, 162, 165
Singh, Gianni Khartar, 161
Singh, Khushwant, 135 n., quoted 149–52, quoted 159 n., quoted 160 n., 167n.
Singh, Master Tara, 159, 161, 167
Singh, Ranjit, 55, 170, 185–86, 365
Sino-Indian conflict (*1962*), 303–04, 308, 519
Sirhind Canal, 67 ff., 71 ff., 120, 204, 206, 385, 444; Project, 176, 317, 377, 380
Sirhind Feeder Canal, 206, 331
Siwaliks, 24 ff., 31, 35, 293, 322, 326, 328, 483
Skardu, 31, 274, 293, 320, 323, 519, 540
Slapper dam site, 320, 325, 523
Slocum, Harvey, 347, 374, 378–79
S-M Link. *See* Sidhnai-Mailsi Link
Soan River, 31, 35 n.
Sodium hazard, 487, 488 n., 498. *See also* Exchangeable-sodium percentage
Soil, 113, 330, 333, 335, 415, 455–56, 464, 466, 475, 486–88, 492, 498, 507,

Index

515–16; conservation, 431, 464; surveys, 335, 464
Soil Conservation Project (West Pakistan), 464
Soil Reclamation Board (West Pakistan), 307, 344, 350, 354, 373, 463, 465, 478, 481–82, 500
Sommers, Davidson, 224–25
Southern Zone (Indus Plains), def. 41, 117, 305, 316, 324, 358, 442, 474–75, 483, 488, 490, 494–95, 499, 504, 507–08
Special Reserve (Indus Basin Development Fund), 302
Specific yield, 492–94, 540. *See also* Storage coefficient
Srinagar, 5, 25, 191, 201, 239, 273, 284
Stable regime (canal), 61
Stamp, Sir William, 453, 511
"Standard acres" (India), 434–35
"Standing wave." *See* "Hydraulic jump"
Standstill Agreement (December 1947), 8, 196, 202
States Reorganisation Act (India, 1956), 366
States Unions (India), 366
Stephens, Ian, 134 n., 141, 145–46, 191, quoted 191 n.
Still pond system, 72
Storage, 82, 114, 211, 236, 238, 240–44, 246–48, 270–74, 283, 285, 292 n., 293, 299, 304, 313, 320, 397, 448, 533–36, 540–41; capacity, 534, 536; off-channel, 285, 299, 304, 313, 536. *See also* Dams
Storage coefficient, 492–93
Strainers, tubewell, 452, 454, 460–63, 470–71, 473. *See also* Screens, tubewell
Sub-Divisional Officers, 387 ff.
"Subsistence holdings," 407 ff., 415, 417–18
Subsoil flow theory (A. N. Khosla), 125
Sugarcane, 76, 113, 332, 391, 394, 513
Sui, 305, 485 n.
Sukkur, 40, 100, 102, 122, 131, 232, 442, 444–45, 488, 495, 507–08; Barrage (Lloyd or Rohri Barrage), 10, 39, 98, 103–05, 107, 108 n., 109–11,

176, 178 n., 215, 330, 432; Project, 15, 110–12, 117–20, 127–28, 214, 216, 237, 243, 245, 292, 336, 393–94, 396, 411
Suleiman Range, 28, 31, 36, 516
Suleimanke (Suleimanki), 176–77, 210, 257–58; headworks (S.V.P.), 6, 95, 97, 124, 176–77, 178 n., 209–10, 271–72, 277, 517; Project (S.V.P.), 271–72, 280, 291
Sulphate-reducing bacteria, 462, 473
Sundarnagar-Sutlej tunnel, 326
Supplemental Agreement. *See* Indus Basin Development Fund Agreement
Surface water, 272–73, 305, 307, 310, 352, 385, 444–45, 495–98, 507, 510–11, 518, 523–24, 534–41, 545; advocates, 503; irrigation, 444, 448, 453, 463, 483–84, 489, 492, 494, 498, 509–10, 513–14, 523, 534, 540, 545; supplies, 536–38
Surface water–groundwater controversy, 503, 534, 540–41
Sutlej River, 6, 8, 15, 25 ff., 32 ff., 71, 80, 85, 87–88, 95, 99, 114, 120, 125, 129, 131, 177–78, 180, 182–83, 185–86, 190, 193, 200, 206–07, 209, 211, 227, 230, 235, 241–42, 256–58, 269, 275, 277, 317–21, 325–26, 330–32, 336, 380, 510, 523; course of, 25 ff., 32 ff.
Sutlej Valley Project, 93 ff., 110–12, 114, 118, 120–21, 127, 129, 176–77, 200–01, 206, 210, 231, 237, 241–42, 256, 342, 396, 445, 447, 453; intensities, 114. *See also* Pakistan Sutlej Valley Canals
S.V.P. *See* Sutlej Valley Project
Swarzenski, W. V., 493
Swat, 35, 163; River, 124, 274, 515, 534
Sylhet District, 158, 163
Symposium on Waterlogging and Salinity (Lahore, October 1963), 493, 498, 502
"System of works," 260, 269, 298–300, 302

T and K. *See* Tipton and Kalmbach
Taccavi loans, 402, 418, 422–23

Tahsil Councils, 387 ff.
Tahsildars, 402, 387 ff.
Tahsils, 165, 186 ff., 387 ff., 519
Talwara, 33, 321–22
TAMS. *See* Tippetts-Abbett-McCarthy-Stratton
Tarbela, 31, 40, 273, 293–94, 299, 307–09, 313–15, 320; "crisis," 277, 295 ff.; Dam, 214, 245, 248, 250, 253, 264, 273–74, 277, 280, 283, 287, 291–92, 298–300, 302–07, 312–16, 324, 347, 356, 502, 523, 526, 529, 533–36, 540, 542, 545; "economic viability," 314, 533; Raised Tarbela Dam, 535; "technical feasibility," 312, 314, 533
Tarn Taran, 184
Tashkent Agreement (January *1966*), 6, 517, 520, 531
Tashkent Conference (January *1966*), 306 n., 315, 522, 531–32
Tatta, 37, 100, 102
Taunsa Barrage, 214, 271, 277, 446; Project, 201, 214–15, 217, 237, 271, 396
Taunsa-Panjnad (T-P) Link, 245, 269
Taxation, 387, 392, 544; in kind, 410. *See also specific types*
T.C.P. *See* Triple Canals Project
T.D.A. *See* Thal Development Authority
Technical assistance, 301 n., 347, 362, 464, 466
Technical services, 346, 426, 428, 502
Techniques, agricultural, 419, 424, 427, 429, 431, 480, 485, 489, 522, 545–46
Technology, 14, 16, 439, 444 ff., 448, 450, 469, 473, 476, 489, 540. *See also* Engineers; Irrigation
Temporary Settlement, 389, 410
Tenants, 403 ff., 412 ff., 417–18, 434–35, 544
Tenure, land, 387 ff., 407, 412 ff., 434, 435 n.
Tethys Sea, 23, 30
Thal Development Authority (T.D.A.), 214, 352, 354, 373, 432
Thal Doab, 39–40, def. 42, 84, 88, 121, 125–26, 175, 214, 275, 335, 442, 466; Lower, 472, 486
Thal Main Line Canal, 128, 334

Thal Project, 121–24, 126 ff., 129–33, 201, 214–15, 232, 237, 242, 271, 275, 334, 339, 393, 396, 453–54, 458, 467
Thar Desert, 206, 212, 317, 319, 328, 330–31, 334, 337
Thein, 34, 238; Dam, 131, 201, 207, 319, 325, 510, 523; dam site, 320, 519
Thermal power, 452–53
Thimayya, Brig., quoted 167 n.
Tibetan Plateau, 24 ff.
Tibetan Sea, 23 ff.
Tinker, Hugh, quoted 438 n.
Tippetts-Abbett-McCarthy-Stratton (TAMS), 244, 303, 313, 315, 358–59
Tipton and Hill, 285, 293, 313, 316, 358
Tipton and Kalmbach, 316, 335, 358–59, 462 n., 473–74, 490, 492–93
T-P Link. *See* Taunsa-Panjnad Link
Training works, 64, 78
Trans-Himalayan stream, 22, 24 ff.
Transition Period, 8, 181, 235–39, 242–43, 247, 249, 255–56, 259, 263, 302, 316, 357; Phase I, 277–78, 280; Phase II, 277–78, 280, 283
Transportation, 84, 87–88, 101, 415. *See also* Navigation; Railways
Trans-Sutlej districts, 56, 185, 365
Trans-Thal links, 545. *See also* Chasma-Jhelum Link; Taunsa-Panjnad Link
Treaty. *See* Indus Waters Treaty
Trench, W. L. C., 122, 133
Trevaskis, Hugh K., 18, 74 n.
Trimmu, 34, 87, 93, 98, 121; headworks, 271, 275, 277, 280, 291; Project, 121–24, 129, 133, 215, 232. *See also* Haveli Project
Trimmu-Sidhnai (T-S) Link, 276, 280
Trimmu-Sidhnai-Islam Link, 256, 269, 271, 275–77. *See also* Trimmu-Sidhnai-Mailsi-Bahawal Link
Trimmu-Sidhnai-Mailsi-Bahawal (T-S-M-B) Link, 256, 271, 276–80, 283. *See also component links*
Tripartite Agreement (Punjab-Bahawalpur-Bikaner, *1919*), 99, 110, 114
Triple Canals Project (T.C.P.), 15–18, 77, 90 ff., 121, 125, 171, 176, 201, 211, 256, 271–72, 275, 291, 445–46

T-S Link. *See* Trimmu-Sidhnai Link
Tsangpo-Brahmaputra, 22–29
T-S-M-B Link. *See* Trimmu-Sidhnai-Mailsi-Bahawal Link
Tubewells, def. 15, 18, 189 n., 213, 250, 270, 301–02, 305, 307, 355, 393, 397, 422, 441, 451–64, 467–73, 477–79, 484, 486–87, 493–95, 498, 502, 509–12, 524, 540–42; design, 452, 470–74, 493–95, 502; drainage, 458, 472, 474, 486–87, 495, 510; irrigation, 453 ff., 458, 472, 474, 509; longevity, 462, 470–74, 510; multiple-bore, 470–71
Tubewells and Drainages component (IBP), 301–04, 308, 311, 359
T.V.A., 219, 222–23, 229, 346, 355, 370, 446 n., 472 n.

UBDC. *See* Upper Bari Doab Canal
UCC. *See* Upper Chenab Canal
UJC. *See* Upper Jhelum Canal
Ujh River, 6, 517
U.K., 225, 248, 296, 300, 303–04, 361, 364, 444, 519, 530–31, 533. *See also* British Government
UN, 6, 219, 221, 463, 521; General Assembly, 525; Security Council, 518, 530; Special Fund, 542
Undersluices, 72, 78
Union Councils, 425
Unit I (BBRP). *See* Beas-Sutlej Link
Unit II (BBRP). *See* Pong Dam
Unit III (BBRP). *See* Rajasthan Canal
United Provinces (U.P.), 54, 82 n., 102, 182, 330, 365, 436, 453, 511
United States Geological Survey (U.S.G.S.), 301, 350, 462 n., 465–67, 474–75, 478, 492–93, 534; team in Pakistan, 466–67, 474, 534
U.P. *See* United Provinces
Uppal, H. L., 510
Upper Bari Doab Canal (UBDC), 34, 60–65, 67, 69–71, 74–76, 81, 85–86, 176–77, 181, 188, 190, 196, 199, 201–02, 209, 256, 385–86. *See also* Lahore Branch; Main Branch; Sabraon Branch, UBDC
Upper Chenab Canal (UCC), 68, 90, 92 n., 209, 217, 276, 291, 458
Upper Indus, def. 40, 540

Upper Indus Link, 244–45
Upper Jhelum Canal (UJC), 90, 274, 276–77, 291, 324, 458–59, 518
Uri, 7, 192
U.S.A., 221, 240, 248, 254, 268, 296, 300, 303–04, 309, 311, 313–14, 316, 322, 330, 361, 364, 465, 473–75, 517, 519, 521–23, 525–26, 528–30, 532–33, 543–546; economic assistance, 240, 306 n.; military assistance, 240, 306 n.; Public Law 480, 240, 254, 309; technical assistance, 240. *See also* Agency for International Development; Bureau of Reclamation; "Food for Peace" Program; United States Geological Survey
U.S. Agency for International Development. *See* Agency for International Development
U.S.G.S. *See* United States Geological Survey
U.S.S.R., 29, 303, 362, 364, 448, 475, 530–32, 534, 542–43, 546

Vale of Kashmir, 25, 191–92, 239
Velocity, critical, 62
Verinag, 257
Veterinary service, 420–21
Viceroy, 55, 58, 67, 110, 135, 144, 153 n.
Victoria, Queen, 55, 365
Village-AID (Pakistan), 423–25, 428, 430, 433, 436, 439, 479, 501
Village Level Workers (India), 436–38
Volumetric assessment, 393

WAPDA (West Pakistan), def. 41, 216, 242, 247, 249–50, 252, 263, 275, 277–78, 280, 287, 294–97, 300, 301 n., 302–04, 307–10, 312–15, 344, 346, 349–63, 373, 375, 421–22, 426–27, 429, 432, 464–75, 477–78, 481–84, 486–90, 492, 503–05, 534; consultants, 250, 253, 315, 360–64, 488, 490, 492, 502–05, 507; consultants' estimates (June *1960*), 297; organization, 352–53; publications, 356
WAPDA master plan for reclamation (May *1961*), 465, 474–75, 478, 482–84, 486–87, 489–90, 502, 504–05, 511

WAPDA Master Plan for Water and Power Development, 316, 474, 490, 504, 539
WAPDA "Program for Waterlogging and Salinity Control in Irrigated Areas of West Pakistan" (May *1961*). *See* WAPDA master plan for reclamation
Warabandi, 393
Ward, Sir Thomas, 118, 122, 230
Warsak Dam, 63, 292 n., 348–49, 373, 446
Washington, D.C., 227, 230, 243, 247, 249, 306 n., 475, 522, 525, 533
WASID (West Pakistan WAPDA), 301 n., 302, 335, 353, 462 n., 466, 472, 474, 478, 493
Water advantage rate, 390–91, 433
Water and Power Development Authority (West Pakistan). *See* WAPDA
Water and Soils Investigation Division (West Pakistan WAPDA). *See* WASID
Water charges. *See* Water rates
Watercourses, 272–73
Water disputes, India-Pakistan, 199 ff.
Water duties, 88, 331, 335, 339
Waterlogging, 15, 88, 126, 244, 269–70, 298, 301–02, 335, 350–51, 372, 452, 454 ff., 467, 469, 475, 477, 482–87, 494, 504, 509–14, 546
Waterlogging Board (*1925*), 457
Waterlogging Enquiry Committee (*1928*), 457
Water-Power, Irrigation, and Navigation Commission (India). *See* Central Water and Power Commission (India)
Water quality, 455–56, 471, 474, 494–95, 498
Water rates, 334, 353, 373, 390–92, 412, 421, 433, 469, 499–500
Water rights, 198 ff.
Water table, 15, 79, 88, 244, 270, 298, 305, 335, 450, 452, 454, 456, 458–59, 463, 468, 479, 486, 494, 509–10, 513, 515, 535–36, 538, 540
Wavell, Lord Archibald, 135, 136 n., 144–46, 149, 153 n., 154, 156
Wavell Plan, 135 n., 146

Wazirabad, 78, 175
Weir-controlled irrigation, 81, def. 111
Weirs, 49, 61, def. 62, 215; shuttered, 78
Well irrigation, 111, 324, 448, 449 n.
Wells, 88, 111, 244, 298, 324, 395, 448–50
West Germany, 248, 296, 303, 362, 472, 543, 546
WJC. *See* Western Jumna Canal
West Pakistan, 6, 117, 176, 211–12, 343–44, 350–51, 353, 432, 480–83, 489, 501, 508–11, 513, 524–25, 533–34, 539–40, 544–46; One Unit Rule, 117; political organization, 343–44
West Pakistan Agricultural Development Corporation (ADC). *See* Agricultural Development Corporation
West Pakistan Engineering Congress, 502
West Pakistan Government. *See* Government of West Pakistan
West Pakistan Land Commission, 415
West Pakistan Land Reforms Regulation. *See* Martial Law Regulation No. 64
West Pakistan Water and Power Development Authority. *See* WAPDA
West Punjab (Pakistan), 5, 7–8, 117, 128, 167, 177, 180, 183, 200–02, 209–11, 214, 216, 245, 513
Western Jumna Canal (WJC), 49, 51, 57 n., 60, 64, 66–67, 74, 75, 120, 319 n., 320, 377, 455–56
Western Rivers, def. 230–31, 234–38, 242–44, 247, 256–60, 262, 268, 270, 273, 292, 304, 519, 535, 540
Wheat, 116, 175, 391, 394, 514, 522, 544
Wheeler, Lt. Gen. Raymond A., 225, 229, 234–35, 239, 243
White House Conference on International Cooperation, 525
White House–Interior Panel on Waterlogging and Salinity in West Pakistan, 301, 463 n., 465. *See also* Revelle Panel; Revelle Report
Wiesner, Jerome B., 301, 475–79
Wiesner Mission, 474, 476–78, 504, 511
Wilson, James, 83, 85, quoted 86, 87, 121

Woods, George D., 310
World Bank, 8, 10, 133, 208, 218, 222–
24, 227–28, 232–33, 238, 241, 247–
55, 259, 262, 264, 268, 270, 275, 277,
295–97, 300, 302–04, 306–07, 309–
10, 312–13, 315–16, 318–19, 322, 342,
352, 358–61, 364, 373, 419, 502–04,
517, 521–23, 526–27, 529–30, 533;
consultants, 251, 297, 360, 364, 490,
503; plan (proposal) of February
1954, 238–39, 241, 244–45
World Court, 219, 221

Wular Lake, 7, 25, 35, 89, 130, 201,
239, 273, 283, 323; storage scheme,
130, 201

XEN. *See* Executive Engineer

Yale University, 491
Young, Popham, 77
Yugoslavia, 359, 361, 546

Zamindars, 389 ff., 399, 410, 434, 451
Zira tahsil, 182–83, 187–88